FOR ORGANS, PIANOS & ELECTRONIC KEYBOARDS

340

Anthology of JAZZ SONGS

GOLD EDITION

ISBN 978-1-4234-9210-8

7777 W. BLUEMOUND RD. P.O. BOX 13819 MILWAUKEE, WI 53213

For all works contained herein:
Unauthorized copying, arranging, adapting, recording, Internet posting, public performance
or other distribution of the printed music in this publication is an infringement of copyright.
Infringers are liable under the law.

E-Z Play® Today Music Notation © 1975 by HAL LEONARD CORPORATION
E-Z PLAY and EASY ELECTRONIC KEYBOARD MUSIC are registered trademarks of HAL LEONARD CORPORATION.

Visit Hal Leonard Online at
www.halleonard.com

(25)	4	Across the Alley from the Alamo	69	Girl Talk
(18) (10)		All of You	76	Gone with the Wind ss
	7	All or Nothing at All	78	Guess Who I Saw Today
(11) (12)		Almost Like Being in Love	81	Harlem Nocturne ss
	14	Always True to You in My Fashion	84	Honeysuckle Rose ss
	20	Angel Eyes	(3) 86	How Are Things in Glocca Morra
(12) (22)		April in Paris ss	88	I Ain't Got Nothin' but the Blues
(7) 24		Autumn Leaves ss	(26) 91	I Can't Get Started with You ss
	26	Bernie's Tune	94	I Don't Stand a Ghost of a Chance
(28)	28	ss The Birth of the Blues — 2/5/14 ss	100	I Got It Bad and That Ain't Good
	30	Body and Soul	97	I Let a Song Go Out of My Heart
	17	C-Jam Blues	102	I Thought About You
ss 32		Caravan ss	105	I Wish I Were in Love Again
(28) ss 34		Come Fly with Me ss	(1) 108	I'll Be Seeing You ss
	38	Cry Me a River	110	I'm Just a Lucky So and So
	40	Dancers in Love	116	I'm Old Fashioned
	47	Day by Day	118	I've Got My Love to Keep Me Warm
	50	Django	(8) 120	I've Got You Under My Skin ss
(16) ss 52		Don't Get Around Much Anymore ss	124	I've Grown Accustomed to Her Face ss
(19) 58		East of the Sun (And West of the Moon)	113	Ill Wind (You're Blowin' Me No Good)
	60	Easy Street	(30) 126	Imagination
	55	Ev'ry Time We Say Goodbye	128	In a Mellow Tone
	62	Falling in Love with Love	(4) 130	In the Mood ss
	64	A Fine Romance	136	It All Depends on You
	66	The Folks Who Live on the Hill	138	It Could Happen to You
	72	From This Moment On	133	It's All Right with Me

(29)	140	It's De-Lovely		200	Rockin' in Rhythm

- (29) 140 It's De-Lovely
- 142 June in January
- (144) Just in Time?
- 146 Just Squeeze Me (But Don't Tease Me)
- 152 The Last Time I Saw Paris *Joanne Weber teaches*
- 149 Lazy Afternoon
- (17) (154) Lazy River
- 156 Let's Face the Music and Dance
- 162 Like Someone in Love
- 164 Love Is a Simple Thing
- 166 Love Letters SS
- 168 Lullaby of the Leaves
- 170 Midnight Sun
- (13) (159) My Foolish Heart
- (14) (172) My Heart Belongs to Daddy
- 174 My Old Flame
- 176 My Shining Hour
- 178 My Ship
- 181 Never Let Me Go
- 184 Ol' Man River SS 2/12/14 *class didn't meet — car problems*
- (30) 186 On a Slow Boat to China
- 188 One Morning in May
- (15) (194) Our Day Will Come SS
- 196 The Party's Over
- 198 Polka Dots and Moonbeams
- (27) 191 The Rainbow Connection SS

- 200 Rockin' in Rhythm
- (23) 203 St. Louis Blues SS
- 208 September Song SS — 1/8/14
- 210 A Sleepin' Bee
- 213 Small World (Gypsy)
- 216 Solitude
- (10) 222 Some Day My Prince Will Come
- (224) Stompin' at the Savoy SS
- 226 Stormy Weather SS — 2/19/14
  (Keeps Rainin' All the Time)
- (5) (228) Tenderly SS
- (22) 230 There Will Never Be Another You
- (6) (232) There's a Small Hotel
- 234 Time After Time
- 236 Too Late Now
- (24) 238 What a Diff'rence a Day Made
- 240 What's New?
- (2) 242 When I Fall in Love SS
- 244 When Sunny Gets Blue
- (21) (219) When You're Smiling SS
  (The Whole World Smiles with You)
- 248 Will You Still Be Mine
- (9) (254) You Are the Sunshine of My Life SS 340
- 251 You Took Advantage of Me
- 256 REGISTRATION GUIDE

Across the Alley from the Alamo

Registration 2
Rhythm: Swing

Words and Music by
Joe Greene

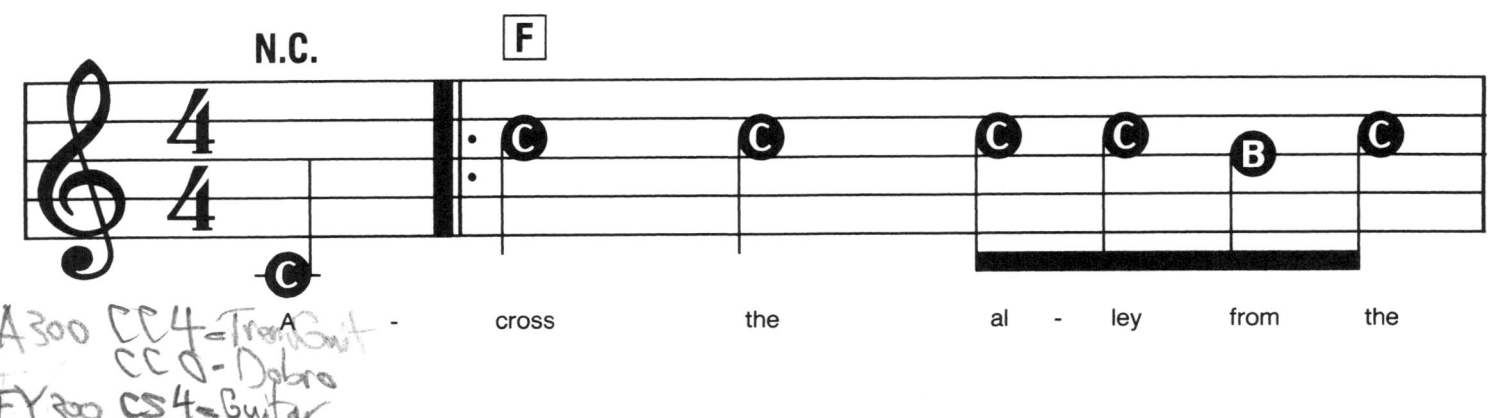

A - cross the al - ley from the

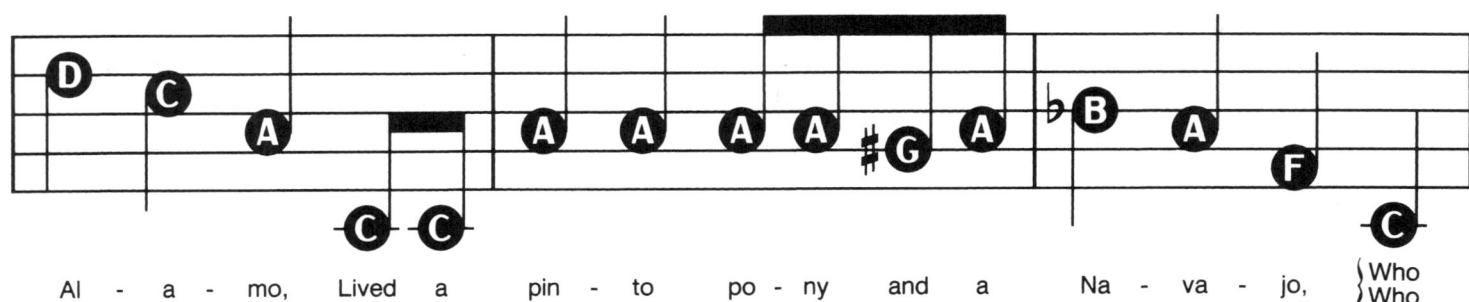

Al - a - mo, Lived a pin - to po - ny and a Na - va - jo, {Who / Who

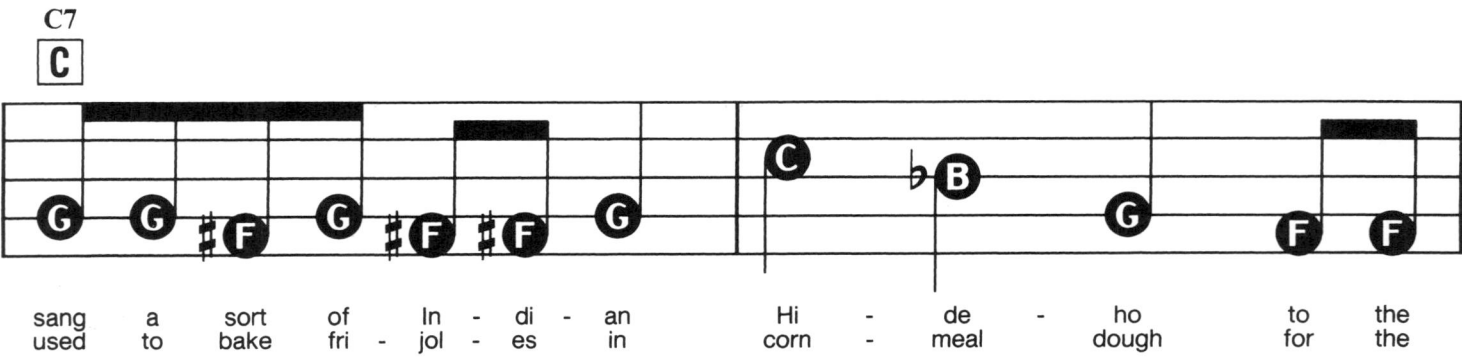

sang a sort of In - di - an Hi - de - ho to the
used to bake fri - jol - es in the corn - meal dough for the

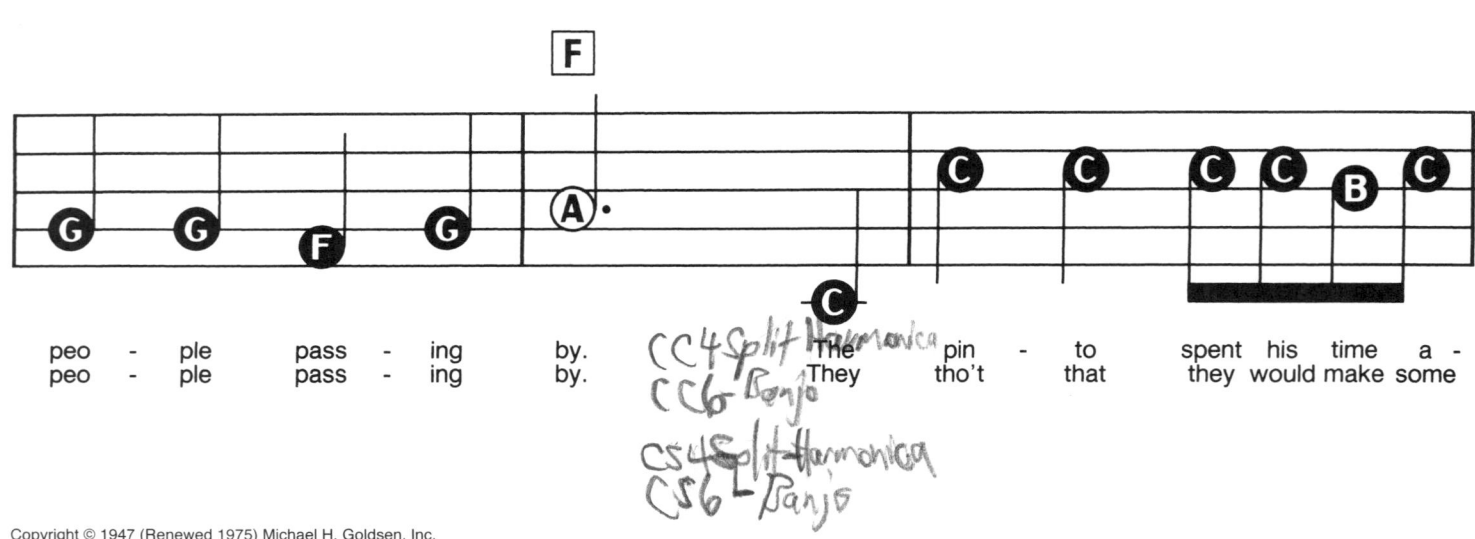

peo - ple pass - ing by. The pin - to spent his time a-
peo - ple pass - ing by. They tho't that they would make some

Copyright © 1947 (Renewed 1975) Michael H. Goldsen, Inc.
International Copyright Secured   All Rights Reserved

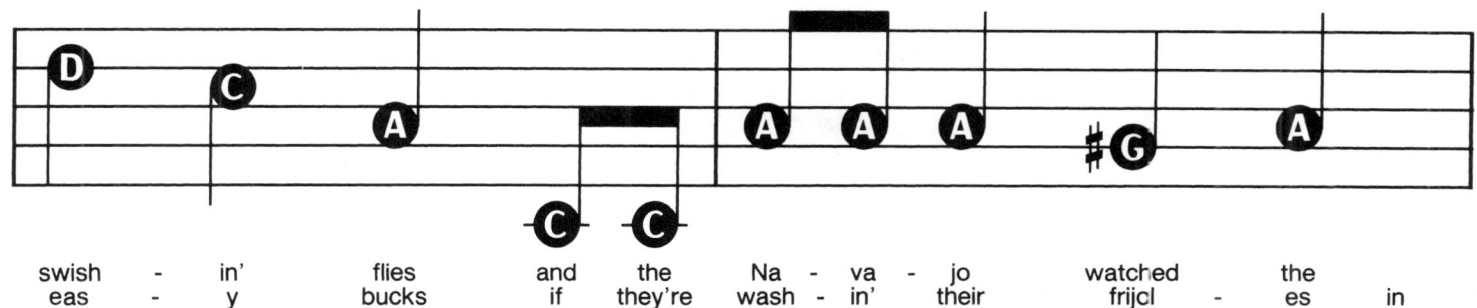
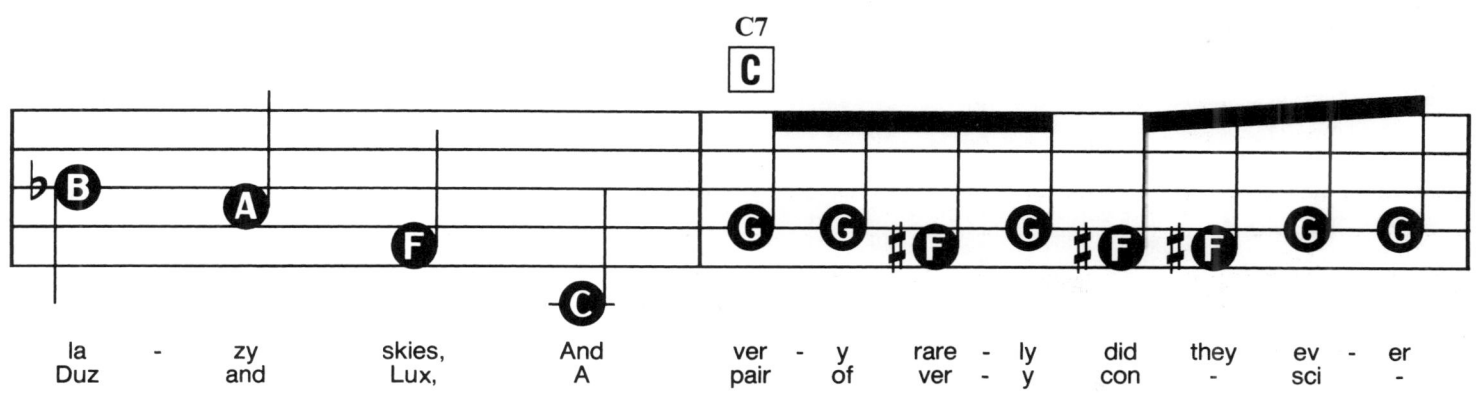
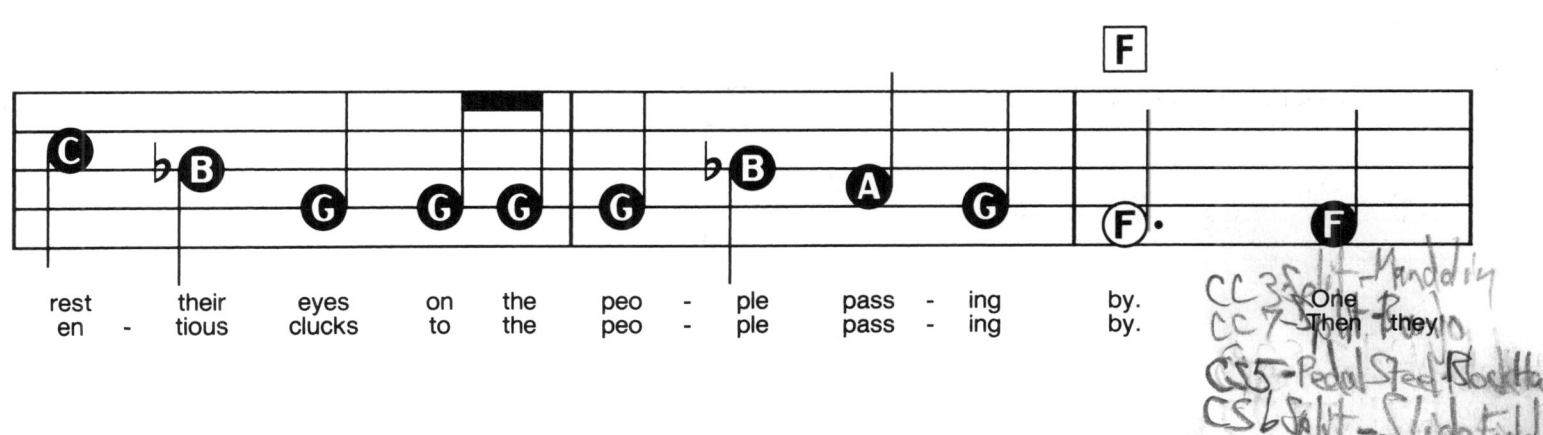
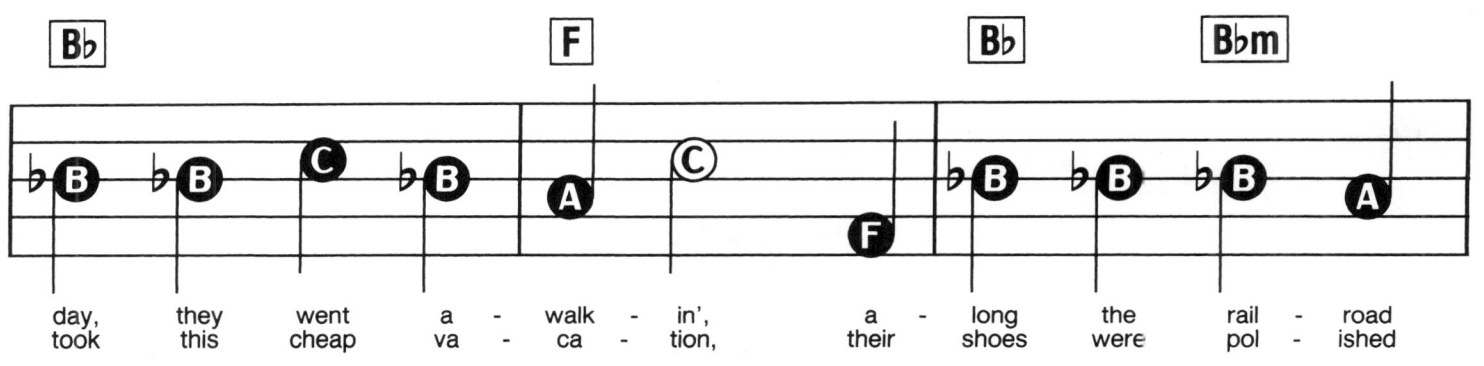

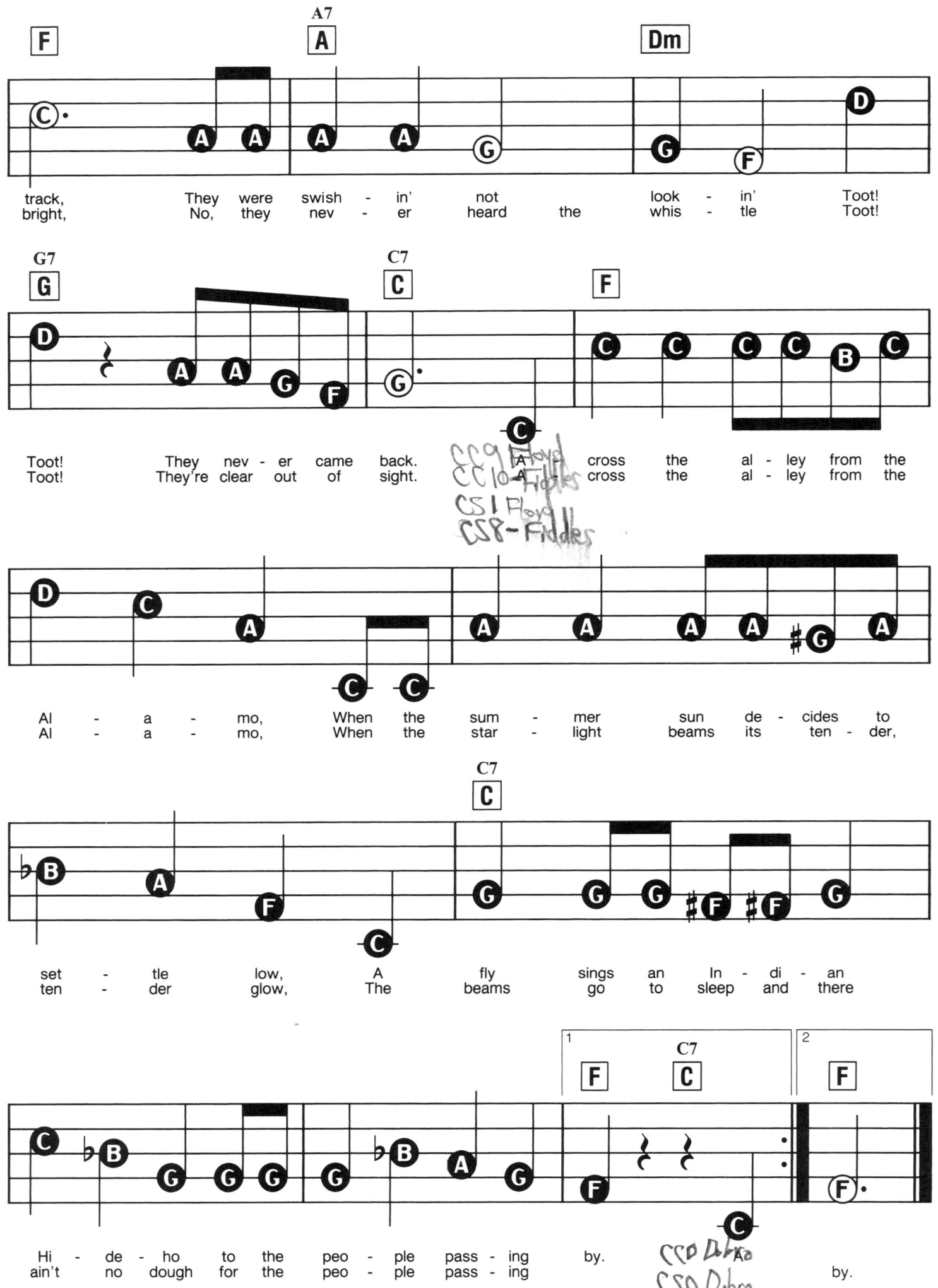

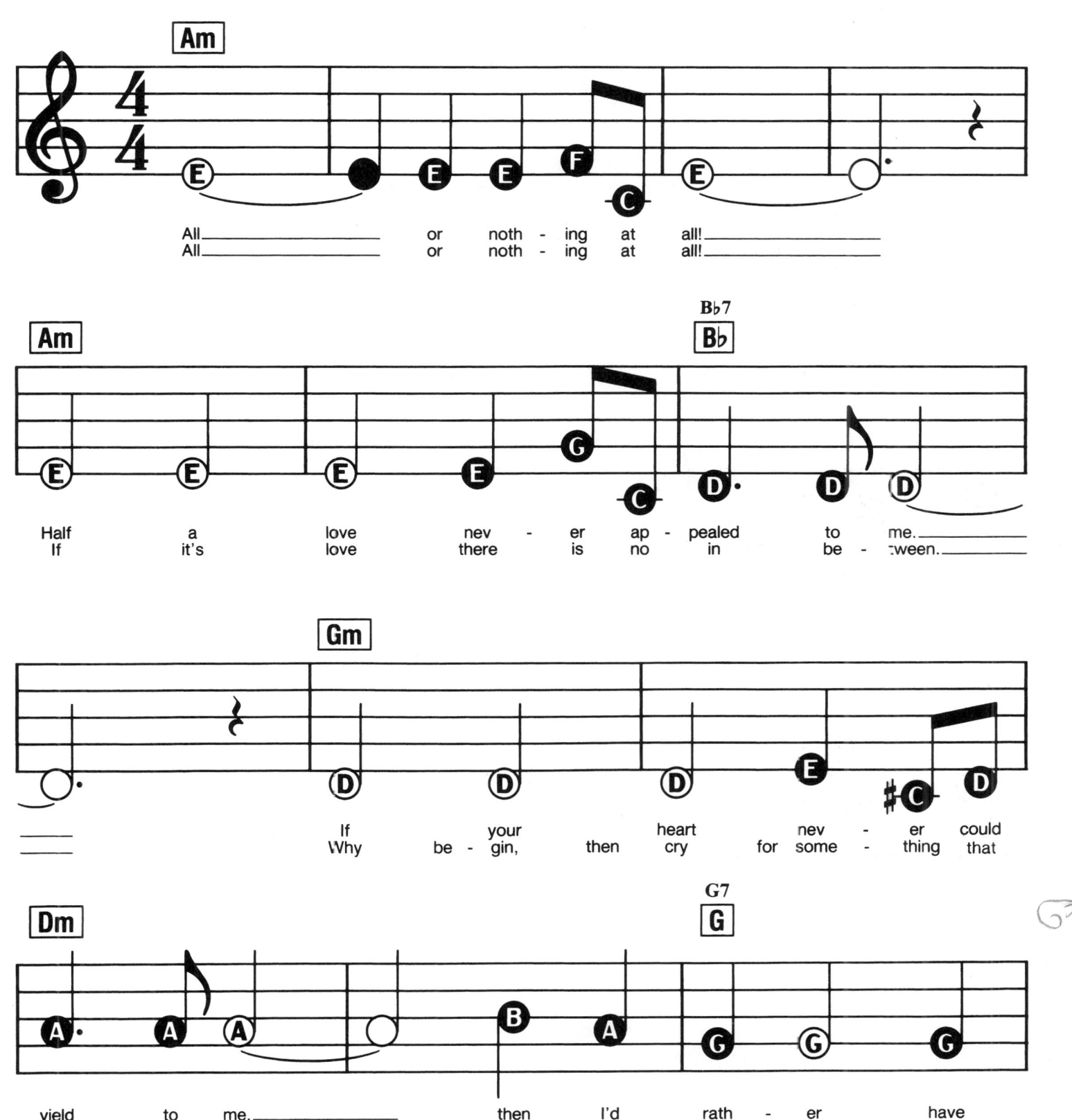

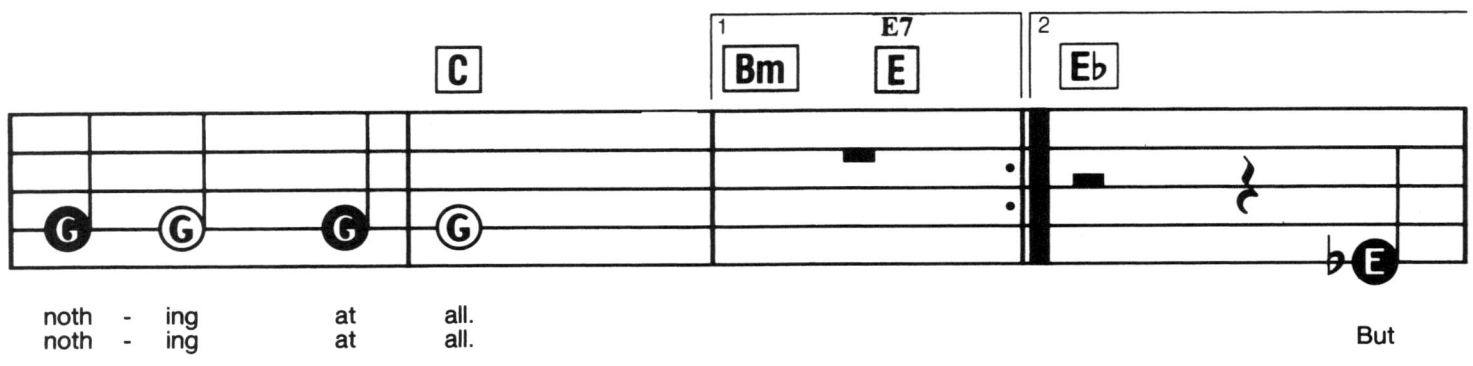
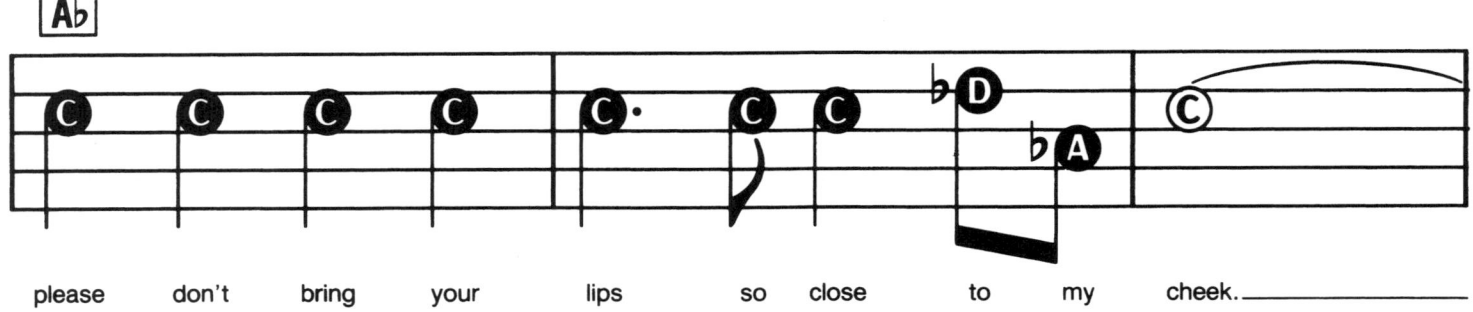
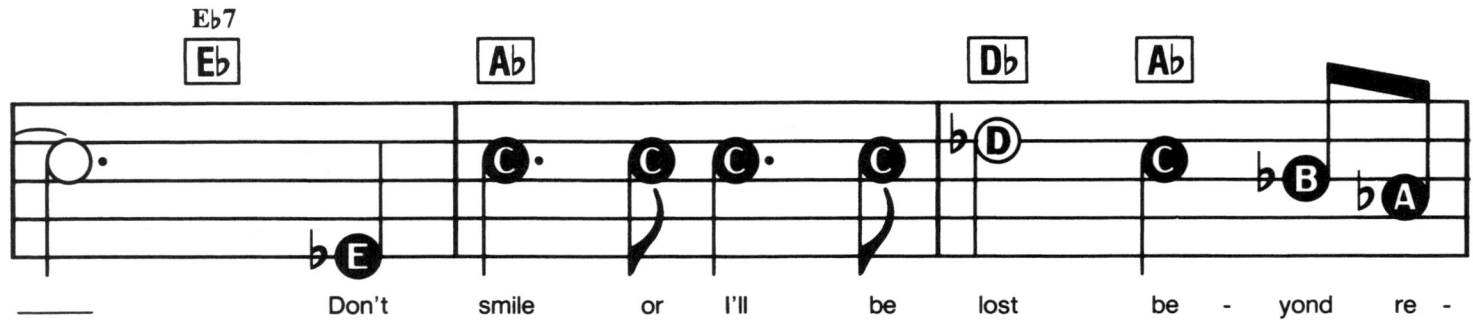
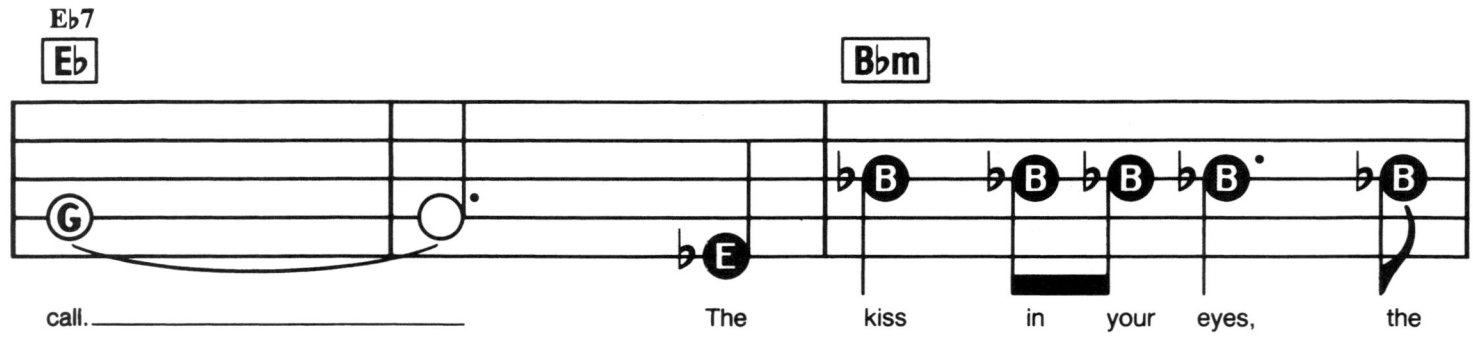
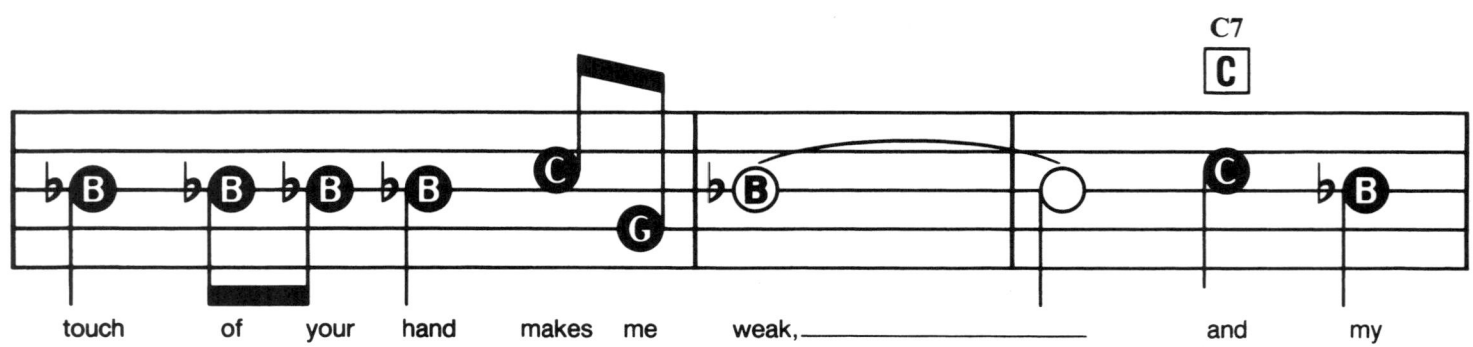

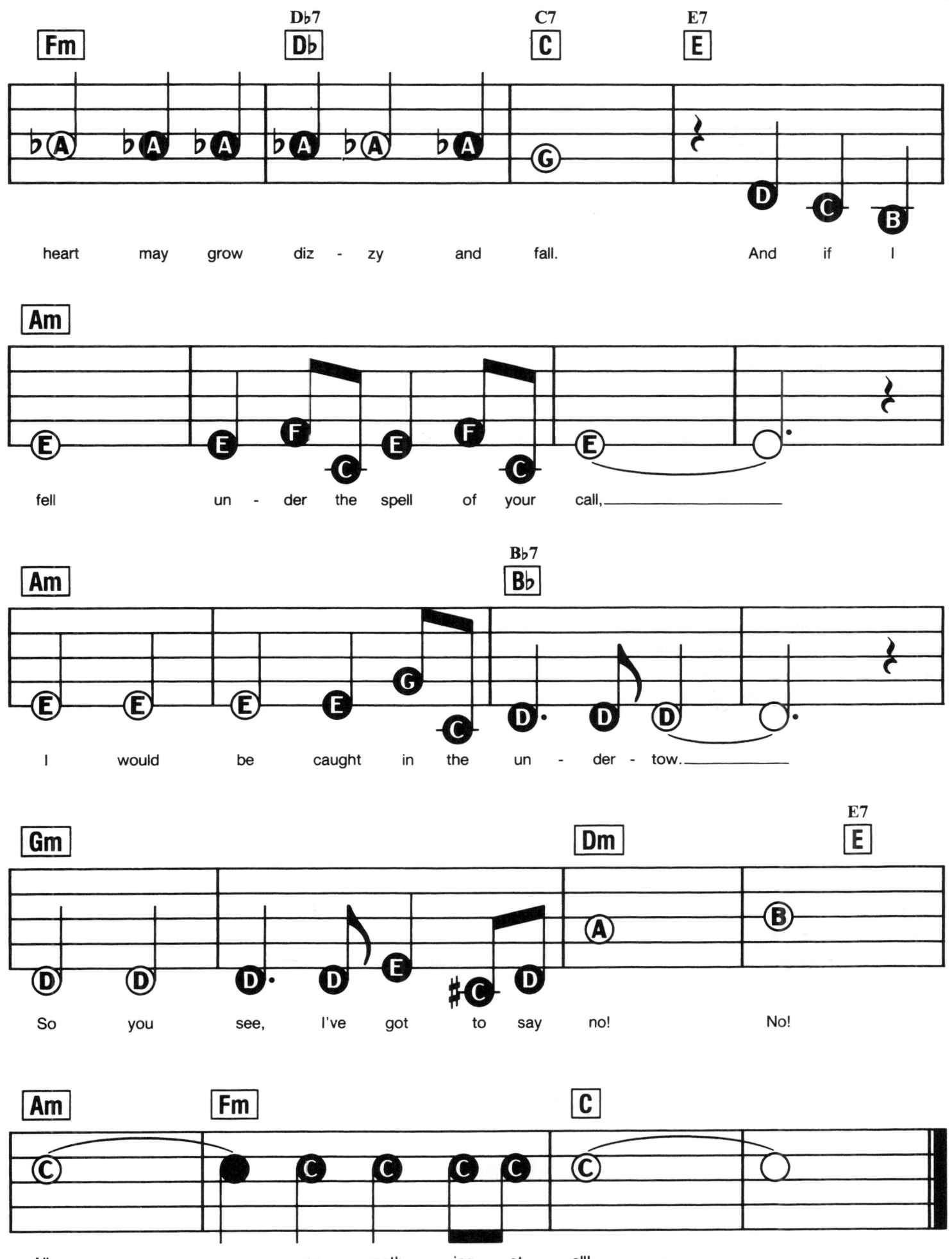

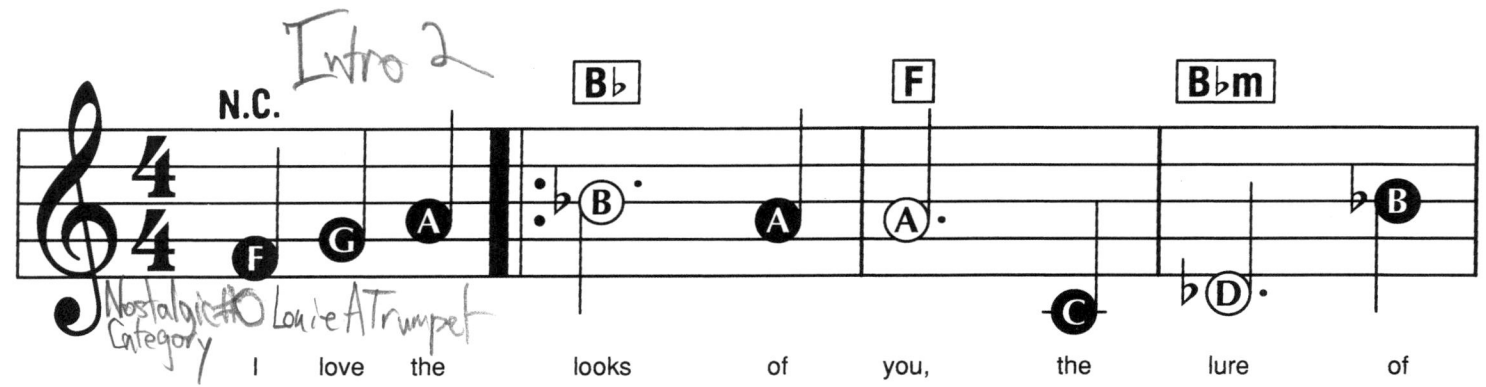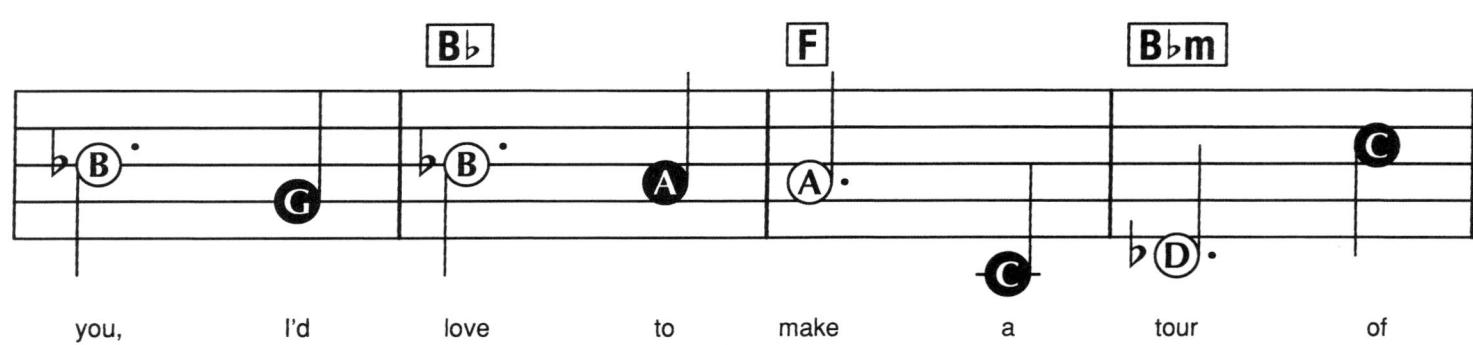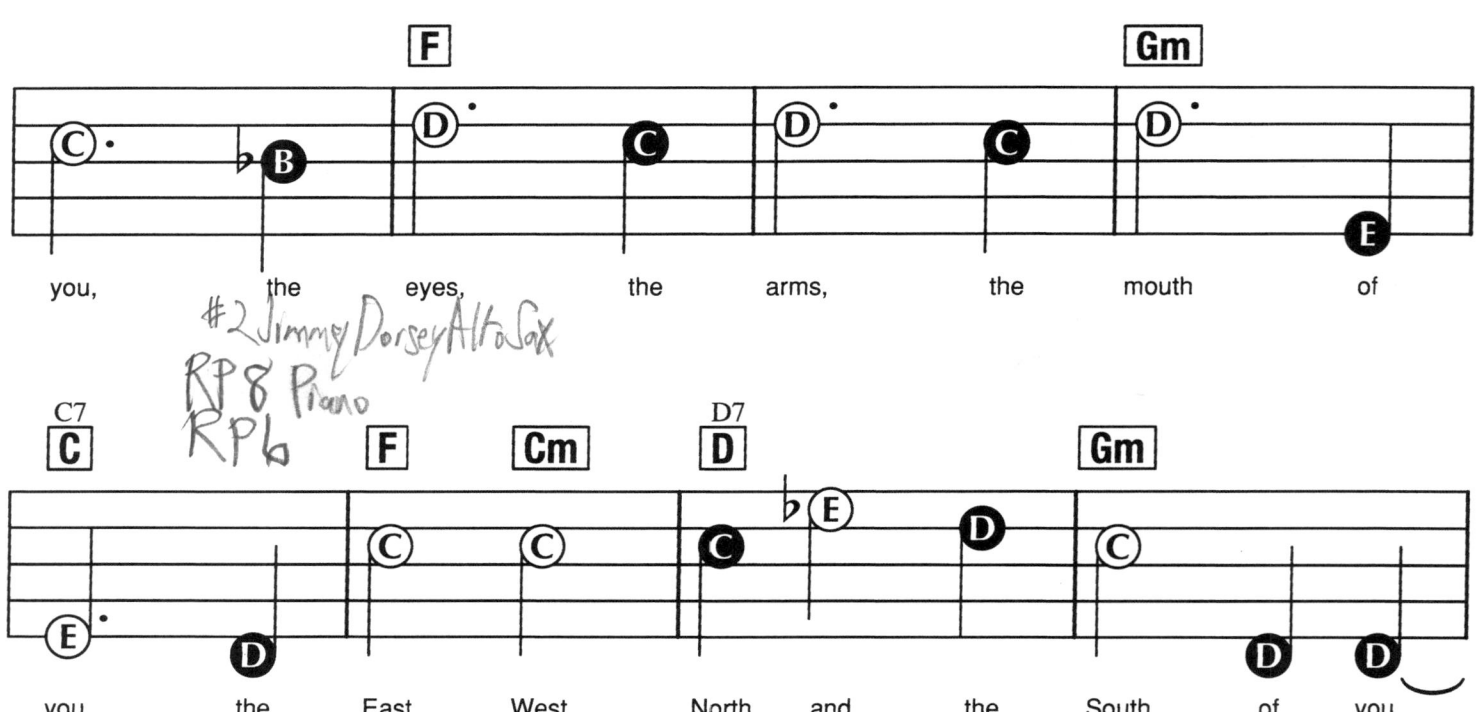

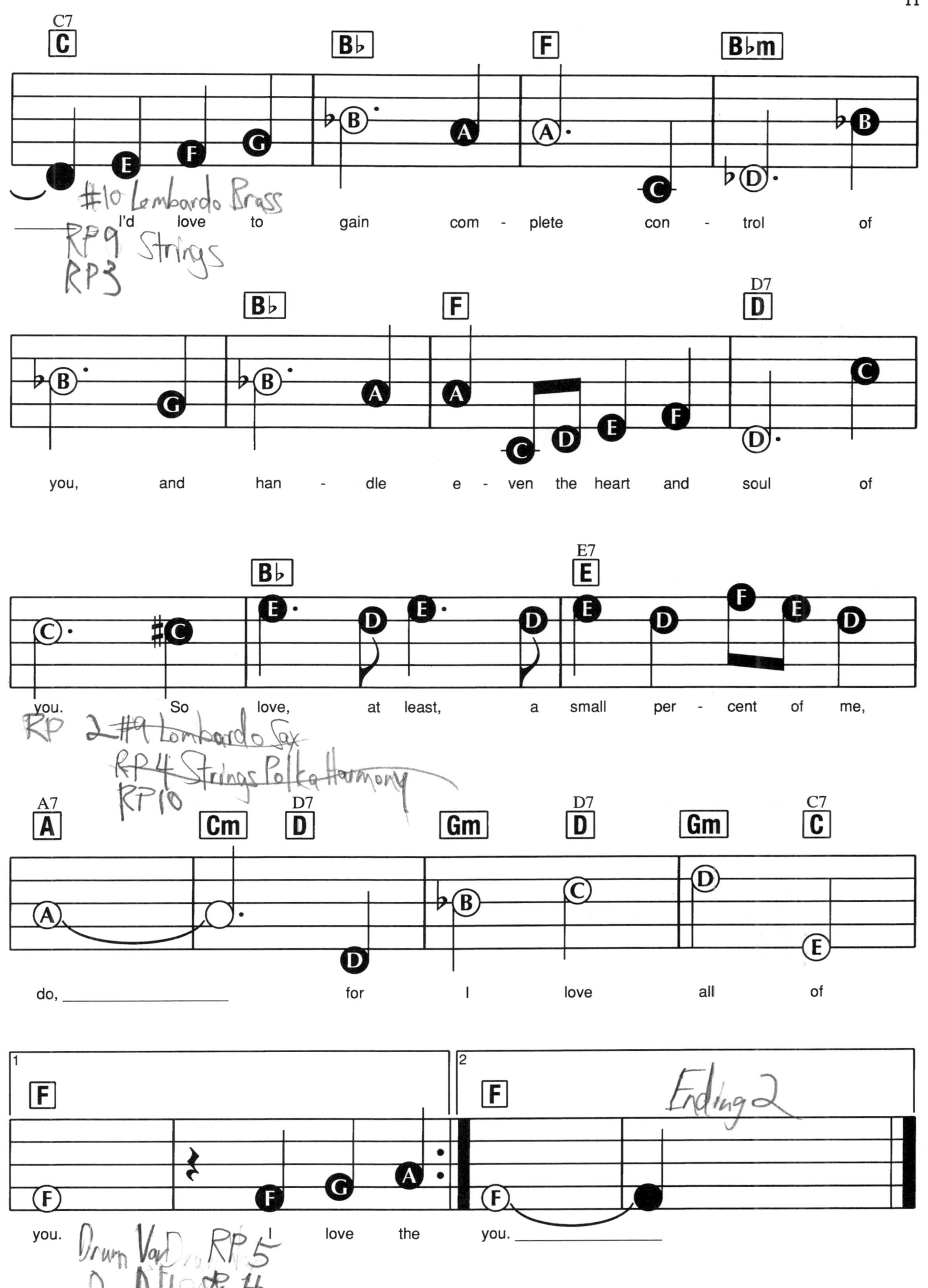

Almost Like Being in Love
from BRIGADOON

Registration 9
Rhythm: Swing

Words by Alan Jay Lerner
Music by Frederick Loewe

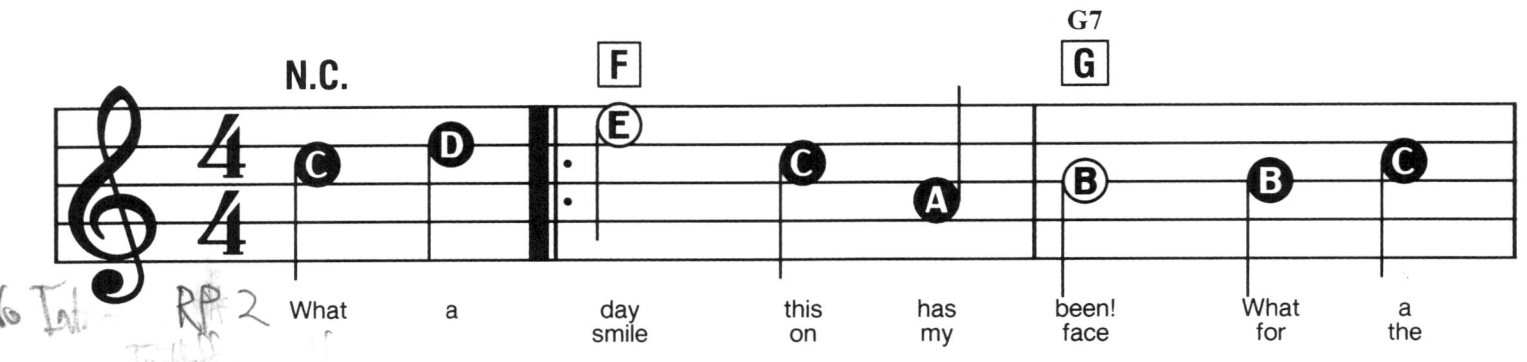

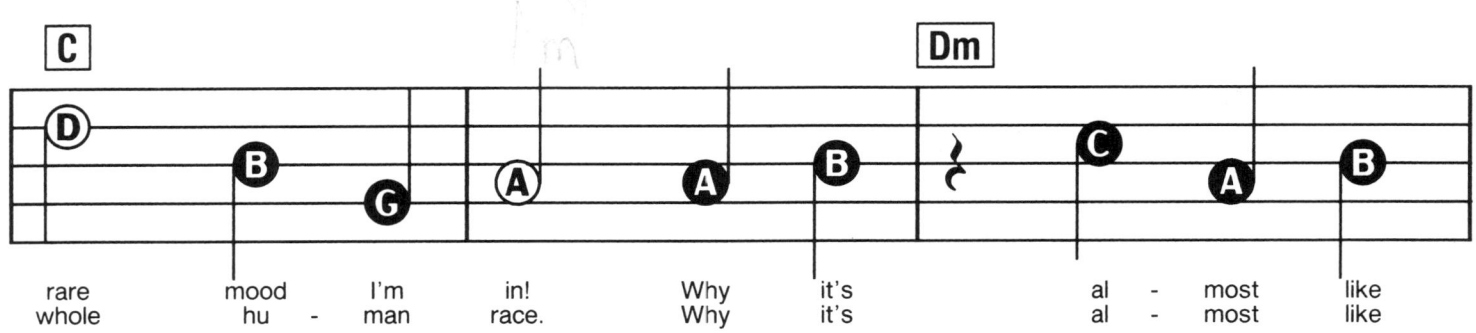

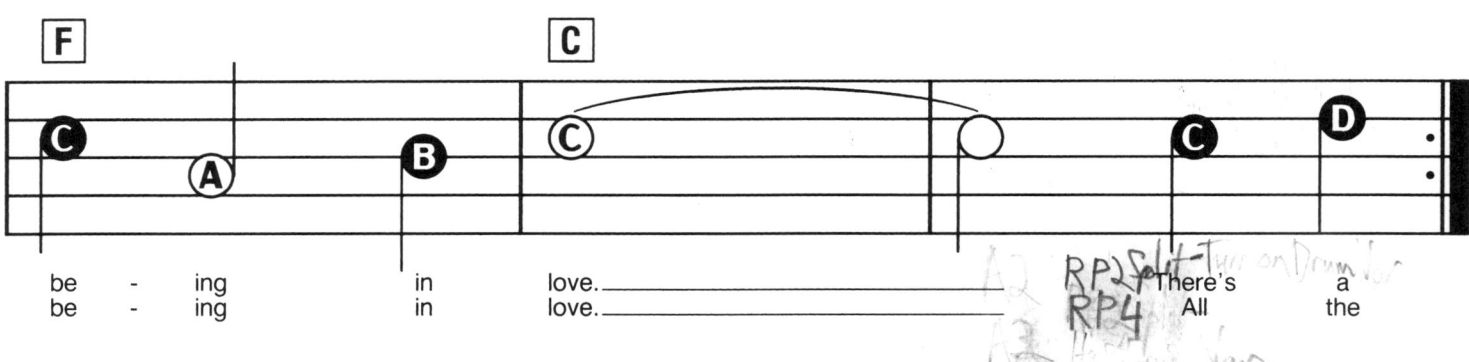

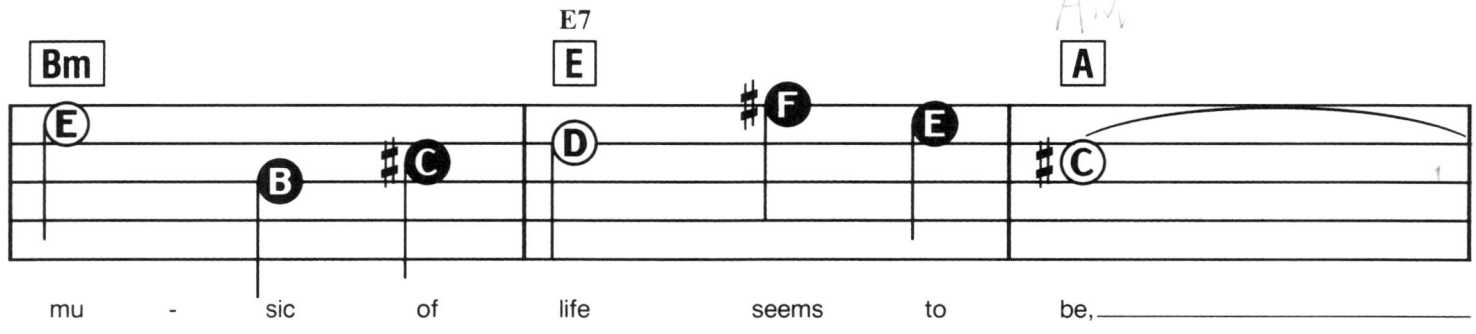

© 1947 (Renewed 1975) THE LERNER HEIRS PUBLISHING DESIGNEE and THE LOEWE FOUNDATION PUBLISHING DESIGNEE
All Rights Controlled and Administered by EMI APRIL MUSIC INC.
All Rights Reserved   International Copyright Secured   Used by Permission

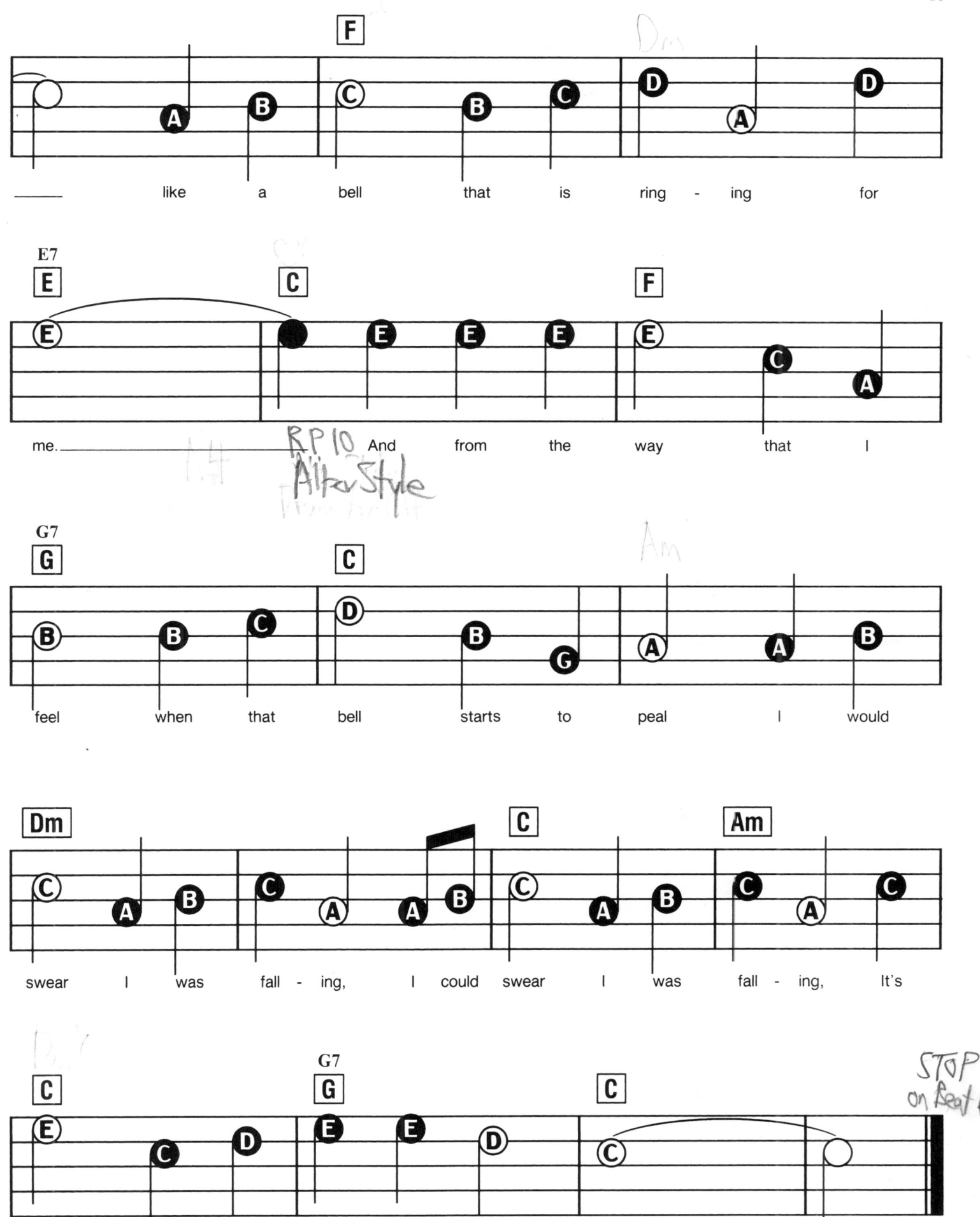

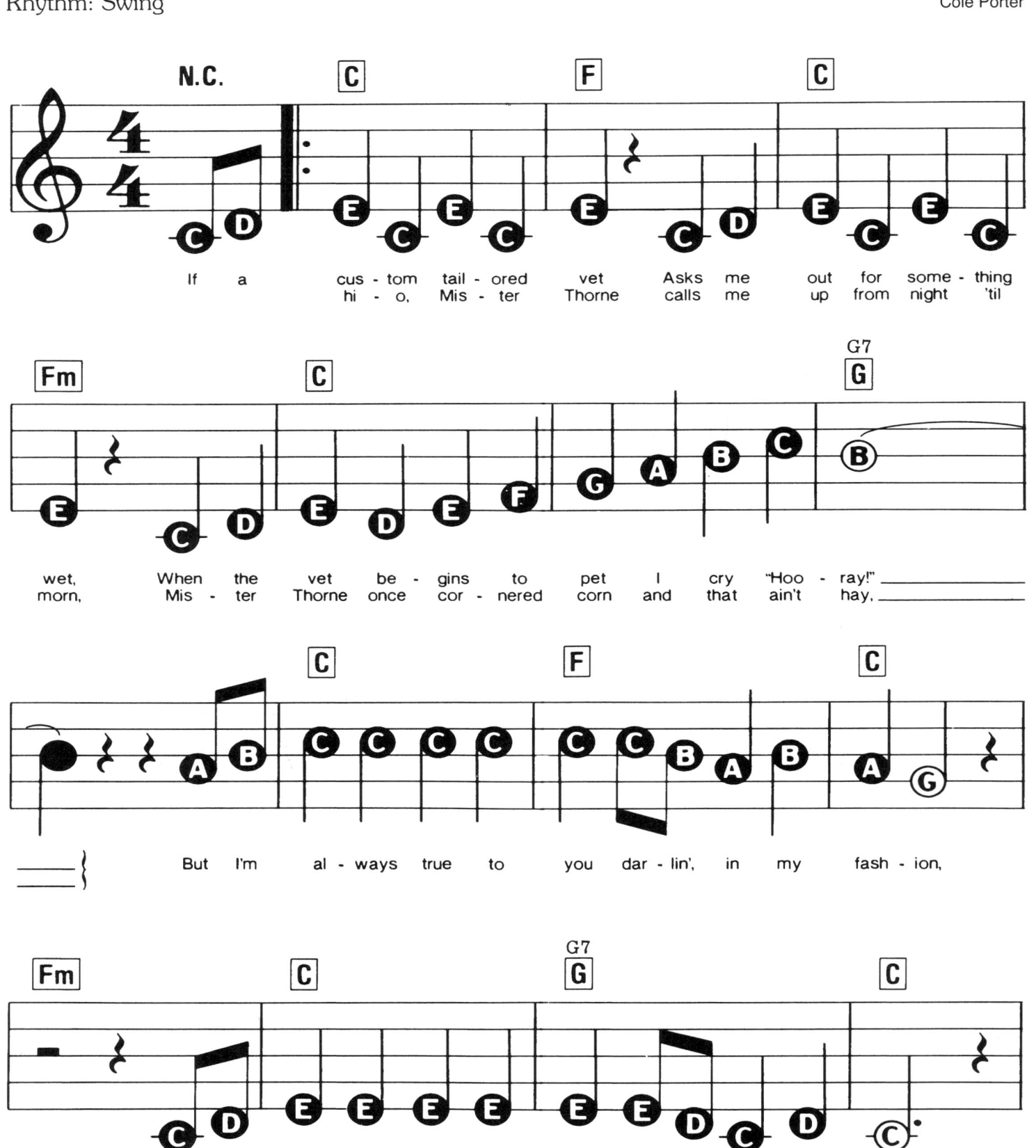

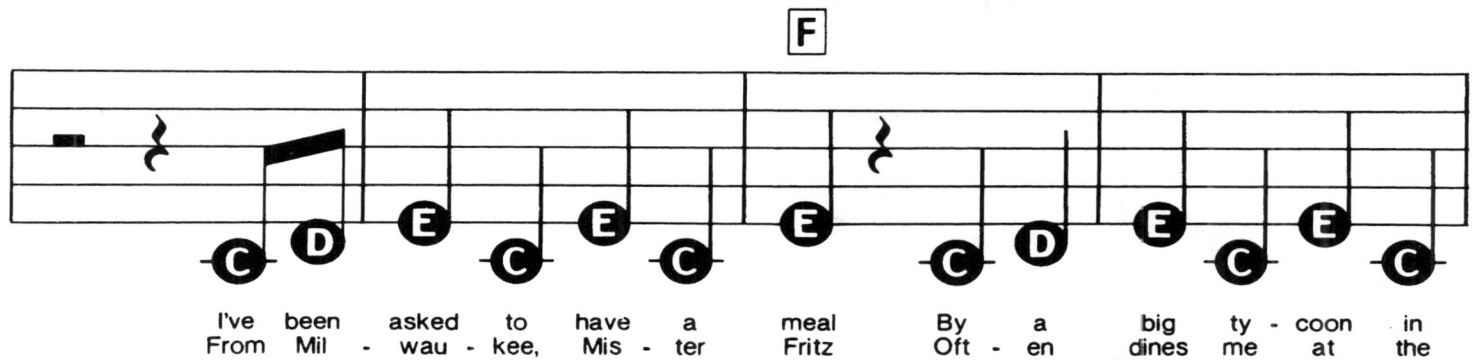
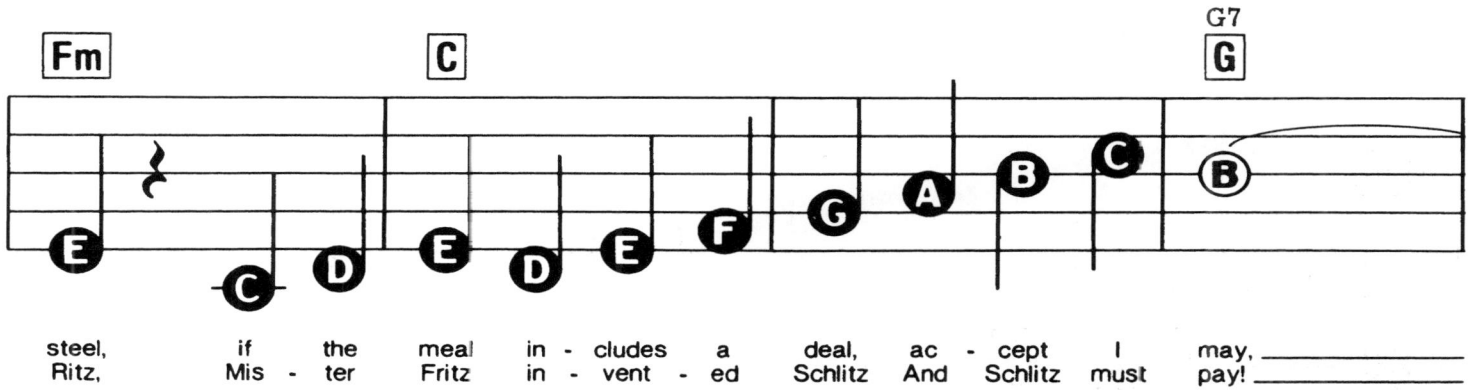
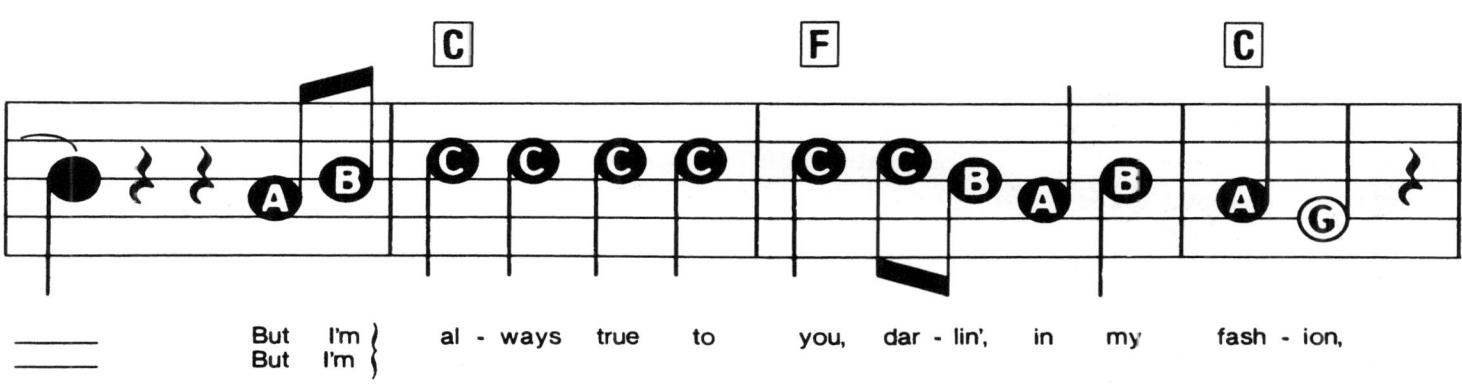
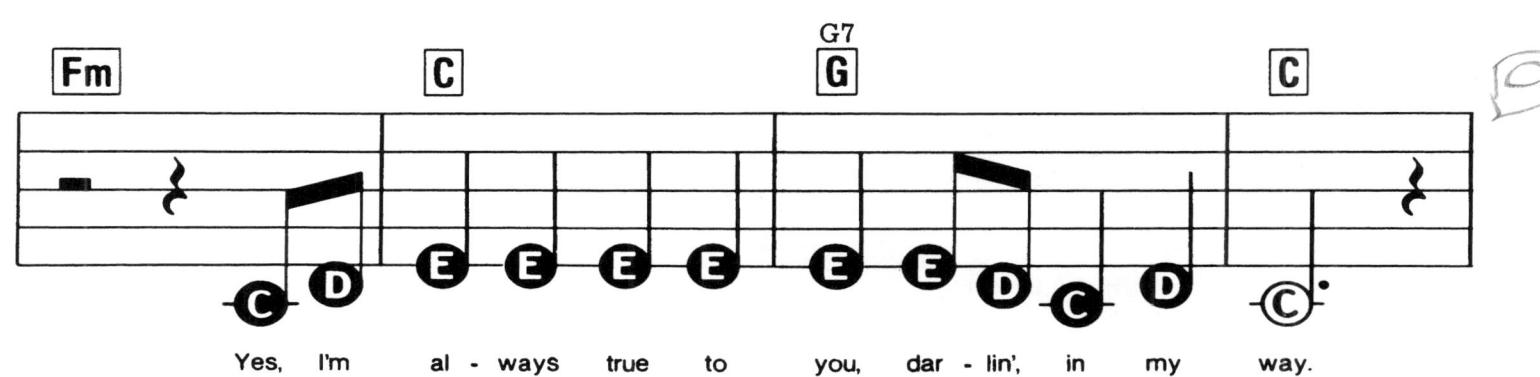

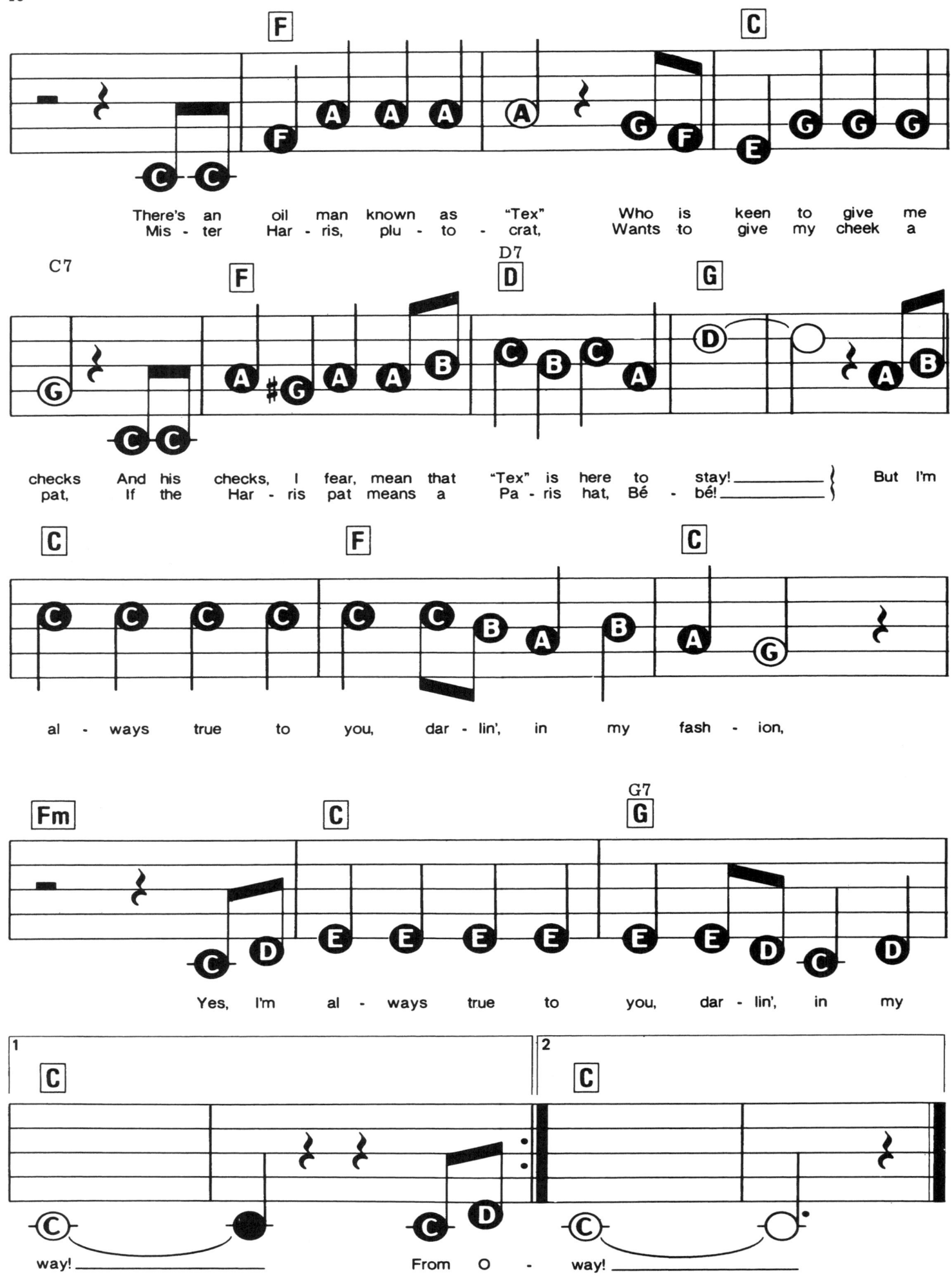

C-Jam Blues

Registration 2
Rhythm: Blues

By Duke Ellington

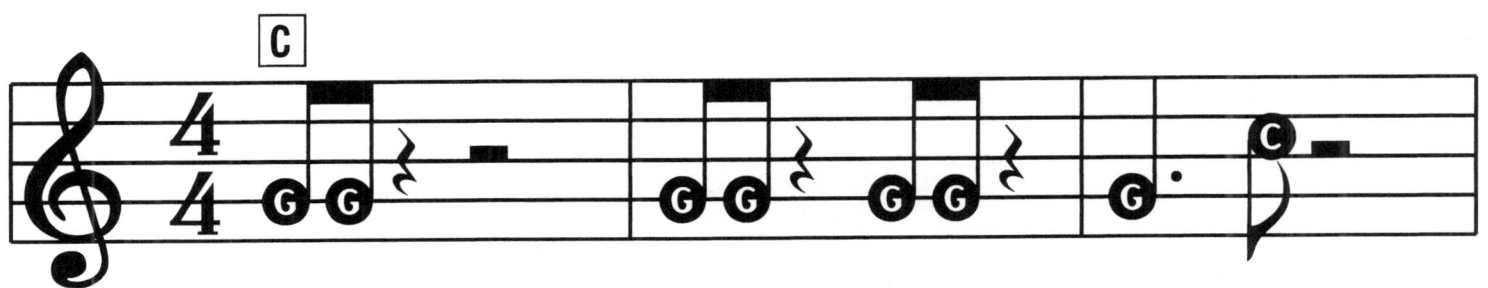
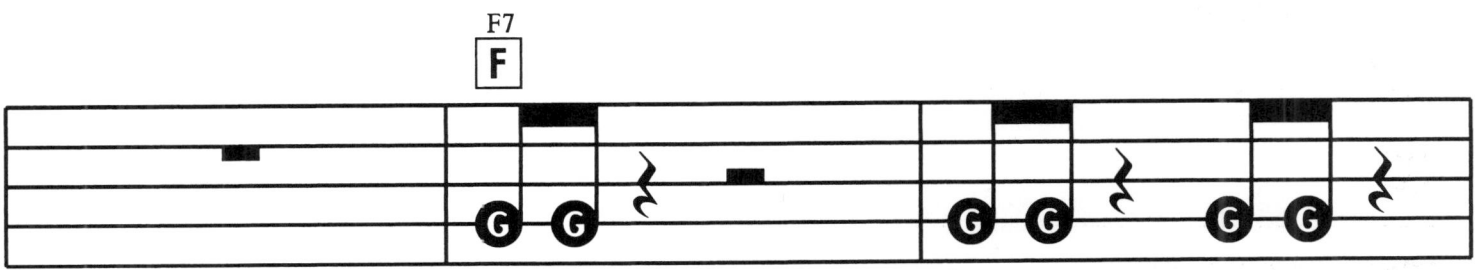
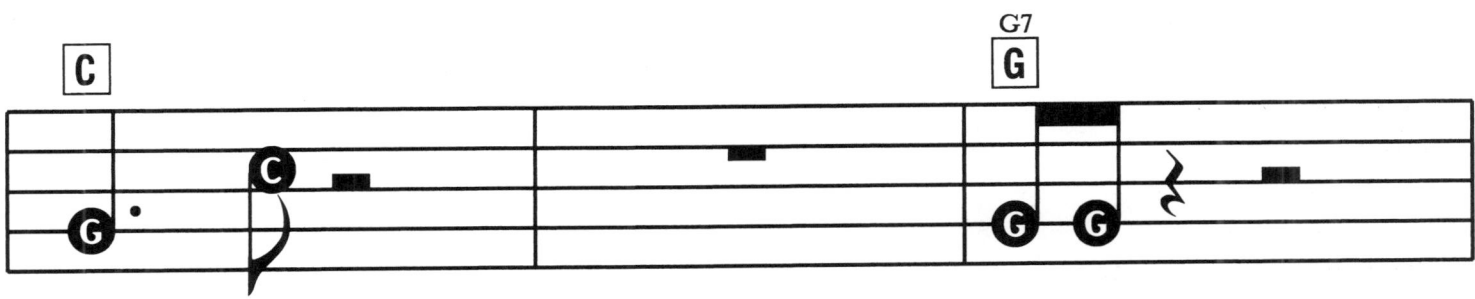
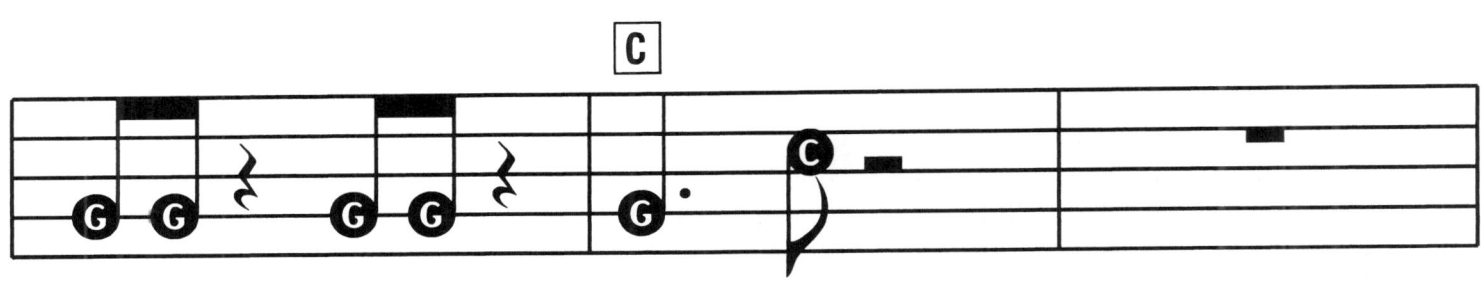

Copyright © 1942 Sony/ATV Music Publishing LLC in the U.S.A.
Copyright Renewed
All Rights Administered by Sony/ATV Music Publishing LLC, 8 Music Square West, Nashville, TN 37203
Rights for the world outside the U.S.A. Administered by EMI Robbins Catalog Inc. (Publishing) and Alfred Publishing Co., Inc. (Print)
International Copyright Secured   All Rights Reserved

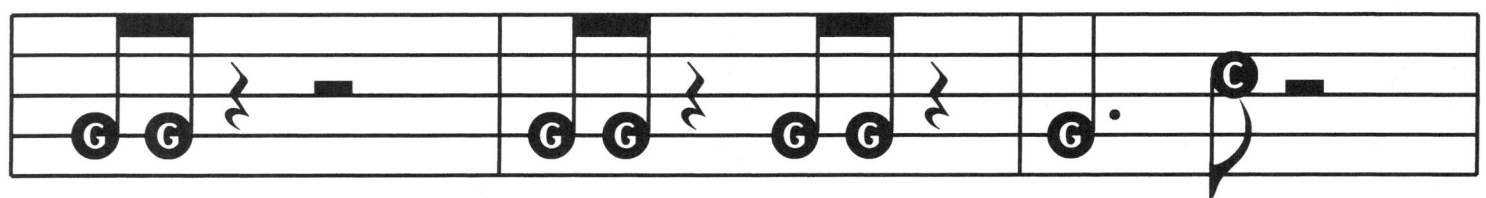
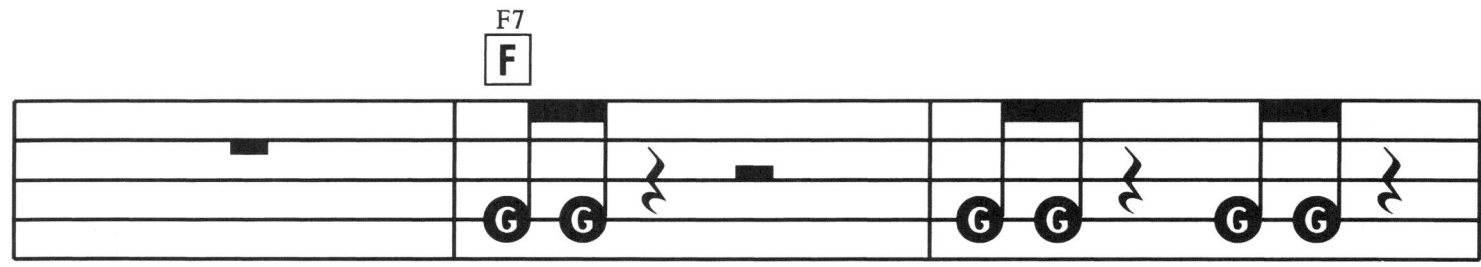
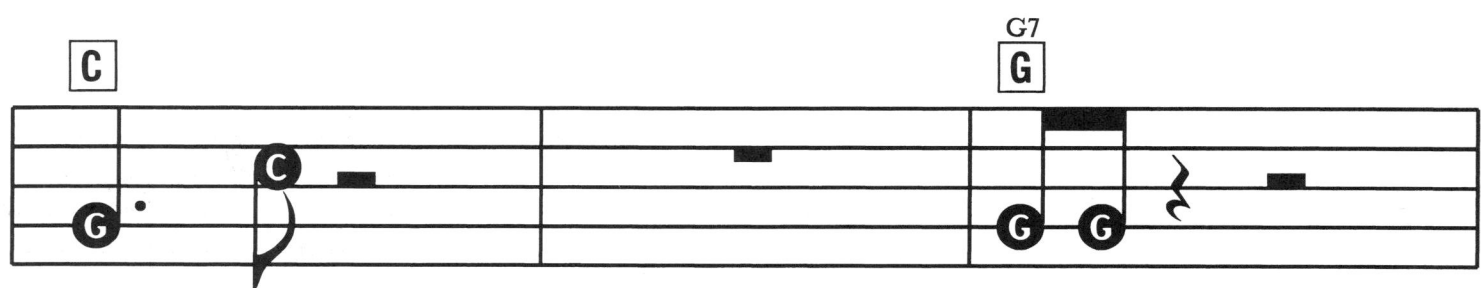
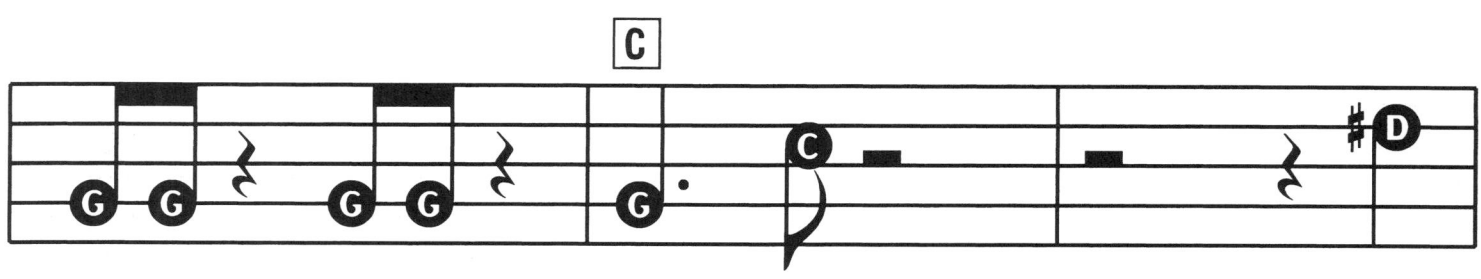
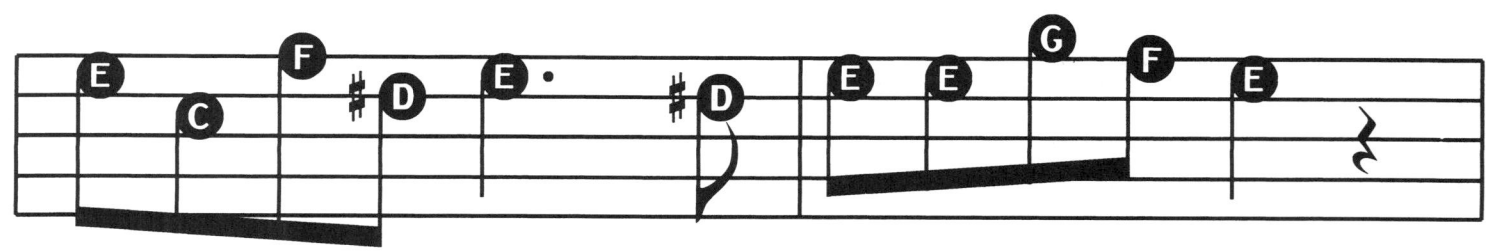

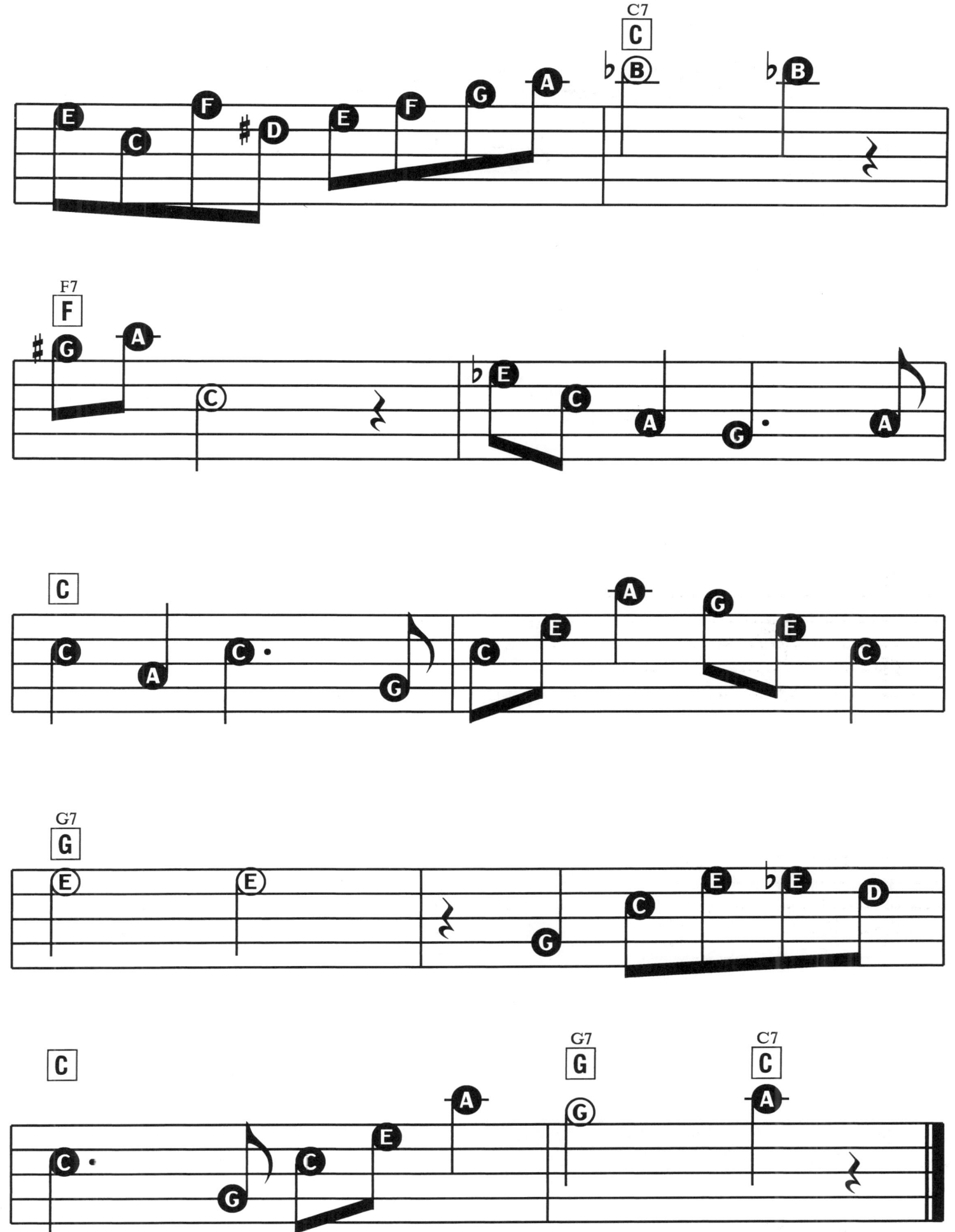

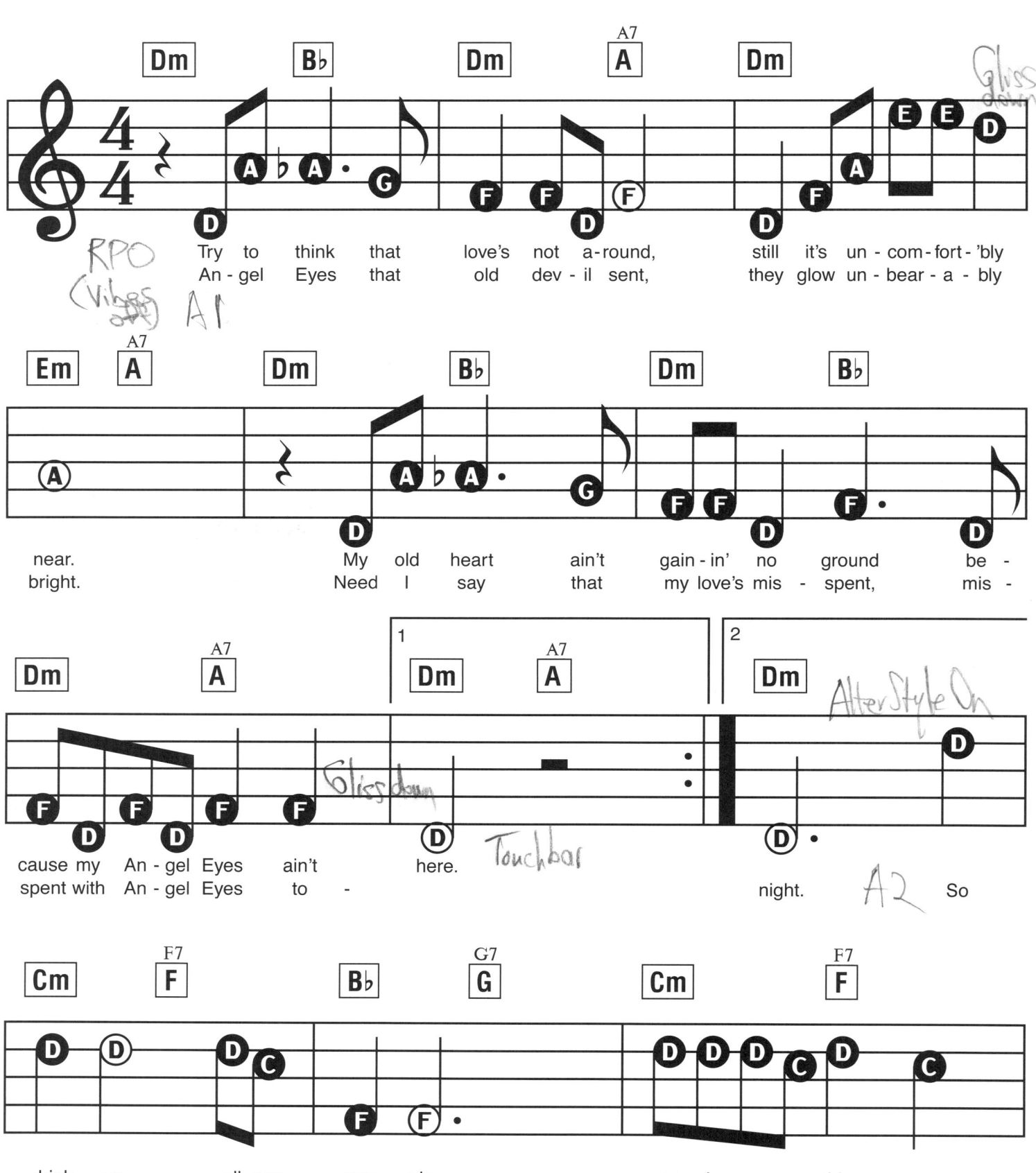

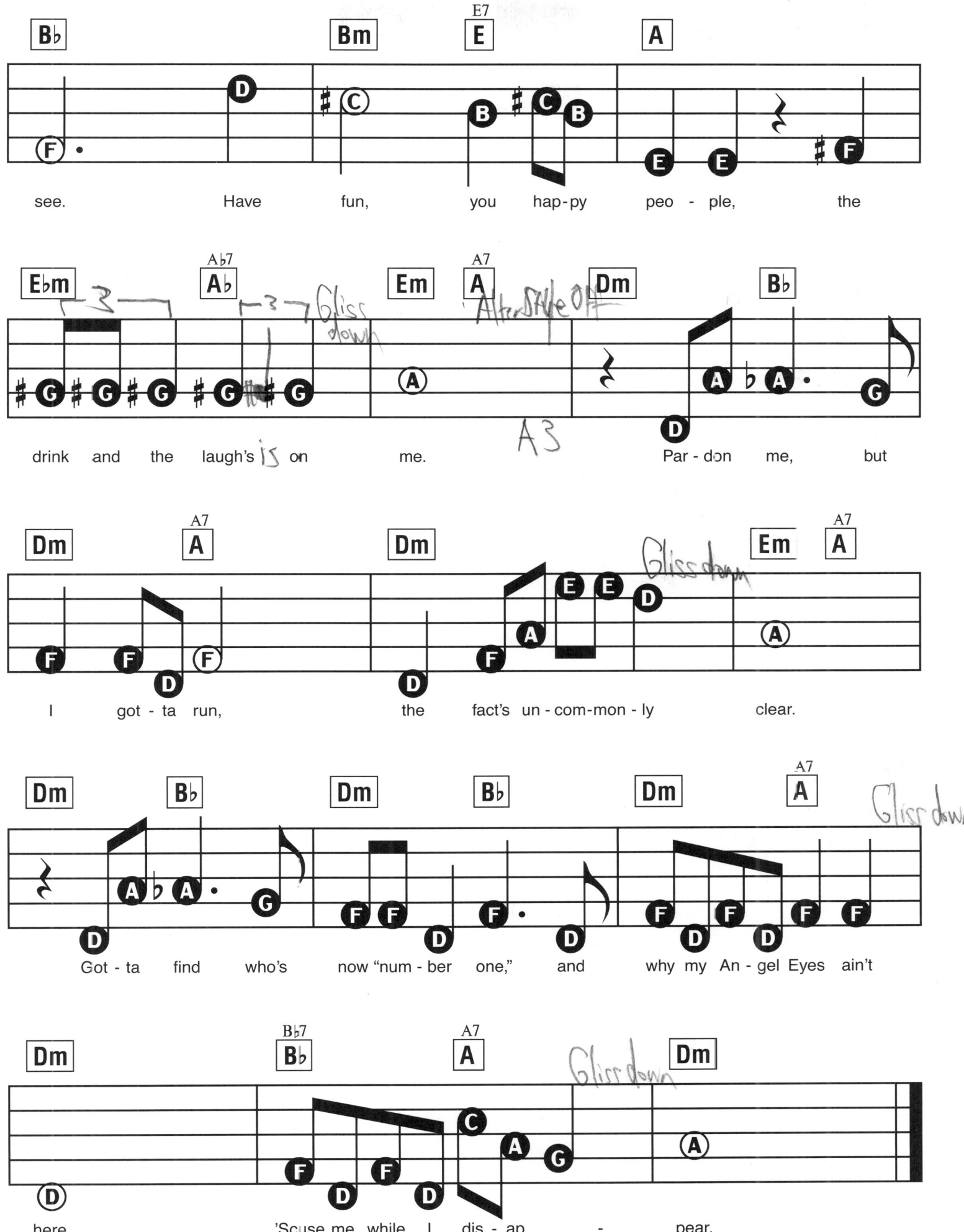

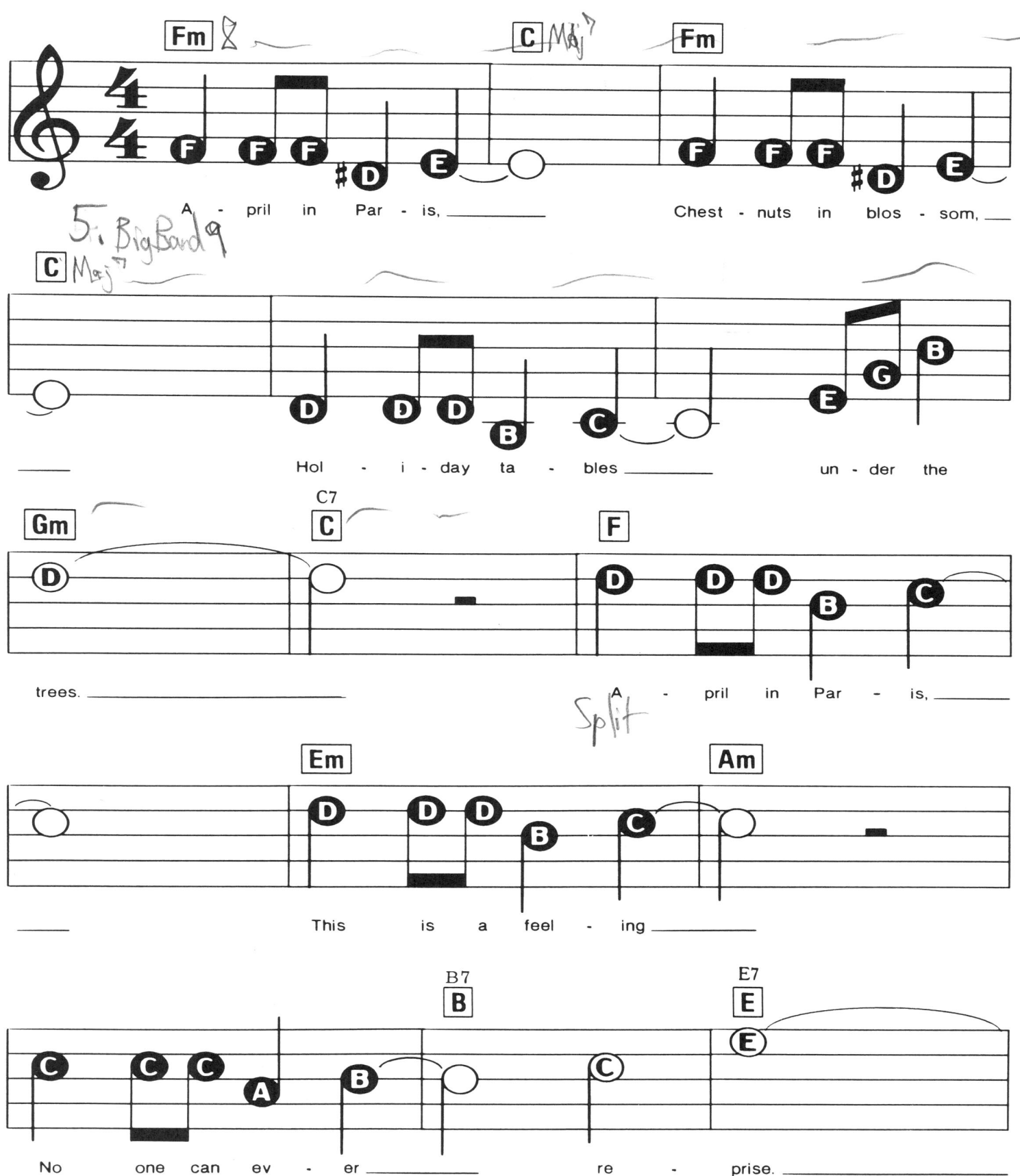

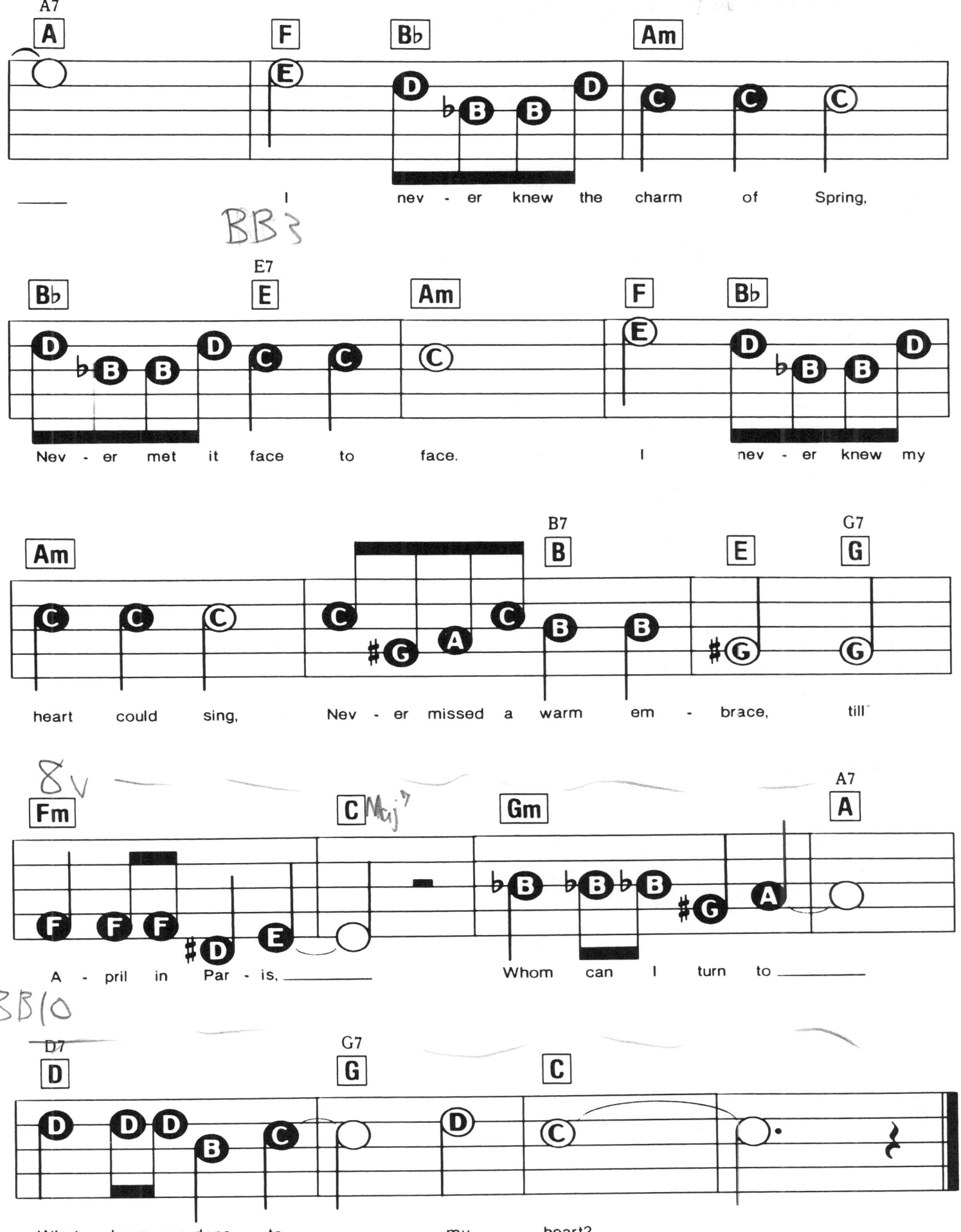

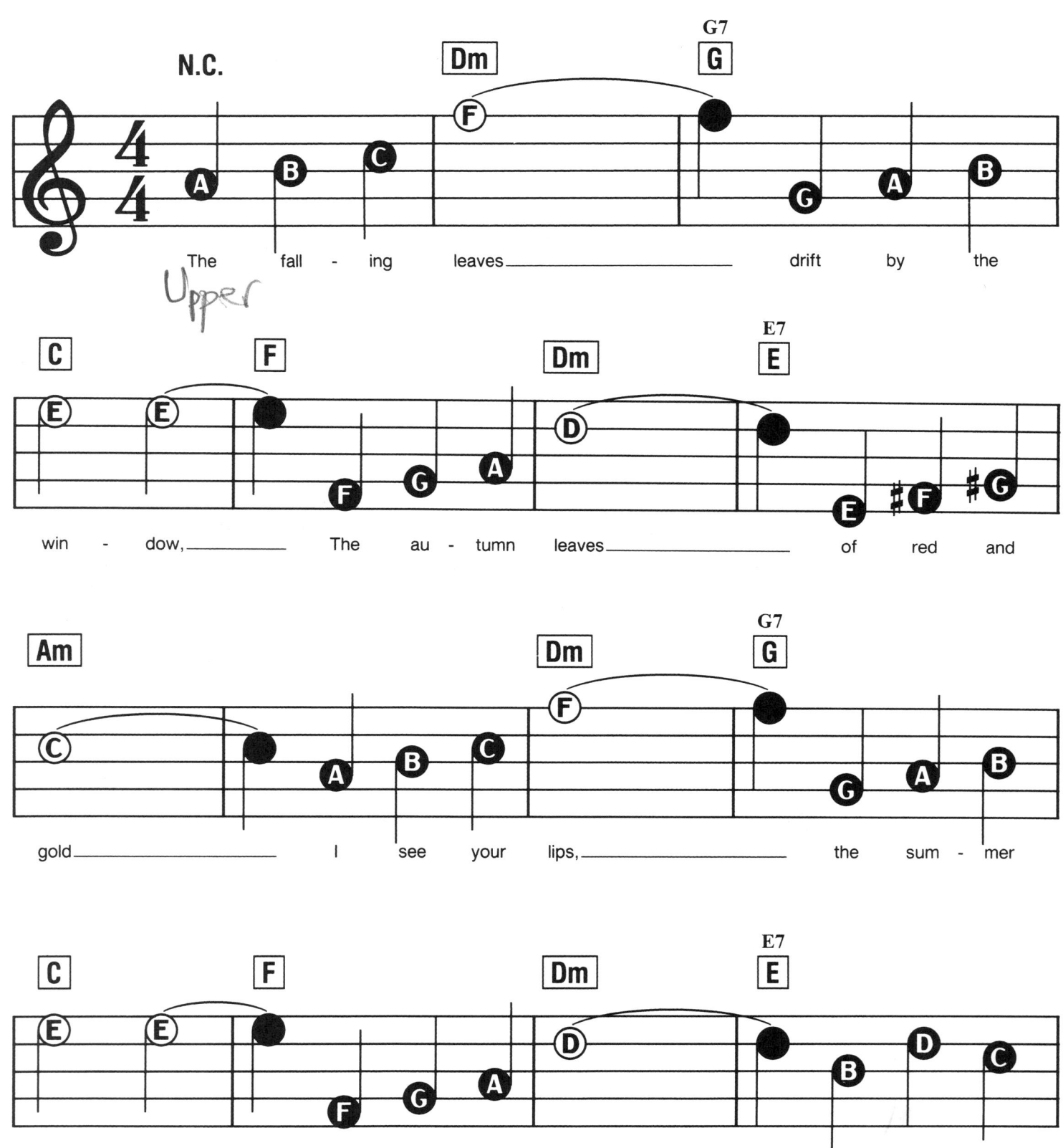

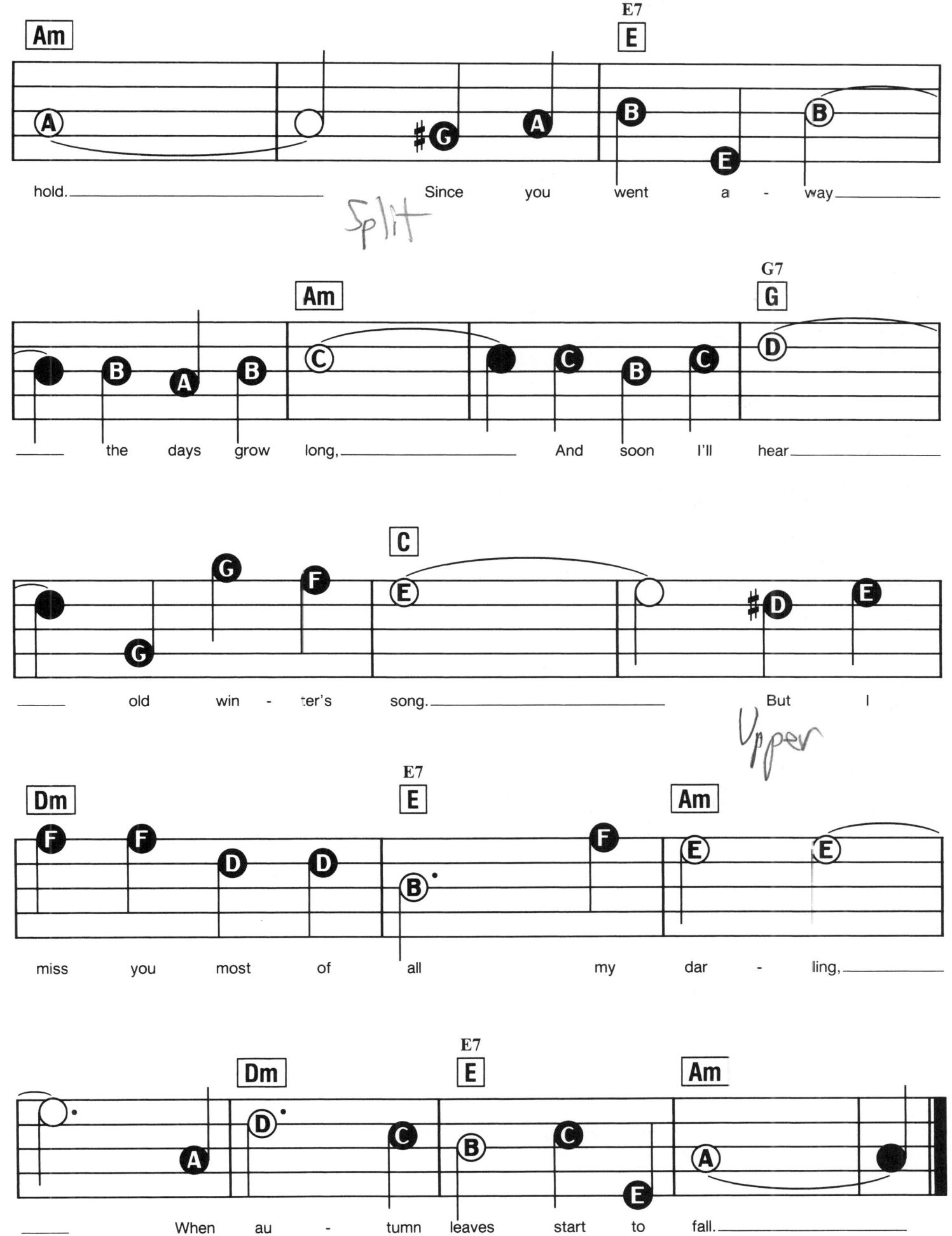

Bernie's Tune

Registration 8
Rhythm: Swing

By Bernie Miller

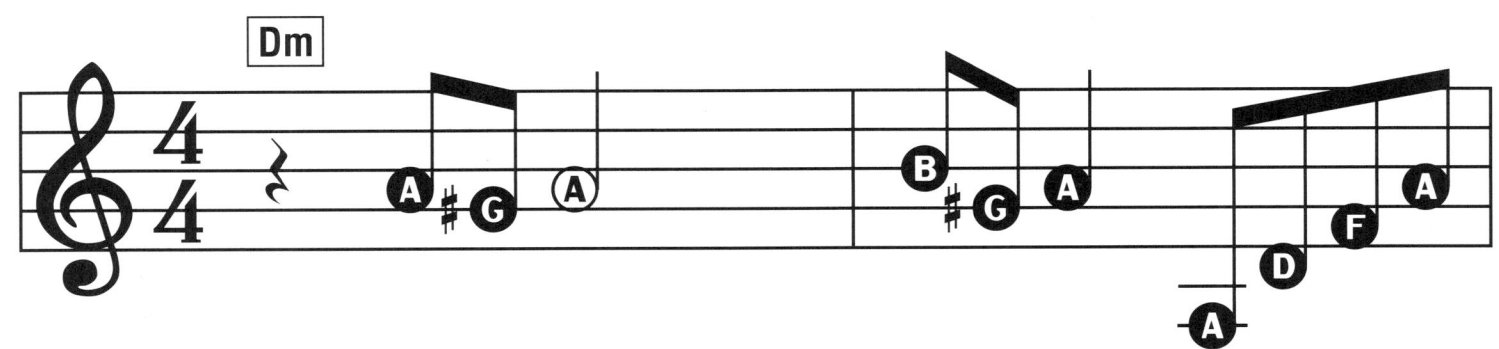
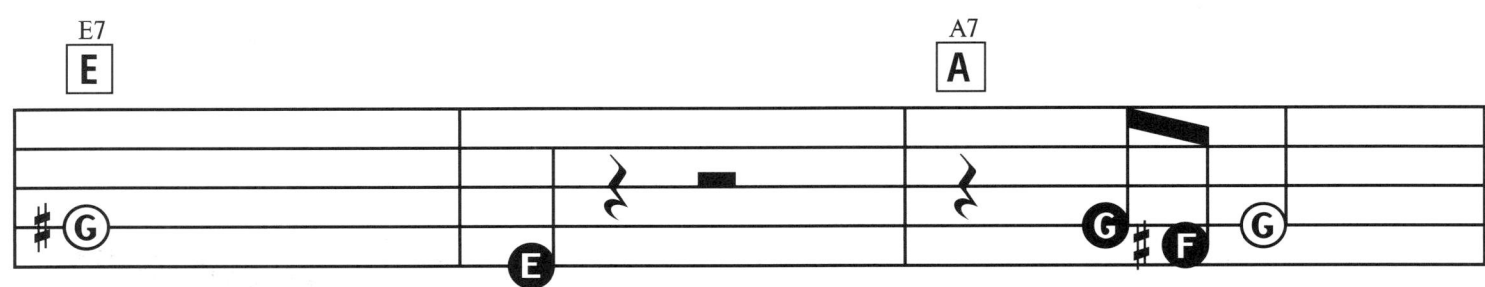
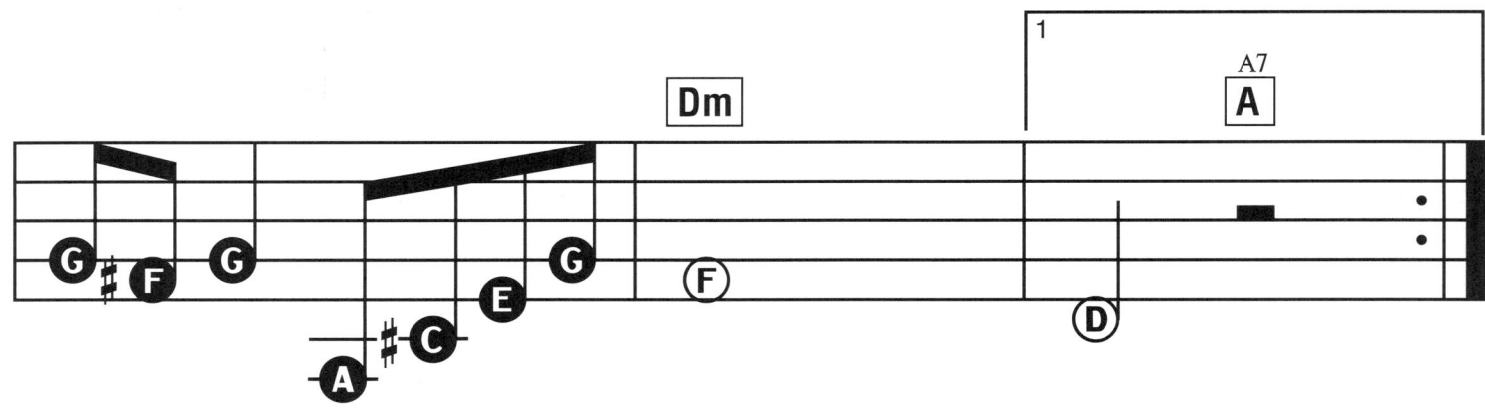
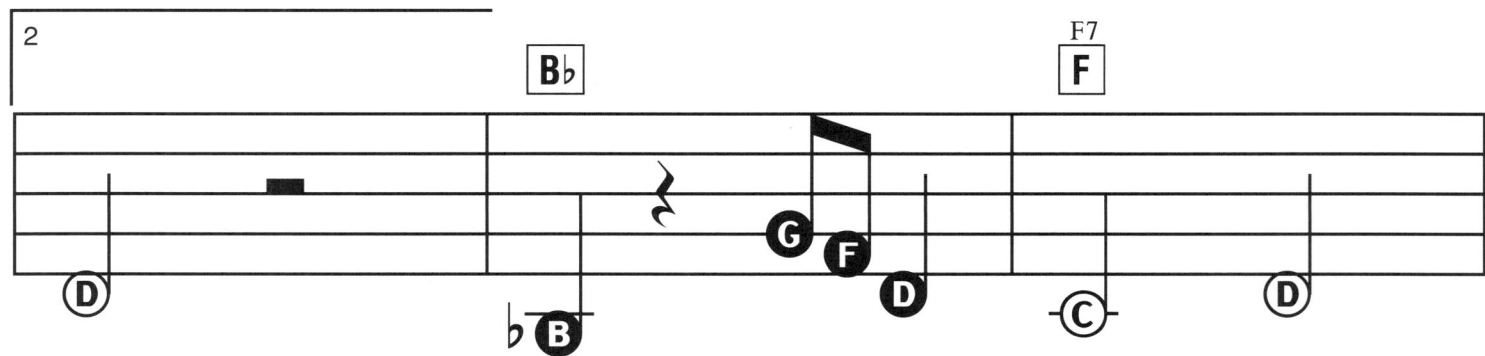

Copyright © 1953, 1954, 1955 (Renewed 1981, 1982, 1983) Atlantic Music Corp.
International Copyright Secured   All Rights Reserved

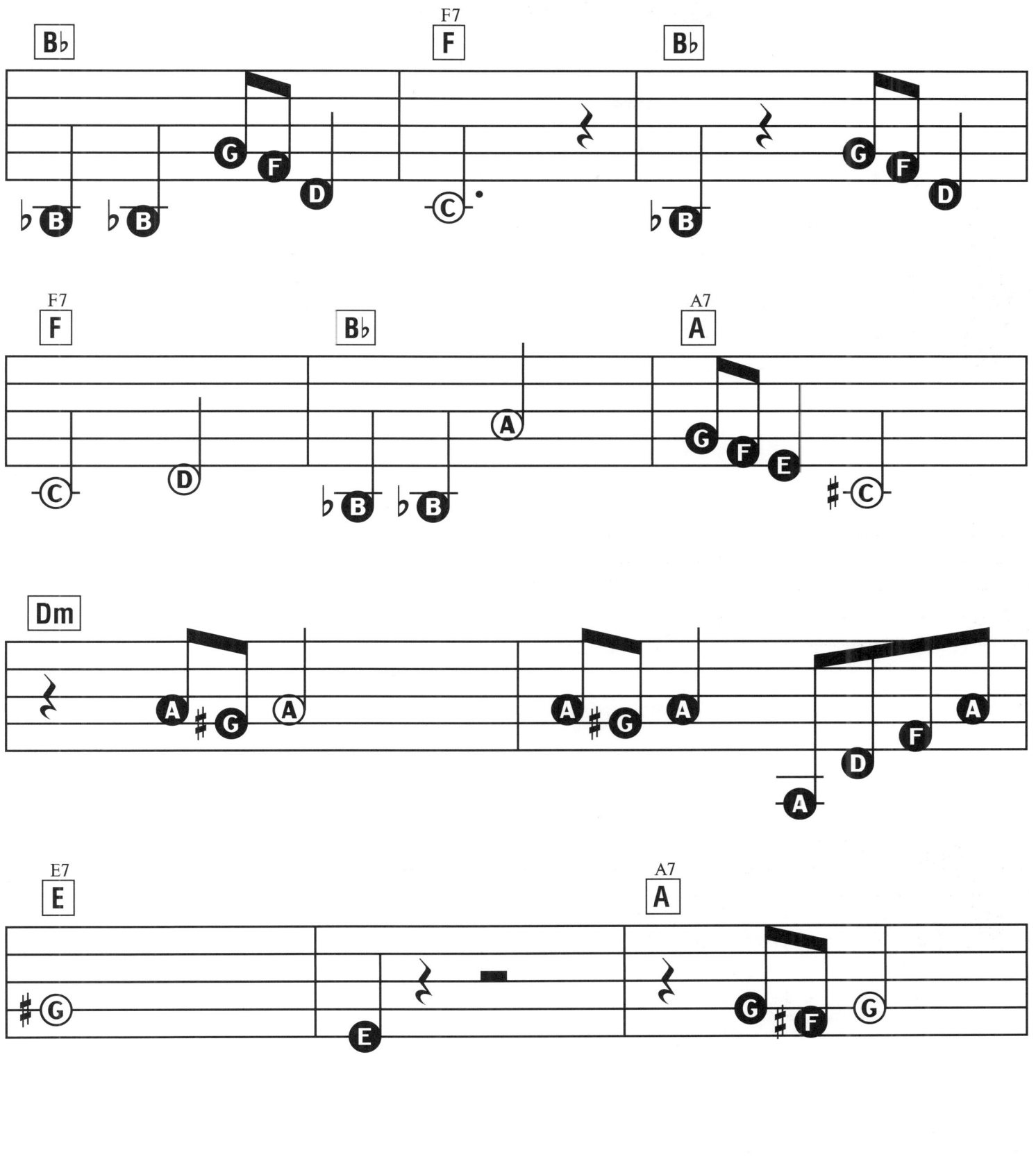

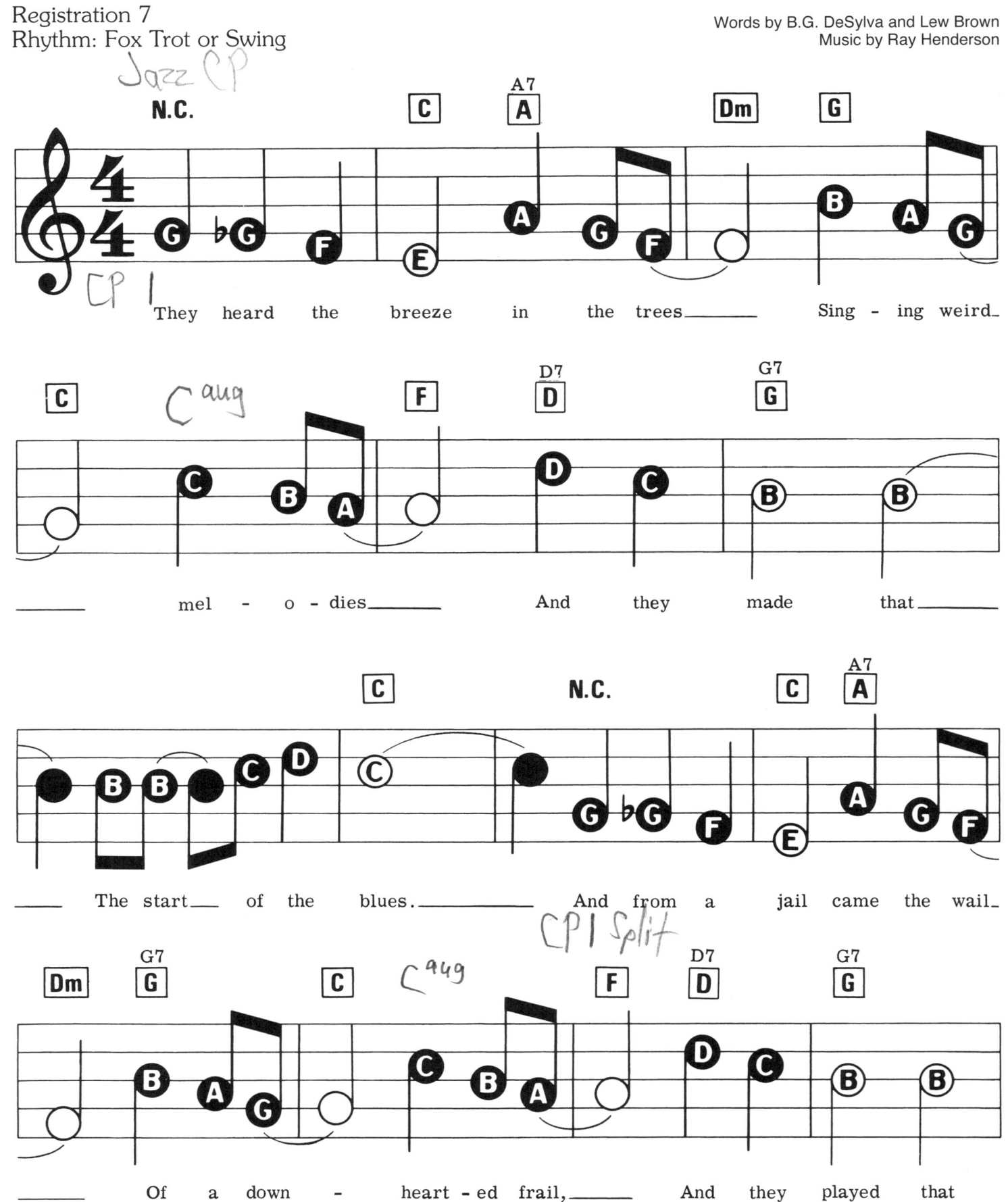

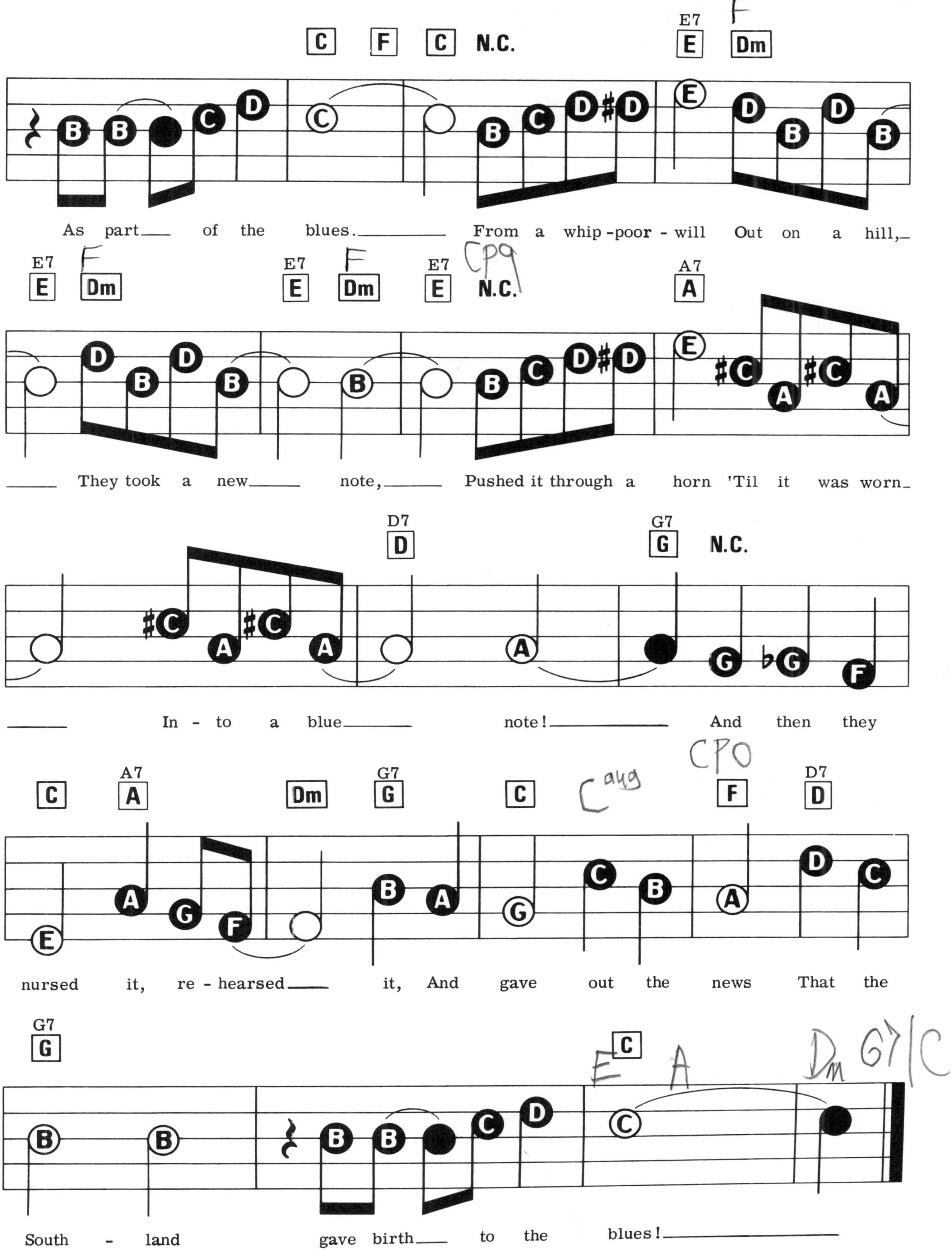
As part of the blues. From a whip-poor-will Out on a hill,
They took a new note, Pushed it through a horn 'Til it was worn
Into a blue note! And then they
nursed it, re-hearsed it, And gave out the news That the
South-land gave birth to the blues!

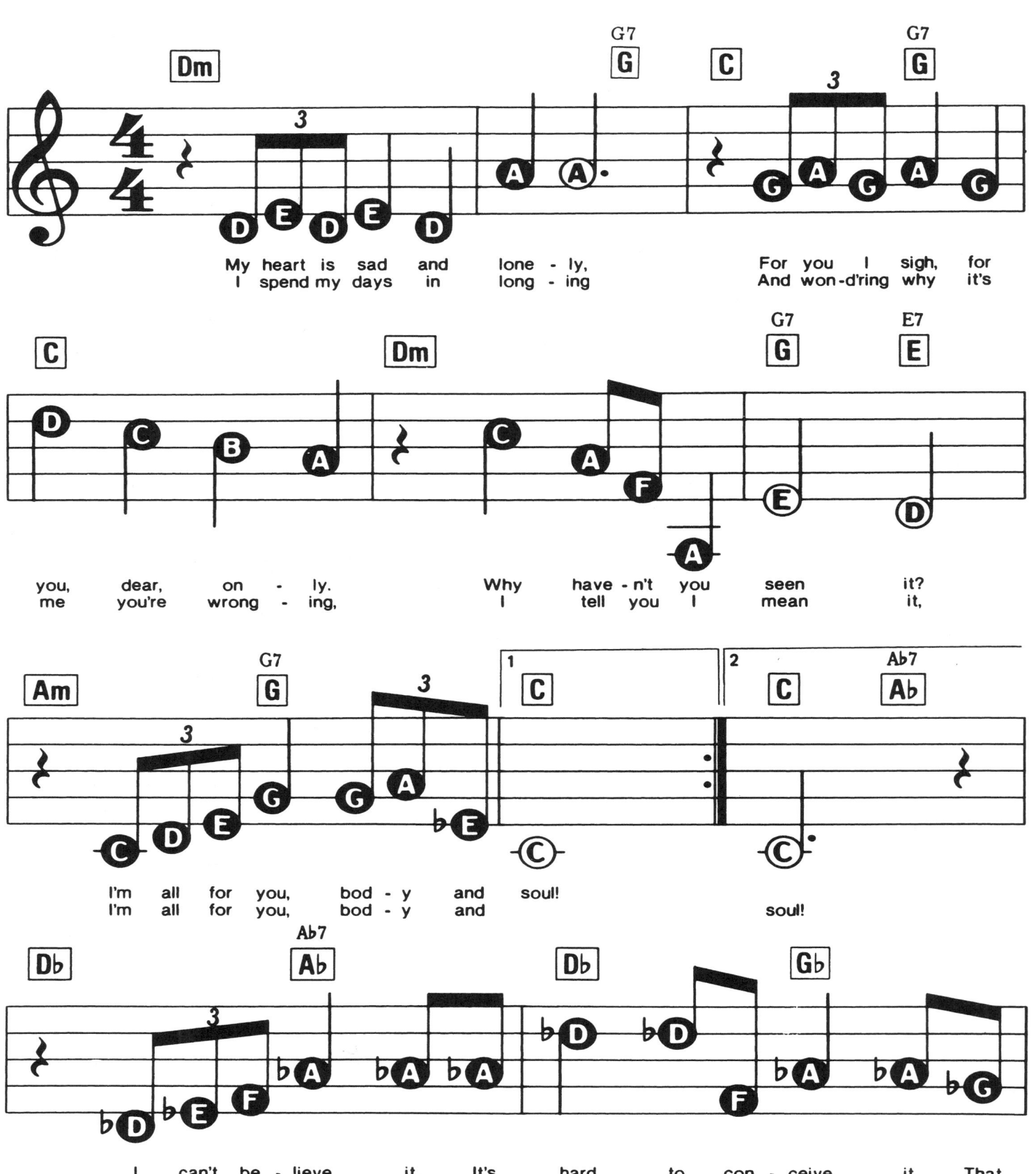

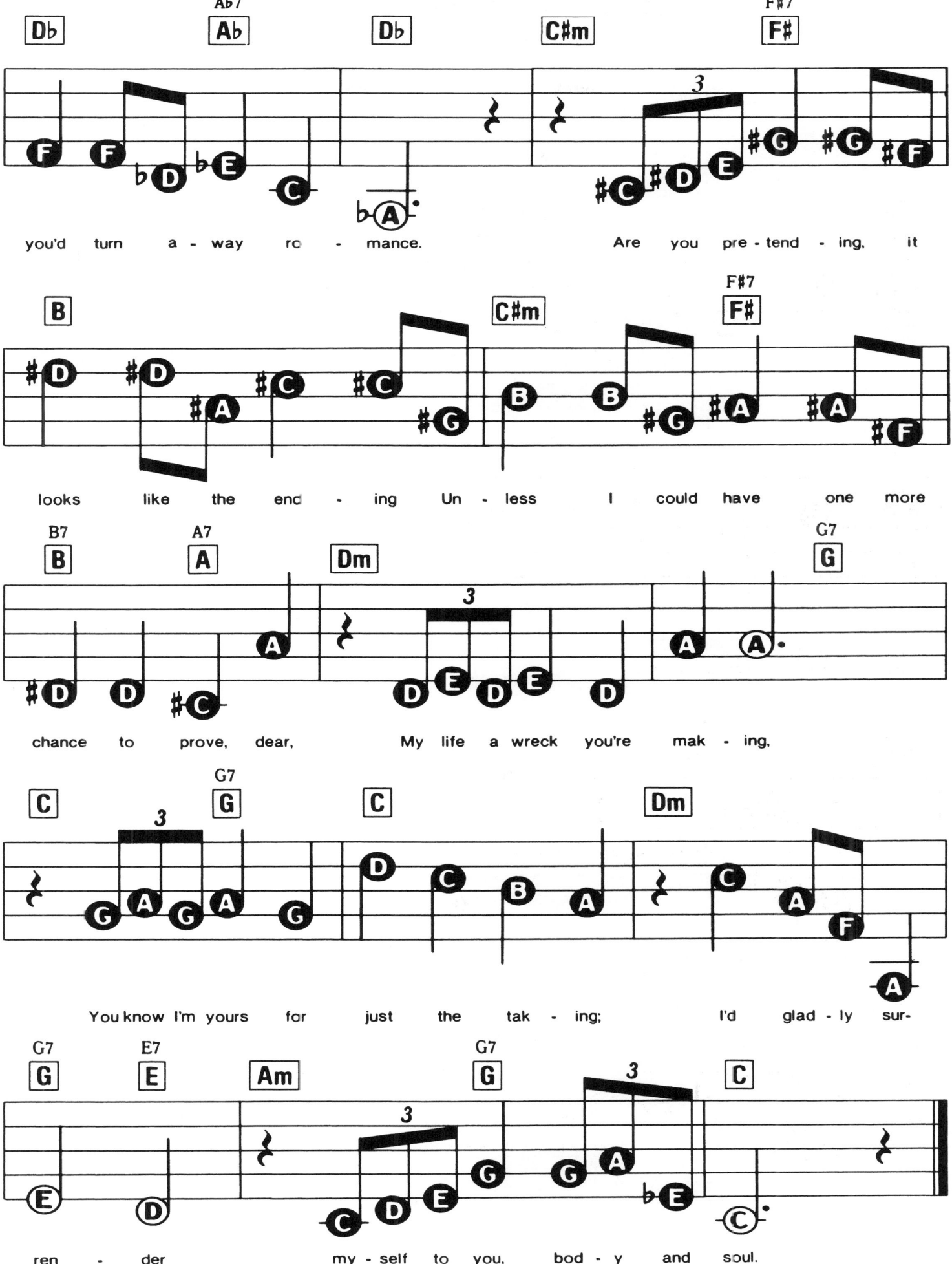

32

Caravan
from SOPHISTICATED LADIES

Registration 7
Rhythm: Ballad or Fox Trot

Words and Music by Duke Ellington,
Irving Mills and Juan Tizol

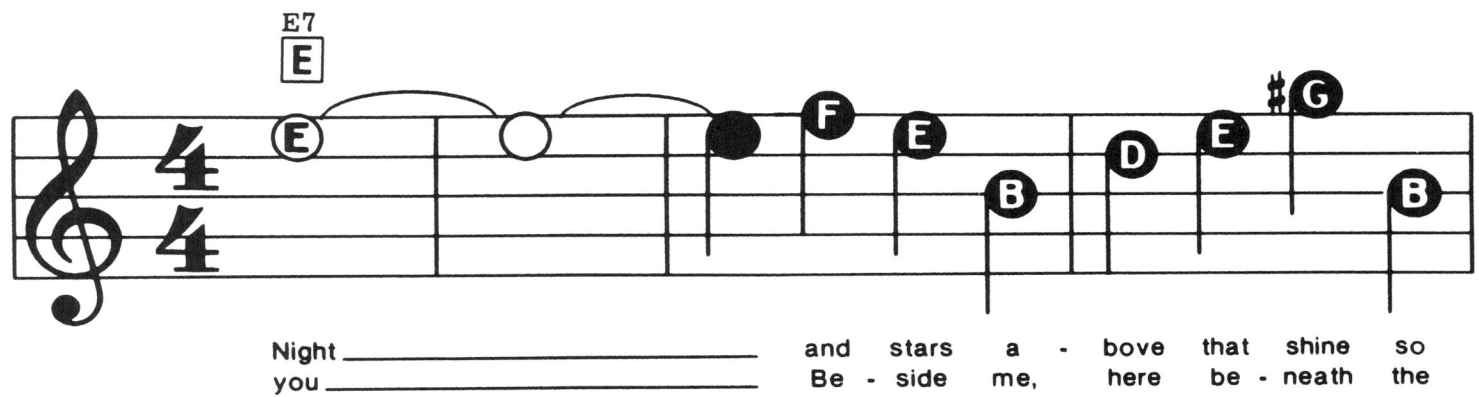

Night _____ and stars a - bove that shine so
you _____ Be - side me, here be - neath the

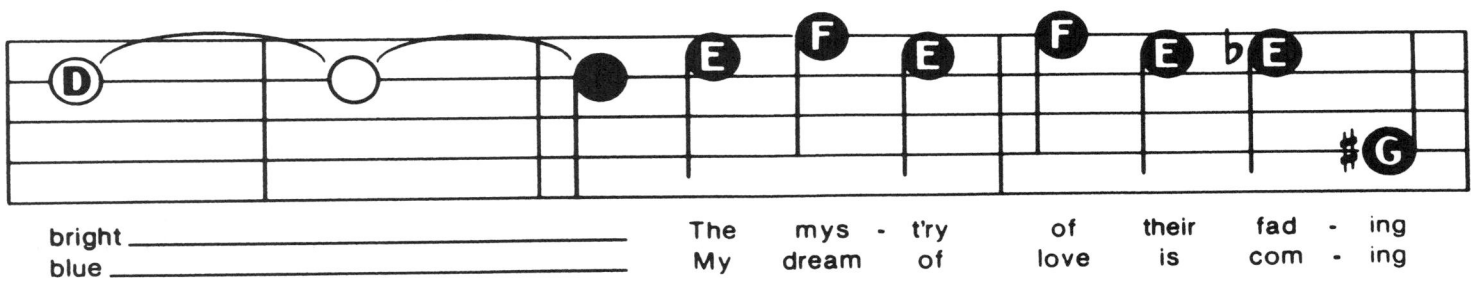

bright _____ The mys - t'ry of their fad - ing
blue _____ My dream of love is com - ing

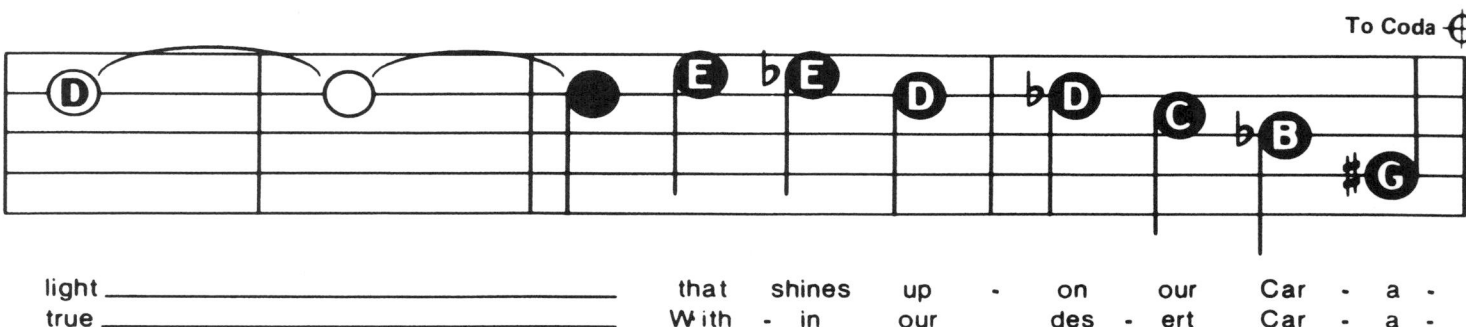

light _____ that shines up - on our Car - a -
true _____ With - in our des - ert Car - a -

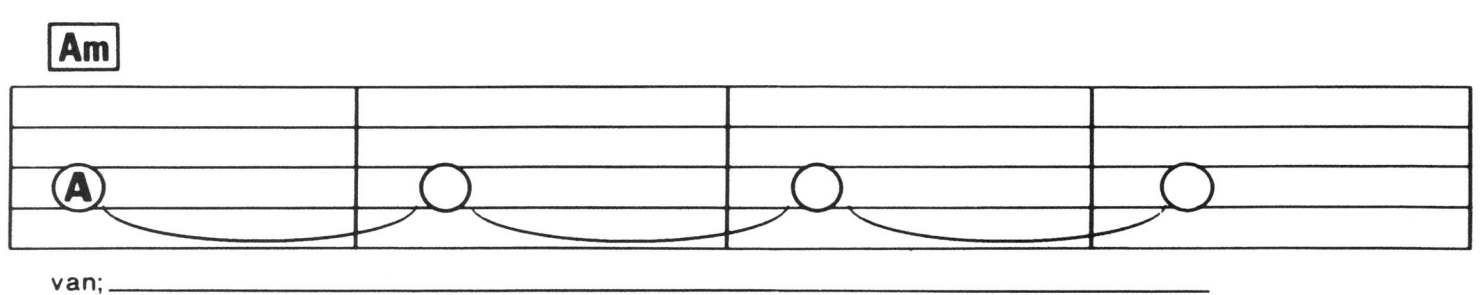

van; _____

Copyright © 1937 Sony/ATV Music Publishing LLC and EMI Mills Music Inc. in the U.S.A.
Copyright Renewed
All Rights on behalf of Sony/ATV Music Publishing LLC Administered by Sony/ATV Music Publishing LLC, 8 Music Square West, Nashville, TN 37203
Rights for the world outside the U.S.A. Administered by EMI Mills Music Inc. (Publishing) and Alfred Publishing Co., Inc. (Print)
International Copyright Secured   All Rights Reserved

340 Jazz

ss Duke Ellington
ss   C-Jam Blues   17
       Caravan   32
       Prelude to a Kiss   40
ss   Don't Get Around Much   52
      I Ain't Got Nothin But the Blues   88

They Didn't Believe Me
Heart Songs 120
2 8' celeste duet
            duet
             Swinging tune
          one voice soft
             swinging feel

100 & Yet it Bad
110 Ain't Just a Lucky
129 On a mellow Tone
146 Just Squeeze me
200 Rockin in Rhythm
217 Solitude

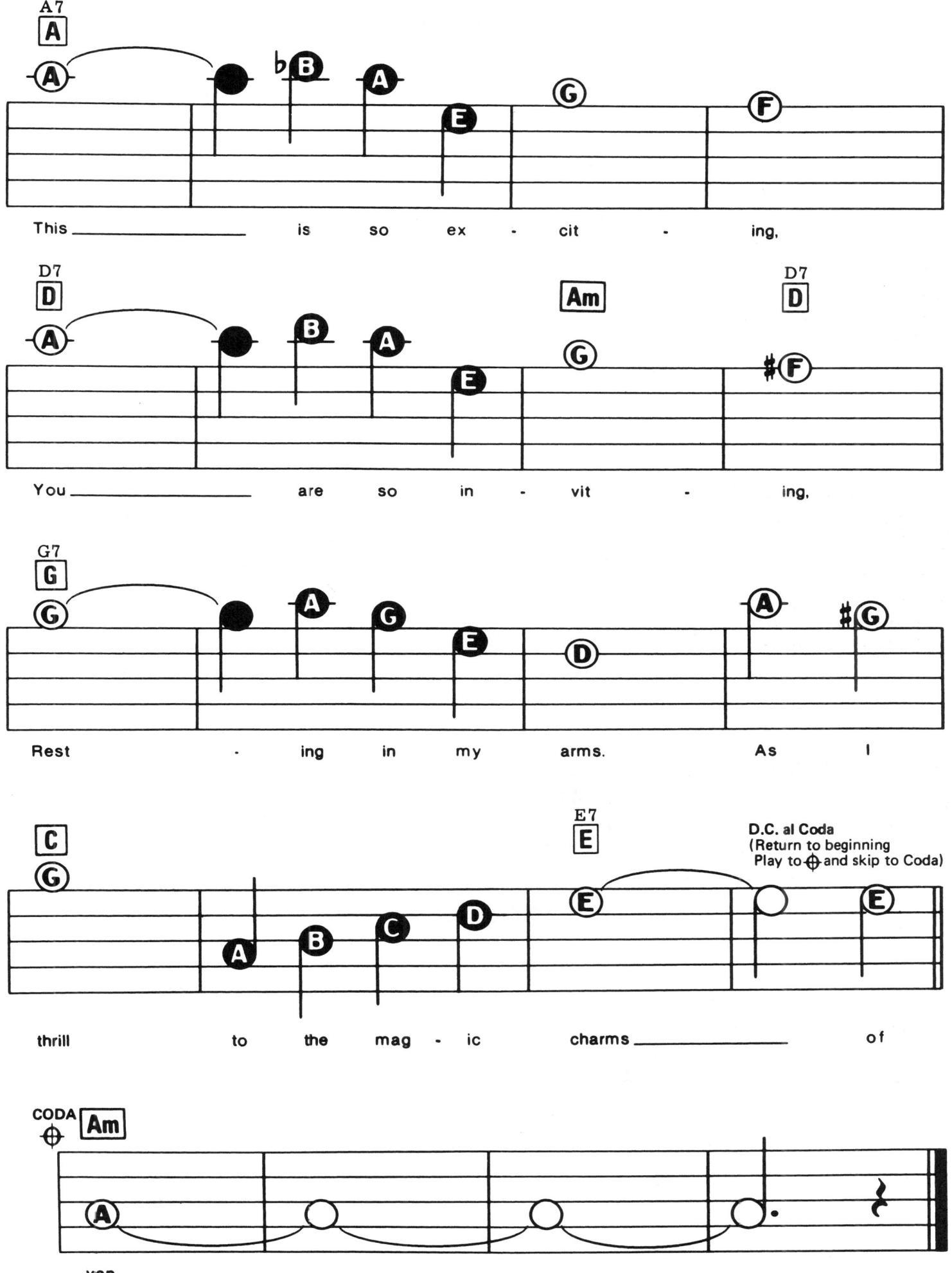

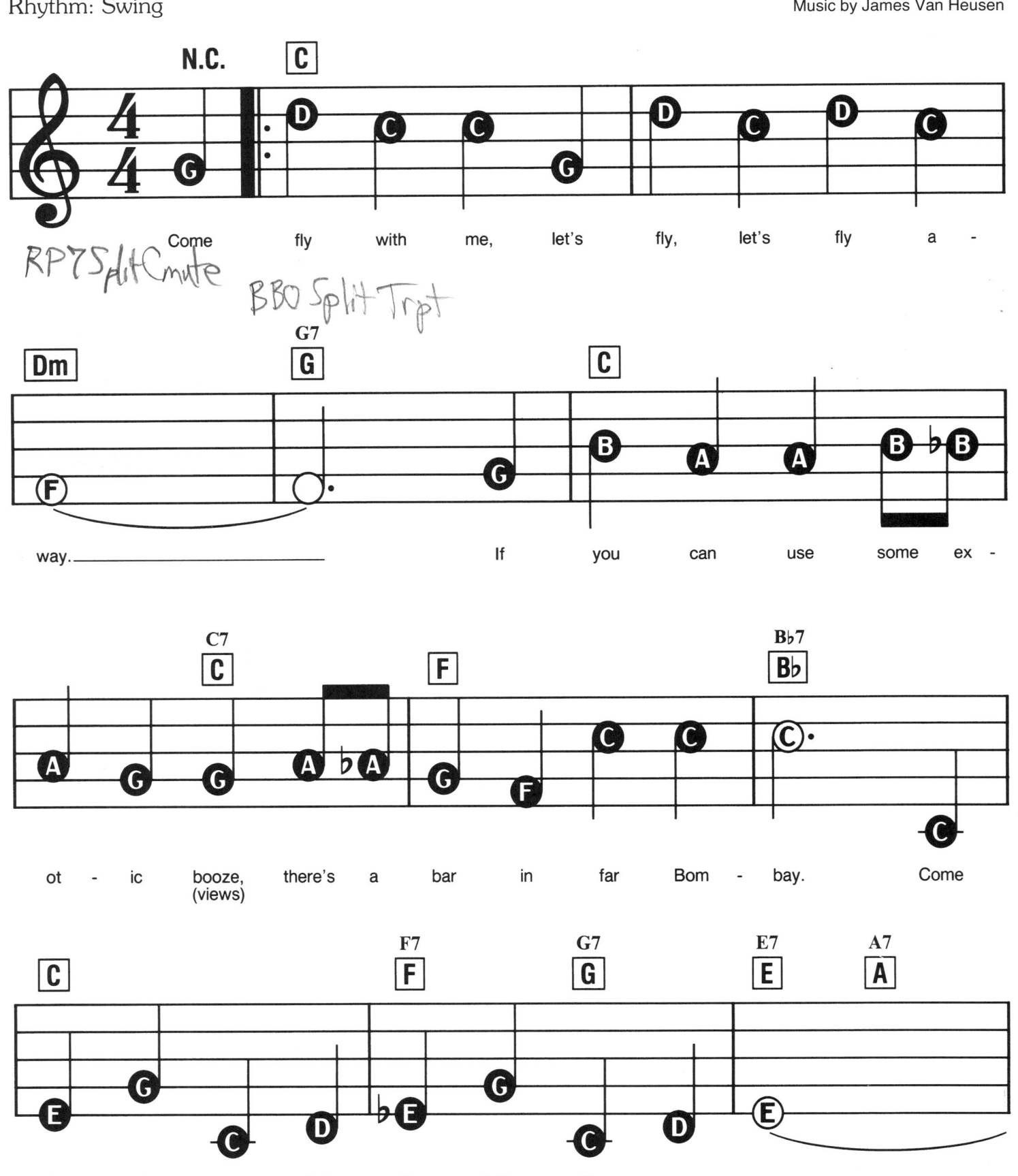

35

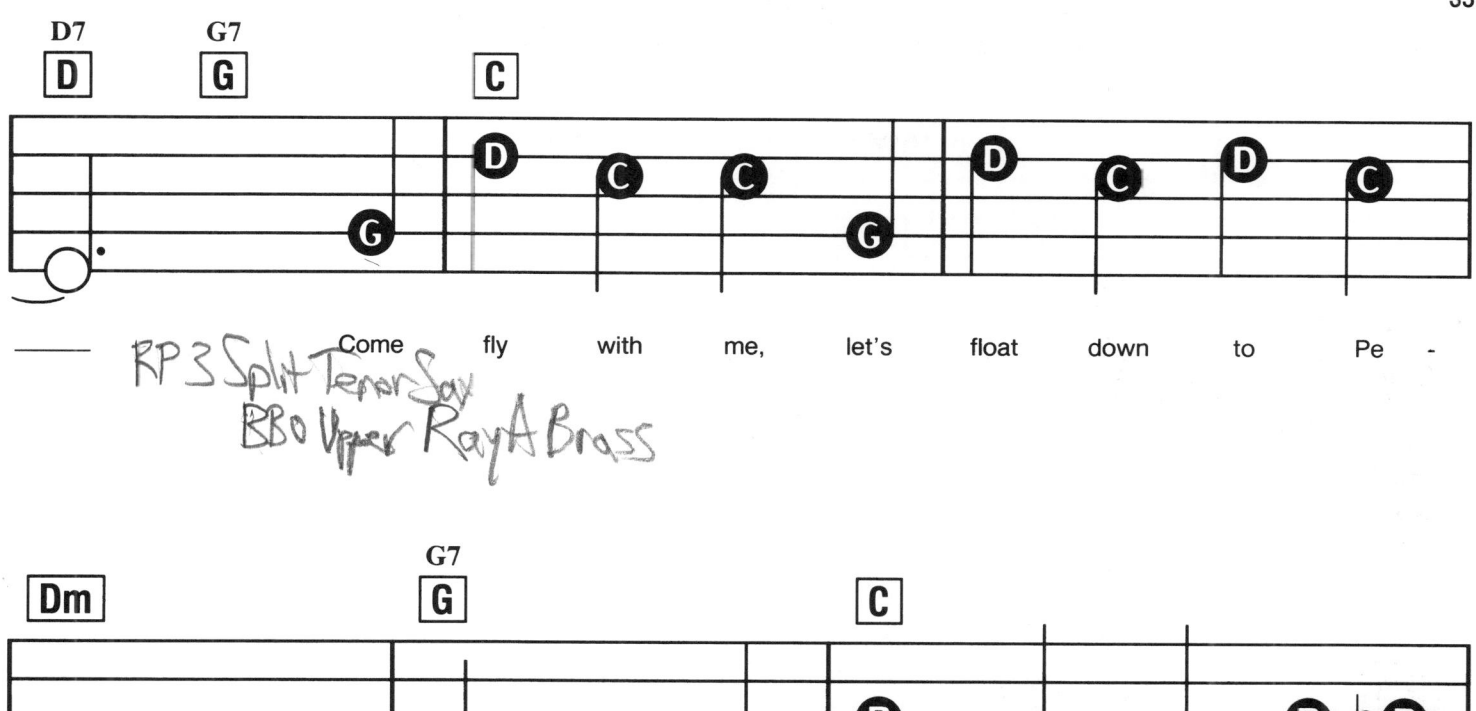

RP3 Split Tenor Sax
BBO Upper RayA Brass

Come fly with me, let's float down to Pe-ru.

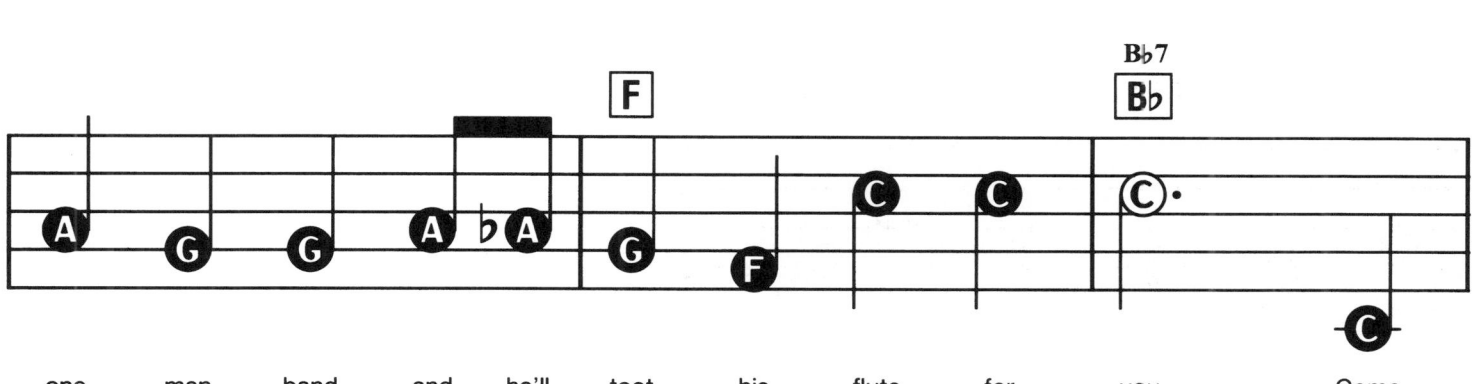

In Lla-ma land there's a one man band and he'll toot his flute for you. Come

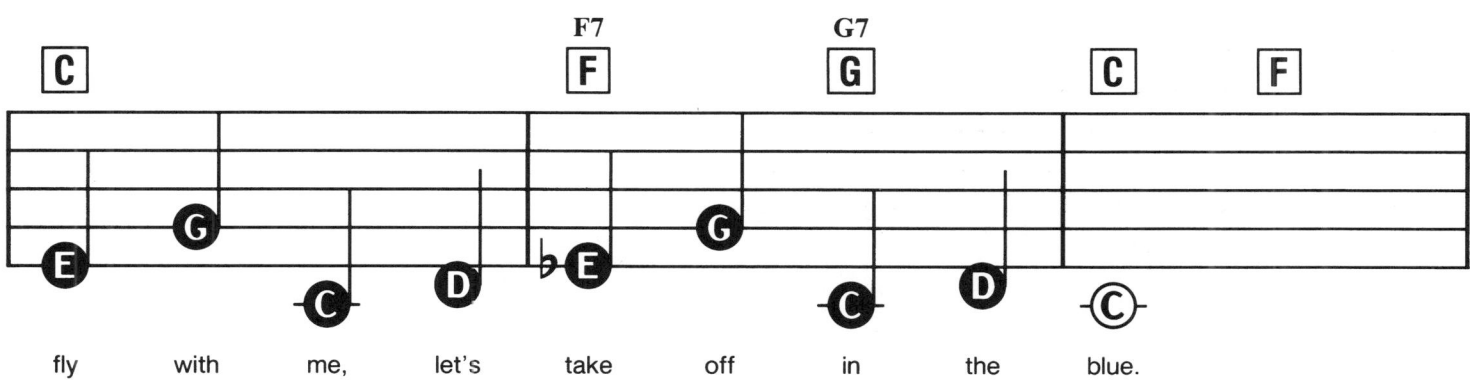

fly with me, let's take off in the blue.

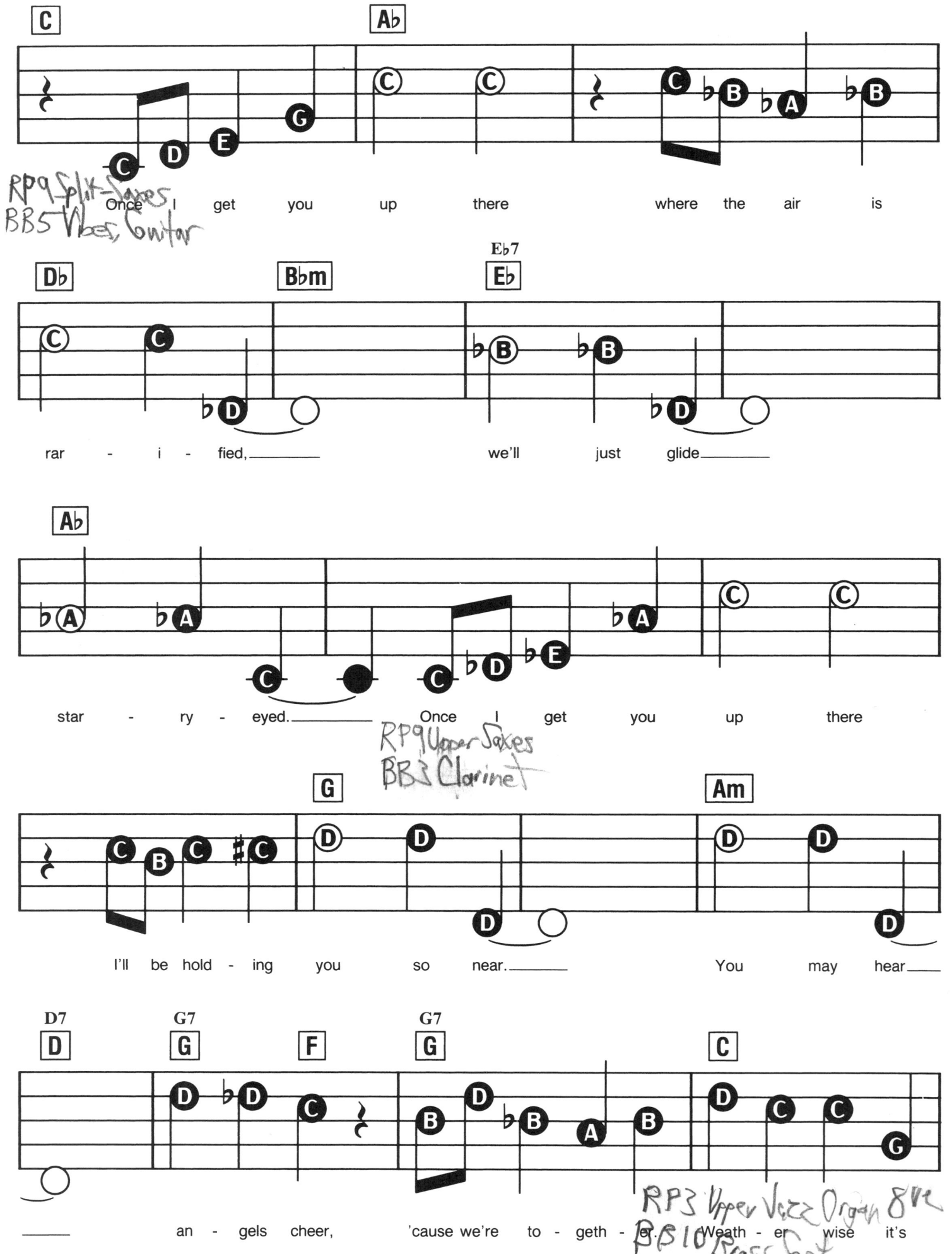

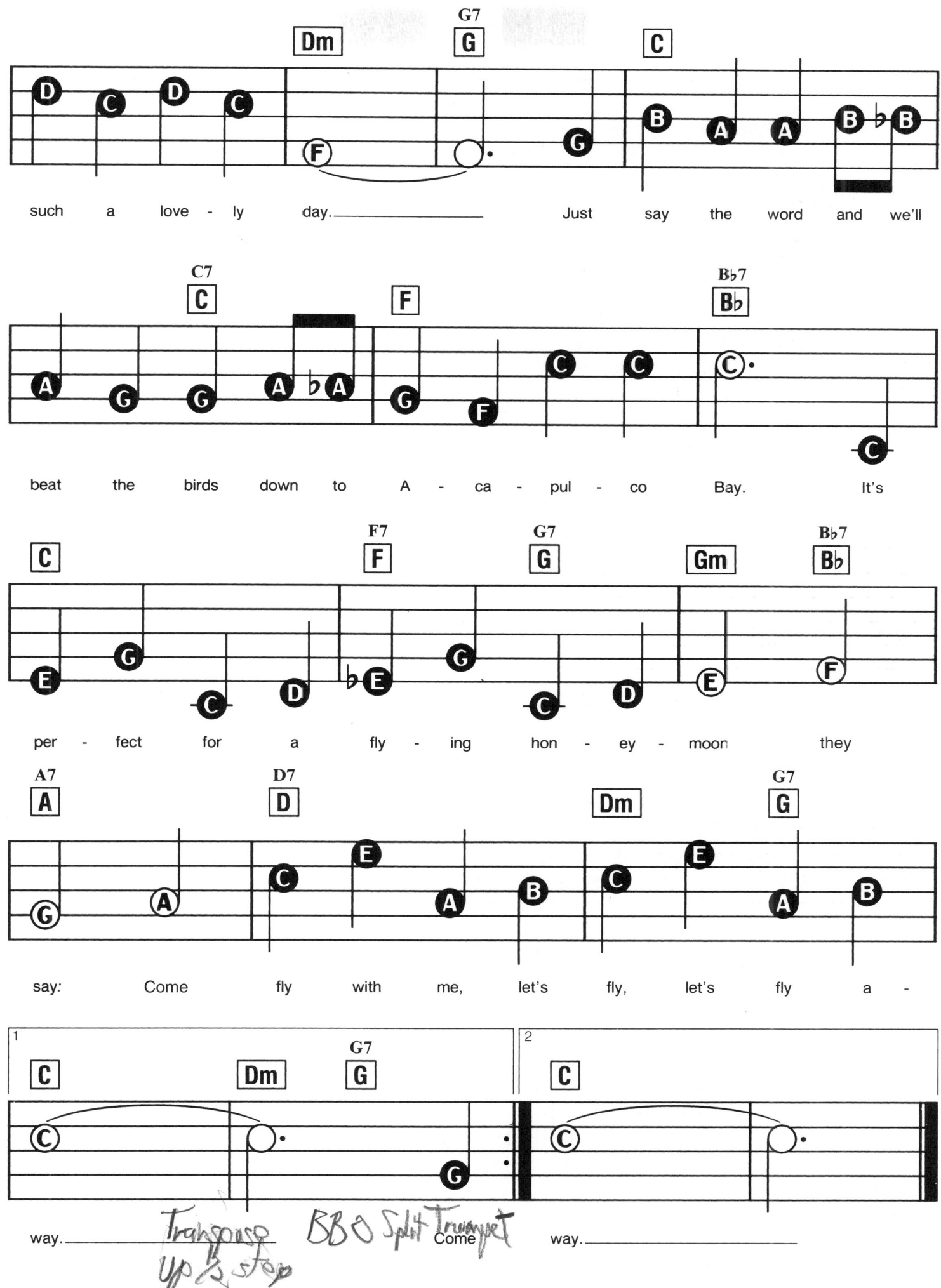

Cry Me a River

Registration 2
Rhythm: Fox Trot

Words and Music by
Arthur Hamilton

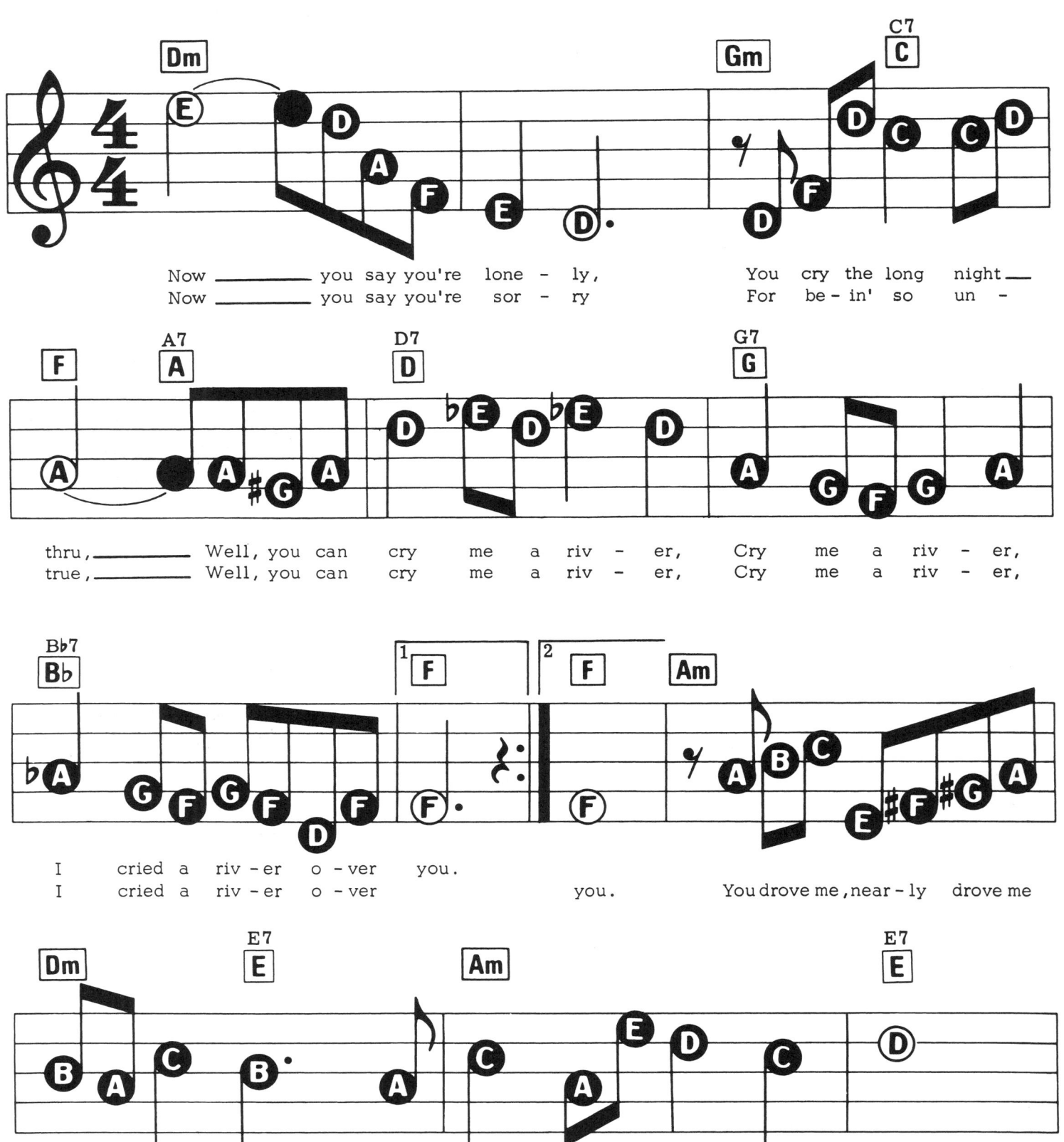

Copyright © 1953, 1955 by Chappell & Co. and Momentum Music
Copyright Renewed
All Rights Administered by Chappell & Co.
International Copyright Secured   All Rights Reserved

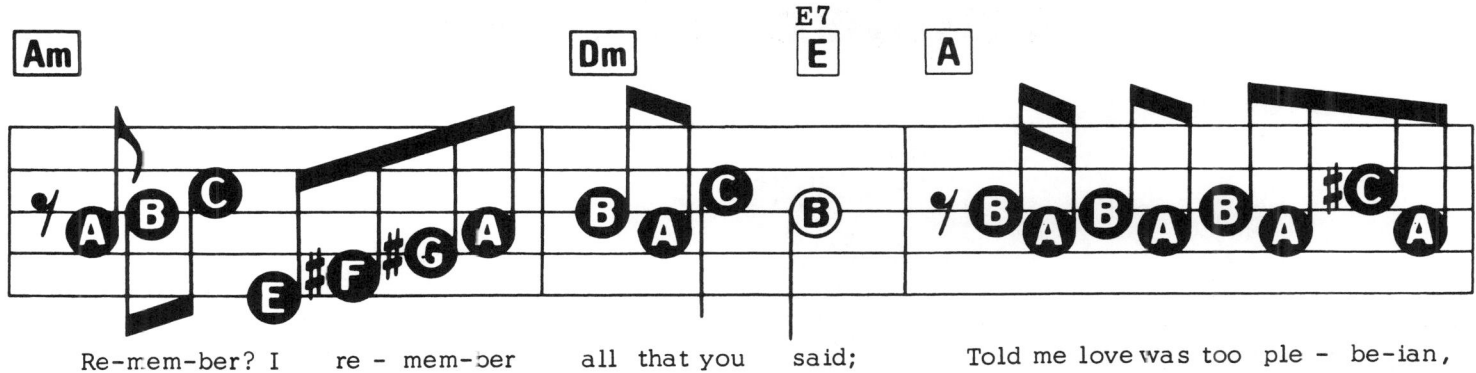
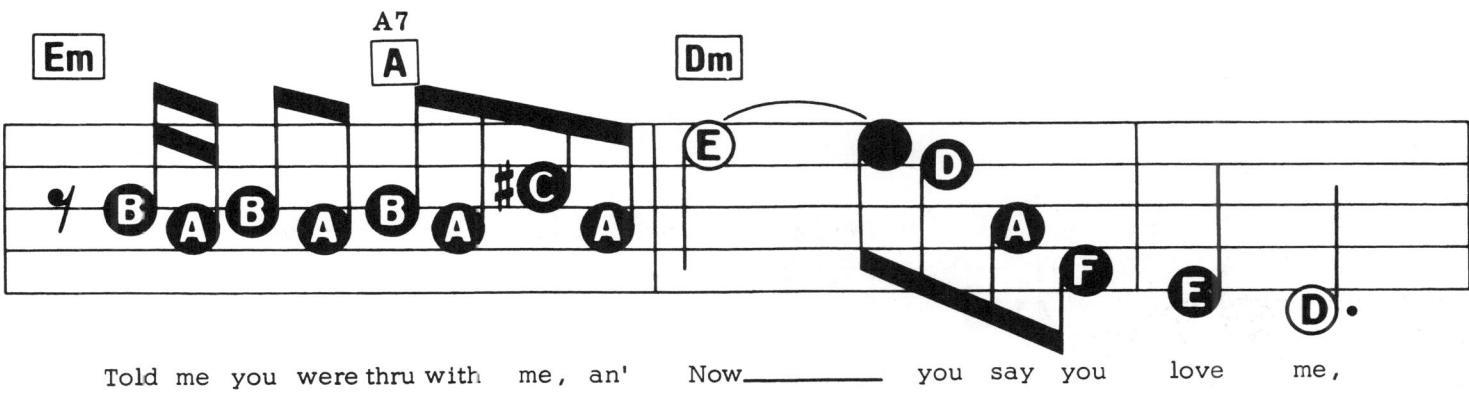
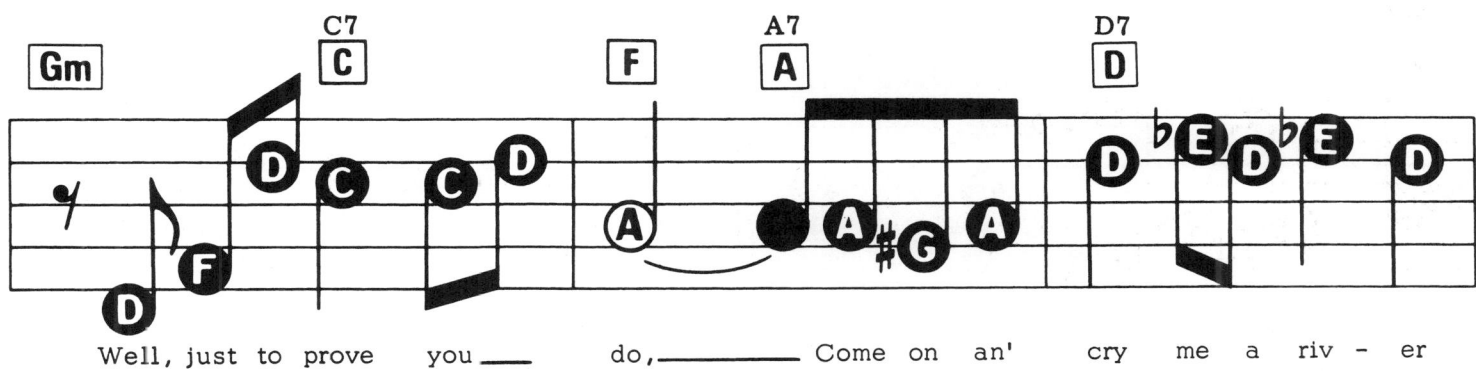
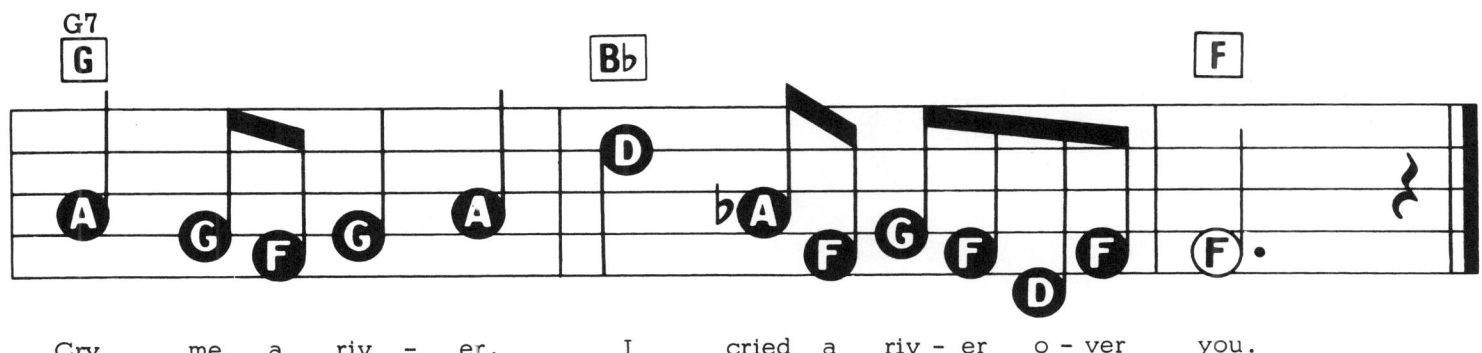

Dancers in Love

Registration 8
Rhythm: Swing

By Duke Ellington

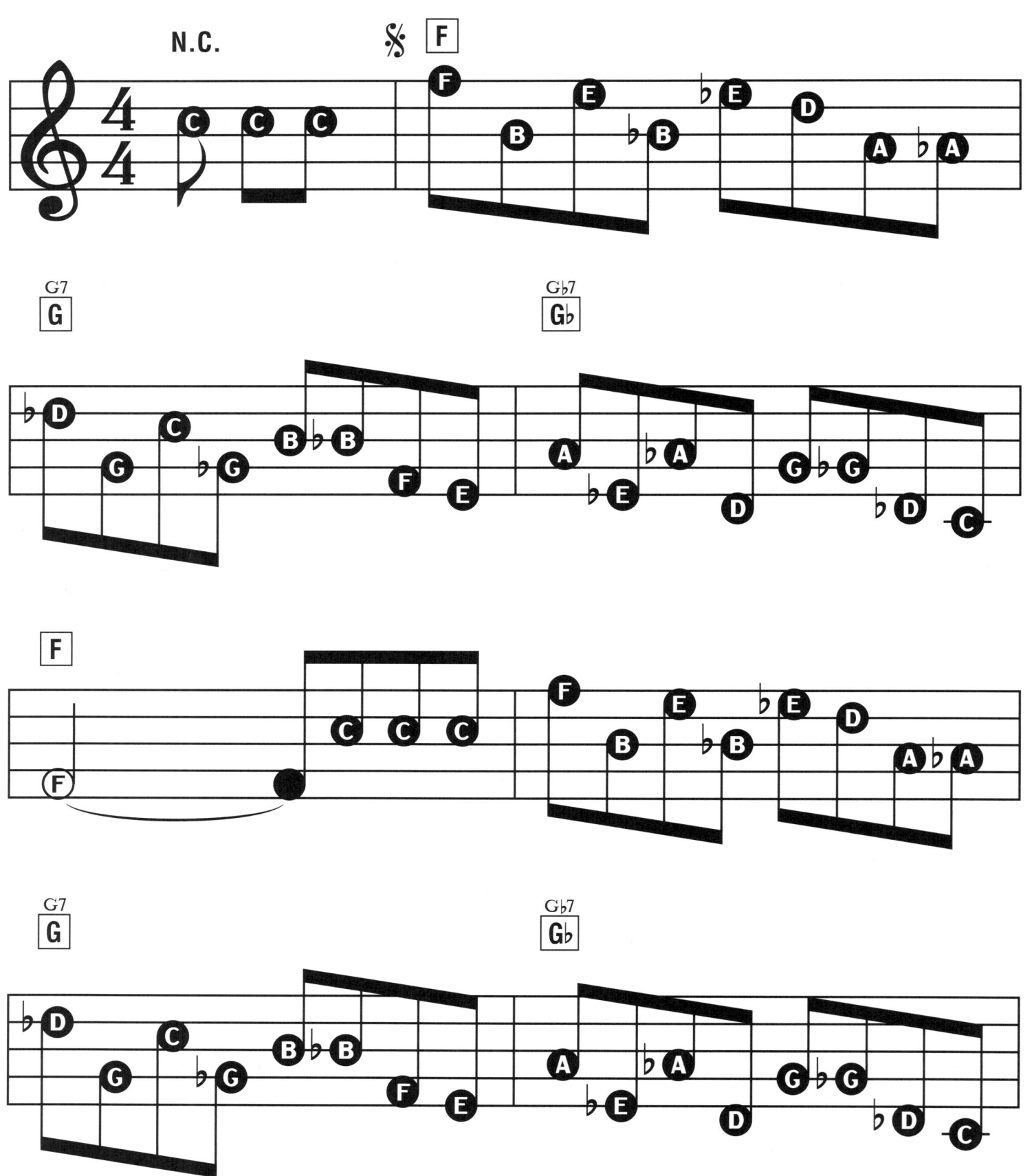

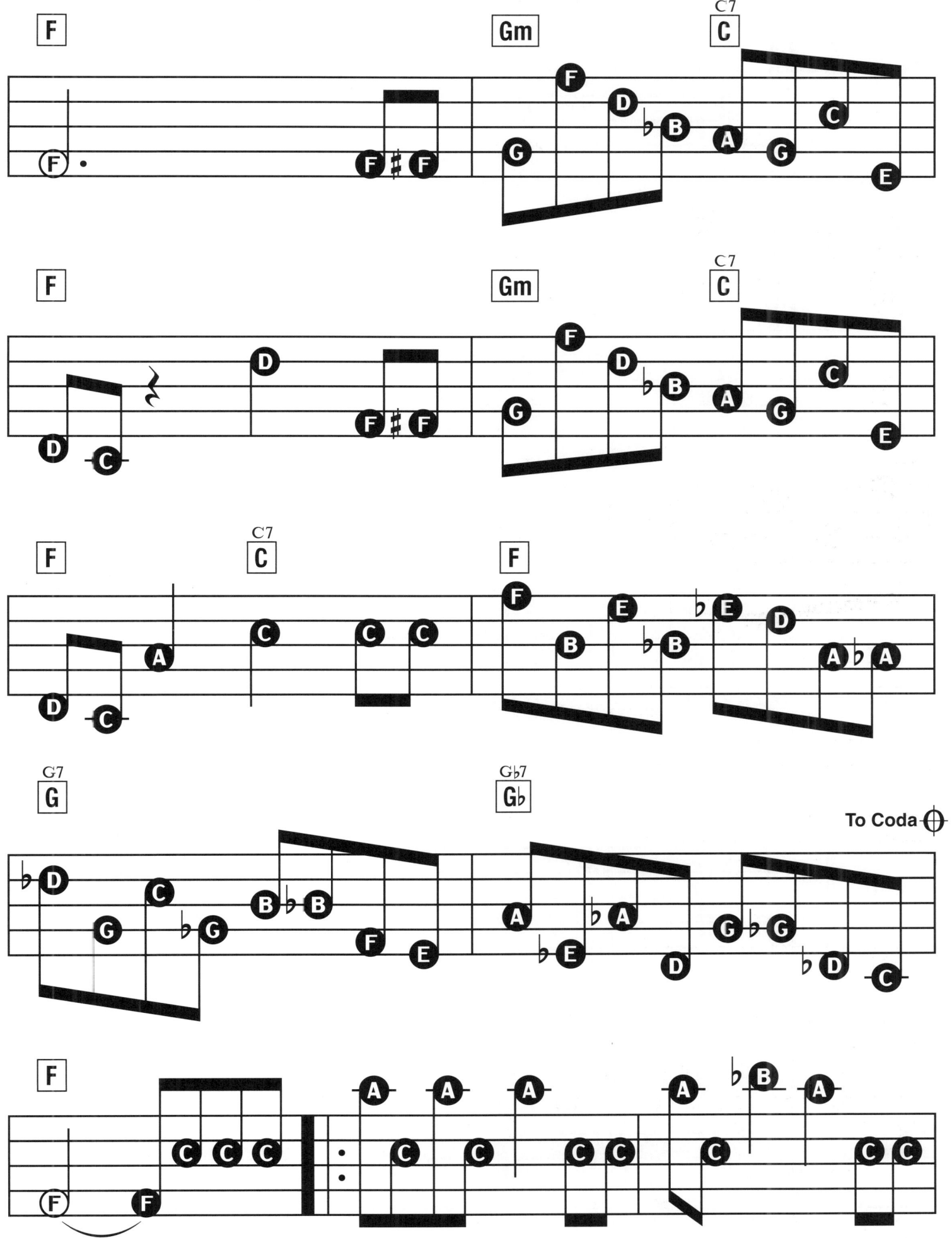

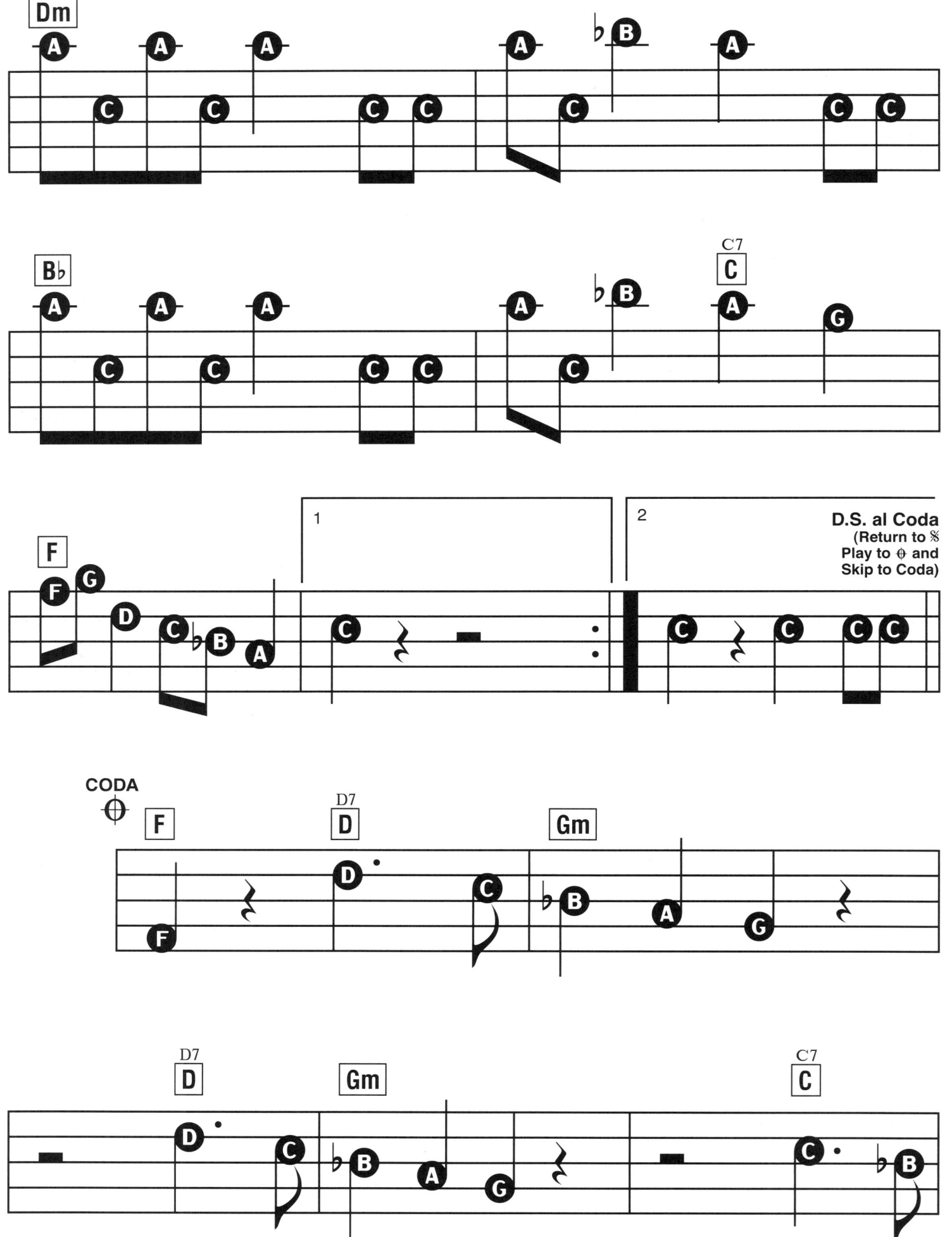

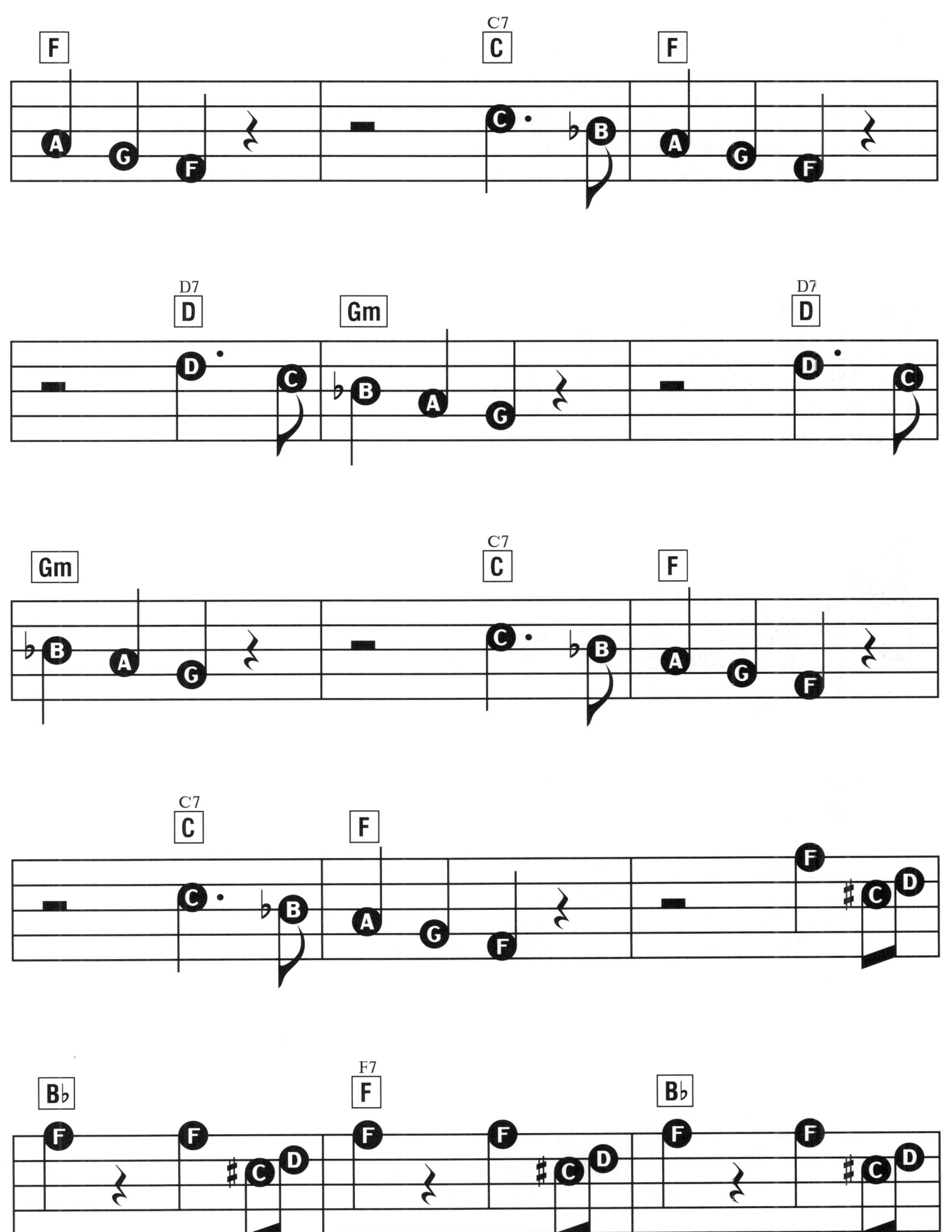

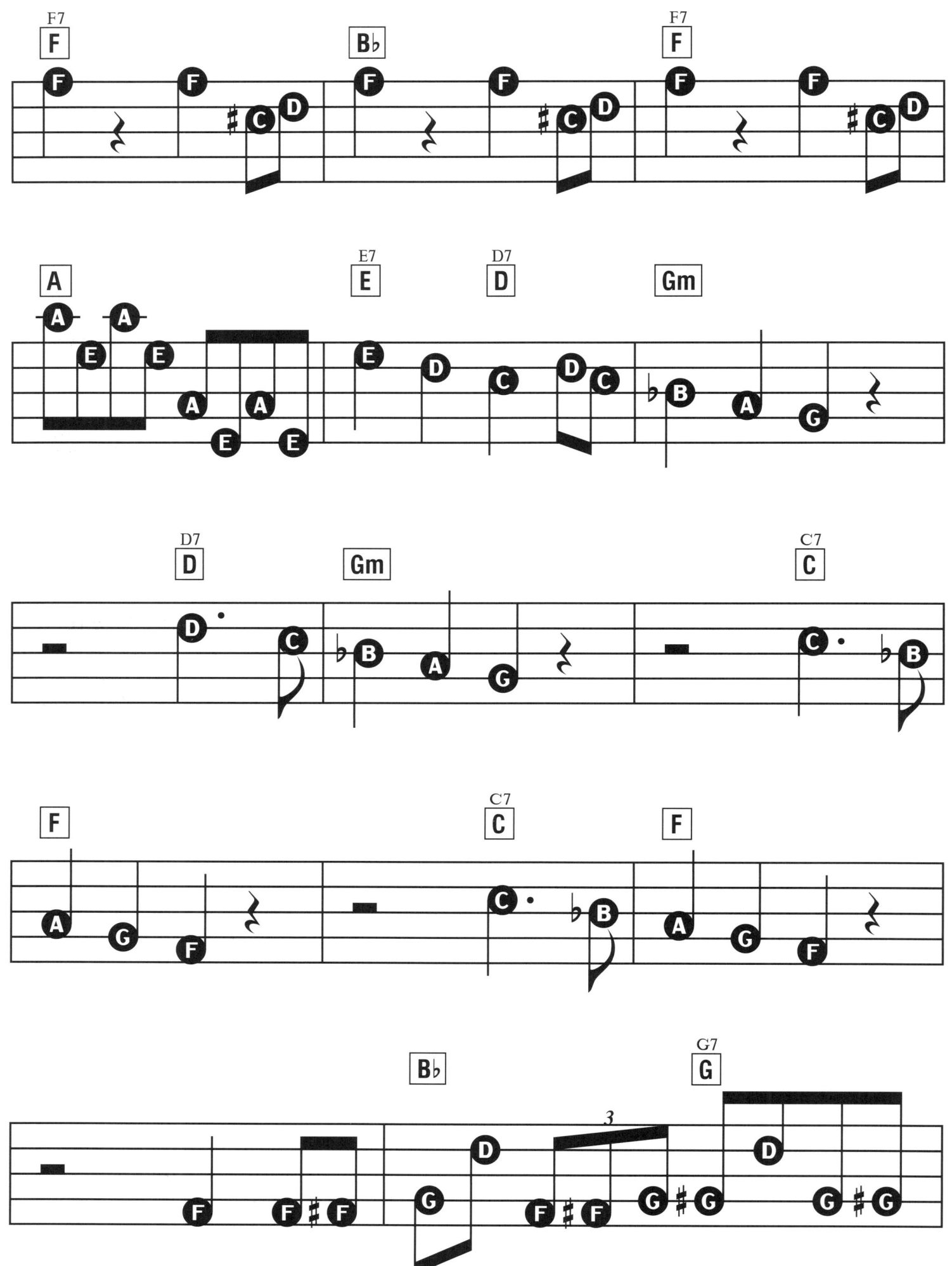

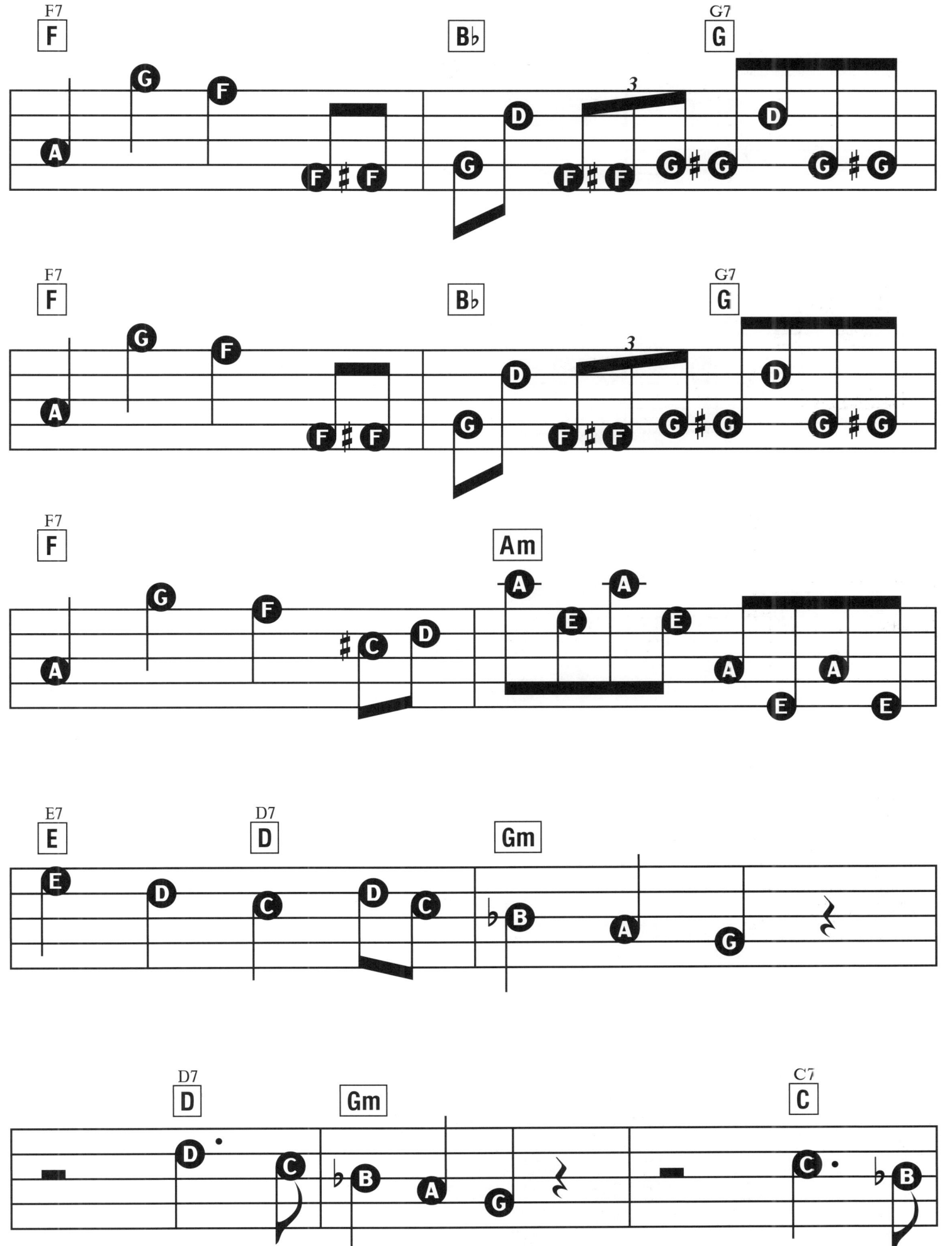

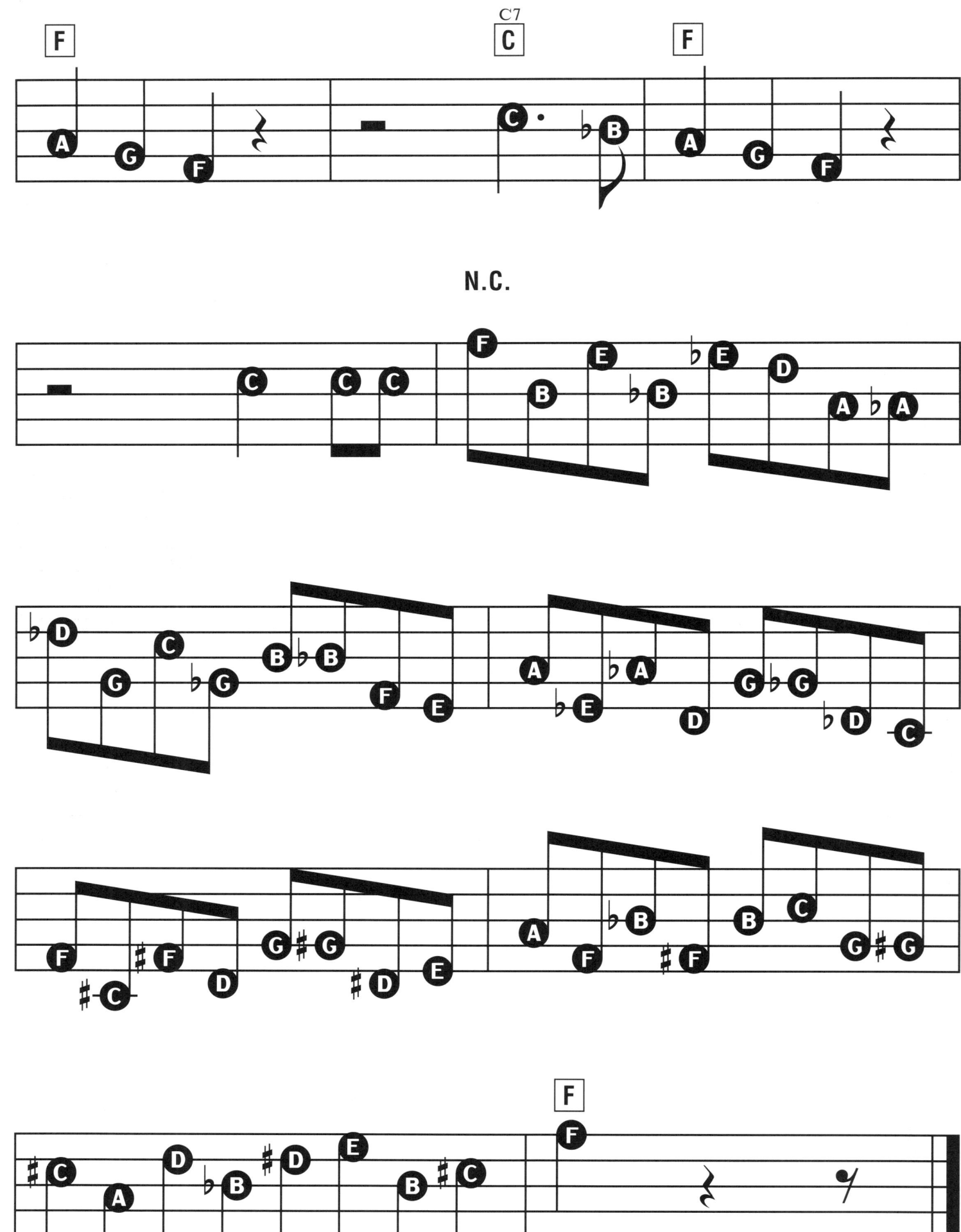

Day by Day
Theme from the Paramount Television Series DAY BY DAY

Registration 4
Rhythm: Swing

Words and Music by Sammy Cahn,
Axel Stordahl and Paul Weston

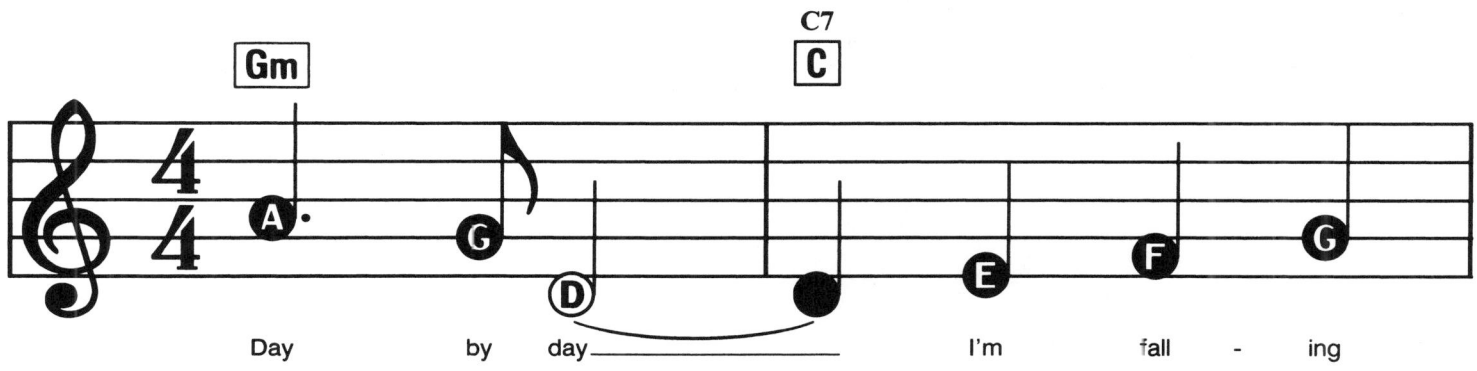

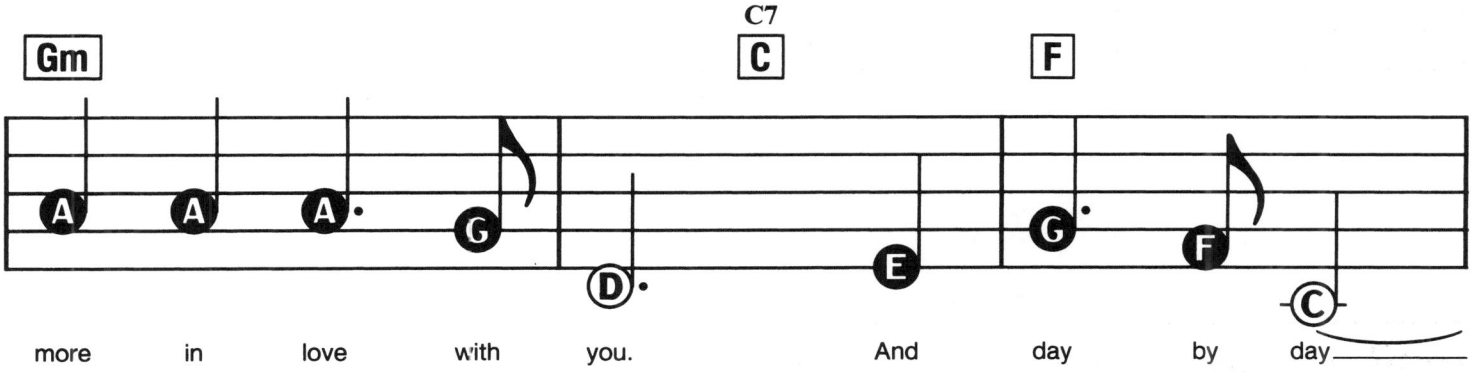

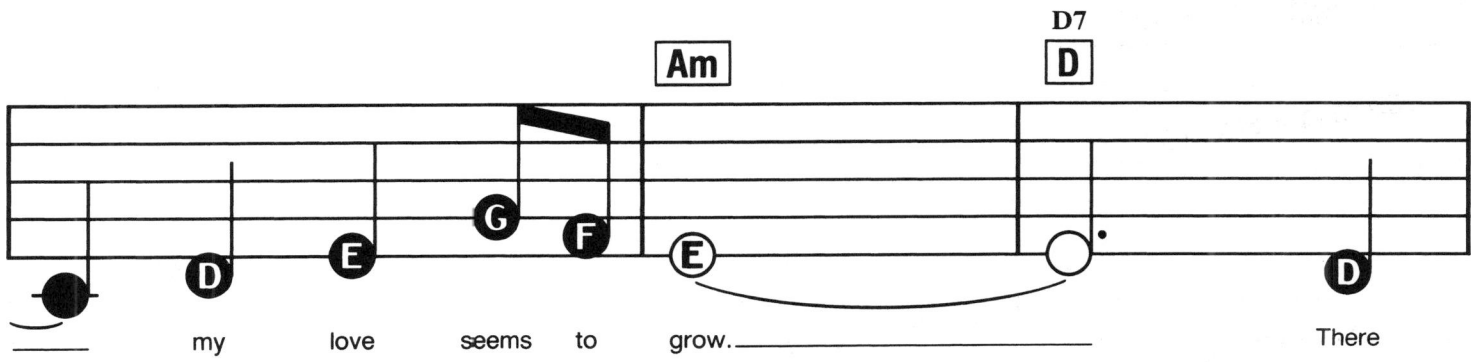

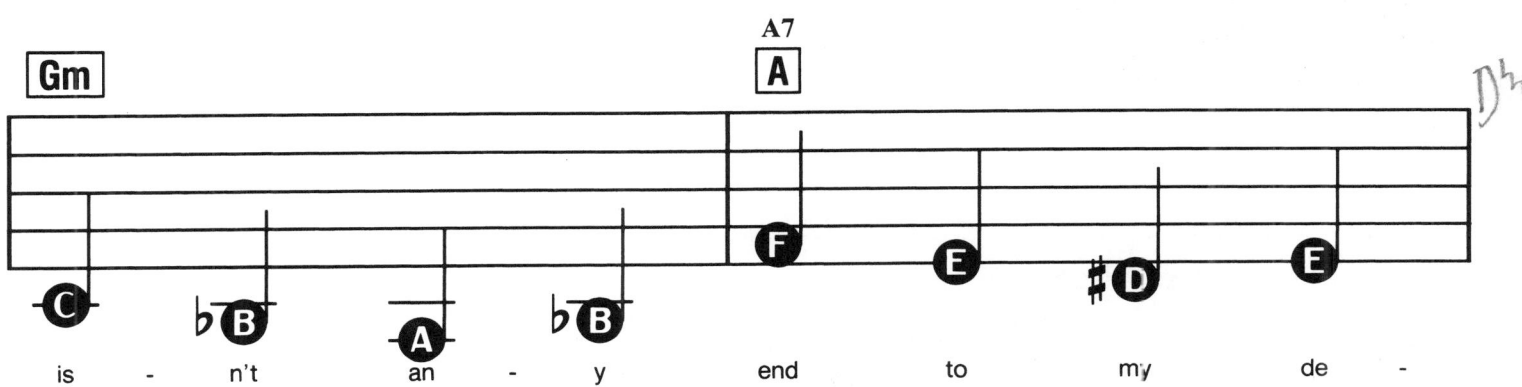

Copyright © 1945 Sony/ATV Music Publishing LLC and Hanover Music Corp.
Copyright Renewed
All Rights on behalf of Sony/ATV Music Publishing LLC Administered by Sony/ATV Music Publishing LLC, 8 Music Square West, Nashville, TN 37203
International Copyright Secured   All Rights Reserved

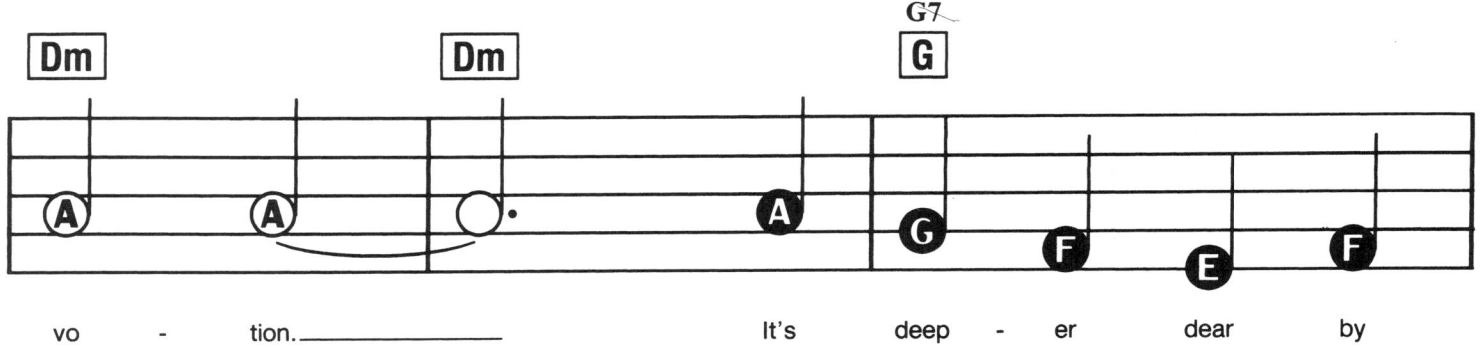
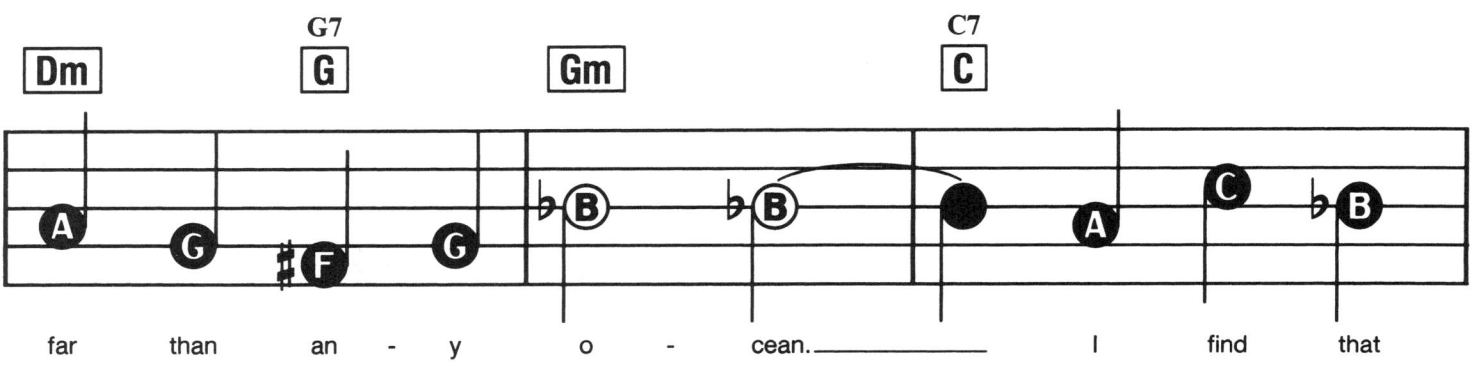
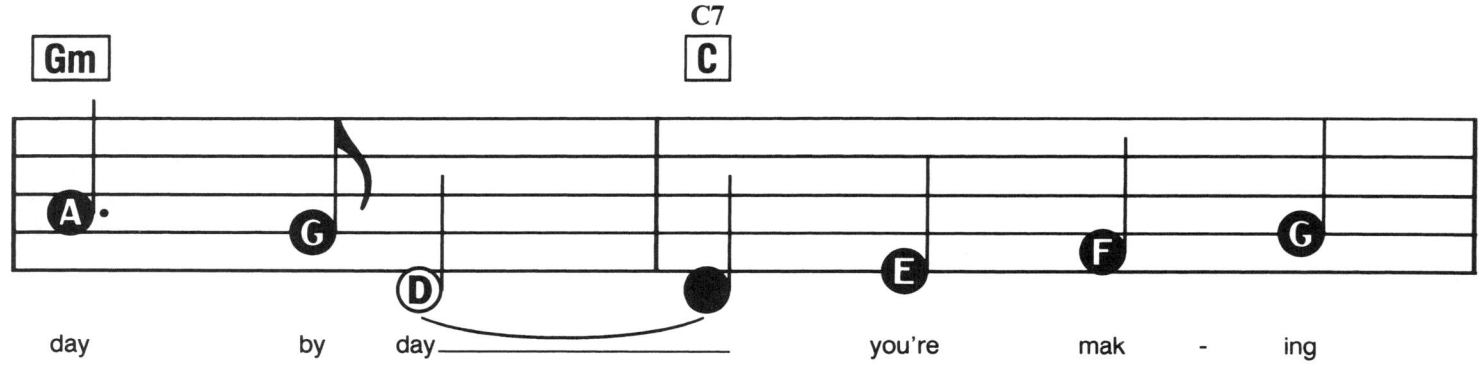
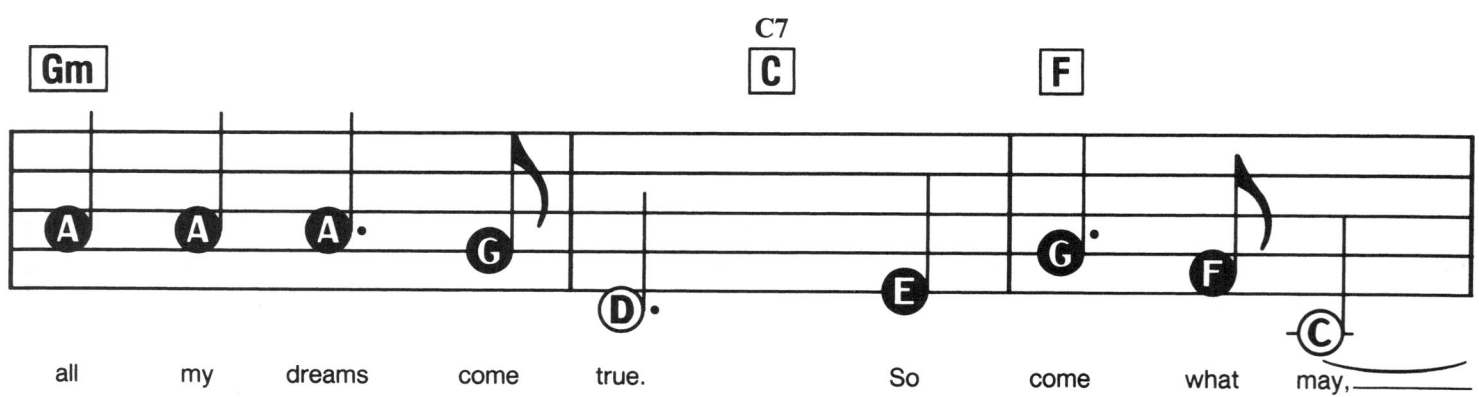

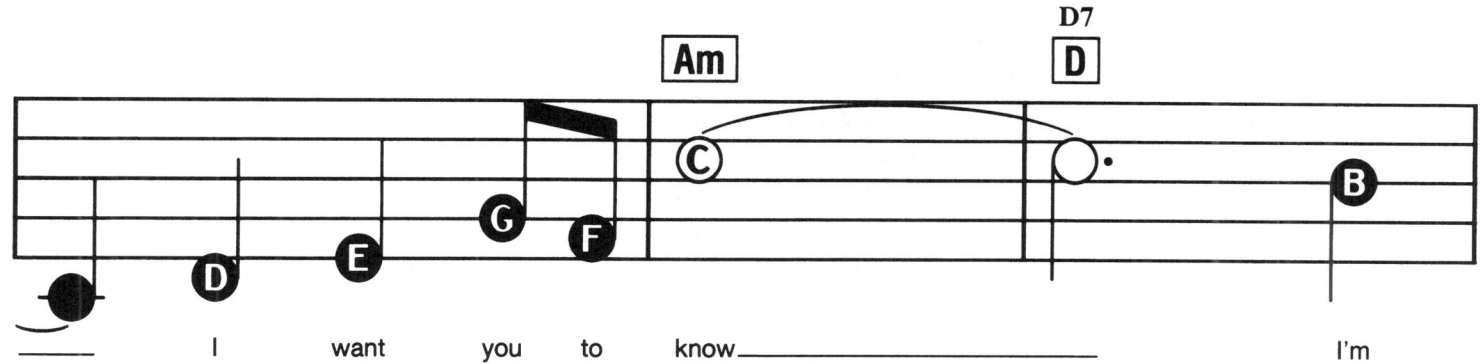
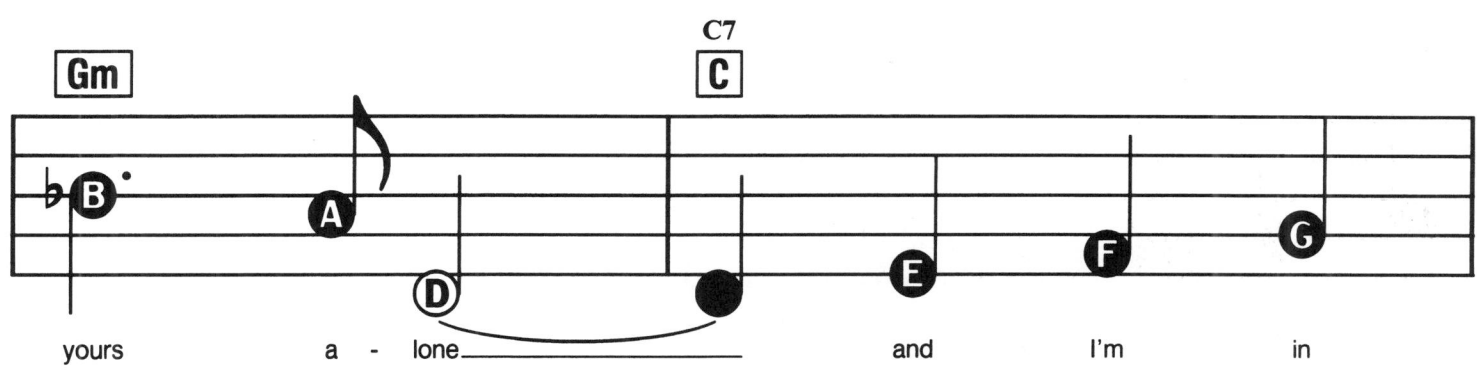
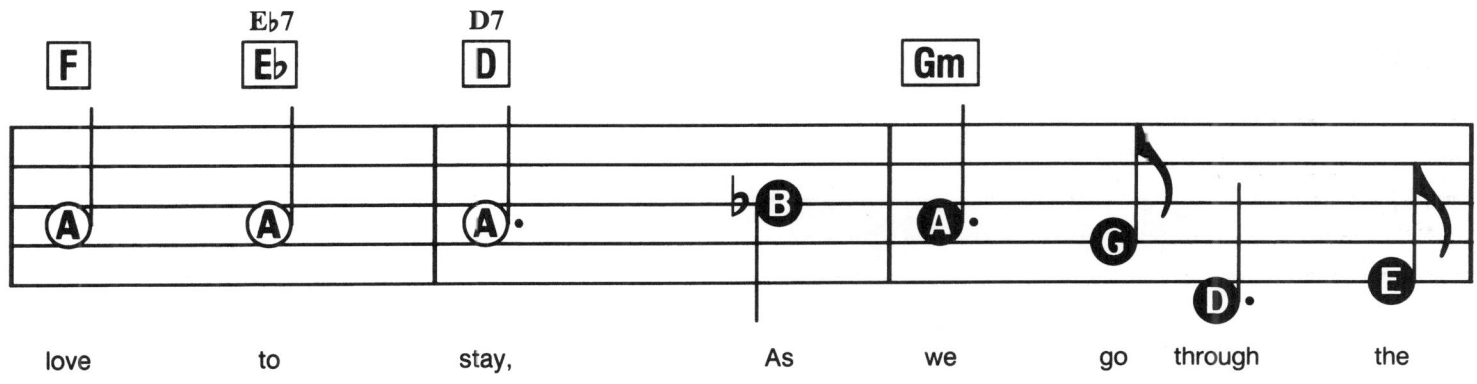
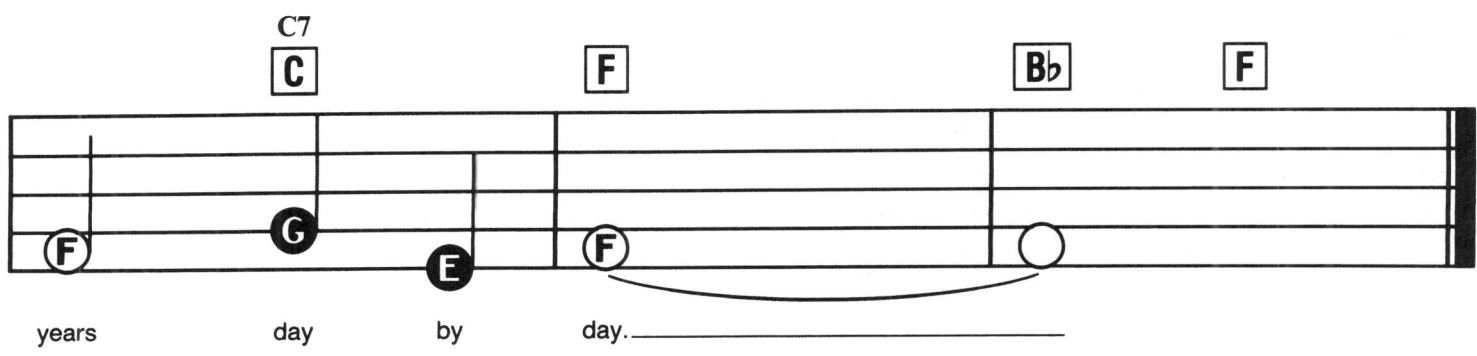

Django

Registration 8
Rhythm: Swing

By John Lewis

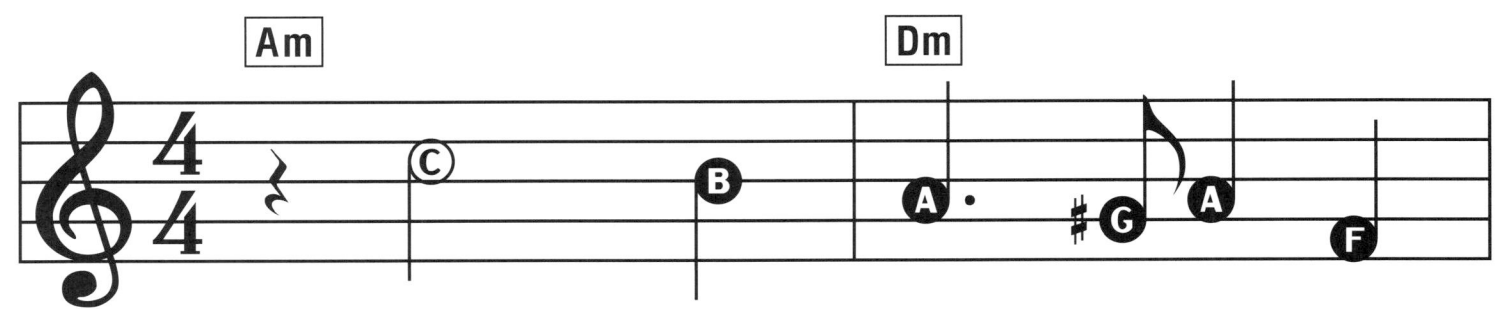

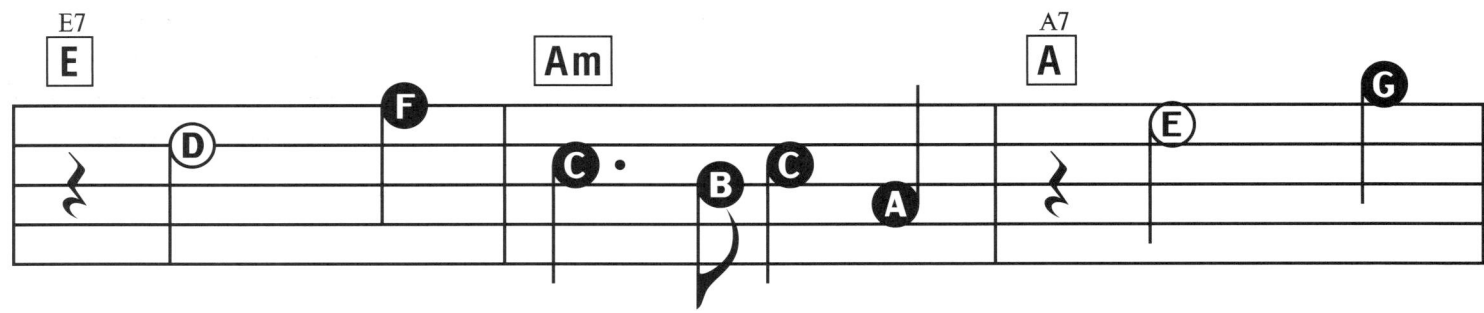

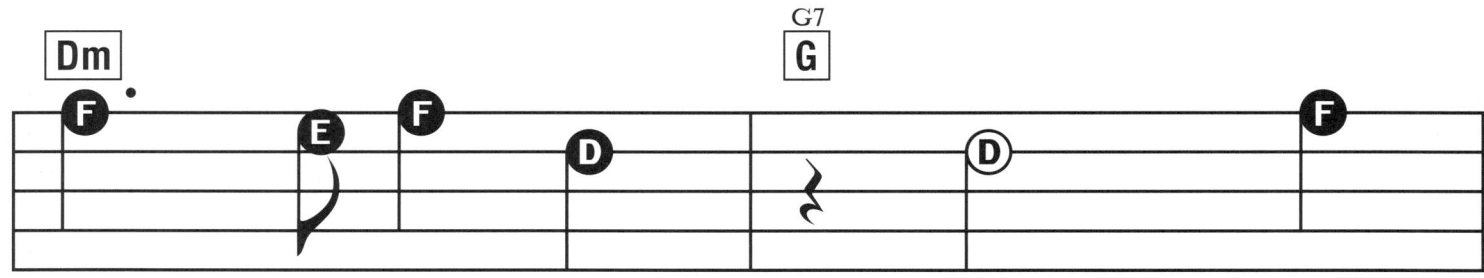

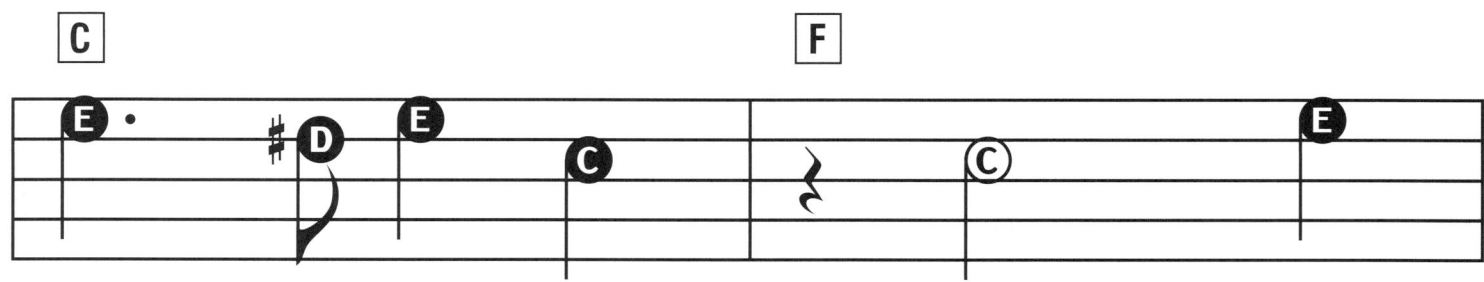

Copyright © 1955 (Renewed 1983) by MJQ Music, Inc.
All Rights Administered by Hal Leonard - Milwin Music Corp.
International Copyright Secured   All Rights Reserved

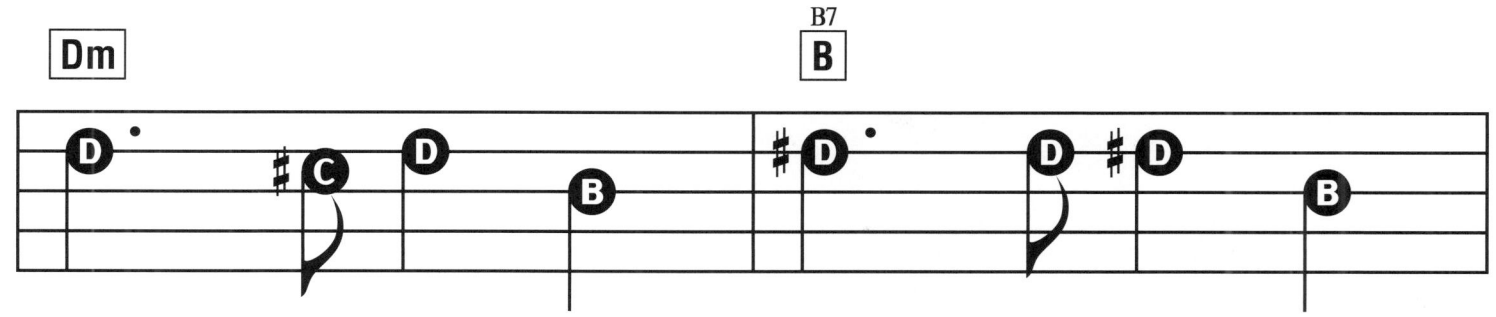
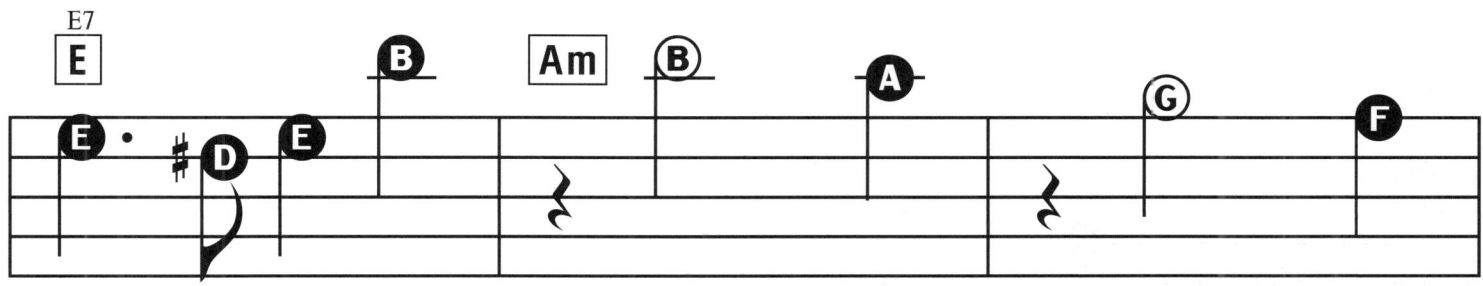
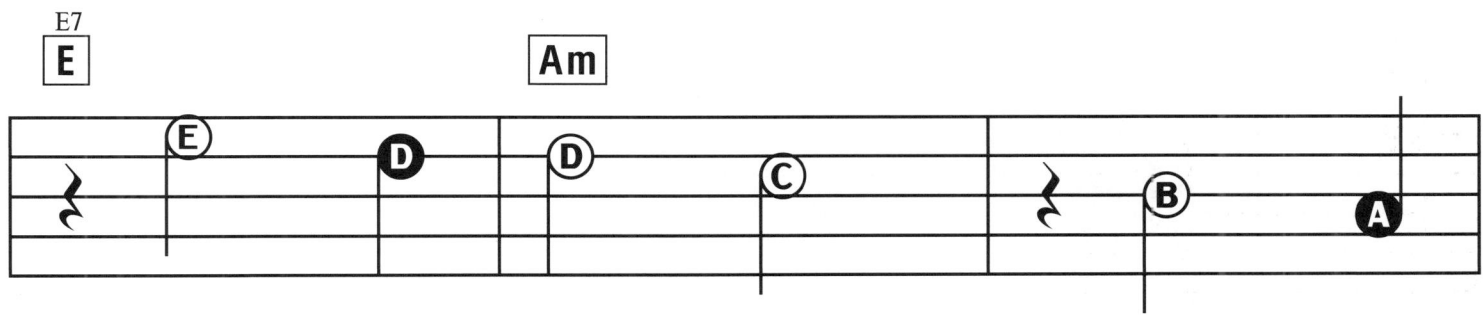
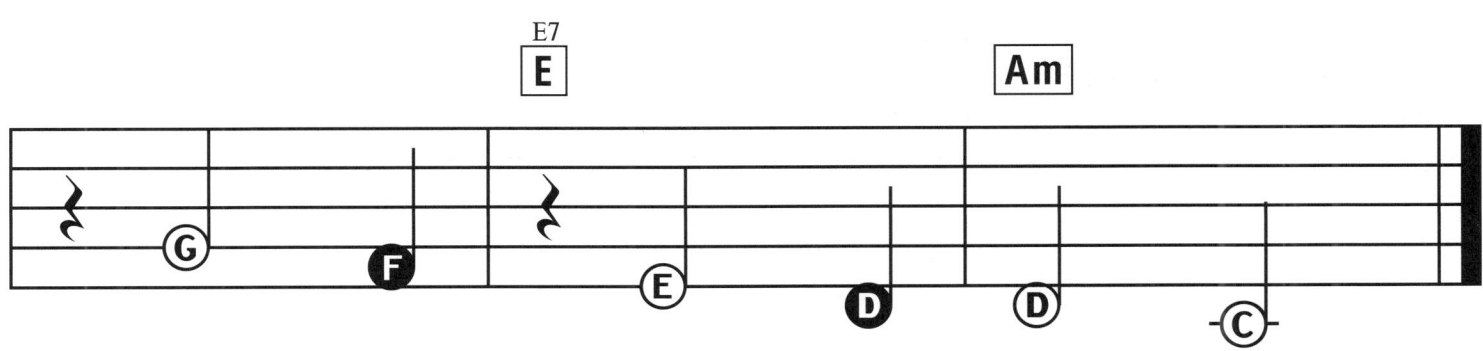

Don't Get Around Much Anymore

Registration 7
Rhythm: Swing

Words and Music by Duke Ellington and Bob Russell

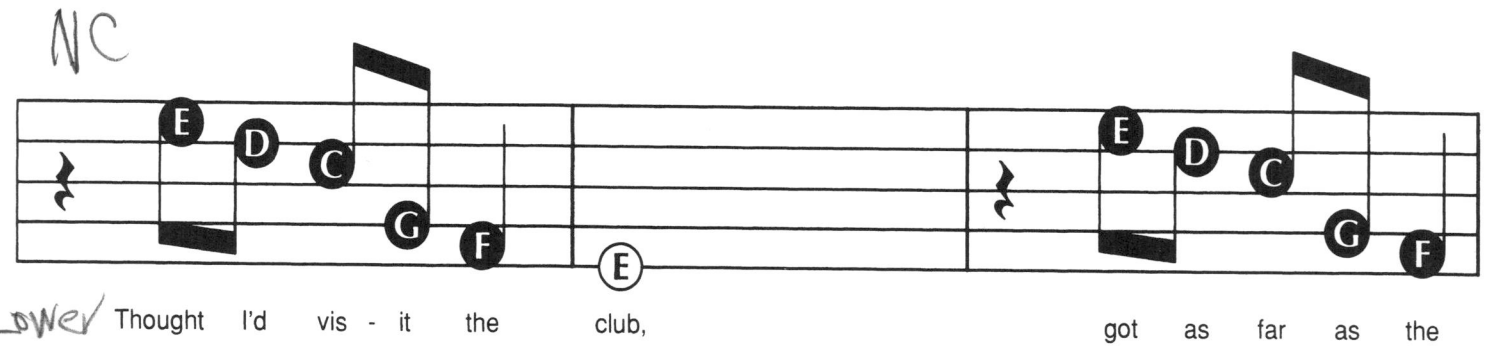

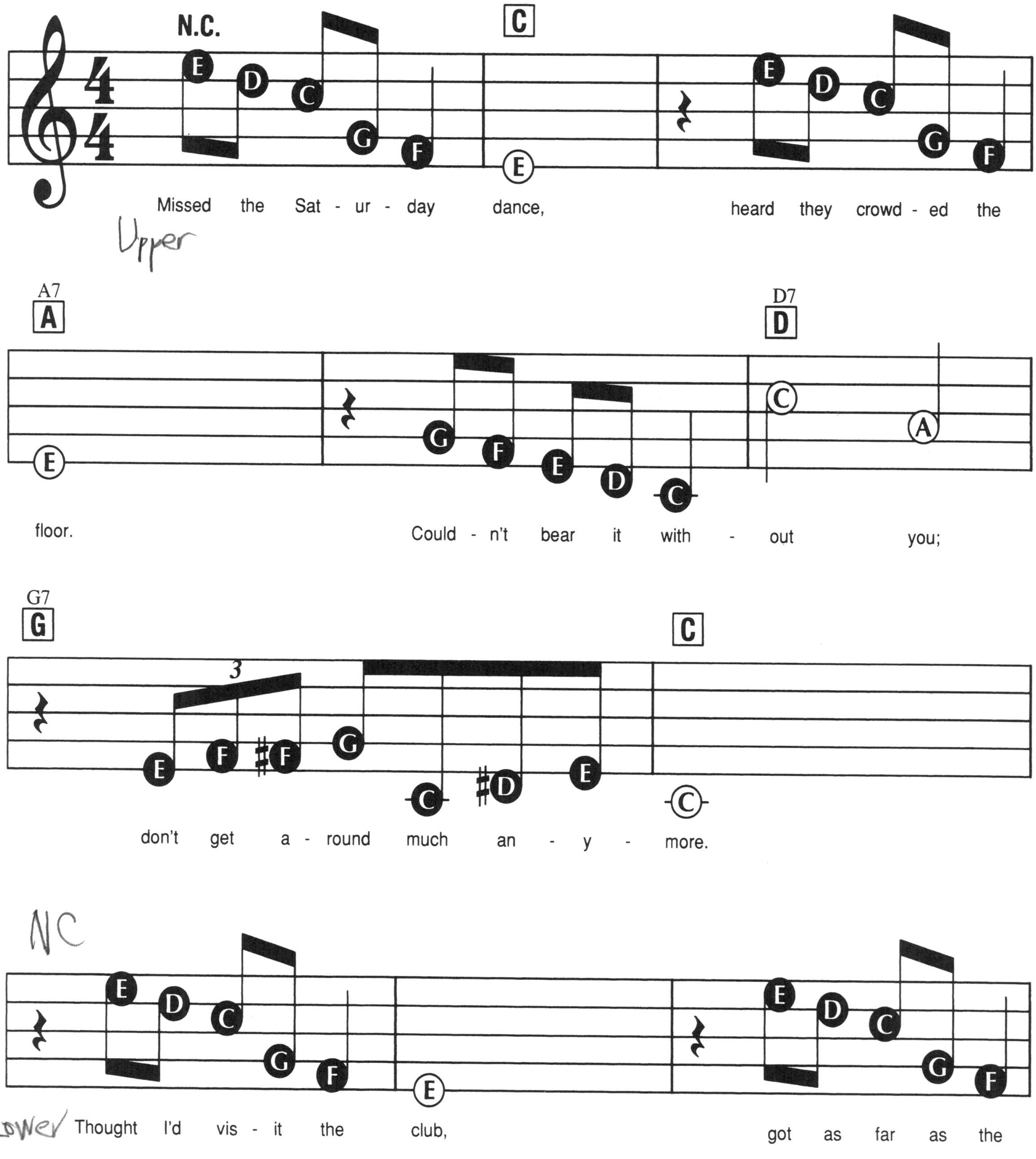

Missed the Sat-ur-day dance, heard they crowd-ed the floor. Could-n't bear it with-out you; don't get a-round much an-y-more.

Thought I'd vis-it the club, got as far as the

Copyright © 1942 Sony/ATV Music Publishing LLC and Music Sales Corporation
Copyright Renewed
All Rights on behalf of Sony/ATV Music Publishing LLC Administered by Sony/ATV Music Publishing LLC,
 8 Music Square West, Nashville, TN 37203
International Copyright Secured   All Rights Reserved

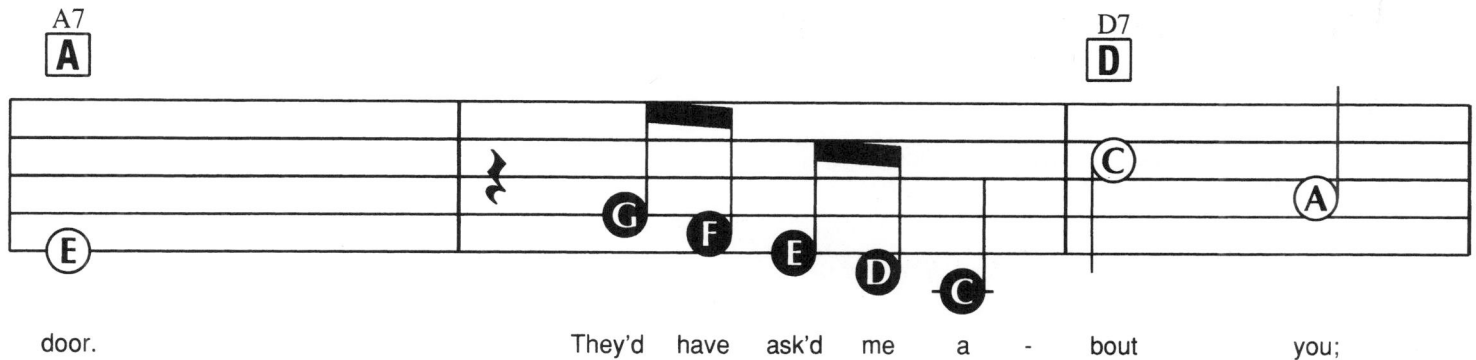
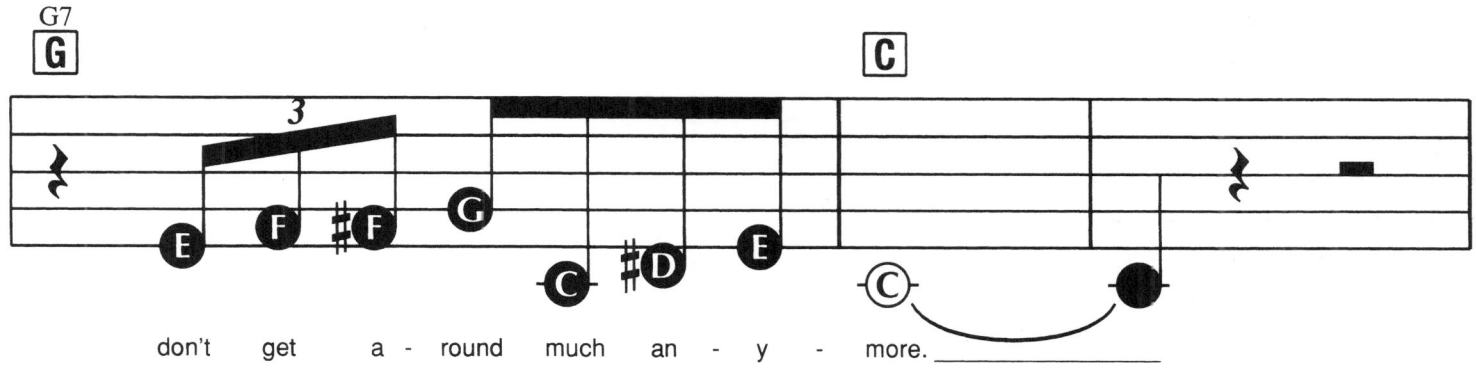
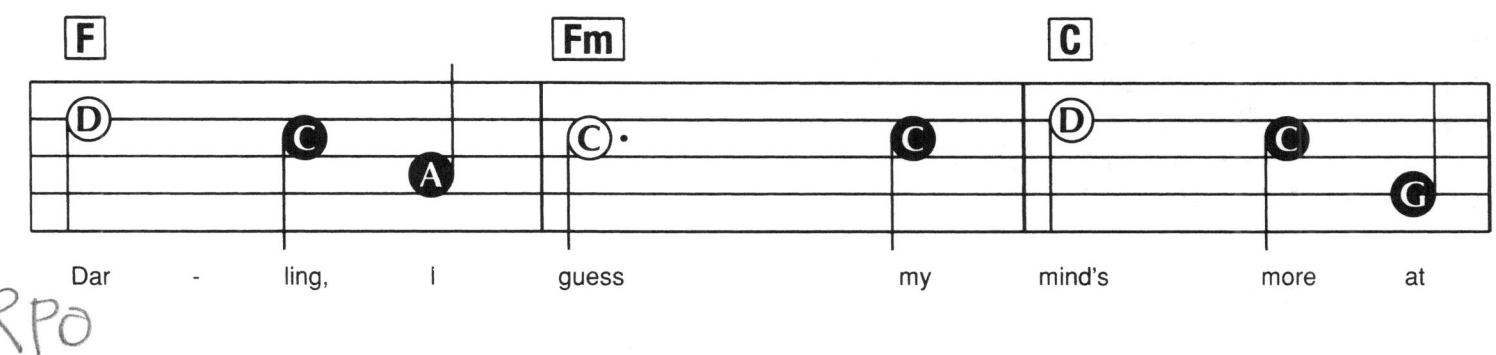
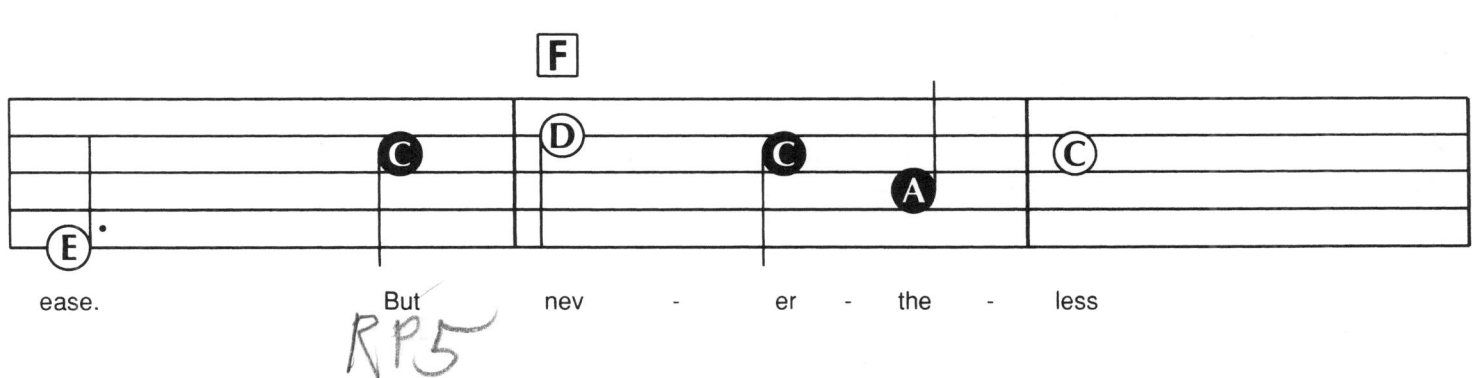

54

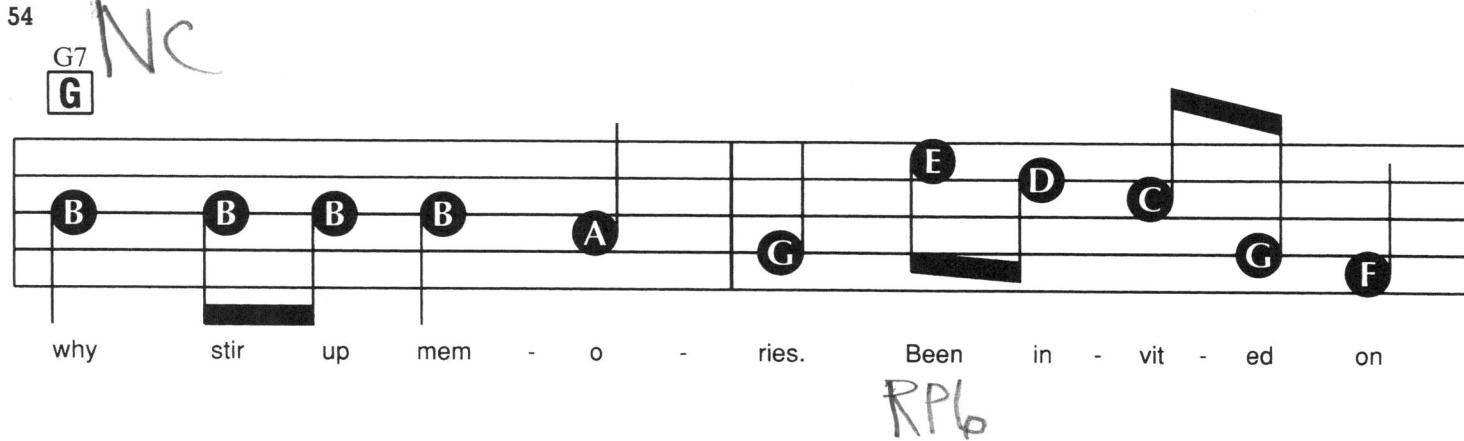

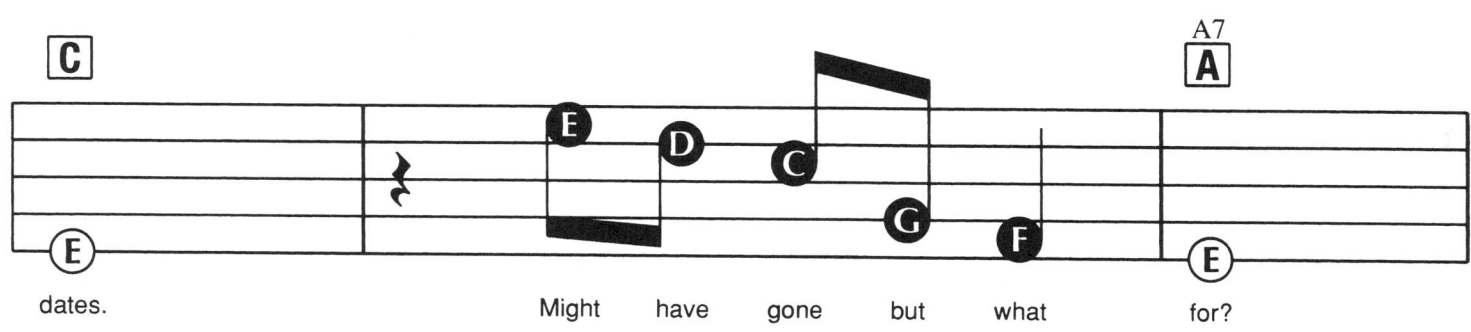

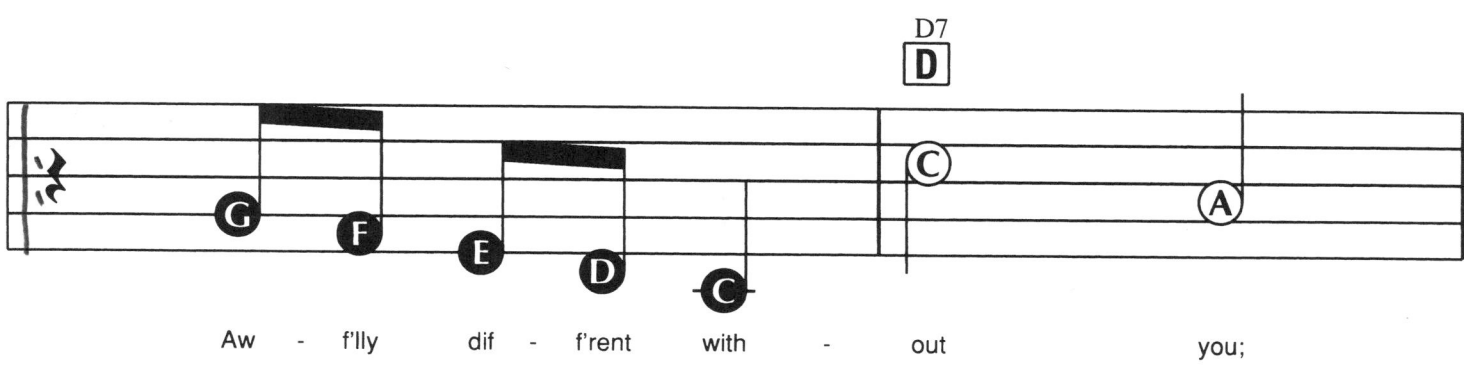

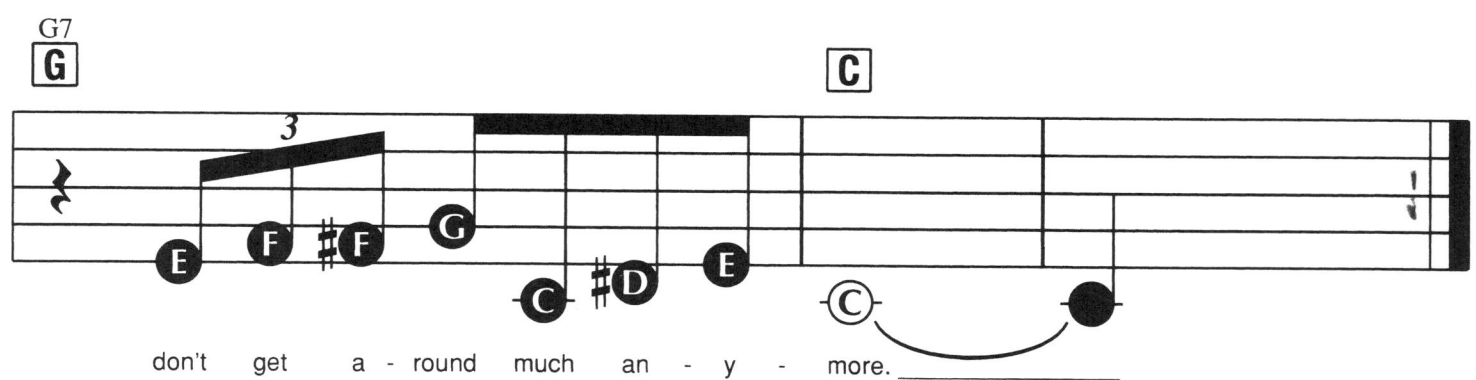

Ev'ry Time We Say Goodbye
from SEVEN LIVELY ARTS

Registration 1
Rhythm: Latin or Bossa Nova

Words and Music by
Cole Porter

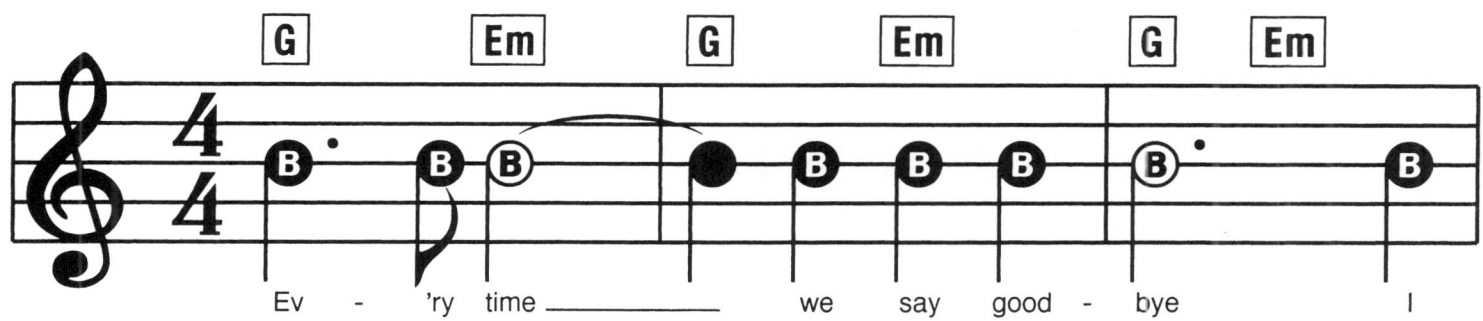

Ev-'ry time _____ we say good-bye I

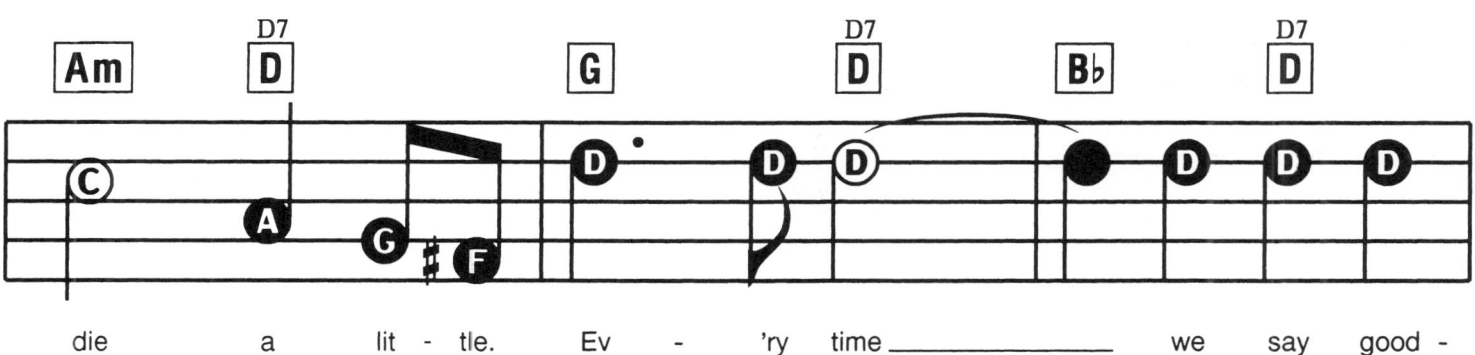

die a lit-tle. Ev-'ry time _____ we say good-

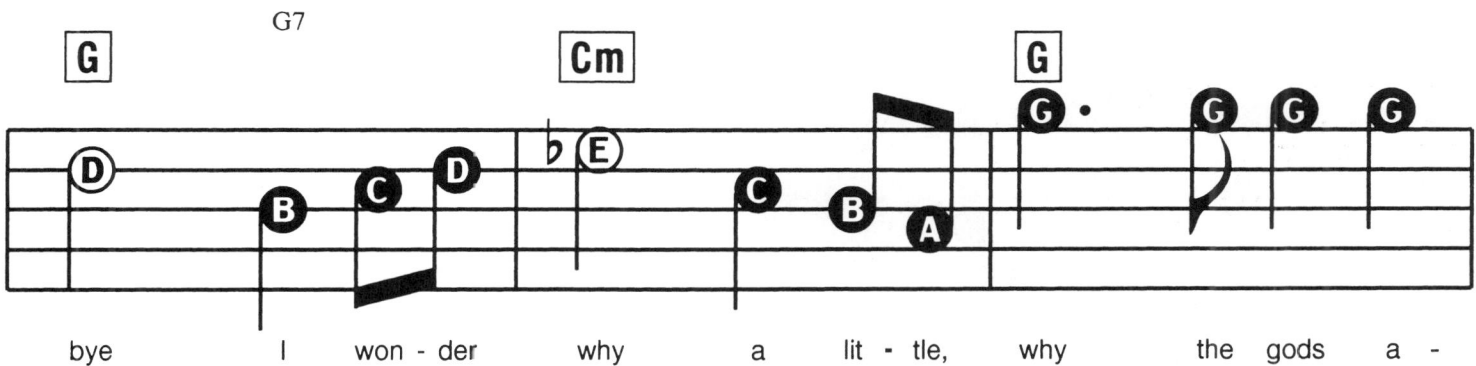

bye I won-der why a lit-tle, why the gods a-

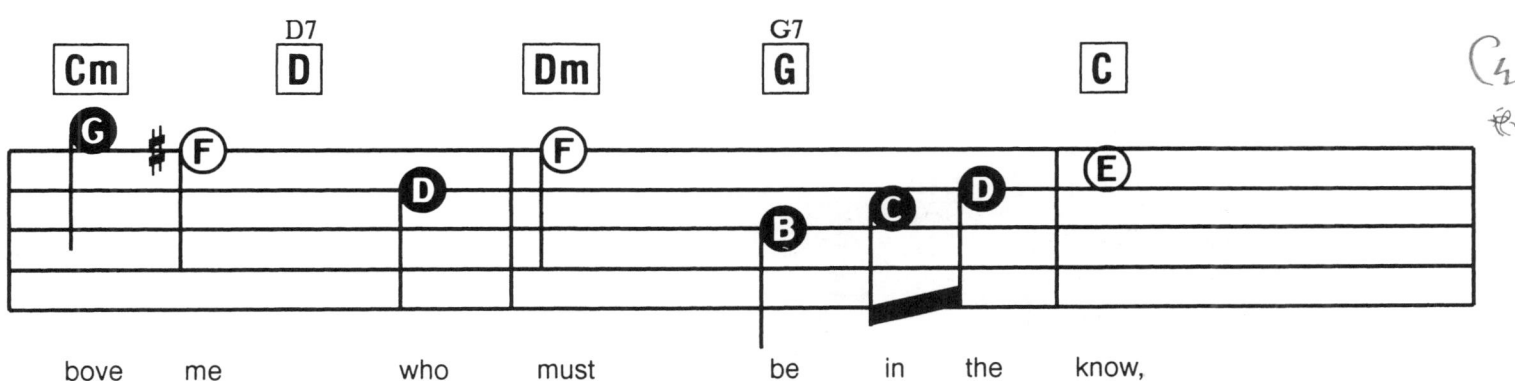

bove me who must be in the know,

Copyright © 1944 by Chappell & Co.
Copyright Renewed, Assigned to John F. Wharton, Trustee of the Cole Porter Musical and Literary Property Trusts
Chappell & Co. owner of publication and allied rights throughout the world
International Copyright Secured All Rights Reserved

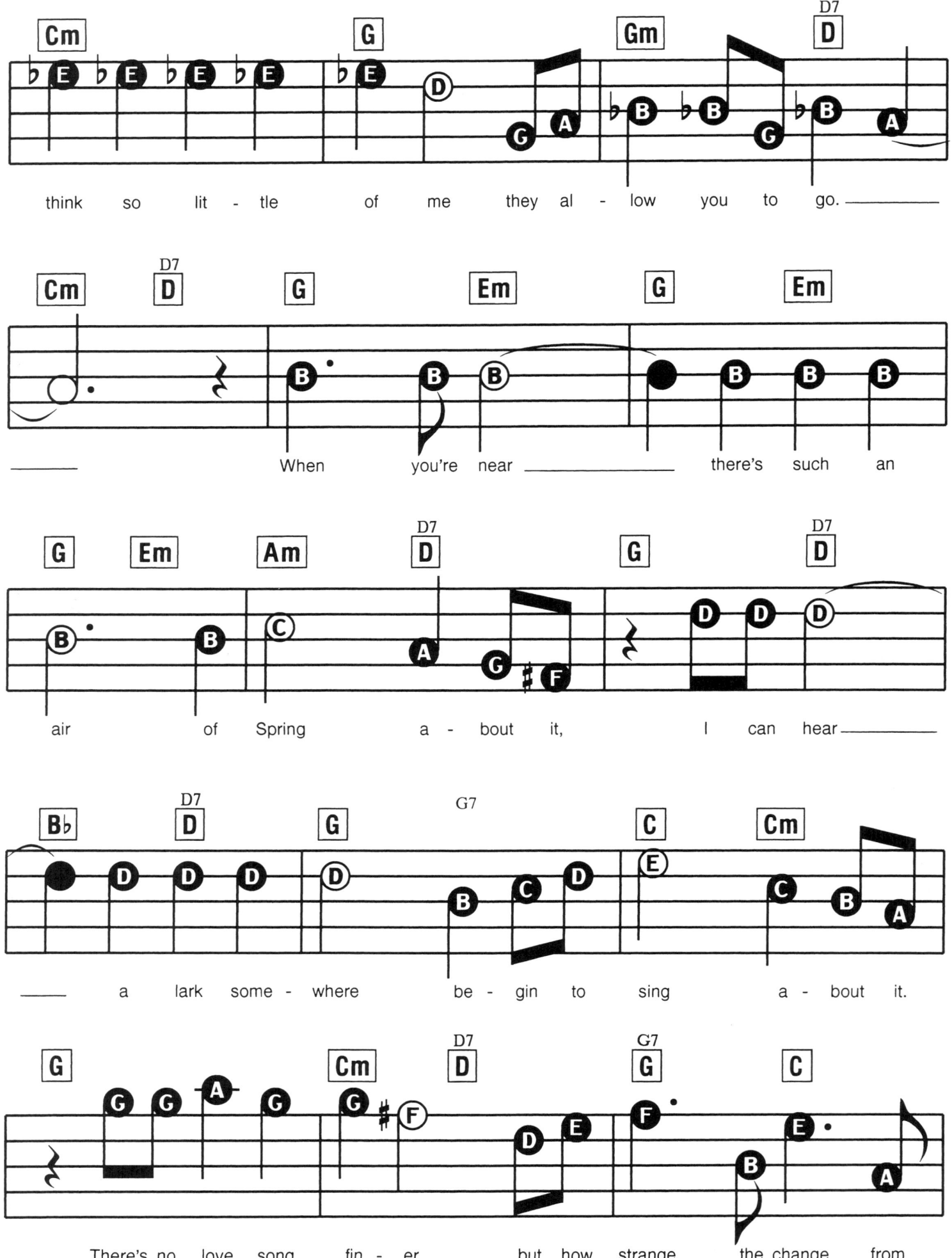

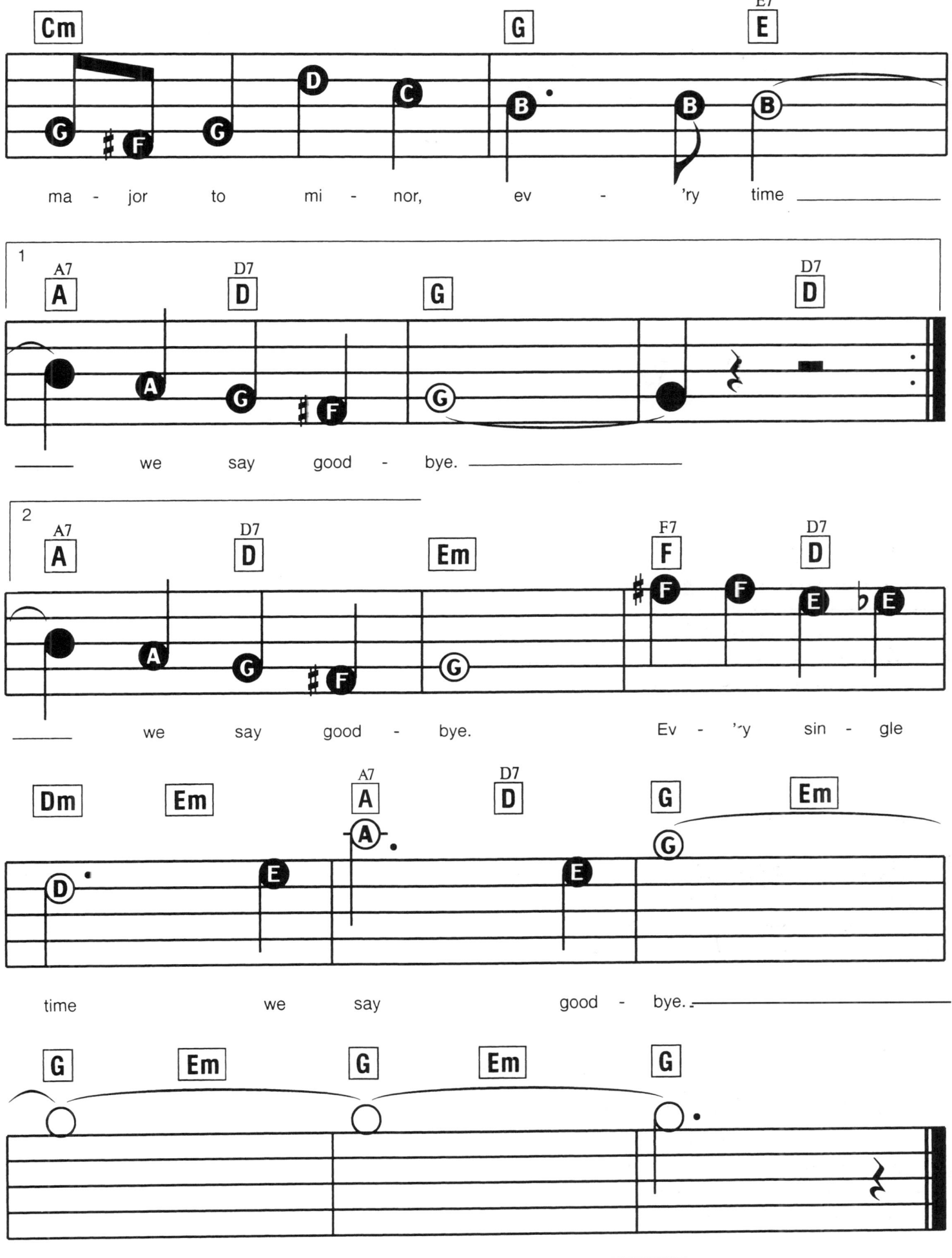

East of the Sun
(And West of the Moon)

Registration 2
Rhythm: Swing or Jazz

Words and Music by
Brooks Bowman

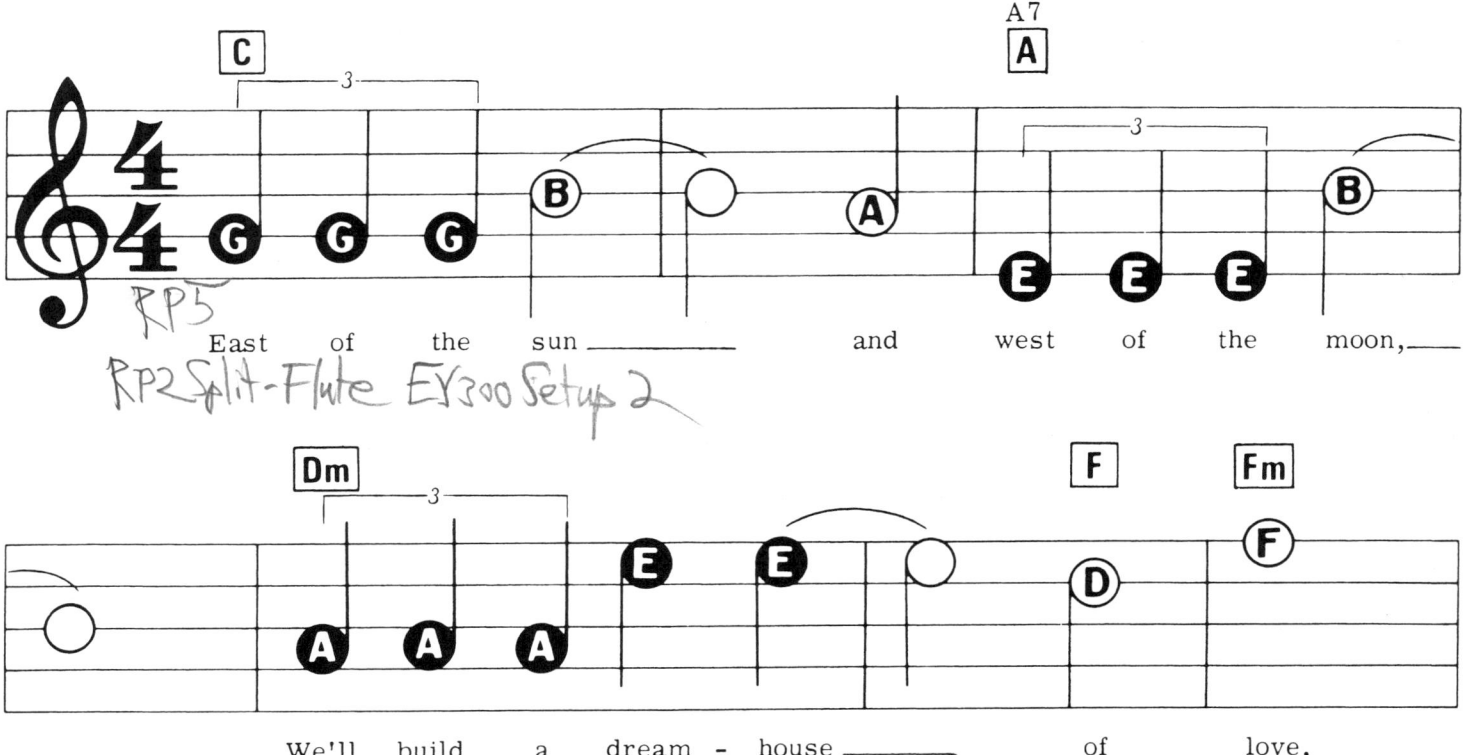

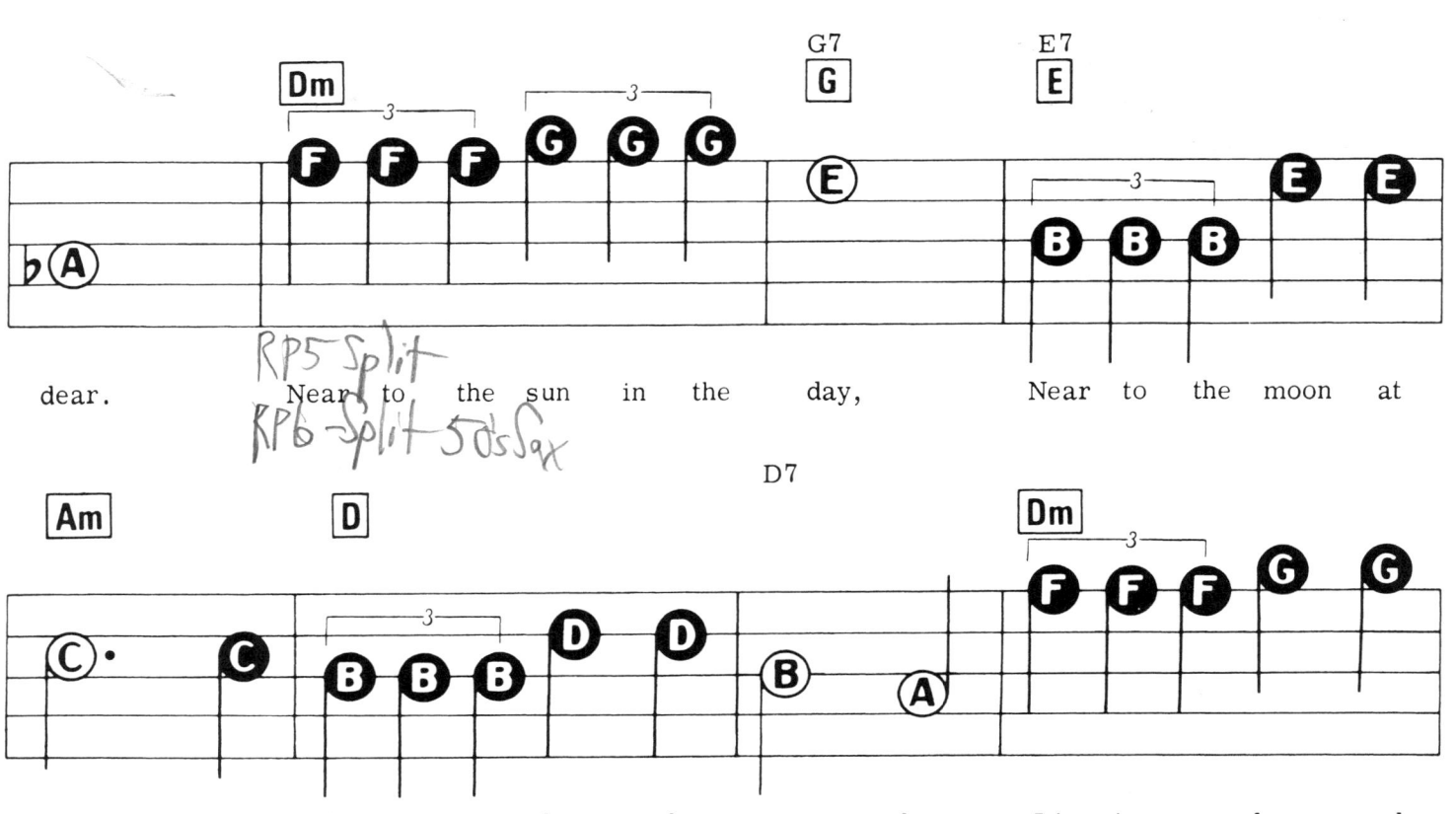

Copyright © 1934 by Chappell & Co.
Copyright Renewed
International Copyright Secured   All Rights Reserved

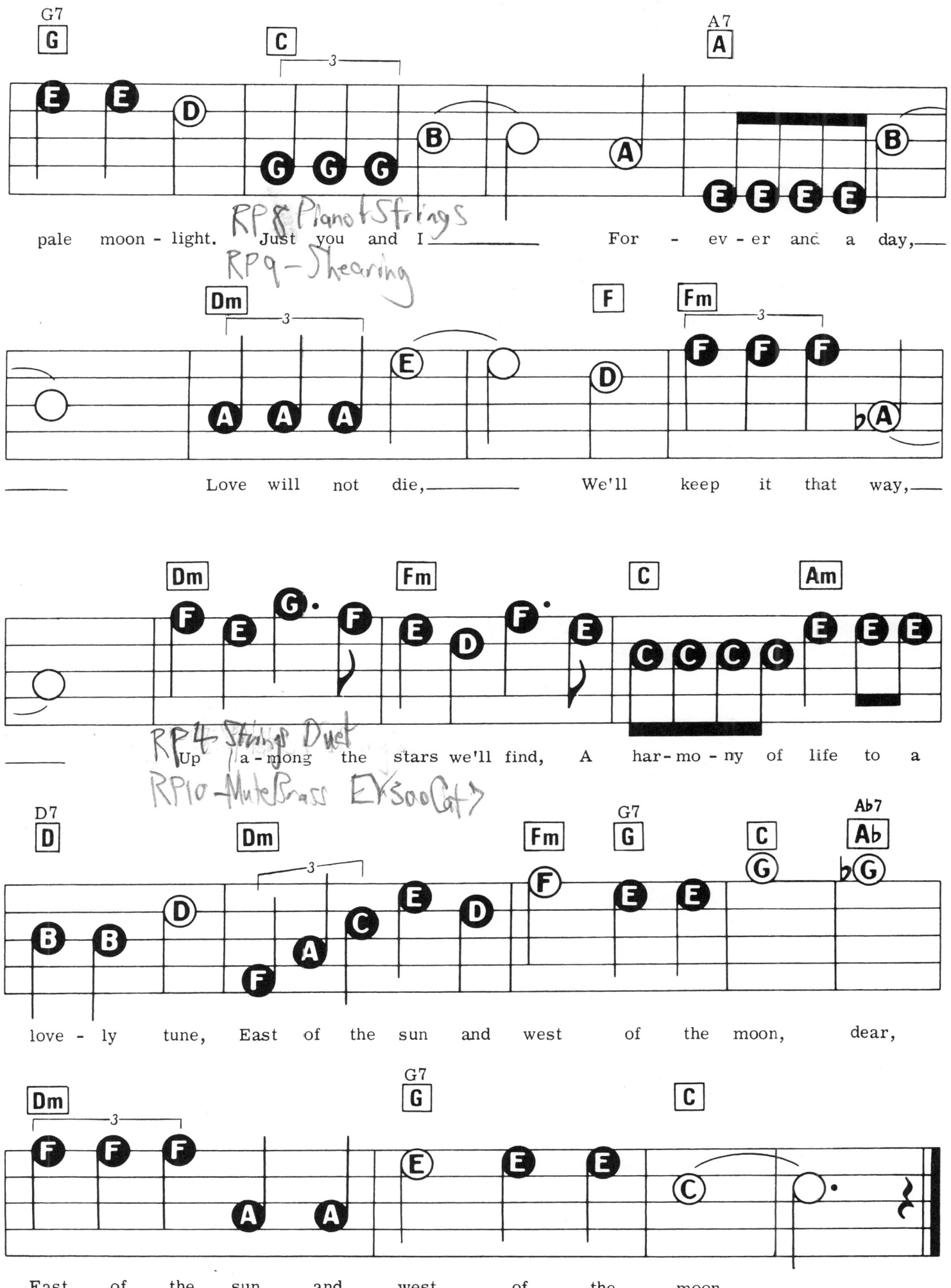

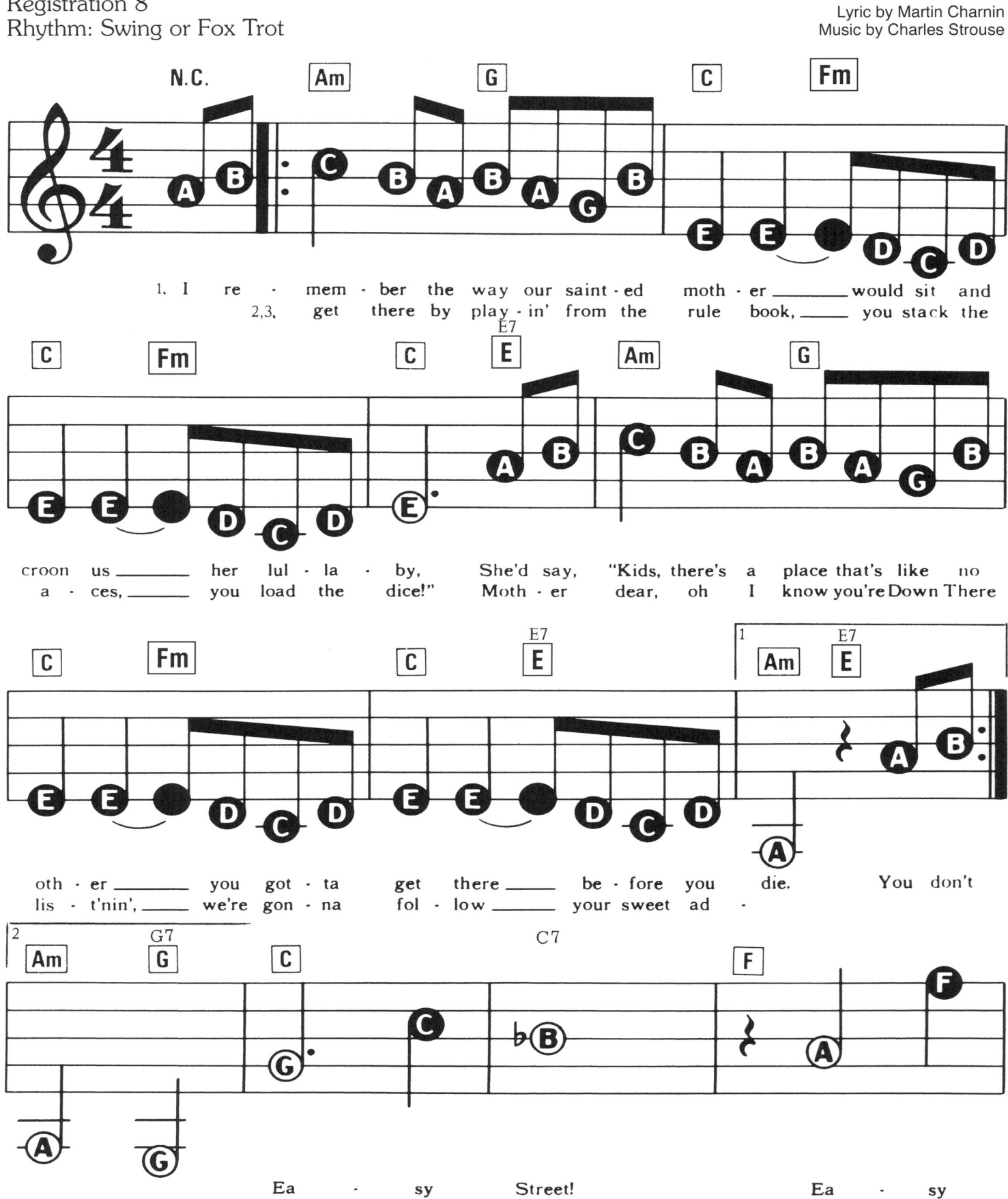

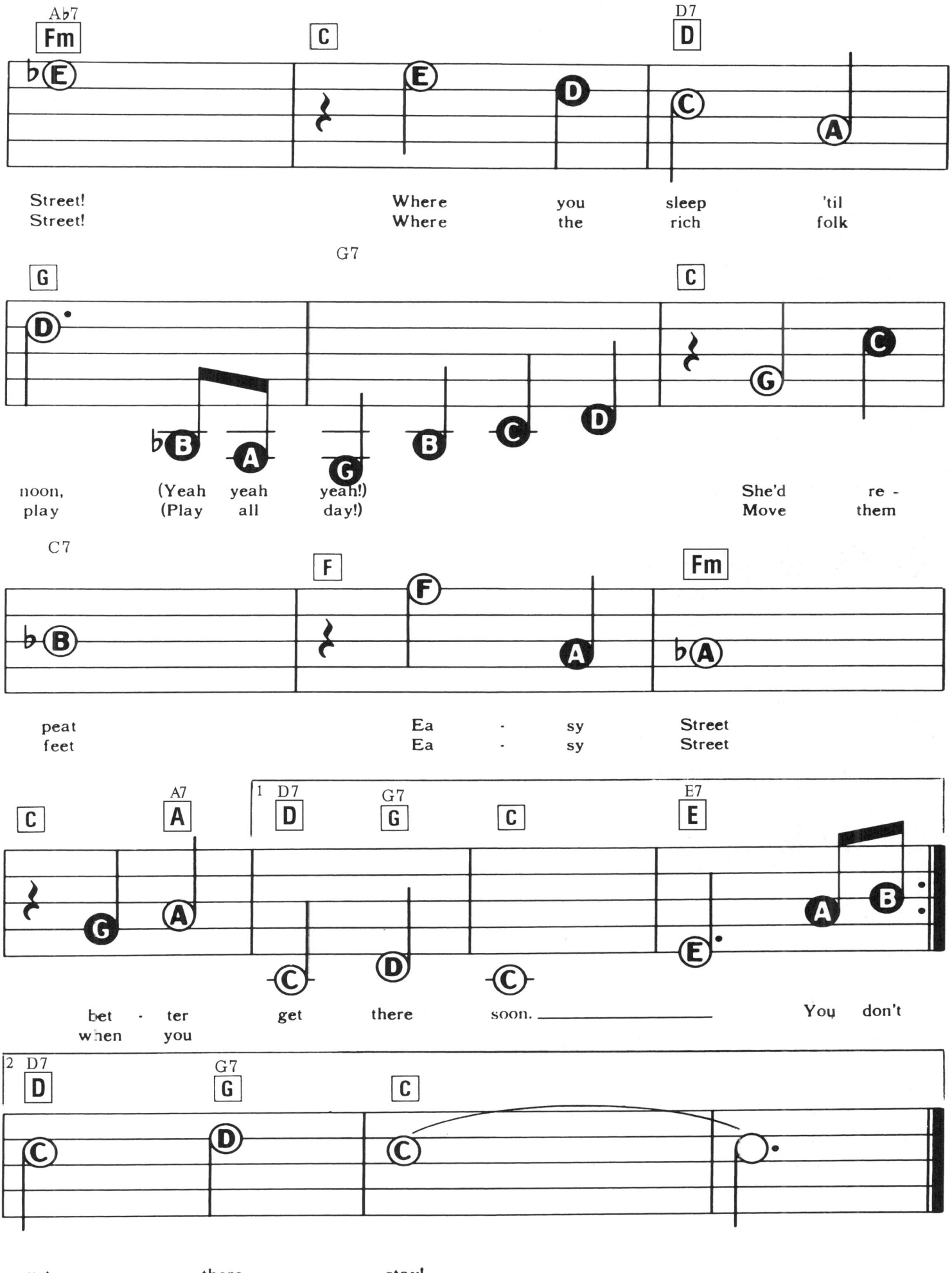

Falling in Love with Love
from THE BOYS FROM SYRACUSE

Registration 5
Rhythm: Waltz

Words by Lorenz Hart
Music by Richard Rodgers

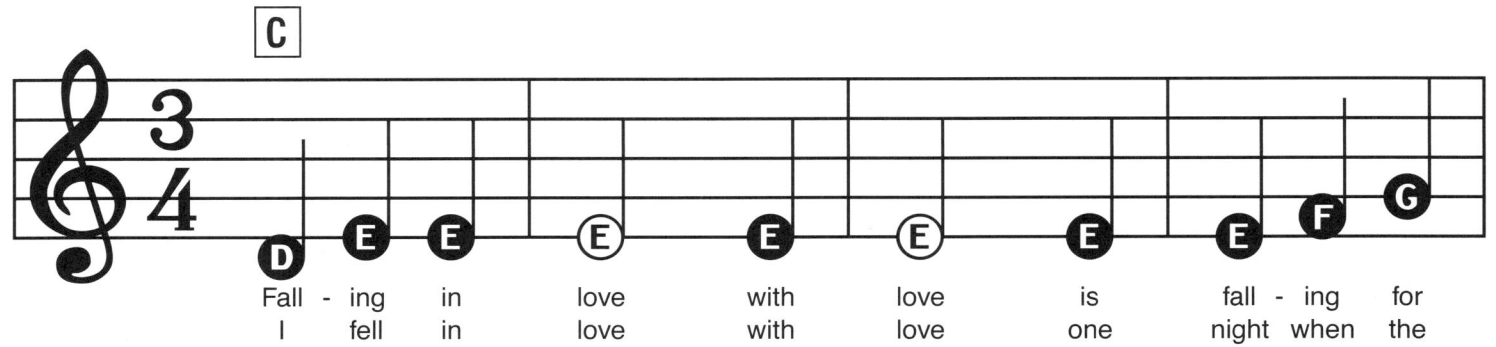

Fall - ing in love with love is fall - ing for
I fell in love with love one night when the

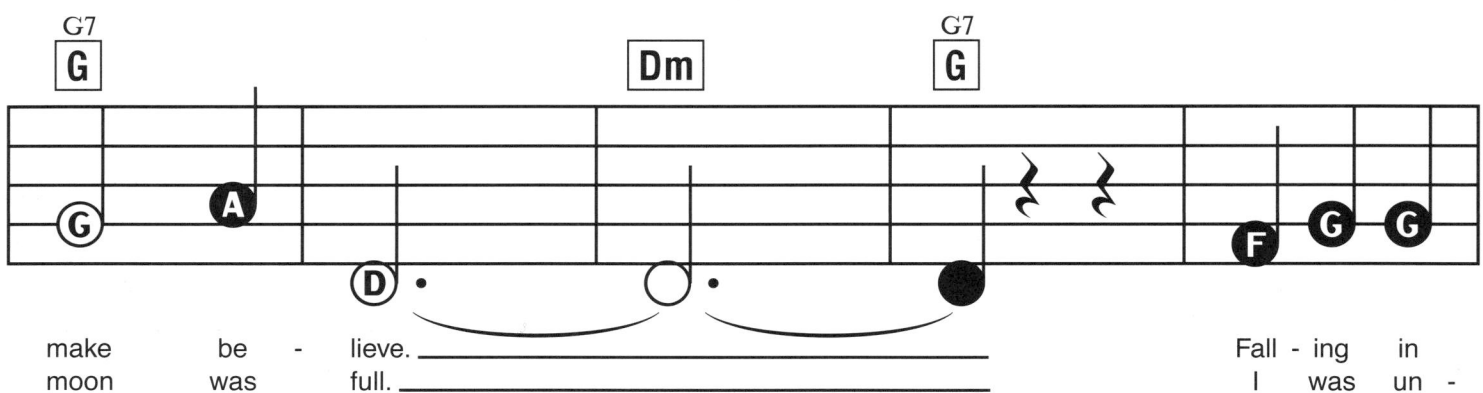

make be - lieve.___ Fall - ing in
moon was full.___ I was un -

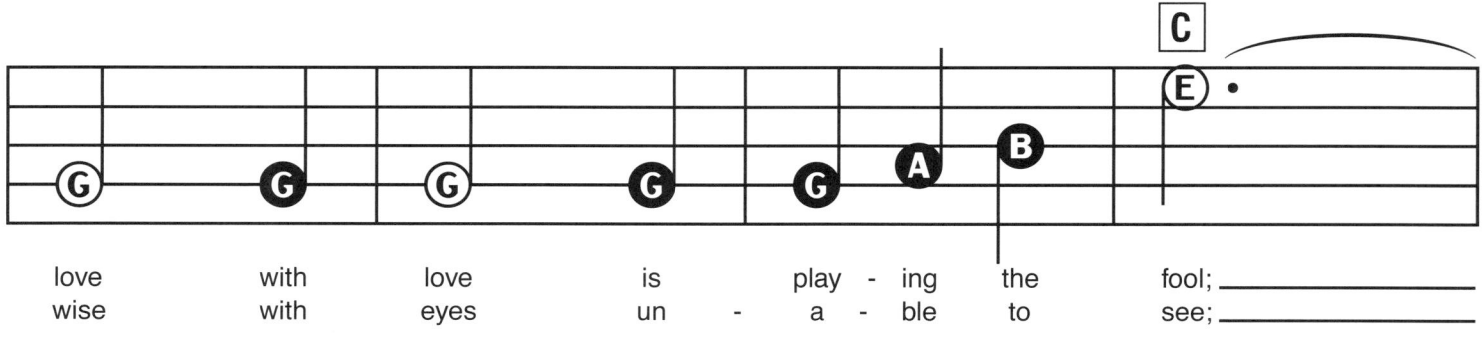

love with love is play - ing the fool;___
wise with eyes un - a - ble to see;___

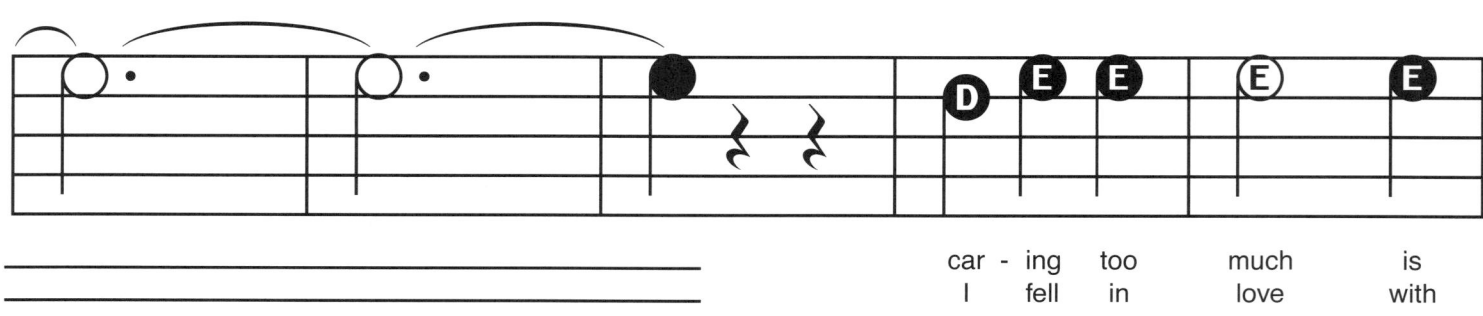

___
___ car - ing too much is
I fell in love with

Copyright © 1938 (Renewed) by Chappell & Co.
Rights for the Extended Renewal Term in the U.S. Controlled by Williamson Music and WB Music Corp. o/b/o The Estate Of Lorenz Hart
International Copyright Secured All Rights Reserved

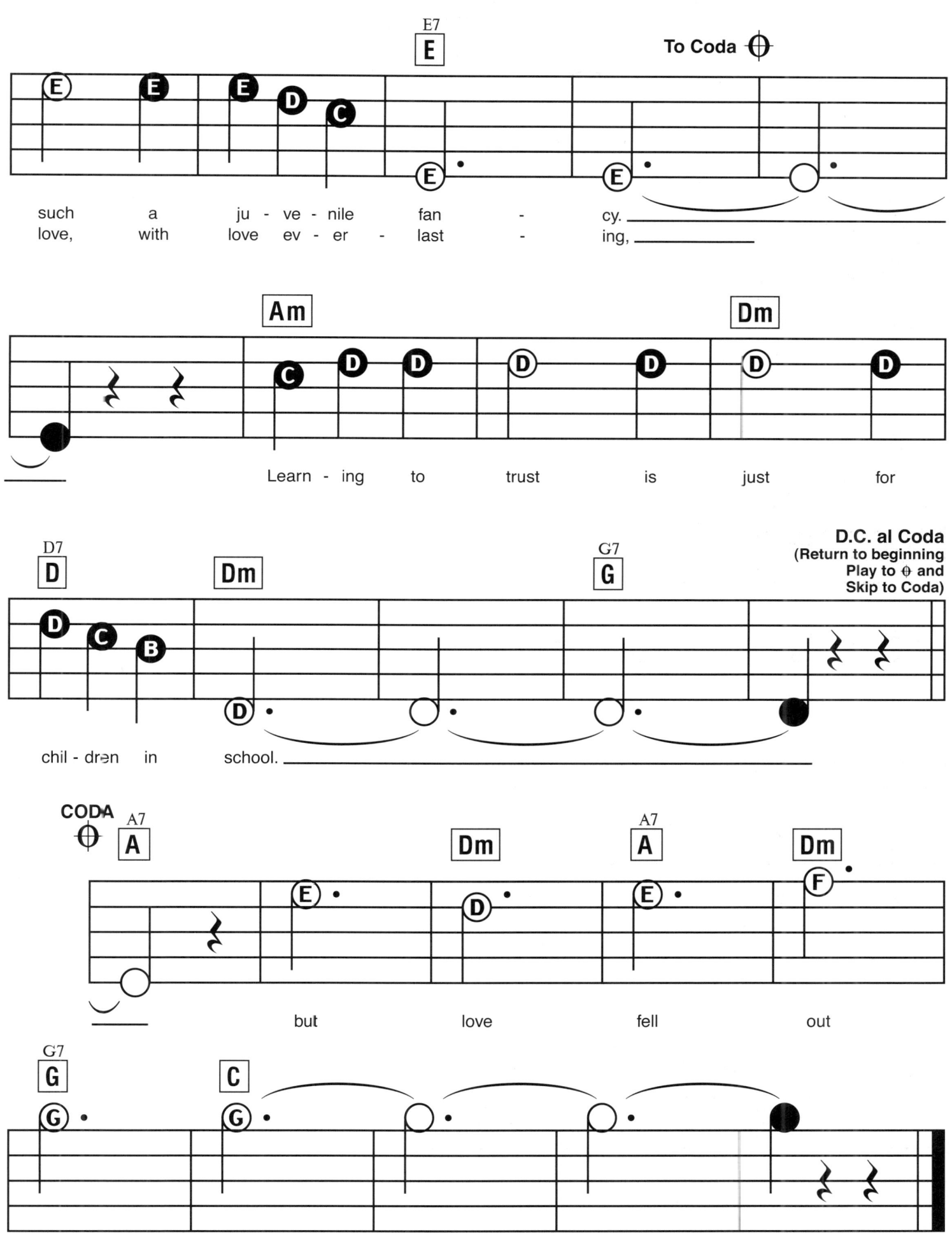

A Fine Romance
from SWING TIME

Registration 2
Rhythm: Ballad or Swing

Words by Dorothy Fields
Music by Jerome Kern

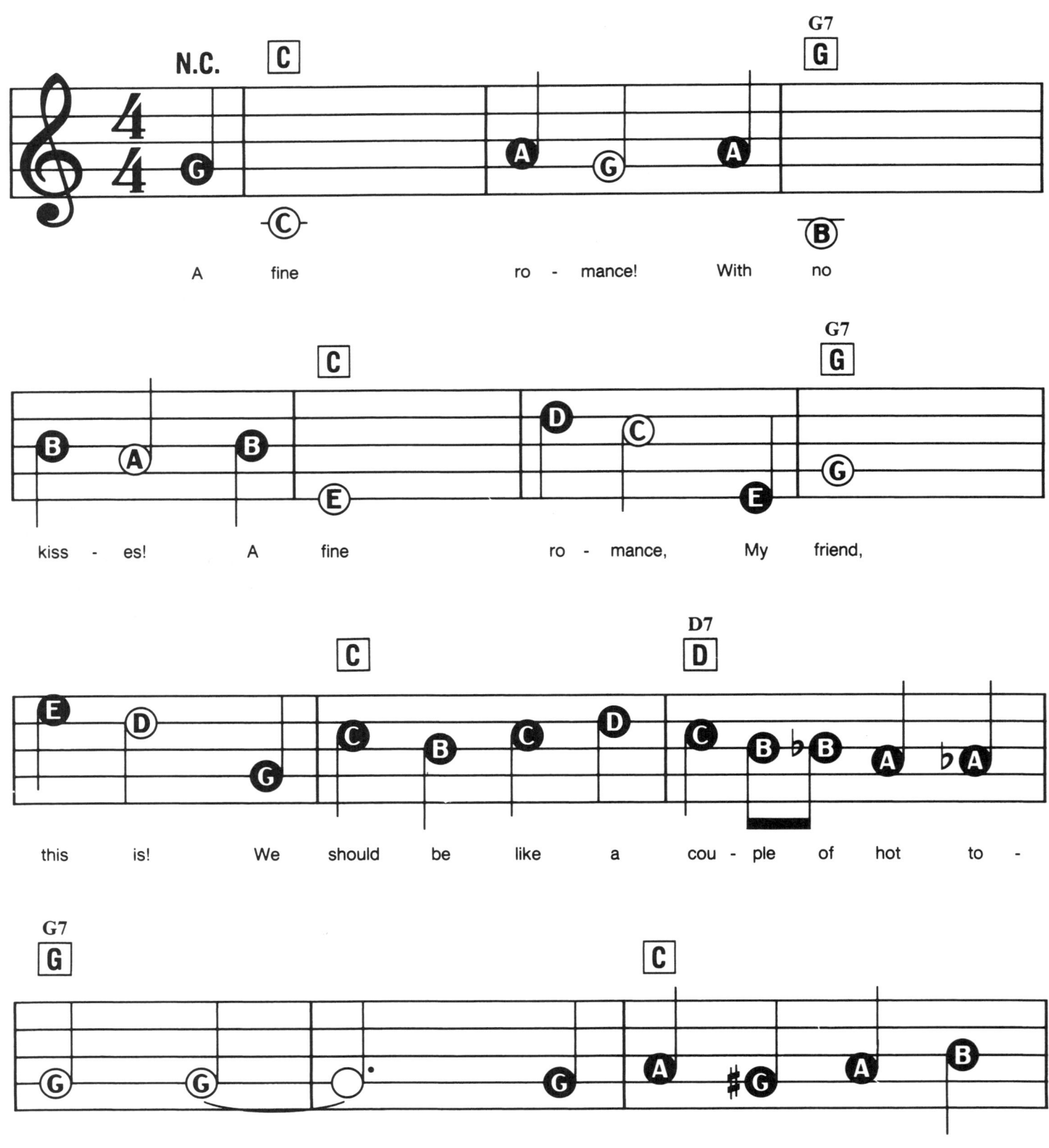

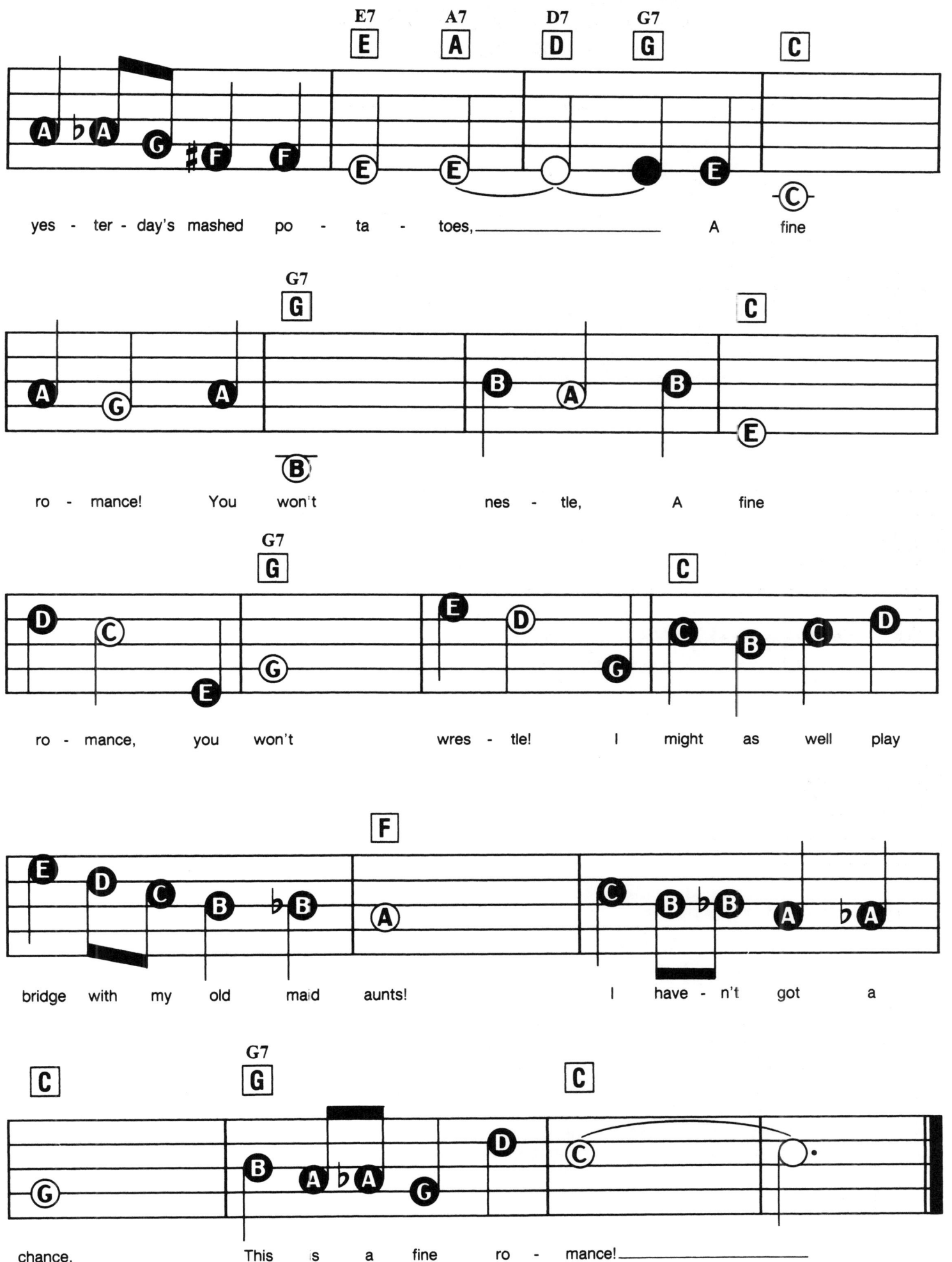

The Folks Who Live on the Hill
from HIGH, WIDE AND HANDSOME

Registration 3
Rhythm: Fox Trot or Swing

Lyrics by Oscar Hammerstein II
Music by Jerome Kern

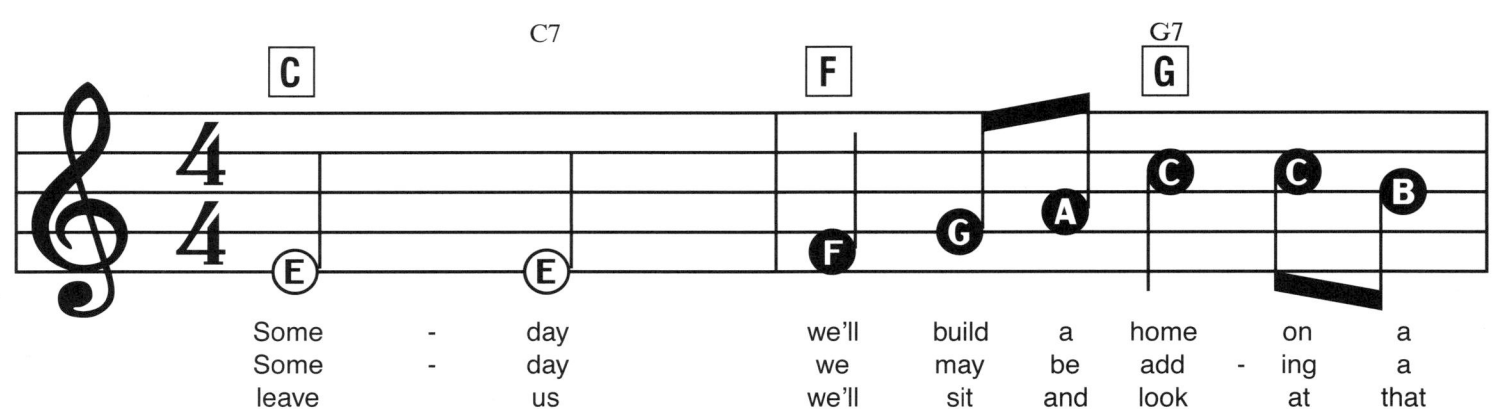

Some - day we'll build a home on a
Some - day we may be add - ing a
leave us we'll sit and look at that

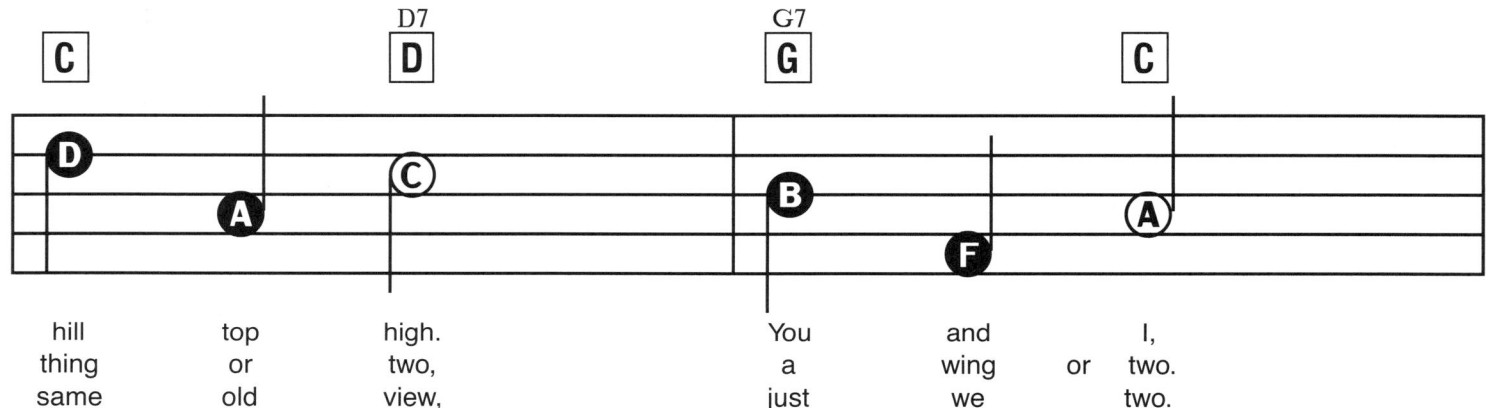

hill top high. You and I,
thing or two, a wing or two.
same old view, just we two.

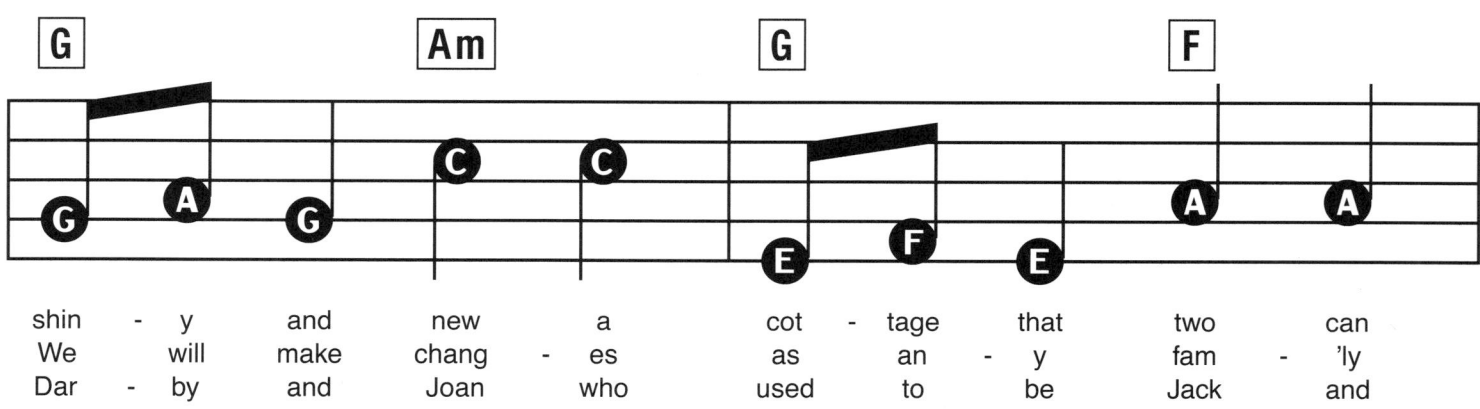

shin - y and new a cot - tage that two can
We will make chang - es as an - y fam - 'ly
Dar - by and Joan who used to be Jack and

Copyright © 1937 UNIVERSAL - POLYGRAM INTERNATIONAL PUBLISHING, INC.
Copyright Renewed
All Rights Reserved   Used by Permission

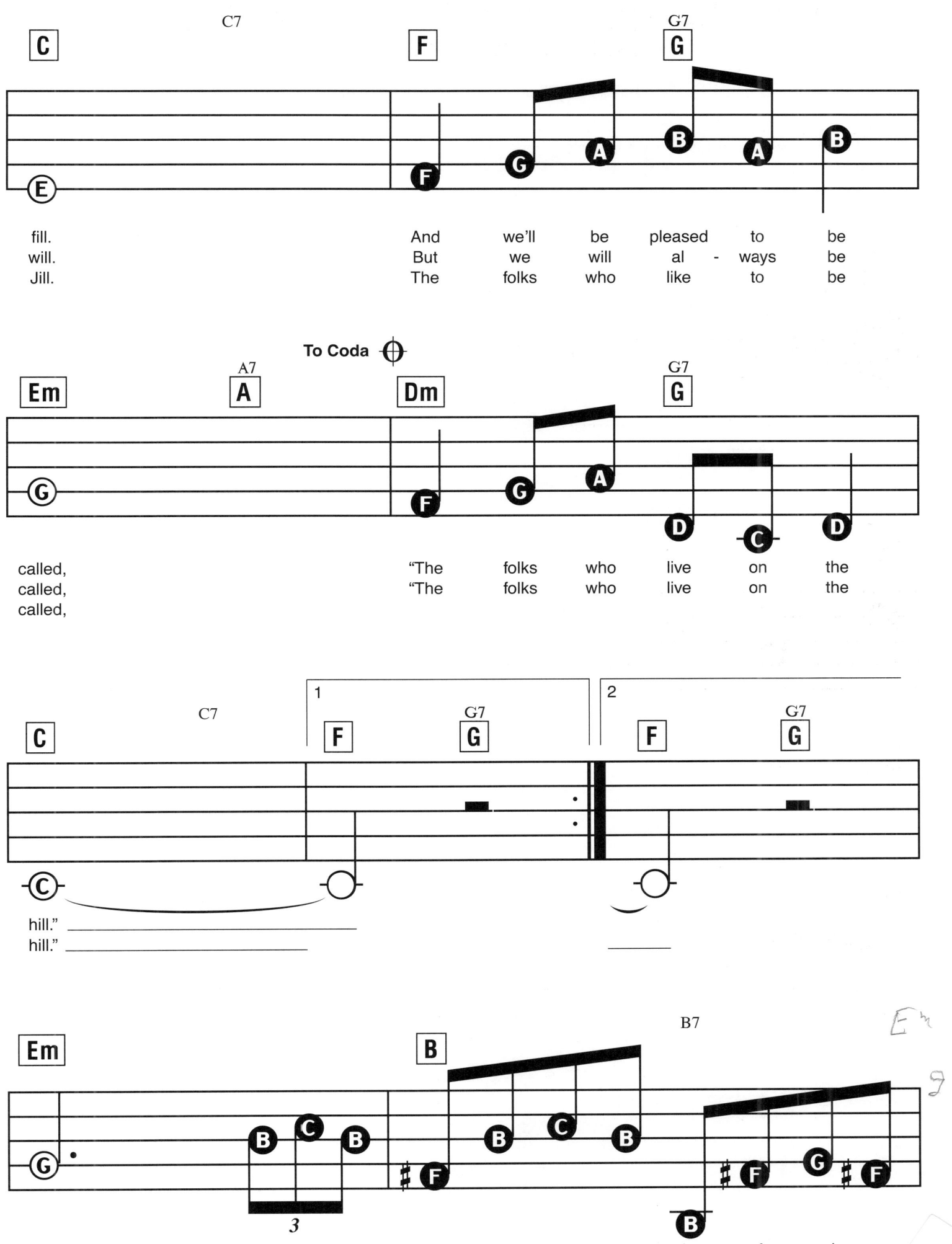

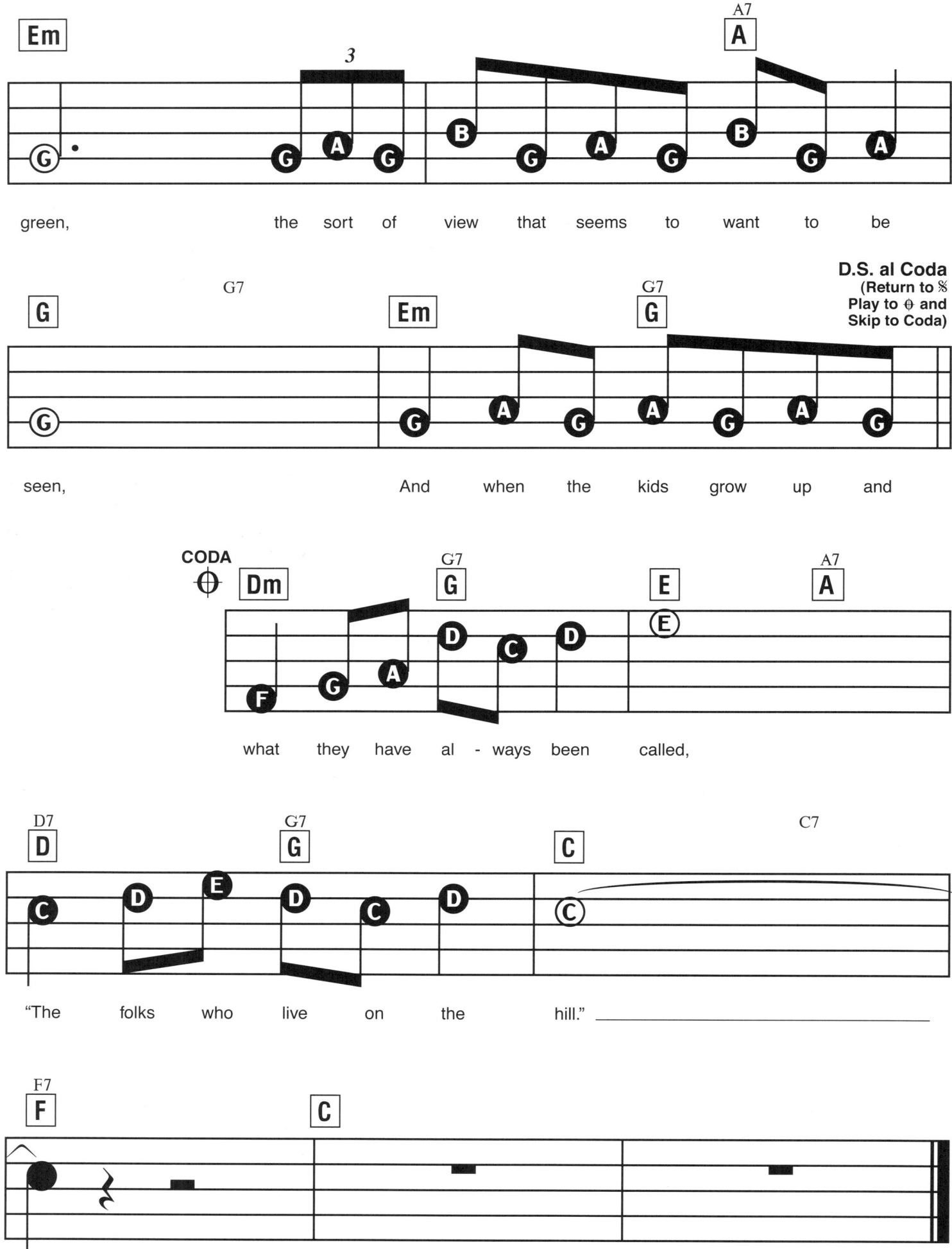

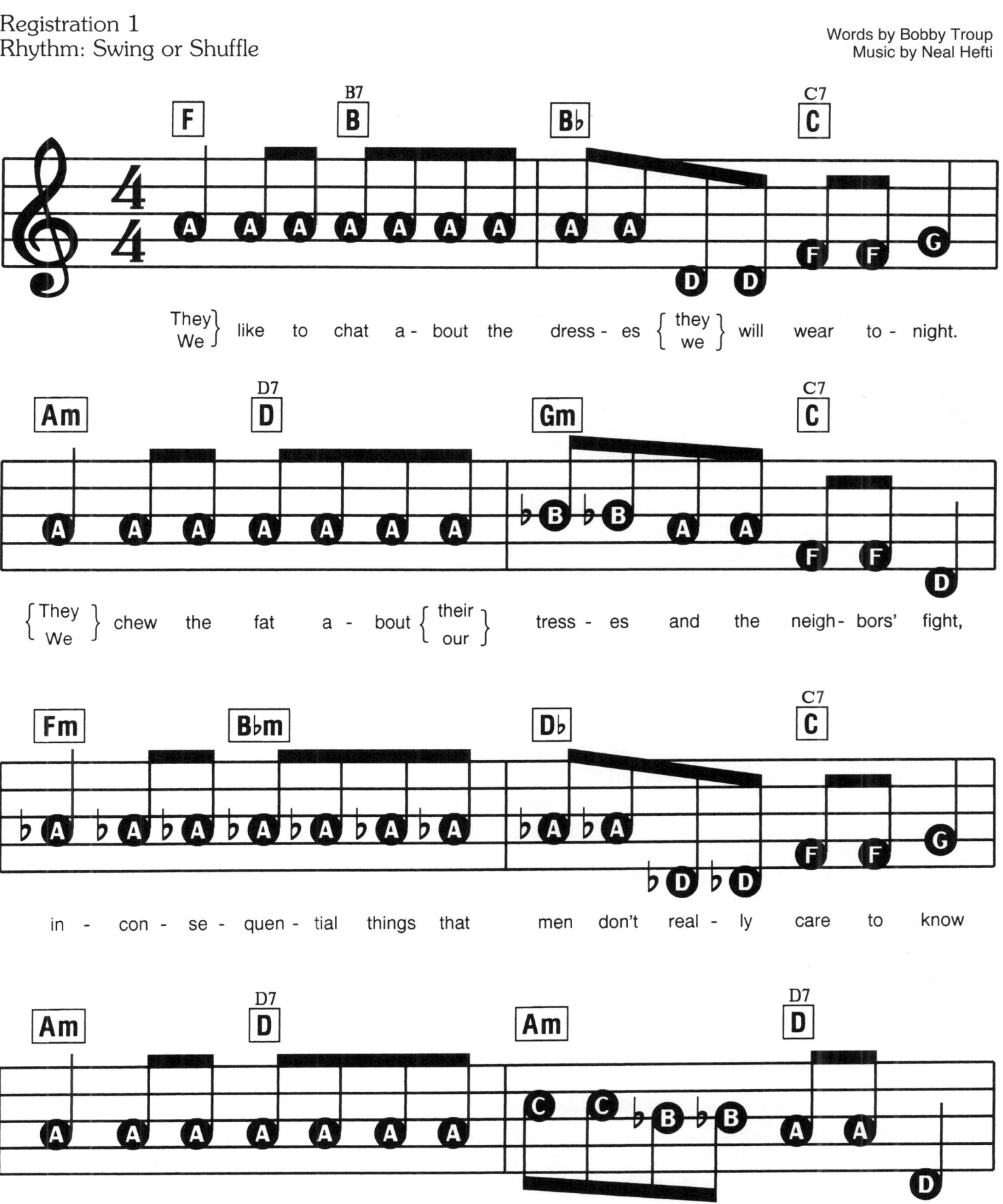

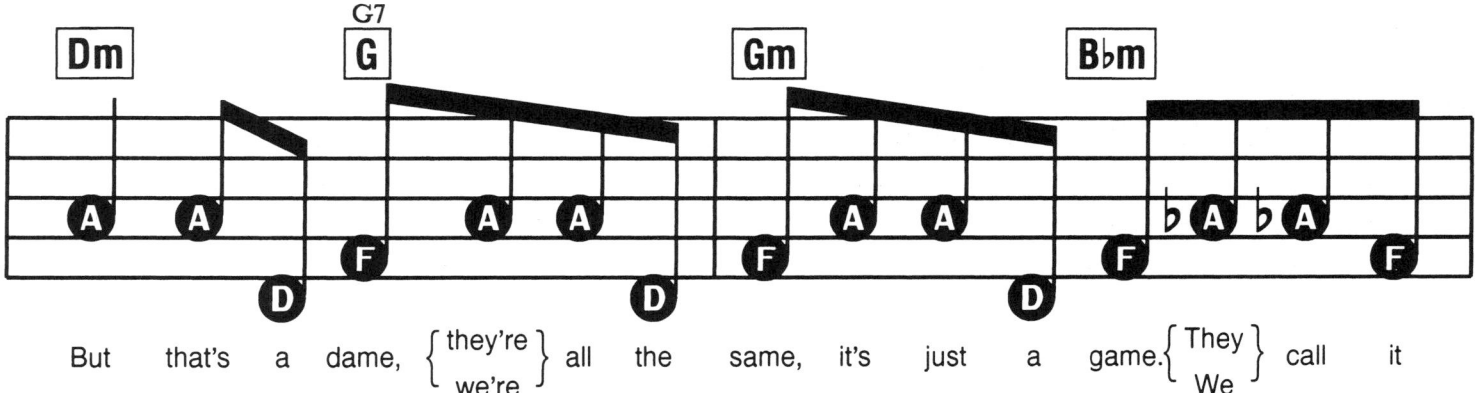
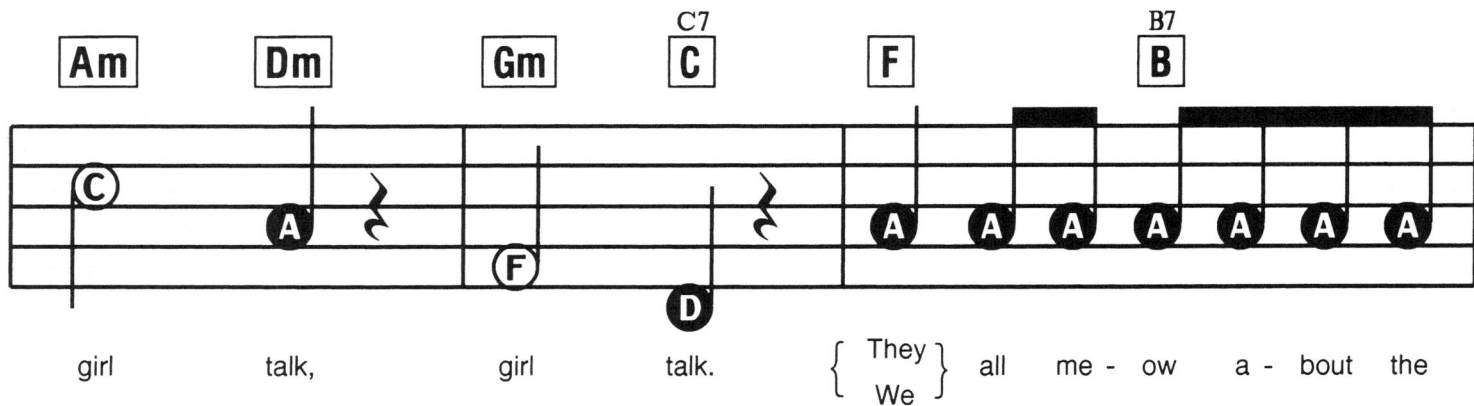
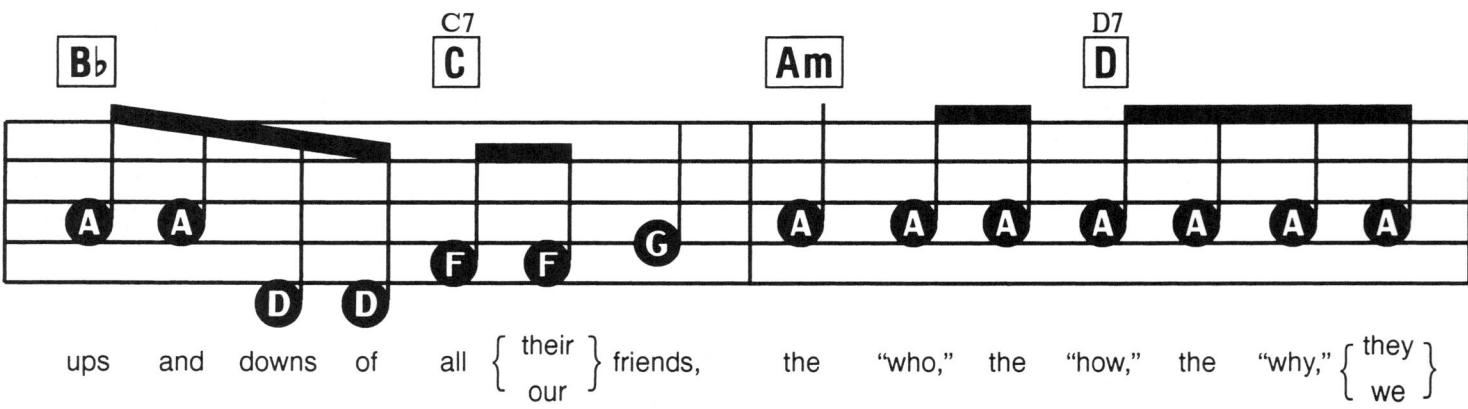
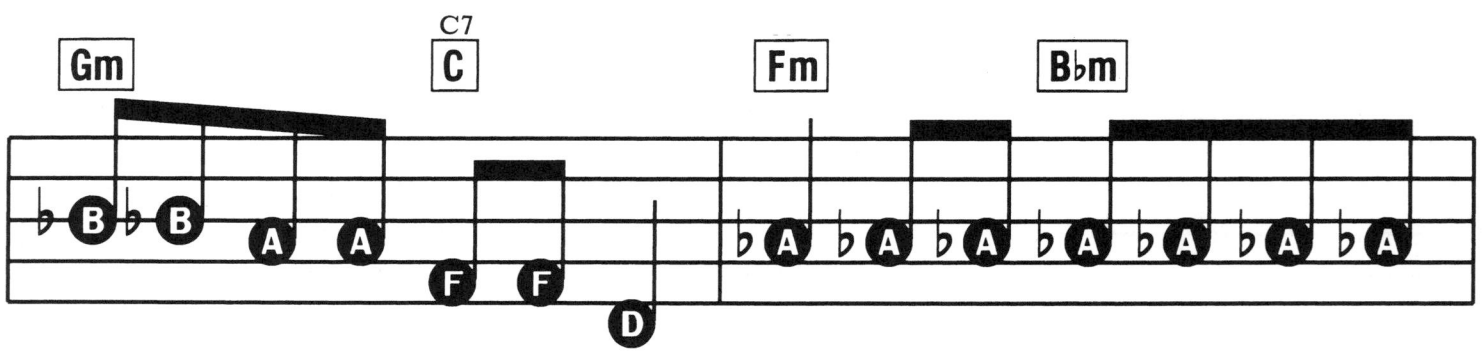

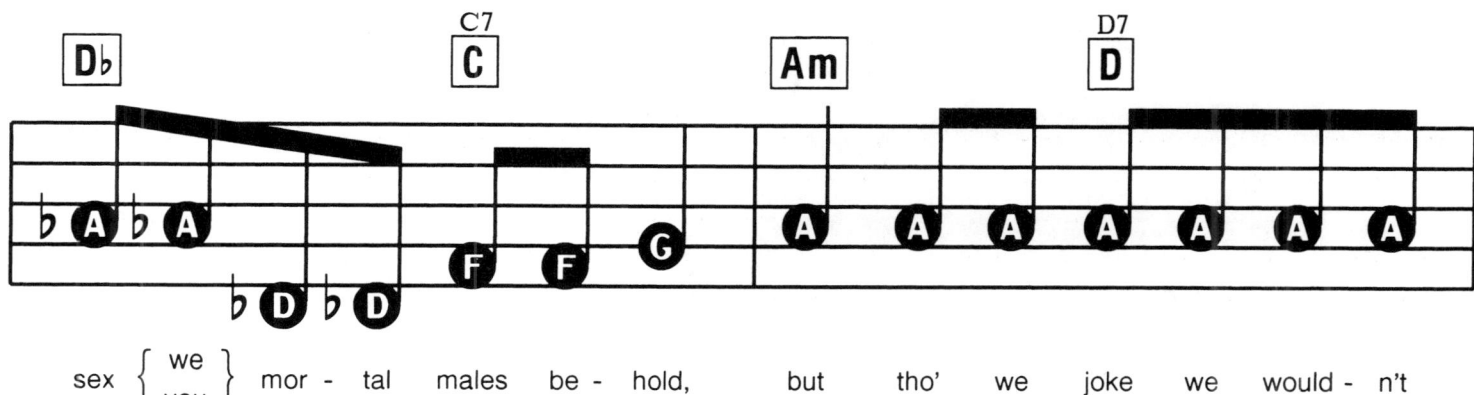
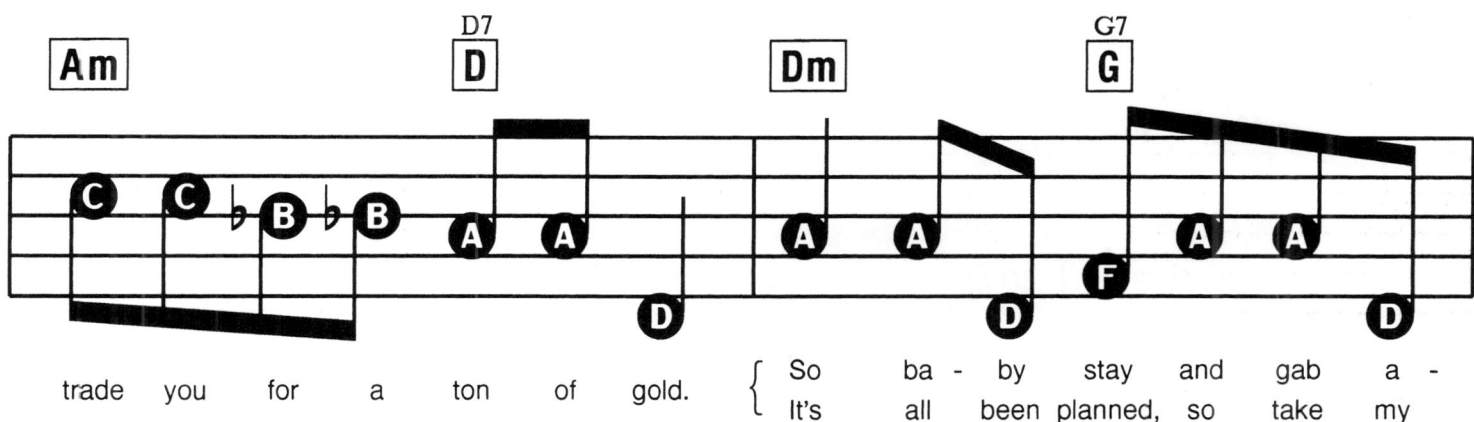
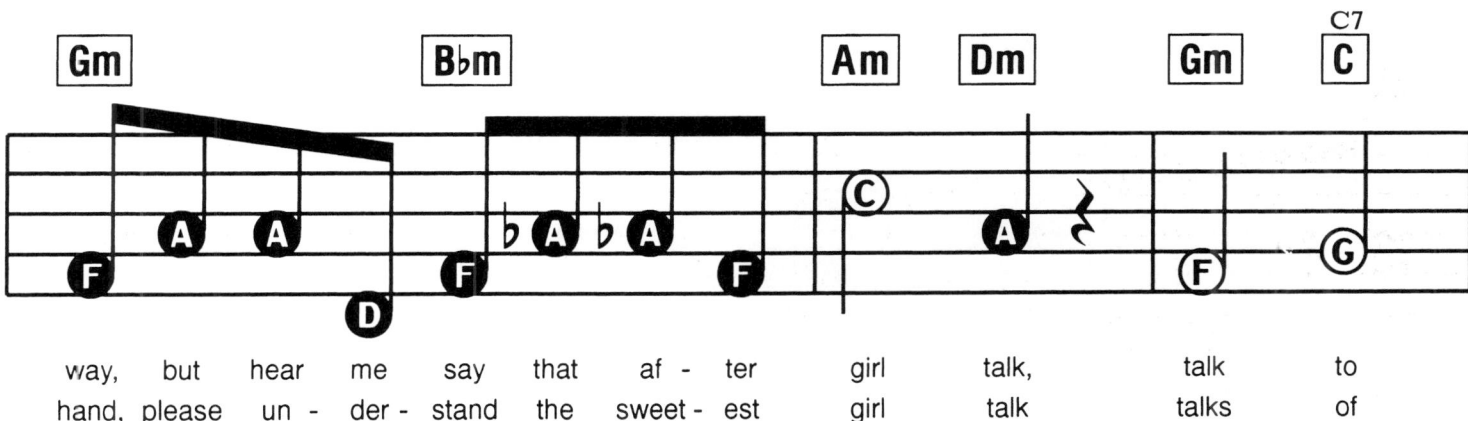
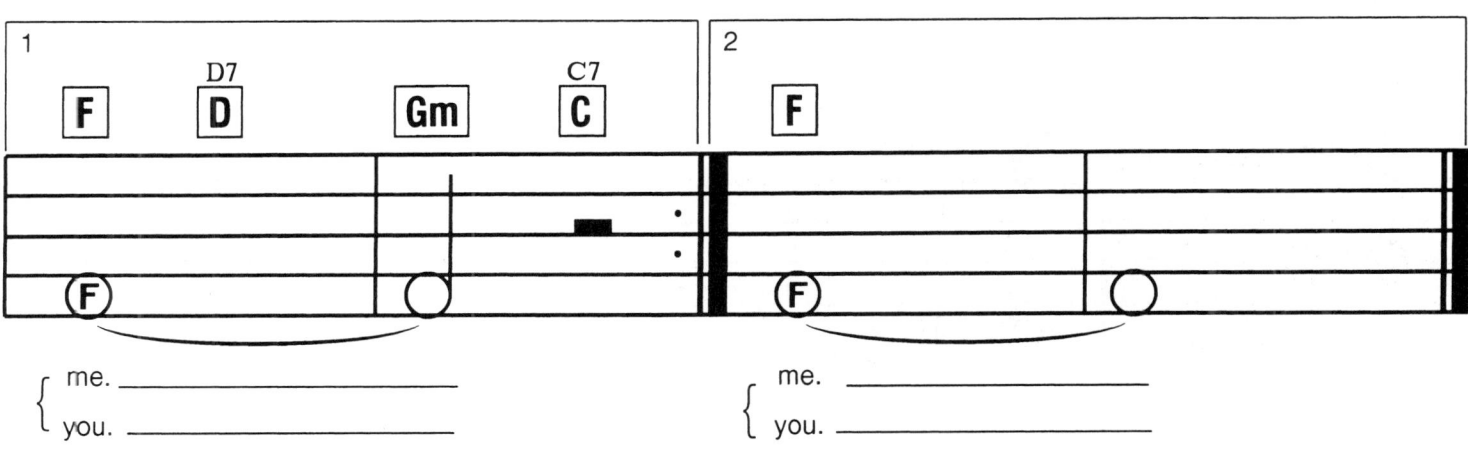

From This Moment On
from OUT OF THIS WORLD

Registration 5
Rhythm: Swing

Words and Music by
Cole Porter

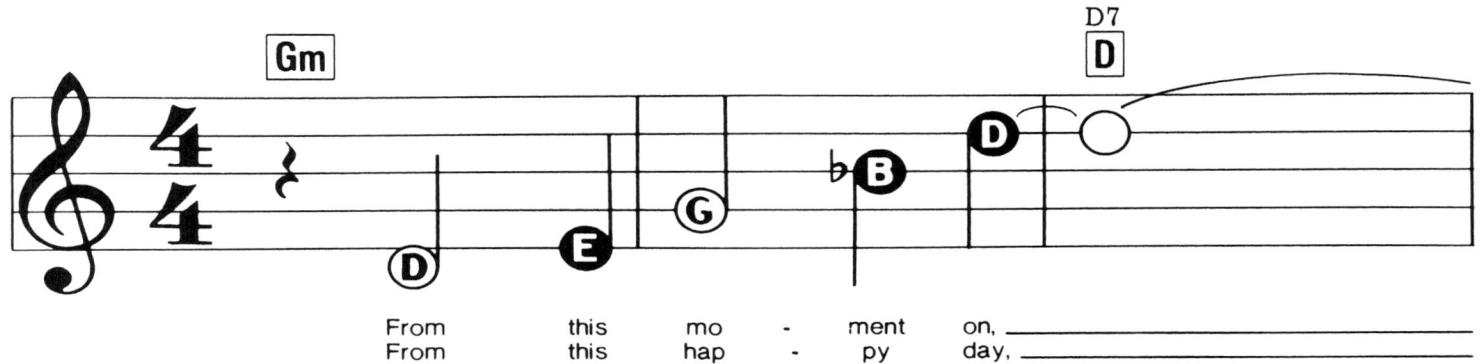

From this mo - ment on, _____
From this hap - py day, _____

you for
no more

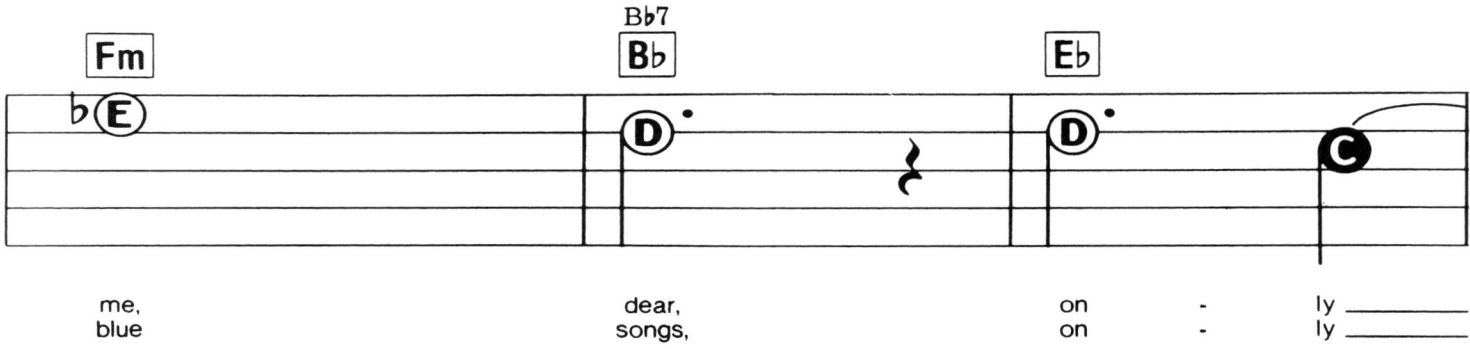

me, dear, on - ly _____
blue songs, on - ly _____

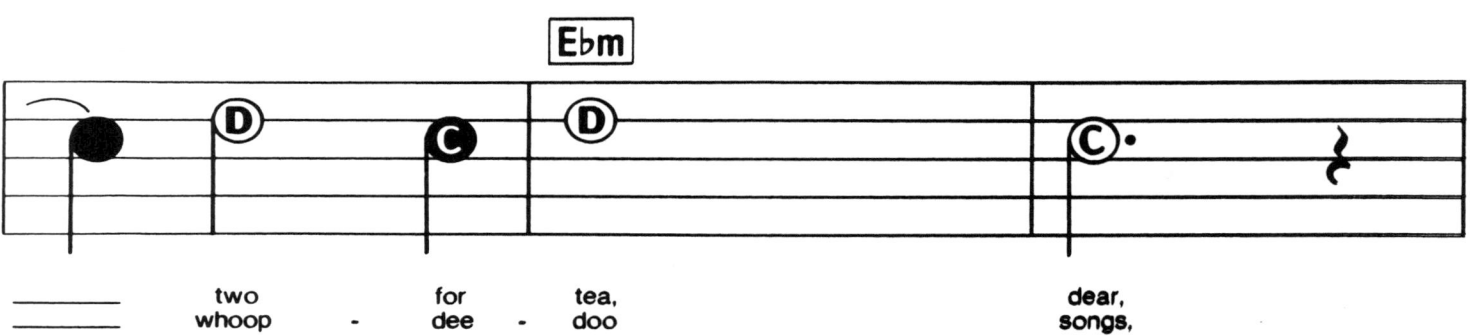

two for tea, dear,
whoop - dee - doo songs,

Copyright © 1950 by Cole Porter
Copyright Renewed, Assigned to Robert H. Montgomery, Trustee of the Cole Porter Musical and Literary Property Trusts
Chappell & Co. owner of publication and allied rights throughout the world
International Copyright Secured   All Rights Reserved

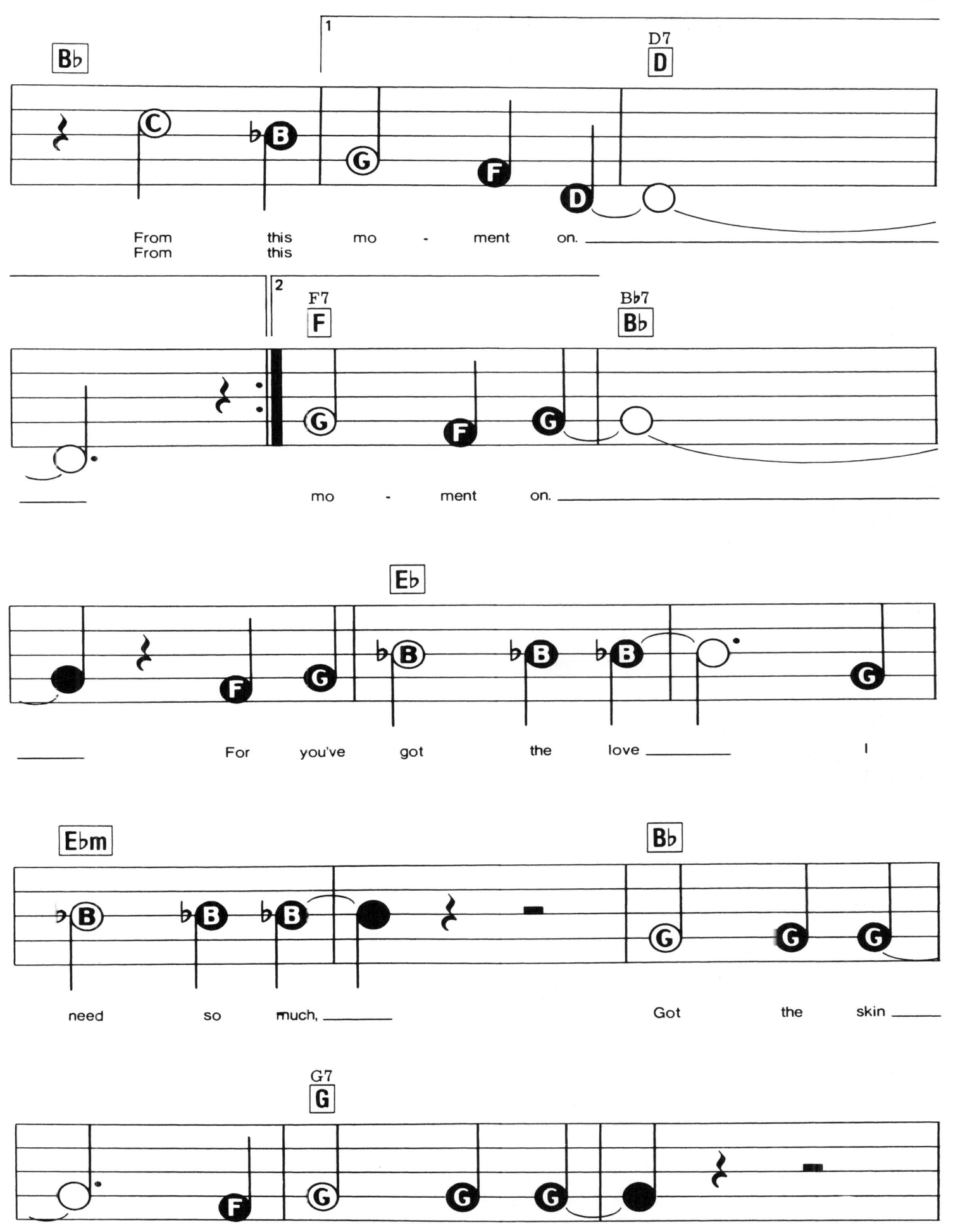

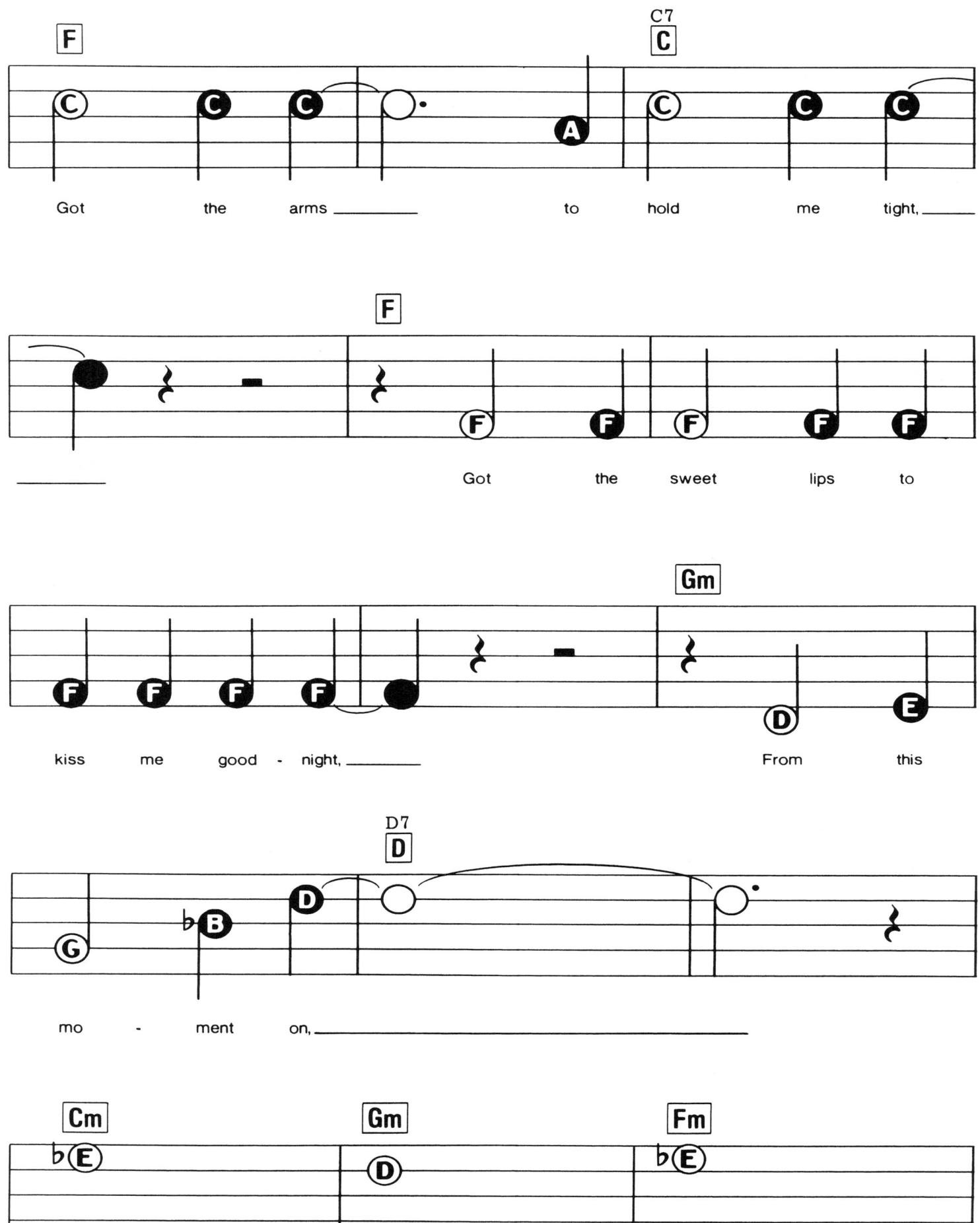

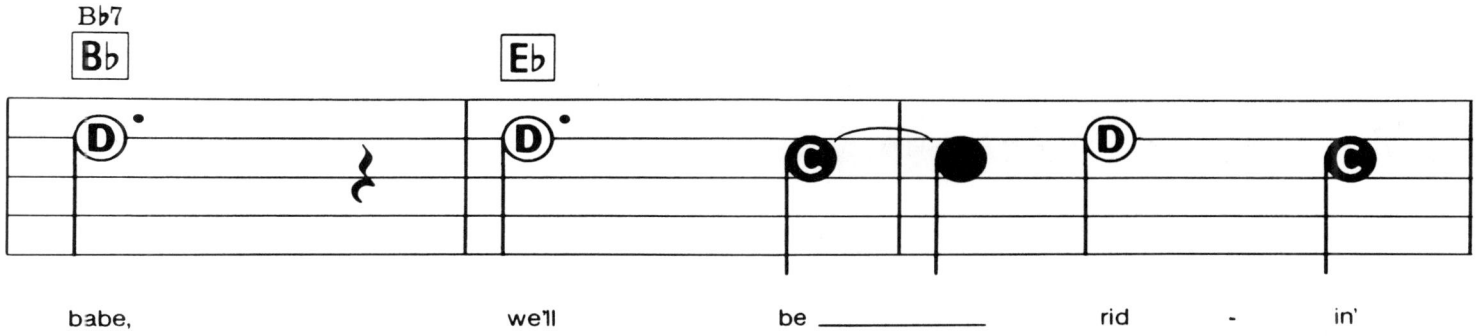
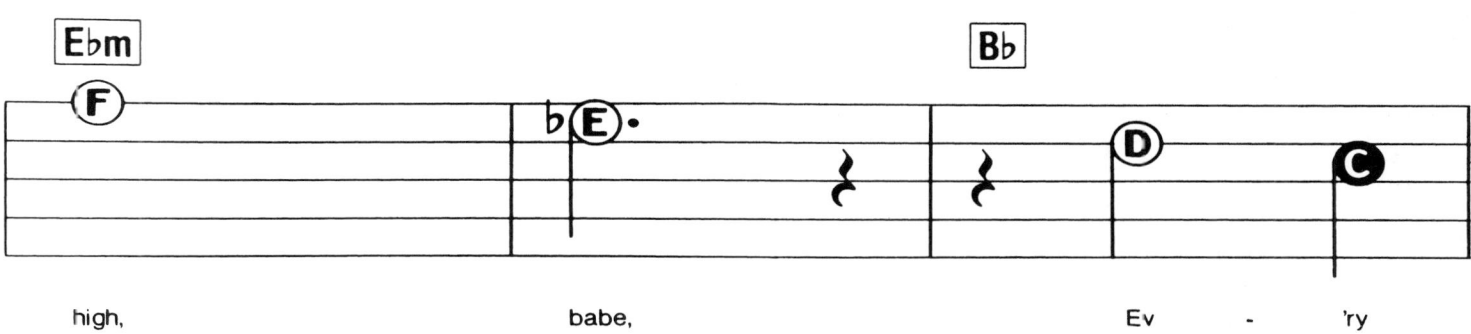
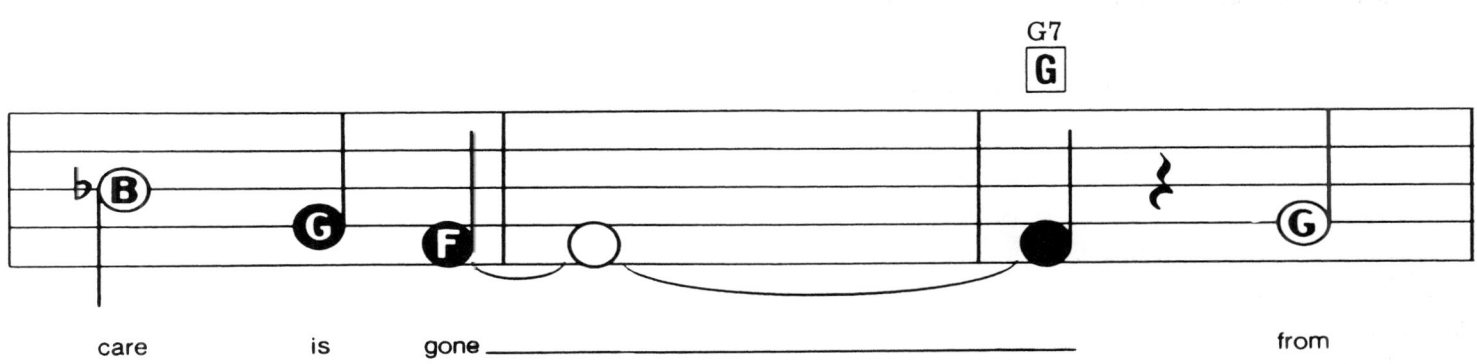
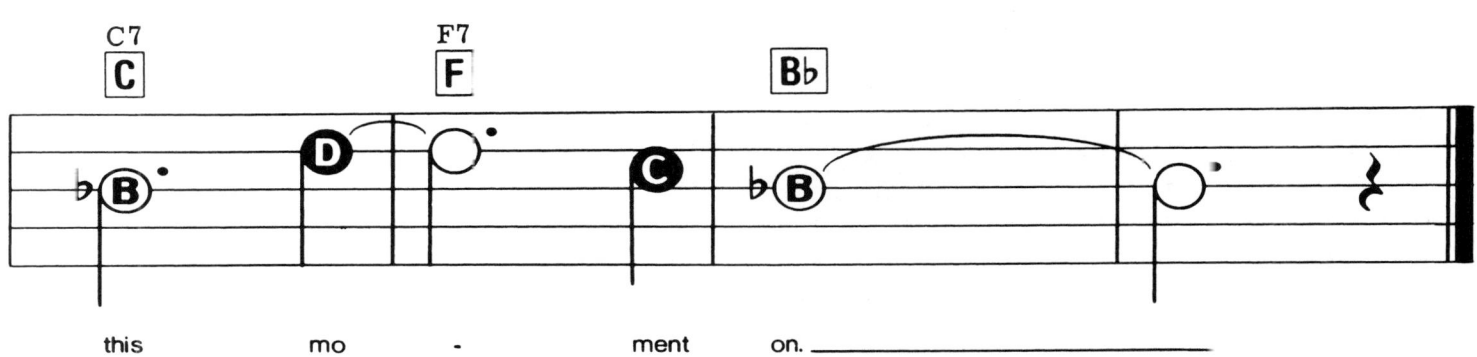

Gone with the Wind

Registration 2
Rhythm: Swing

Words and Music by Herb Magidson
and Allie Wrubel

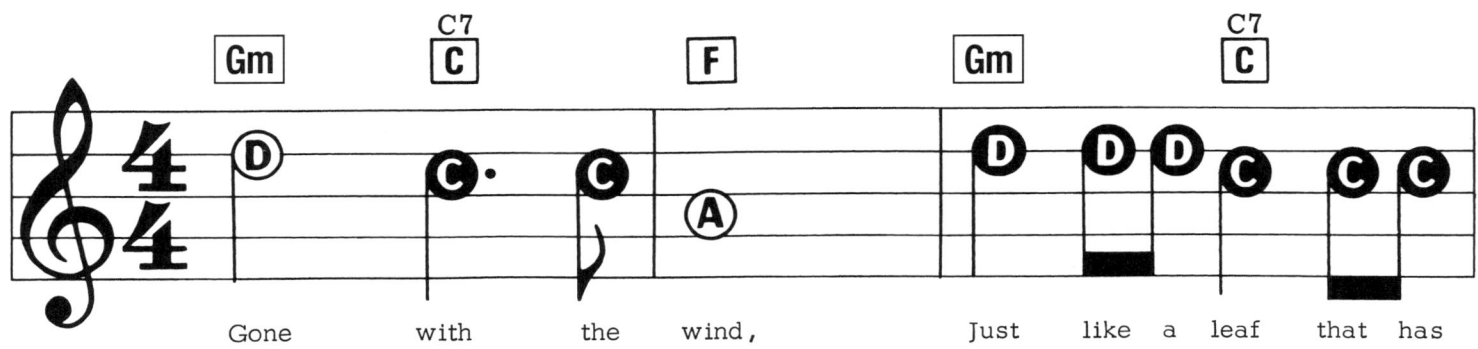
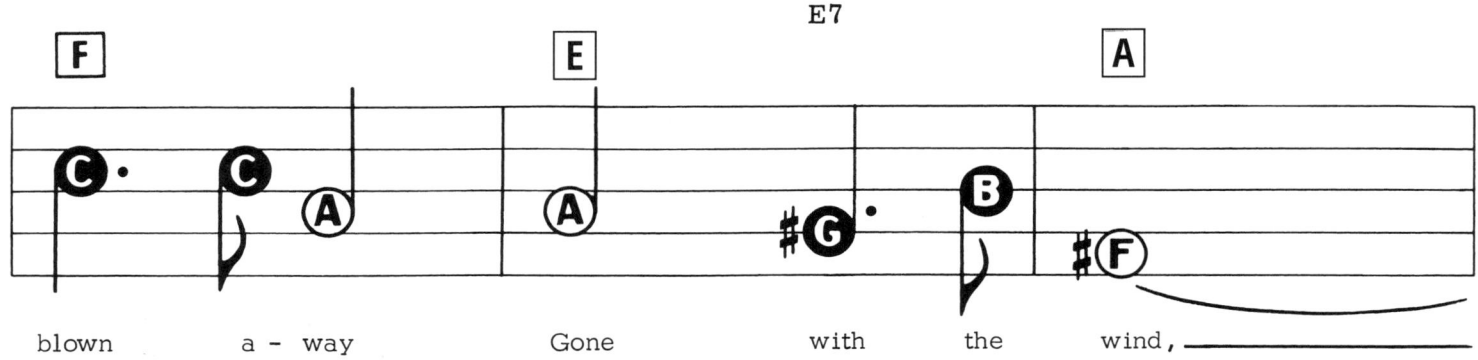
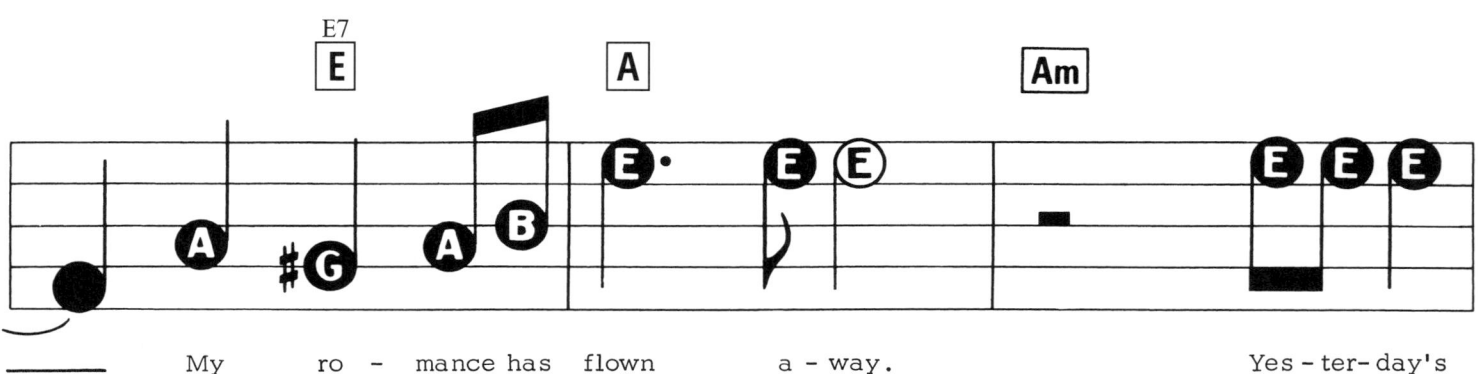
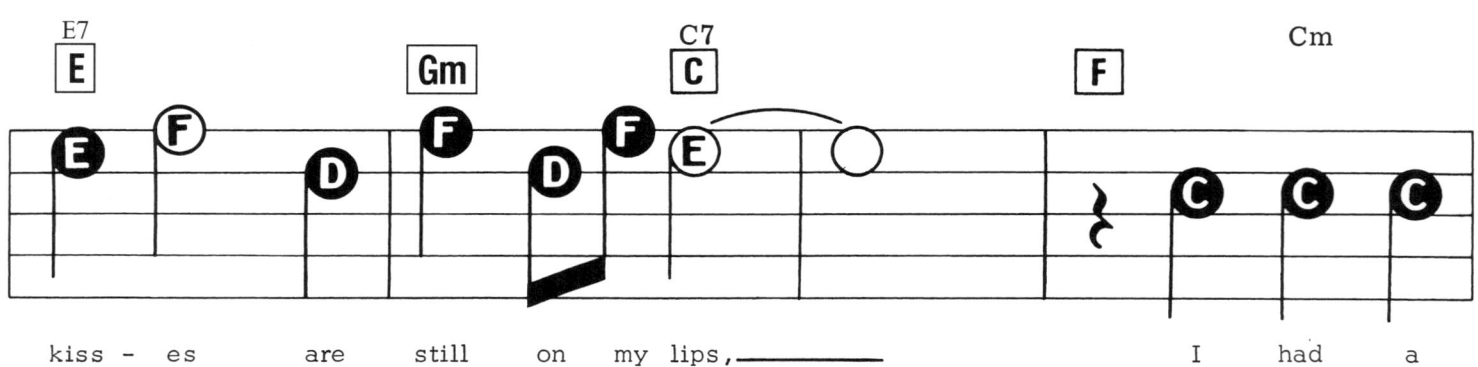

Copyright © 1937 by Bourne Co. (ASCAP)
Copyright Renewed
International Copyright Secured   All Rights Reserved

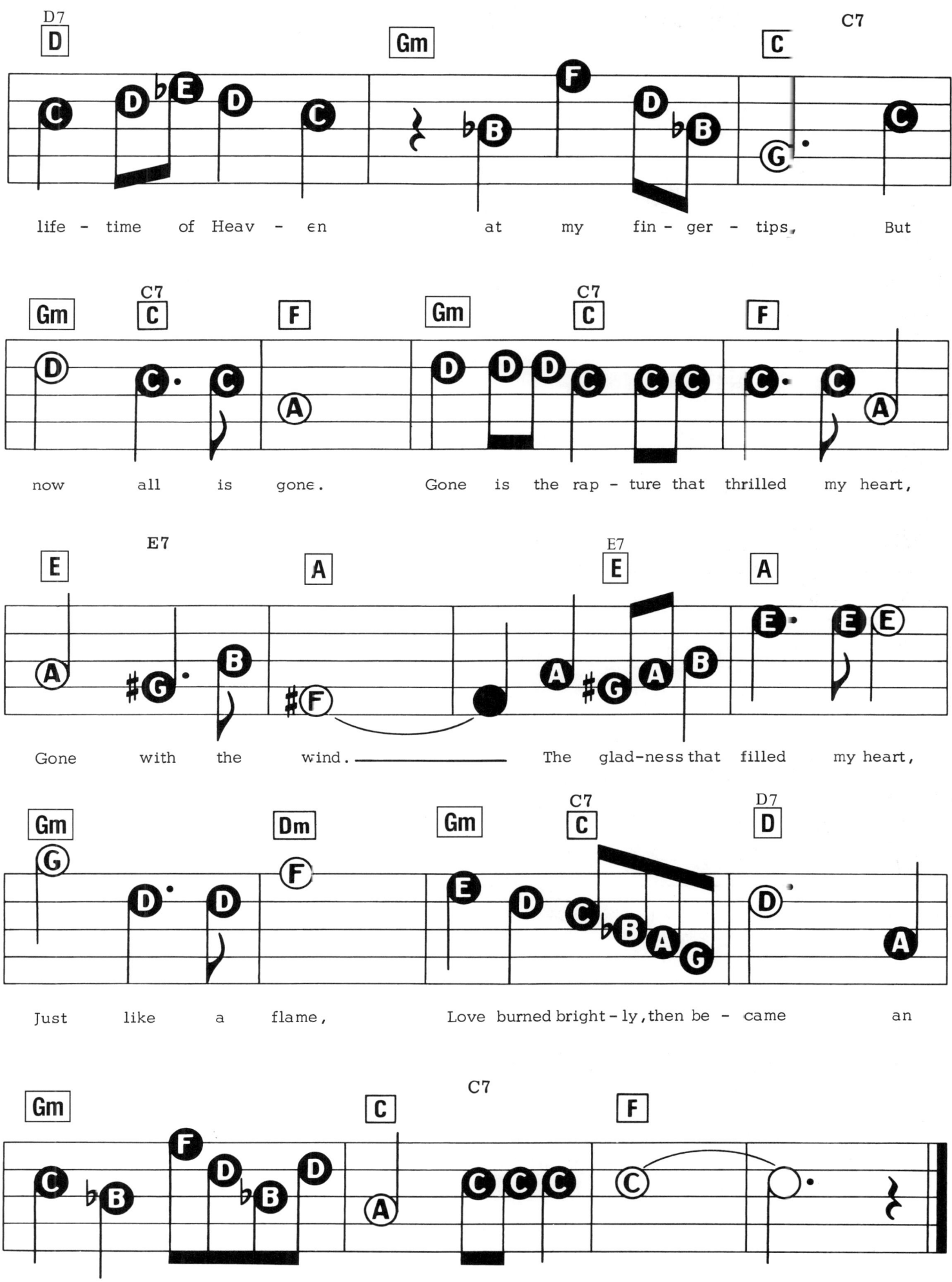

Guess Who I Saw Today

Registration 1
Rhythm: Ballad or Fox Trot

Words and Music by Murray Grand
and Elisse Boyd

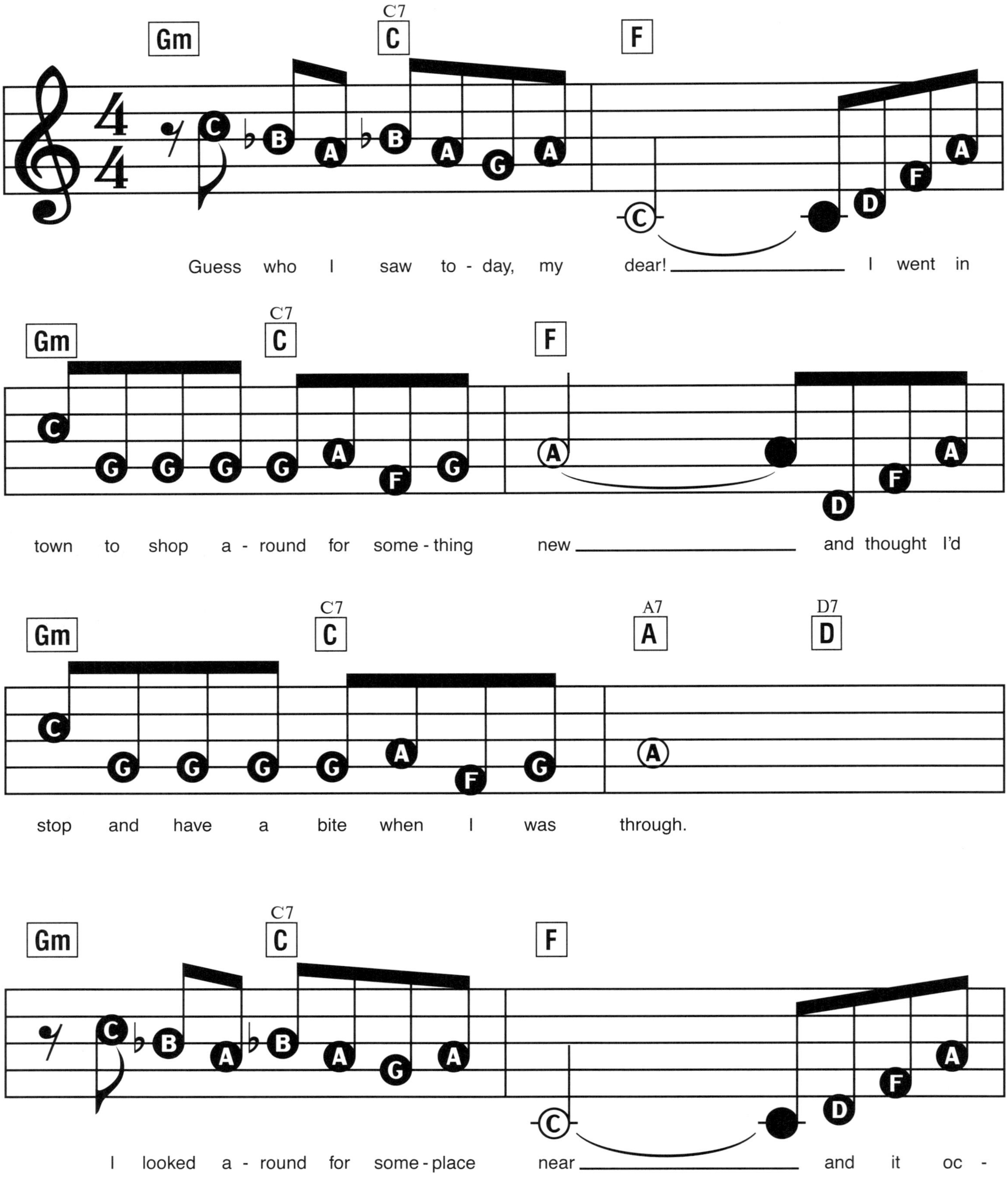

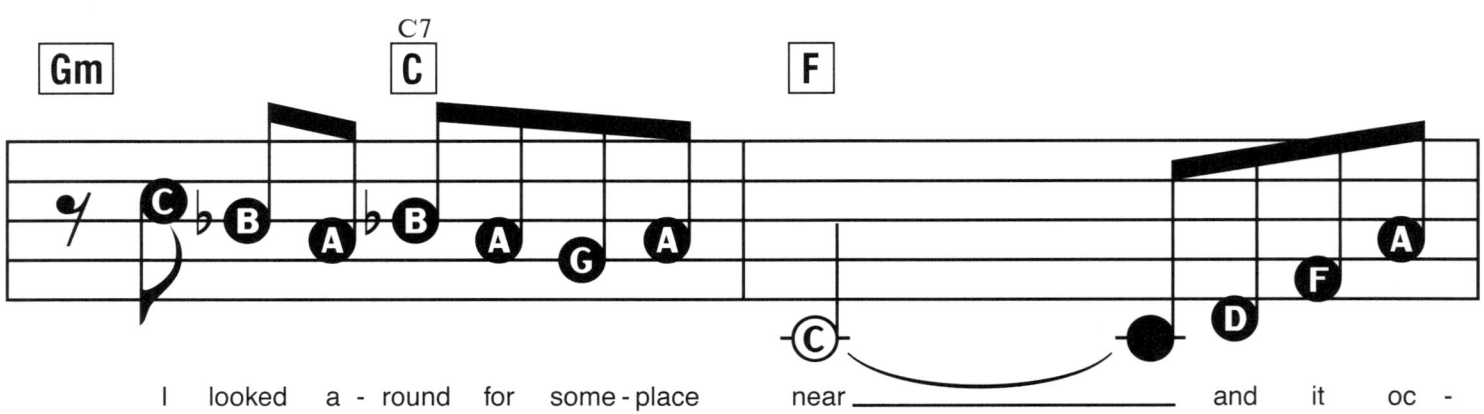

Guess who I saw to-day, my dear! _____ I went in town to shop a-round for some-thing new _____ and thought I'd stop and have a bite when I was through. I looked a-round for some-place near _____ and it oc-

Copyright © 1952 by Santly-Joy Select
Copyright Renewed. Assigned to R.C. Jay Publishing Inc.
All Rights Administered by Chappell & Co.
International Copyright Secured   All Rights Reserved

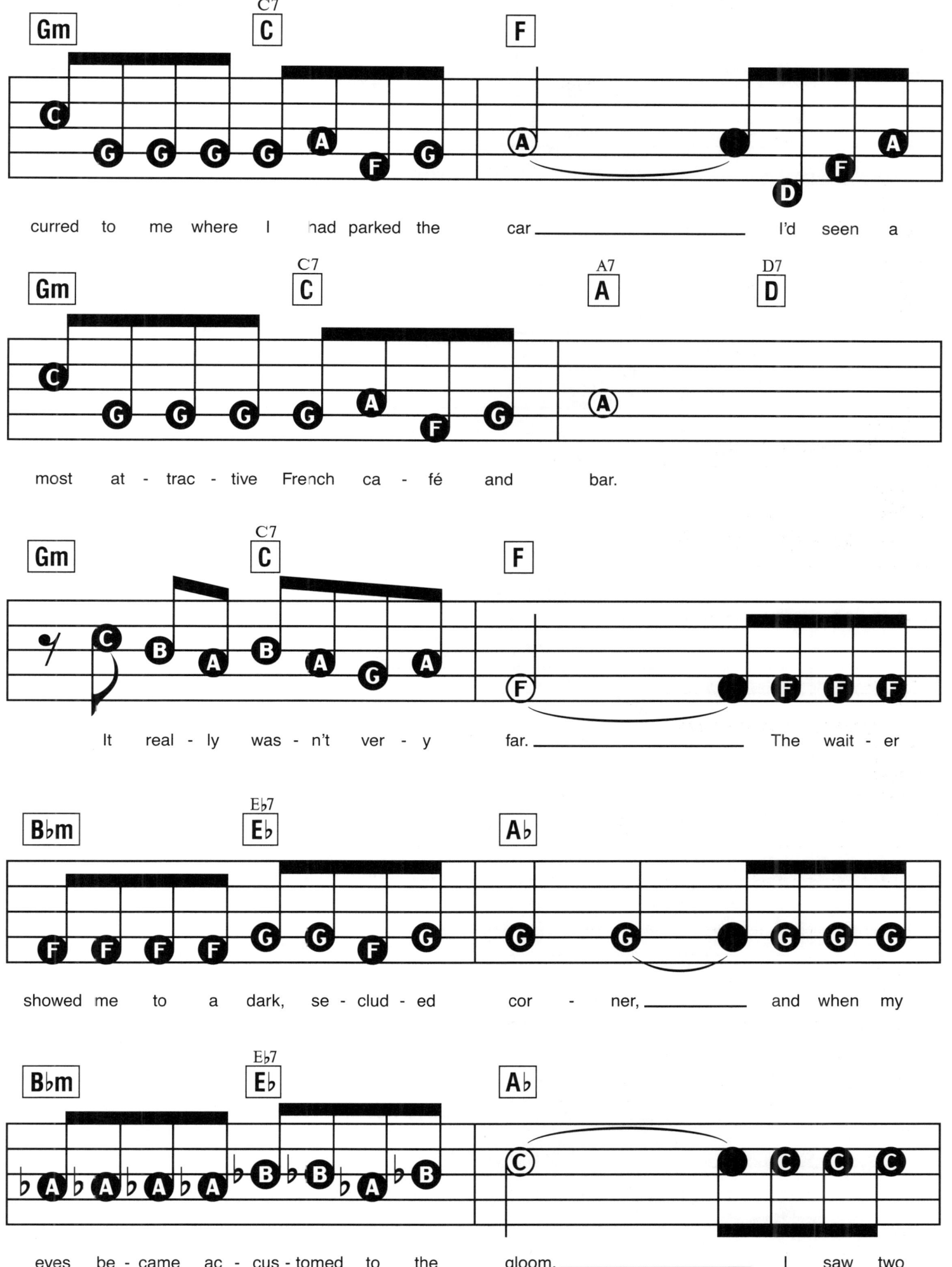

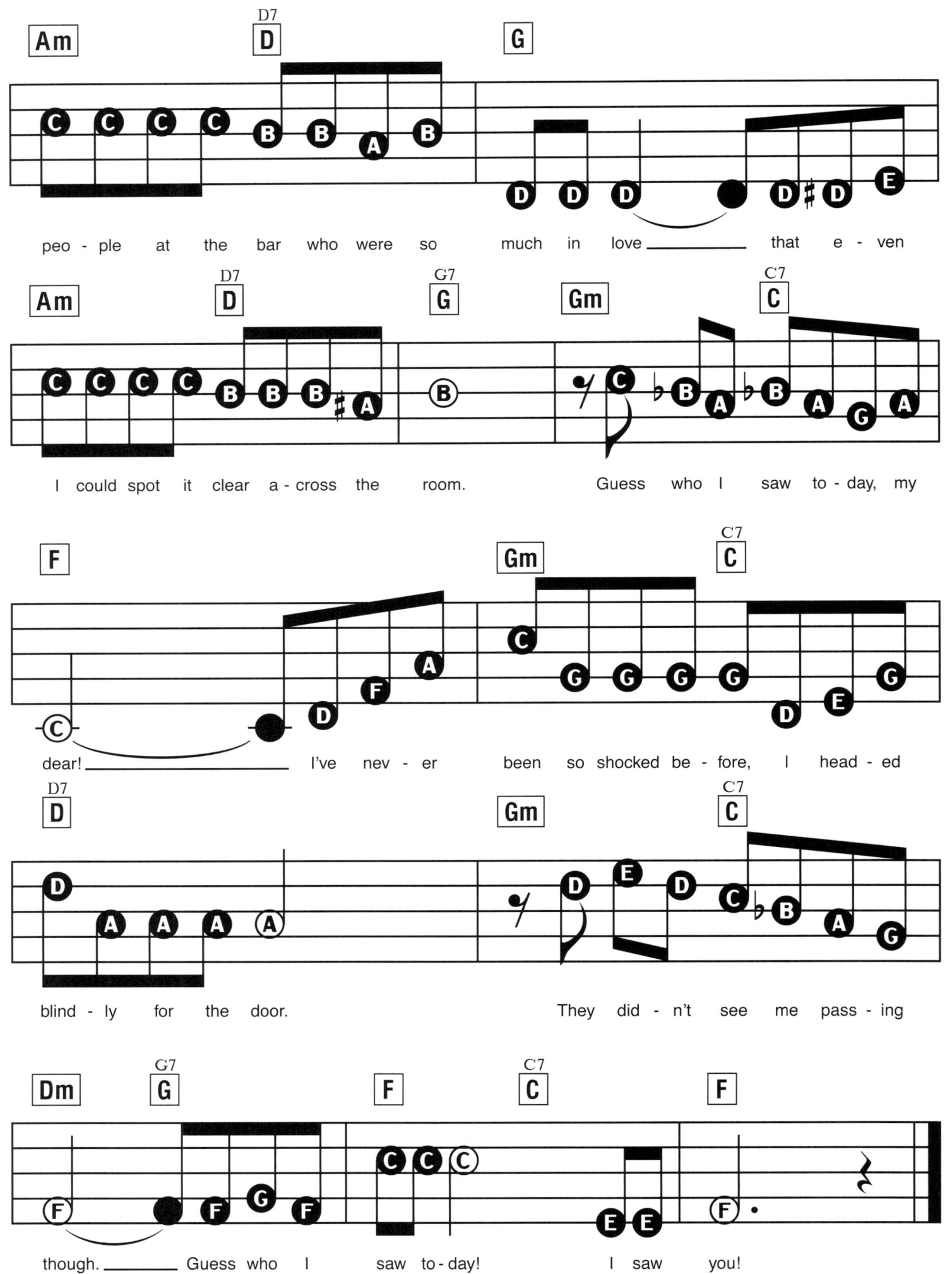

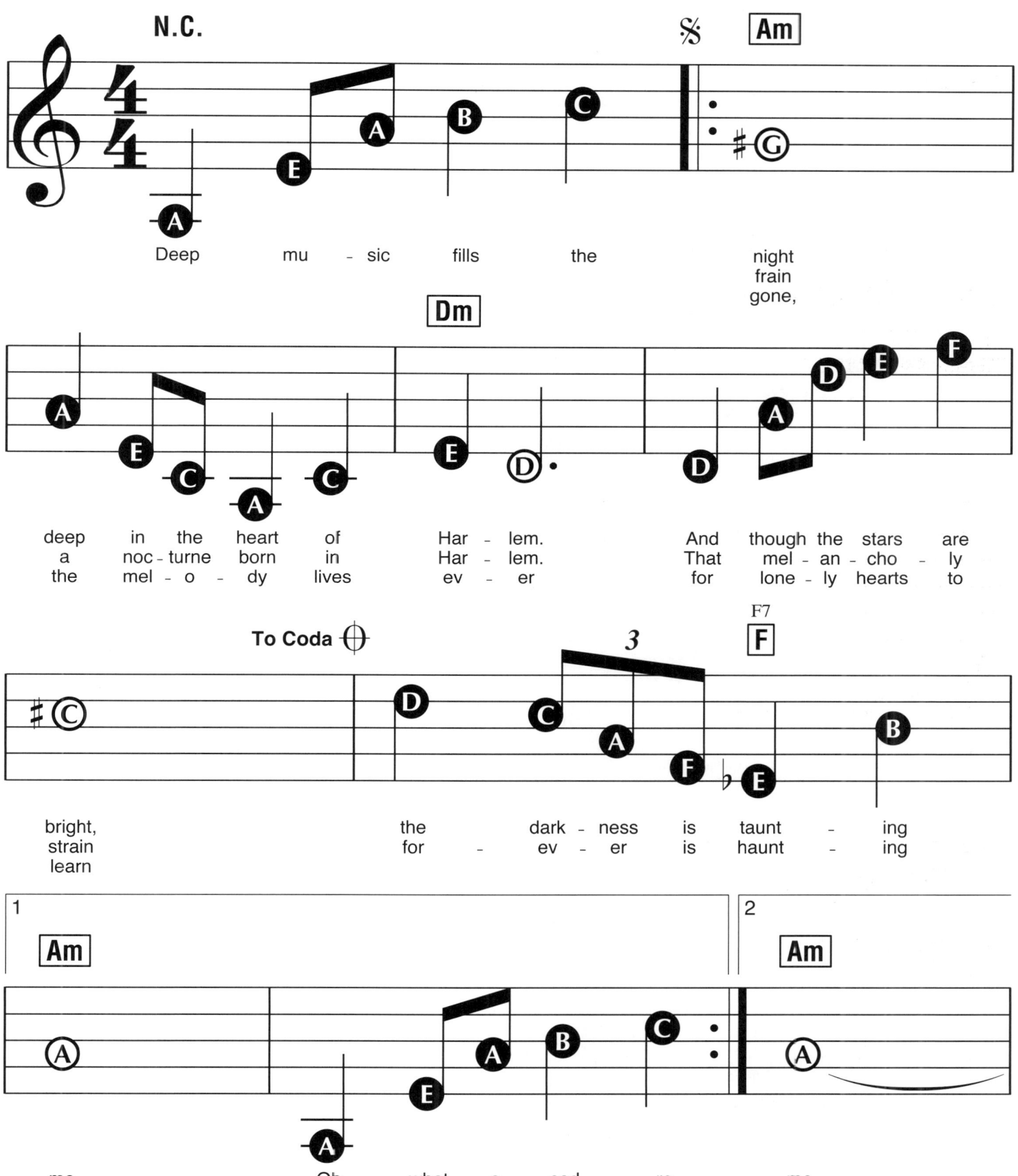

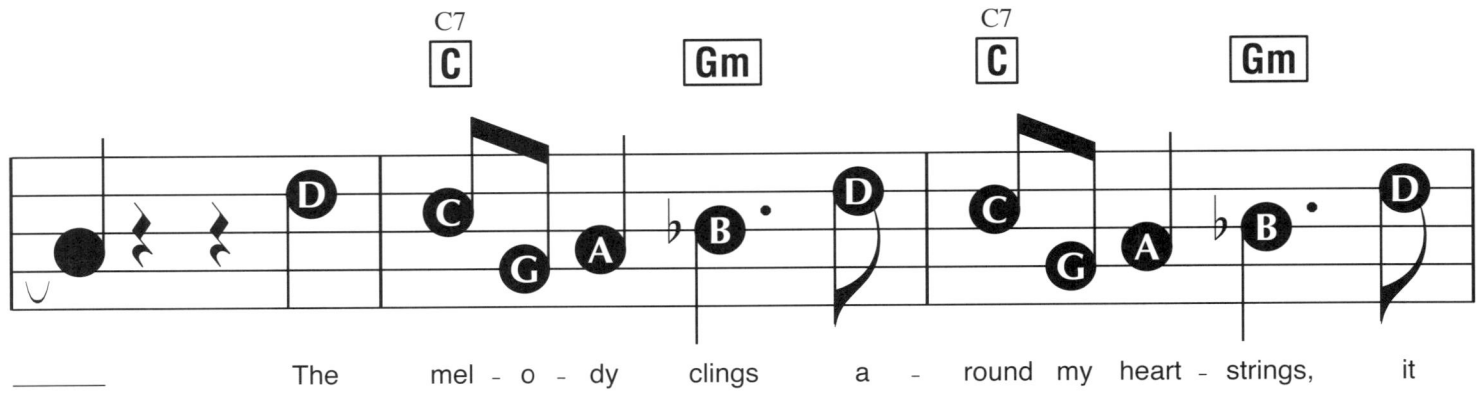
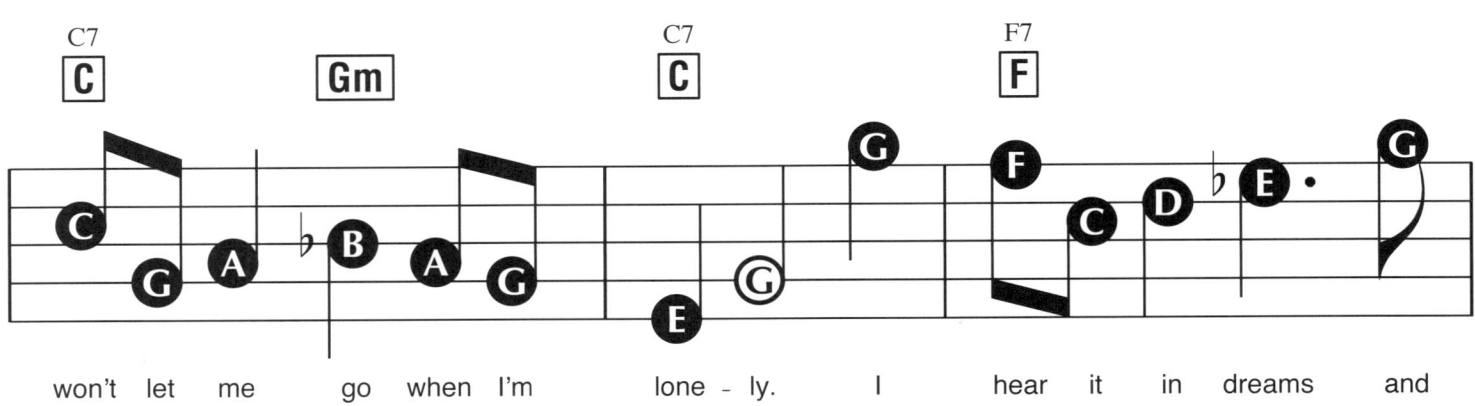
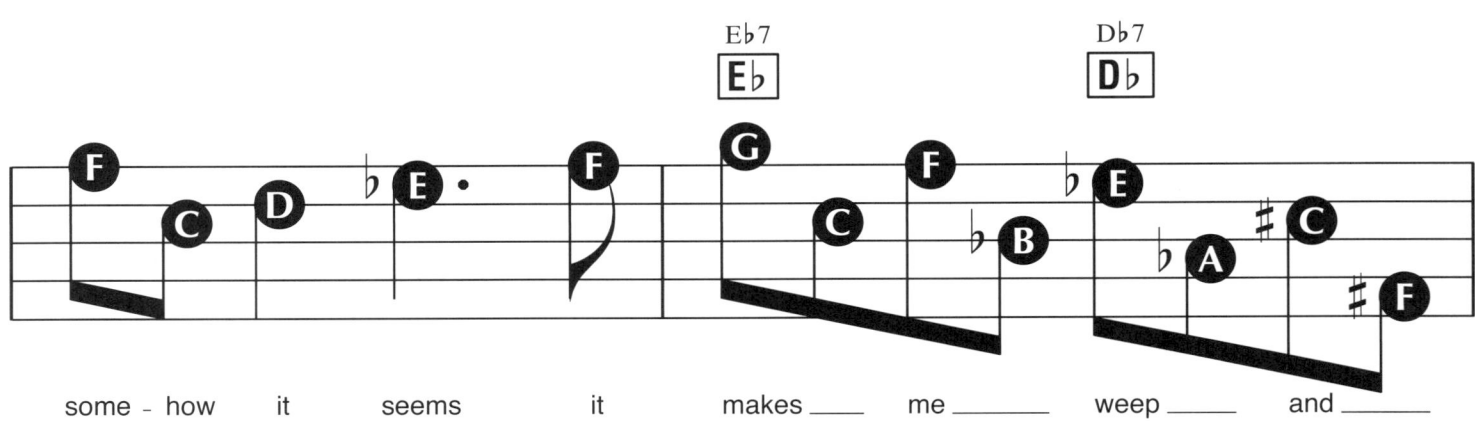
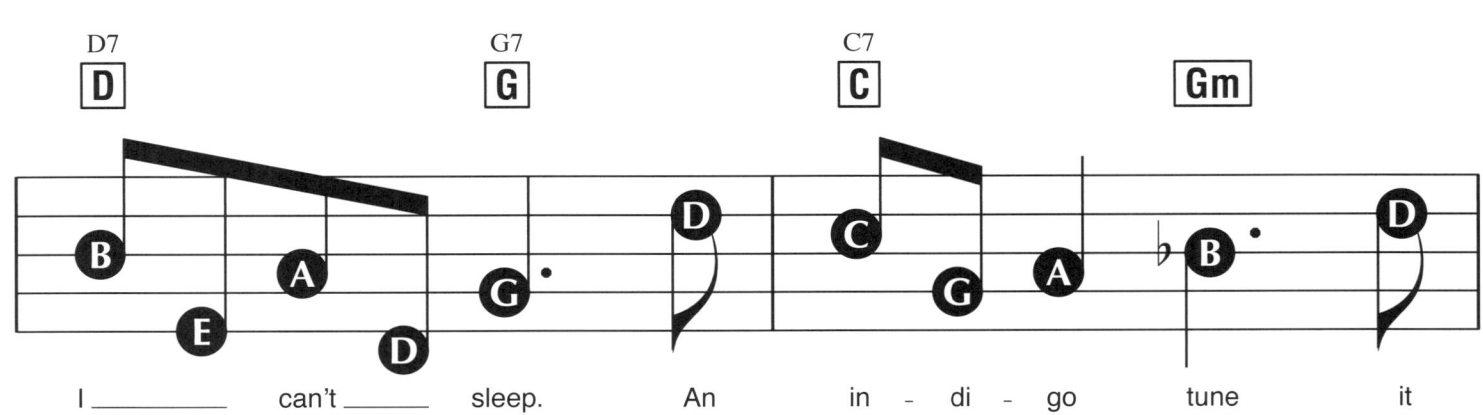

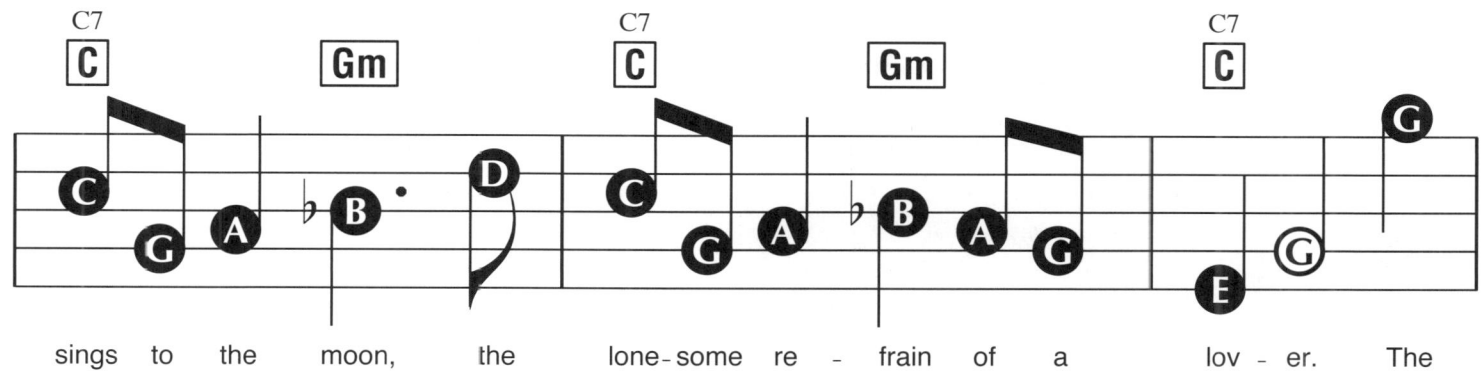
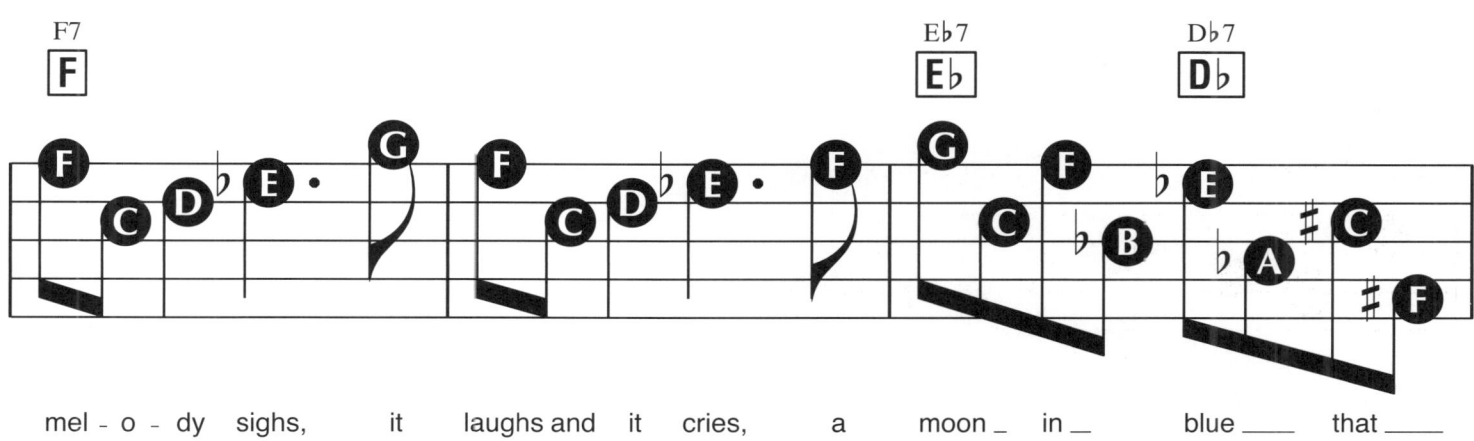
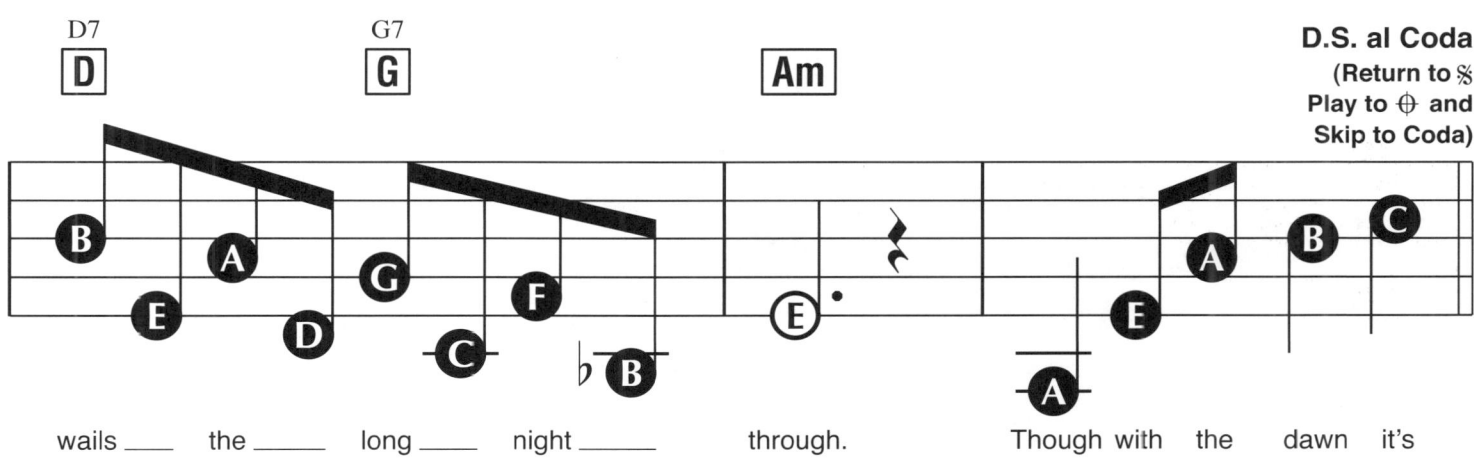
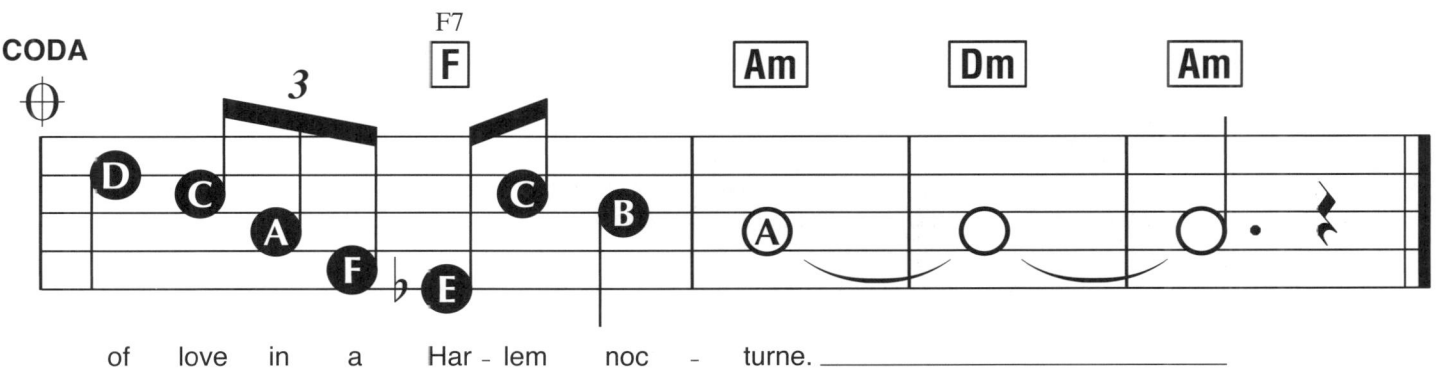

Honeysuckle Rose
from AIN'T MISBEHAVIN'
from TIN PAN ALLEY

Registration 4
Rhythm: Fox Trot or Swing

Words by Andy Razaf
Music by Thomas "Fats" Waller

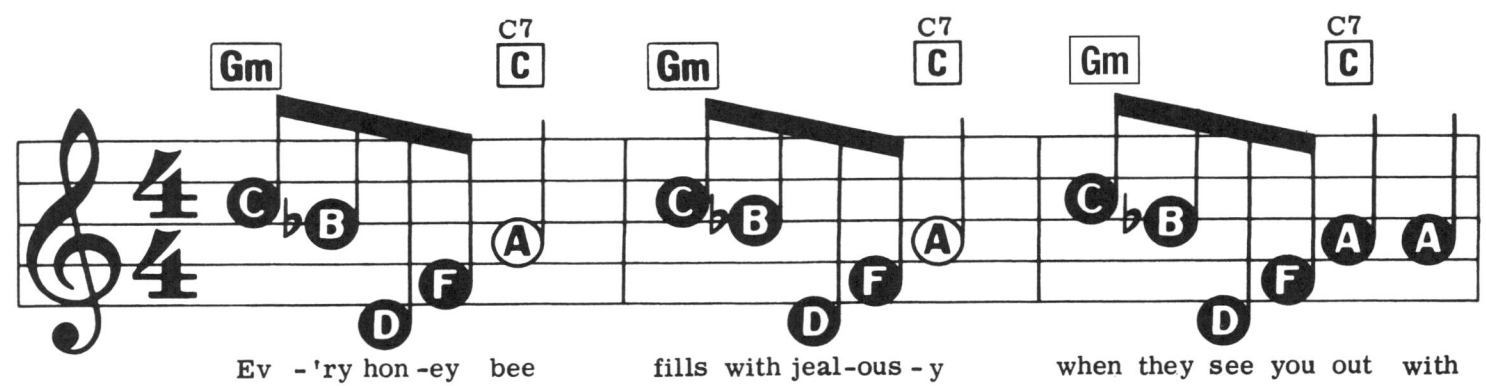

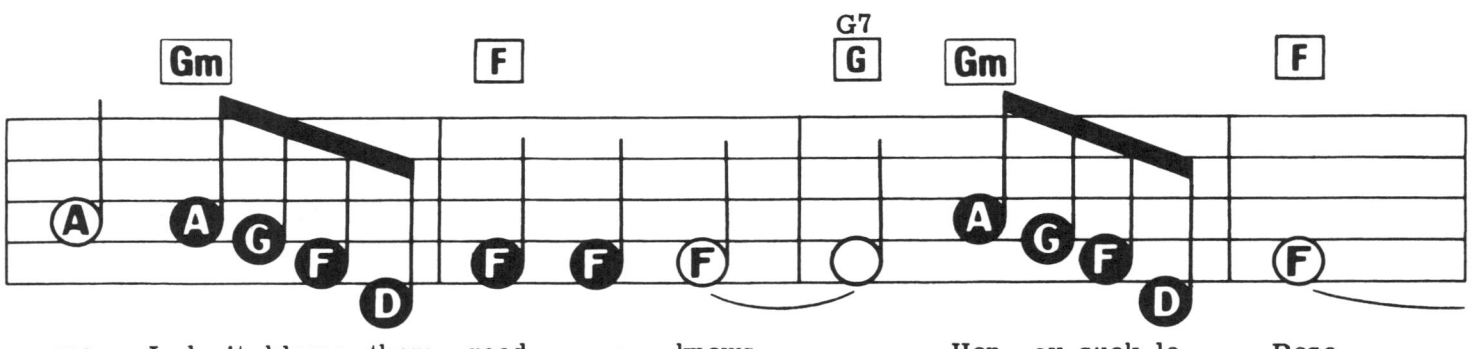

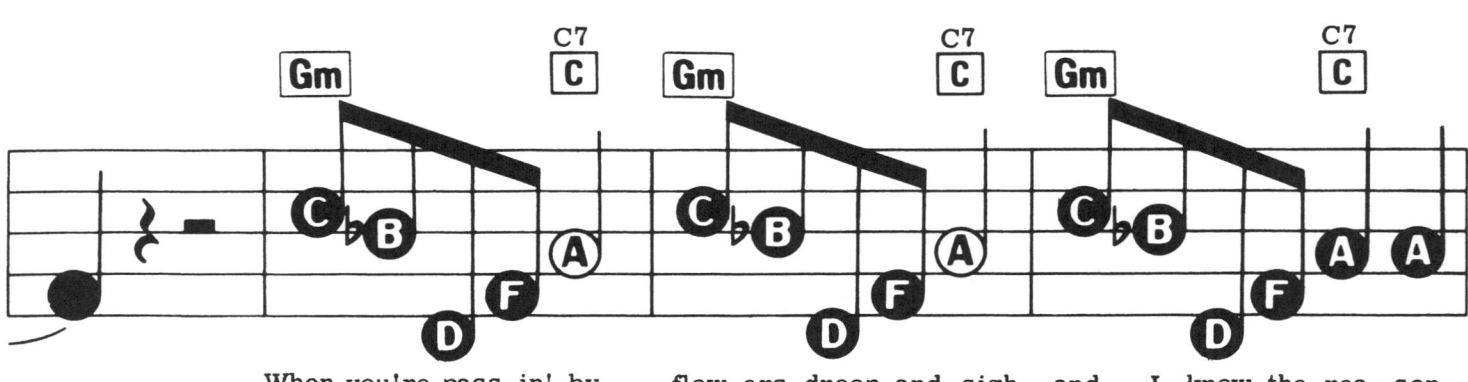

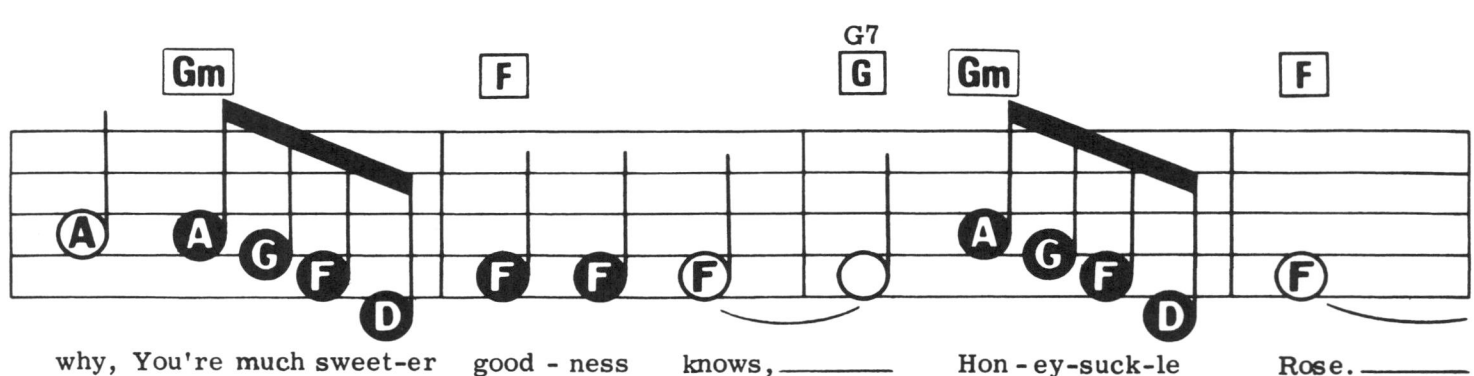

Copyright © 1929 by Chappell & Co. and Razaf Music Co. in the United States
Copyright Renewed
All Rights for Razaf Music Co. Administered by The Songwriters Guild Of America
International Copyright Secured   All Rights Reserved

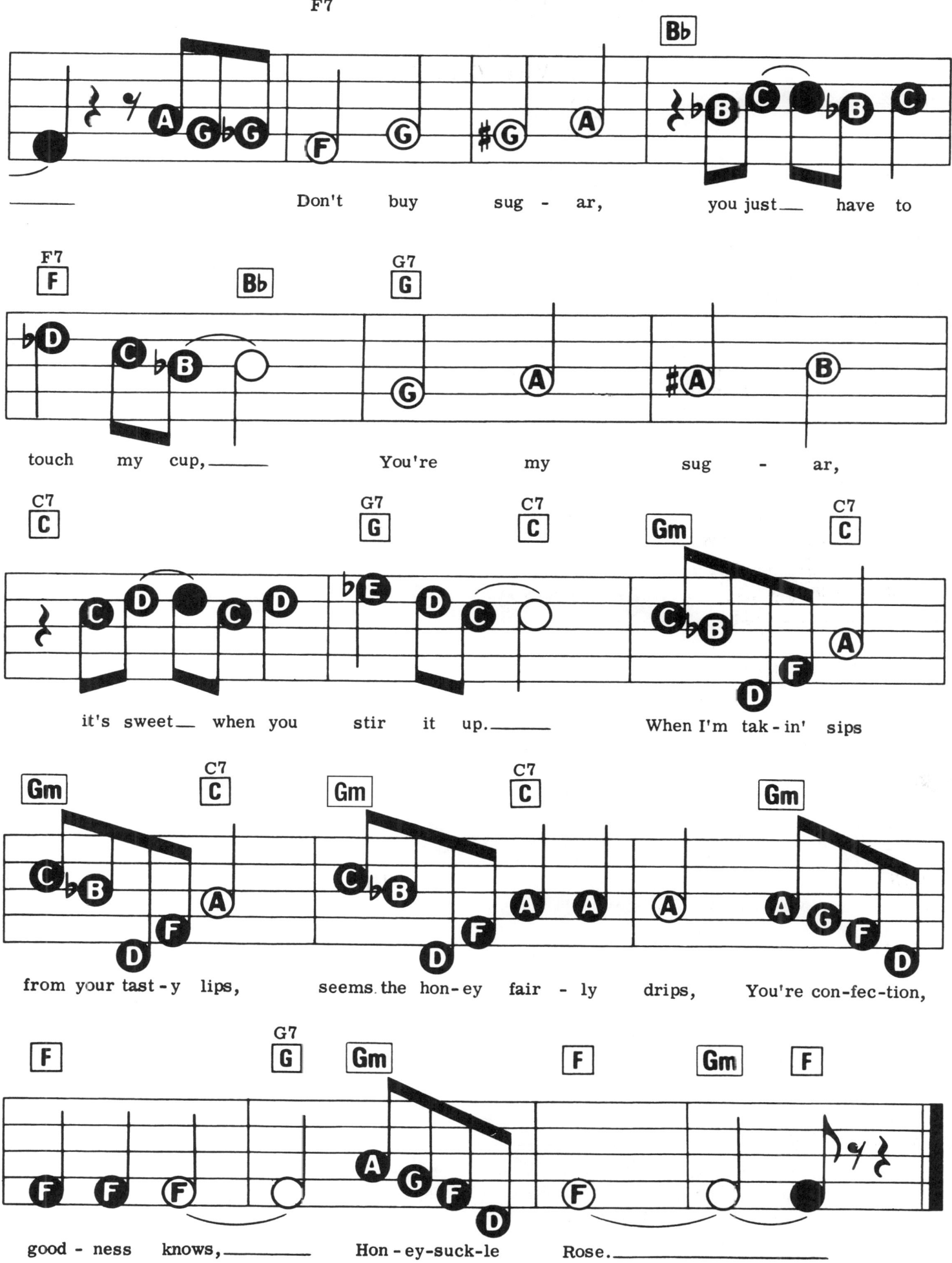

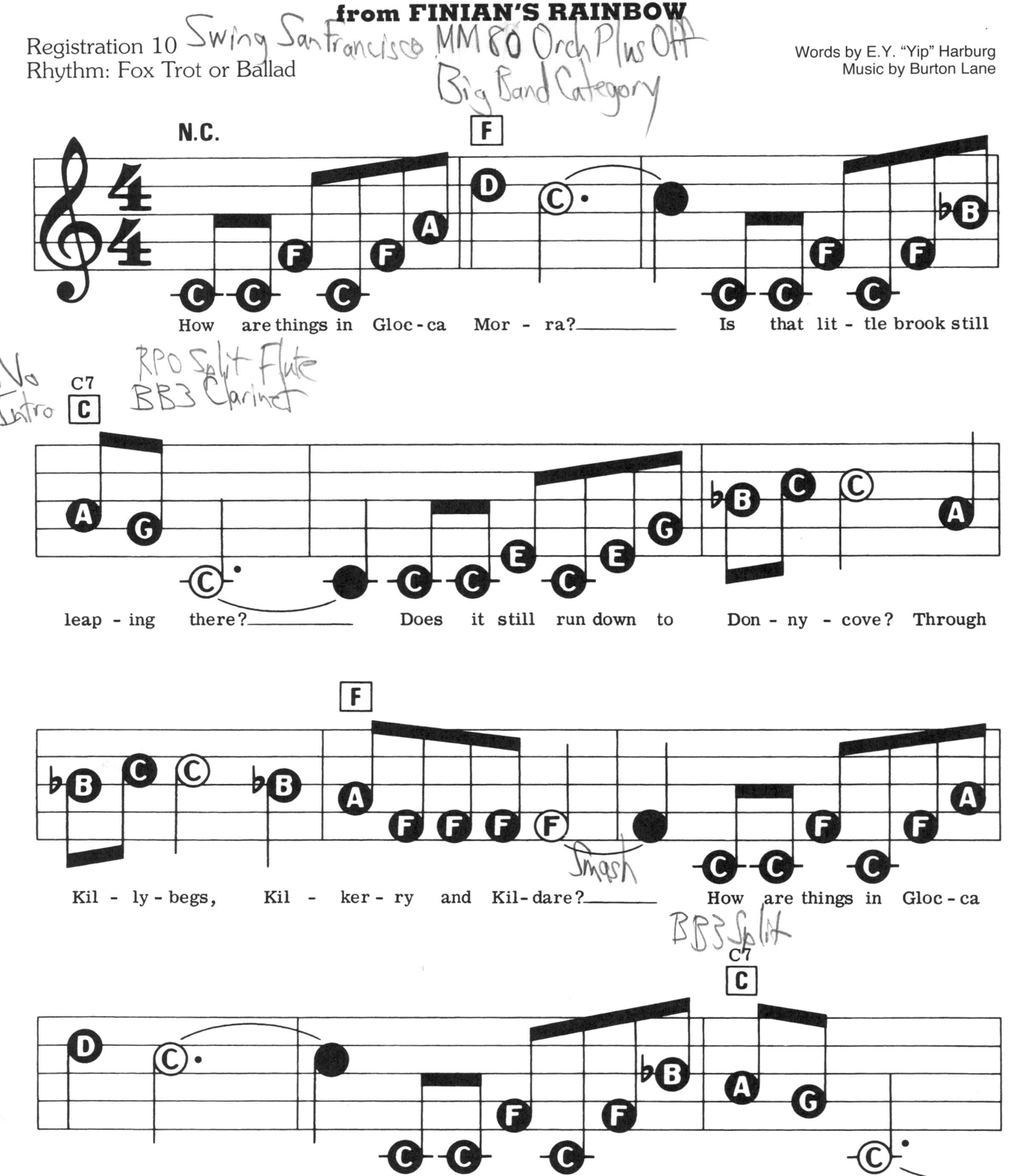

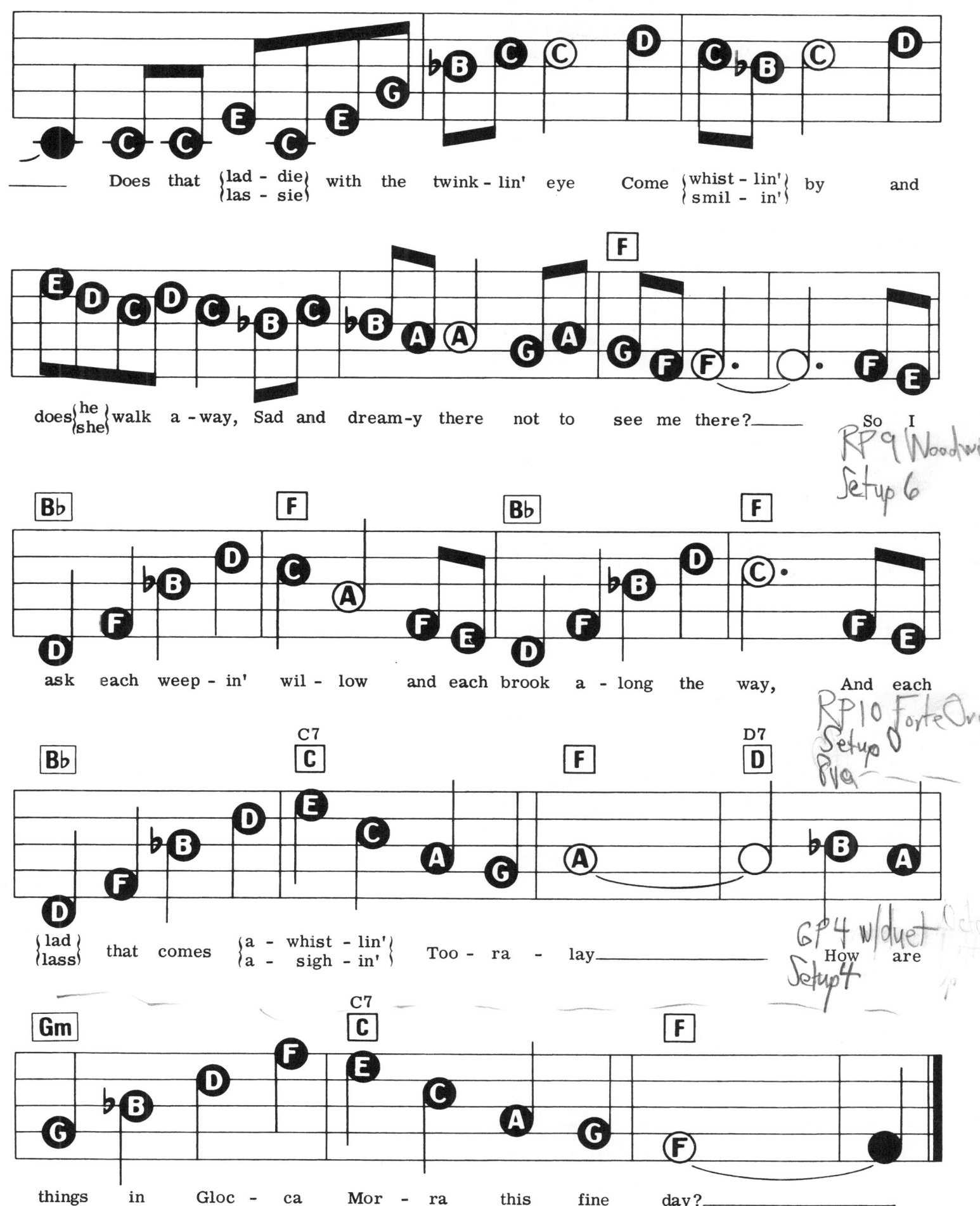

I Ain't Got Nothin' but the Blues

Registration 7
Rhythm: Swing

Words by Don George
Music by Duke Ellington

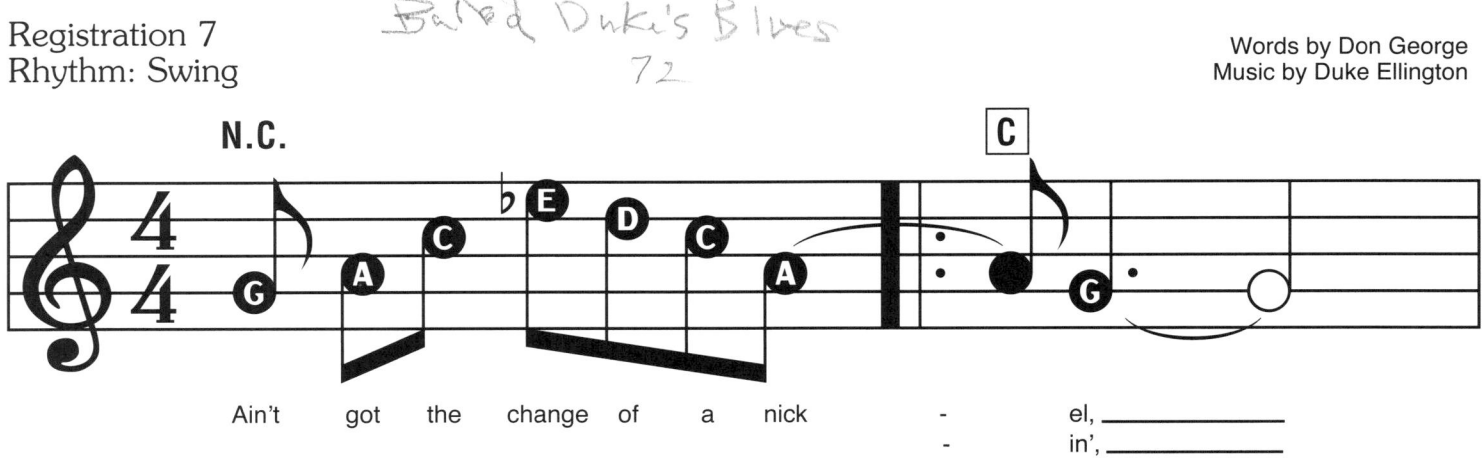

Ain't got the change of a nick - el, _____
- in', _____

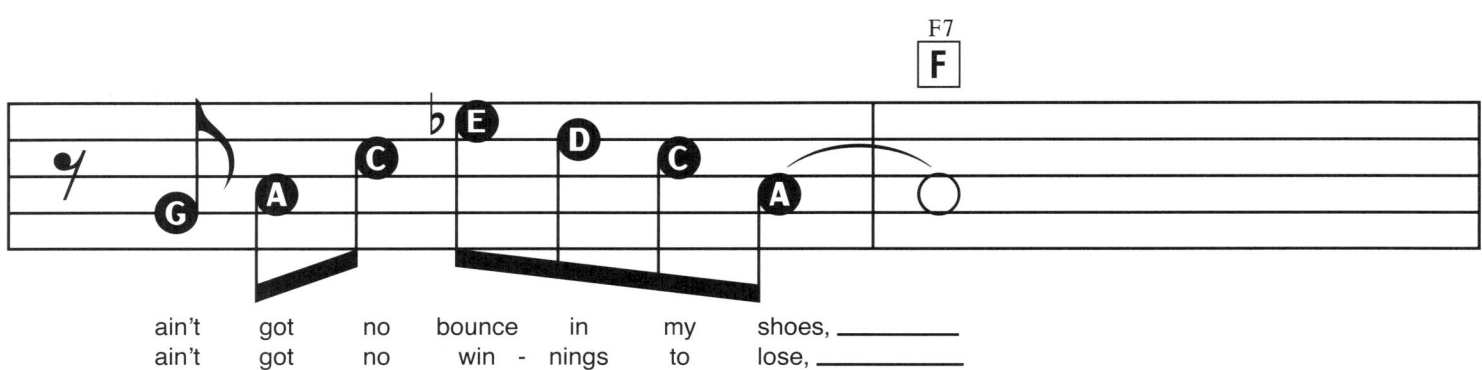

ain't got no bounce in my shoes, _____
ain't got no win - nings to lose, _____

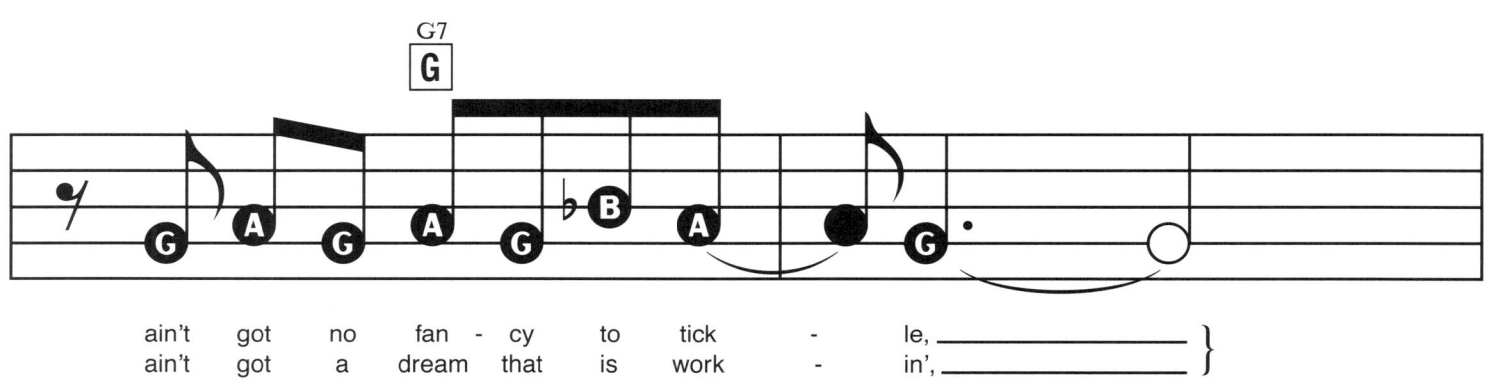

ain't got no fan - cy to tick - le, _____
ain't got a dream that is work - in', _____

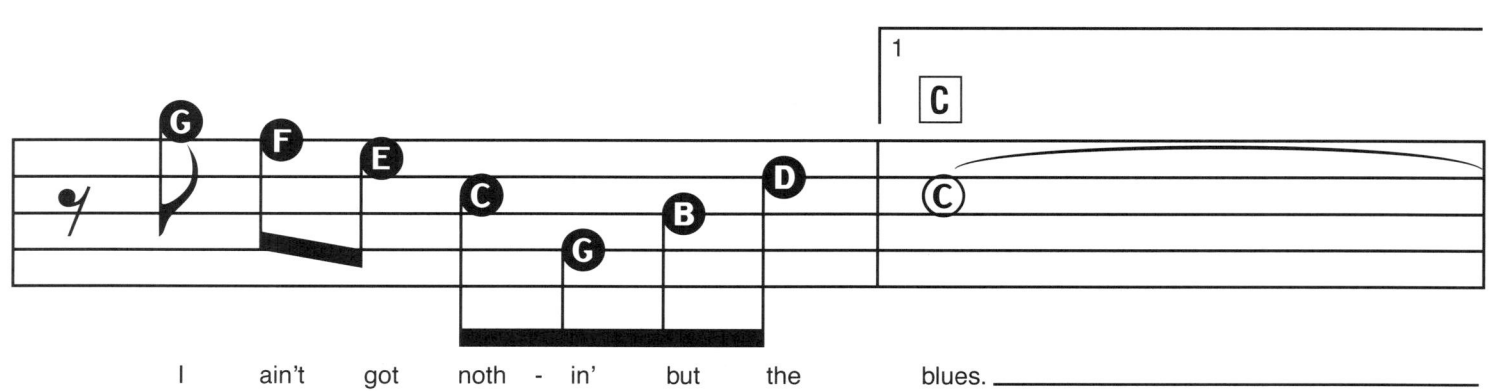

I ain't got noth - in' but the blues. _____

Copyright © 1944 Sony/ATV Music Publishing LLC, Tempo Music, Inc. c/o Music Sales Corporation and Ricki Music Co. in the U.S.A.
Copyright Renewed
All Rights on behalf of Sony/ATV Music Publishing LLC Administered by Sony/ATV Music Publishing LLC,
8 Music Square West, Nashville, TN 37203
Rights for the world outside the U.S.A. Controlled by Ricki Music Co.
International Copyright Secured   All Rights Reserved

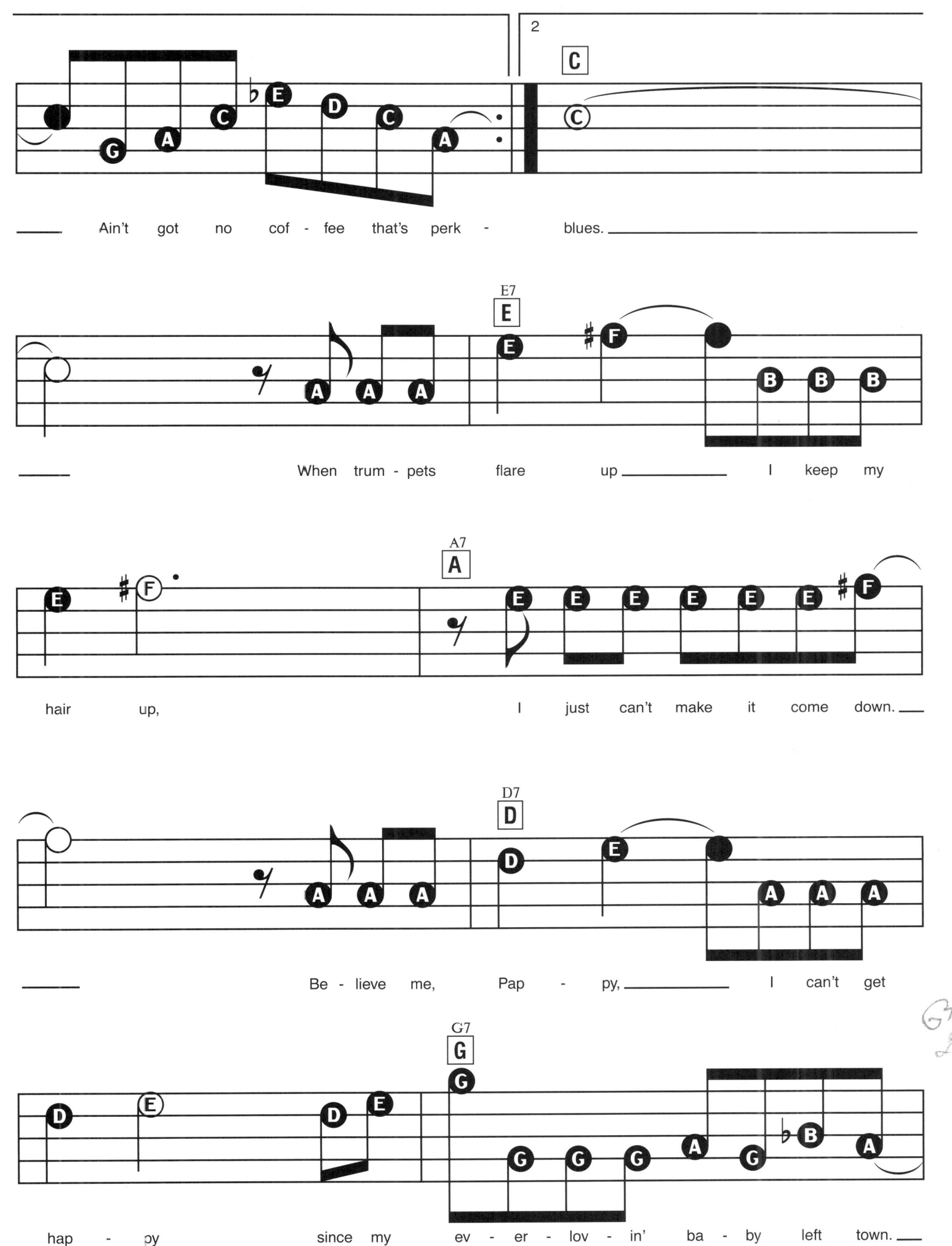

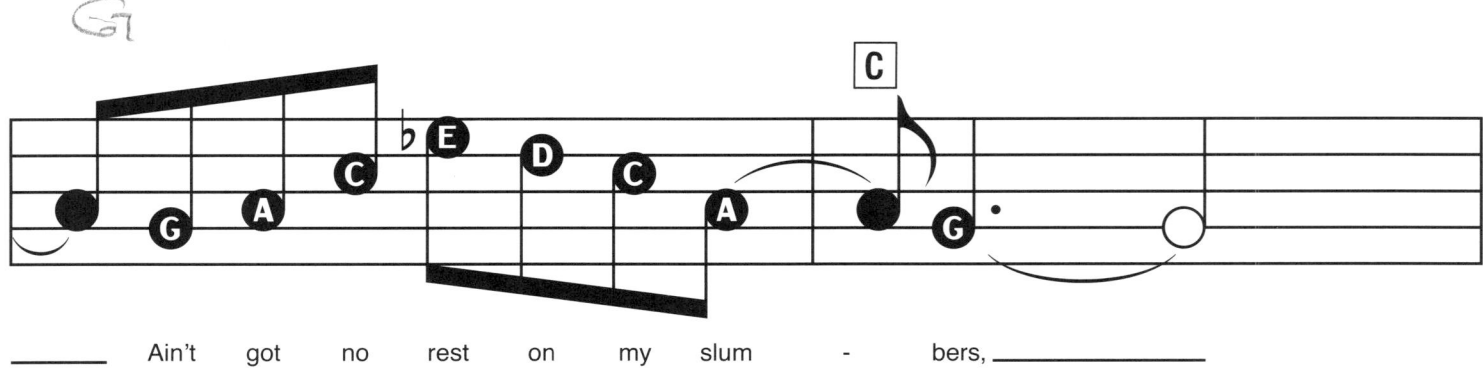
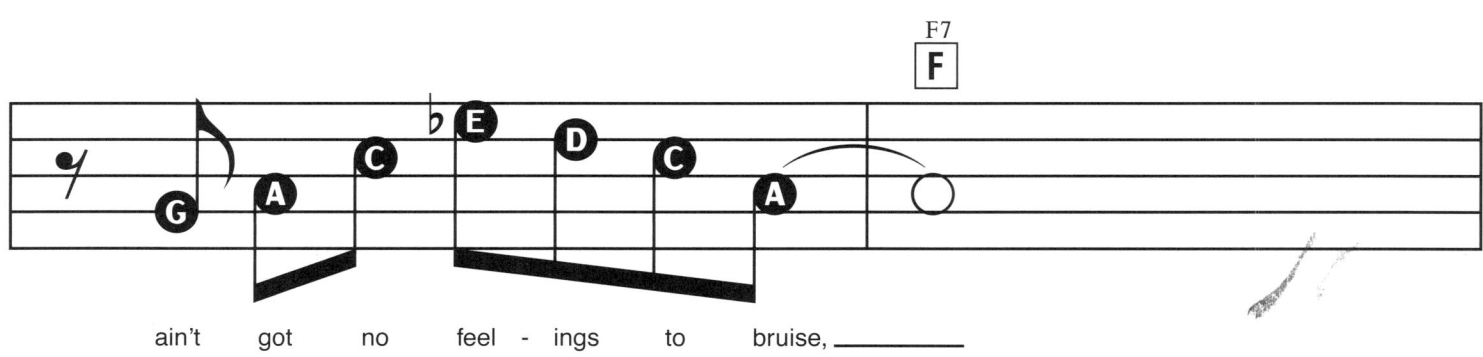
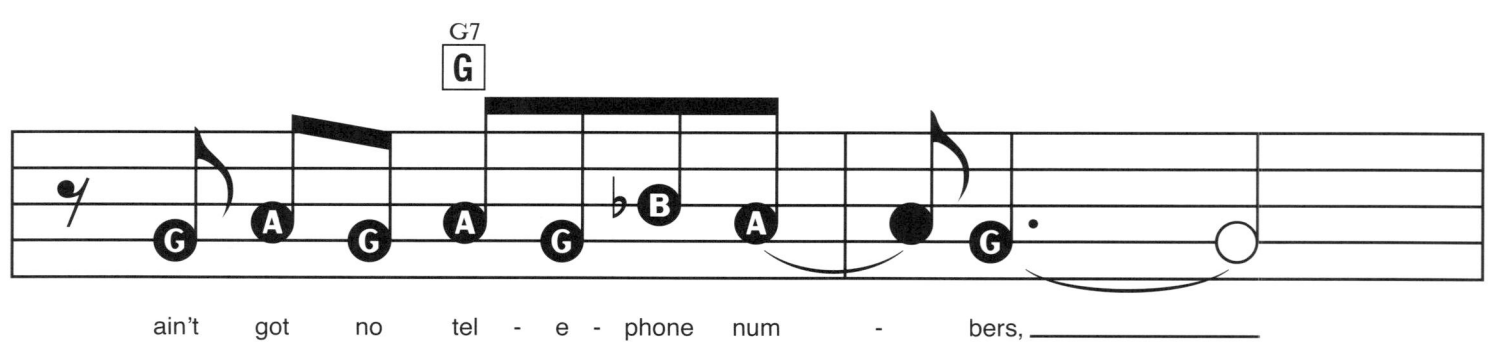
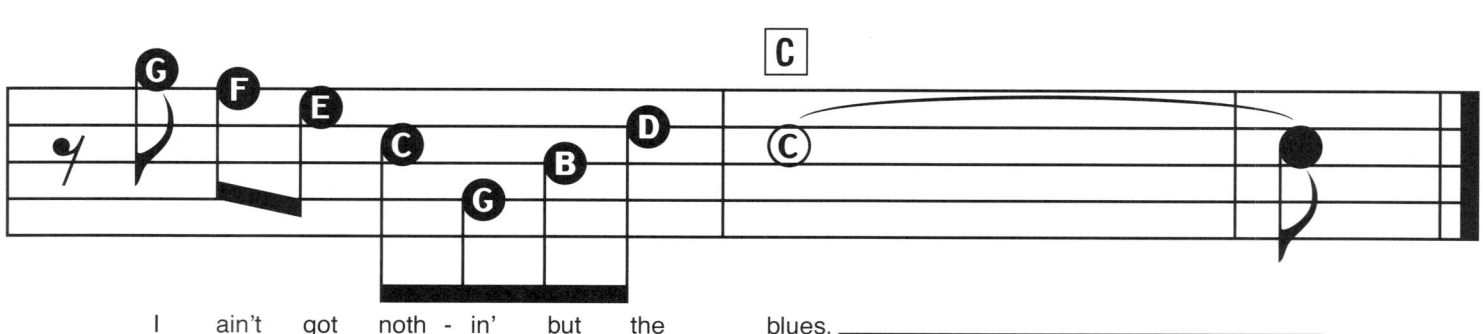

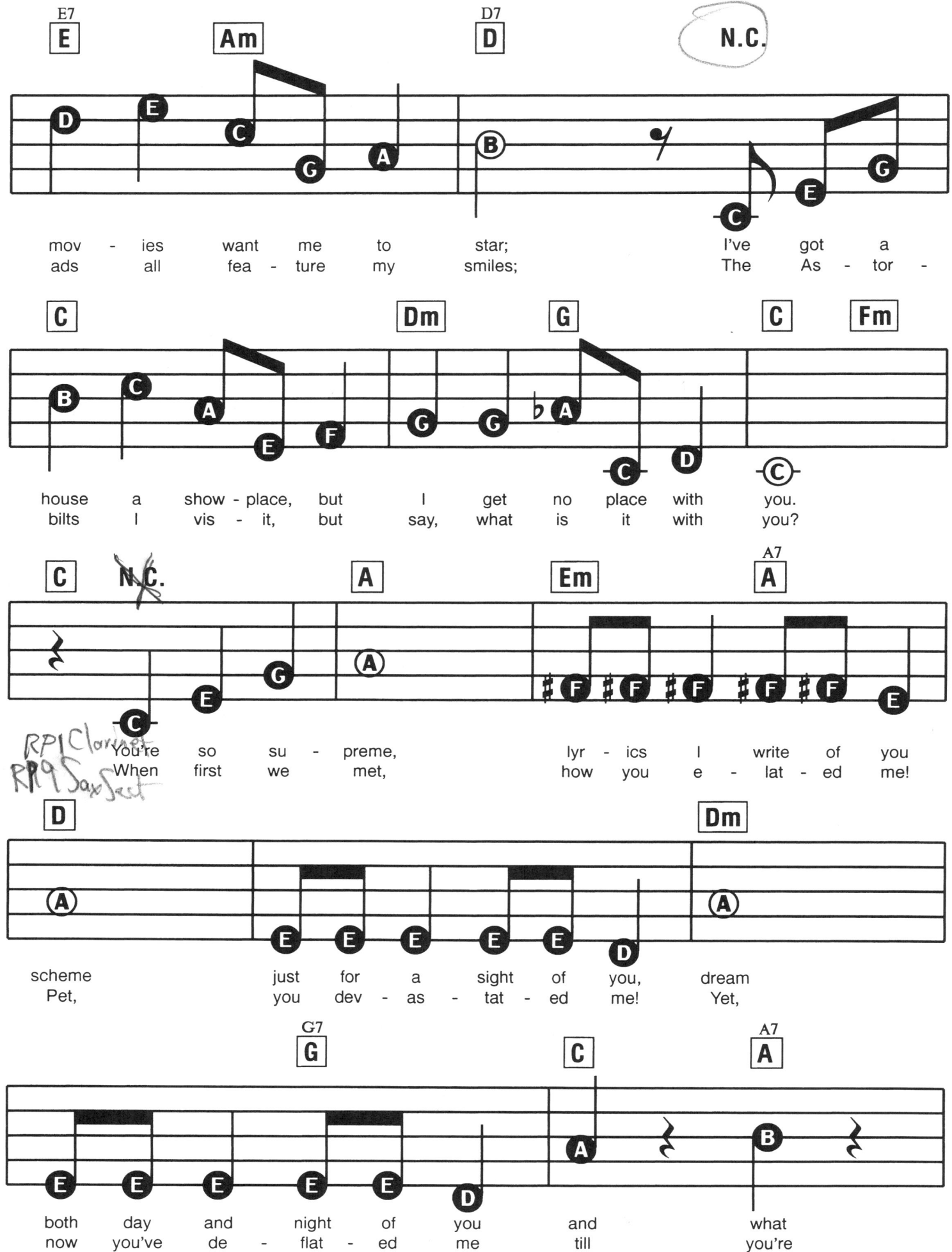

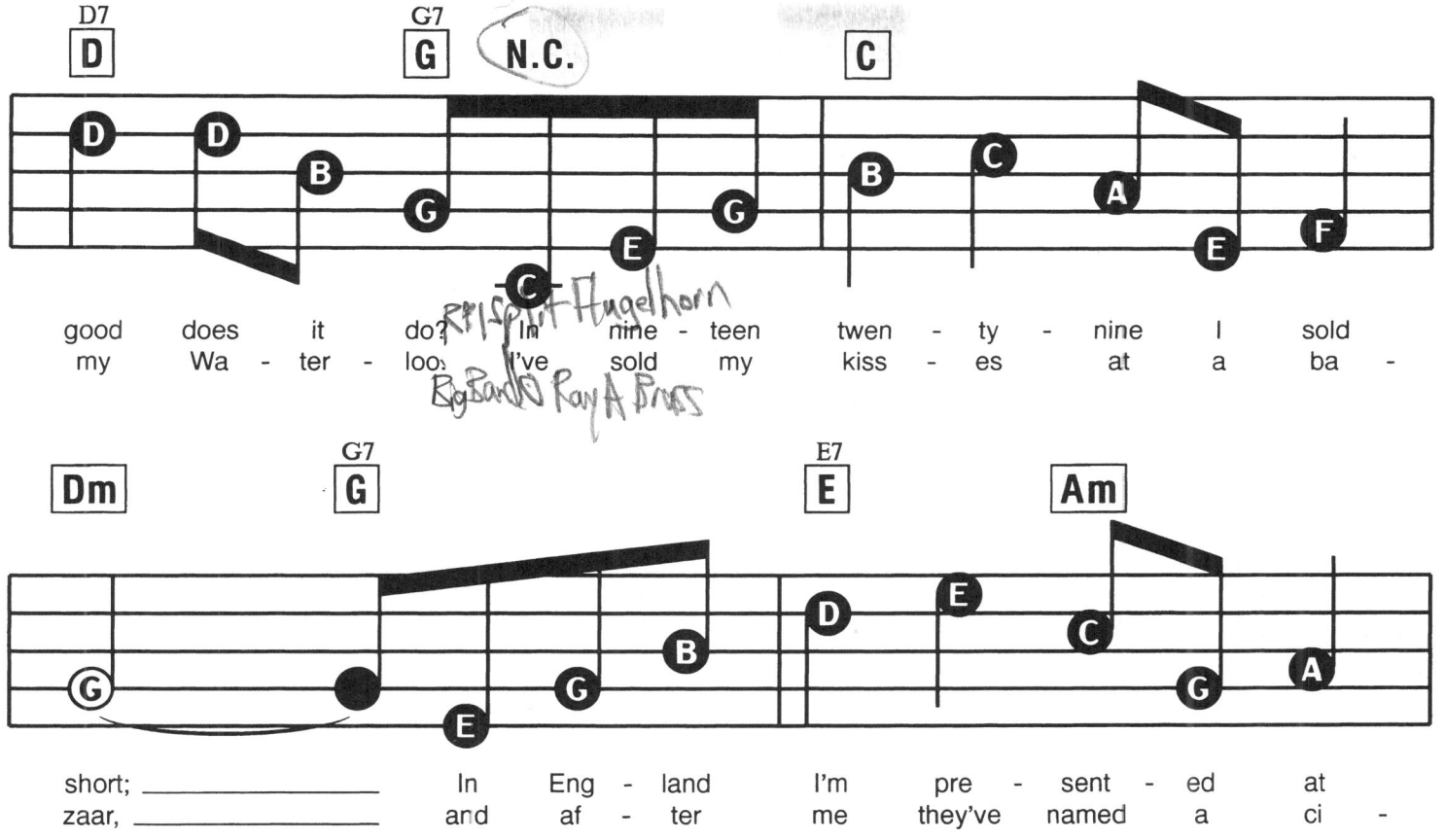
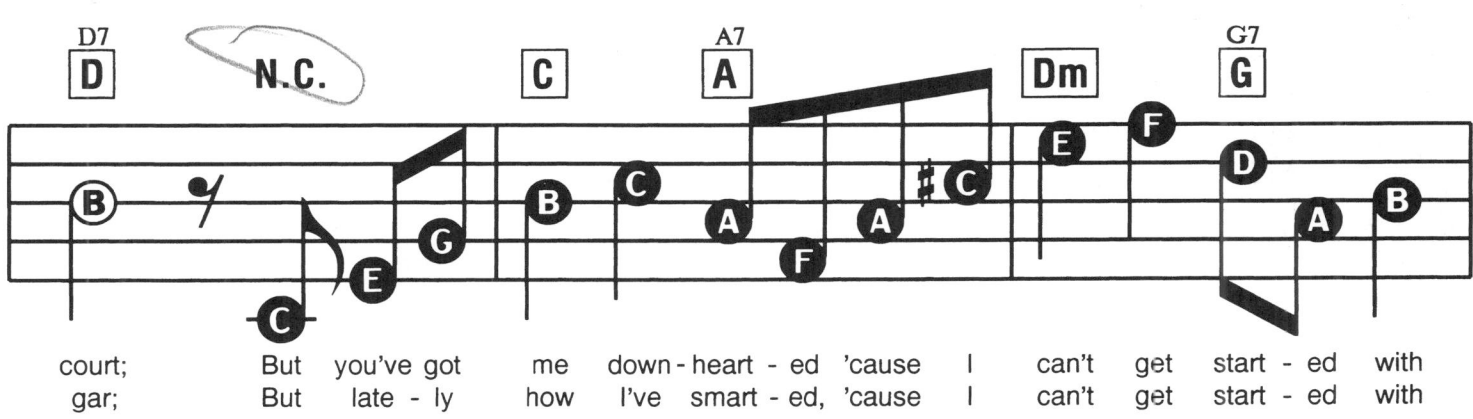
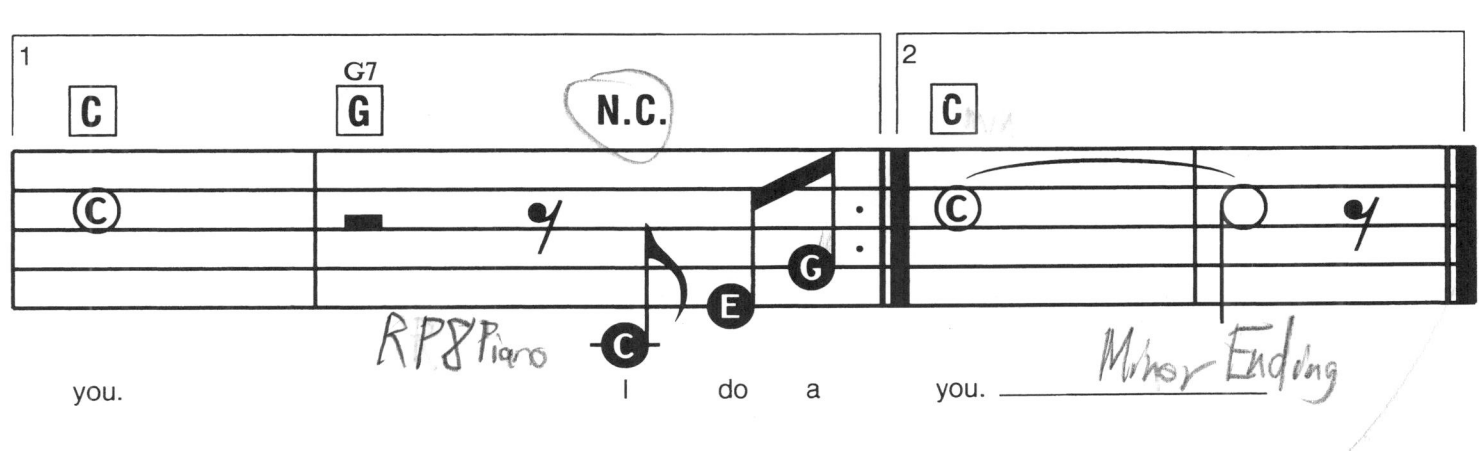

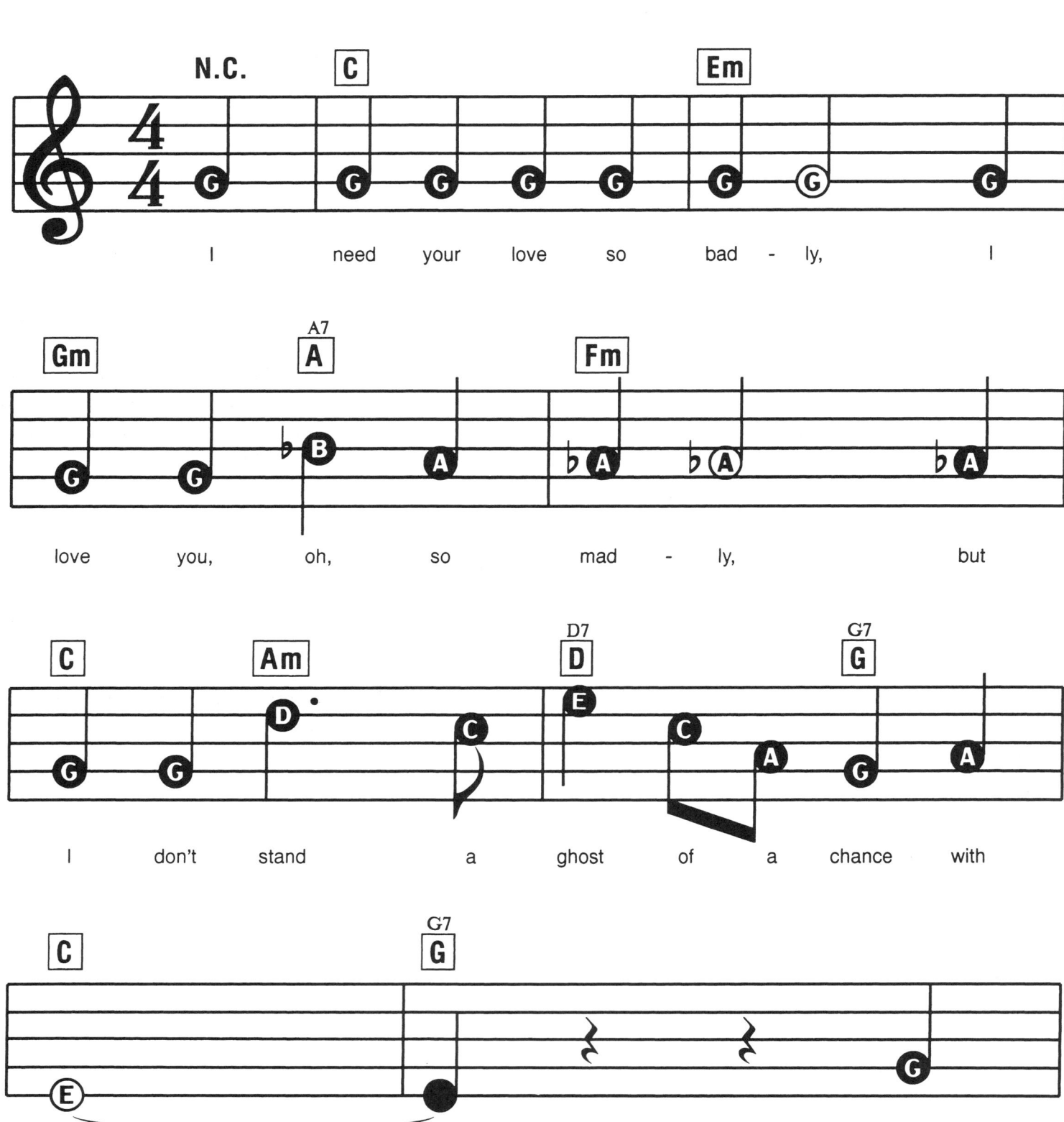

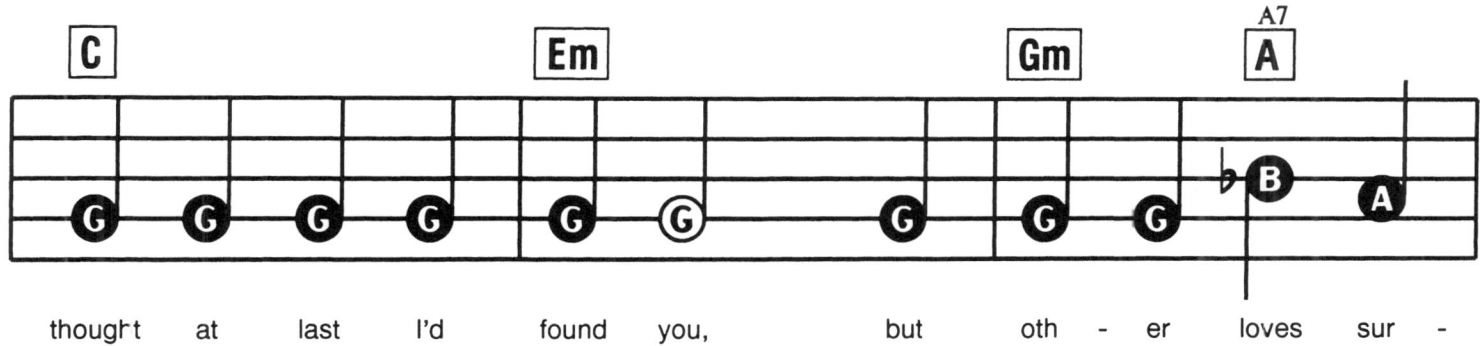
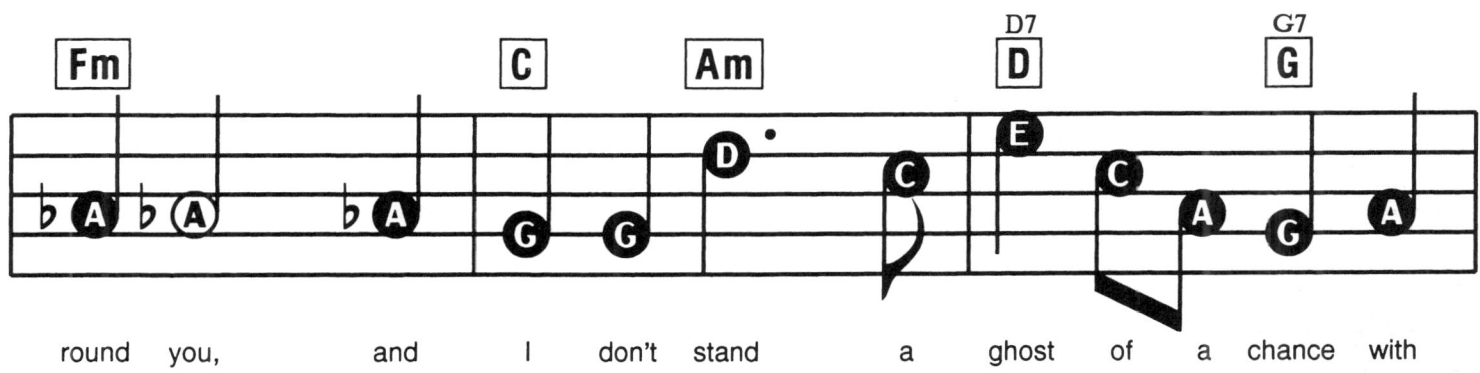
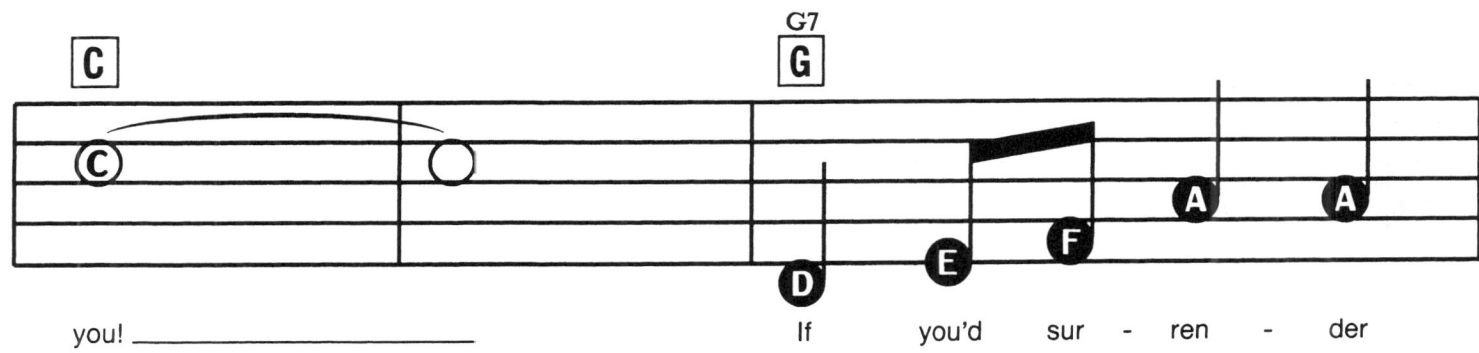
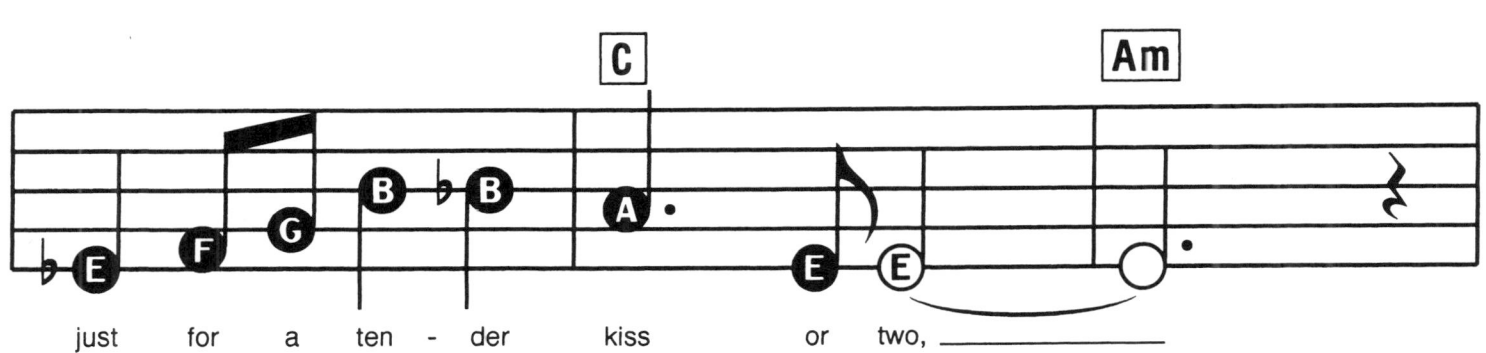

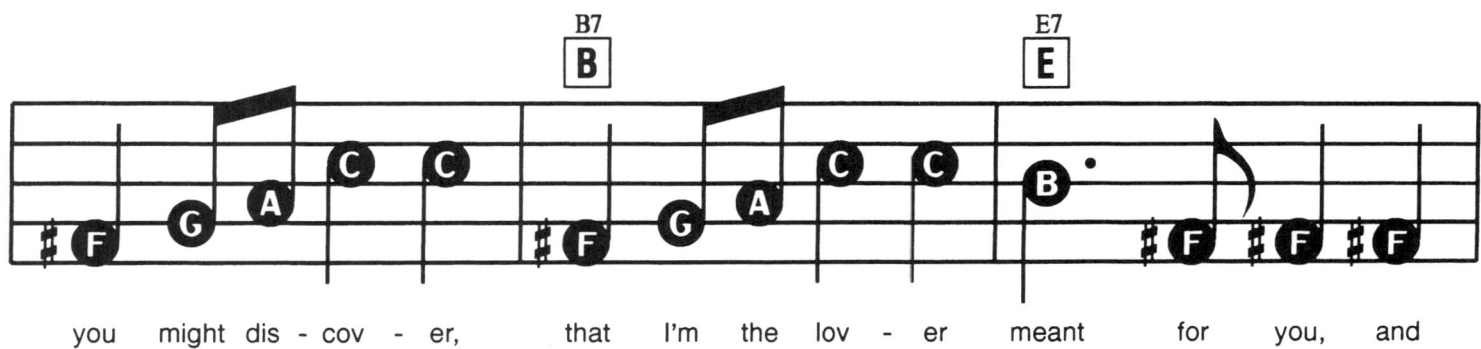
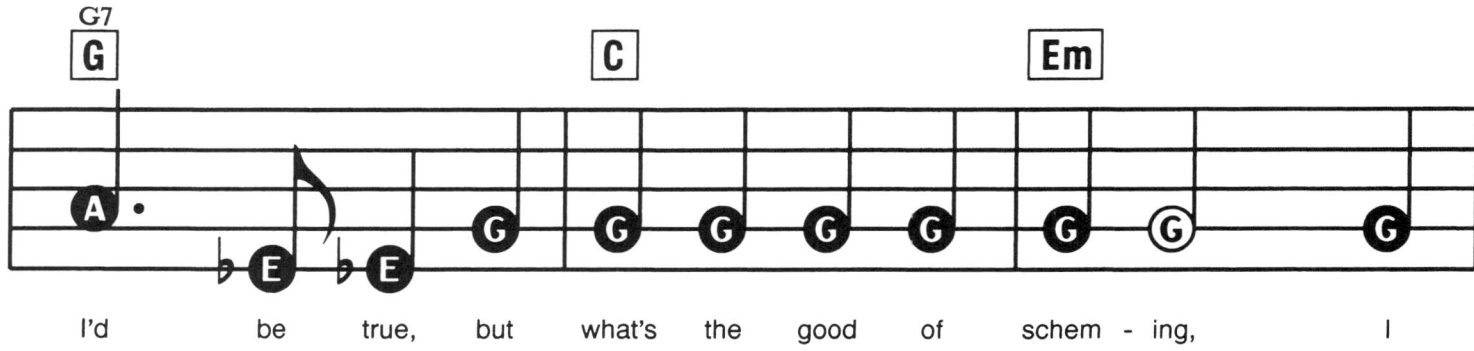
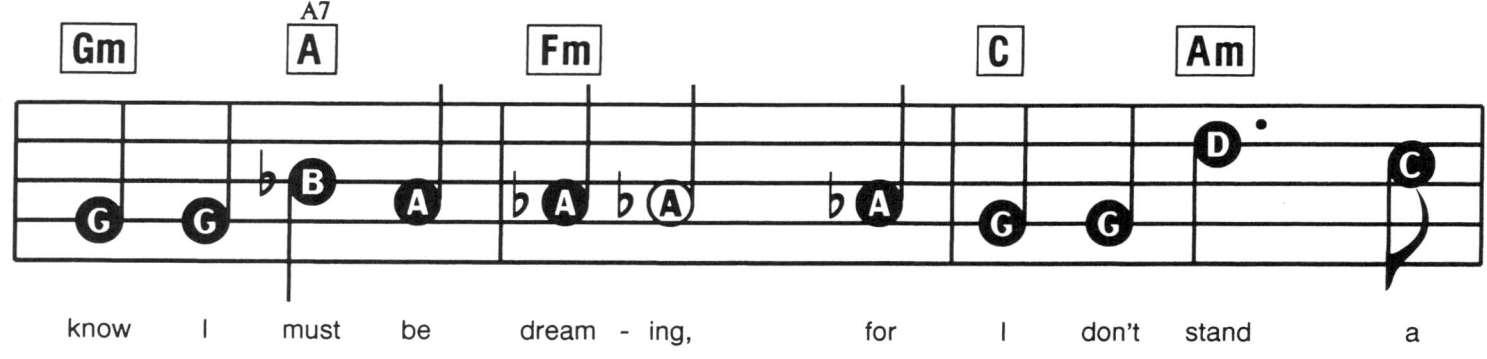
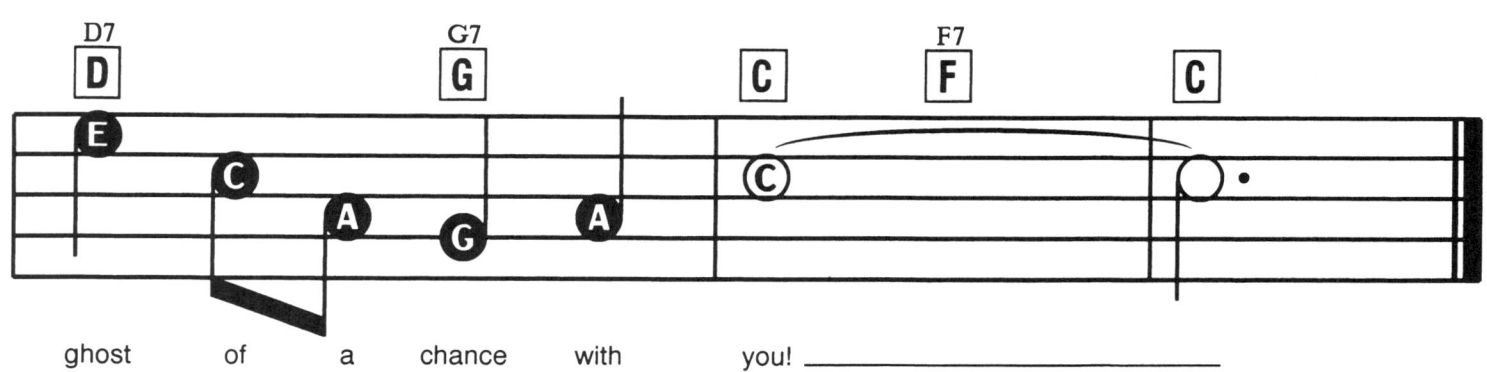

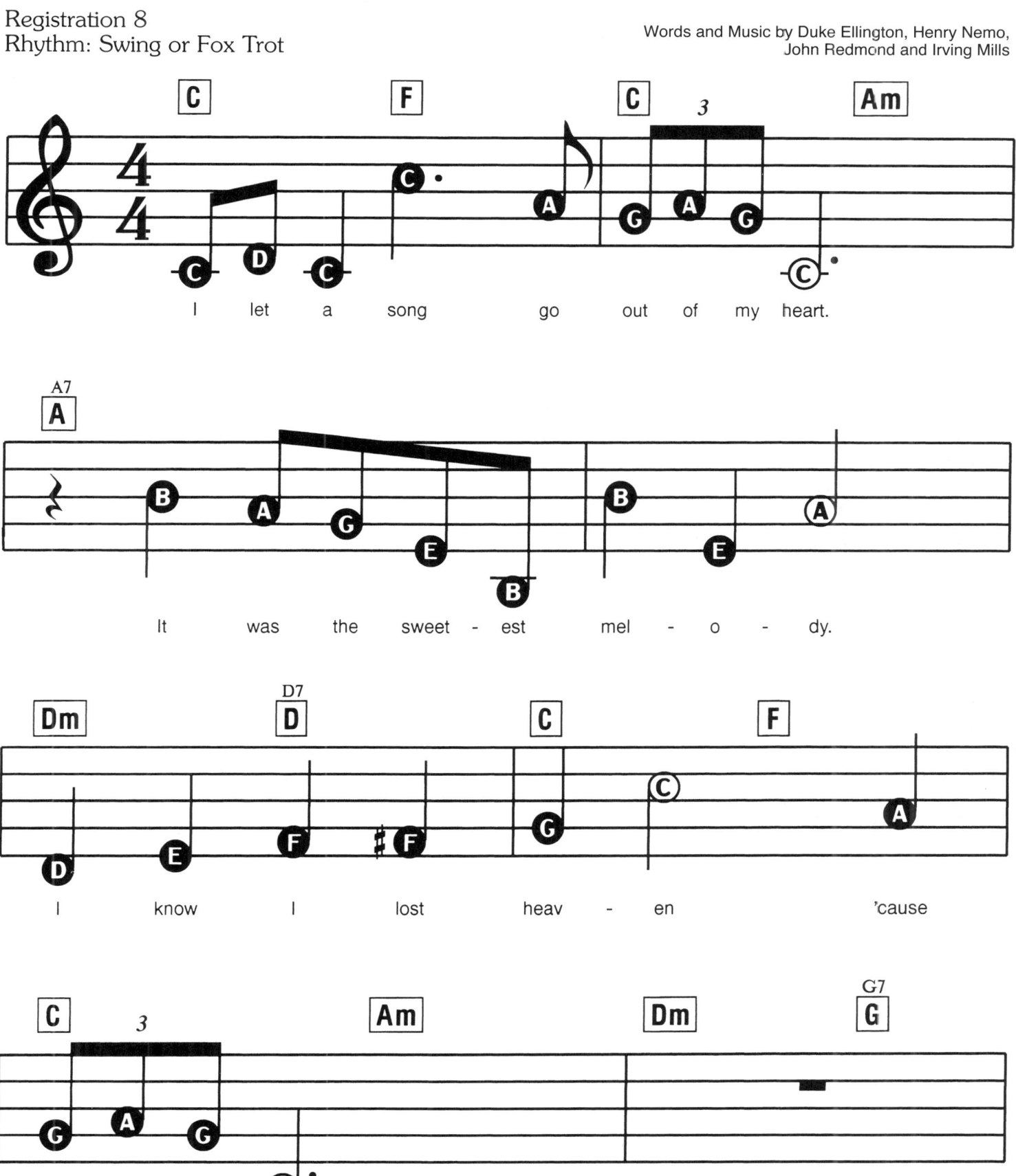

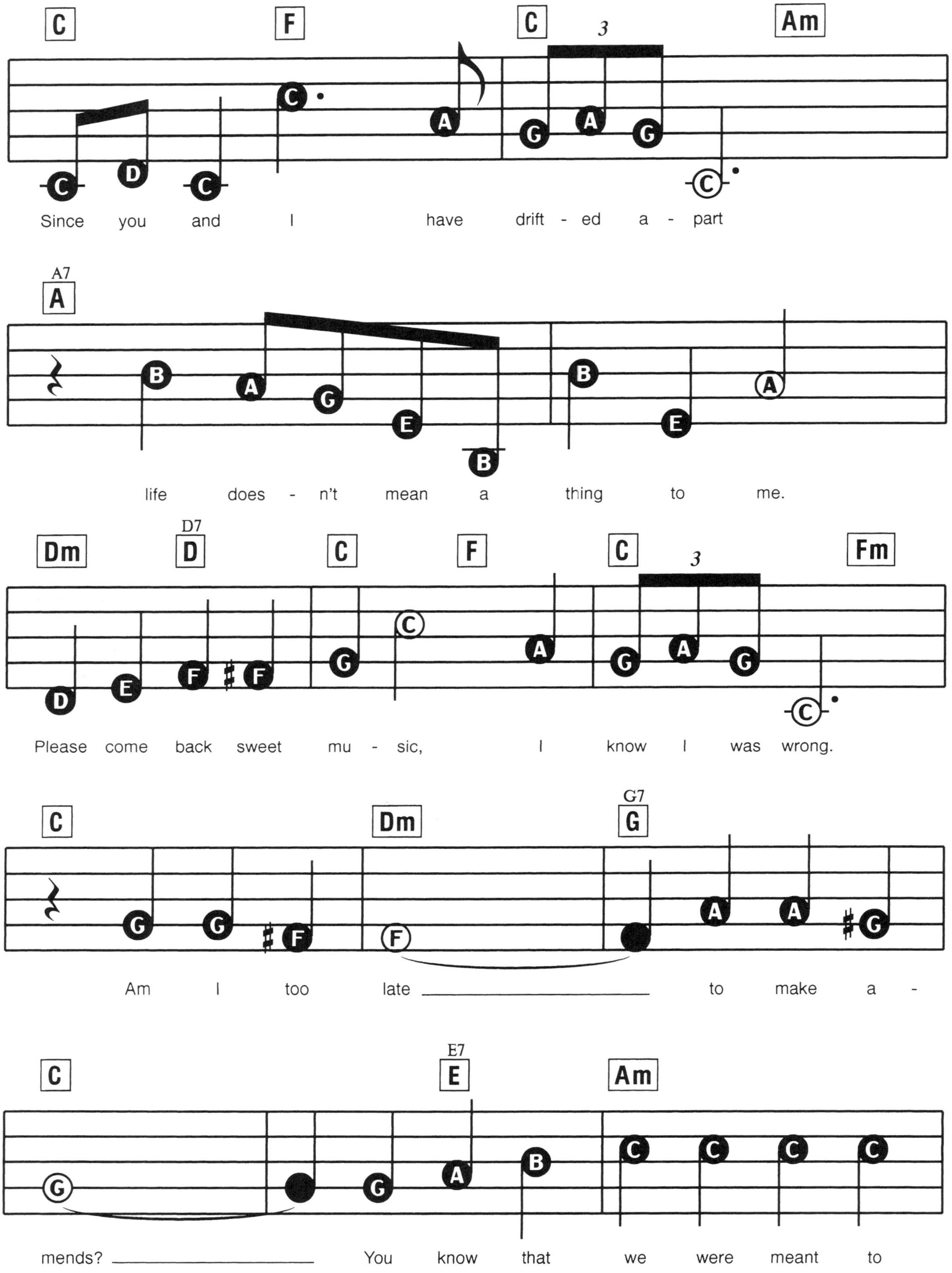
C F C Am
Since you and I have drift - ed a - part
A7 A
life does - n't mean a thing to me.
Dm D7 D C F C Fm
Please come back sweet mu - sic, I know I was wrong.
C Dm G7 G
Am I too late to make a -
C E7 E Am
mends? You know that we were meant to

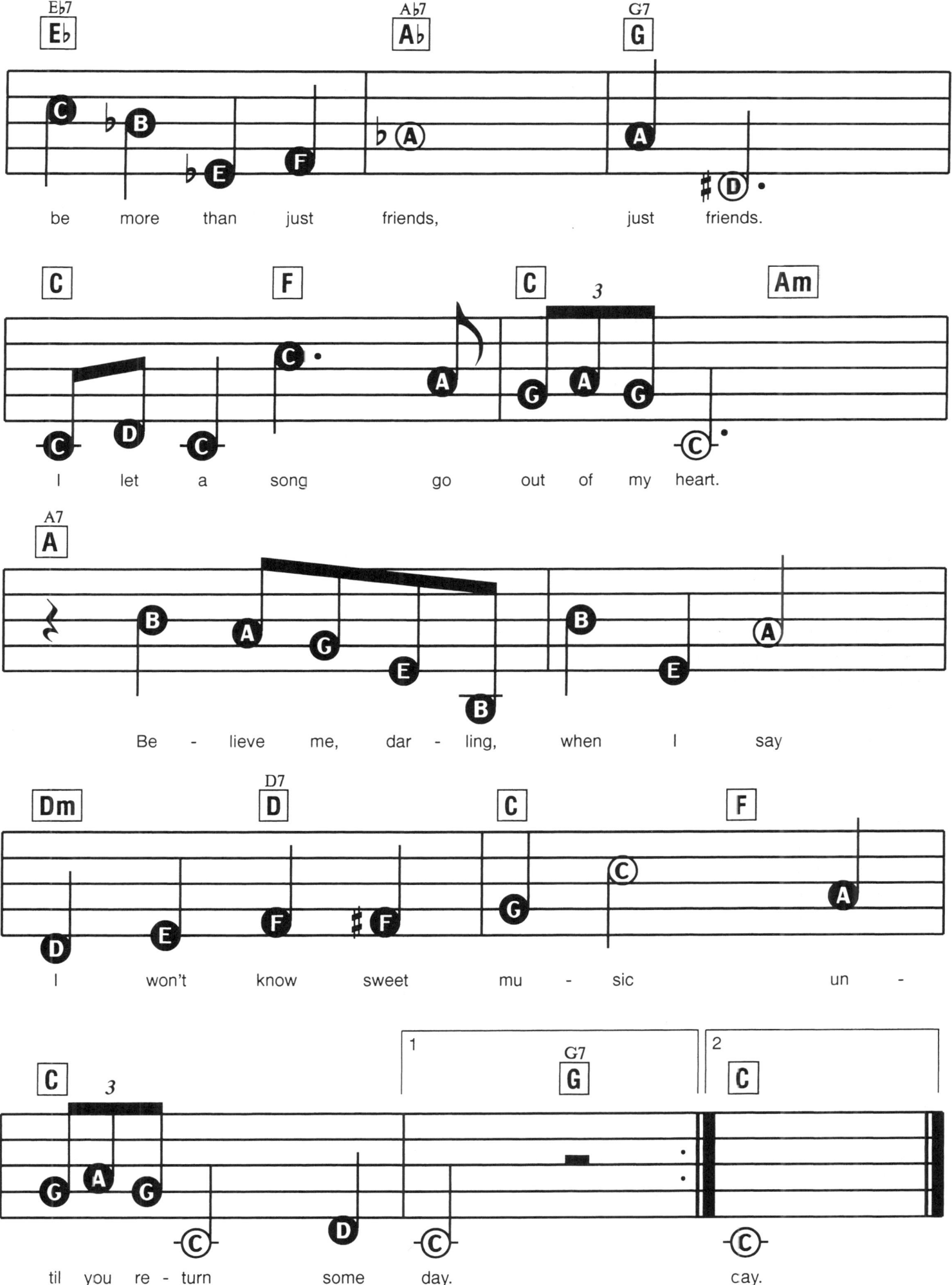

I Got It Bad and That Ain't Good

Registration 6
Rhythm: Ballad

Words by Paul Francis Webster
Music by Duke Ellington

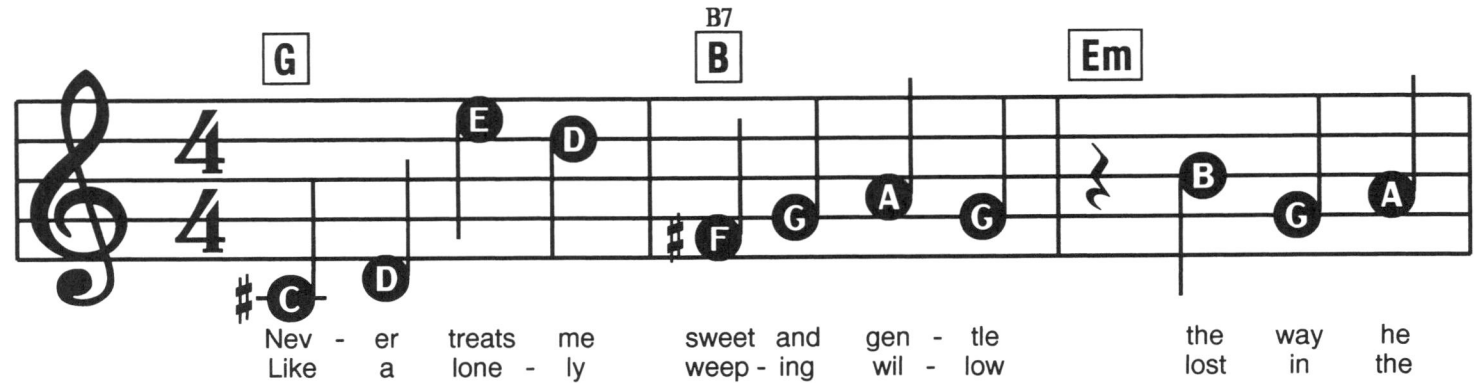

Nev - er treats me sweet and gen - tle the way he should;
Like a lone - ly weep - ing wil - low lost in the wood,

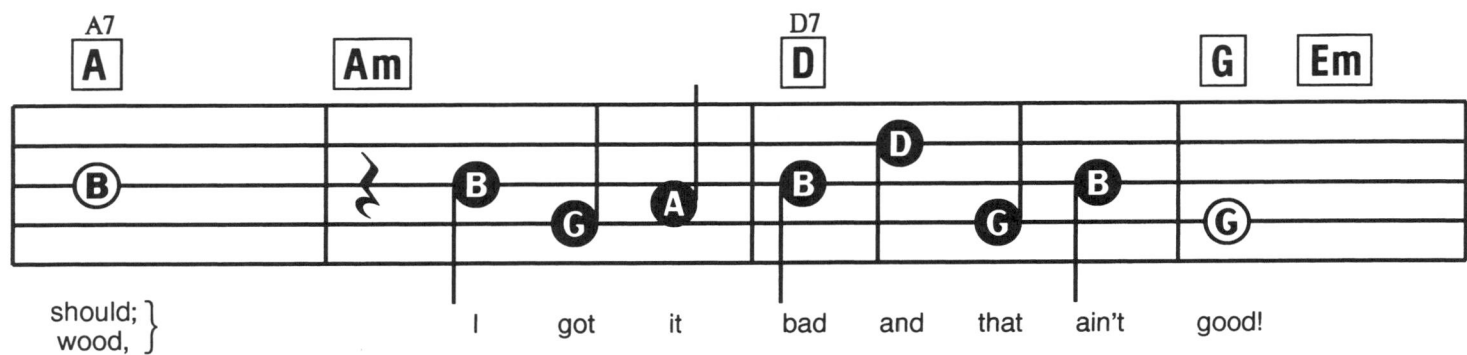

I got it bad and that ain't good!

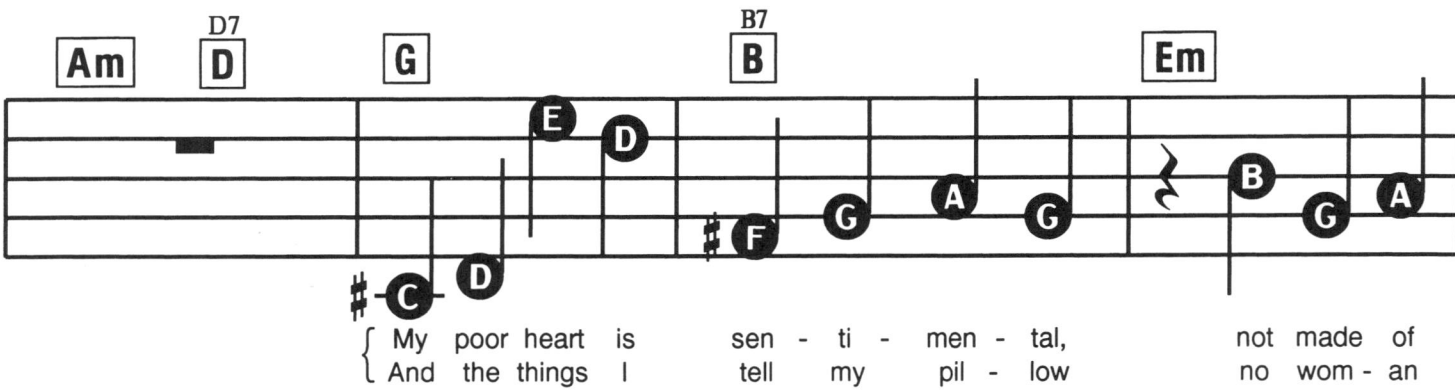

My poor heart is sen - ti - men - tal, not made of wood.
And the things I tell my pil - low no wom - an

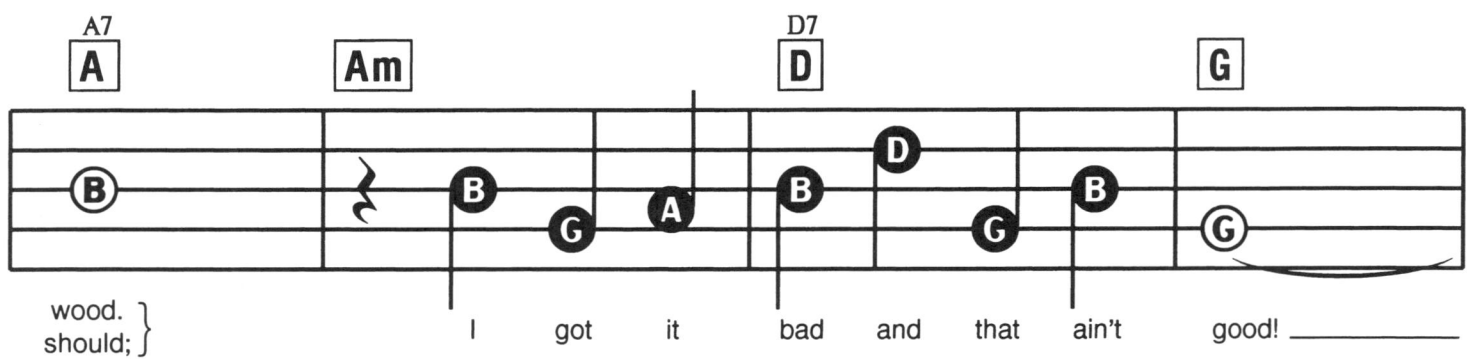

wood. should;
I got it bad and that ain't good! _____

Copyright © 1941 Sony/ATV Music Publishing LLC and Webster Music Co. in the U.S.A.
Copyright Renewed
All Rights on behalf of Sony/ATV Music Publishing LLC Administered by Sony/ATV Music Publishing LLC, 8 Music Square West, Nashville, TN 37203
Rights for the world outside the U.S.A. Administered by EMI Robbins Catalog Inc. (Publishing) and Alfred Publishing Co., Inc. (Print)
International Copyright Secured   All Rights Reserved

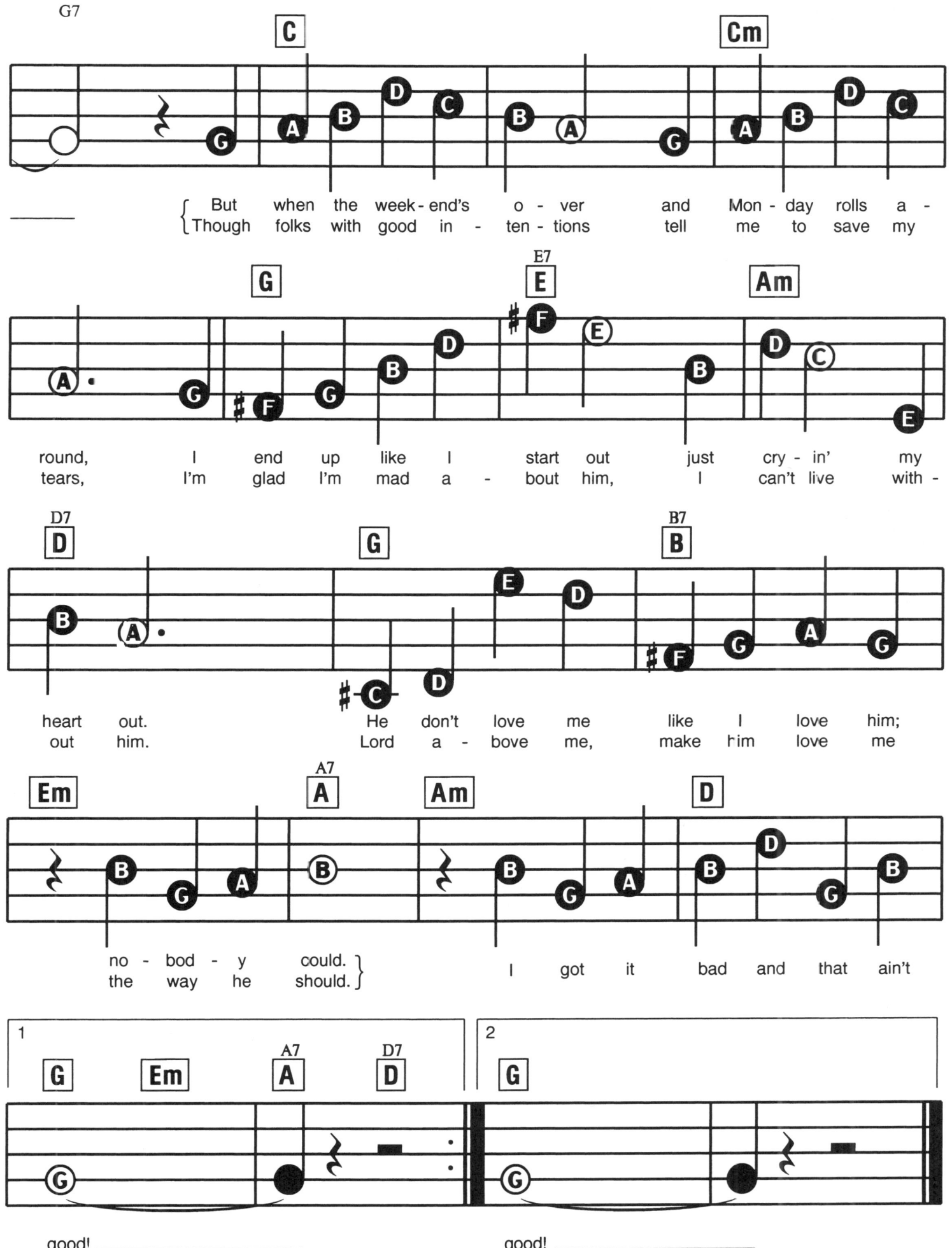

I Thought About You

Registration 2
Rhythm: Swing

Words by Johnny Mercer
Music by Jimmy Van Heusen

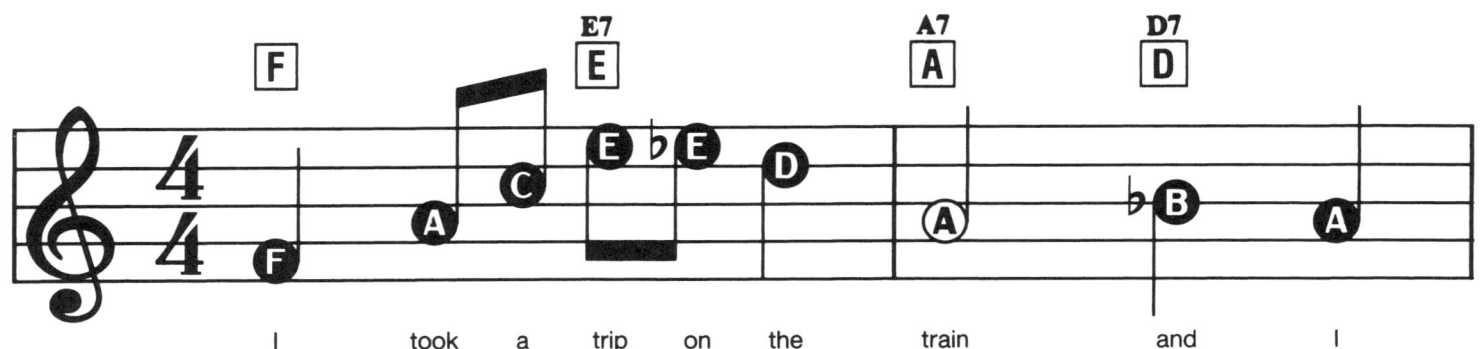

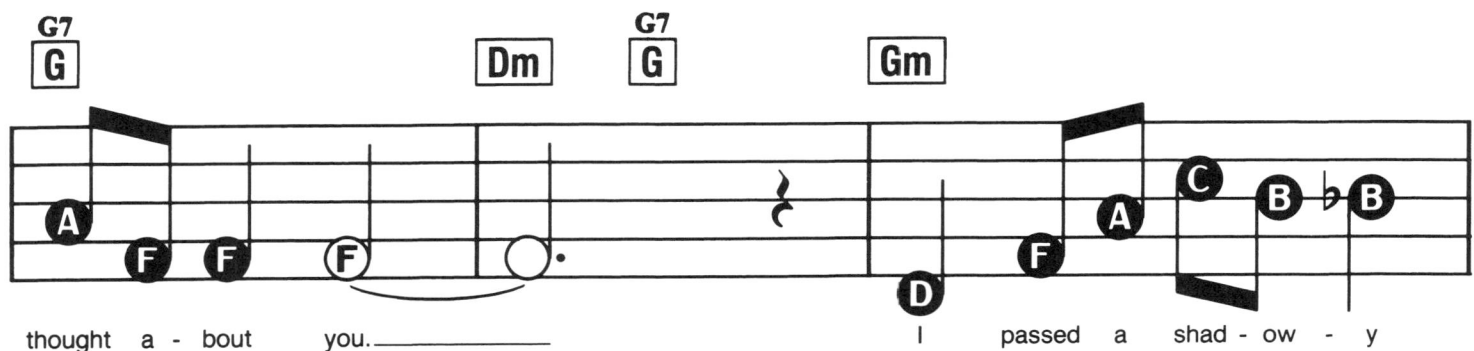

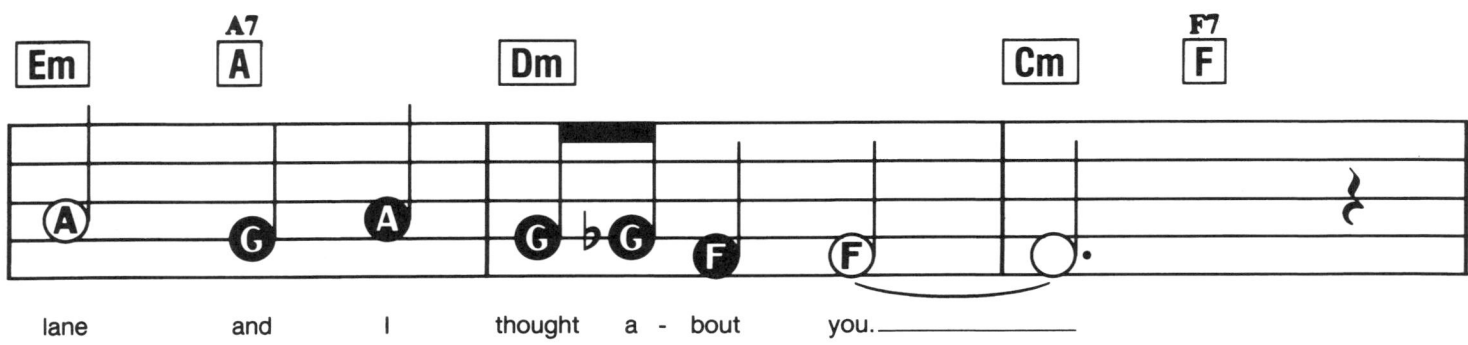

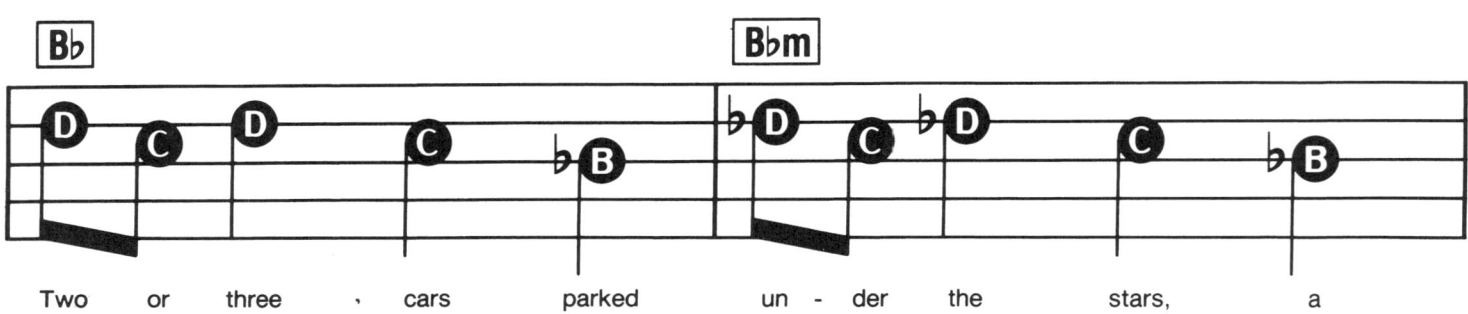

Copyright © 1939 by Range Road Music Inc., Jerry Leiber Music, Mike Stoller Music and The Johnny Mercer Foundation
Copyright Renewed; extended term of Copyright deriving from Jimmy Van Heusen assigned and effective October 13, 1995 to Range Road Music Inc., Jerry Leiber Music and Mike Stoller Music
All Rights for Jerry Leiber Music and Mike Stoller Music Administered by Range Road Music Inc.
All Rights for The Johnny Mercer Foundation Administered by WB Music Corp.
International Copyright Secured   All Rights Reserved
Used by Permission

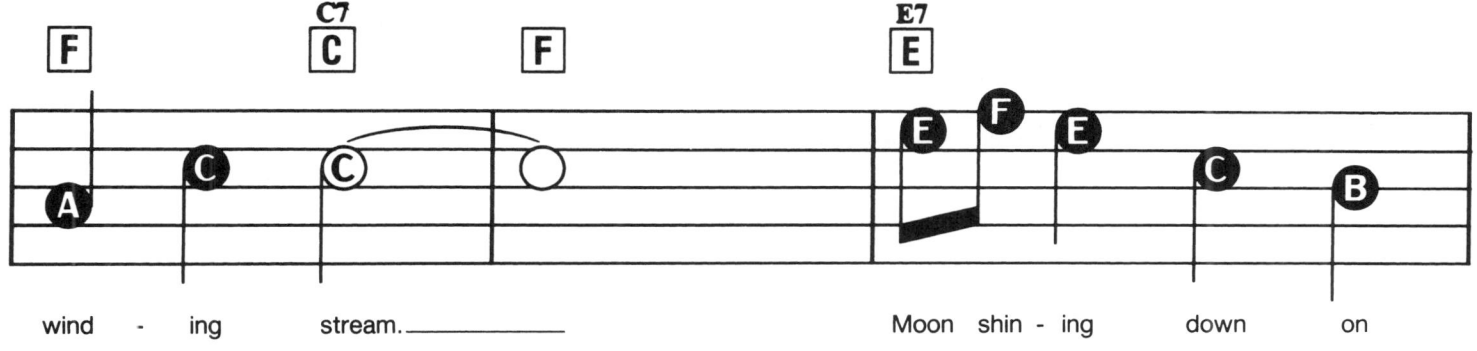
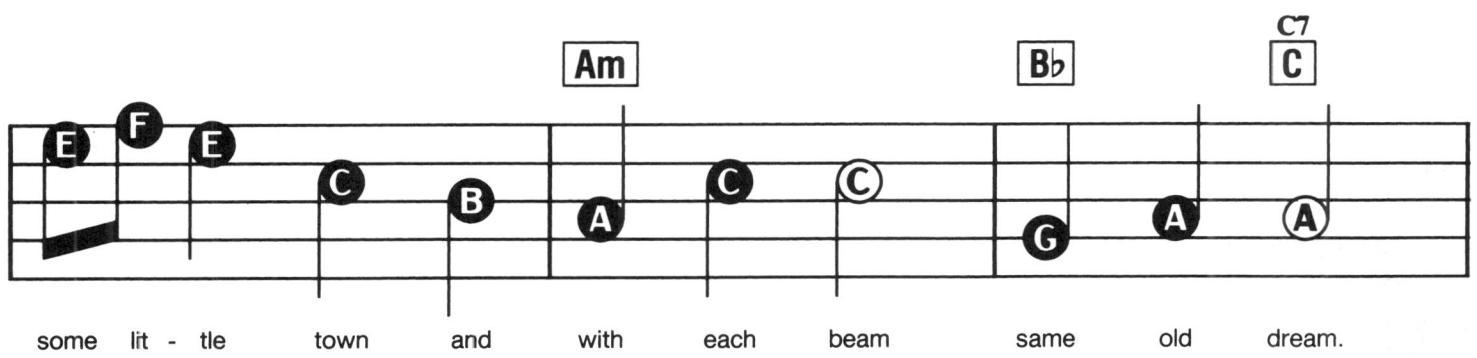
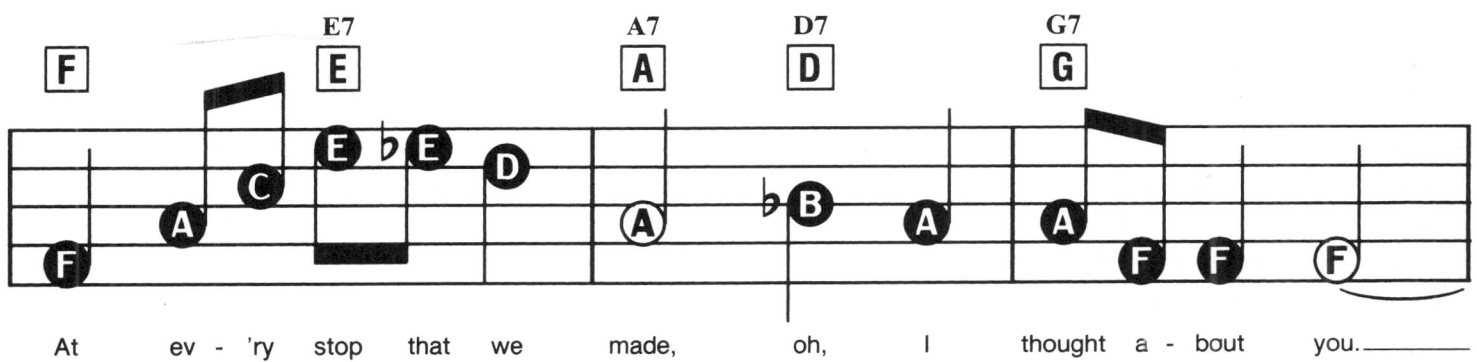
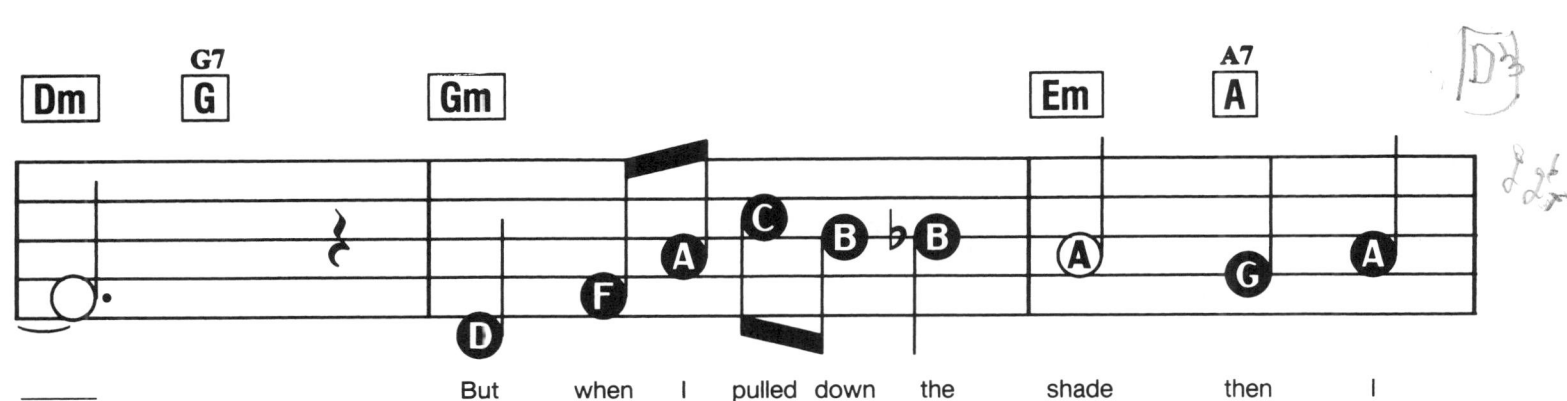

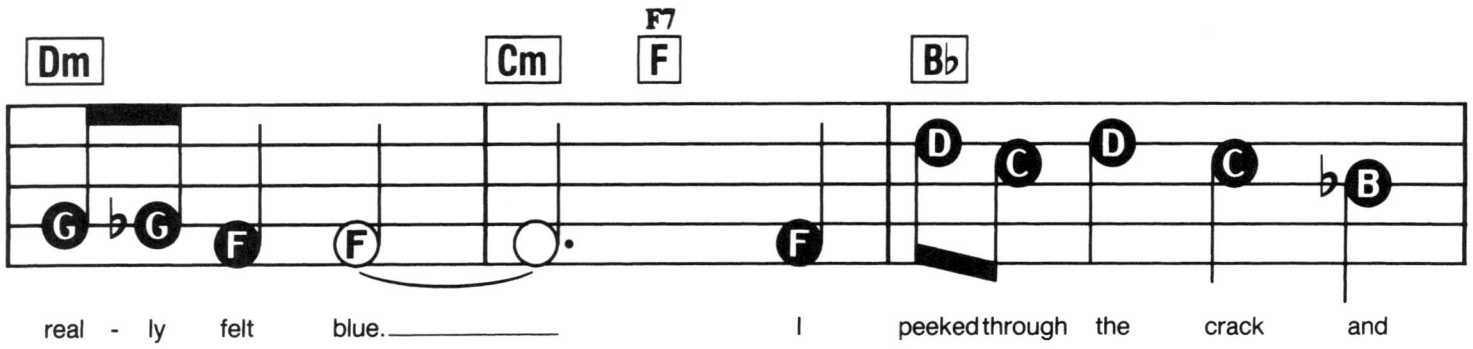
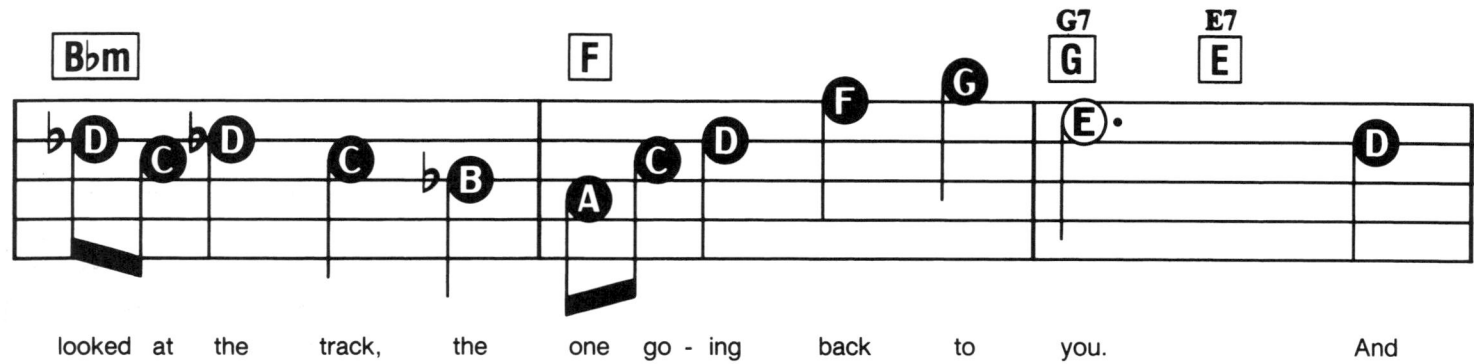
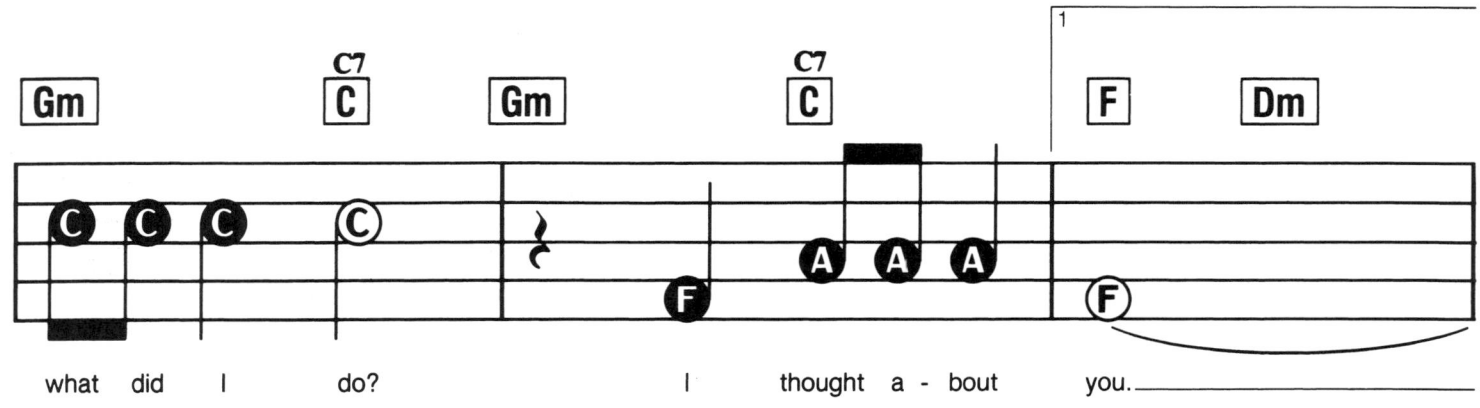
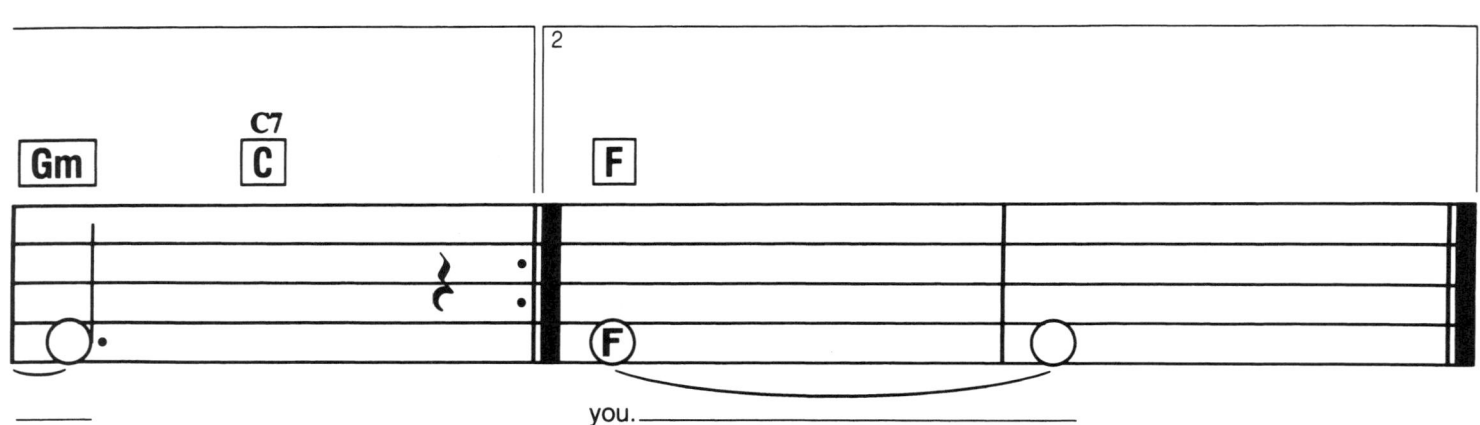

I Wish I Were in Love Again
from BABES IN ARMS

Registration 7
Rhythm: Swing

Words by Lorenz Hart
Music by Richard Rodgers

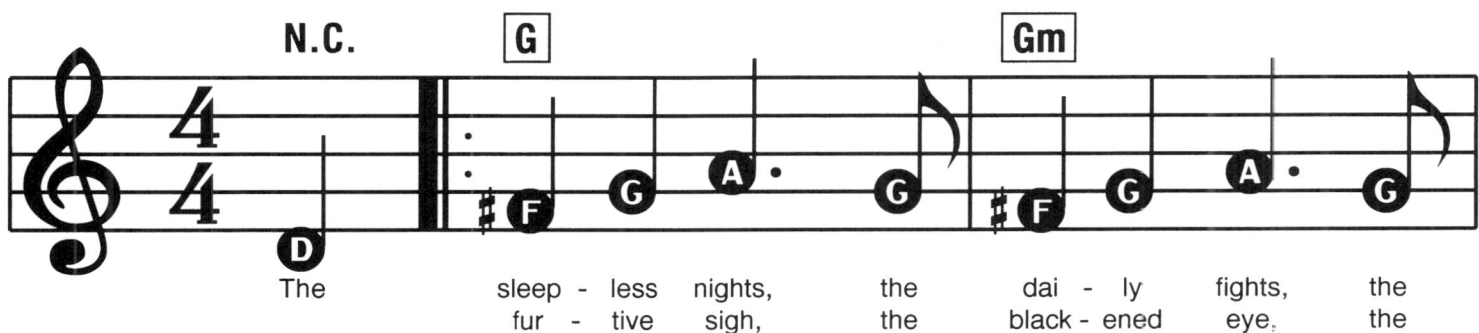
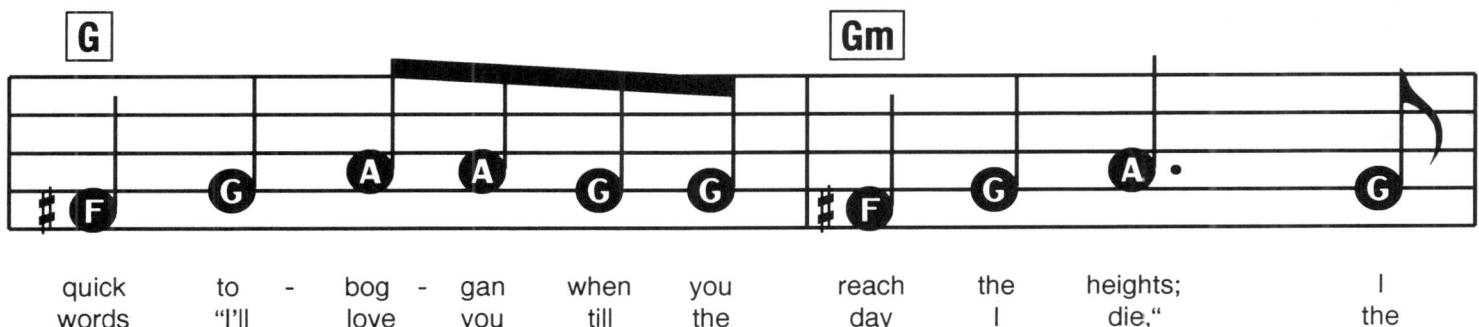
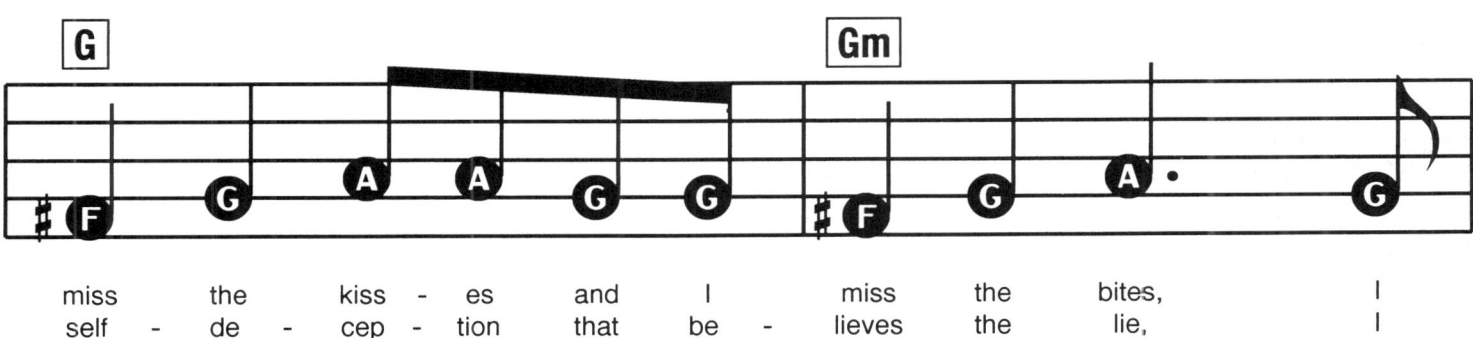
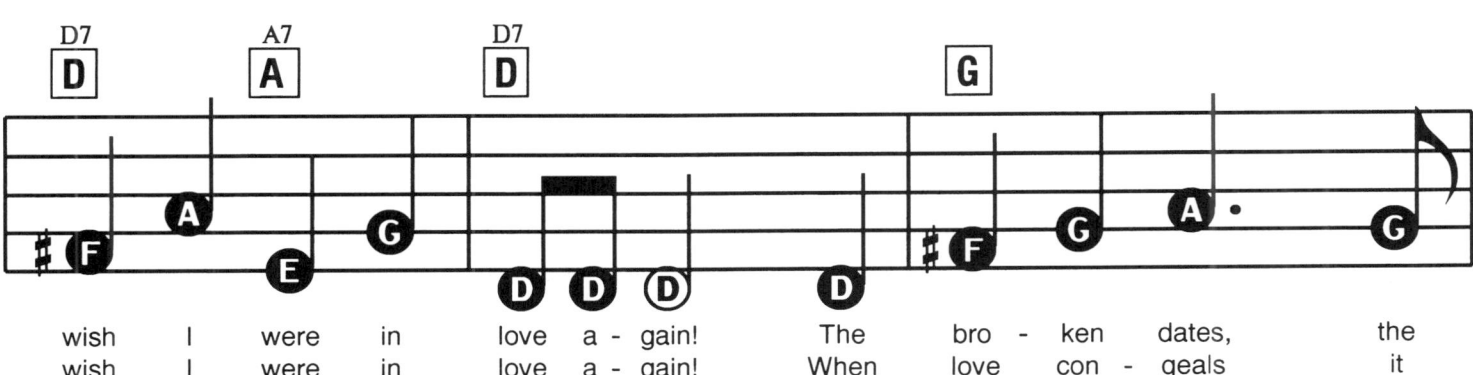

Copyright © 1937 (Renewed) by Chappell & Co.
Rights for the Extended Renewal Term in the U.S. Controlled by Williamson Music and WB Music Corp. o/b/o The Estate Of Lorenz Hart
International Copyright Secured   All Rights Reserved

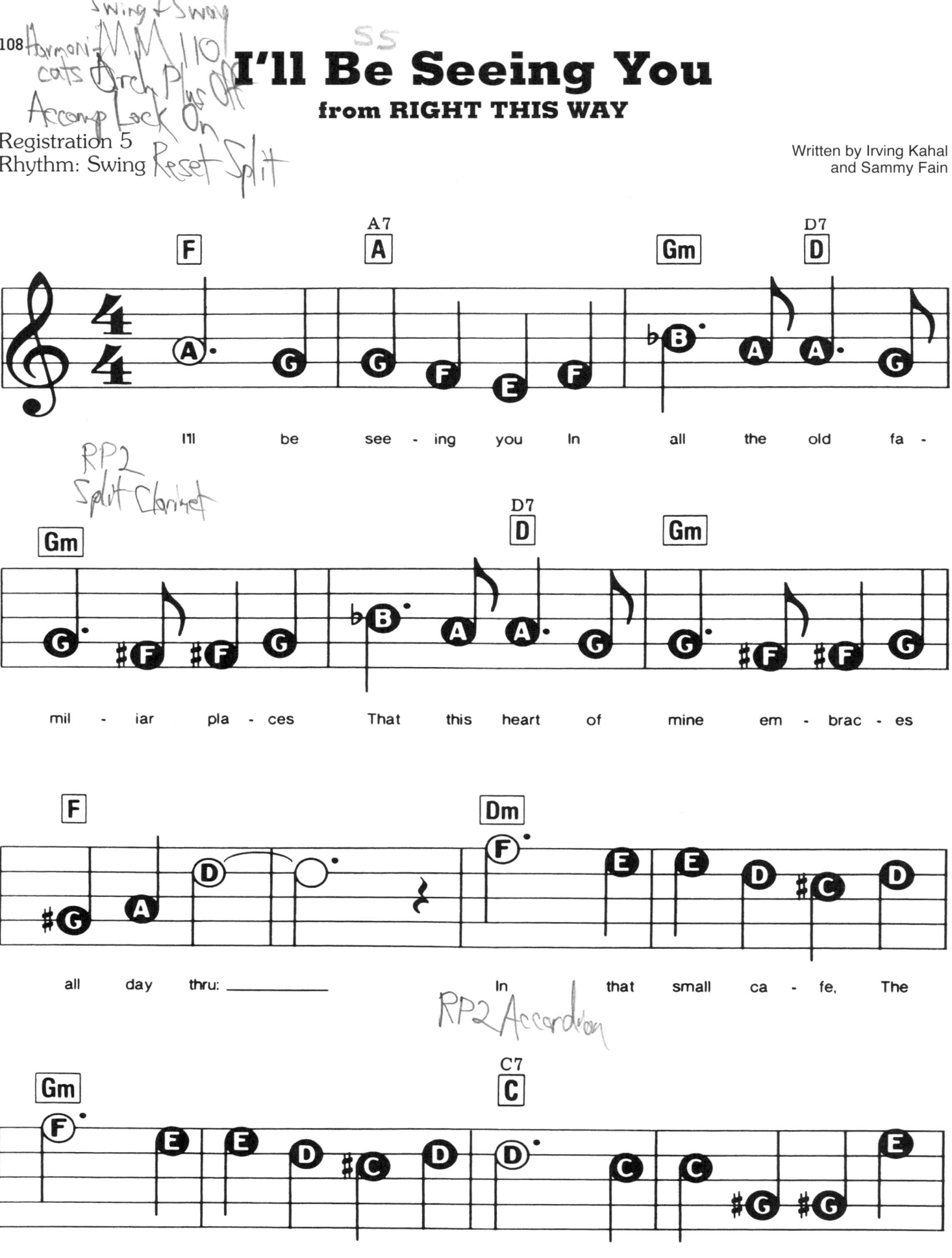

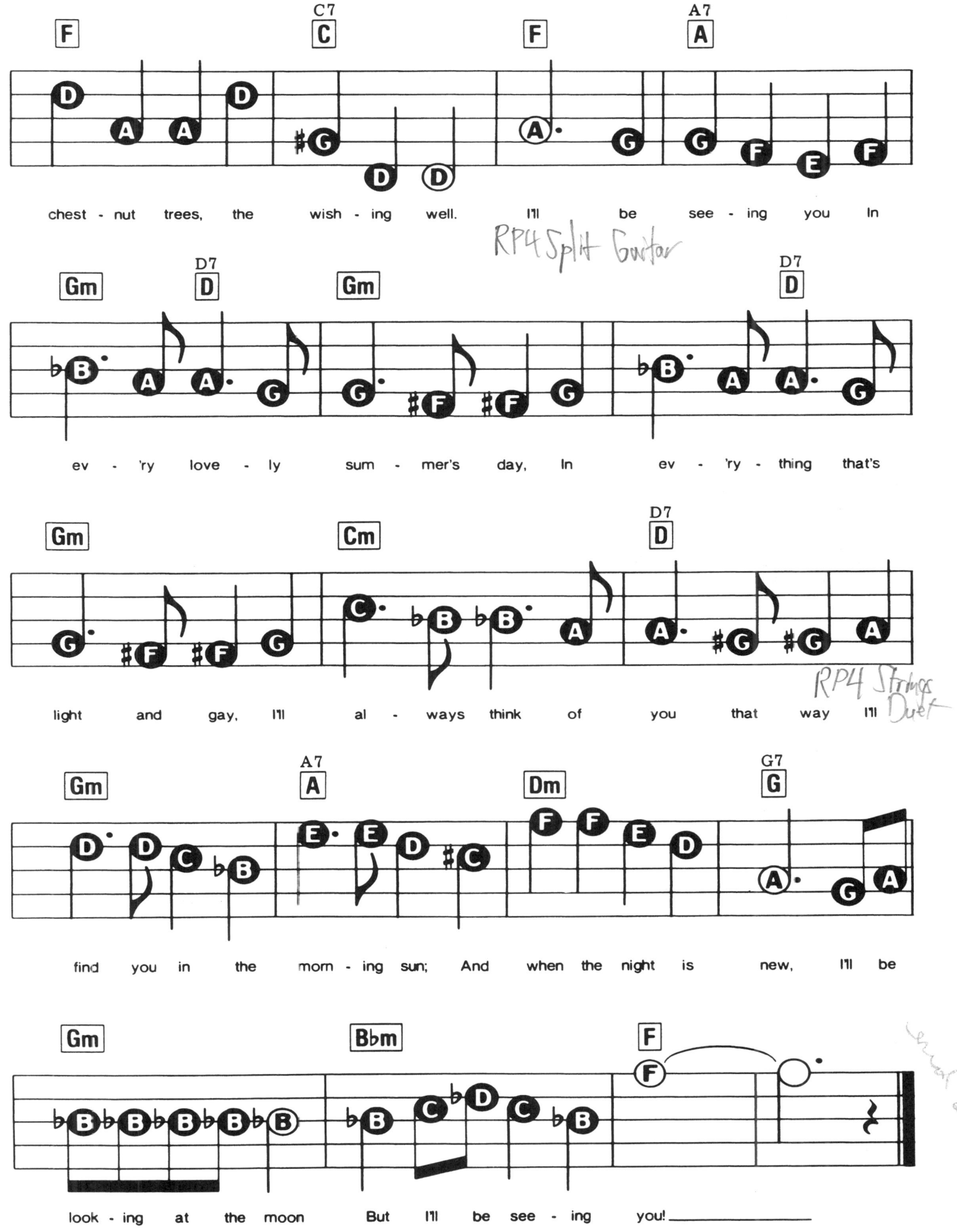

I'm Just a Lucky So and So

Registration 4
Rhythm: Fox Trot or Swing

Words by Mack David
Music by Duke Ellington

As I walk down the street seems ev-'ry-one I meet gives me a friend-ly "Hel-lo." I guess I'm just a luck-y so-and-so. _____ The birds in ev-'ry tree are all so neigh-bor-ly,

Copyright © 1945 Sony/ATV Music Publishing LLC and Universal - PolyGram International Publishing, Inc. in the U.S.A.
Copyright Renewed
All Rights on behalf of Sony/ATV Music Publishing LLC Administered by Sony/ATV Music Publishing LLC, 8 Music Square West, Nashville, TN 37203
International Copyright Secured   All Rights Reserved

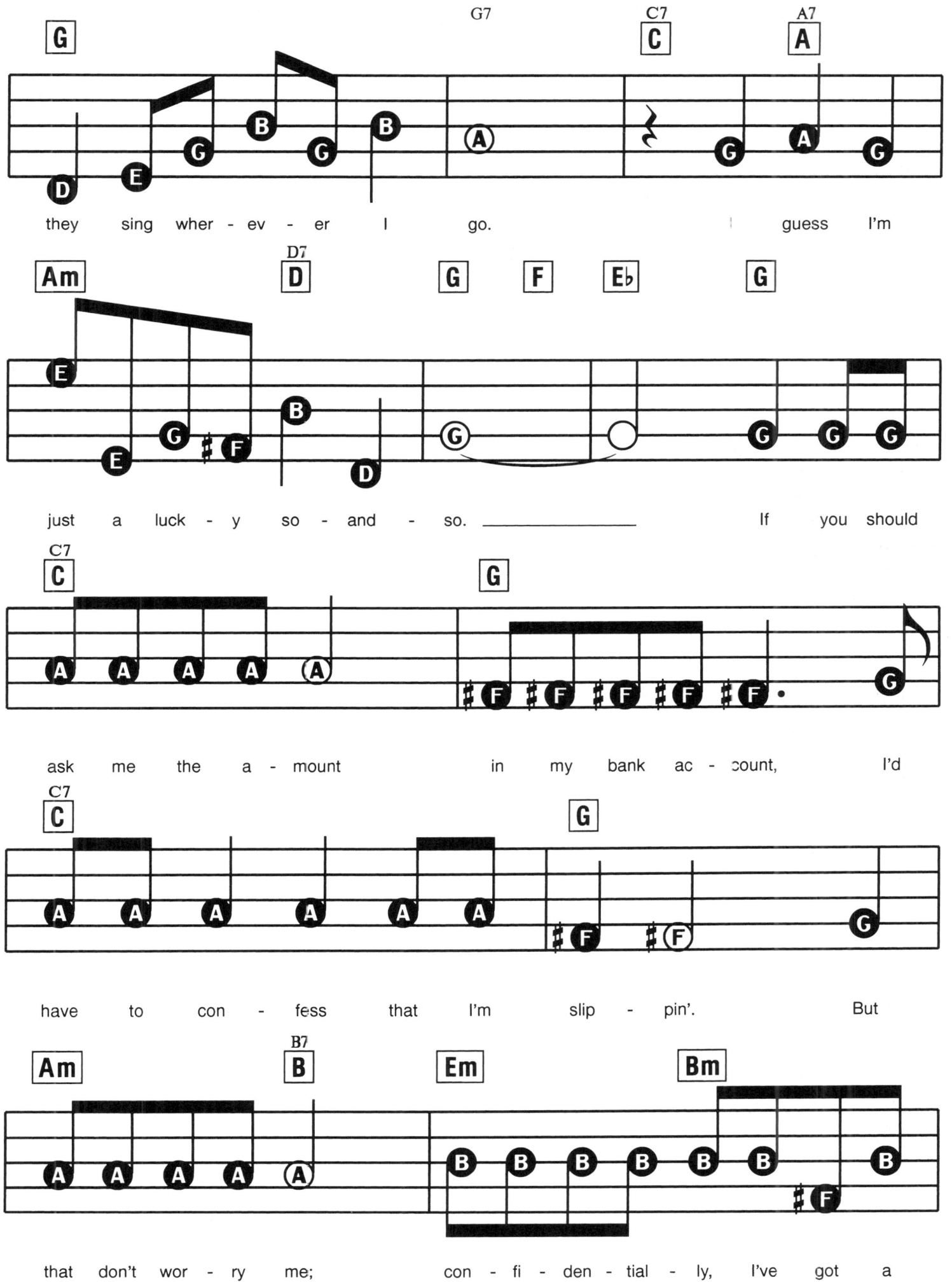

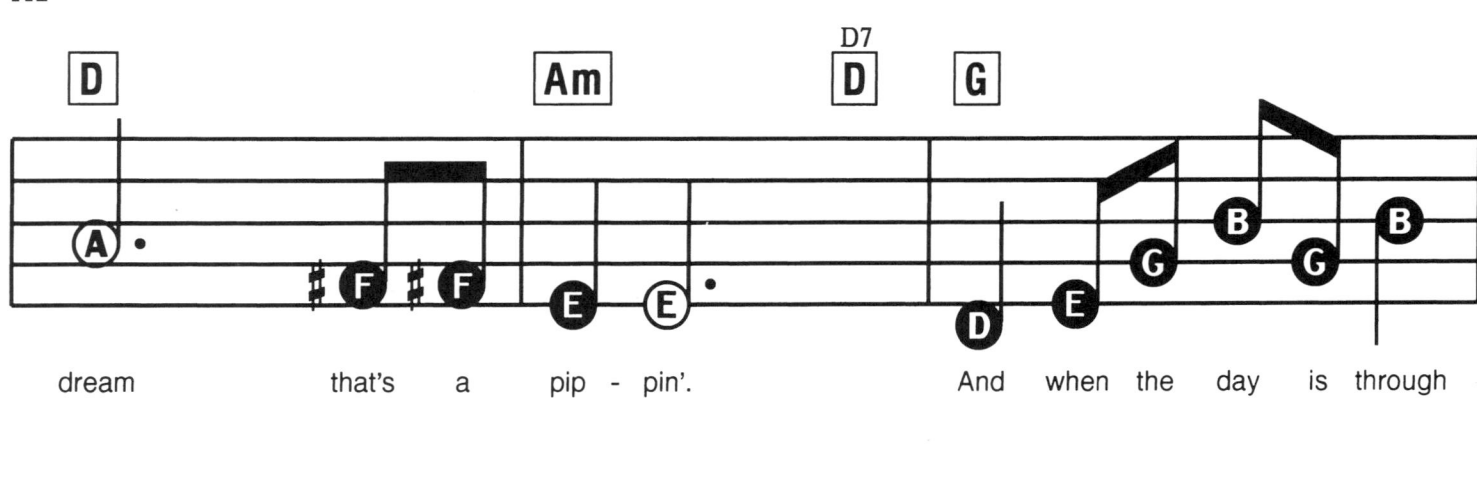
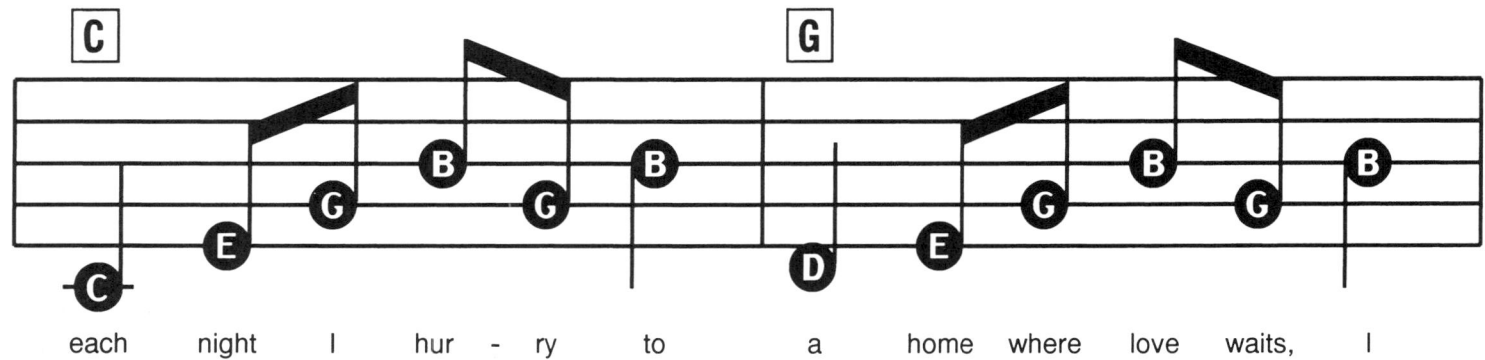
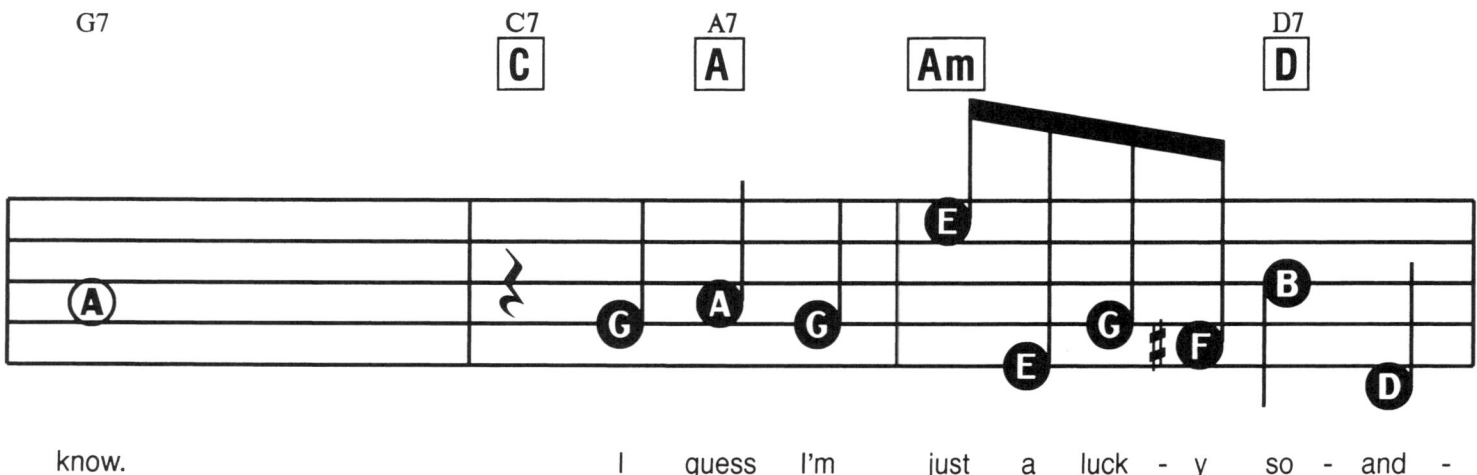
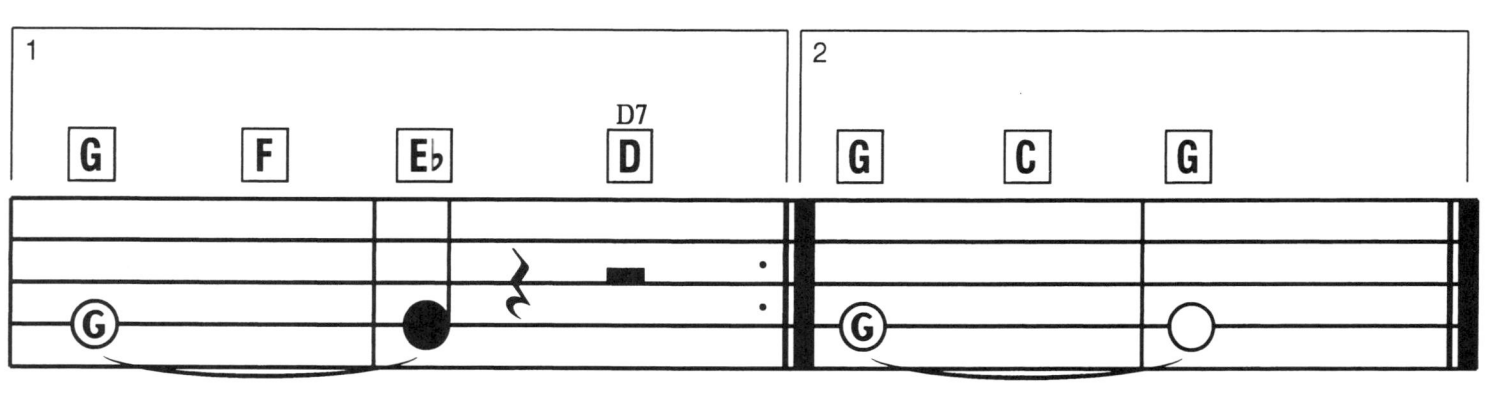

Ill Wind
(You're Blowin' Me No Good)
from COTTON CLUB PARADE

Registration 2
Rhythm: Ballad

Lyric by Ted Koehler
Music by Harold Arlen

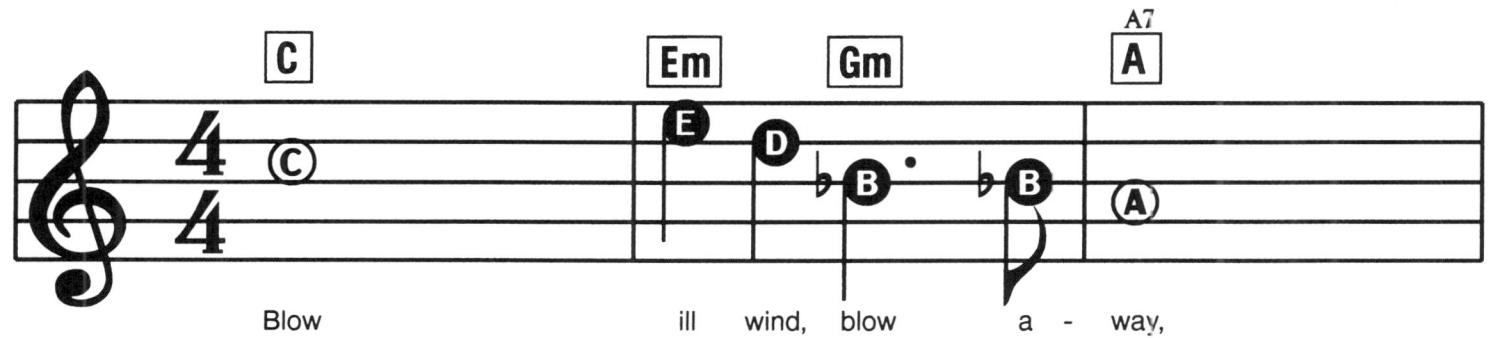

Blow ill wind, blow a - way,

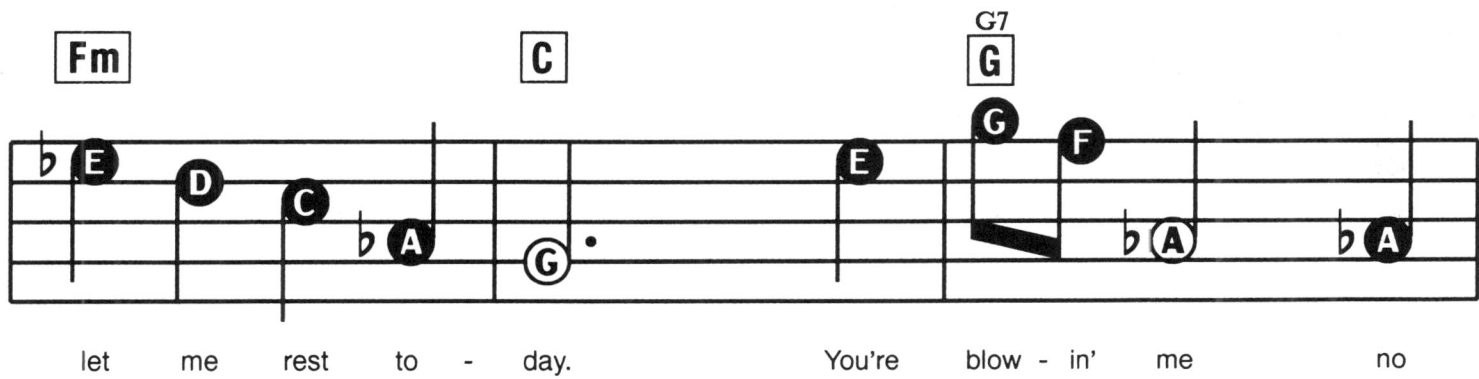

let me rest to - day. You're blow - in' me no

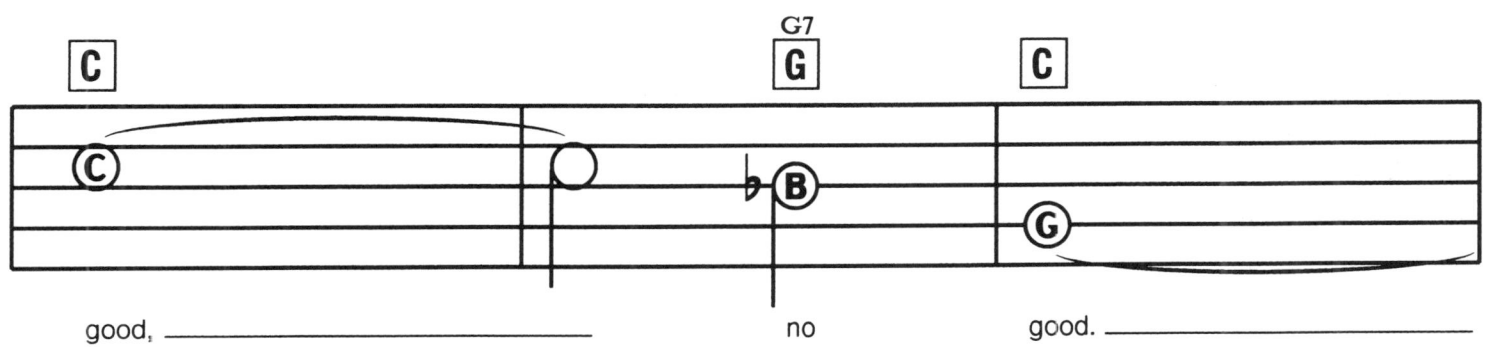

good, _____ no good. _____

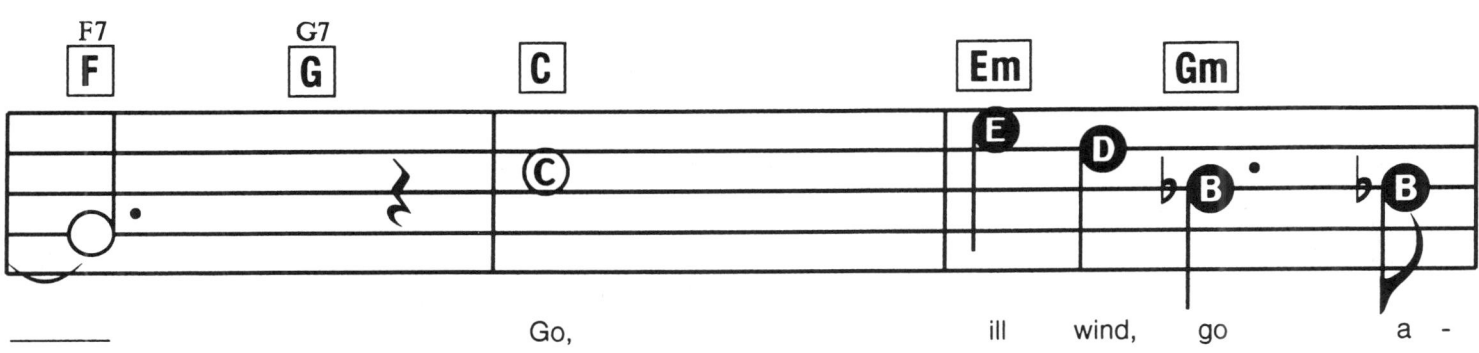

Go, ill wind, go a -

© 1934 (Renewed 1962) FRED AHLERT MUSIC GROUP (ASCAP) and TED KOEHLER MUSIC CO.
(ASCAP)/Administered by BUG MUSIC and S.A. MUSIC CO.
All Rights Reserved   Used by Permission

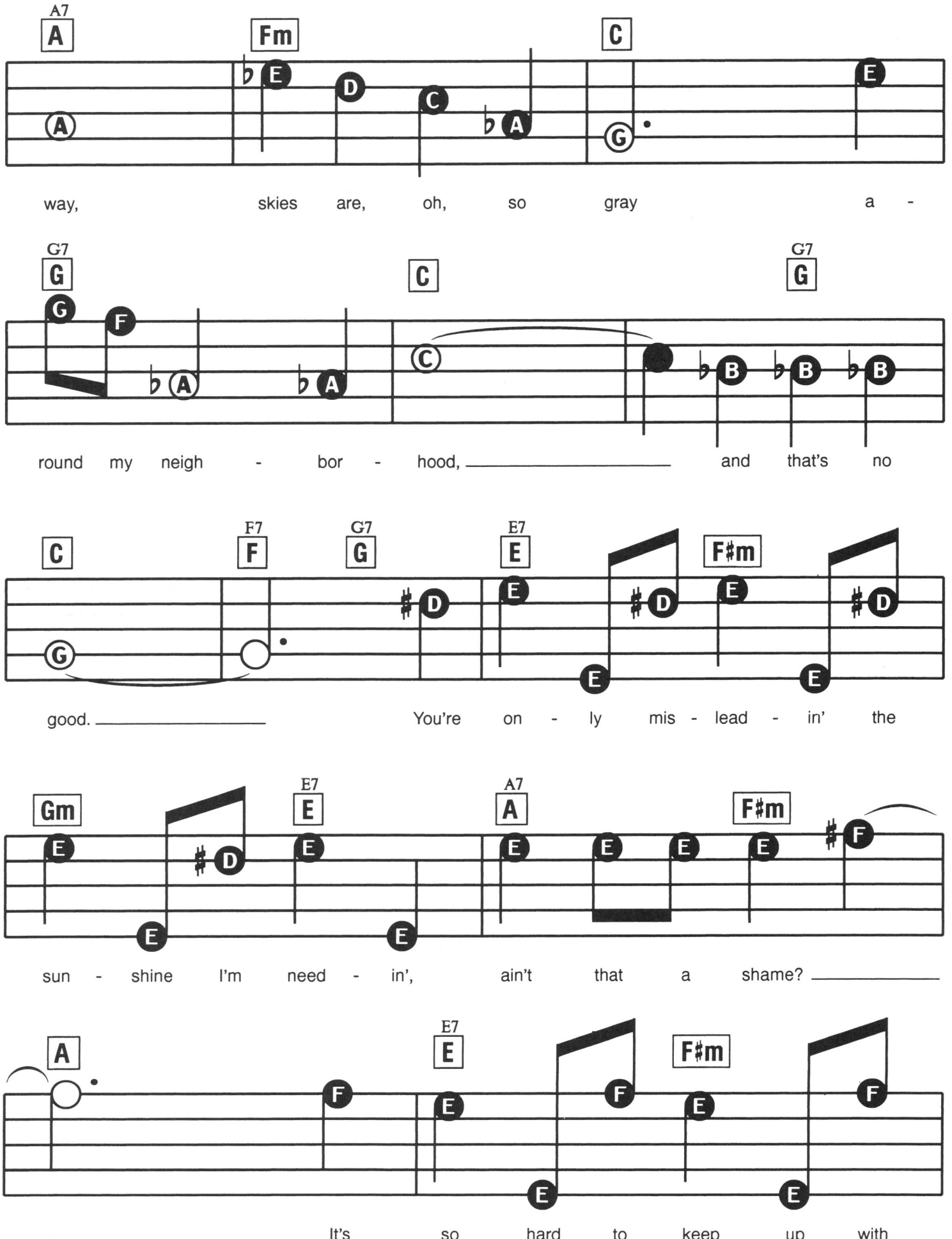

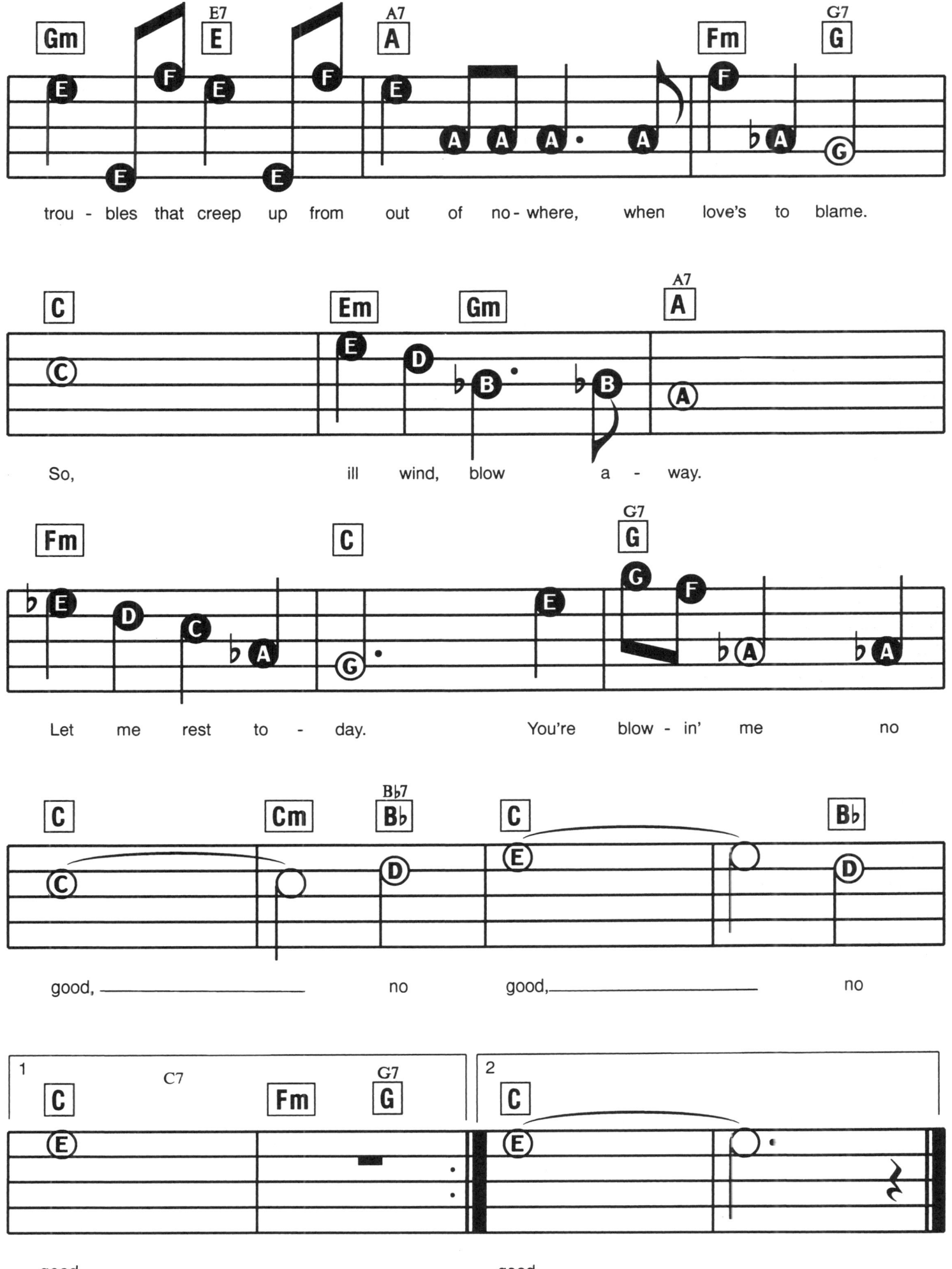

I'm Old Fashioned
from YOU WERE NEVER LOVELIER

Registration 5
Rhythm: Fox Trot or Ballad

Words by Johnny Mercer
Music by Jerome Kern

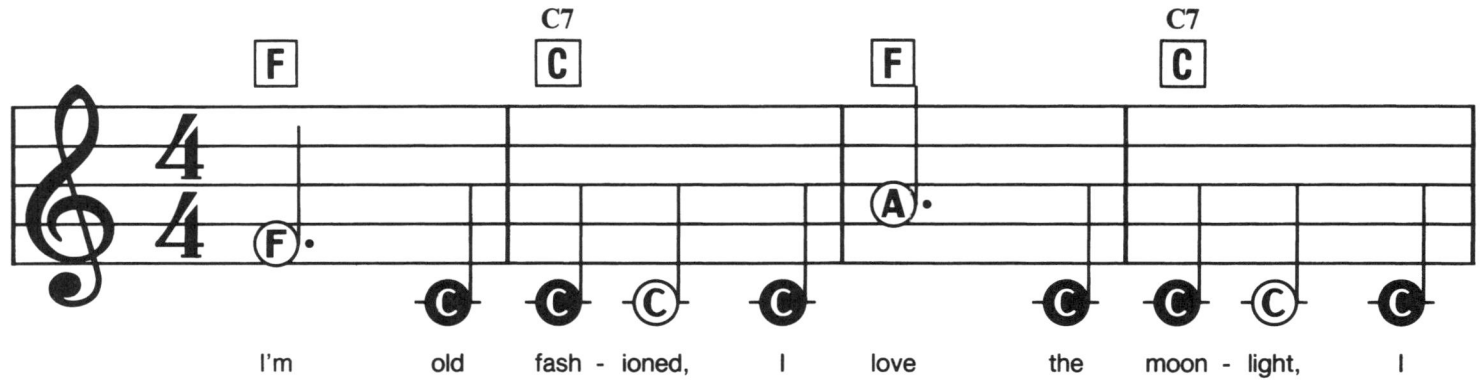

I'm old fash-ioned, I love the moon-light, I

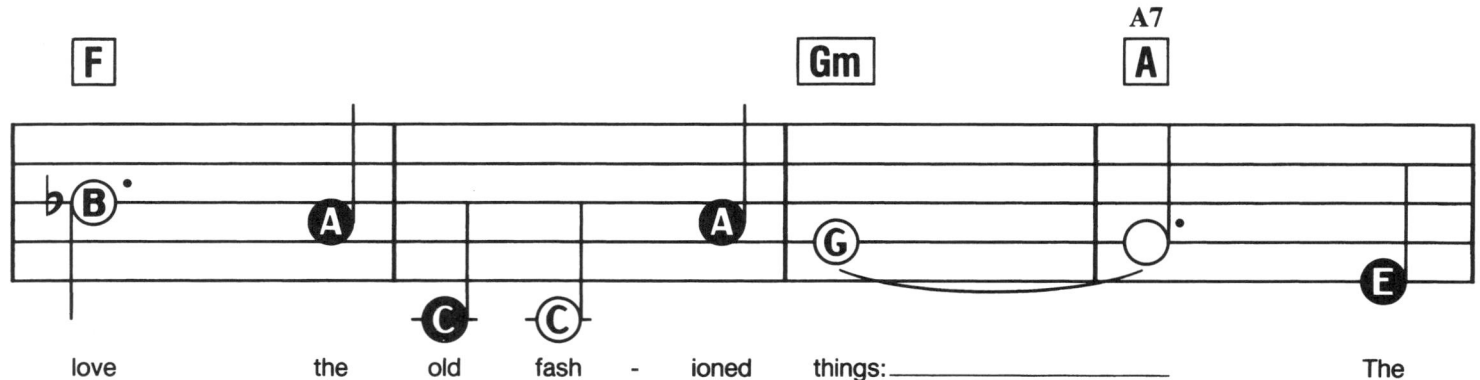

love the old fash-ioned things: The

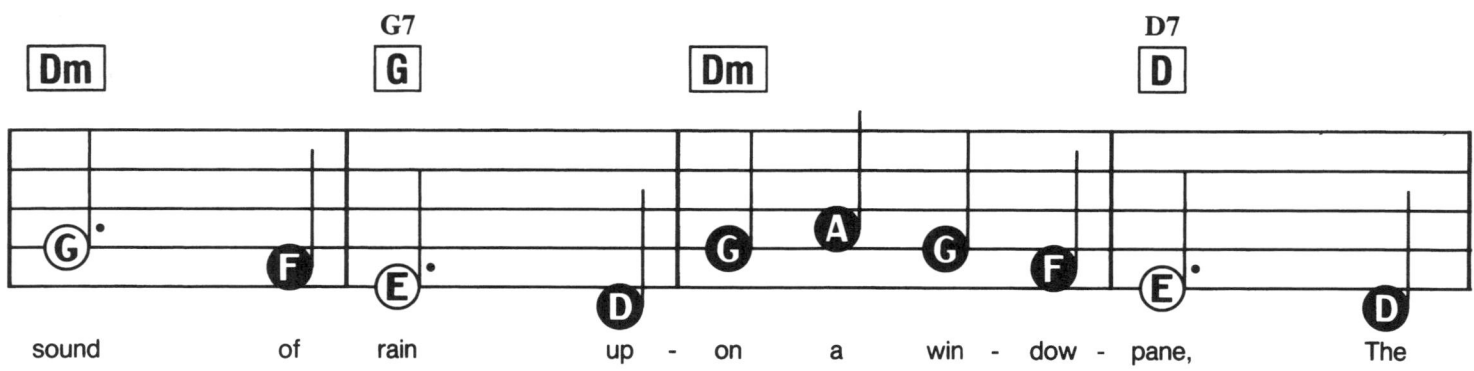

sound of rain up-on a win-dow-pane, The

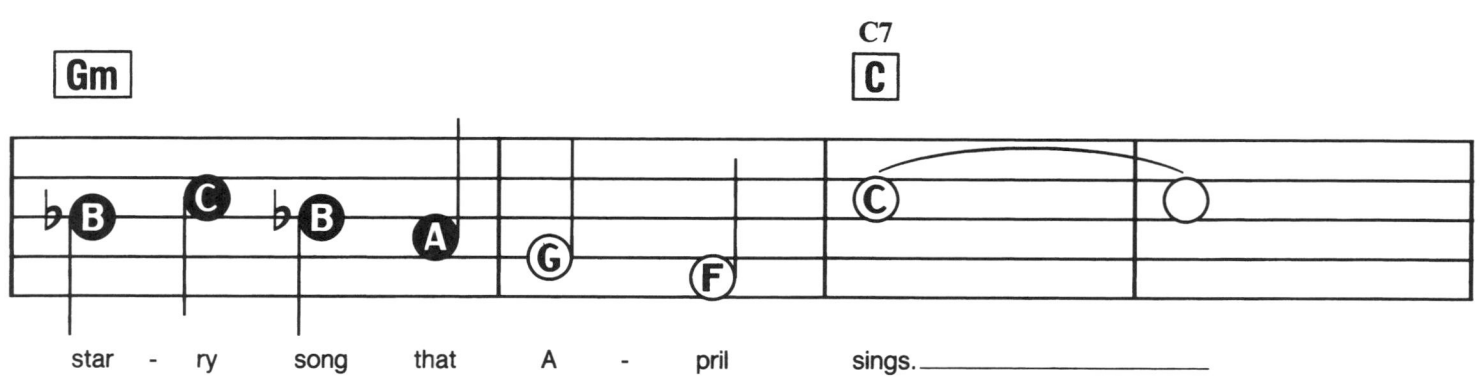

star-ry song that A-pril sings.

Copyright © 1942 UNIVERSAL - POLYGRAM INTERNATIONAL PUBLISHING, INC.
Copyright Renewed
All Rights Reserved   Used by Permission

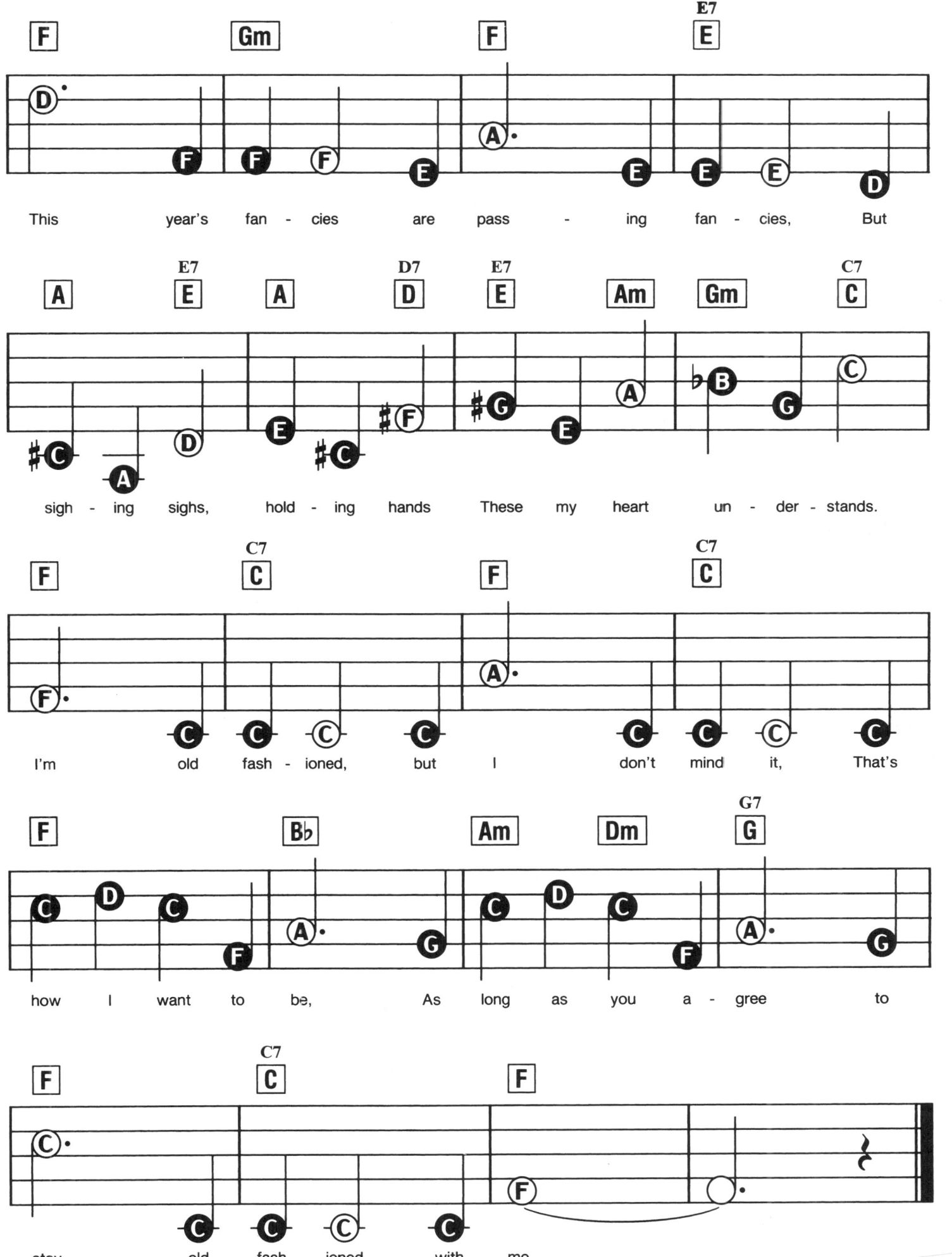

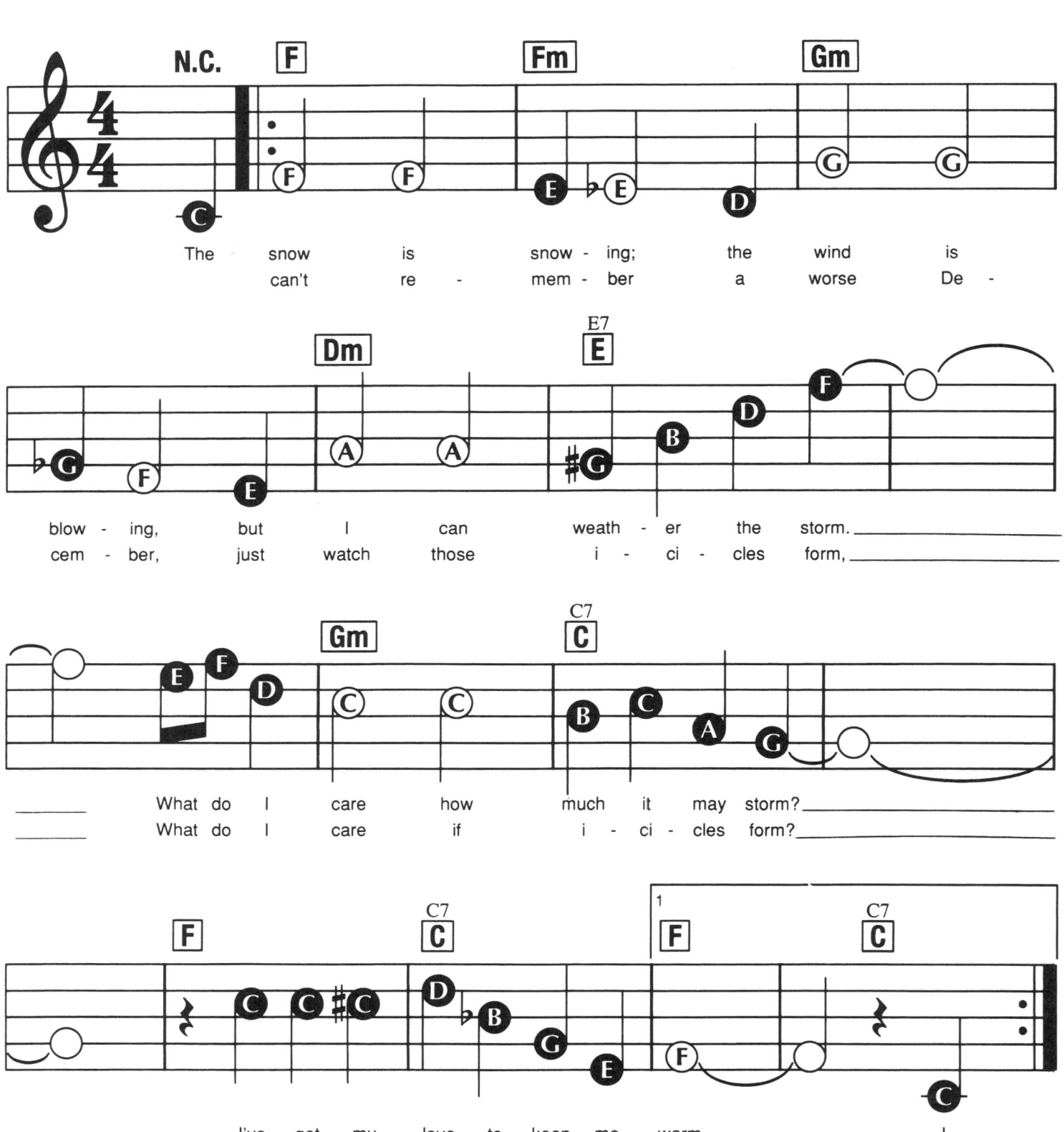

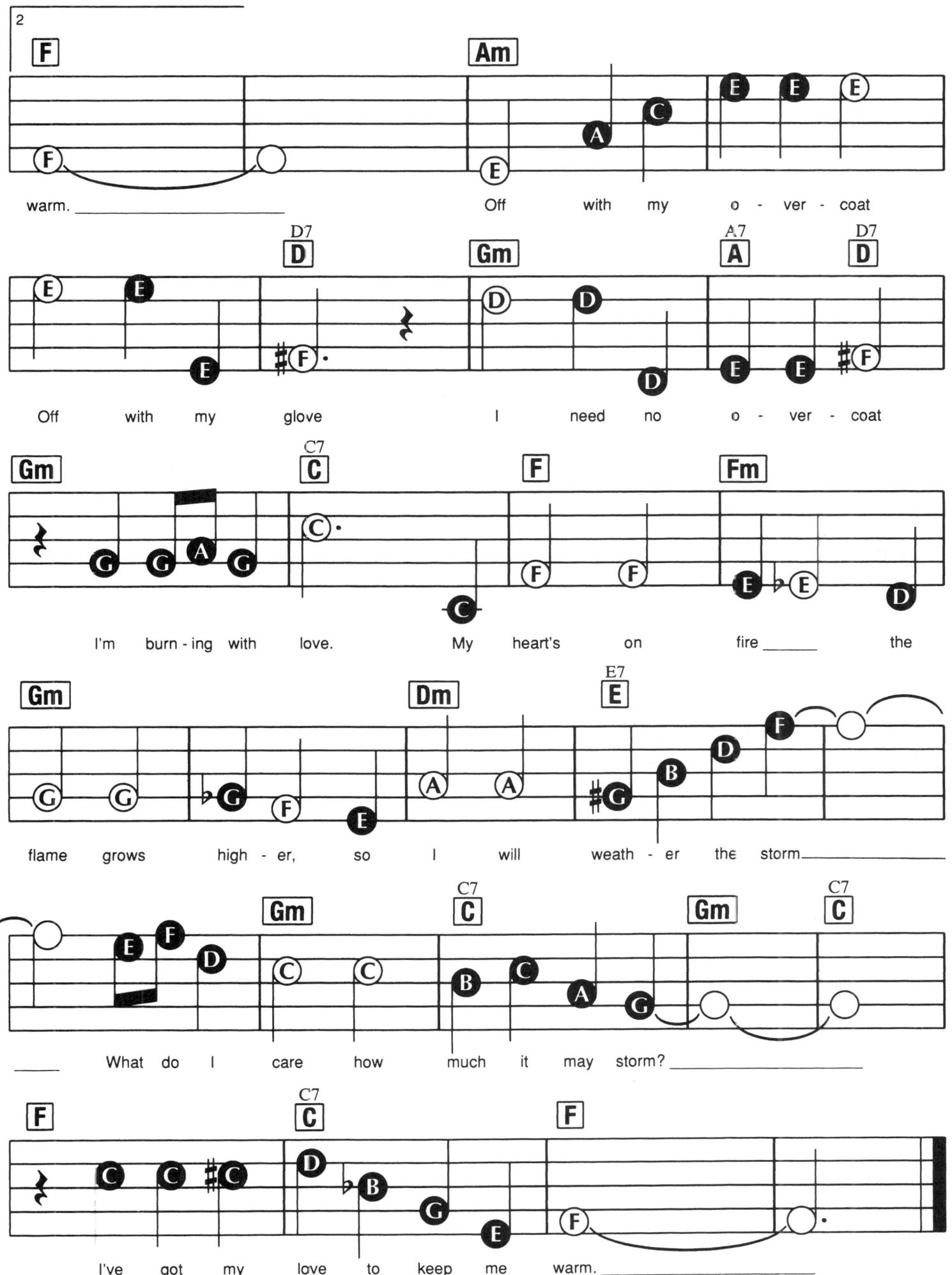

I've Got You Under My Skin
from BORN TO DANCE

Registration 5
Rhythm: Ballad or Fox Trot

Words and Music by
Cole Porter

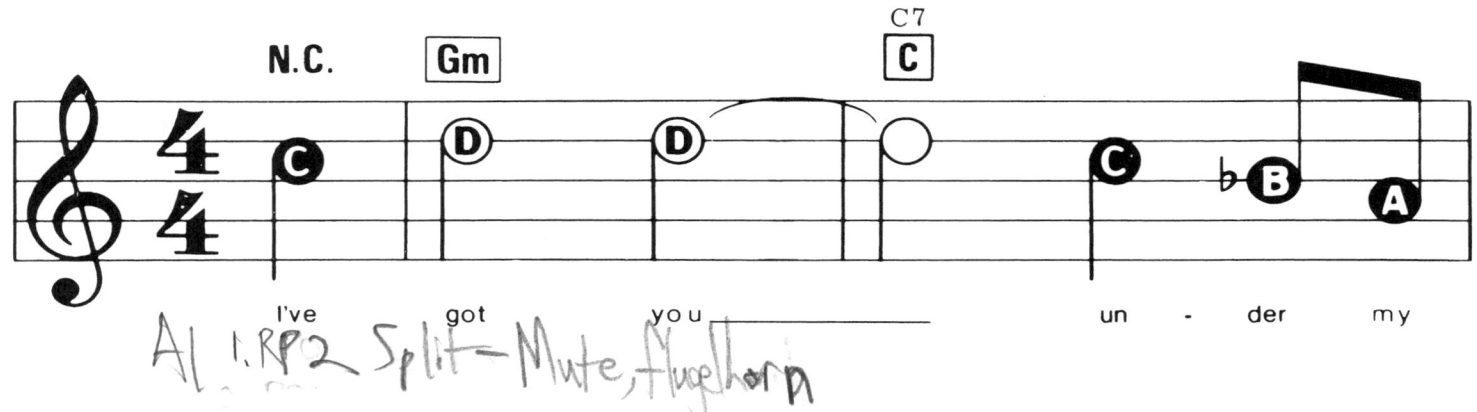

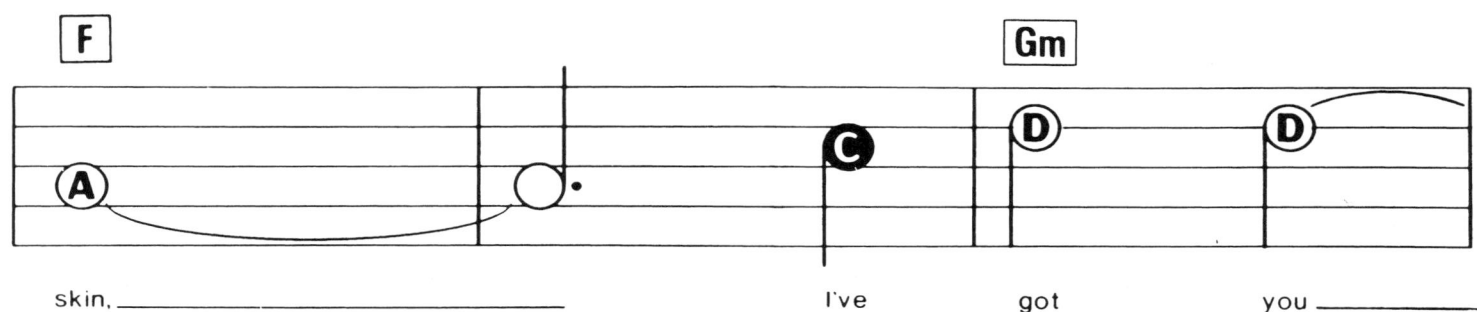

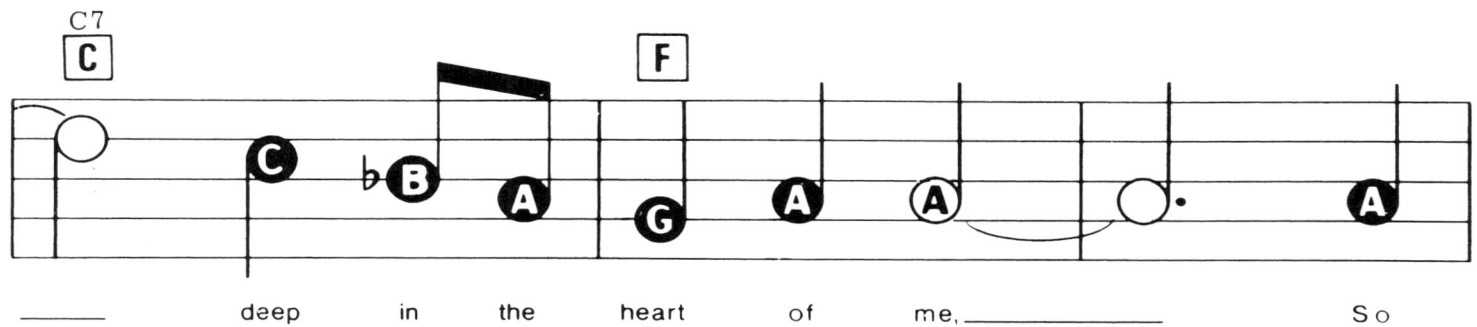

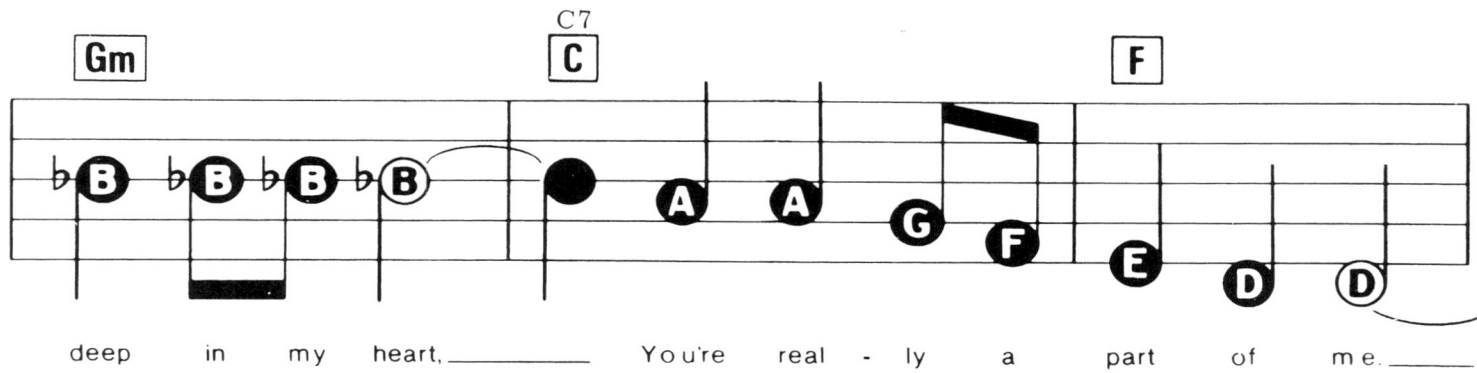

Copyright © 1936 by Chappell & Co.
Copyright Renewed, Assigned to Robert H. Montgomery, Trustee of the Cole Porter Musical and Literary Property Trusts
Chappell & Co. owner of publication and allied rights throughout the world
International Copyright Secured   All Rights Reserved

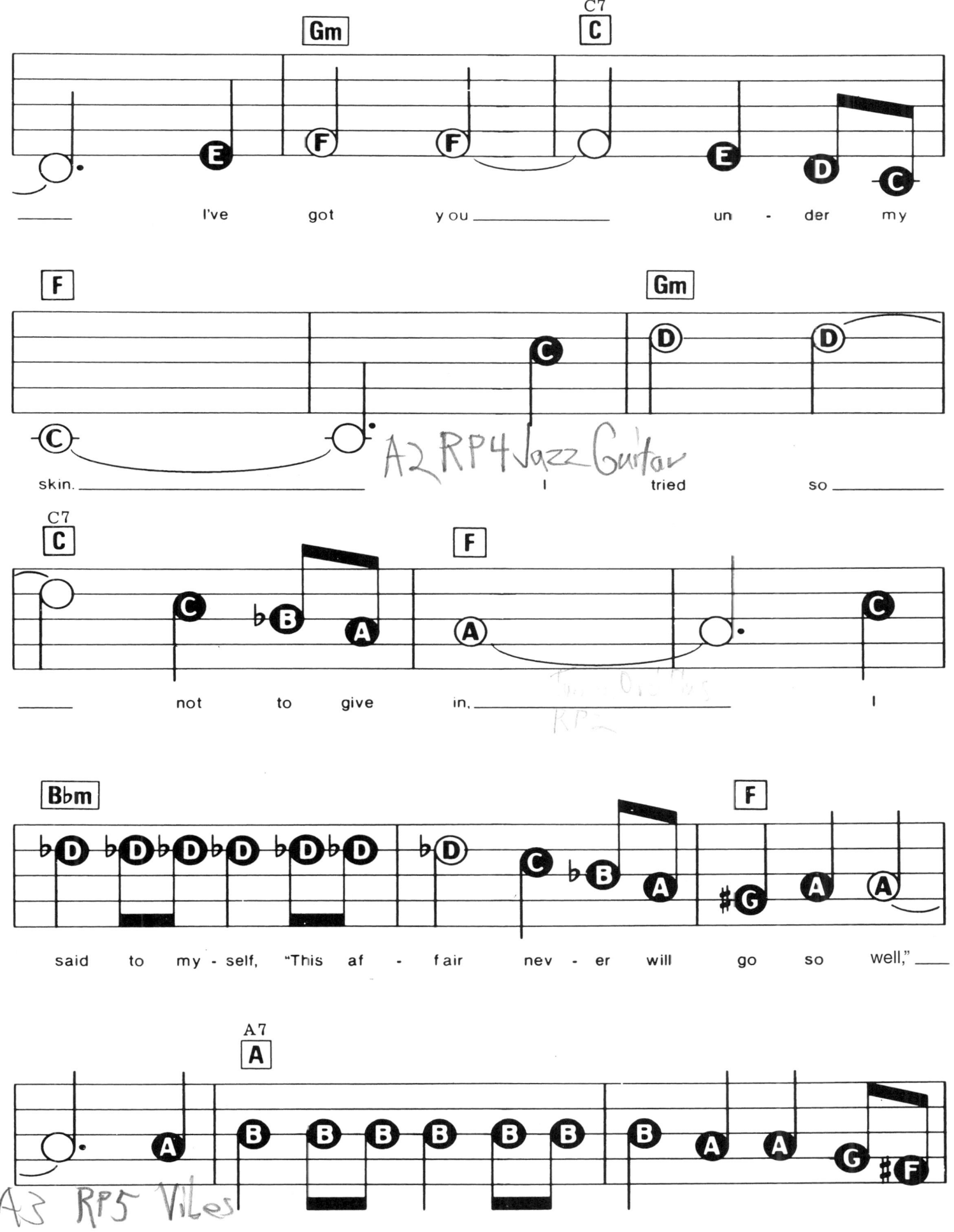

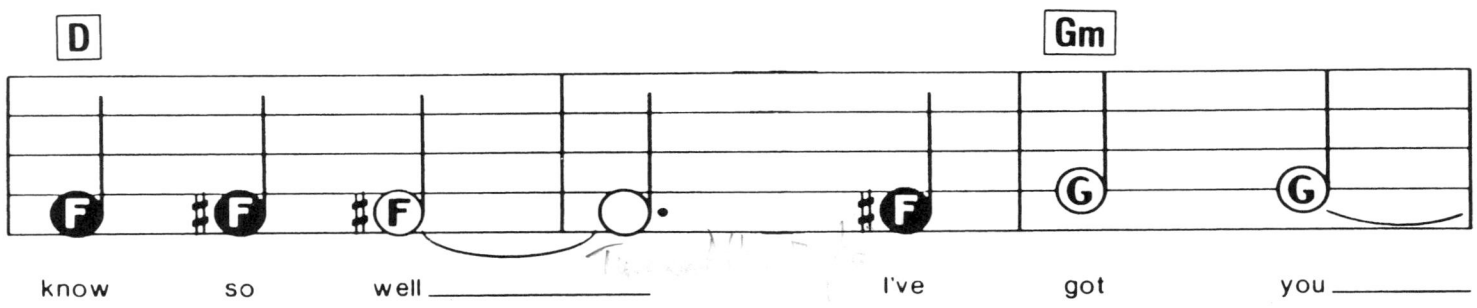
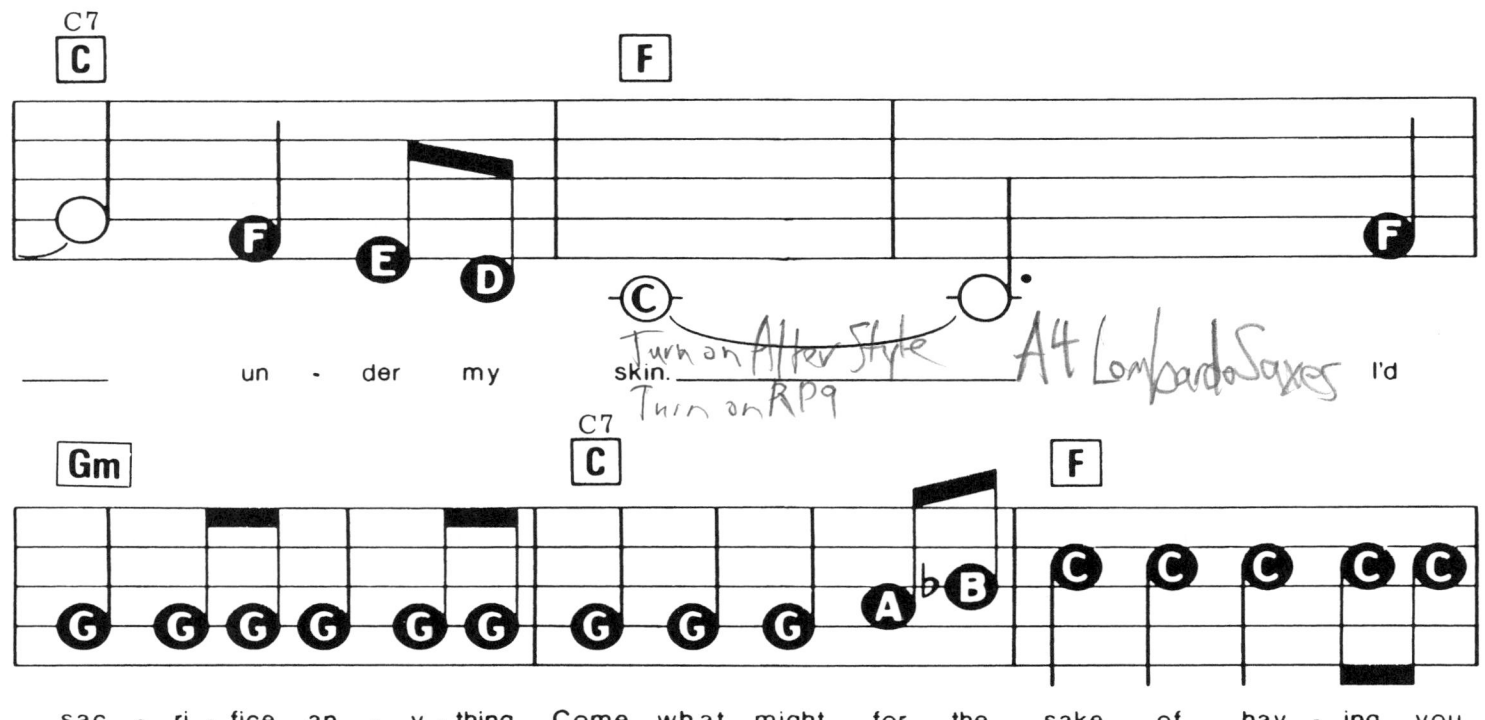
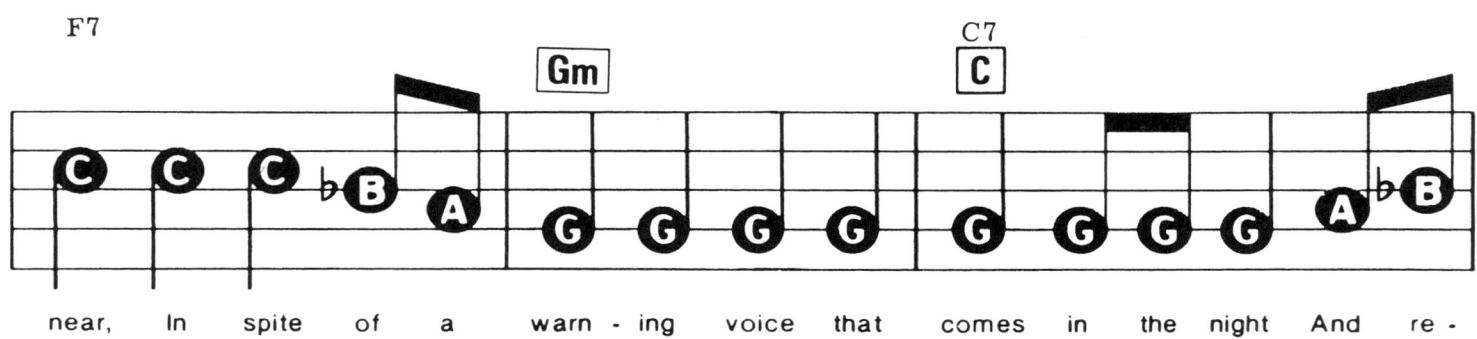
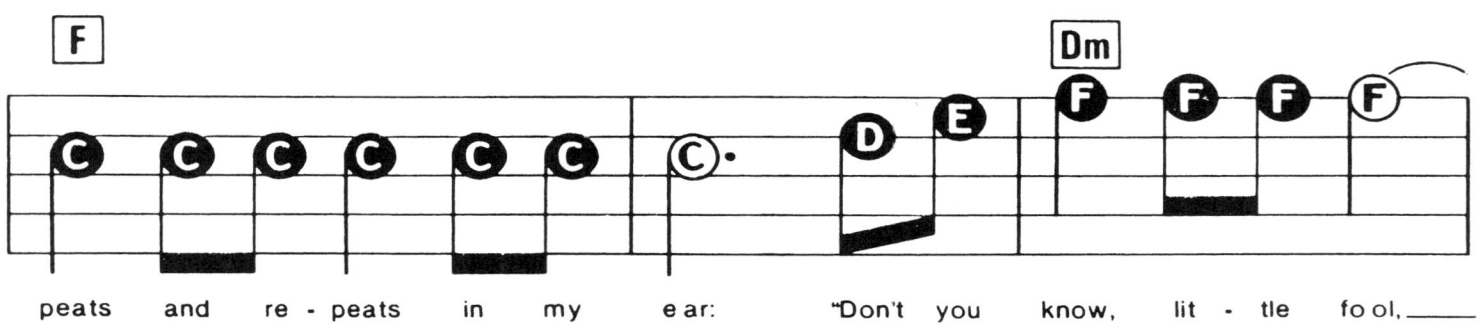

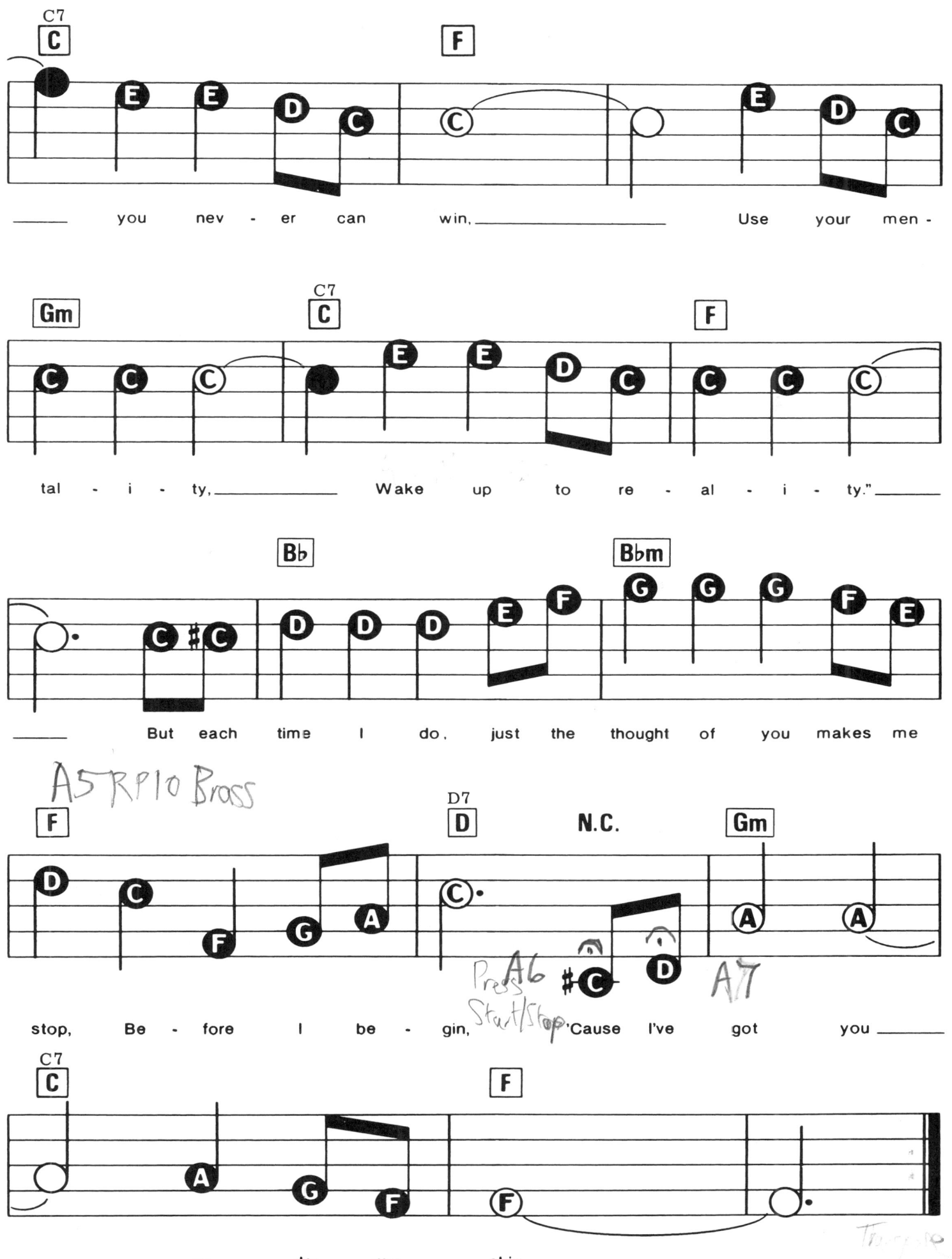

I've Grown Accustomed to Her Face
from MY FAIR LADY

Registration 10
Rhythm: Fox Trot

Words by Alan Jay Lerner
Music by Frederick Loewe

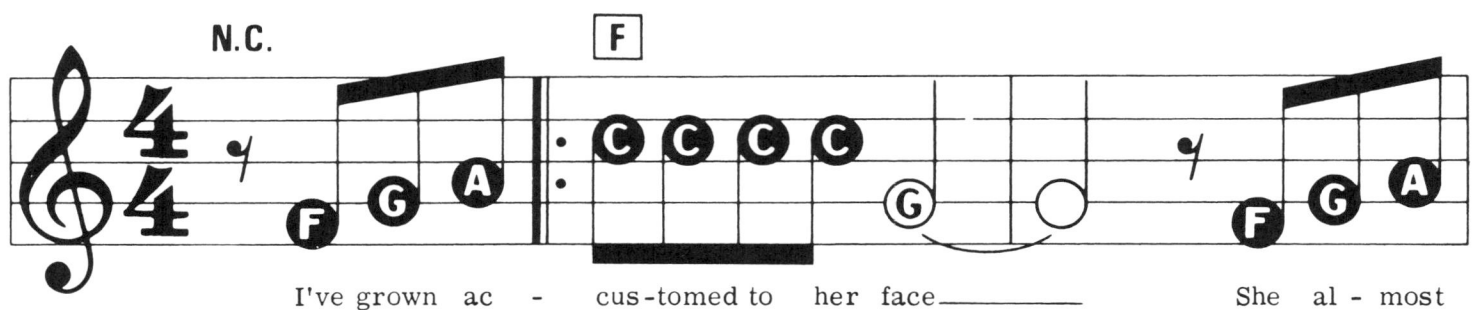

I've grown ac - cus-tomed to her face___ She al - most

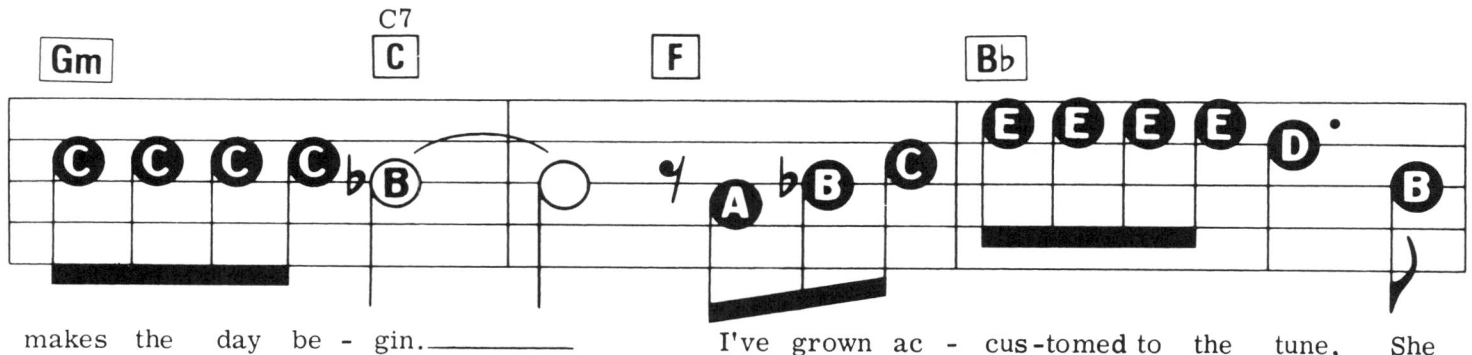

makes the day be - gin.___ I've grown ac - cus-tomed to the tune, She

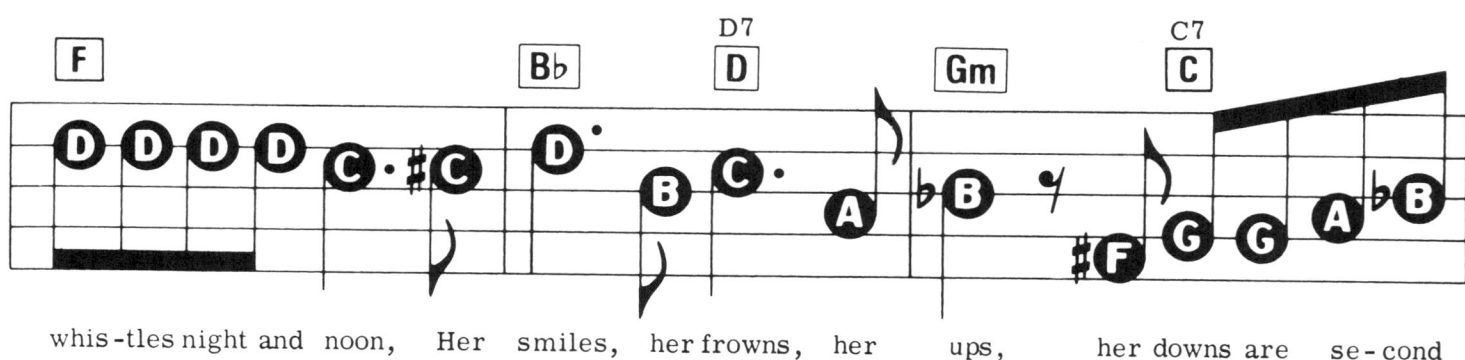

whis-tles night and noon, Her smiles, her frowns, her ups, her downs are se - cond

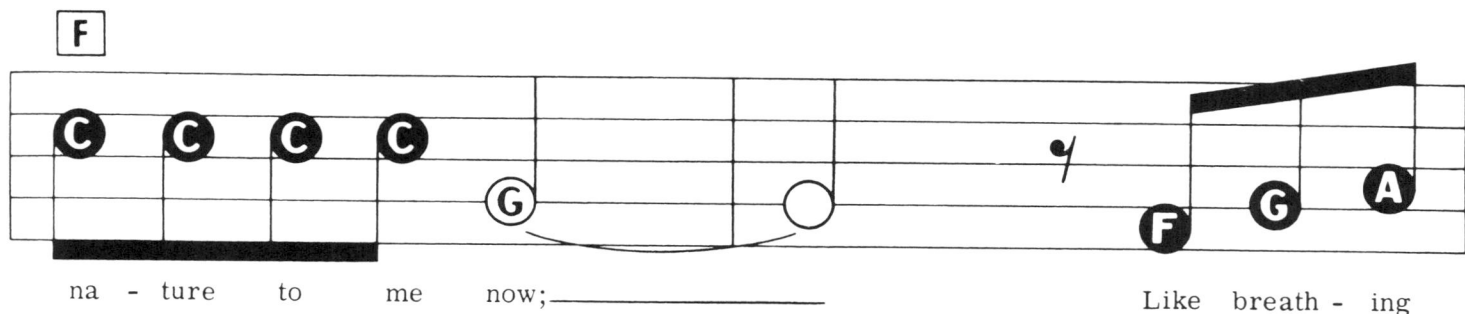

na - ture to me now;___ Like breath - ing

Copyright © 1956 by Alan Jay Lerner and Frederick Loewe
Copyright Renewed
Chappell & Co. owner of publication and allied rights throughout the world
International Copyright Secured   All Rights Reserved

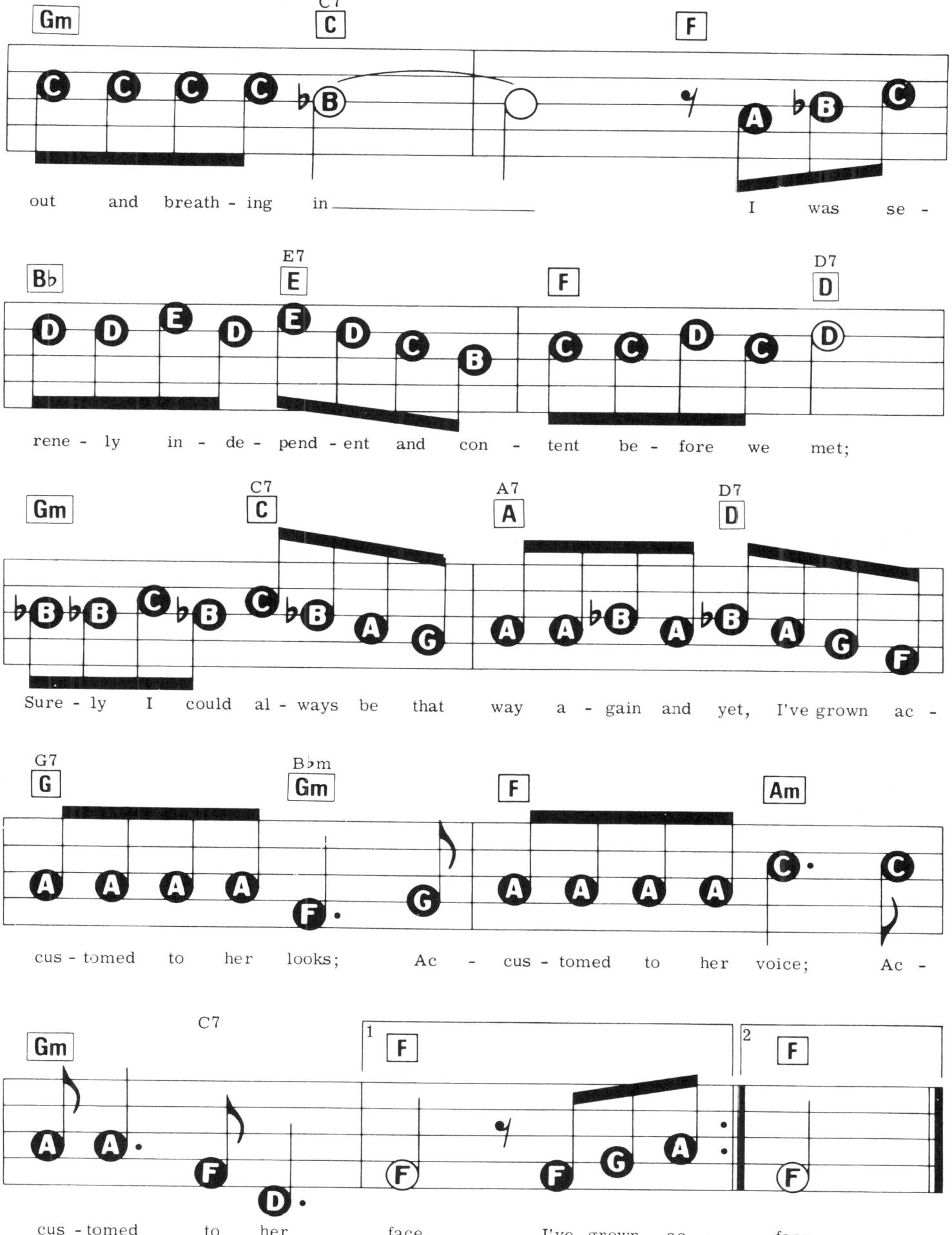

Imagination

Registration 4
Rhythm: Fox Trot

Words by Johnny Burke
Music by Jimmy Van Heusen

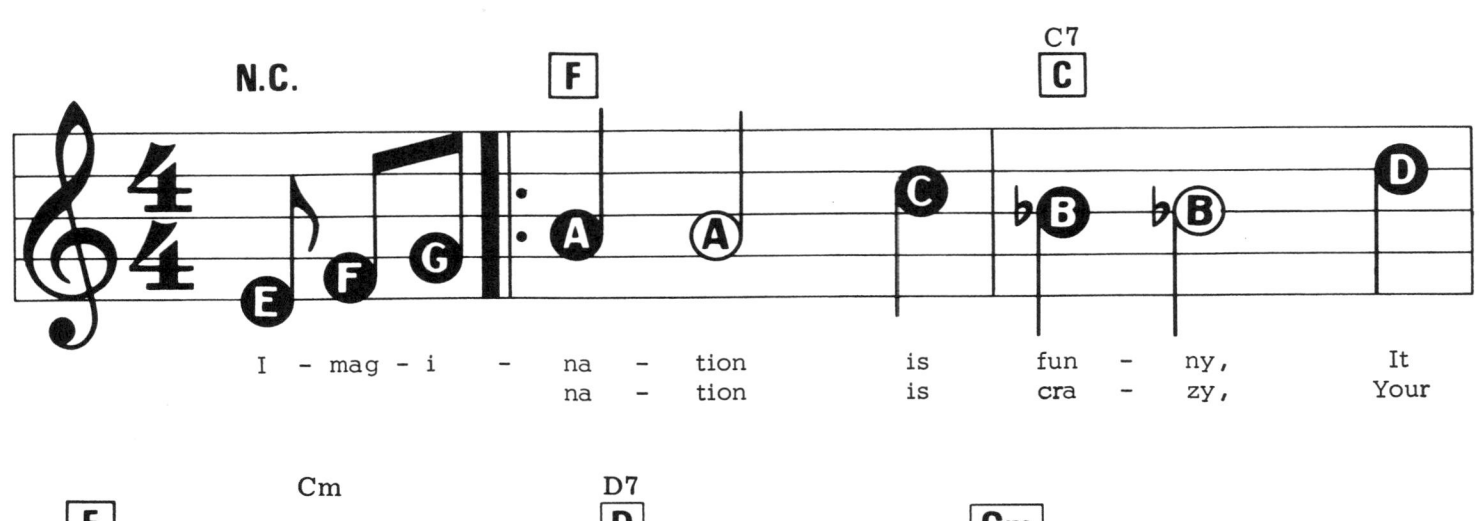
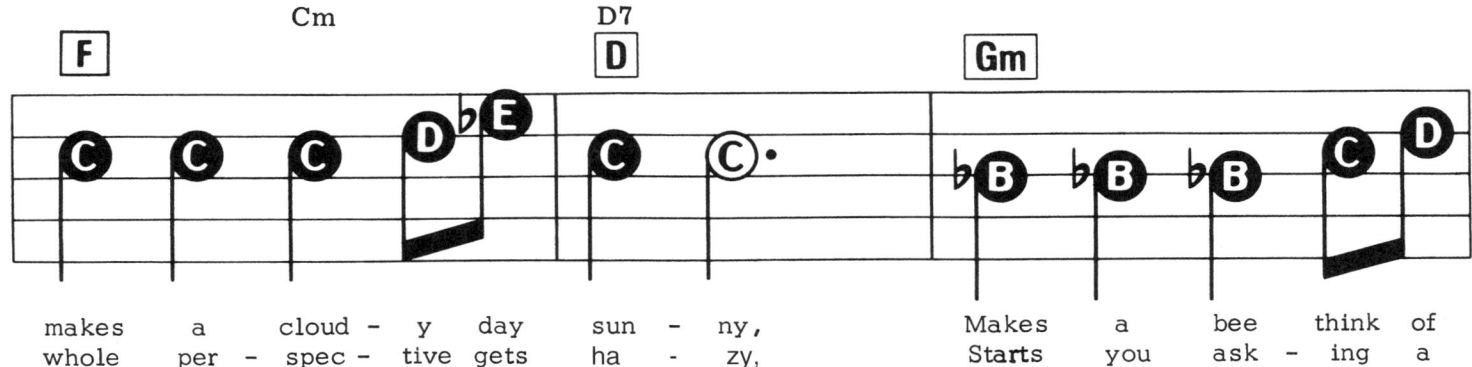
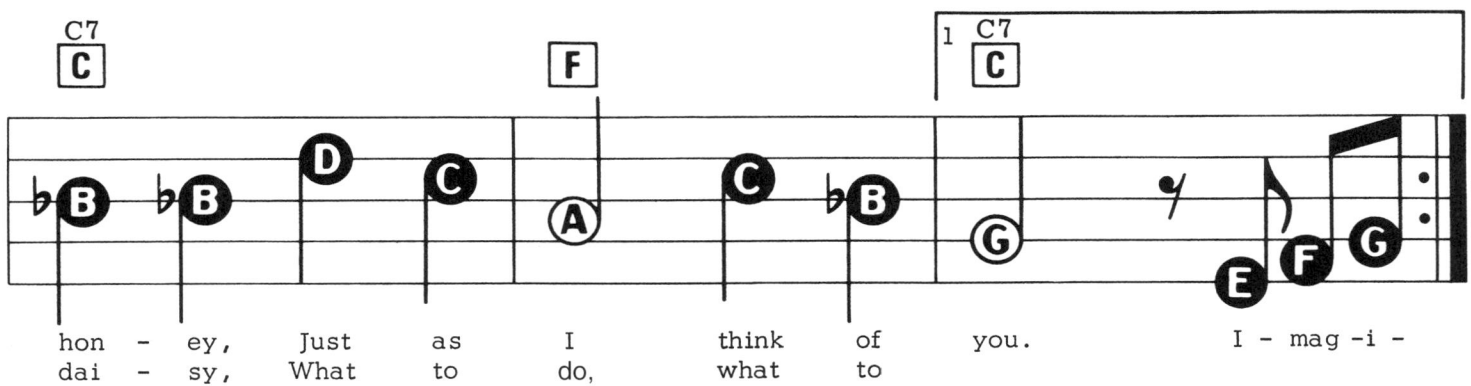
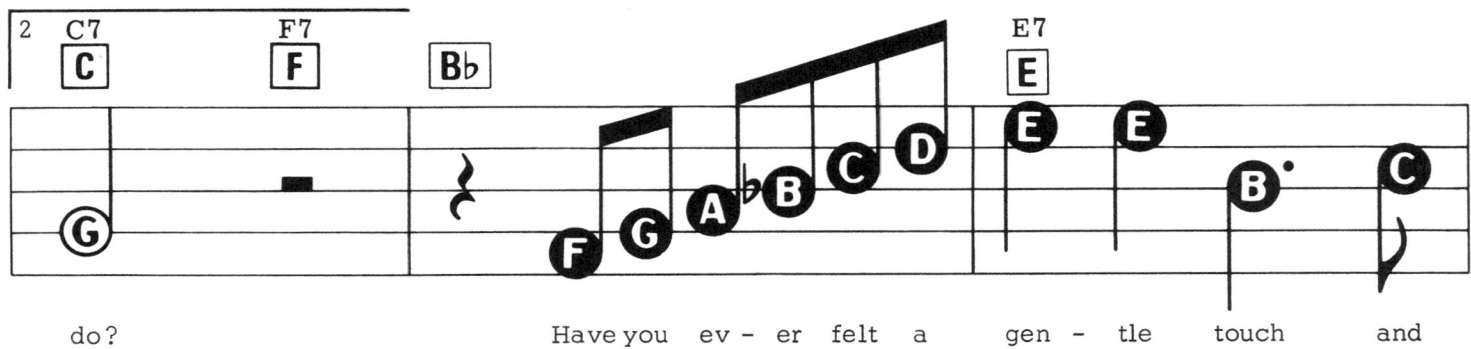

Copyright © 1939, 1949 by Bourne Co. (ASCAP), Marke Music Publishing Co., Inc., Limerick Music, My Dad's Songs, Inc. and Reganesque Music
Copyright Renewed
All Rights for Marke Music Publishing Co., Inc. Administered by Universal Music - MGB Songs
All Rights for Limerick Music, My Dad's Songs, Inc. and Reganesque Music Administered by Spirit Two Music, Inc.
International Copyright Secured   All Rights Reserved

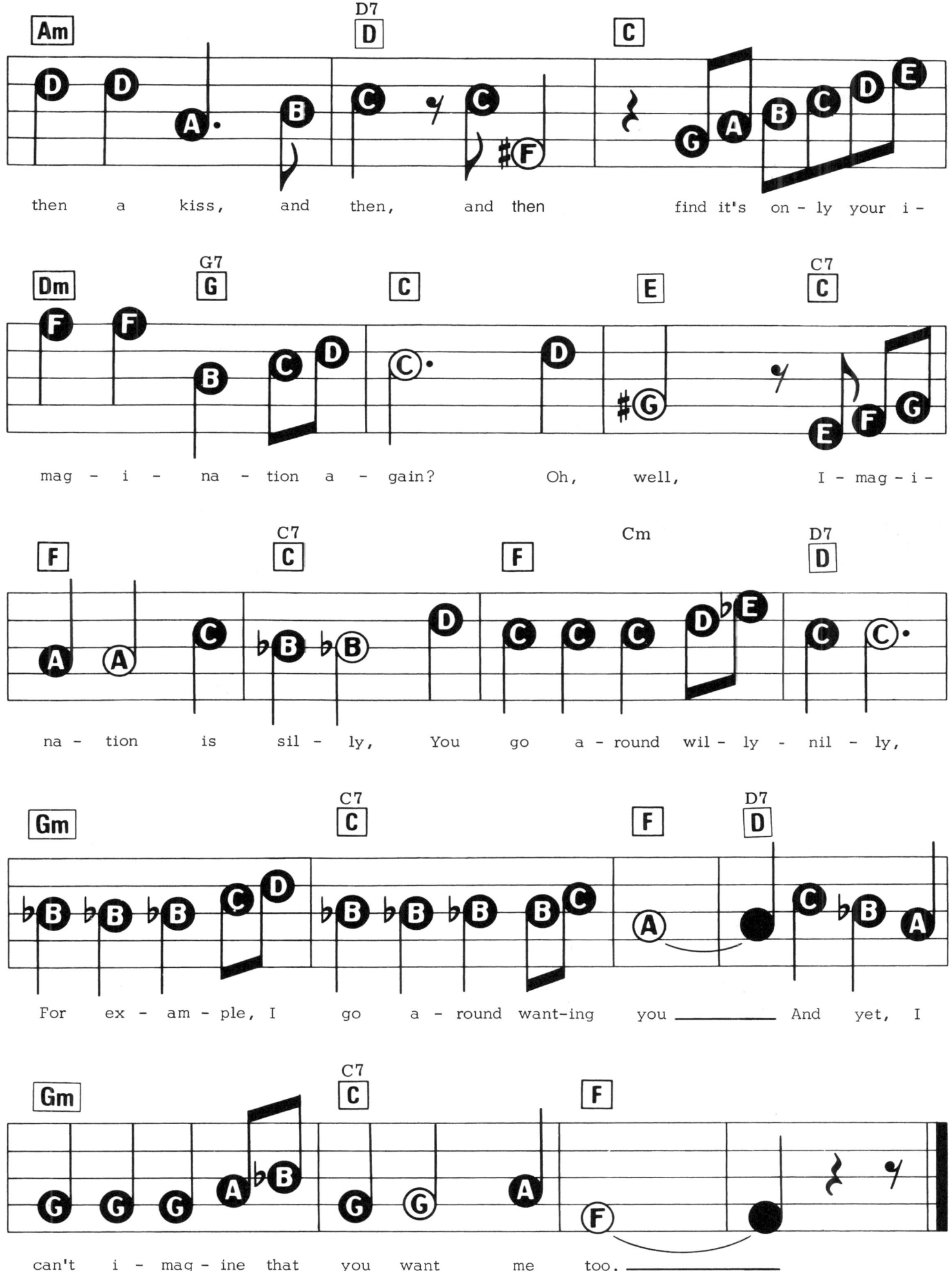

In a Mellow Tone

Registration 4
Rhythm: Swing or Fox Trot

Words by Milt Gabler
Music by Duke Ellington

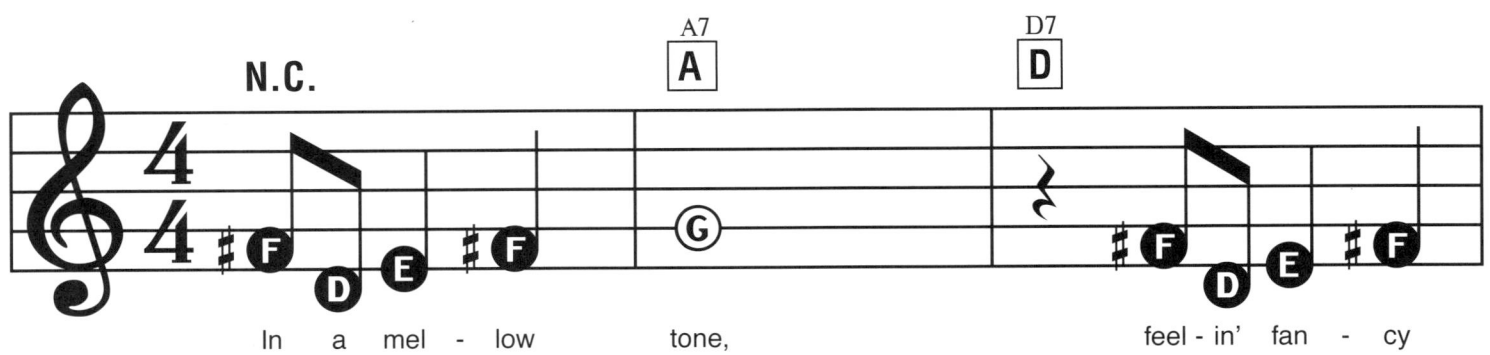

In a mel - low tone, feel - in' fan - cy

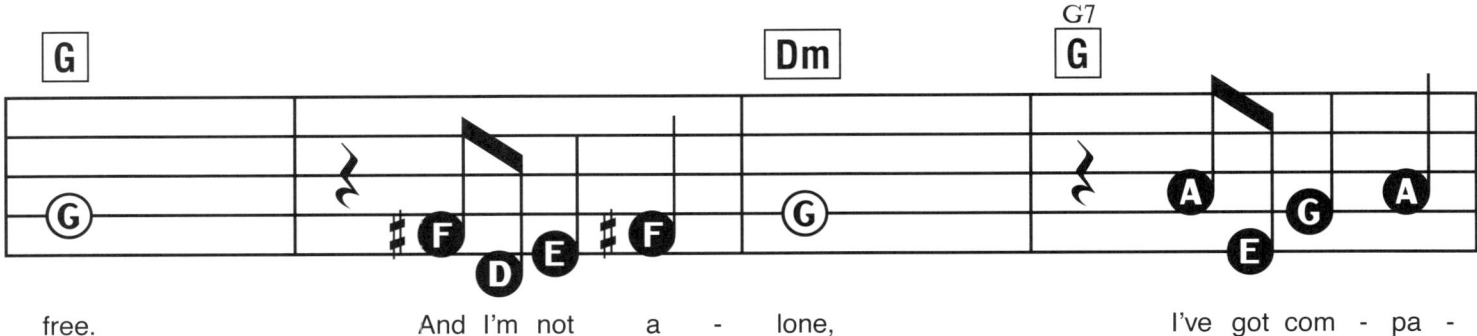

free. And I'm not a - lone, I've got com - pa -

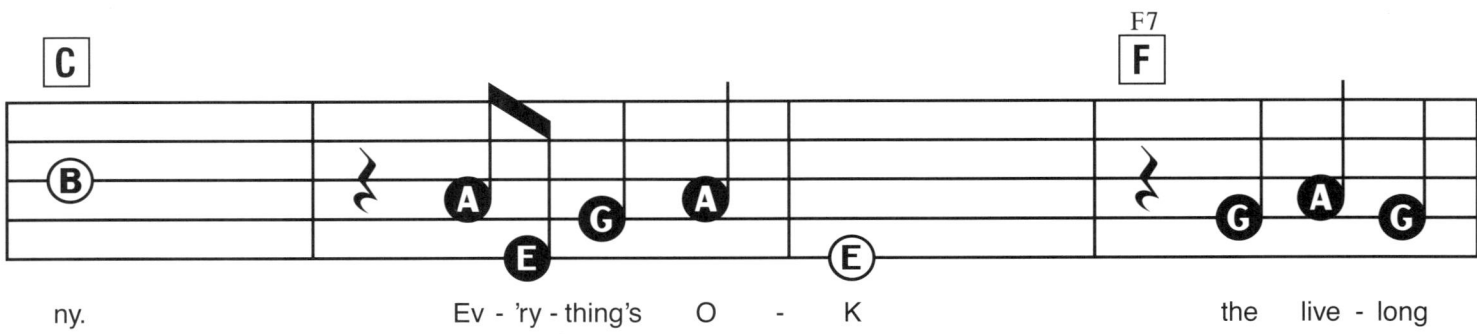

ny. Ev - 'ry - thing's O - K the live - long

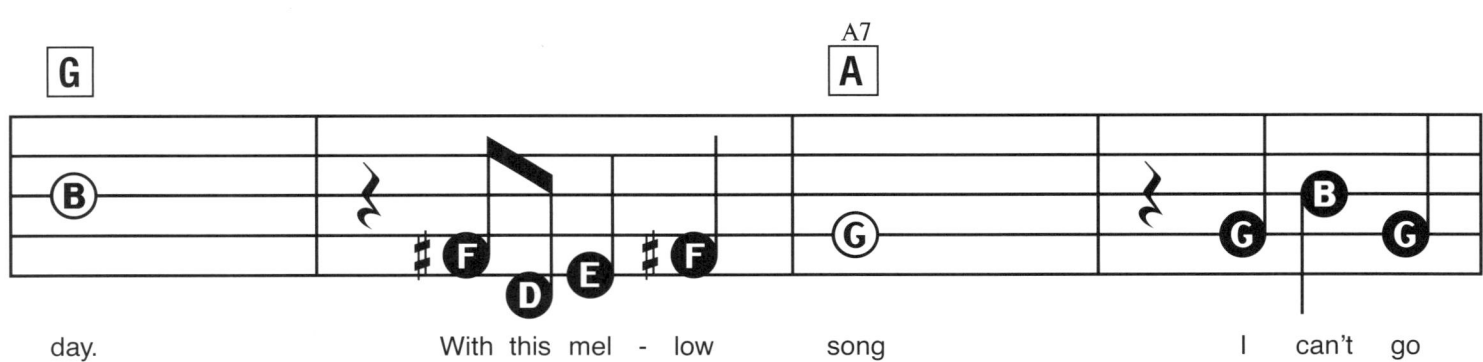

day. With this mel - low song I can't go

Copyright © 1955 Sony/ATV Music Publishing LLC and EMI Robbins Catalog Inc. in the U.S.A.
Copyright Renewed
All Rights on behalf of Sony/ATV Music Publishing LLC Administered by Sony/ATV Music Publishing LLC, 8 Music Square West, Nashville, TN 37203
Rights for the world outside the U.S.A. Administered by EMI Robbins Catalog Inc. (Publishing) and Alfred Publishing Co., Inc. (Print)
International Copyright Secured   All Rights Reserved

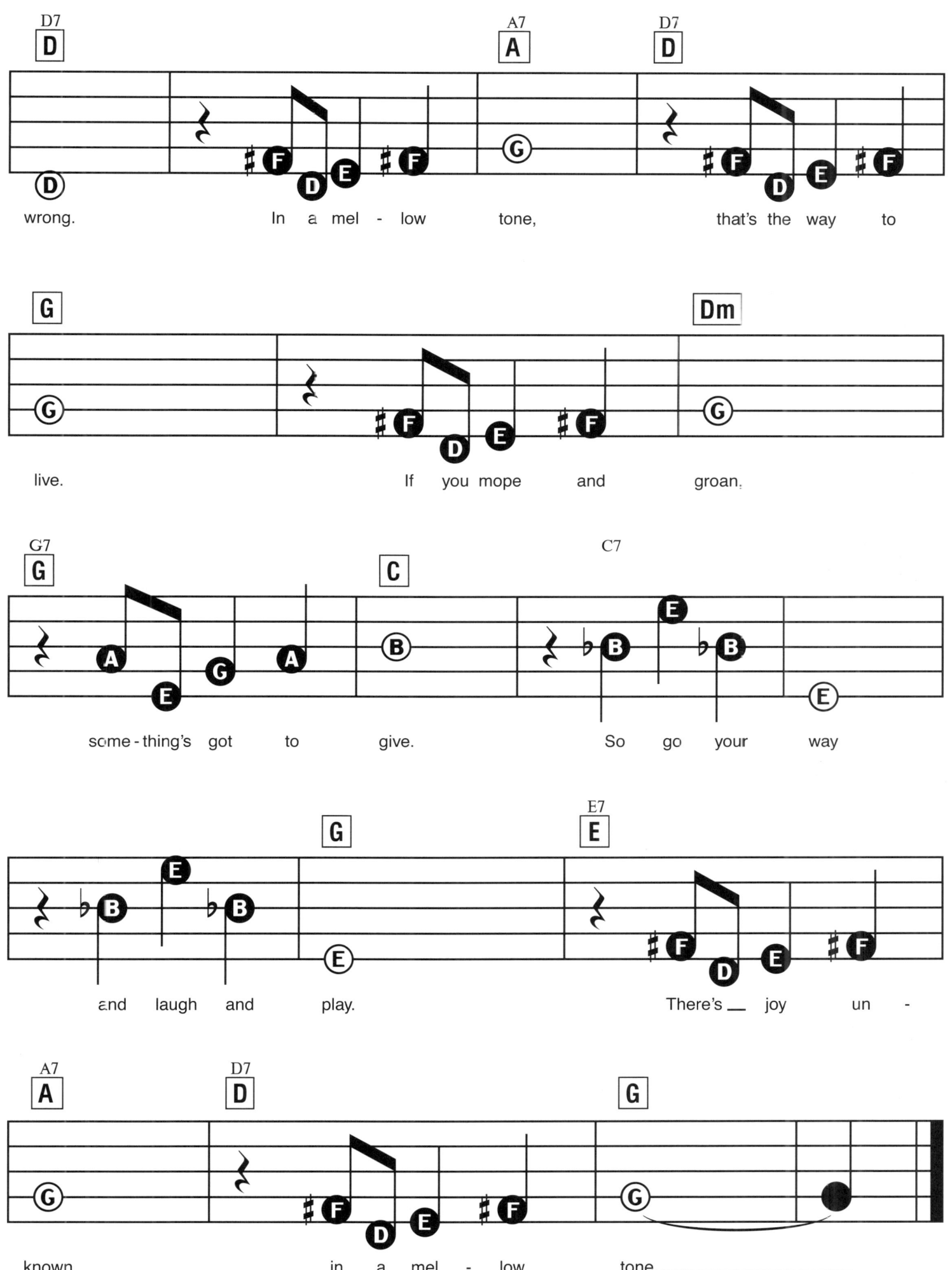

130

Big Band-Swing Band

In the Mood

55

Registration 8
Rhythm: Swing

By Joe Garland

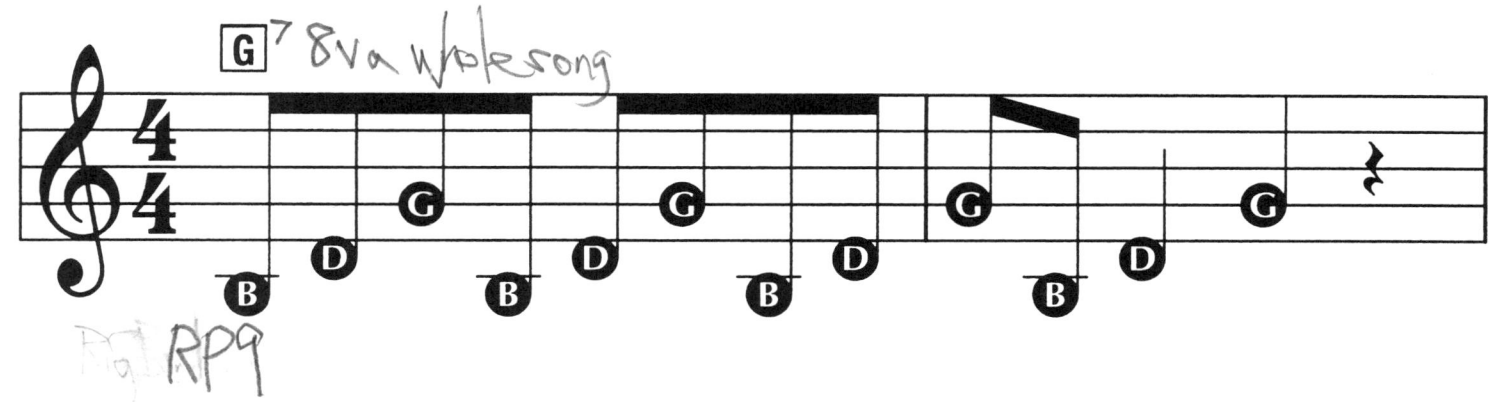

Pg. RP9

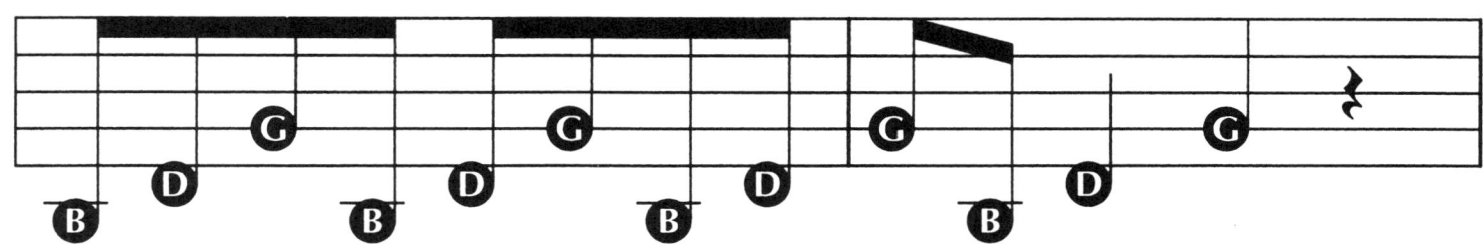

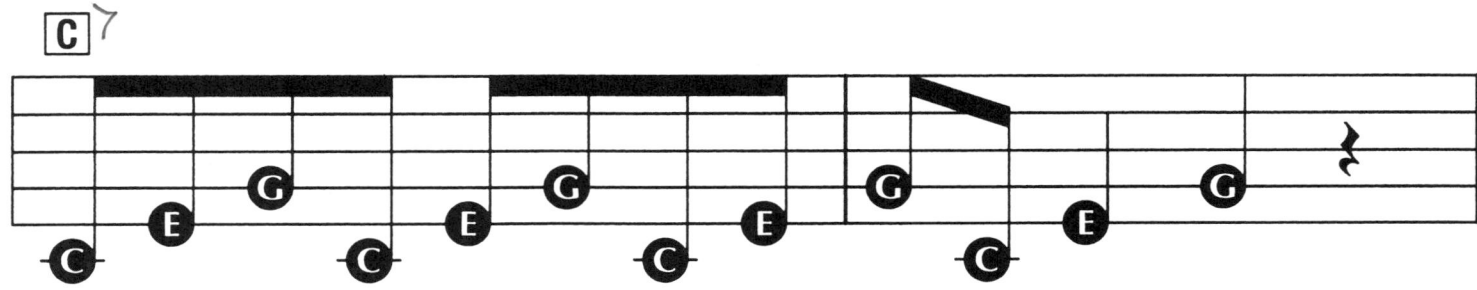

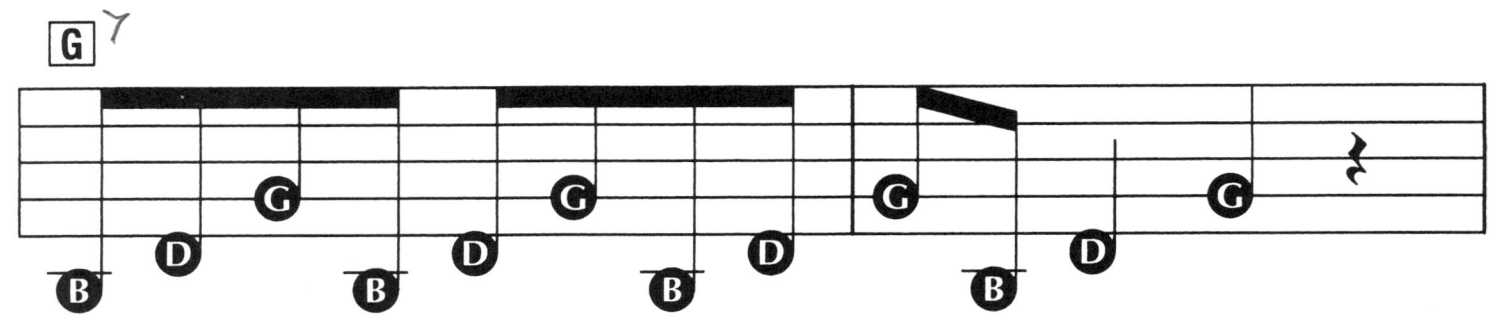

Copyright © 1939, 1960 Shapiro, Bernstein & Co., Inc., New York
Copyright Renewed
International Copyright Secured   All Rights Reserved
Used by Permission

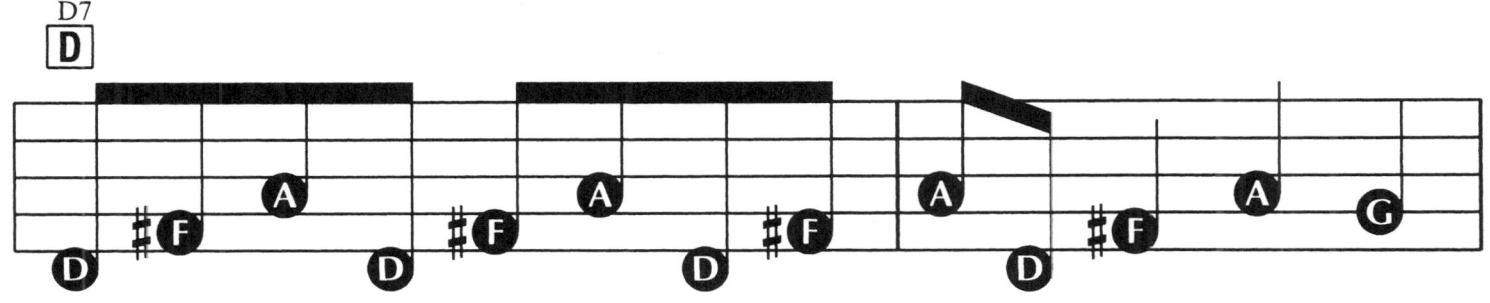
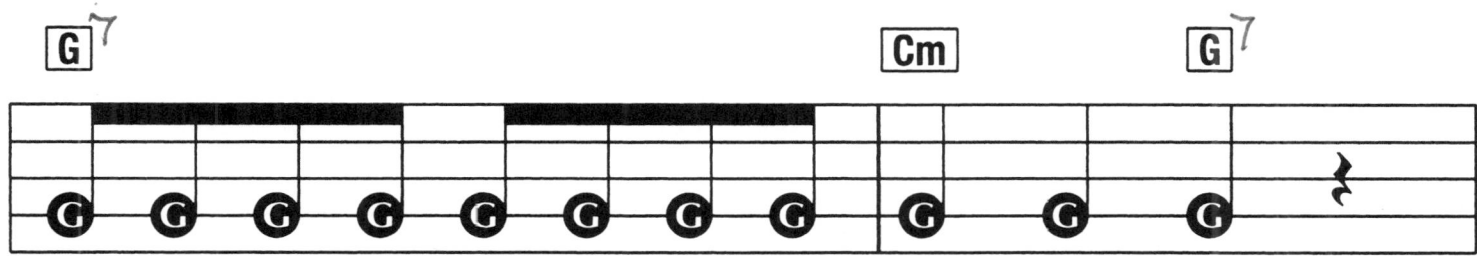
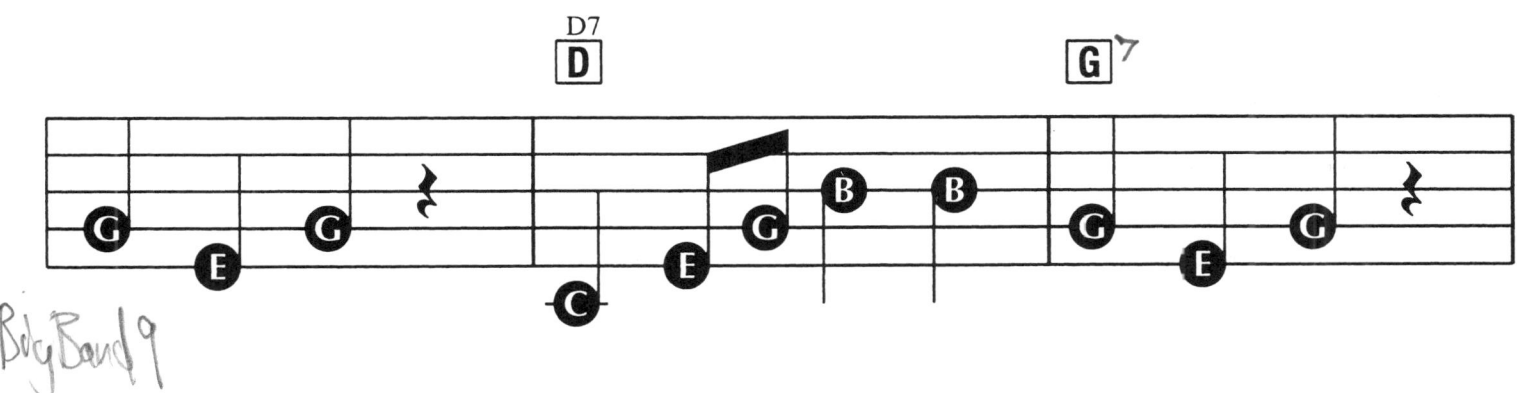

BigBand 9

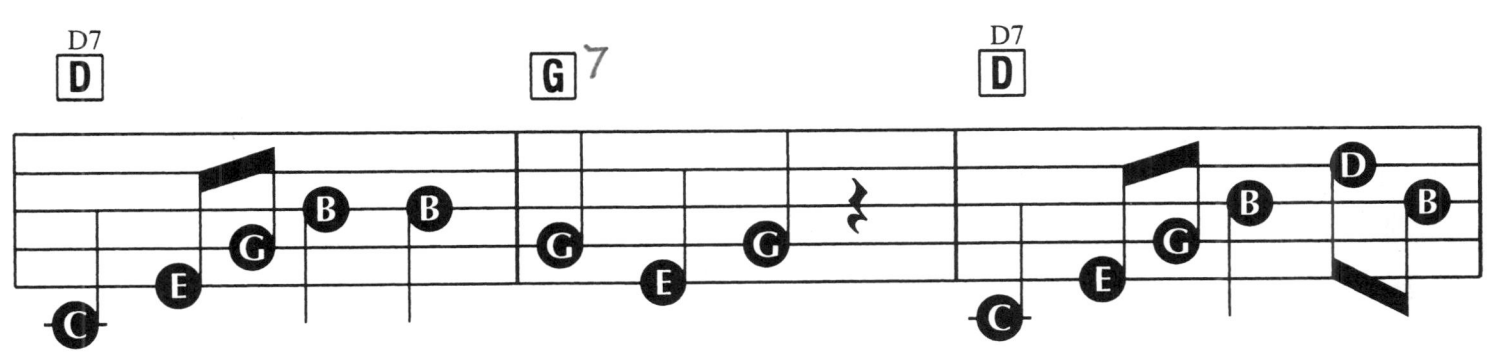

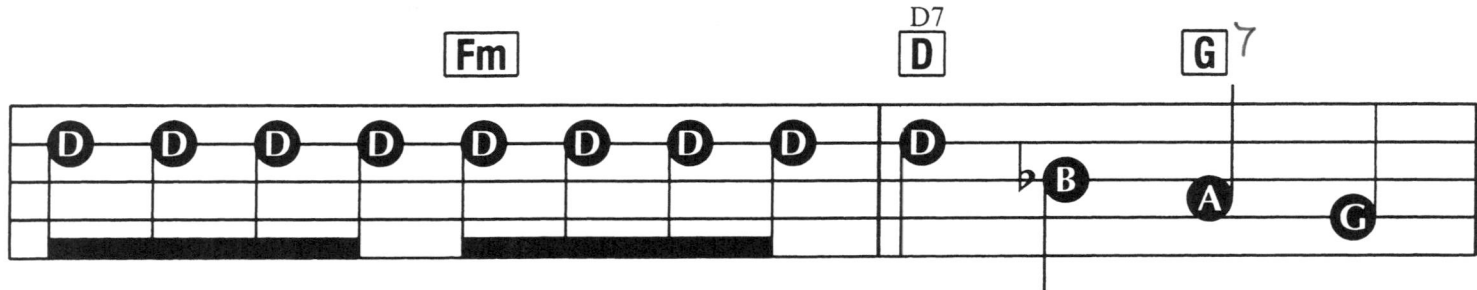
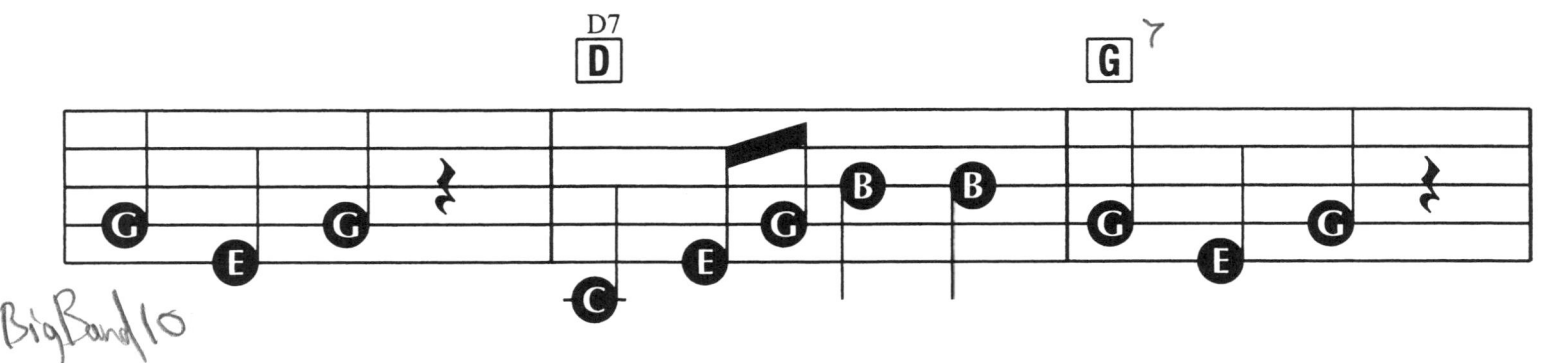

BigBand 10

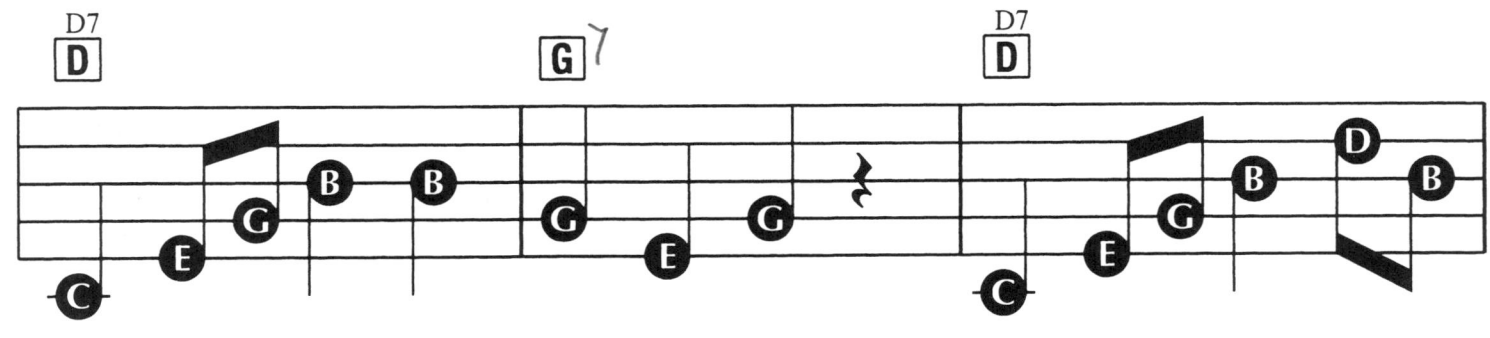
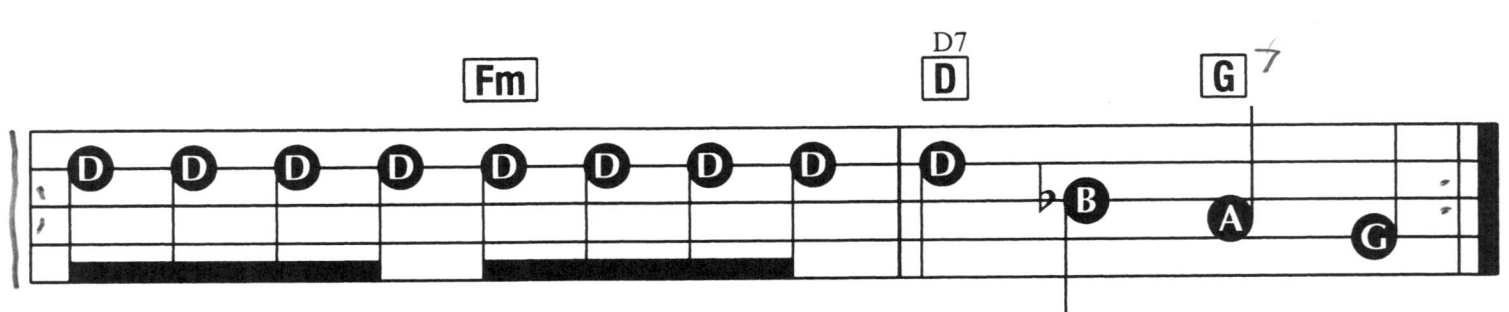

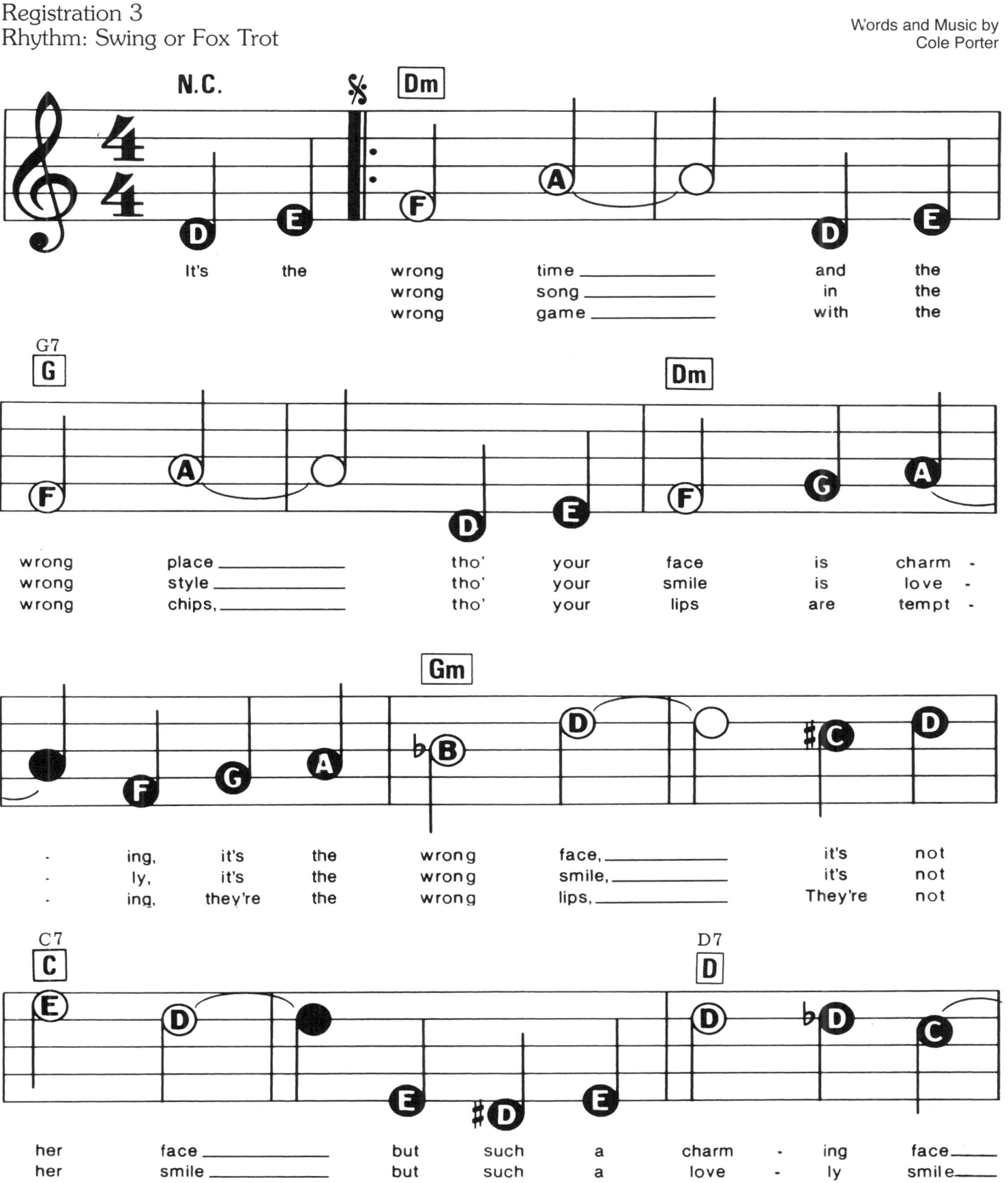

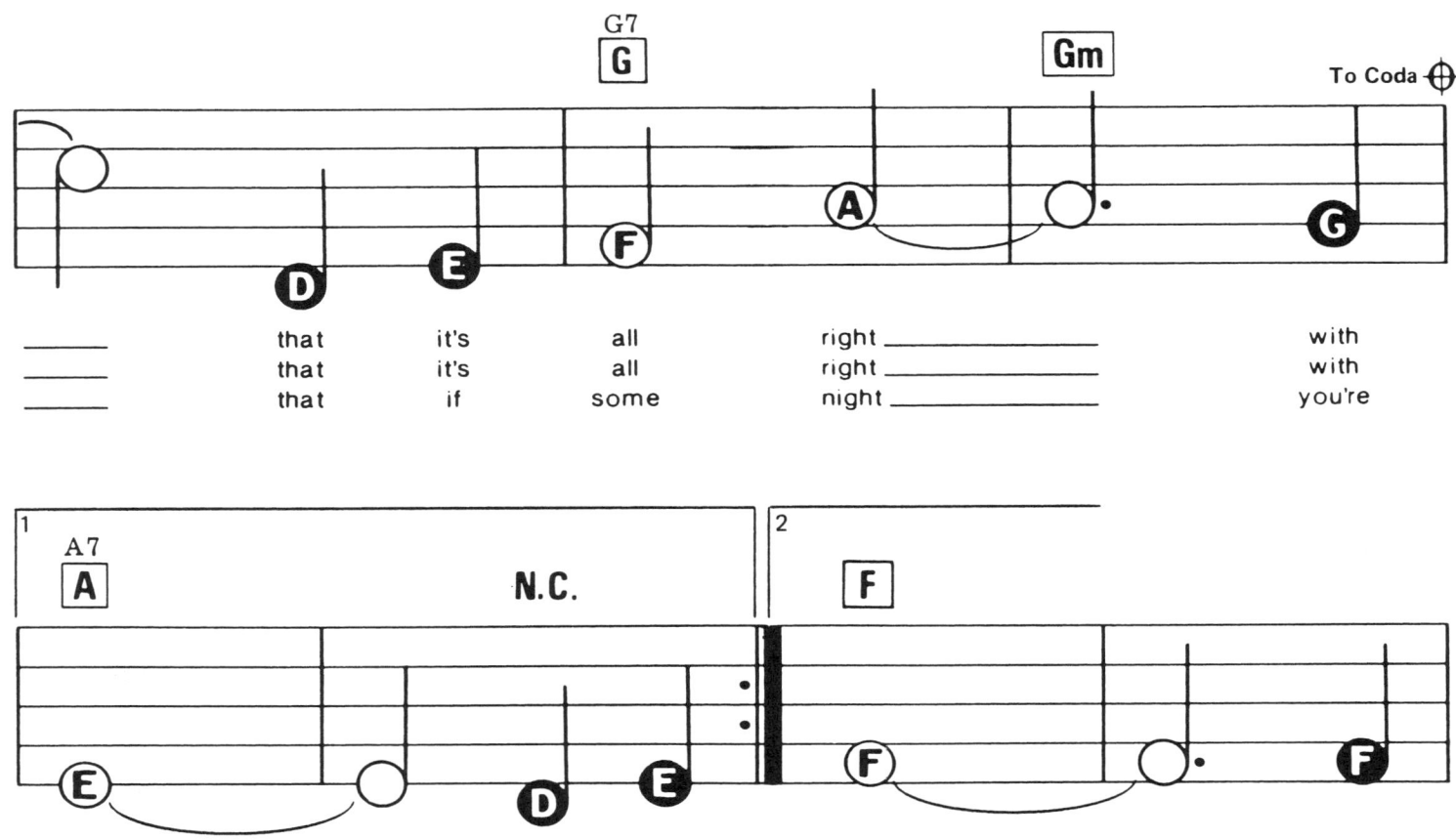
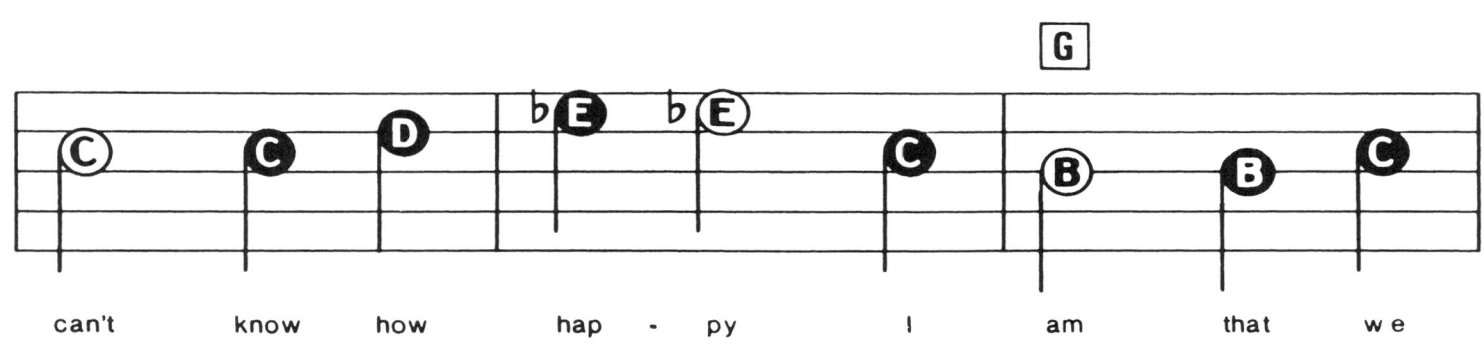
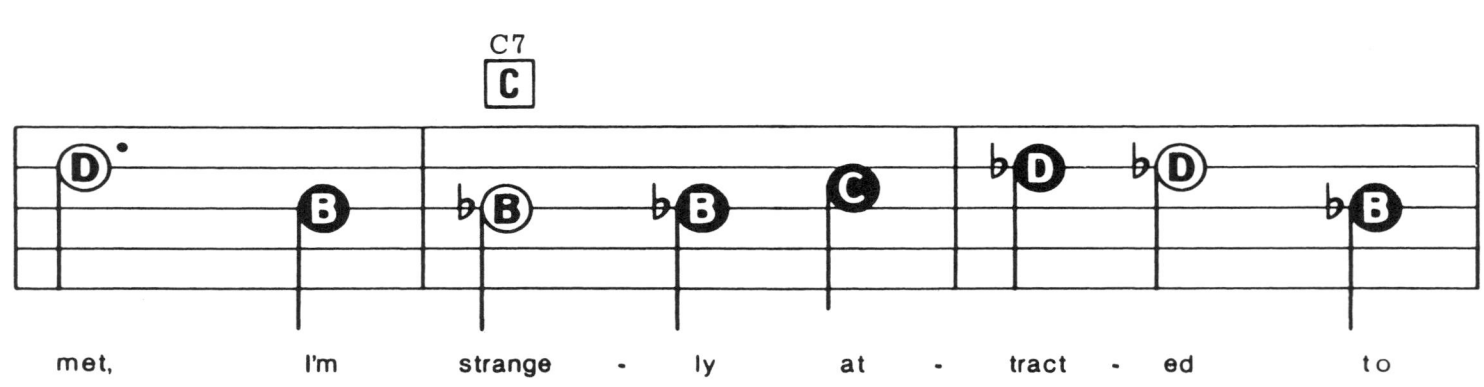

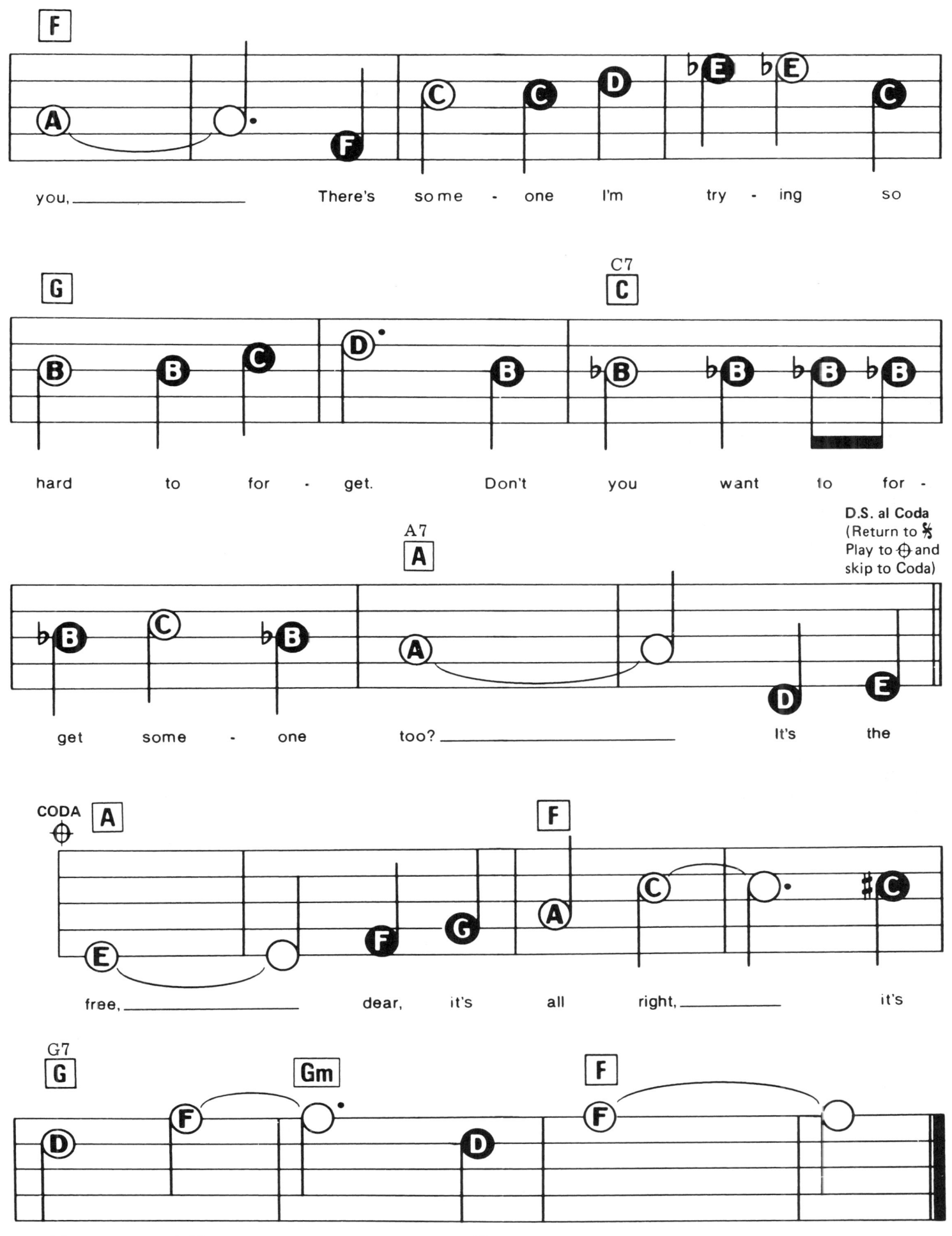

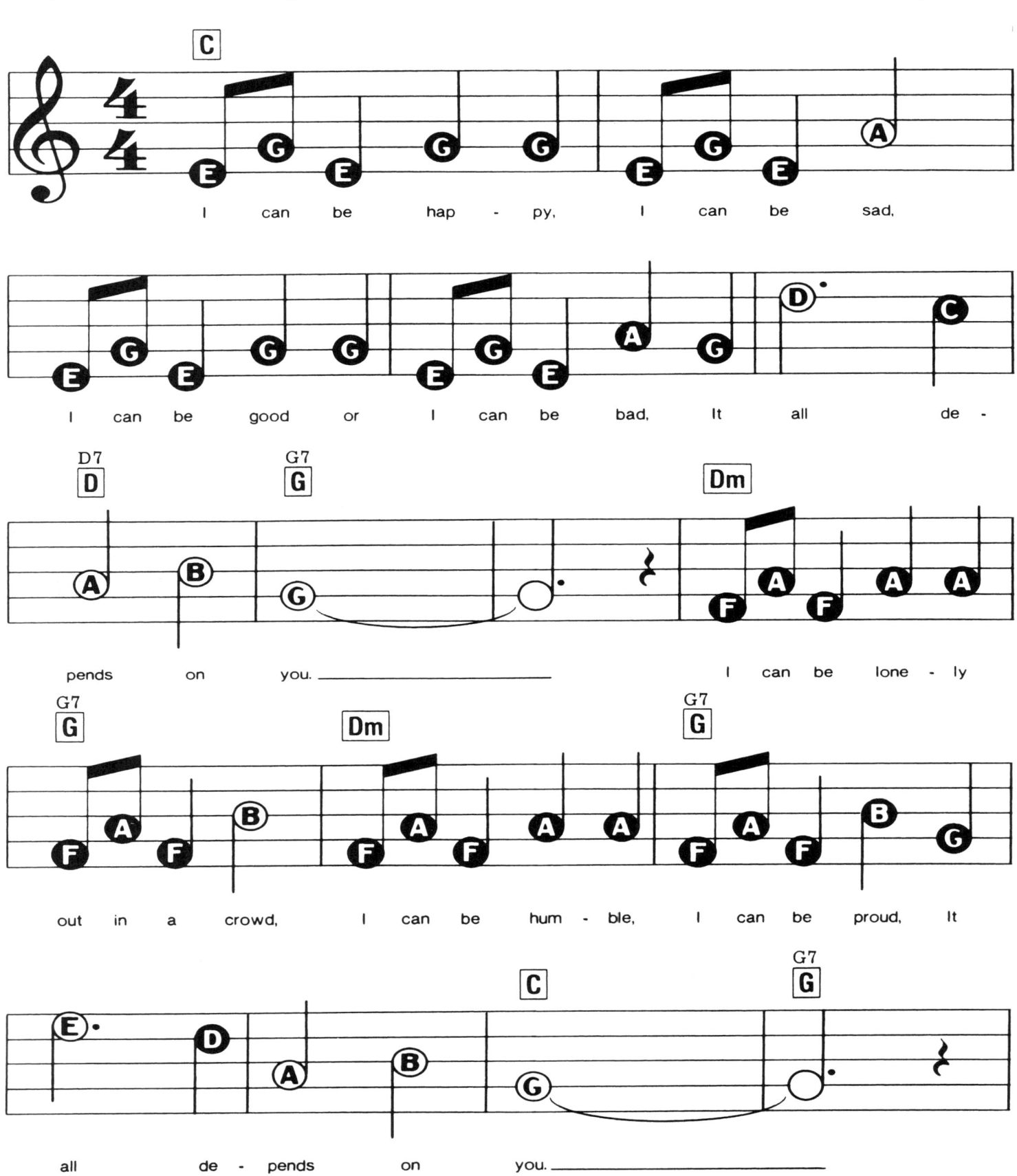

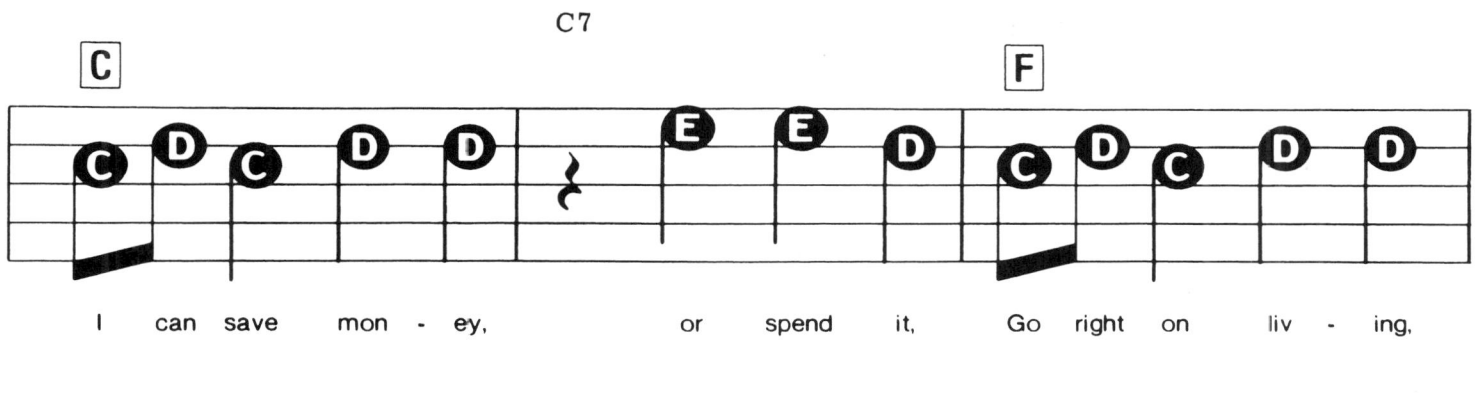
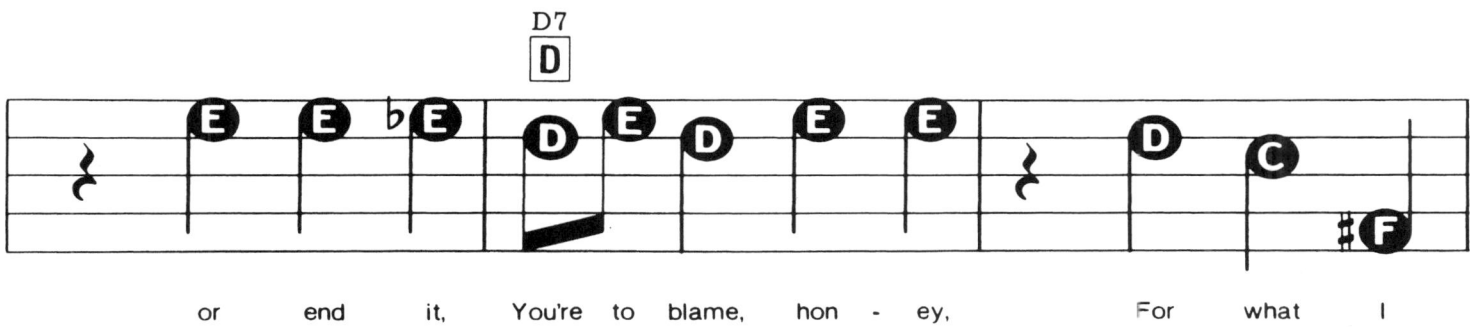
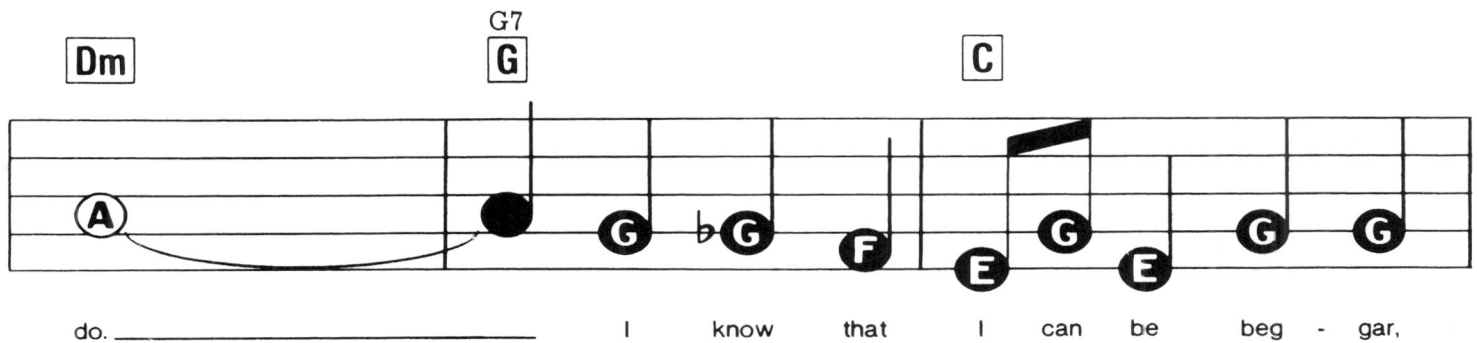
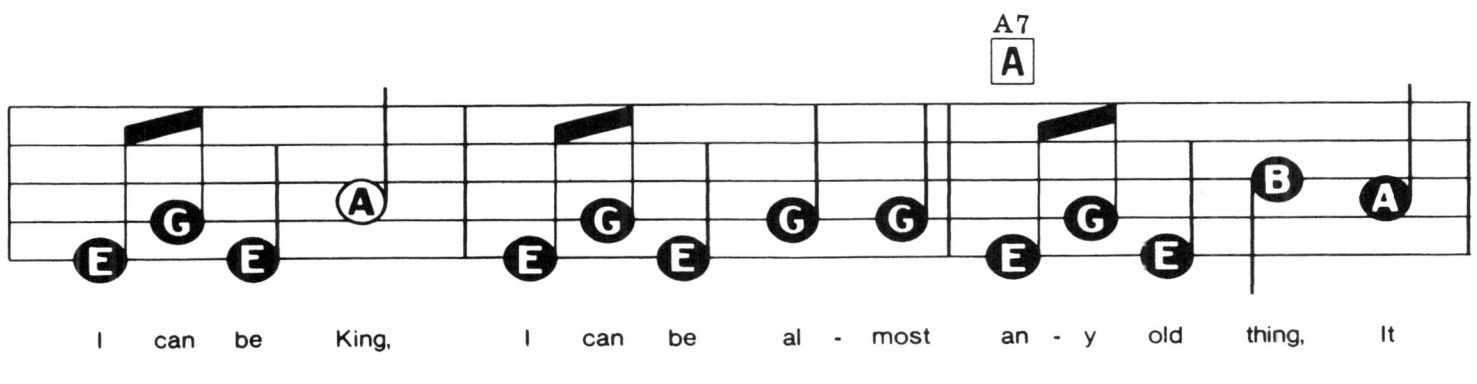
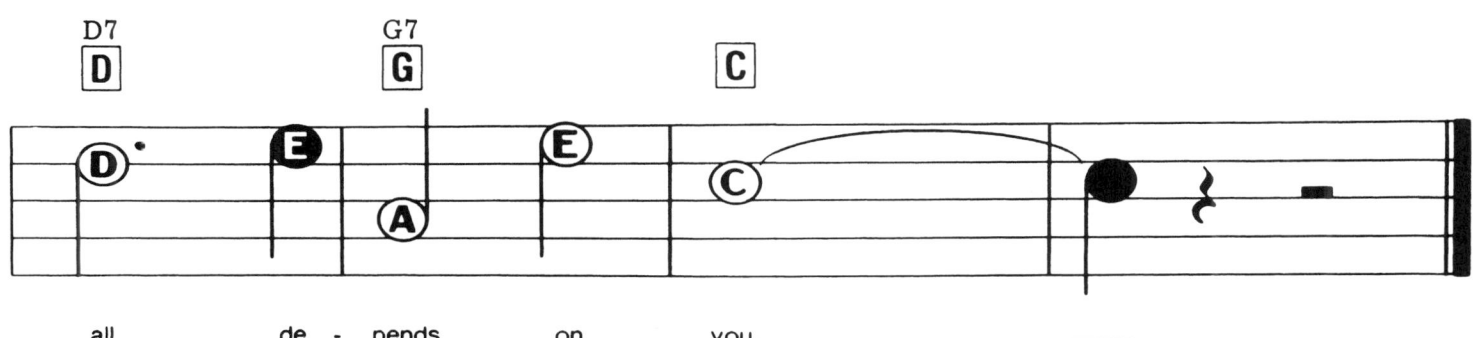

It Could Happen to You
from the Paramount Picture AND THE ANGELS SING

Registration 10
Rhythm: Swing

Words by Johnny Burke
Music by James Van Heusen

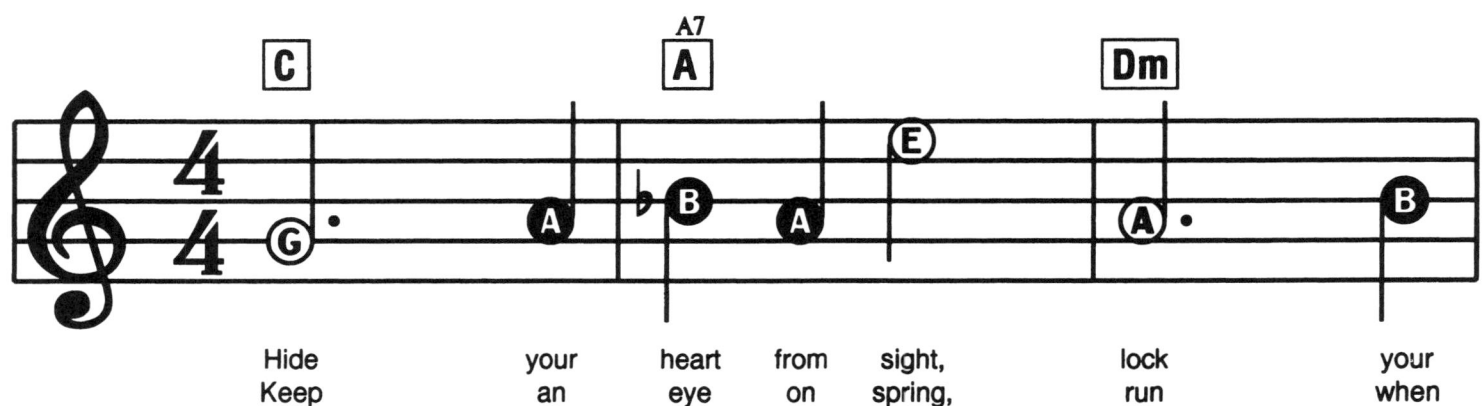

Hide your heart from sight, lock your
Keep an eye on spring, run when

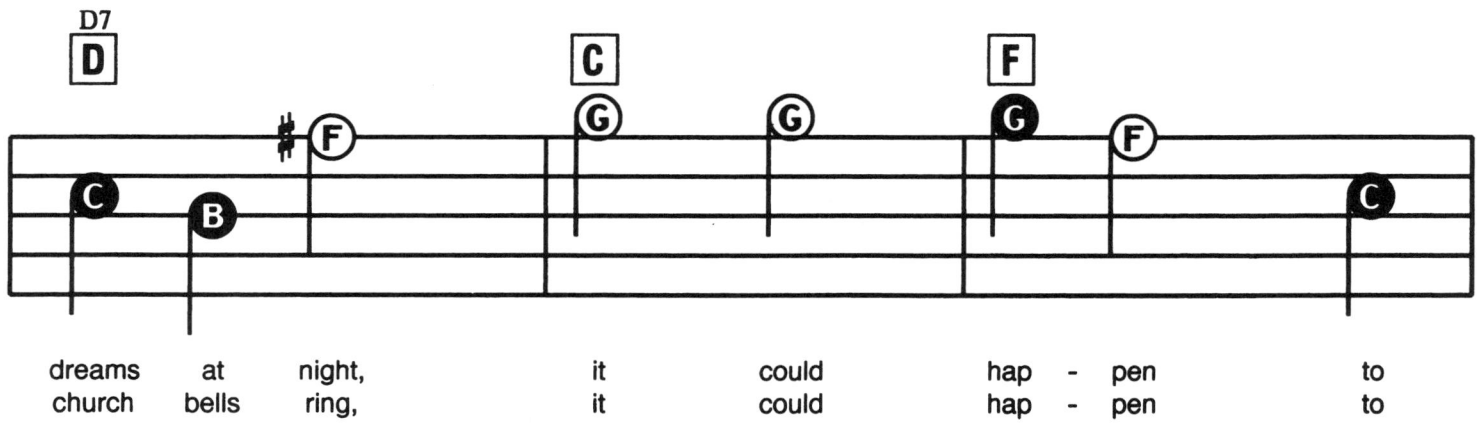

dreams at night, it could hap - pen to
church bells ring, it could hap - pen to

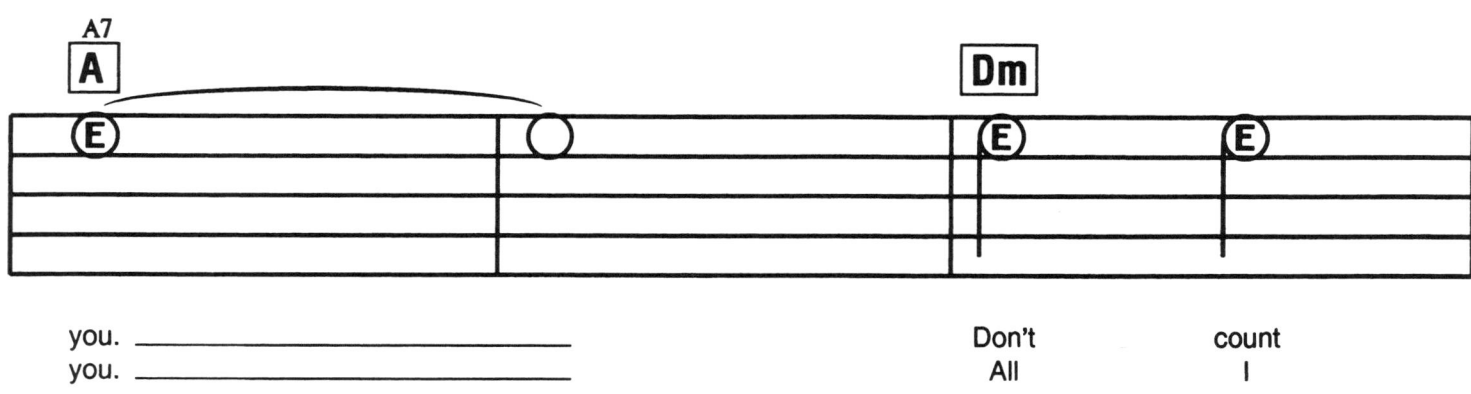

you.
you. Don't count
All I

Copyright © 1944 Sony/ATV Music Publishing LLC
Copyright Renewed
All Rights Administered by Sony/ATV Music Publishing LLC, 8 Music Square West, Nashville, TN 37203
International Copyright Secured All Rights Reserved

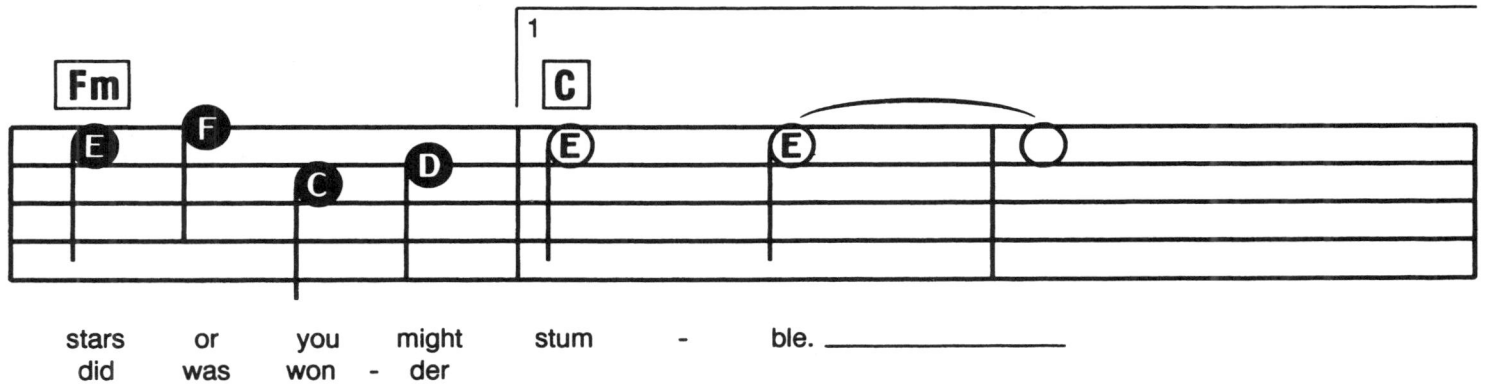
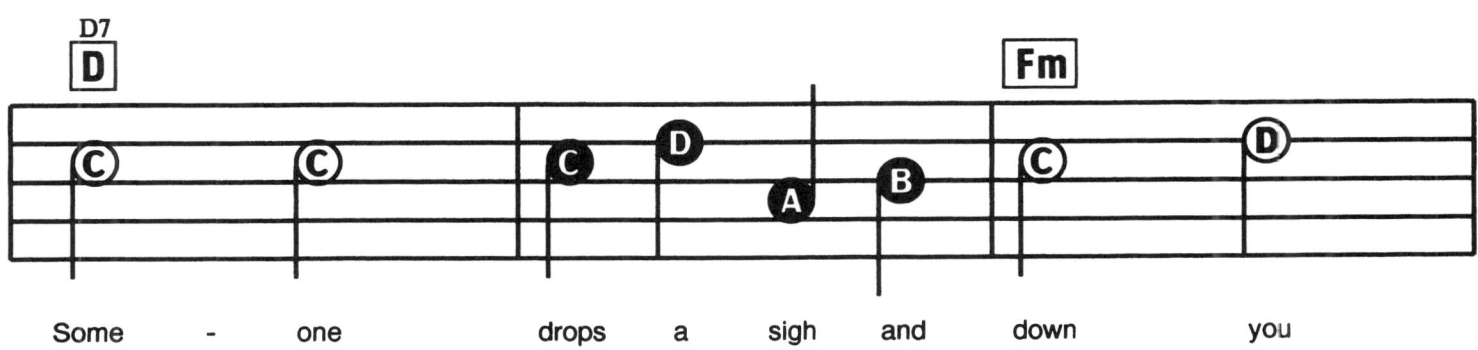
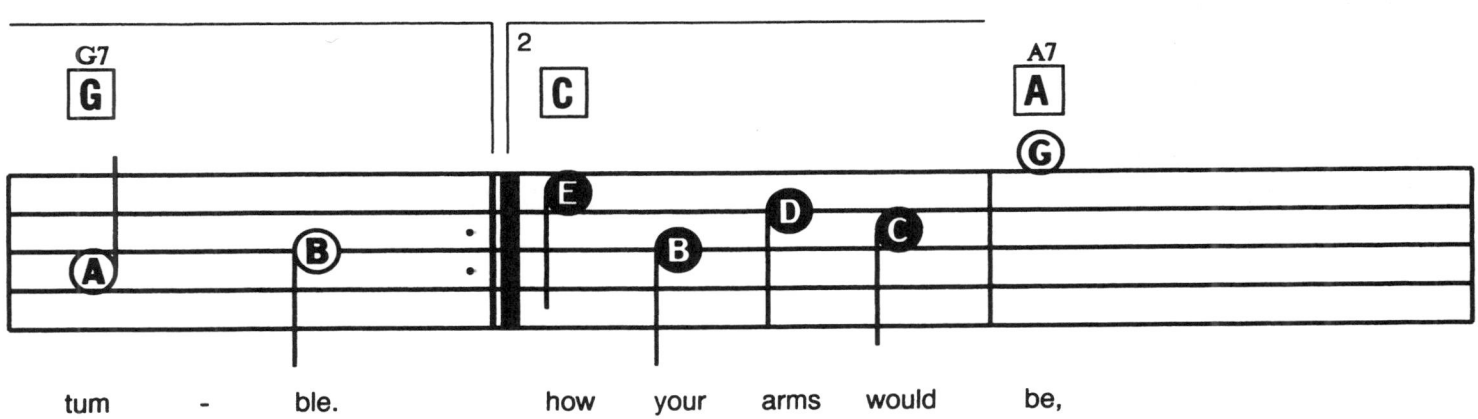
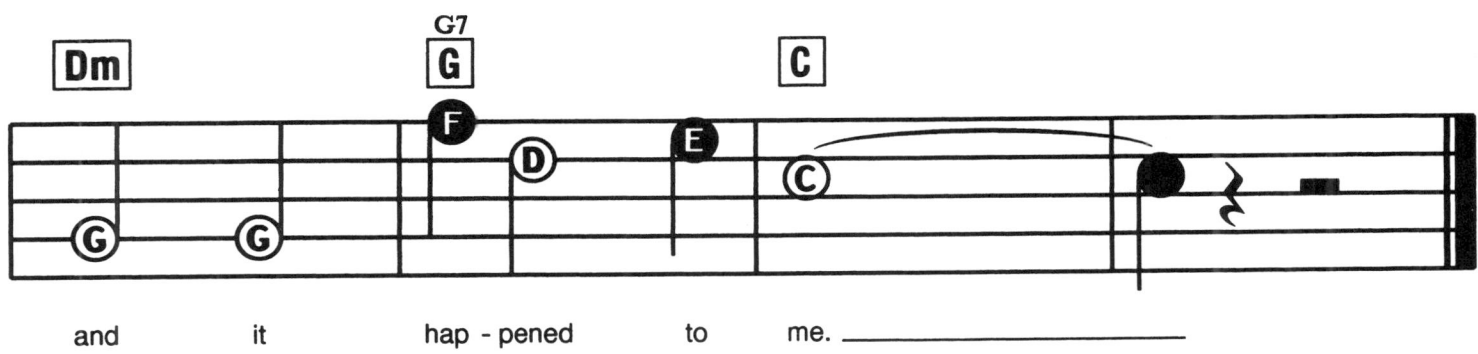

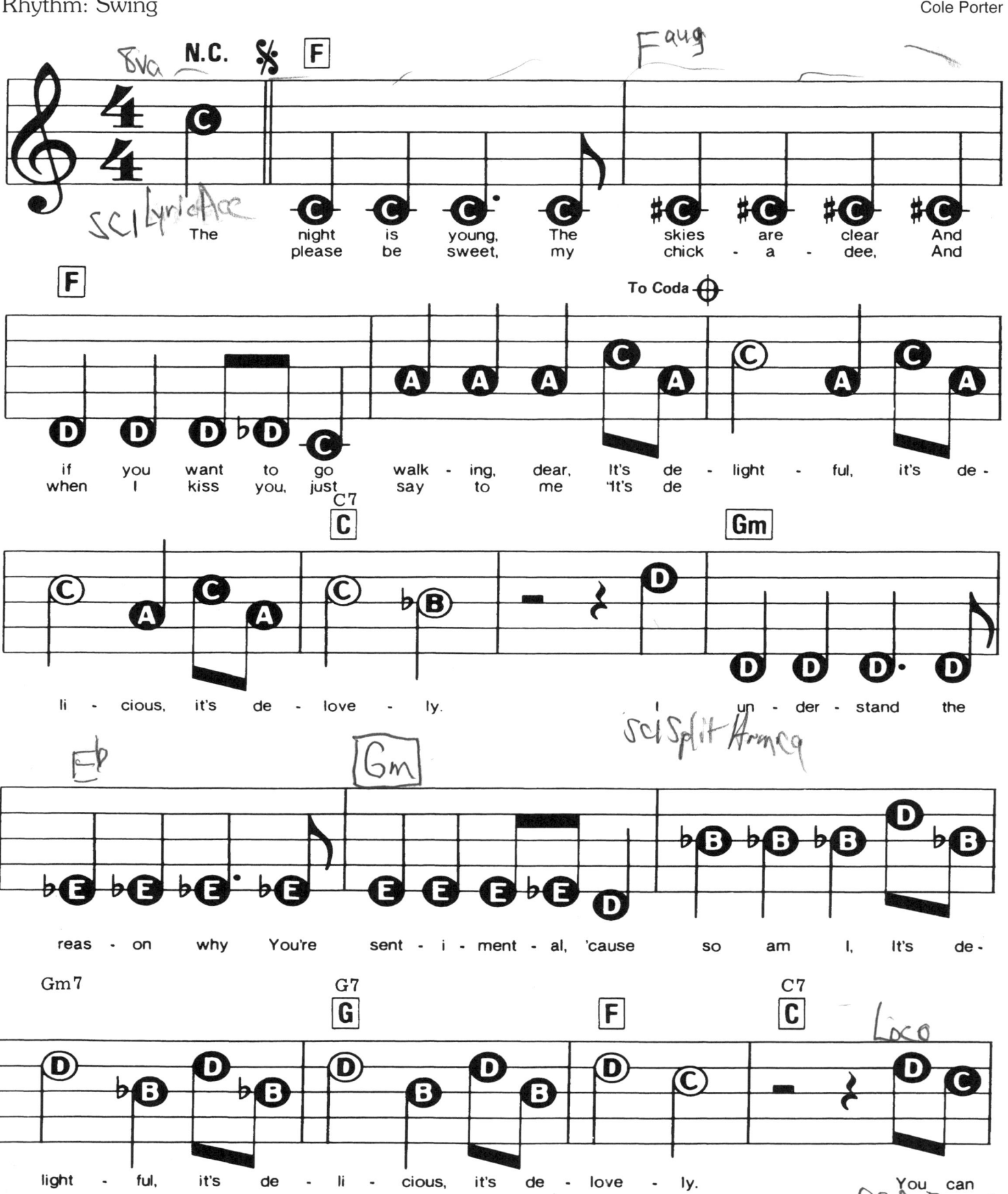

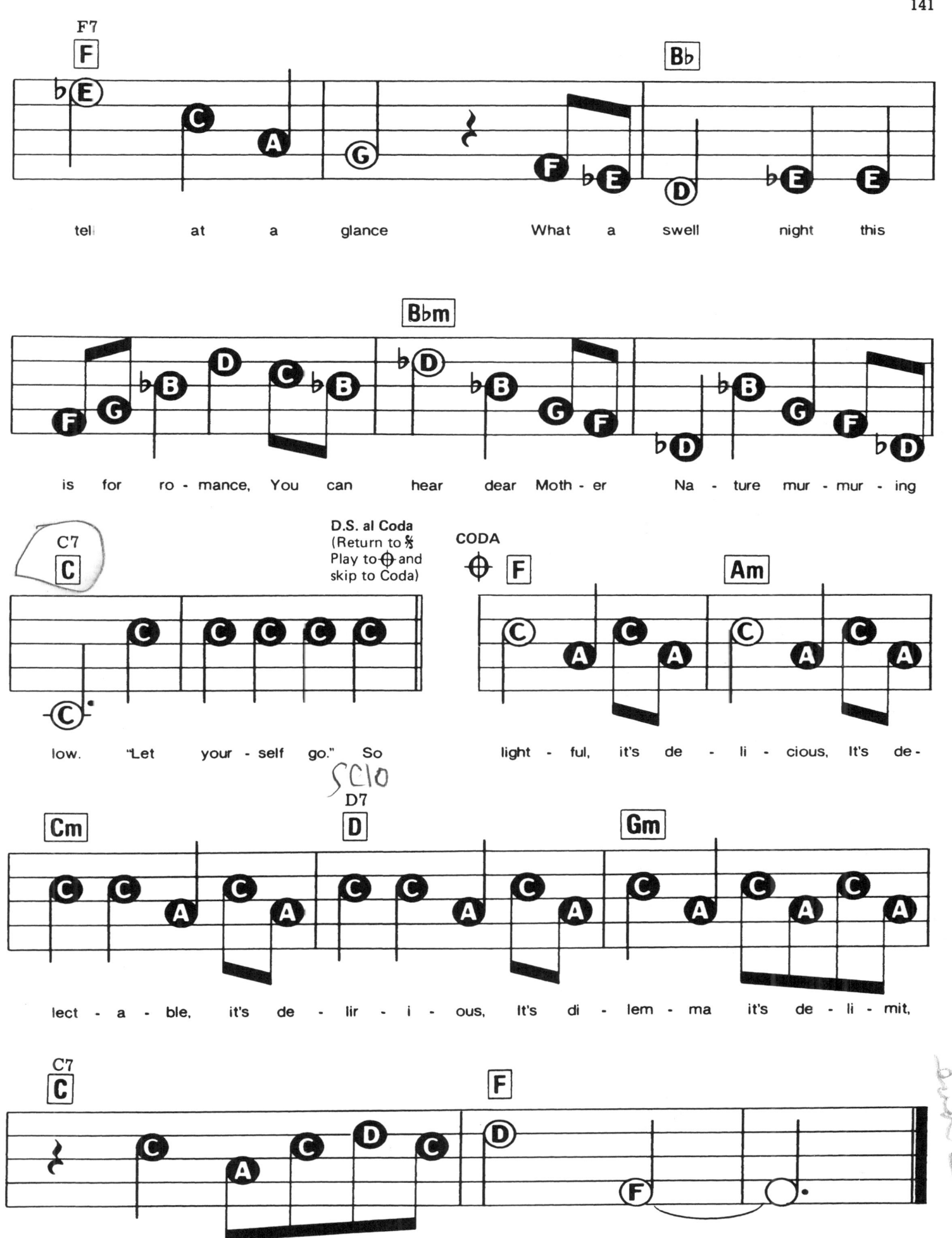

June in January
from the Paramount Picture HERE IS MY HEART

Registration 2
Rhythm: Fox Trot

Words and Music by Leo Robin
and Ralph Rainger

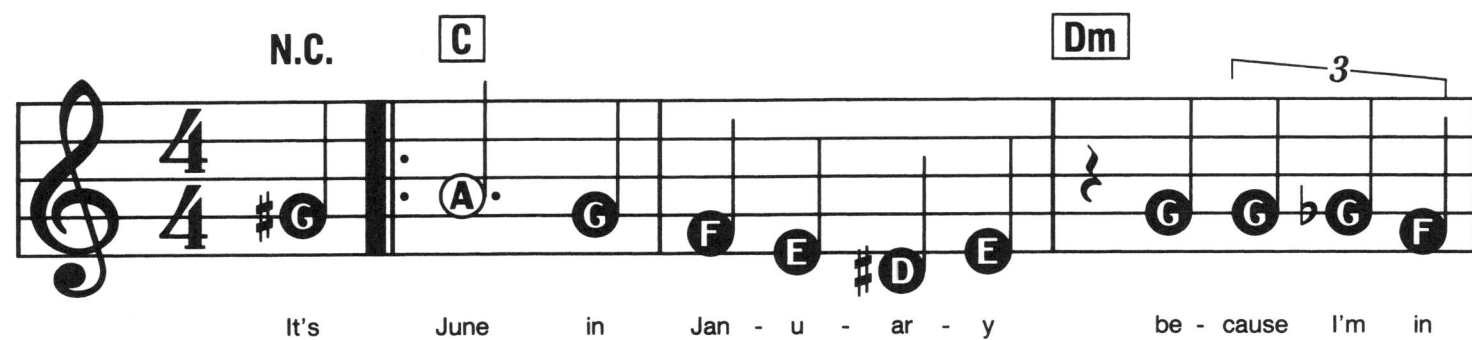

It's June in Jan - u - ar - y be - cause I'm in

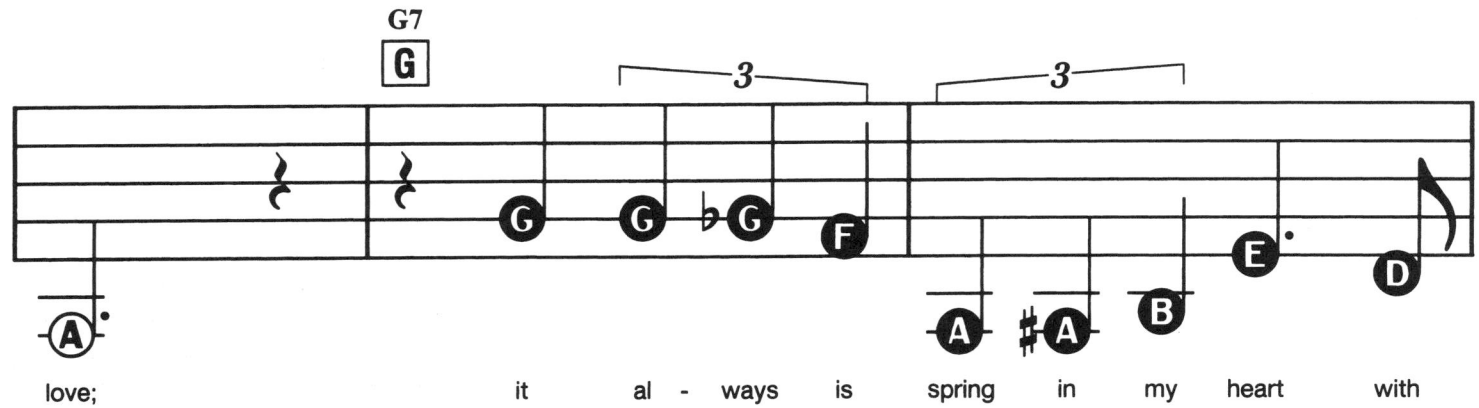

love; it al - ways is spring in my heart with

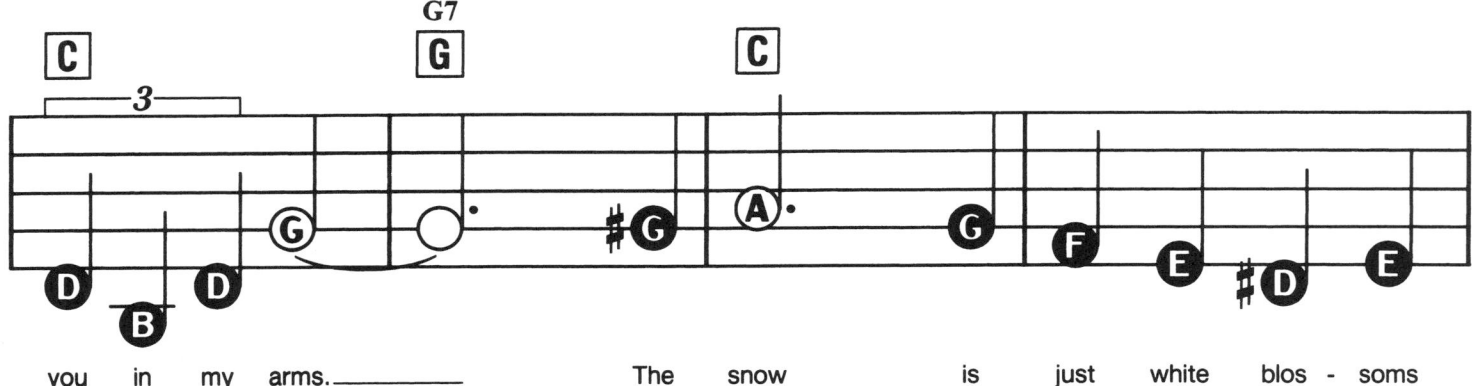

you in my arms.___ The snow is just white blos - soms

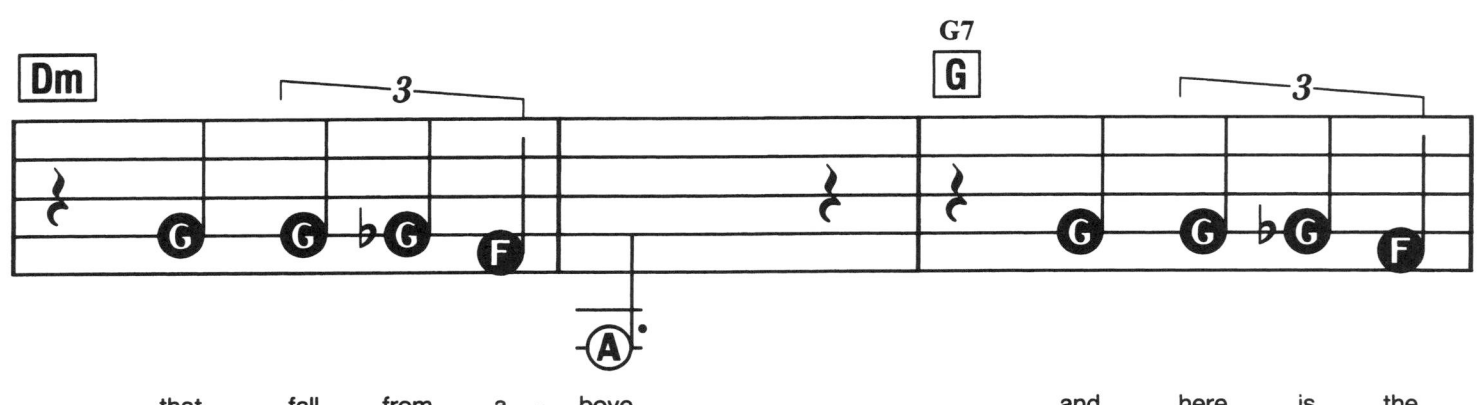

that fall from a - bove, and here is the

Copyright © 1934 Sony/ATV Music Publishing LLC
Copyright Renewed
All Rights Administered by Sony/ATV Music Publishing LLC, 8 Music Square West, Nashville, TN 37203
International Copyright Secured All Rights Reserved

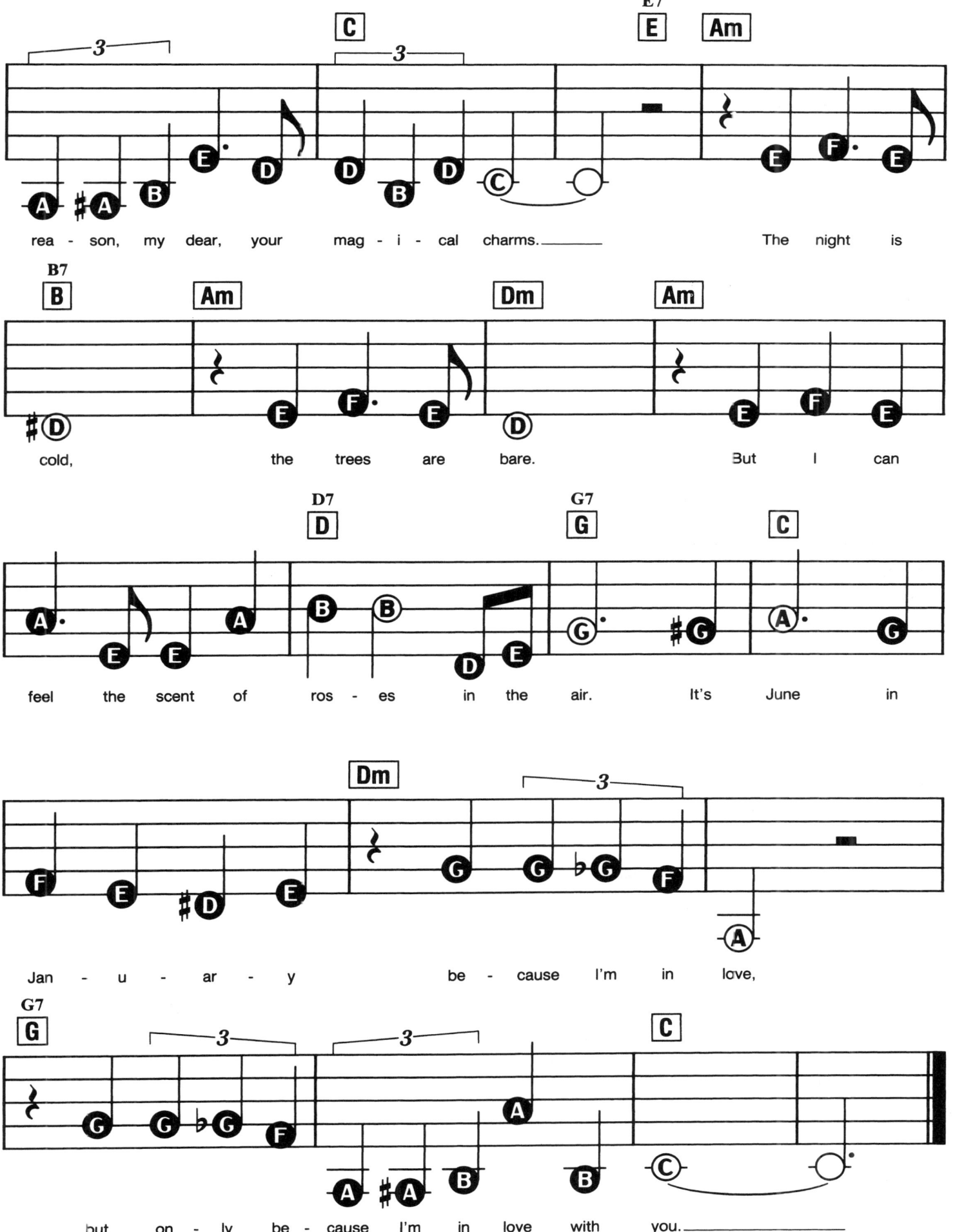

Big Band-Swing Band

Just in Time
from BELLS ARE RINGING

Registration 2
Rhythm: Fox Trot or Swing

Words by Betty Comden and Adolph Green
Music by Jule Styne

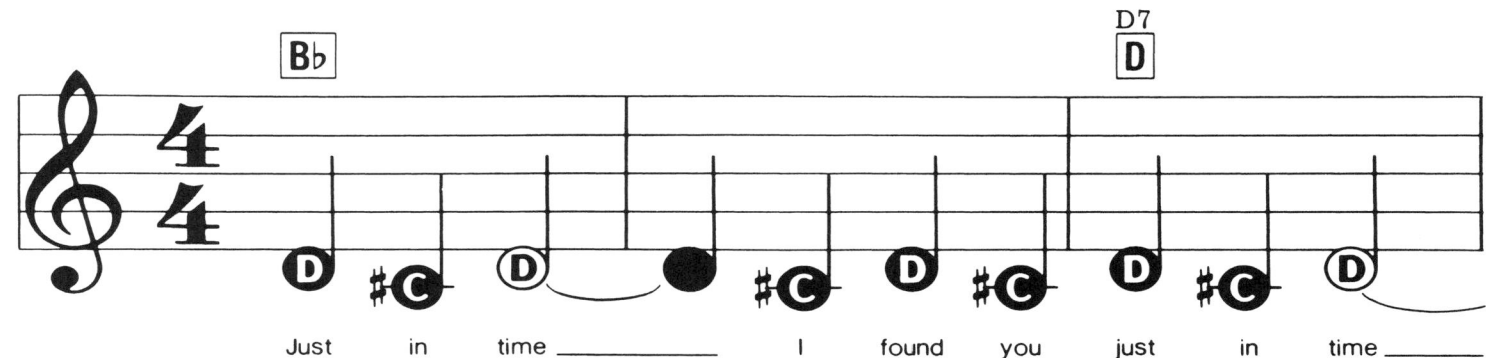

Just in time ____ I found you just in time ____

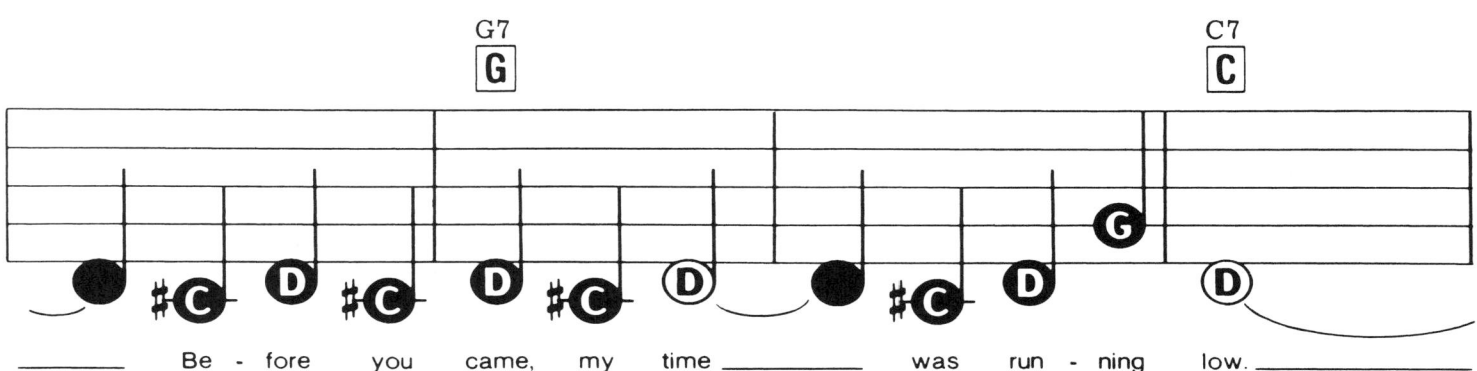

____ Be - fore you came, my time ____ was run - ning low. ____

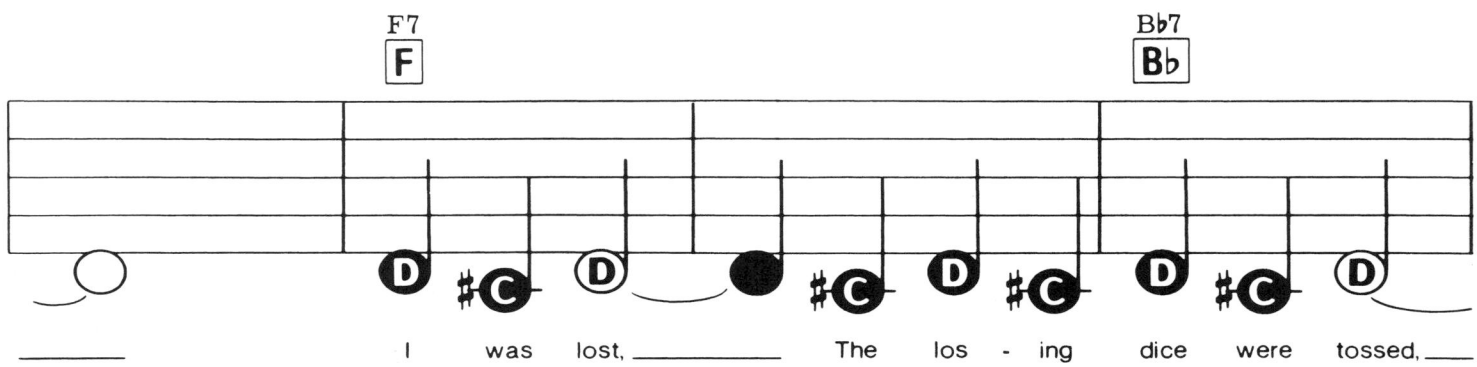

____ I was lost, ____ The los - ing dice were tossed, ____

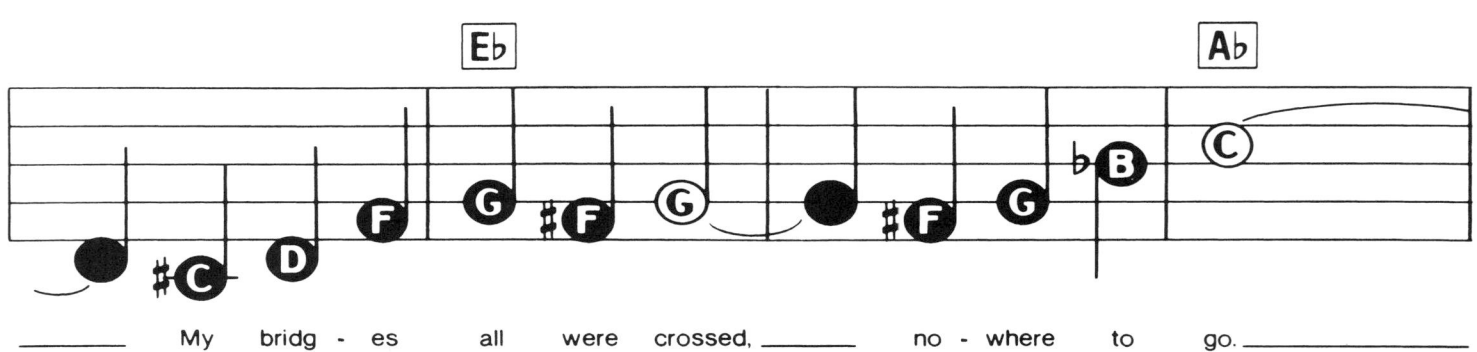

____ My bridg - es all were crossed, ____ no - where to go. ____

Copyright © 1956 by Betty Comden, Adolph Green and Jule Styne
Copyright Renewed
Stratford Music Corporation, owner of publication and allied rights throughout the world
Chappell & Co., Administrator
International Copyright Secured   All Rights Reserved

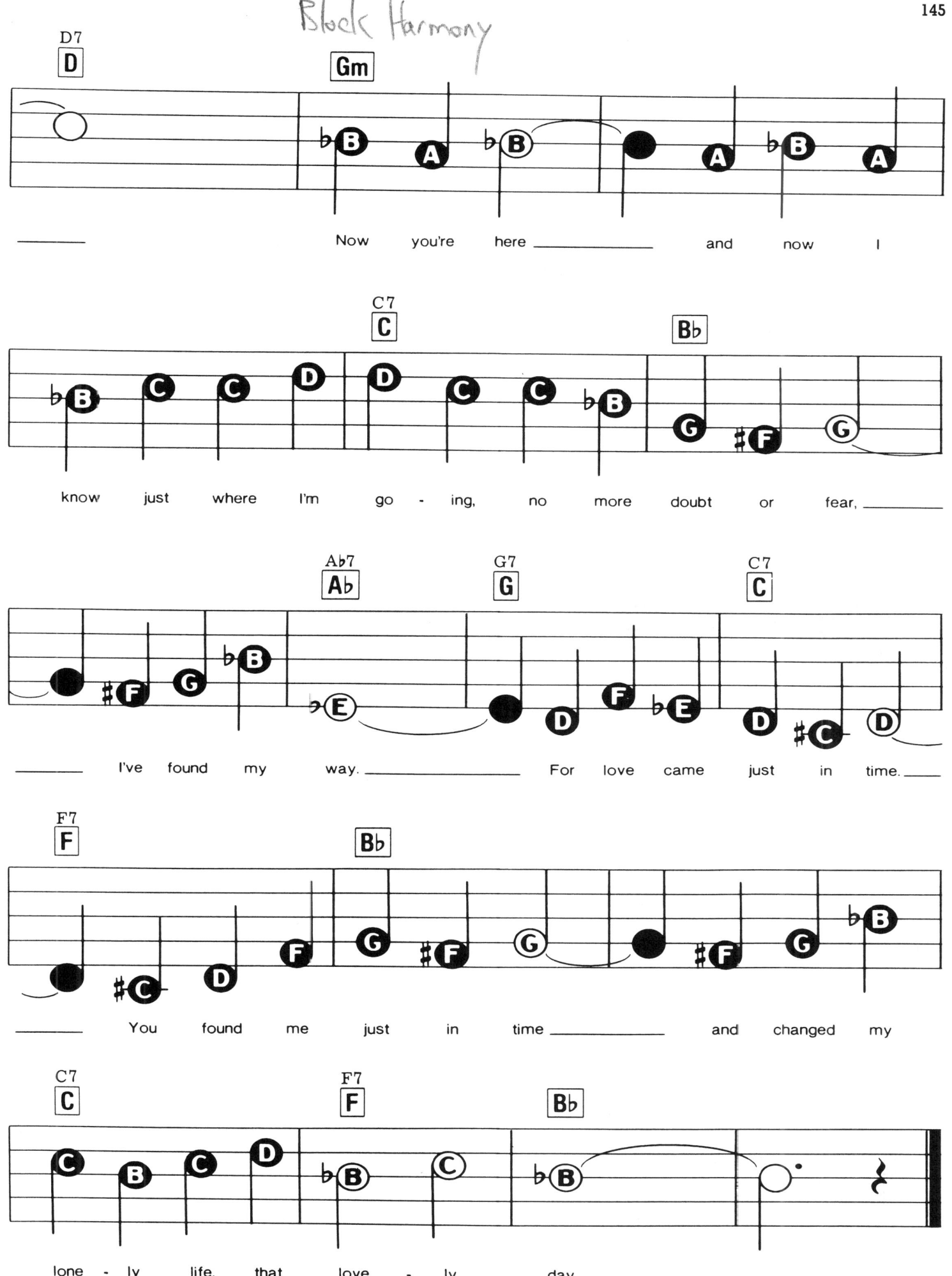

Block Harmony

Just Squeeze Me
(But Don't Tease Me)

Registration 7
Rhythm: Swing or Fox Trot

Words by Lee Gaines
Music by Duke Ellington

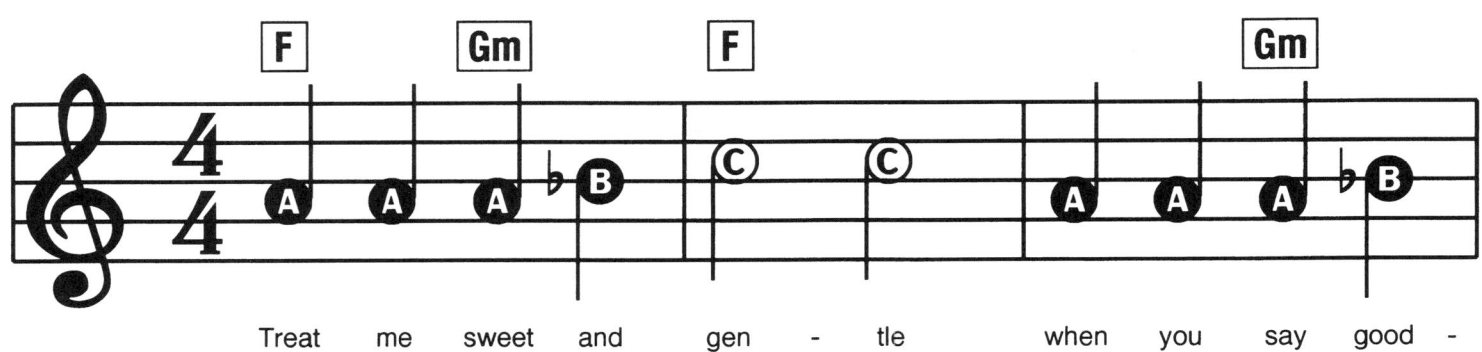

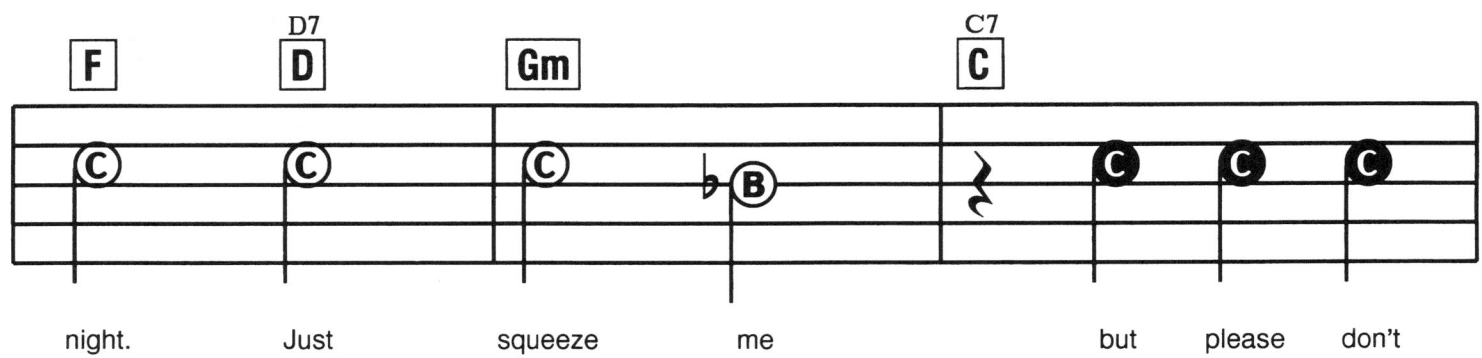

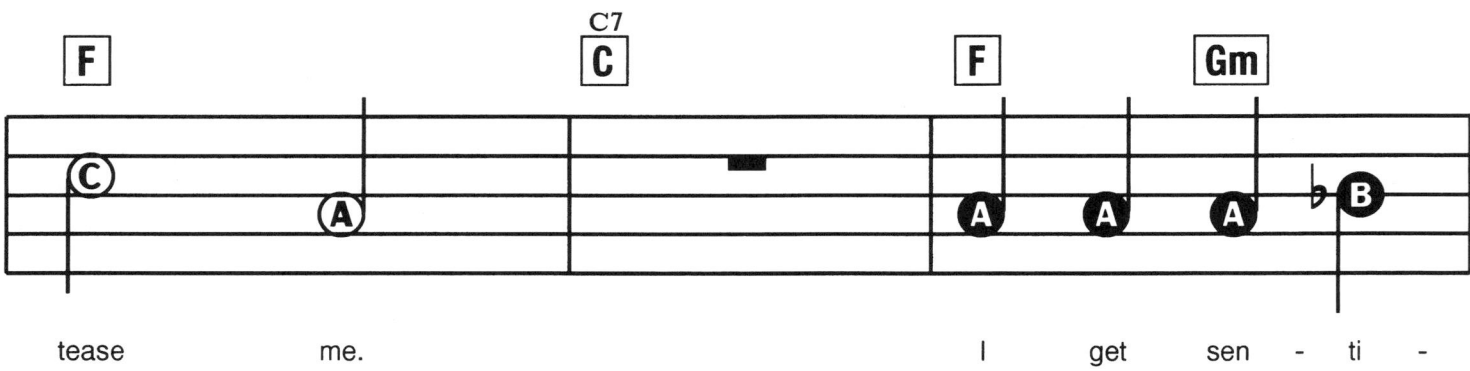

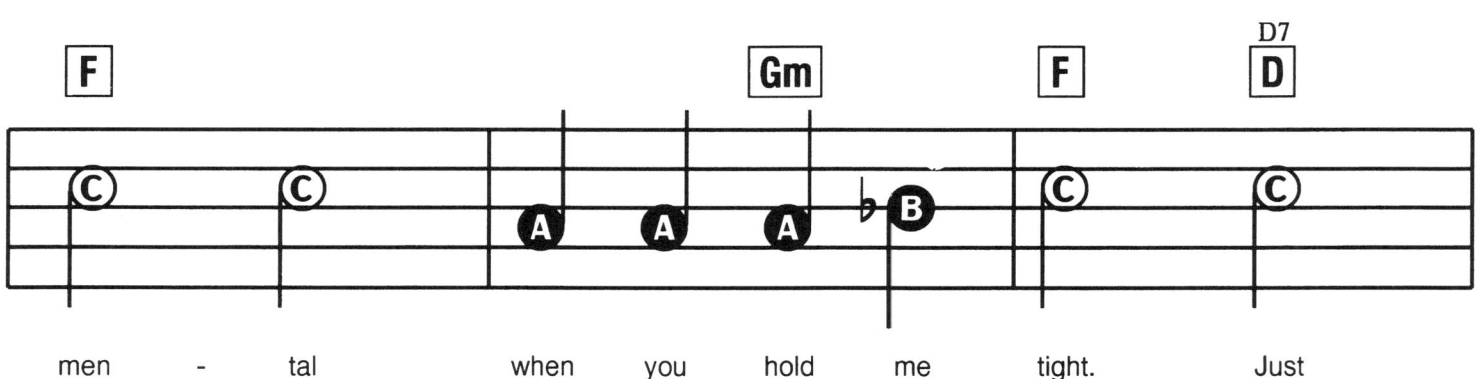

Copyright © 1946 Sony/ATV Music Publishing LLC and EMI Robbins Catalog Inc. in the U.S.A.
Copyright Renewed
All Rights on behalf of Sony/ATV Music Publishing LLC Administered by Sony/ATV Music Publishing LLC, 8 Music Square West, Nashville, TN 37203
Rights for the world outside the U.S.A. Administered by EMI Robbins Catalog Inc. (Publishing) and Alfred Publishing Co., Inc. (Print)
International Copyright Secured   All Rights Reserved

147

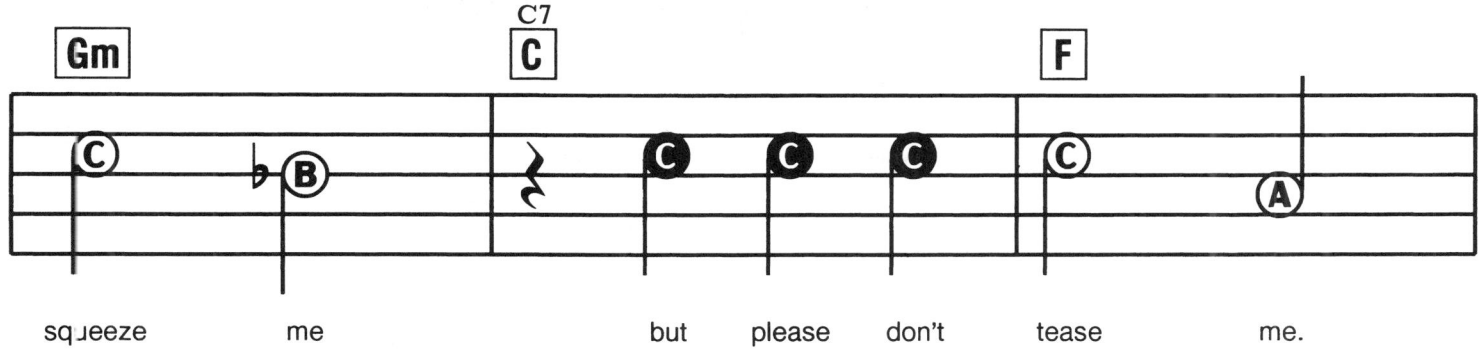

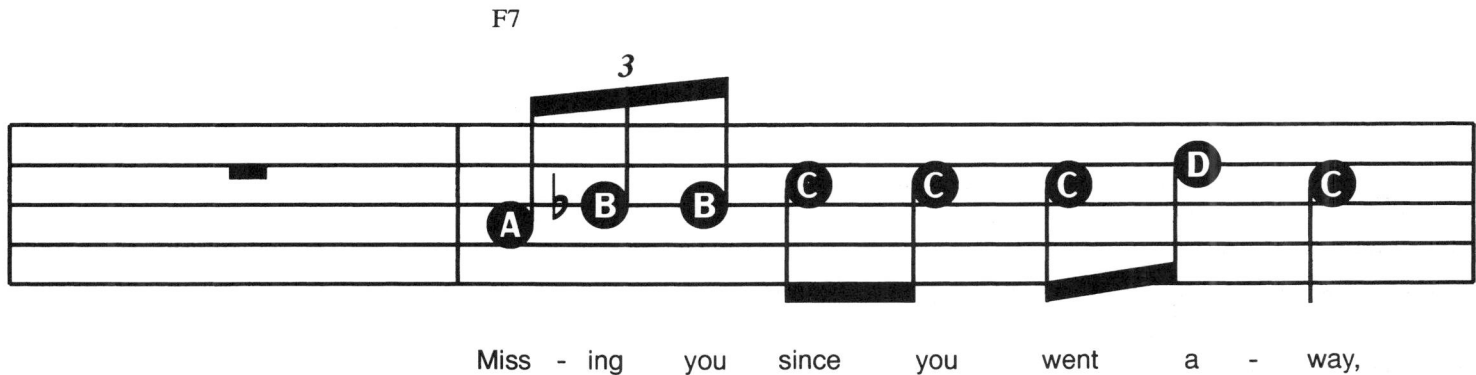

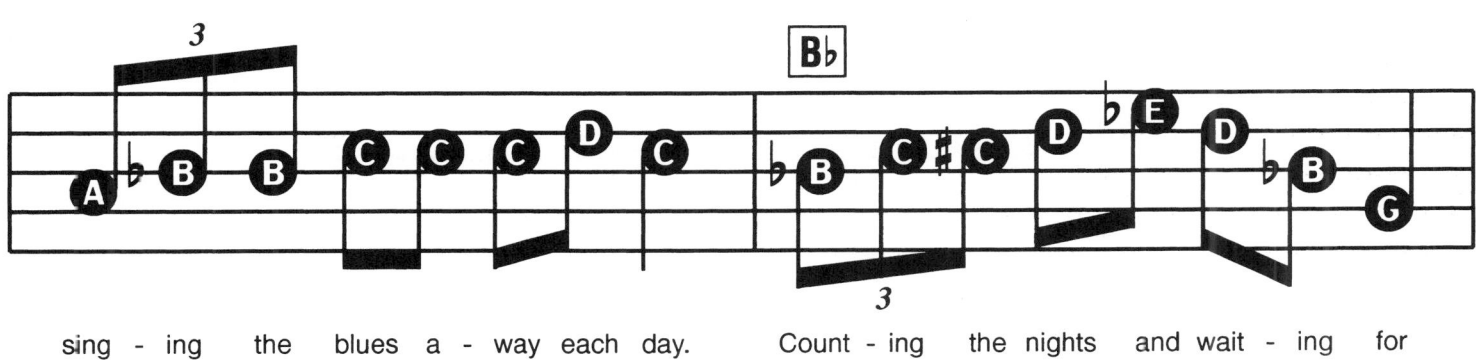

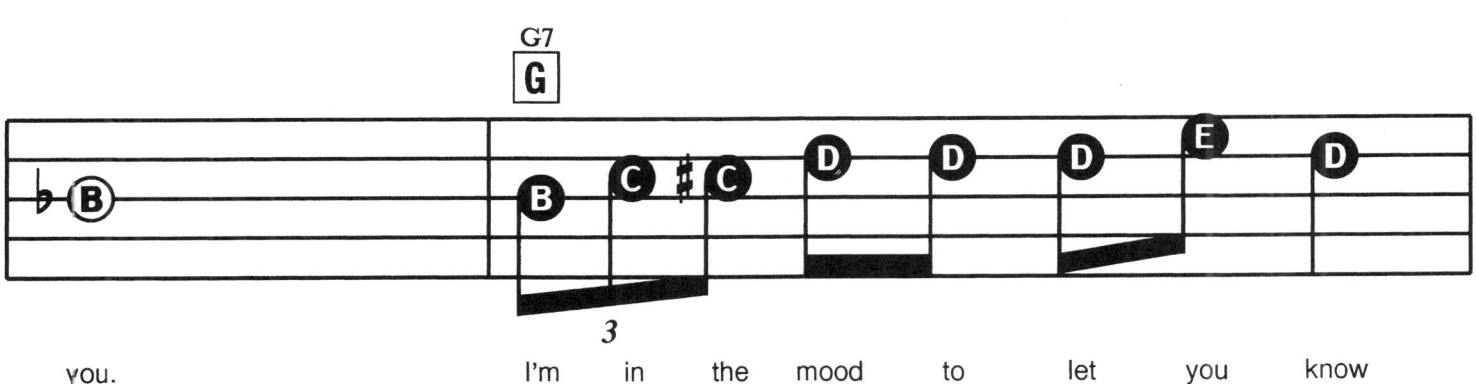

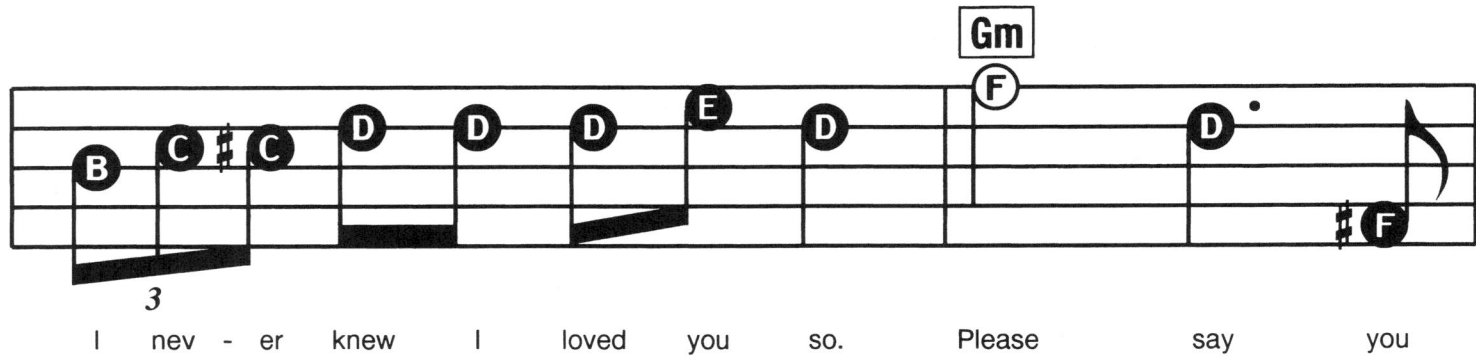
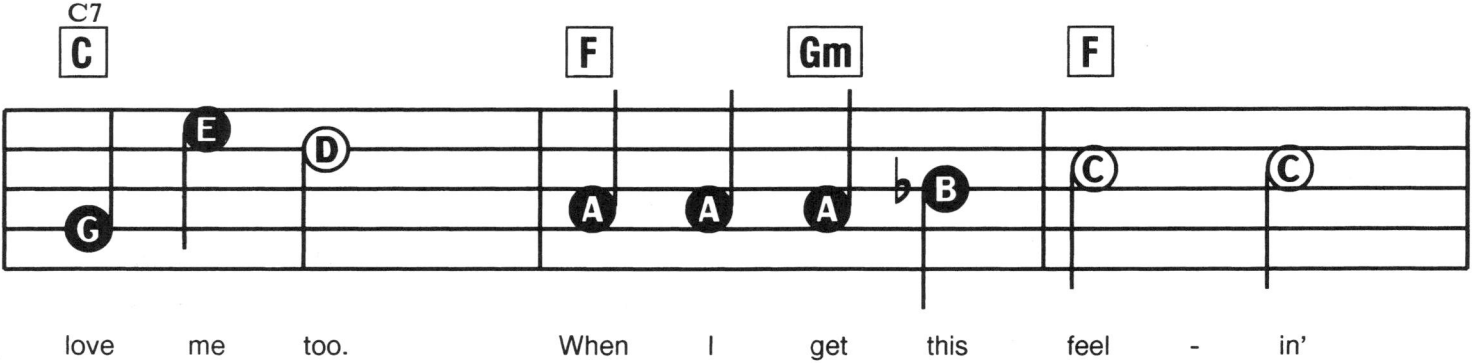
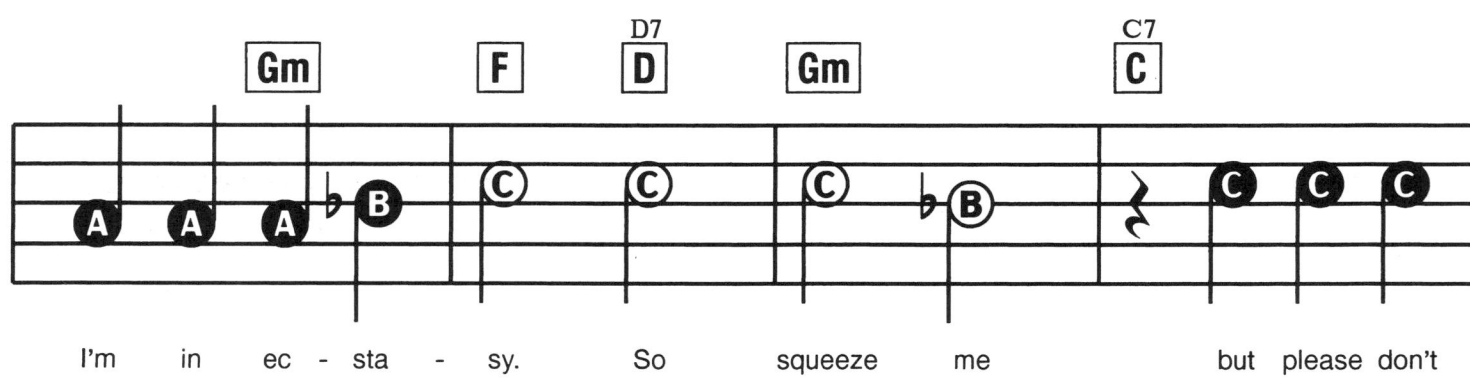
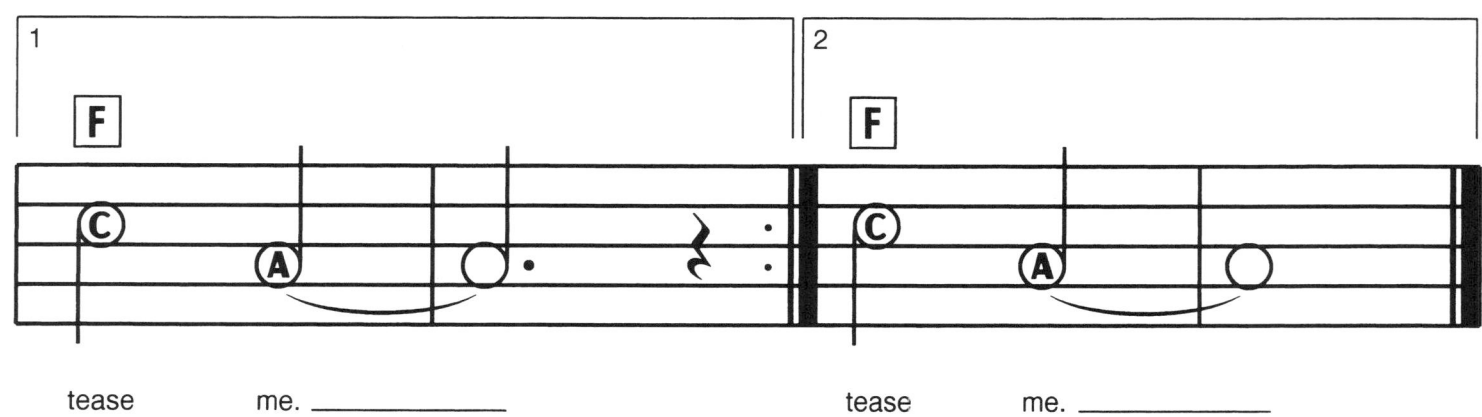

Lazy Afternoon
from THE GOLDEN APPLE

Registration 9
Rhythm: Pops or 8-Beat

Words and Music by John Latouche
and Jerome Moross

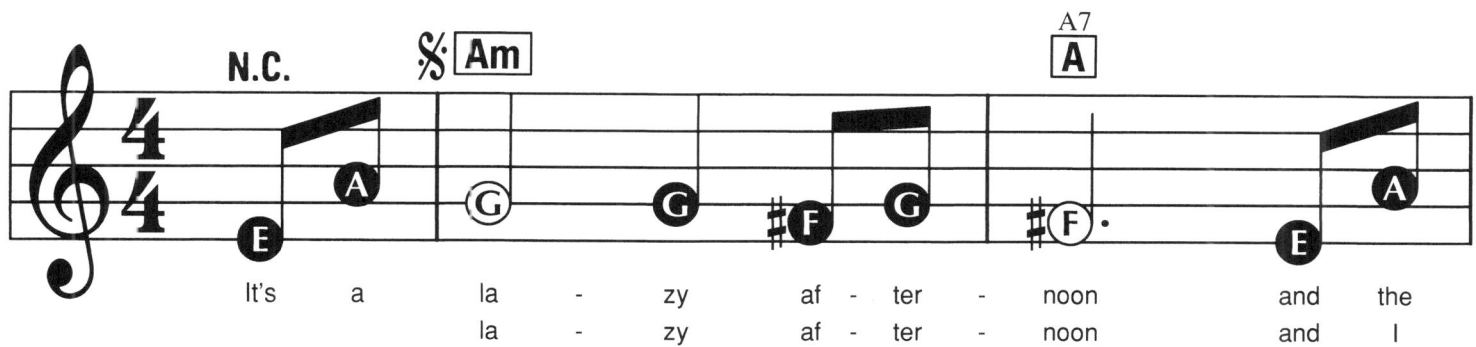
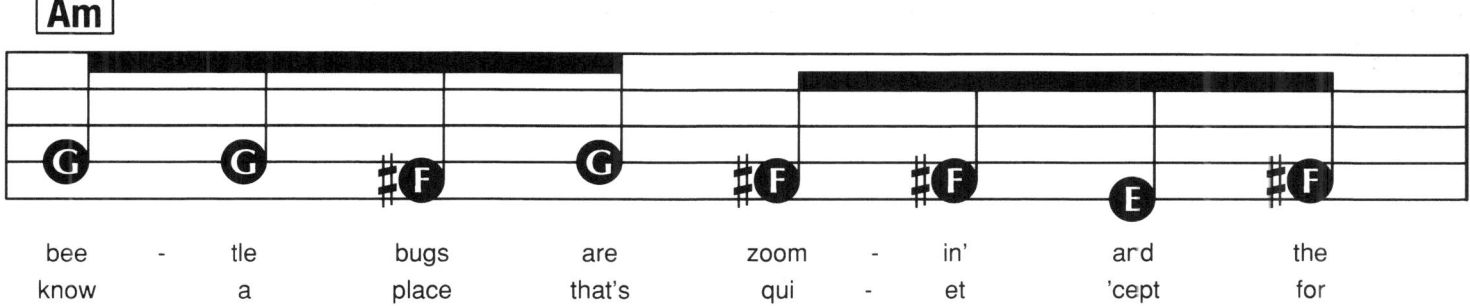
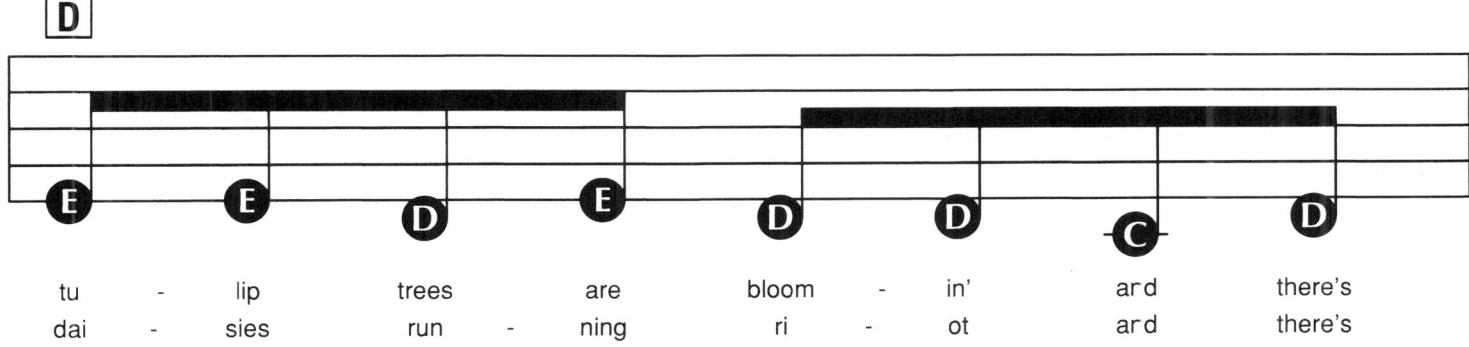
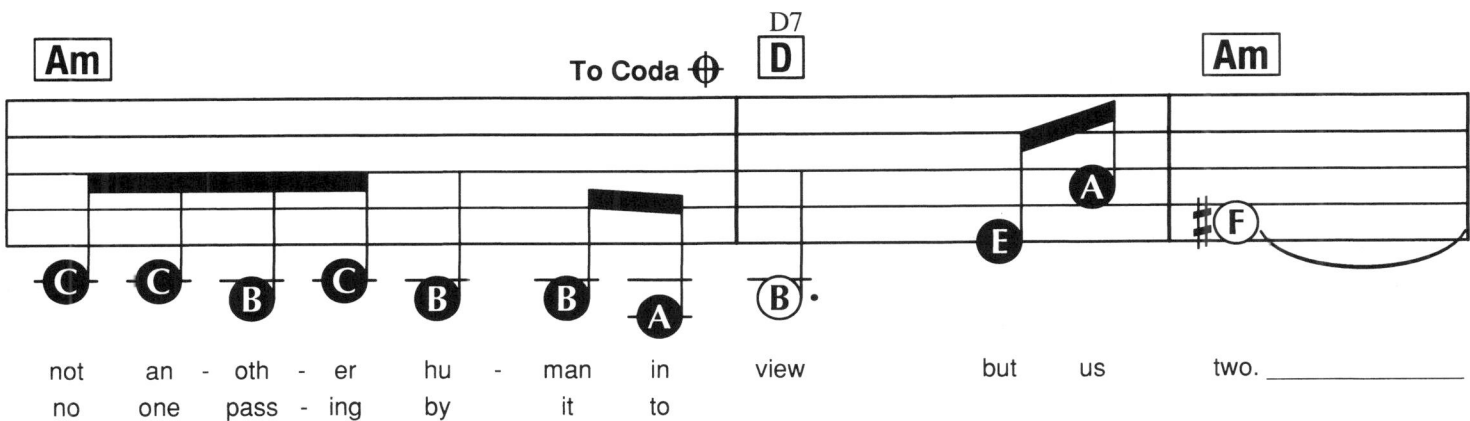

Copyright © 1954 by Chappell & Co. and Sony/ATV Music Publishing LLC
Copyright Renewed
All Rights on behalf of Sony/ATV Music Publishing LLC Administered by Sony/ATV Music Publishing LLC, 8 Music Square West, Nashville, TN 37203
International Copyright Secured   All Rights Reserved

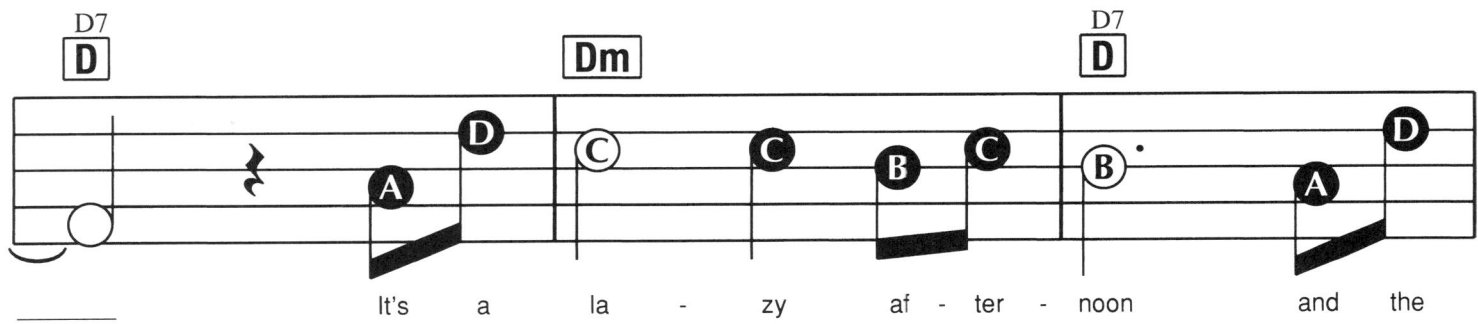
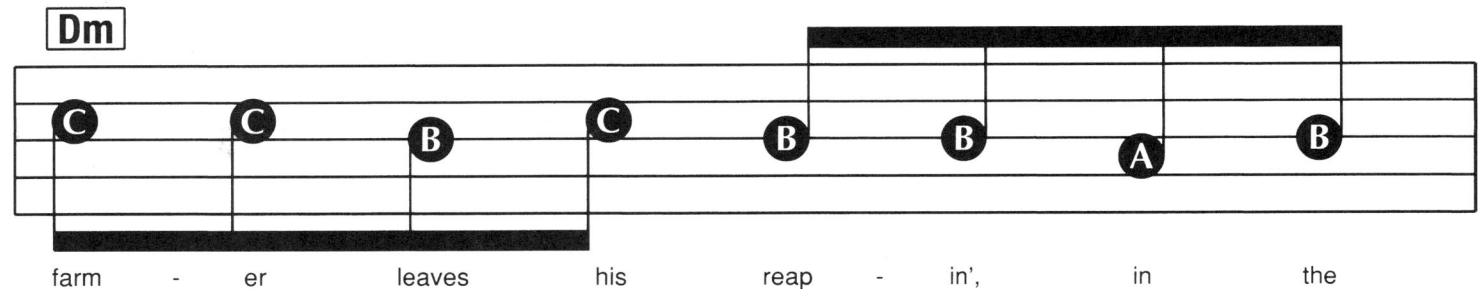
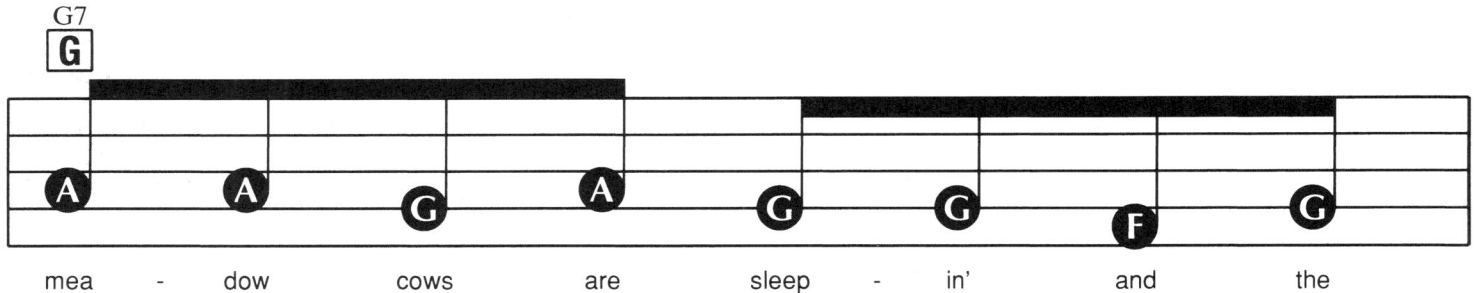
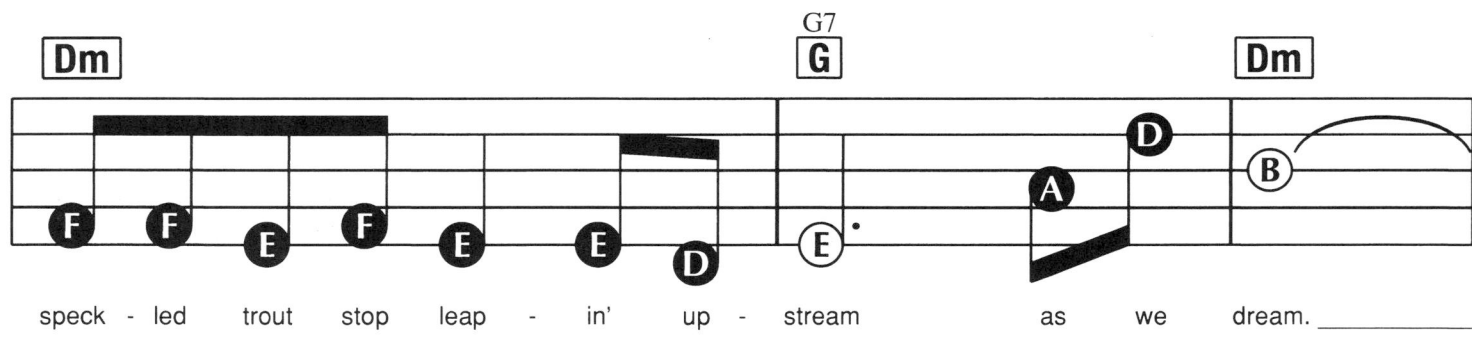
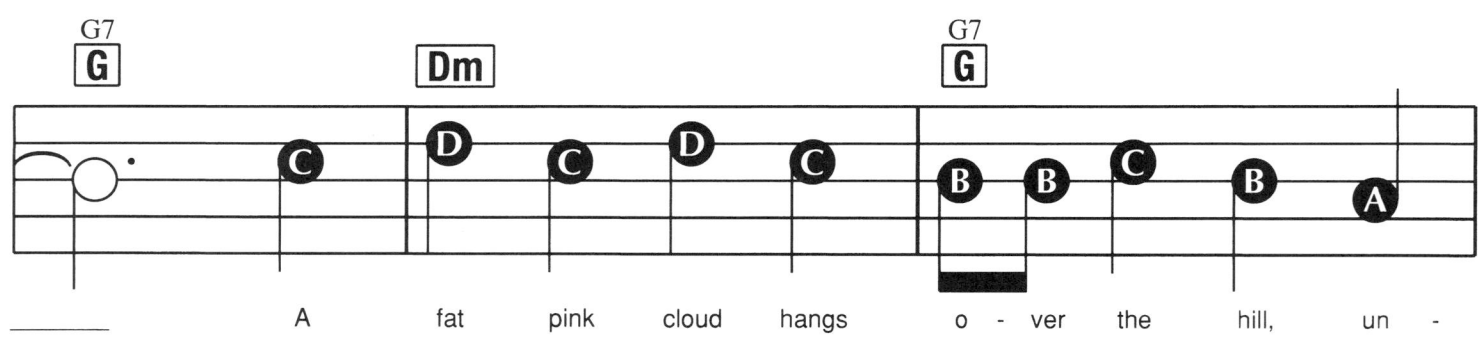

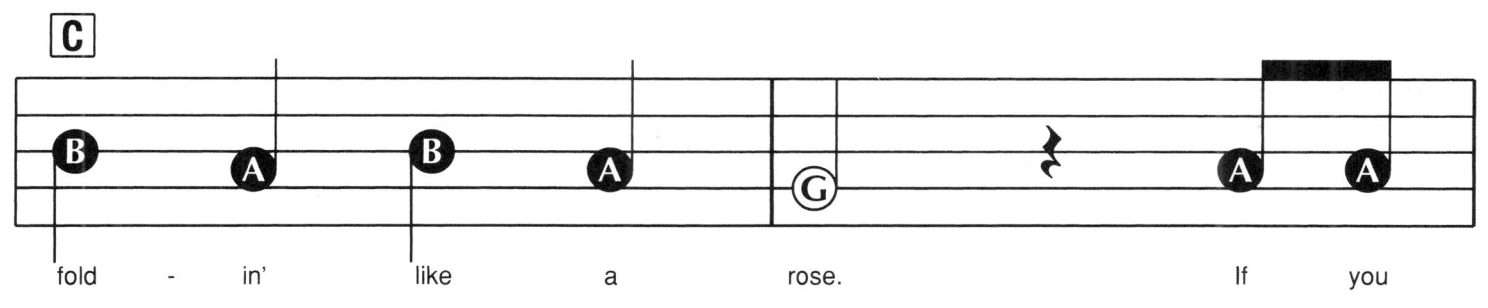
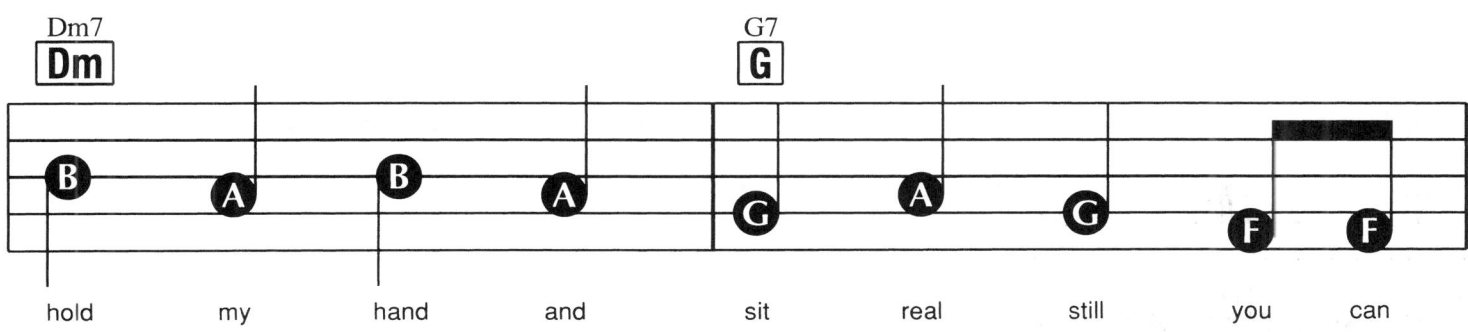
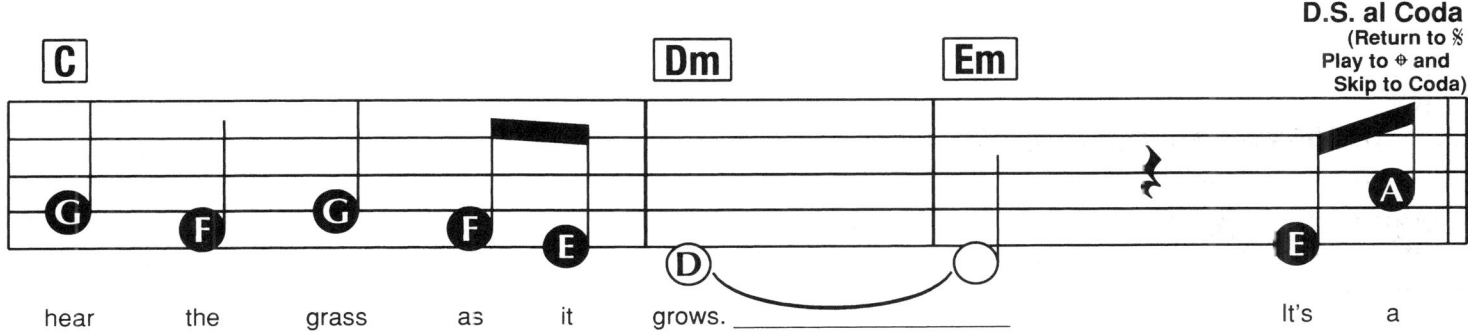
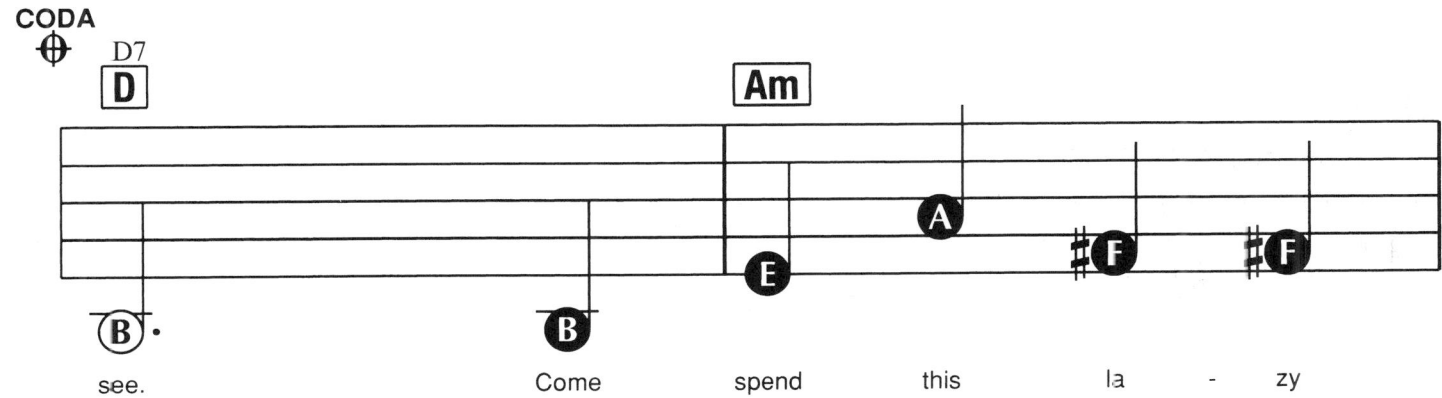
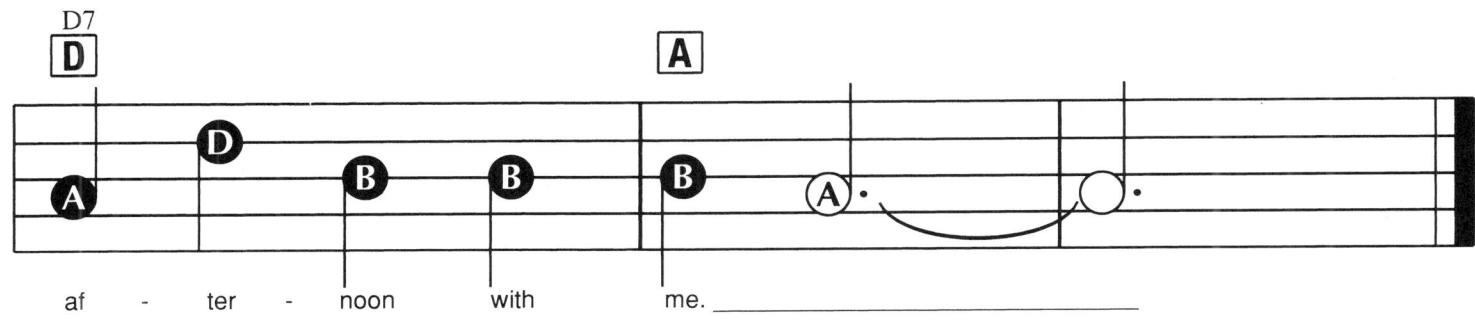

The Last Time I Saw Paris

from LADY, BE GOOD
from TILL THE CLOUDS ROLL BY

Registration 10
Rhythm: Ballad or Swing

Lyrics by Oscar Hammerstein II
Music by Jerome Kern

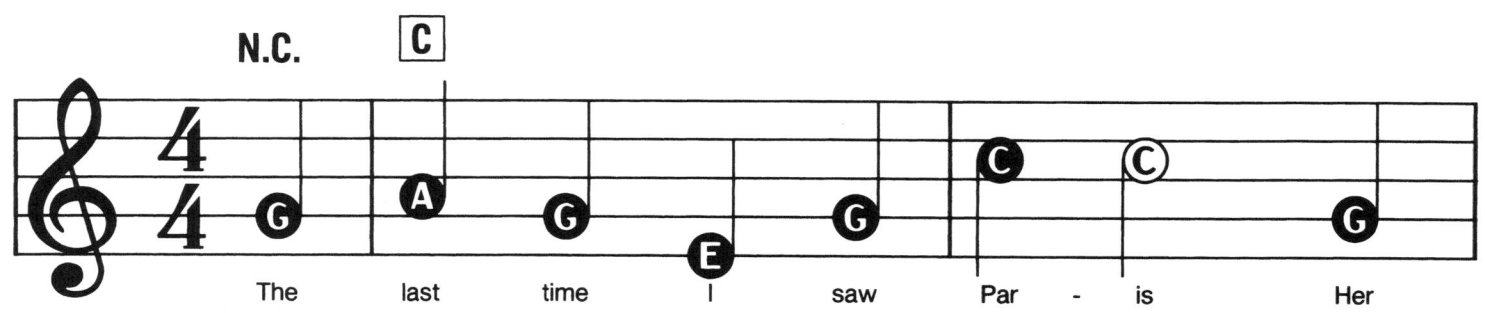

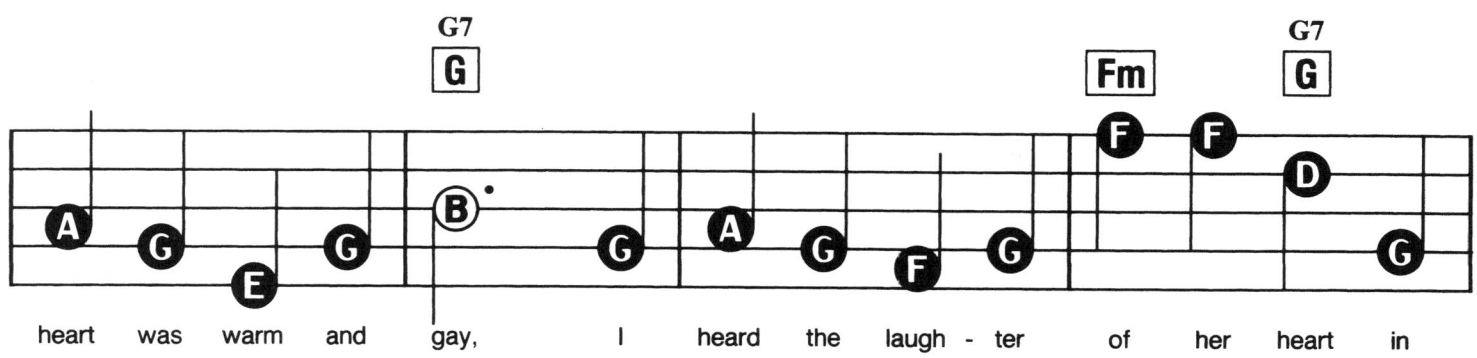

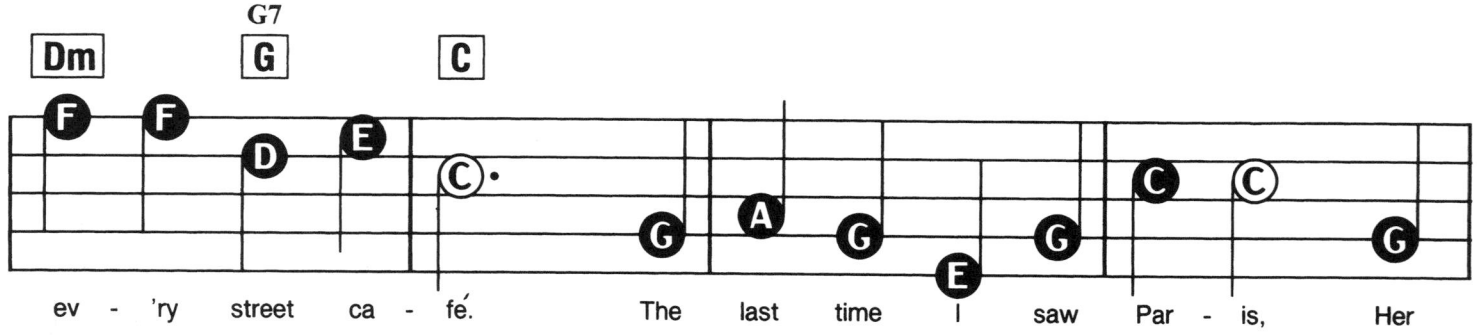

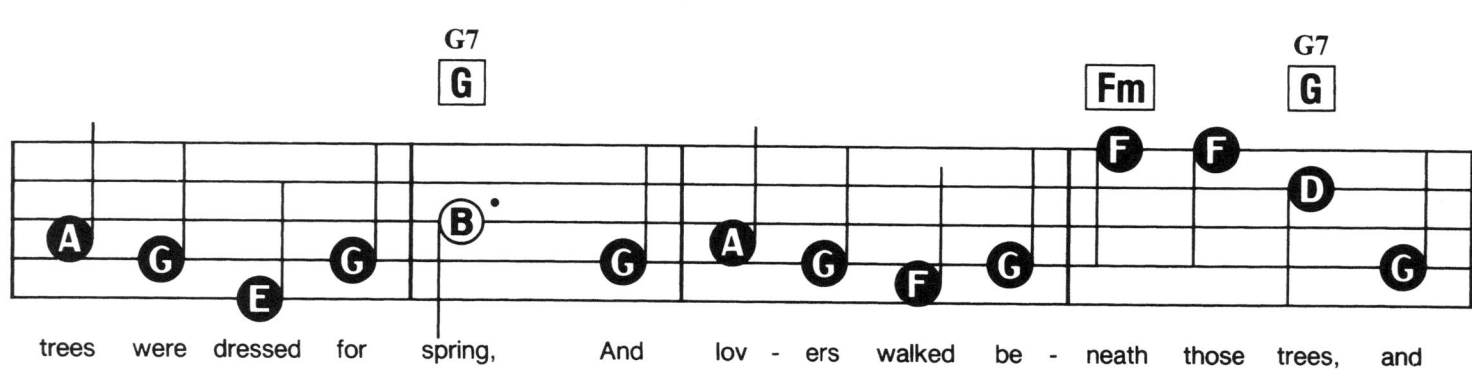

Copyright © 1940 UNIVERSAL - POLYGRAM INTERNATIONAL PUBLISHING, INC.
Copyright Renewed
All Rights Reserved   Used by Permission

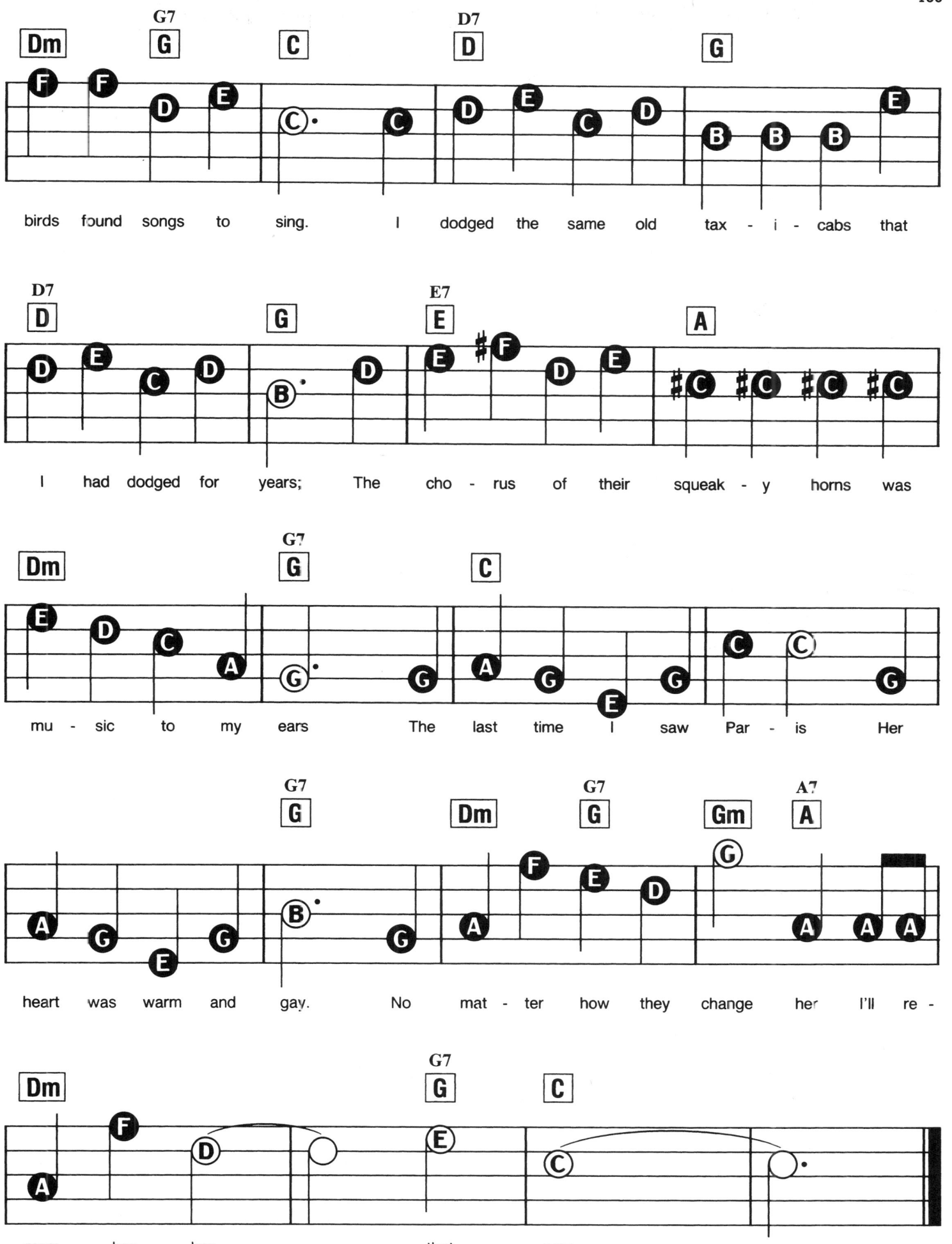

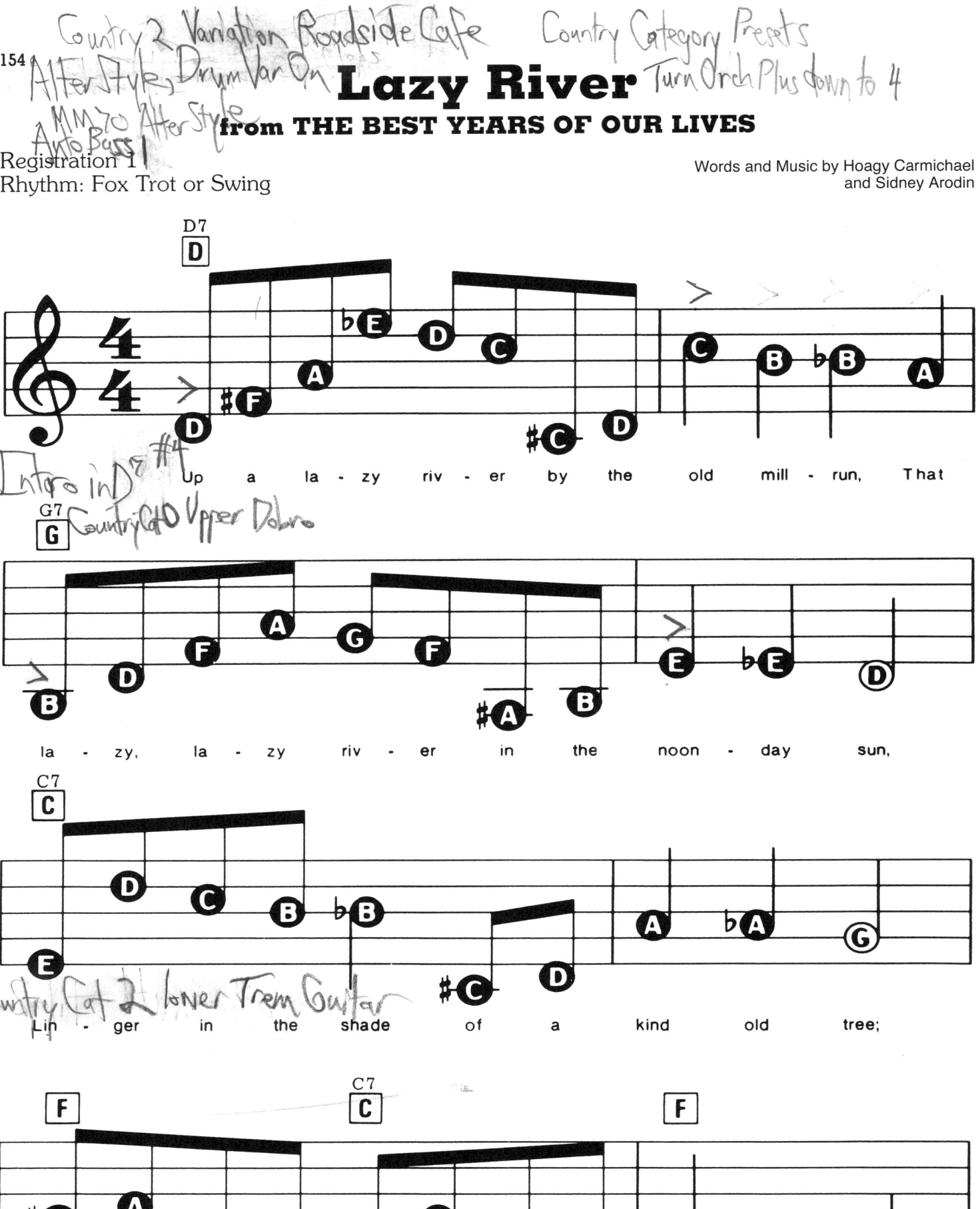

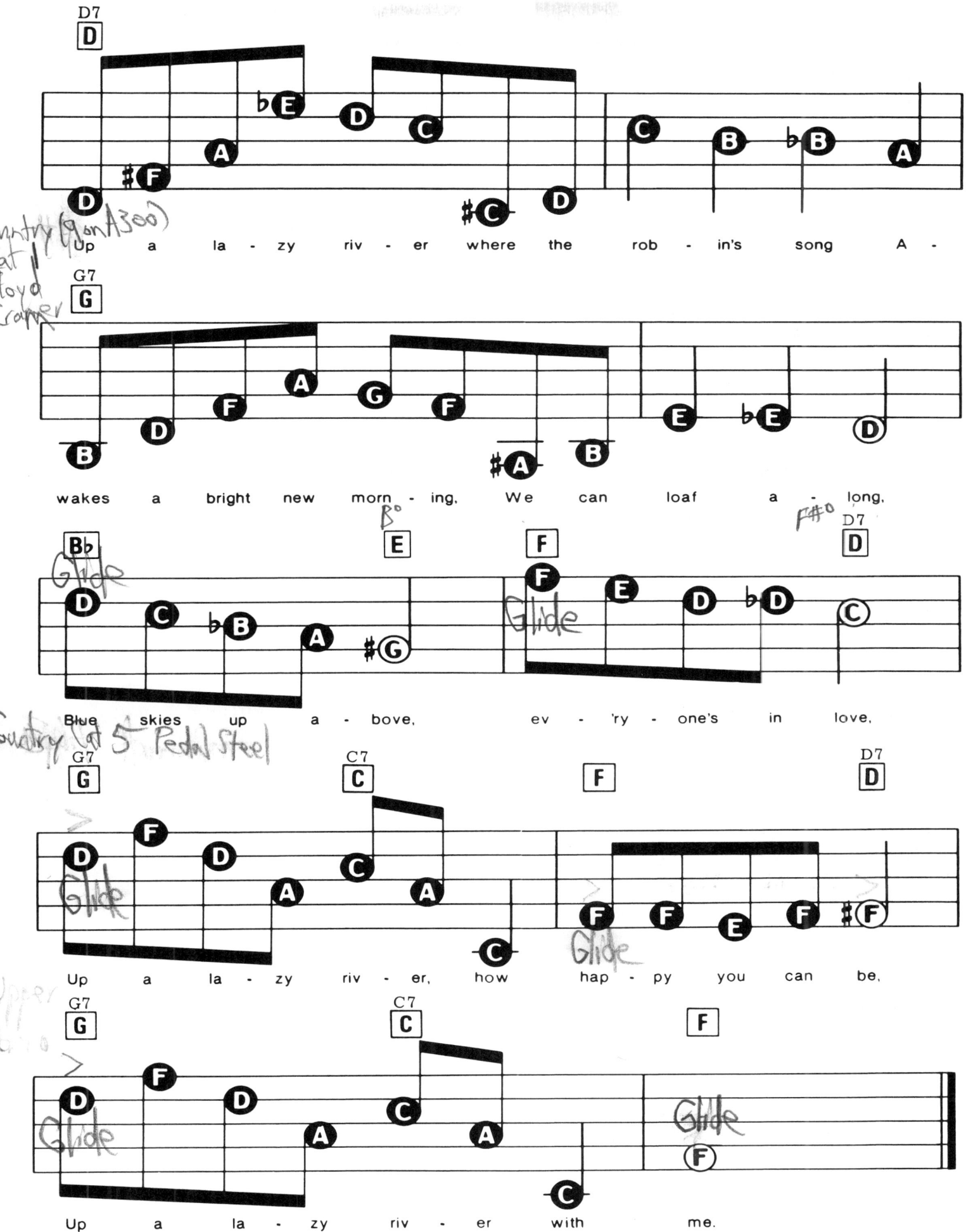

Let's Face the Music and Dance
from the Motion Picture FOLLOW THE FLEET

Registration 3
Rhythm: Swing or Ballad

Words and Music by
Irving Berlin

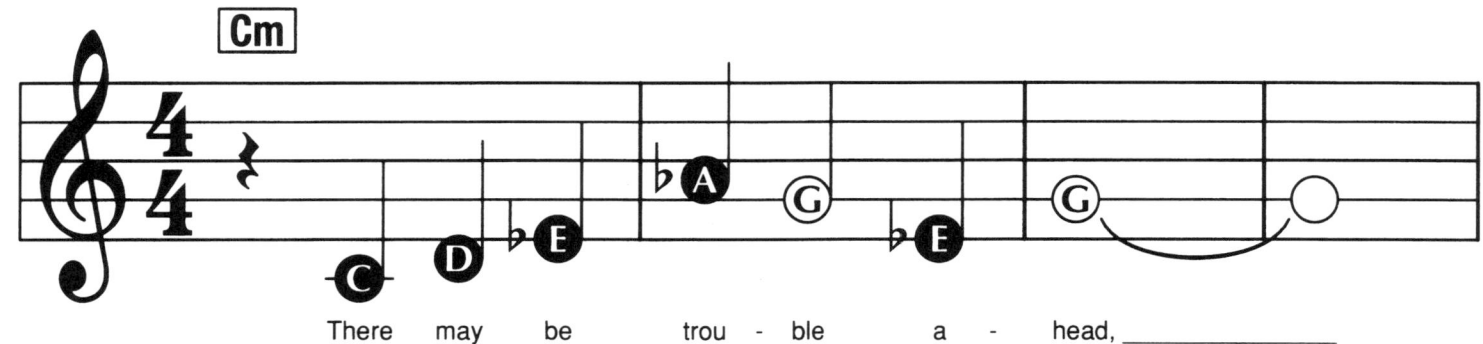

There may be trou - ble a - head, _____

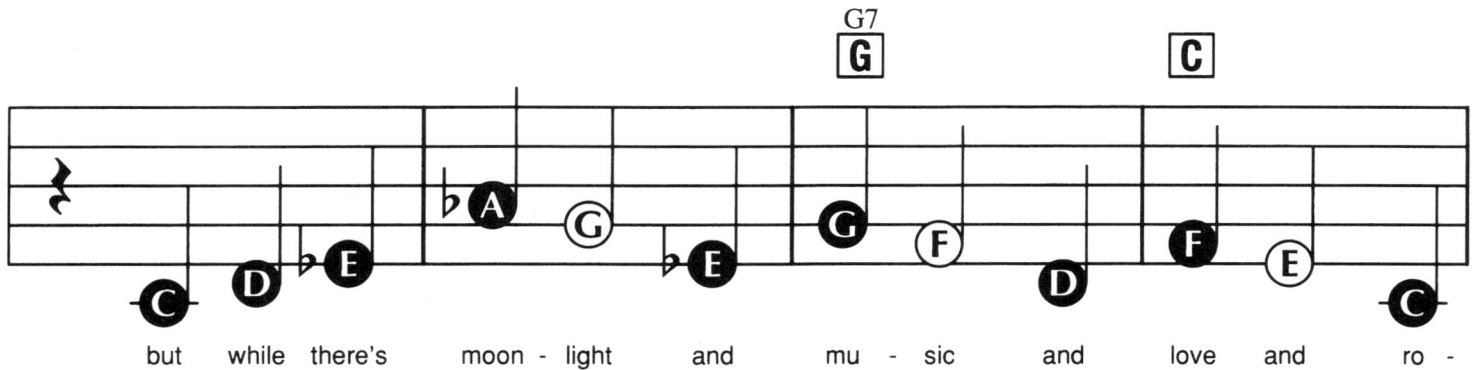

but while there's moon - light and mu - sic and love and ro -

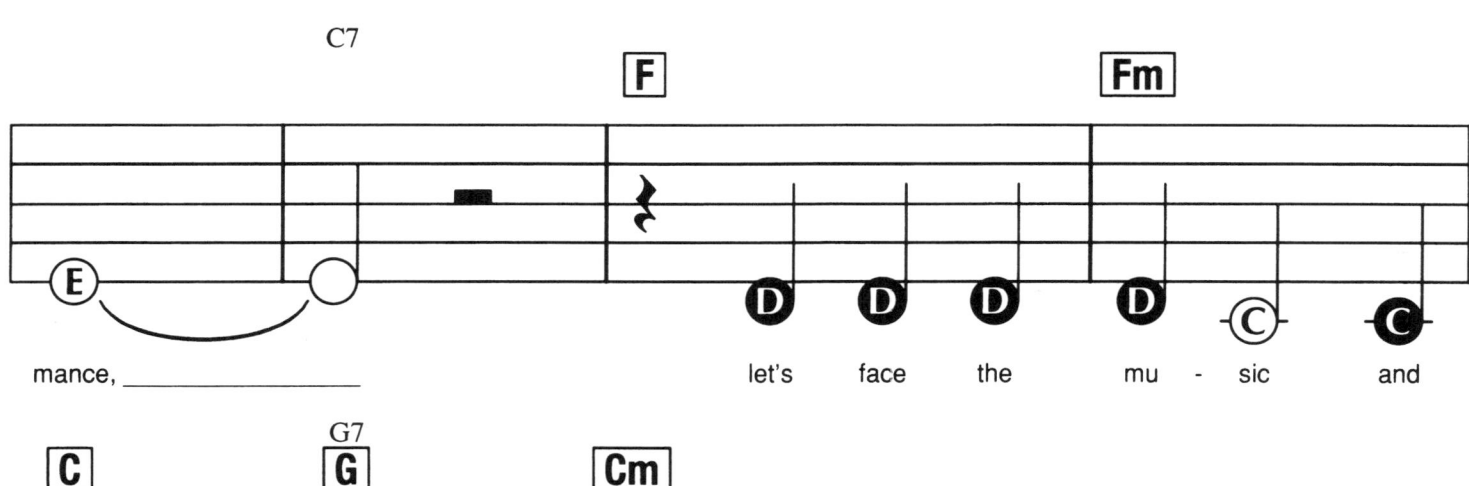

mance, _____ let's face the mu - sic and

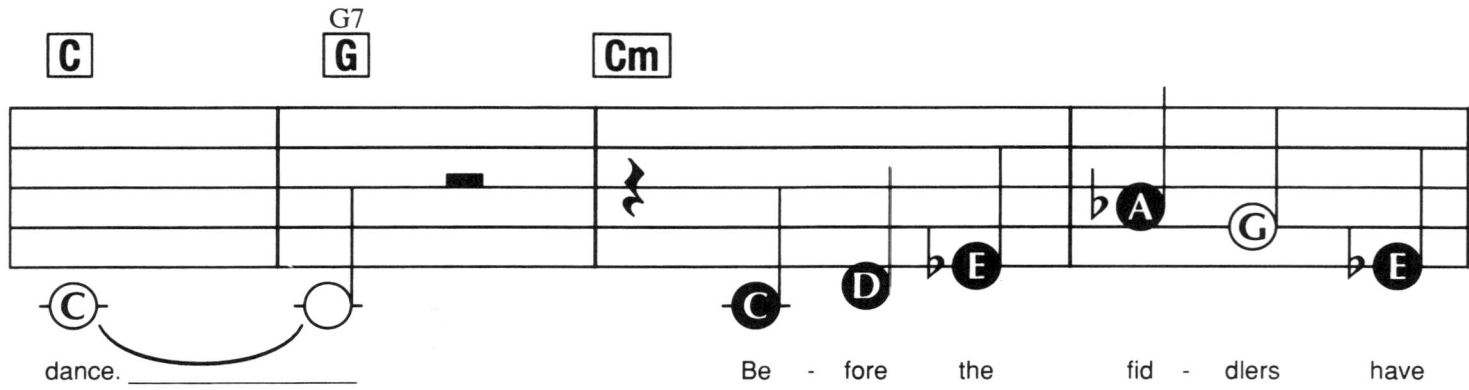

dance. _____ Be - fore the fid - dlers have

© Copyright 1935, 1936 by Irving Berlin
Copyright Renewed
International Copyright Secured   All Rights Reserved

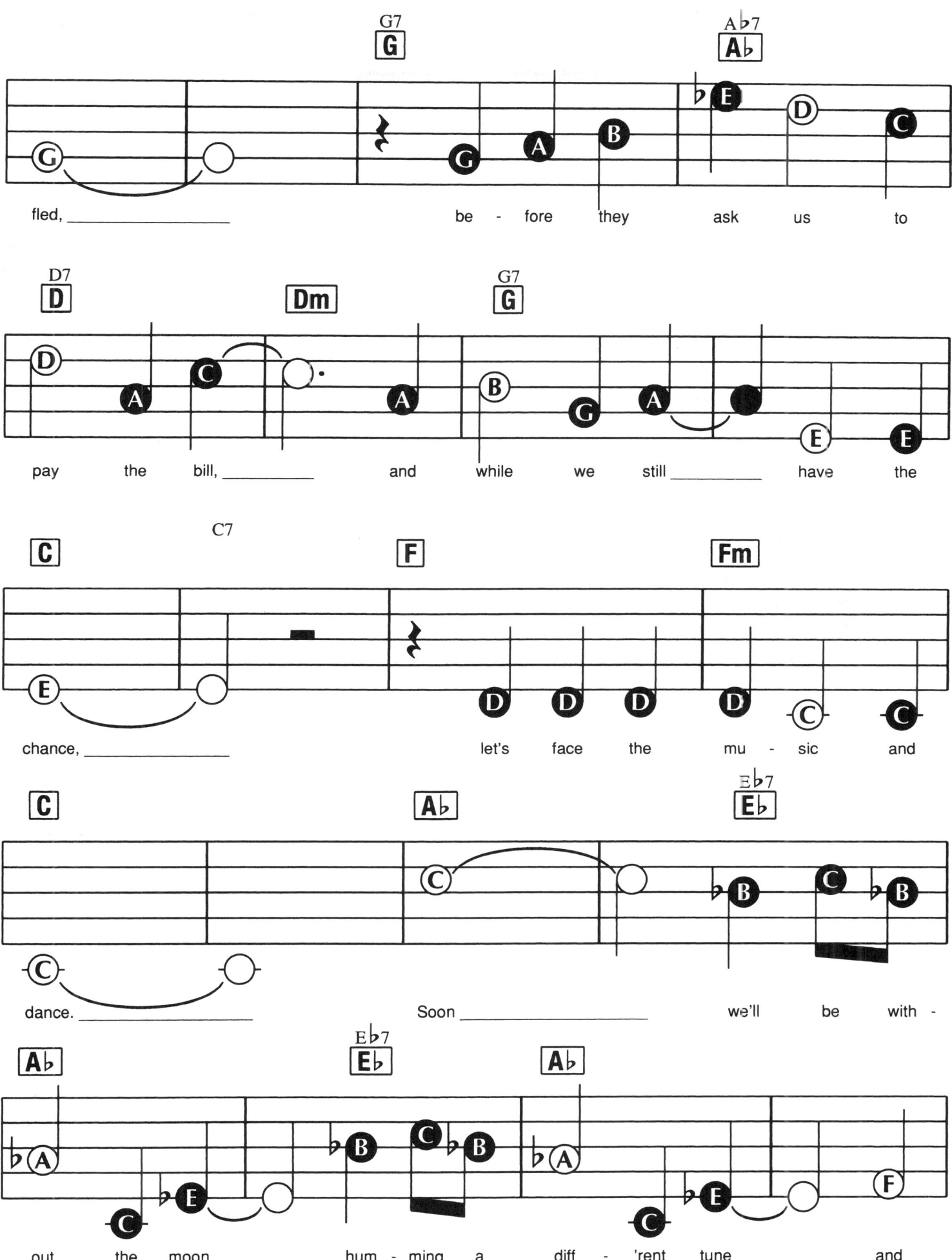

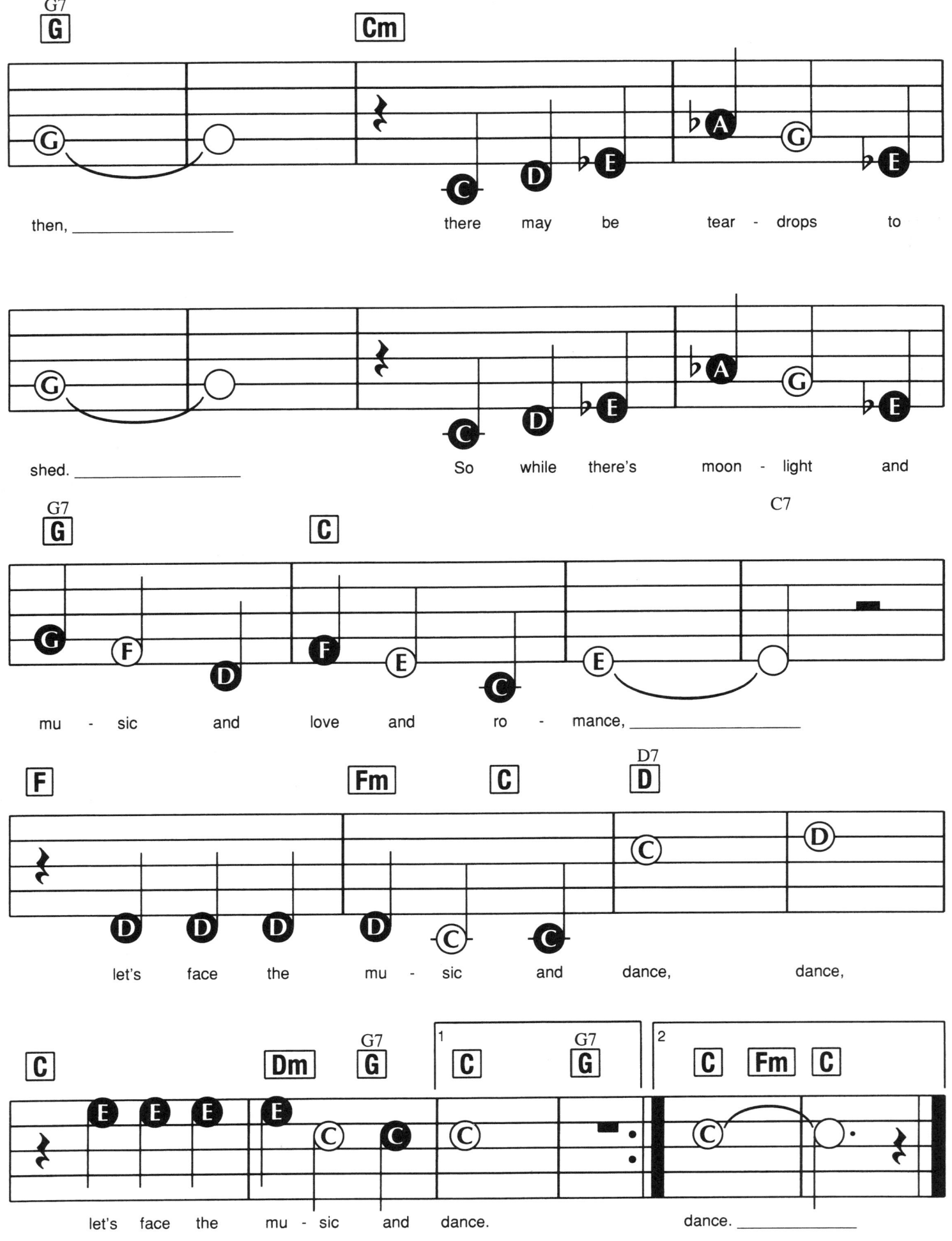

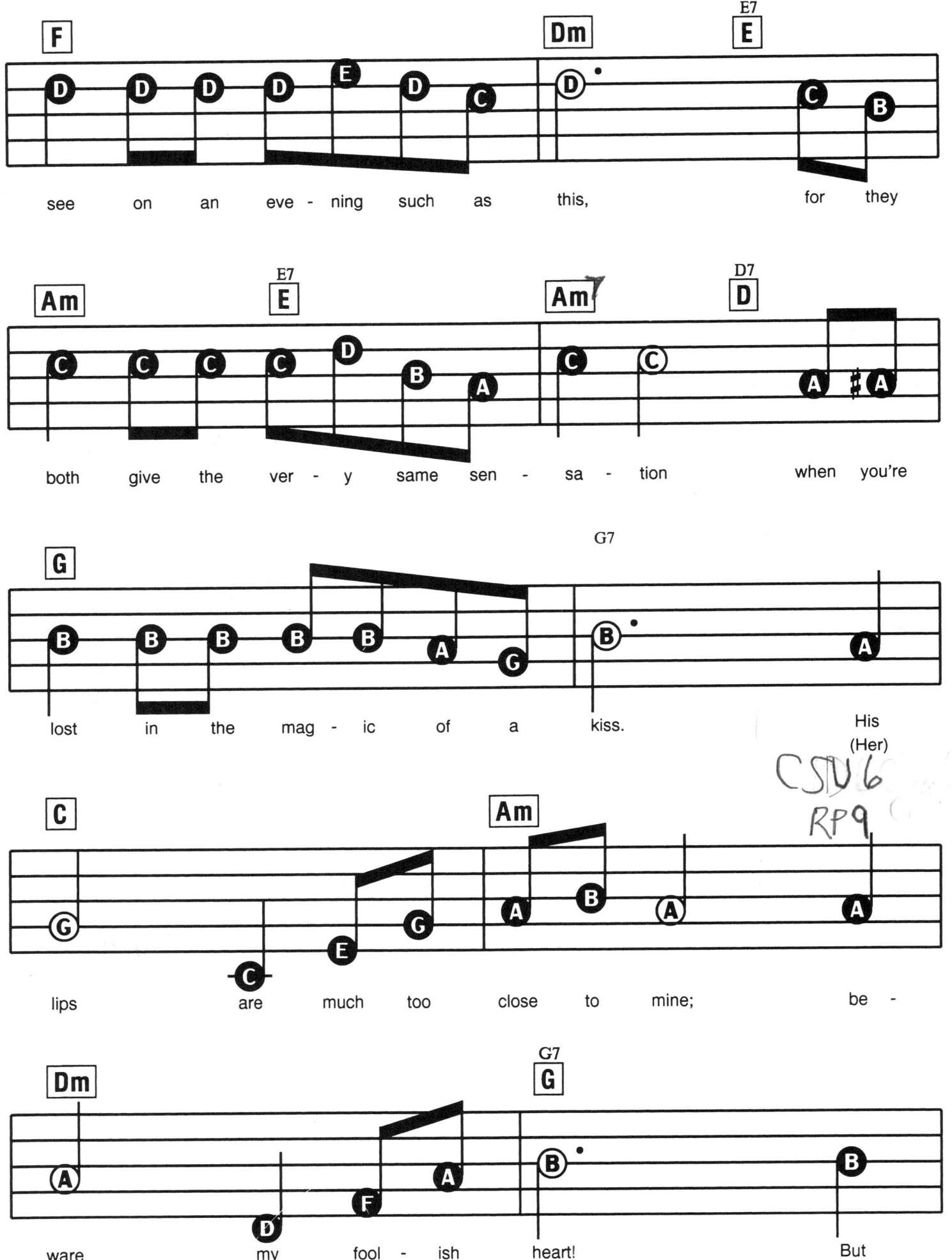

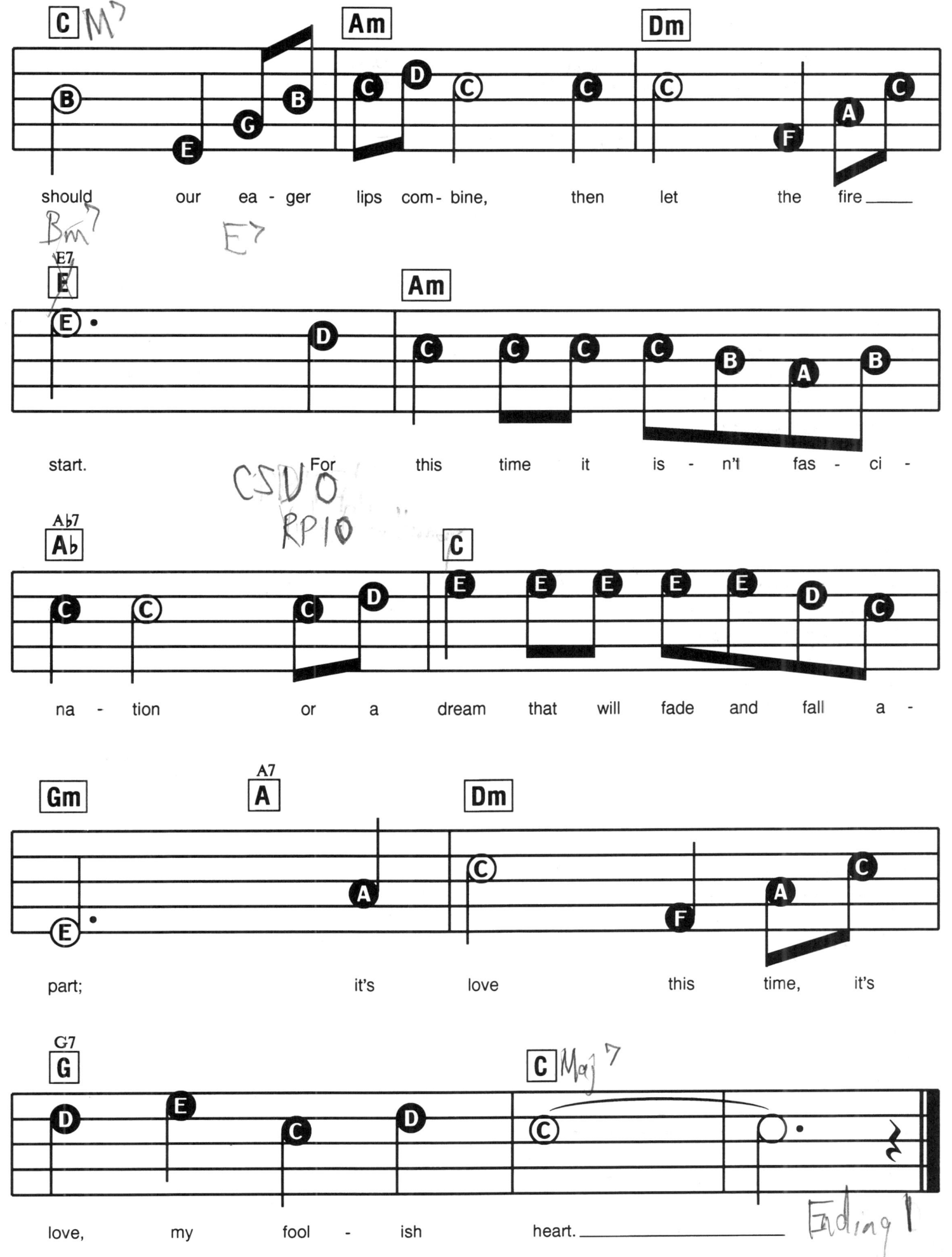

Like Someone in Love

Registration 2
Rhythm: Fox Trot or Swing

Words by Johnny Burke
Music by Jimmy Van Heusen

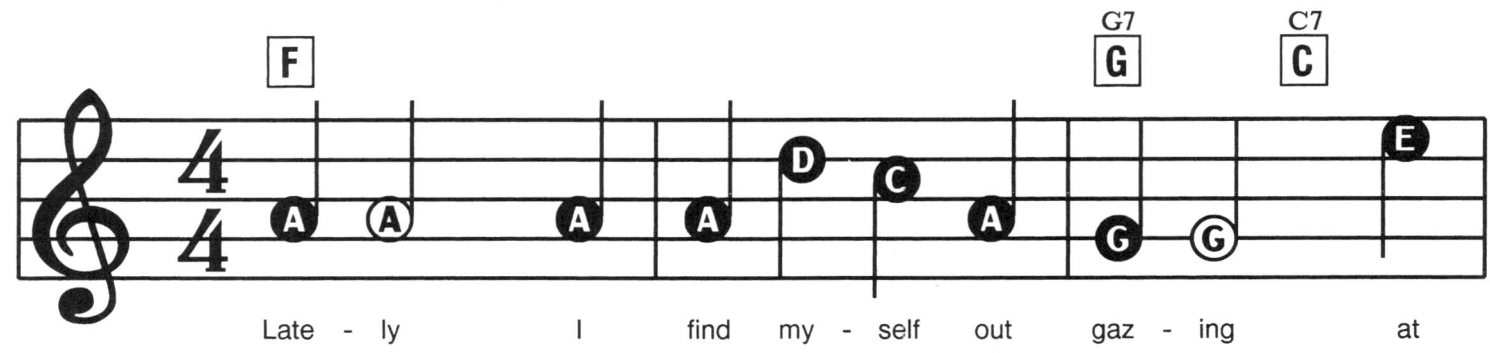

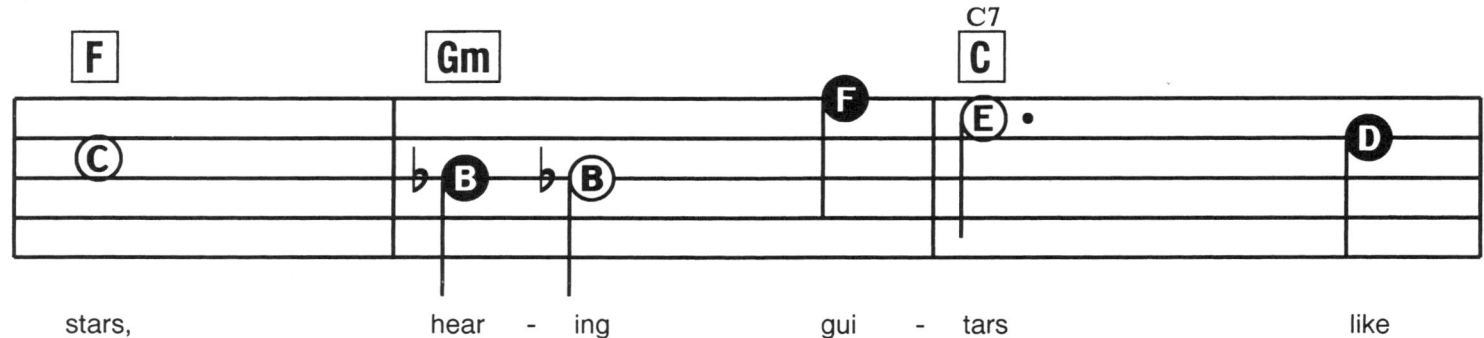

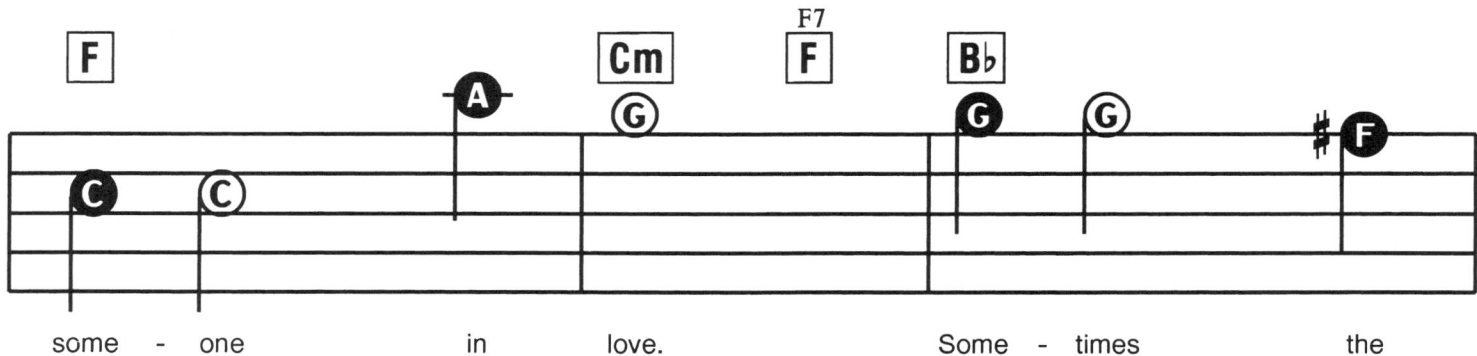

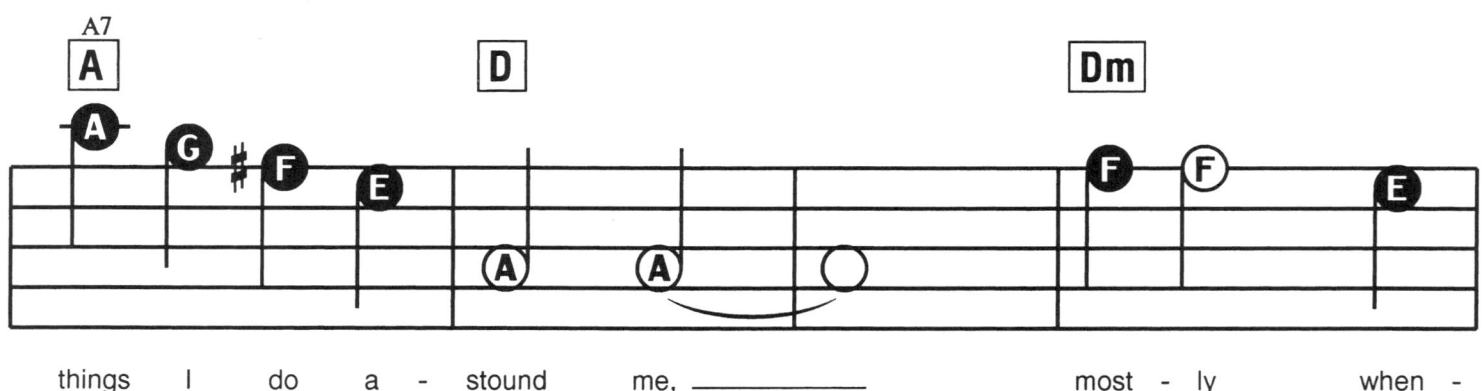

Copyright © 1944 by Burke & Van Heusen Inc., a division of Bourne Co. (ASCAP) and Dorsey Bros. Music, A Division of Music Sales Corporation
Copyright Renewed
International Copyright Secured   All Rights Reserved

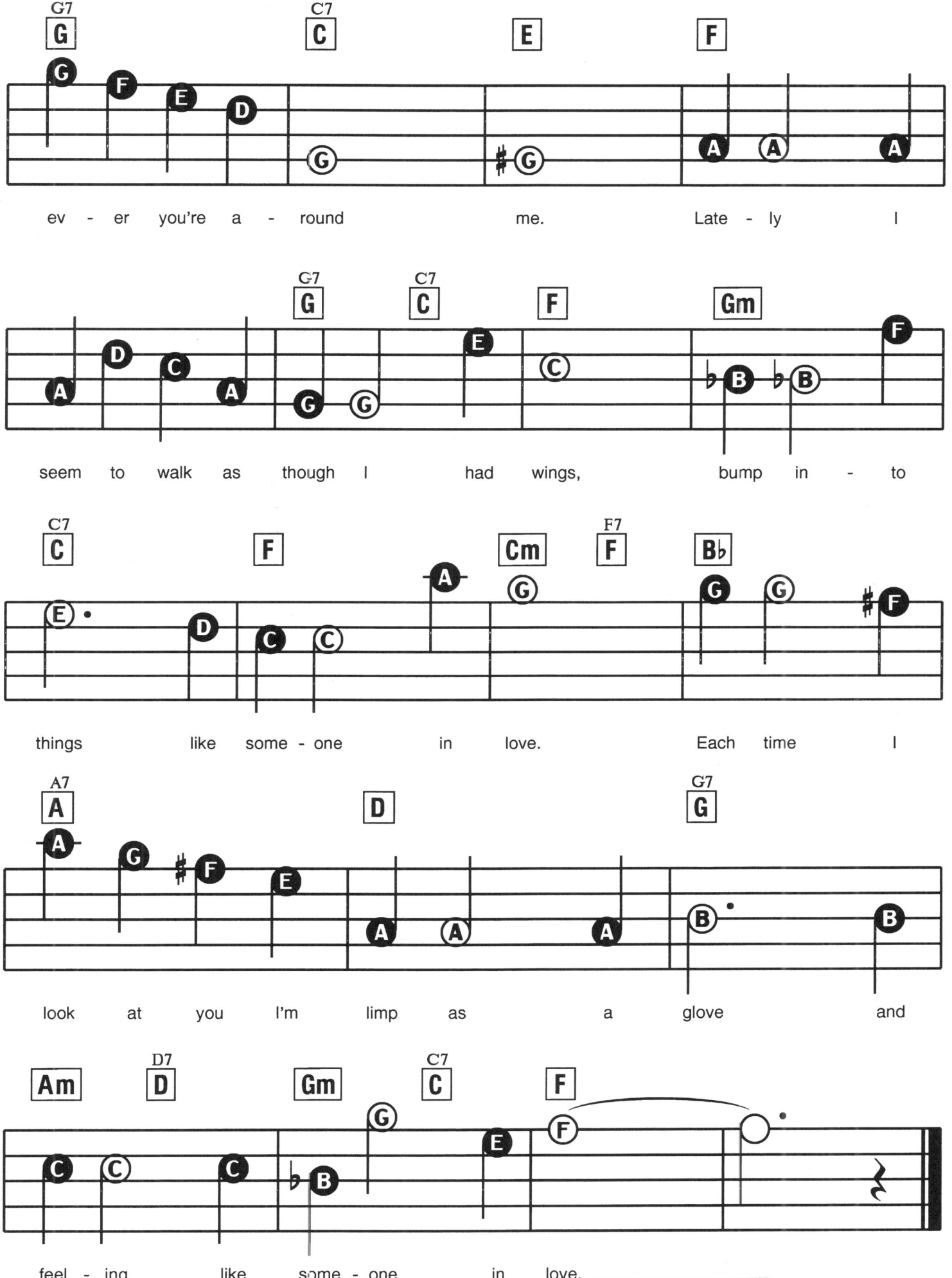

Love Is a Simple Thing

Registration 4
Rhythm: Fox Trot

Words by June Carroll
Music by Arthur Siegel

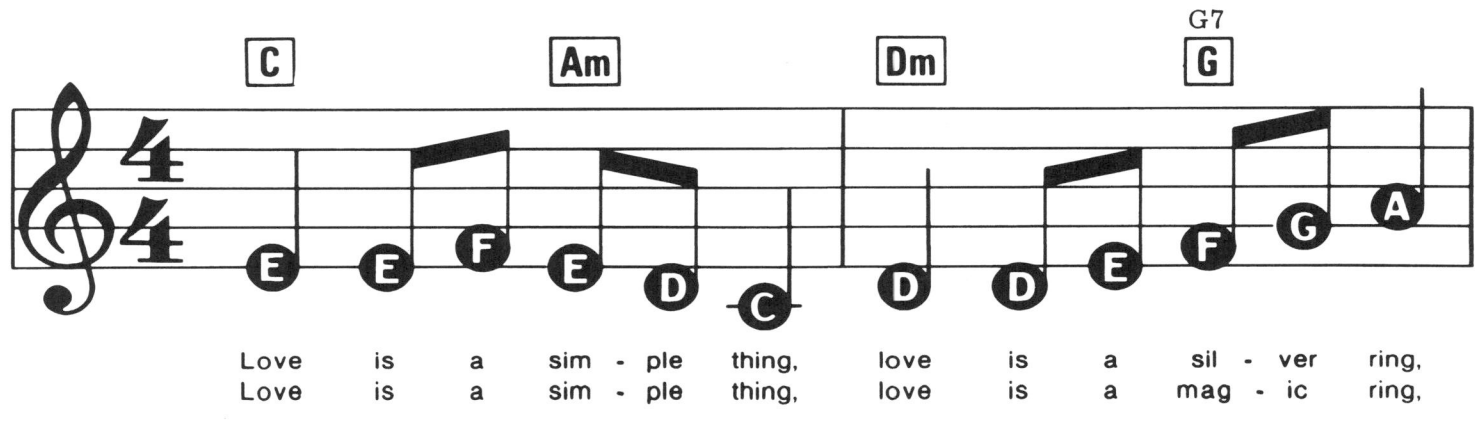
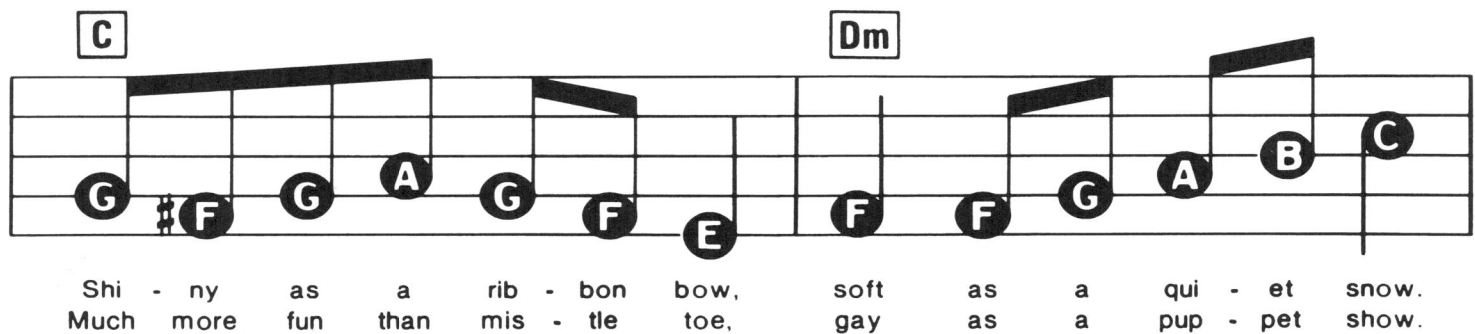
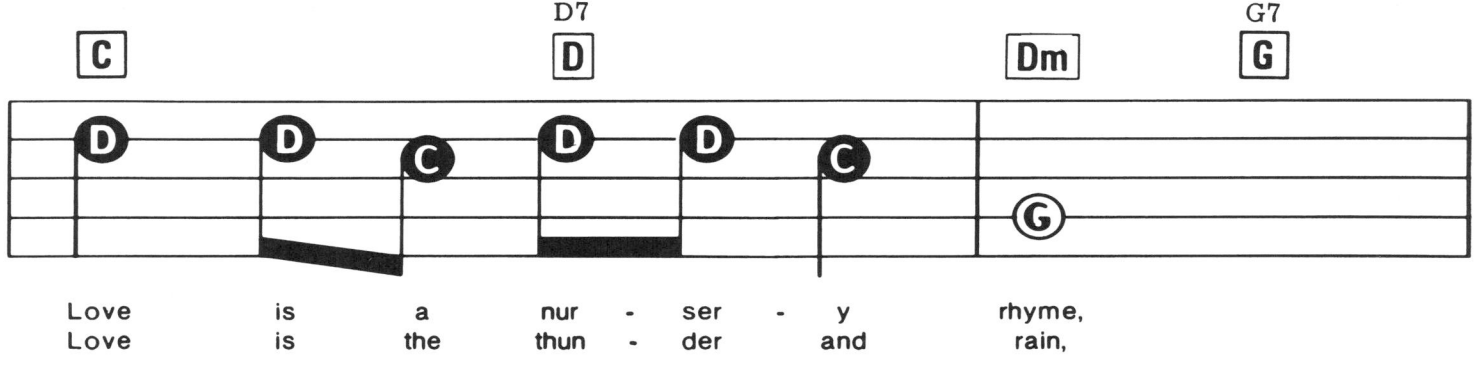
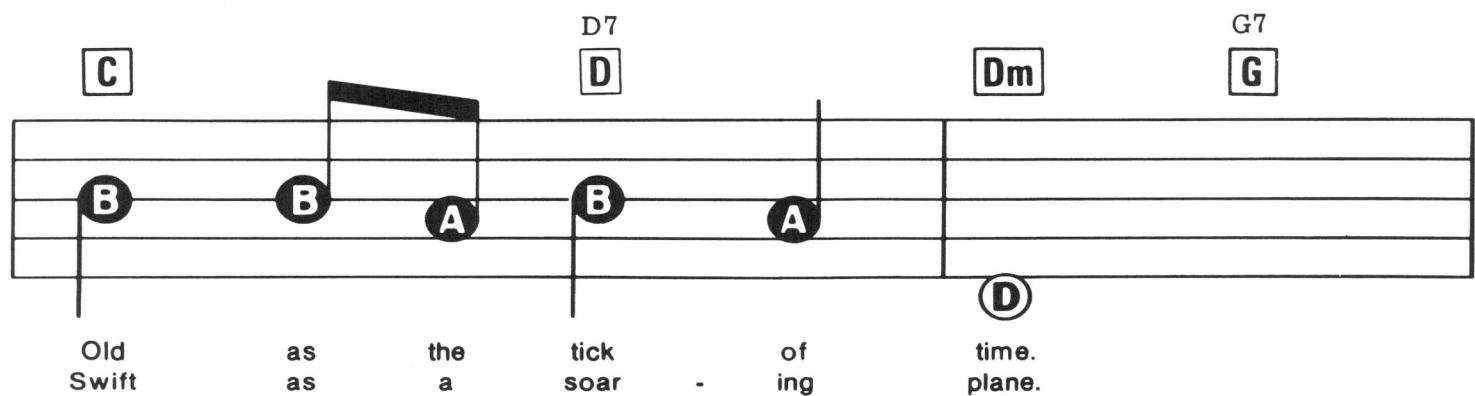

Copyright © 1952 by Chappell & Co.
Copyright Renewed
International Copyright Secured   All Rights Reserved

Love Letters
Theme from the Paramount Picture LOVE LETTERS

Registration 1
Rhythm: Swing

Words by Edward Heyman
Music by Victor Young

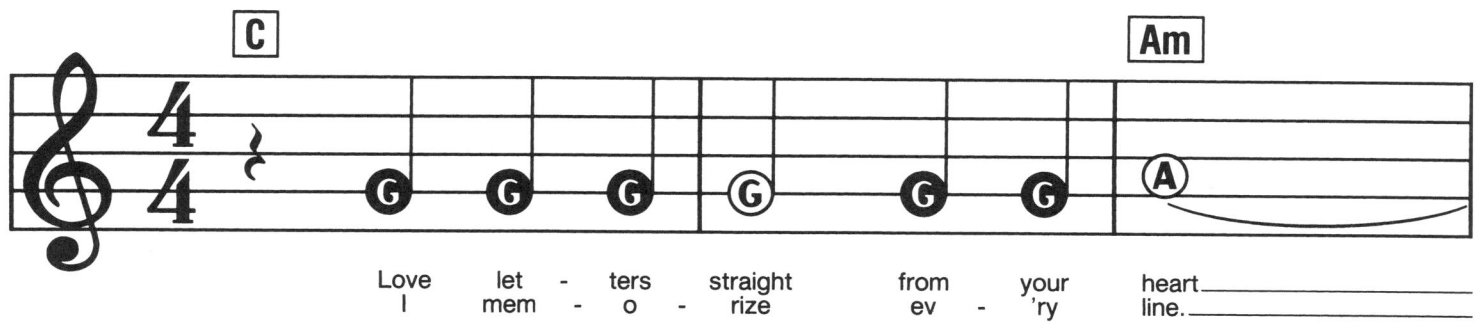

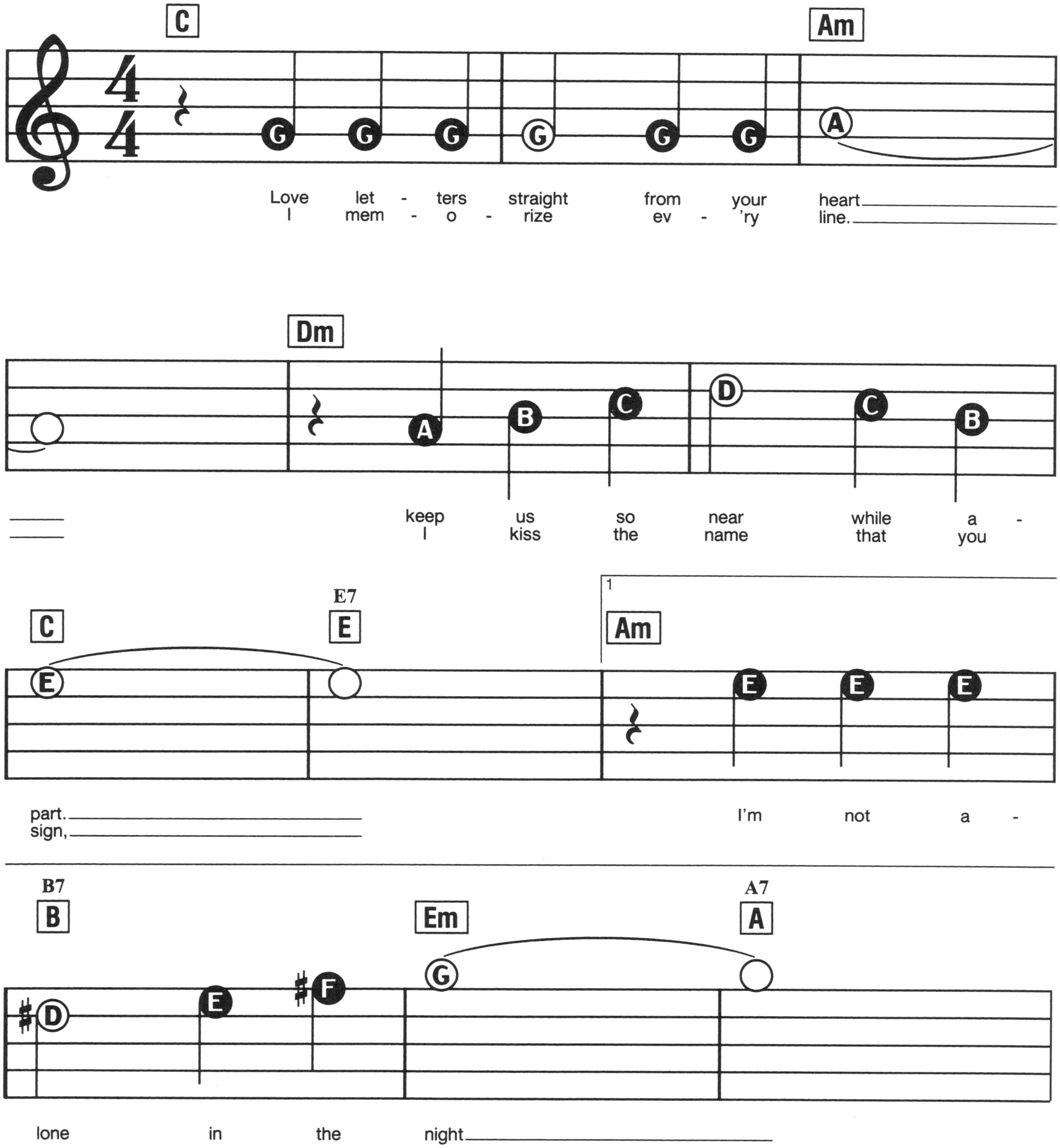

Love let-ters straight from your heart
I mem-o-rize ev-'ry line.

keep us so near while a-
I kiss the name that you

part.
sign,

I'm not a-

lone in the night

Copyright © 1945 Sony/ATV Music Publishing LLC
Copyright Renewed
All Rights Administered by Sony/ATV Music Publishing LLC, 8 Music Square West, Nashville, TN 37203
International Copyright Secured   All Rights Reserved

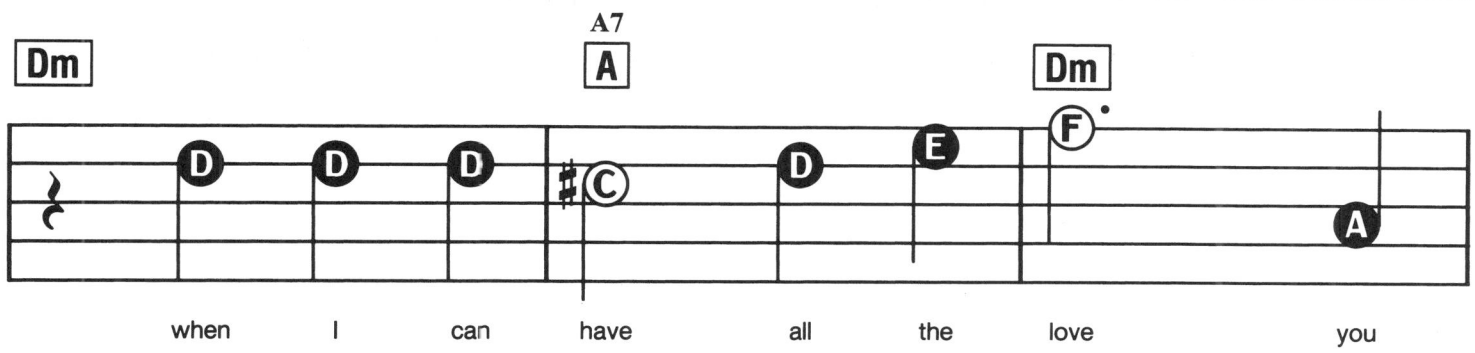
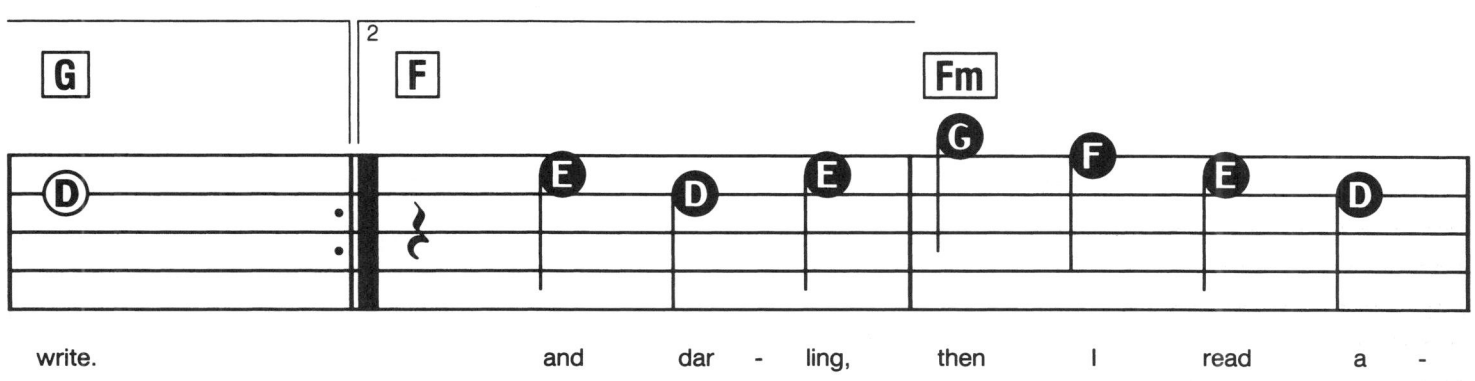
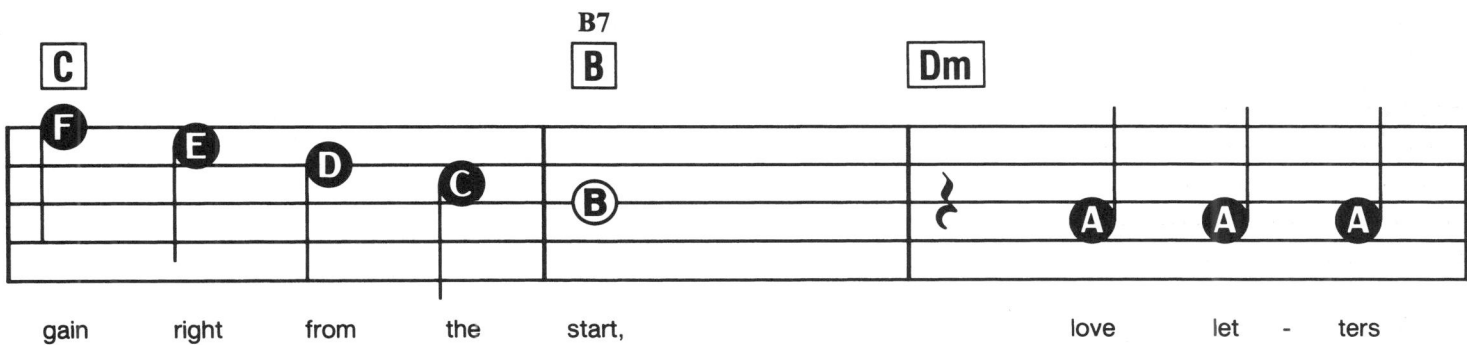
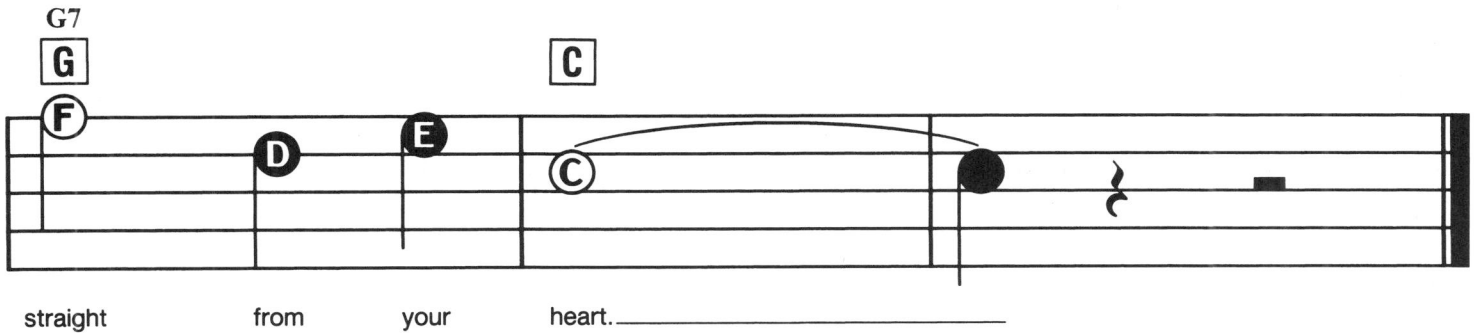

Lullaby of the Leaves

Registration 10
Rhythm: Fox Trot or Swing

Words by Joe Young
Music by Bernice Petkere

Cra-dle me where south-ern skies can watch me with a mil-lion eyes, Oh sing me to sleep, Lul-la-by of the leaves. Cov-er me with hea-ven's blue and let me dream a dream or two, Oh sing me to sleep, Lul-la-by of the leaves. I'm breez-ing a-long, a-long with the breeze, I'm

© 1932 IRVING BERLIN, INC.
© Renewed WAROCK CORP. and BOURNE CO. (ASCAP)
All Rights Reserved

D
hear - ing a song, a song thru the trees, Ooh ooh ooh ooh ooh
Gm
ooh. That pine mel - o - dy car - ess - ing the shore, Fa -
D
mil - iar to me, I've heard it be - fore ooh ooh ooh ooh
A7 Dm A7 D7
That's south-land, don't I feel it in my soul, and don't I know I've
Gm A7 Dm
reached my goal, Oh sing me to sleep, Lul - la - by of the leaves.

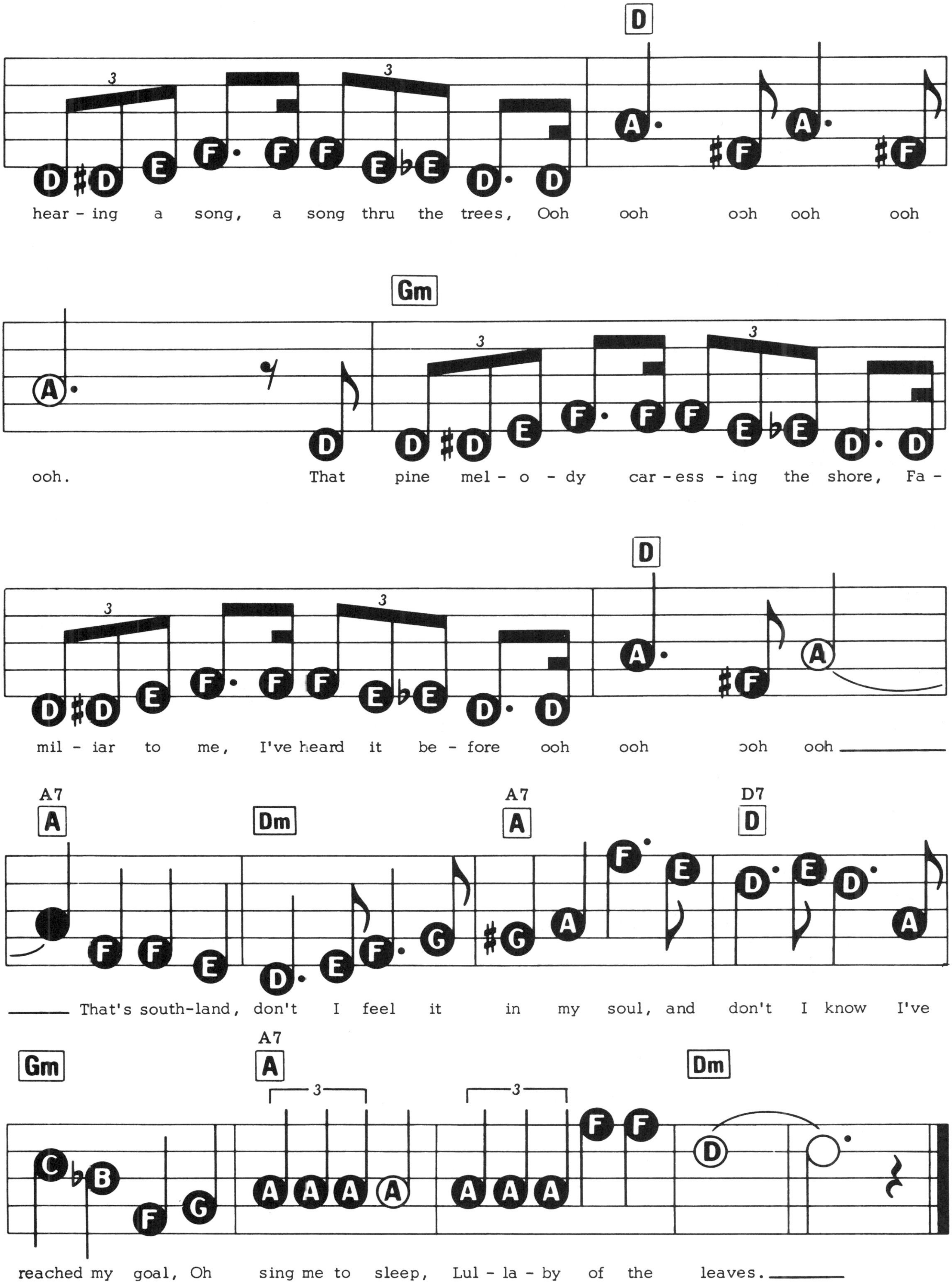

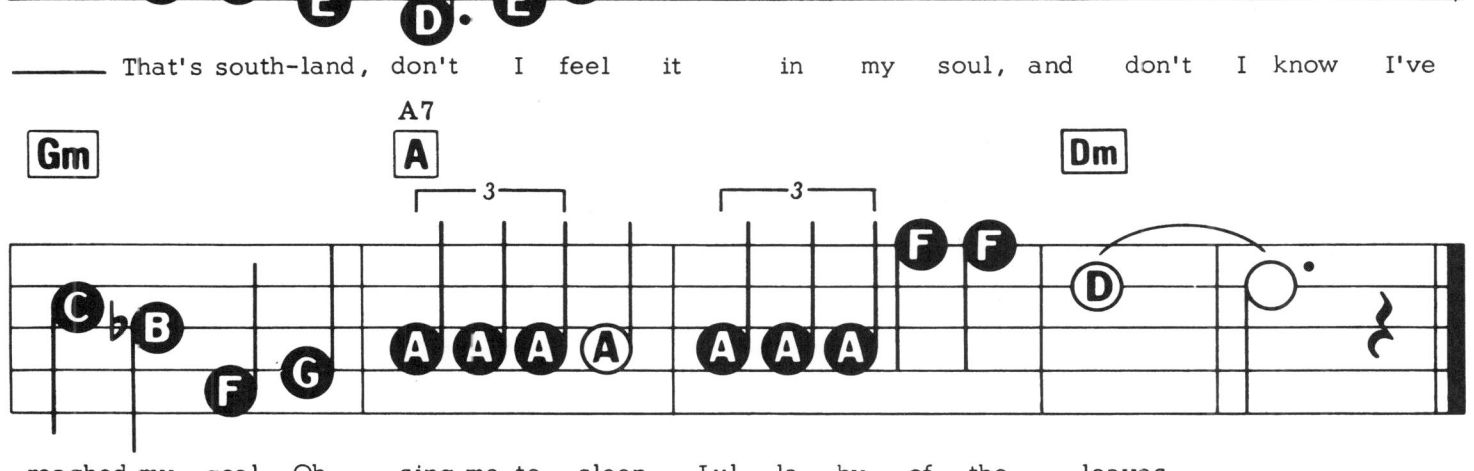

Midnight Sun

Registration 2
Rhythm: Fox Trot or Ballad

Words and Music by Lionel Hampton,
Sonny Burke and Johnny Mercer

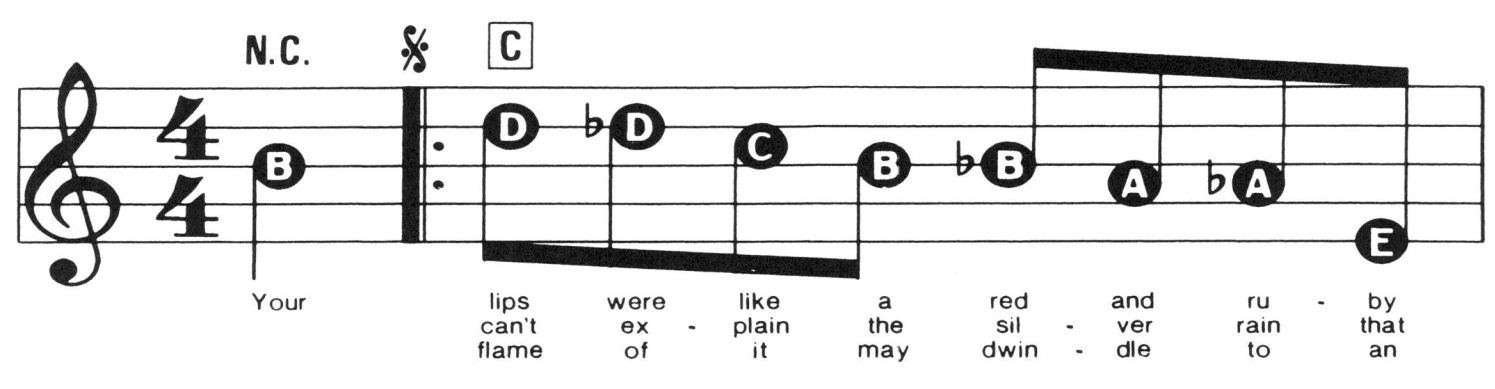

Your
lips were like a red and ru - by
can't ex - plain the sil - ver rain that
flame of it may dwin - dle to an

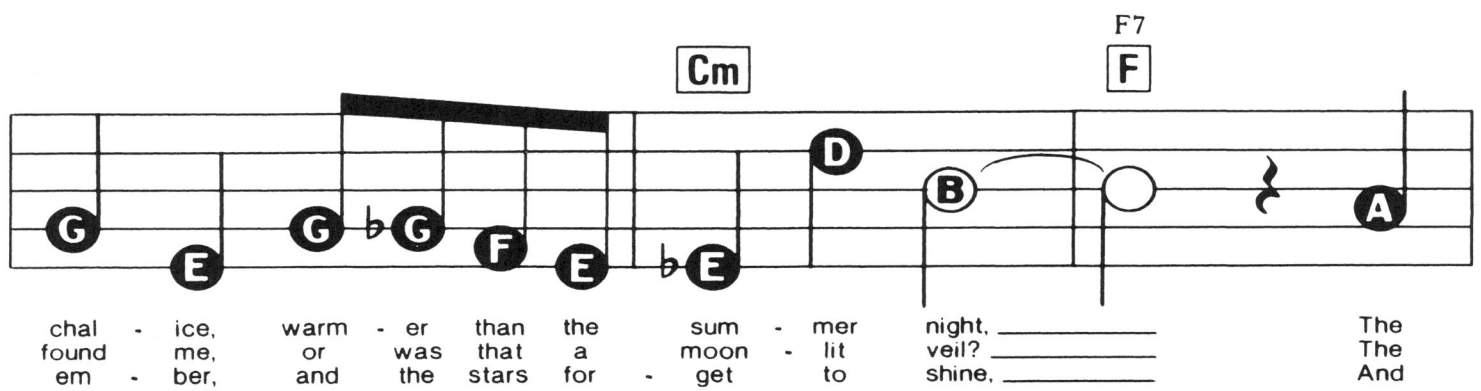

chal - ice, warm - er than the sum - mer night, ___ The
found me, or was that a moon - lit veil? ___ The
em - ber, and the stars for - get to shine, ___ And

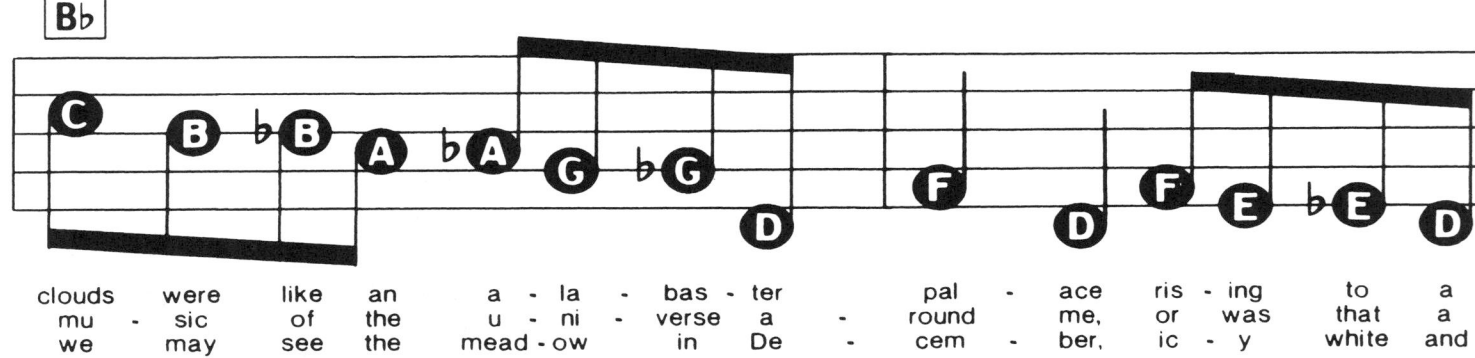

clouds were like an a - la - bas - ter pal - ace ris - ing to a
mu - sic of the u - ni - verse a - round me, or was that a
we may see the mead - ow in De - cem - ber, ic - y white and

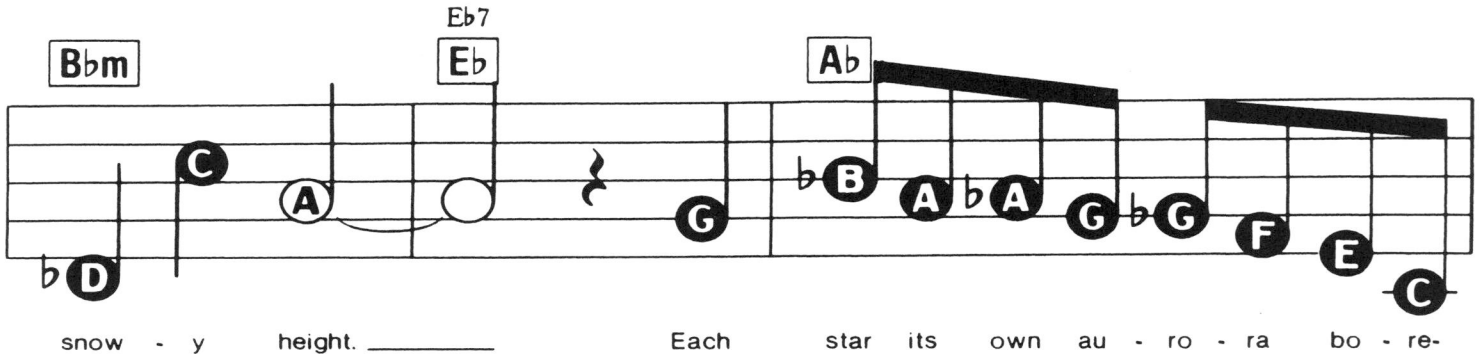

snow - y height. ___ Each star its own au - ro - ra bo - re -
night - in - gale? ___ And then your arms mi - rac - u - lous - ly
crys - tal - line. ___ But, oh, my dar - ling al - ways I'll re -

Copyright © 1947 (Renewed) by Regent Music Corporation (BMI) and Crystal Music Publishers, Inc. (ASCAP)
International Copyright Secured All Rights Reserved
Used by Permission

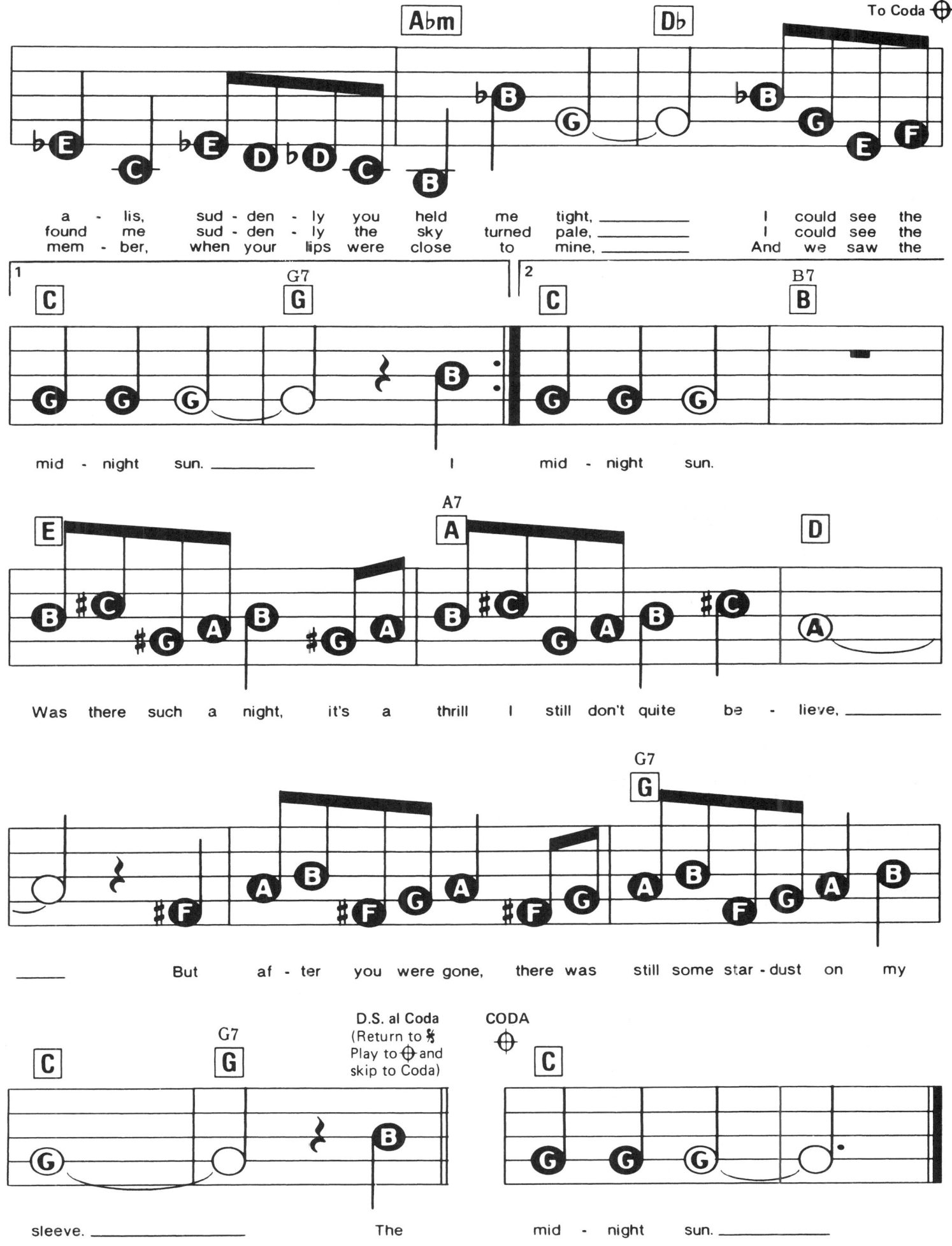

My Heart Belongs to Daddy
from LEAVE IT TO ME

Registration 7
Rhythm: Swing or Jazz

Words and Music by
Cole Porter

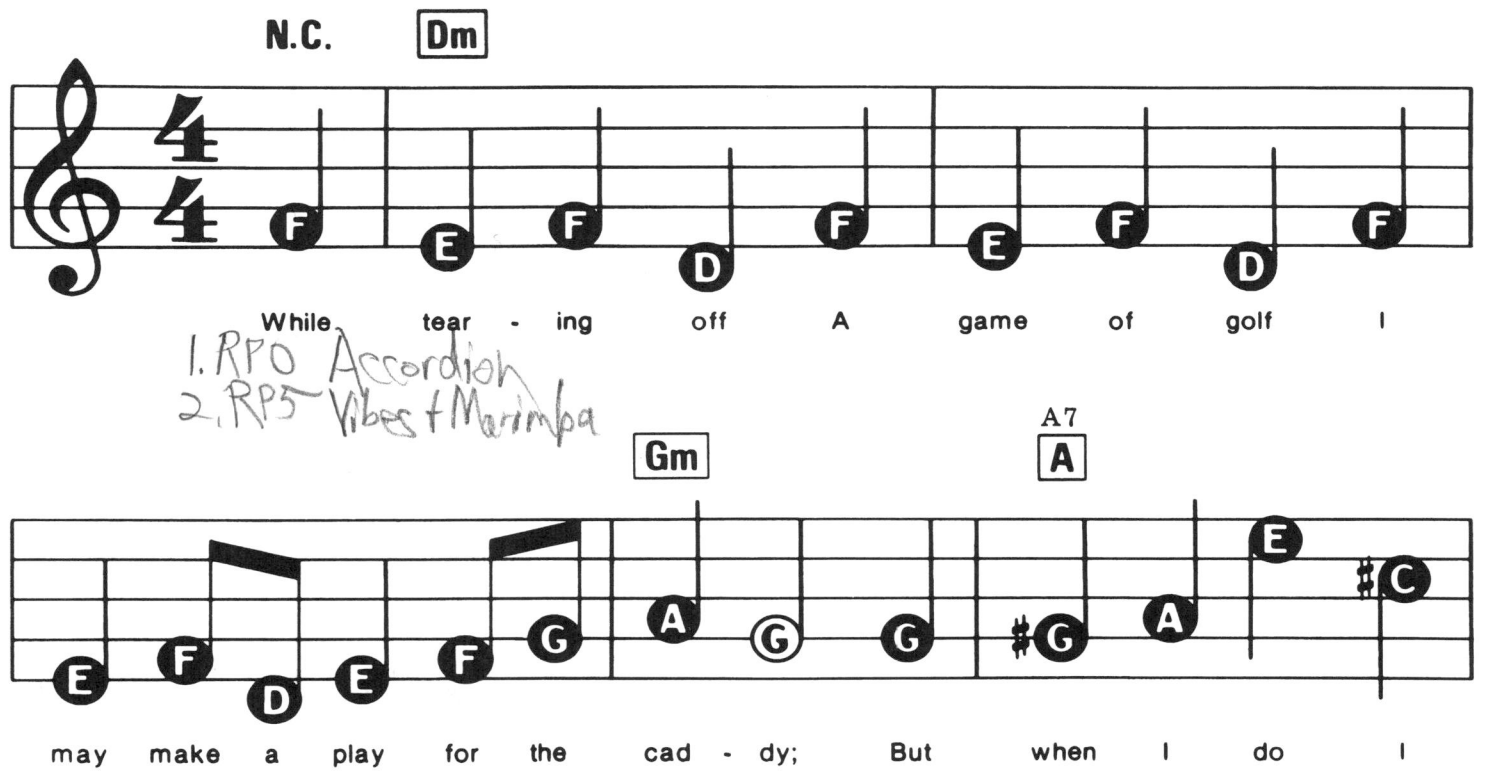

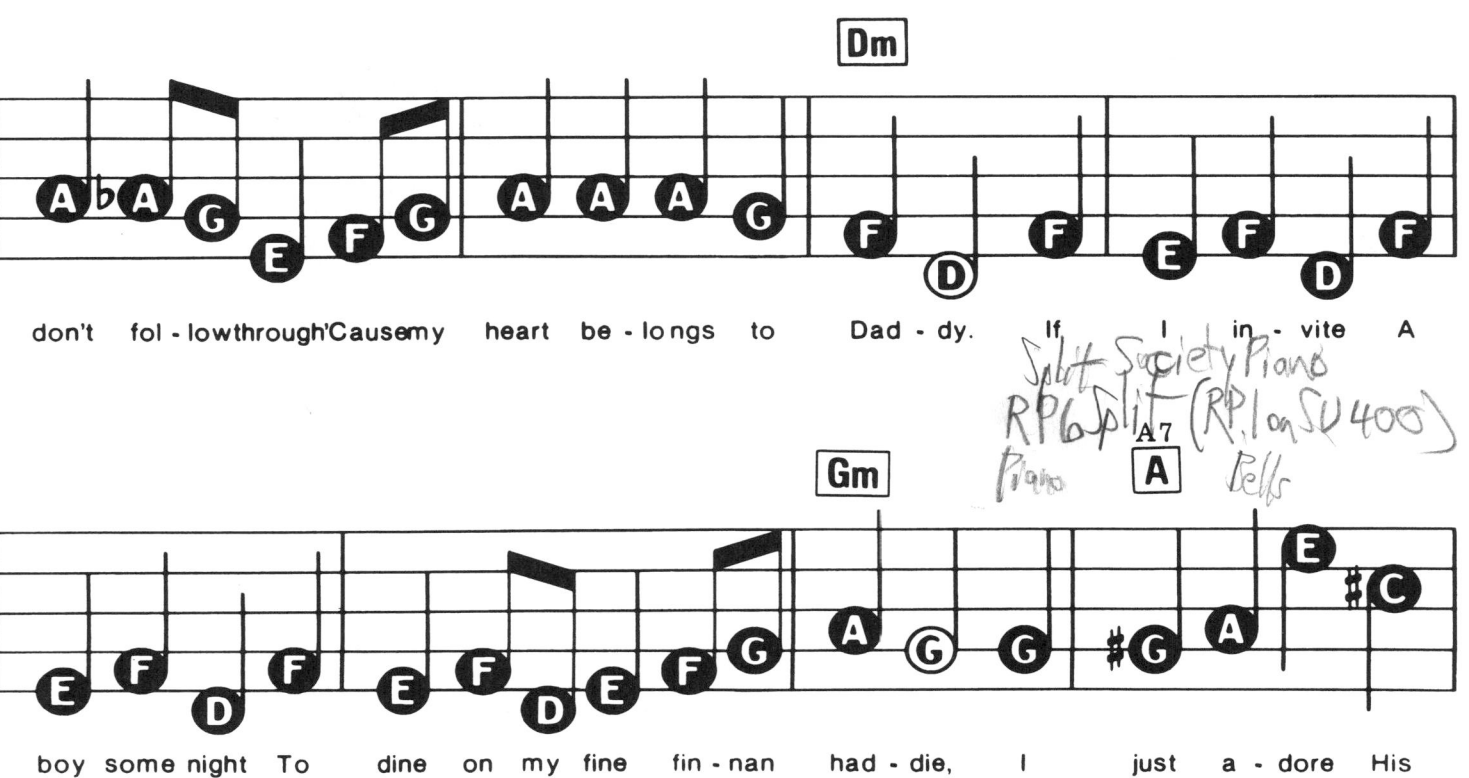

Copyright © 1938 by Chappell & Co.
Copyright Renewed, Assigned to Robert H. Montgomery, Trustee of the Cole Porter Musical and Literary Property Trusts
Chappell & Co. owner of publication and allied rights throughout the world
International Copyright Secured   All Rights Reserved

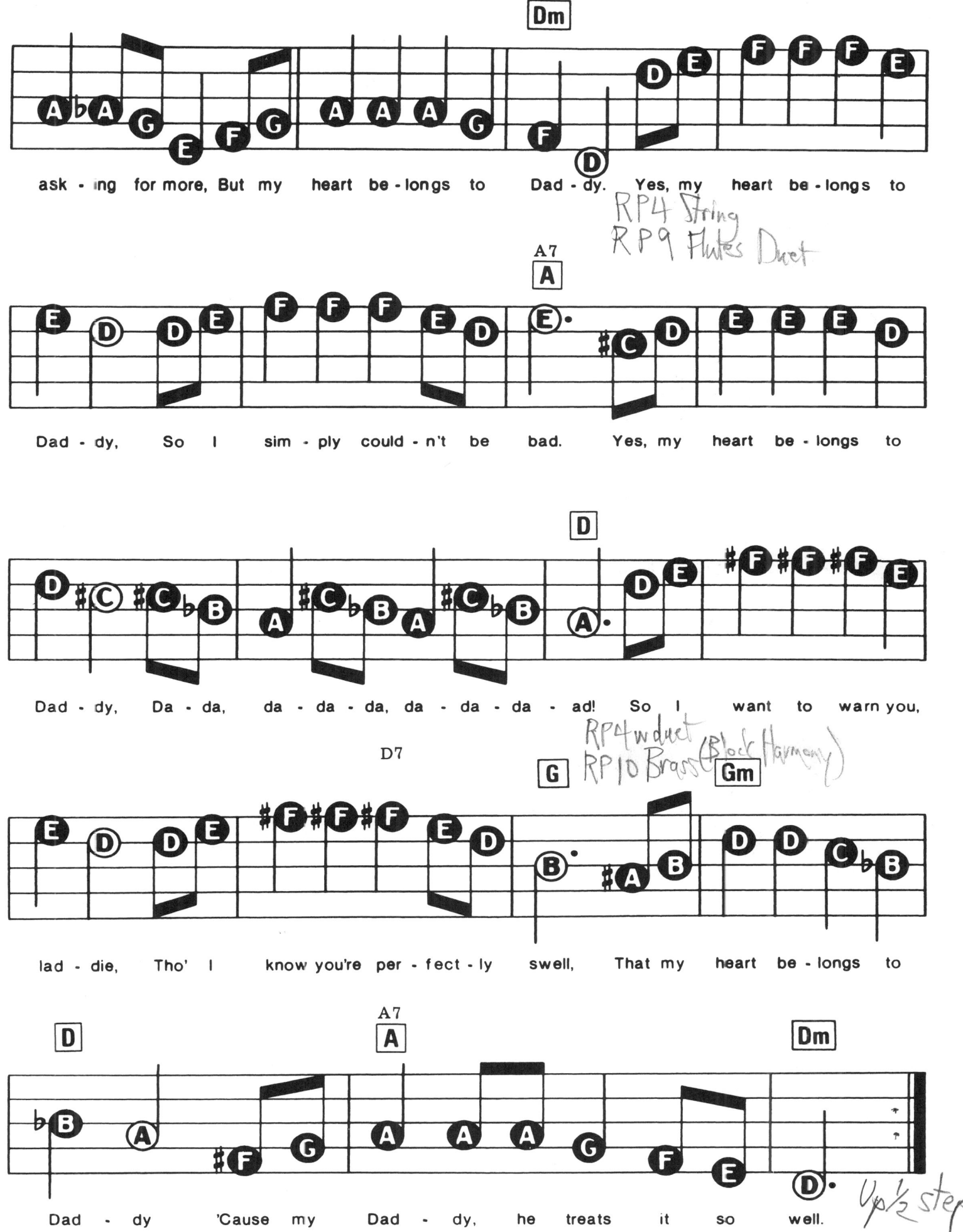

My Old Flame
from the Paramount Picture BELLE OF THE NINETIES

Registration 4
Rhythm: Swing

Words and Music by Arthur Johnston
and Sam Coslow

My old flame, I can't even think of his name,
but it's funny now and then how my thoughts go flashing back again to my old flame.

My old flame, my new lovers all seem too tame,
for I haven't now met a gent so magnificent or elegant as my old flame.

I've met so many who had fascinatin' ways, a fascinatin' gaze in their

Copyright © 1934 Sony/ATV Music Publishing LLC
Copyright Renewed
All Rights Administered by Sony/ATV Music Publishing LLC, 8 Music Square West, Nashville, TN 37203
International Copyright Secured   All Rights Reserved

My Shining Hour
from the Motion Picture THE SKY'S THE LIMIT

Registration 7
Rhythm: Fox Trot or Swing

Lyric by Johnny Mercer
Music by Harold Arlen

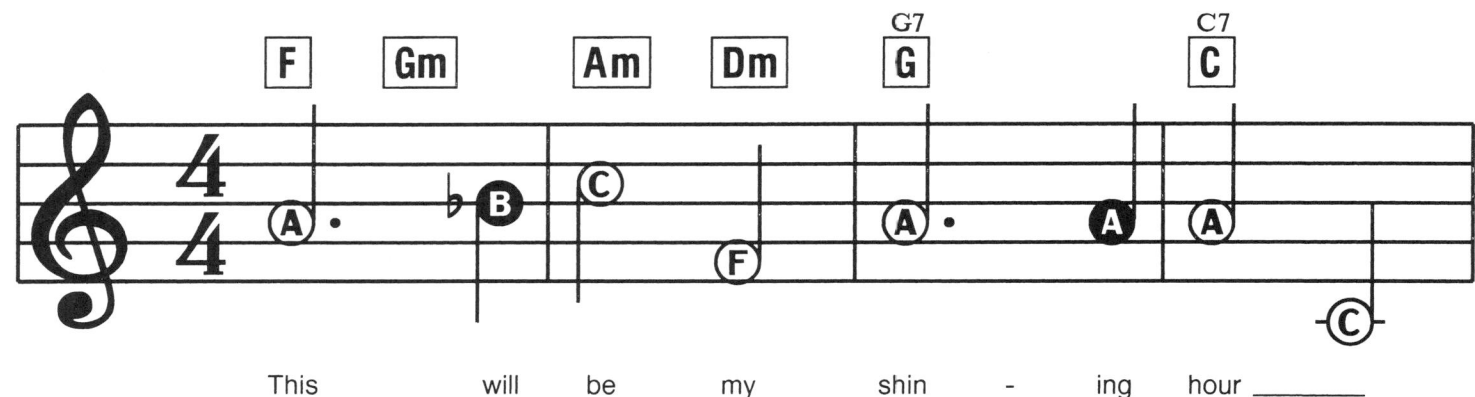

This will be my shin - ing hour

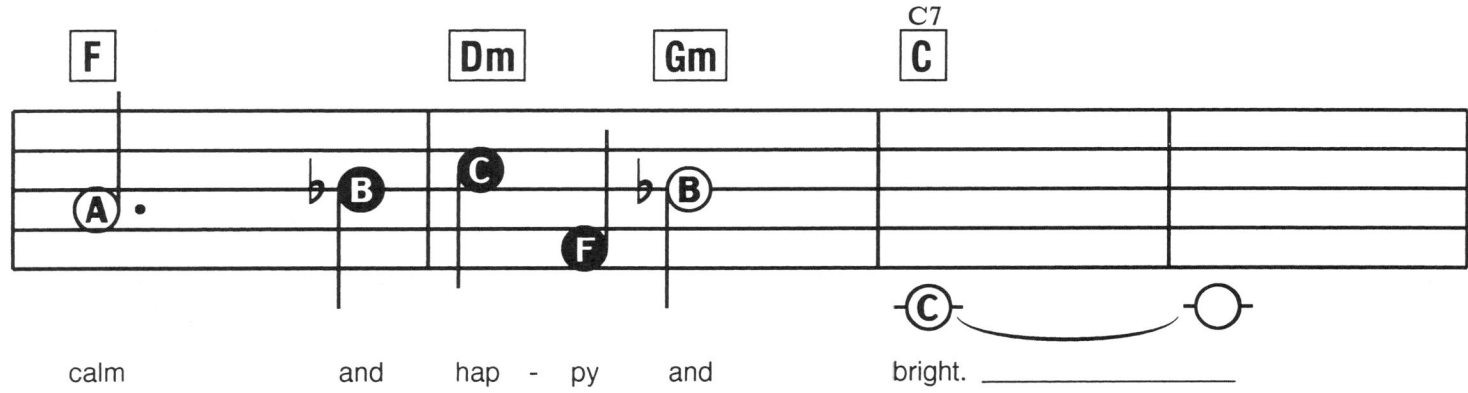

calm and hap - py and bright.

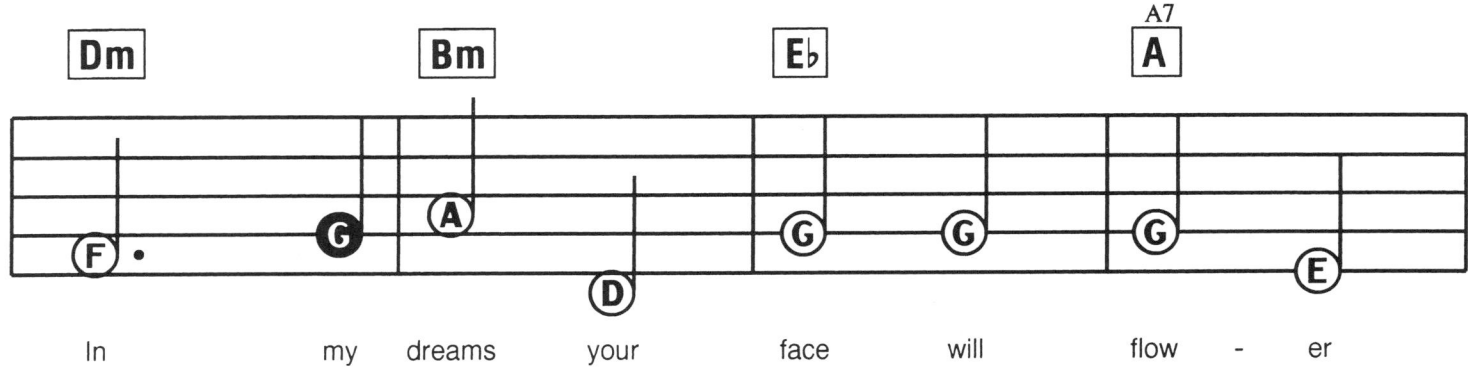

In my dreams your face will flow - er

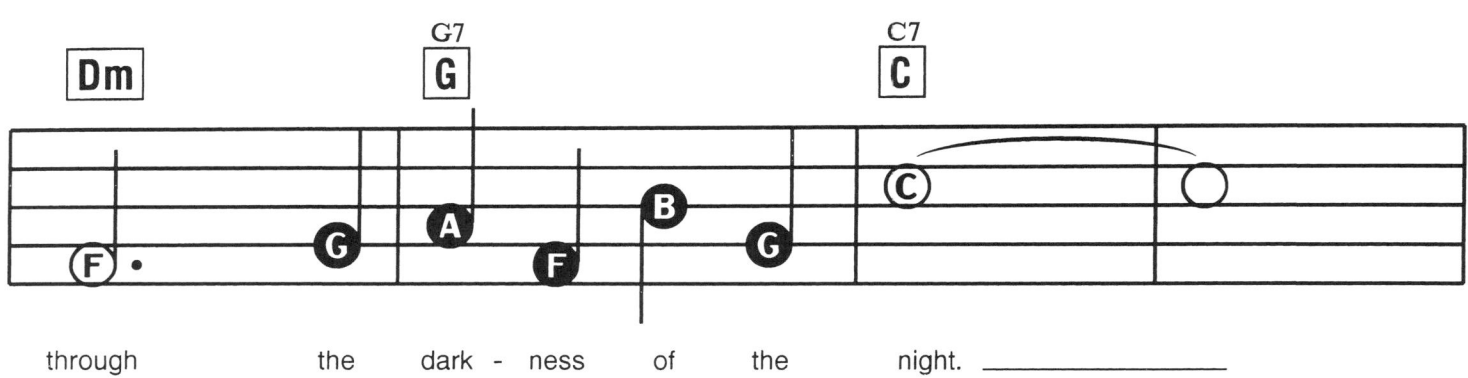

through the dark - ness of the night.

© 1943 (Renewed) HARWIN MUSIC CO.
All Rights Reserved

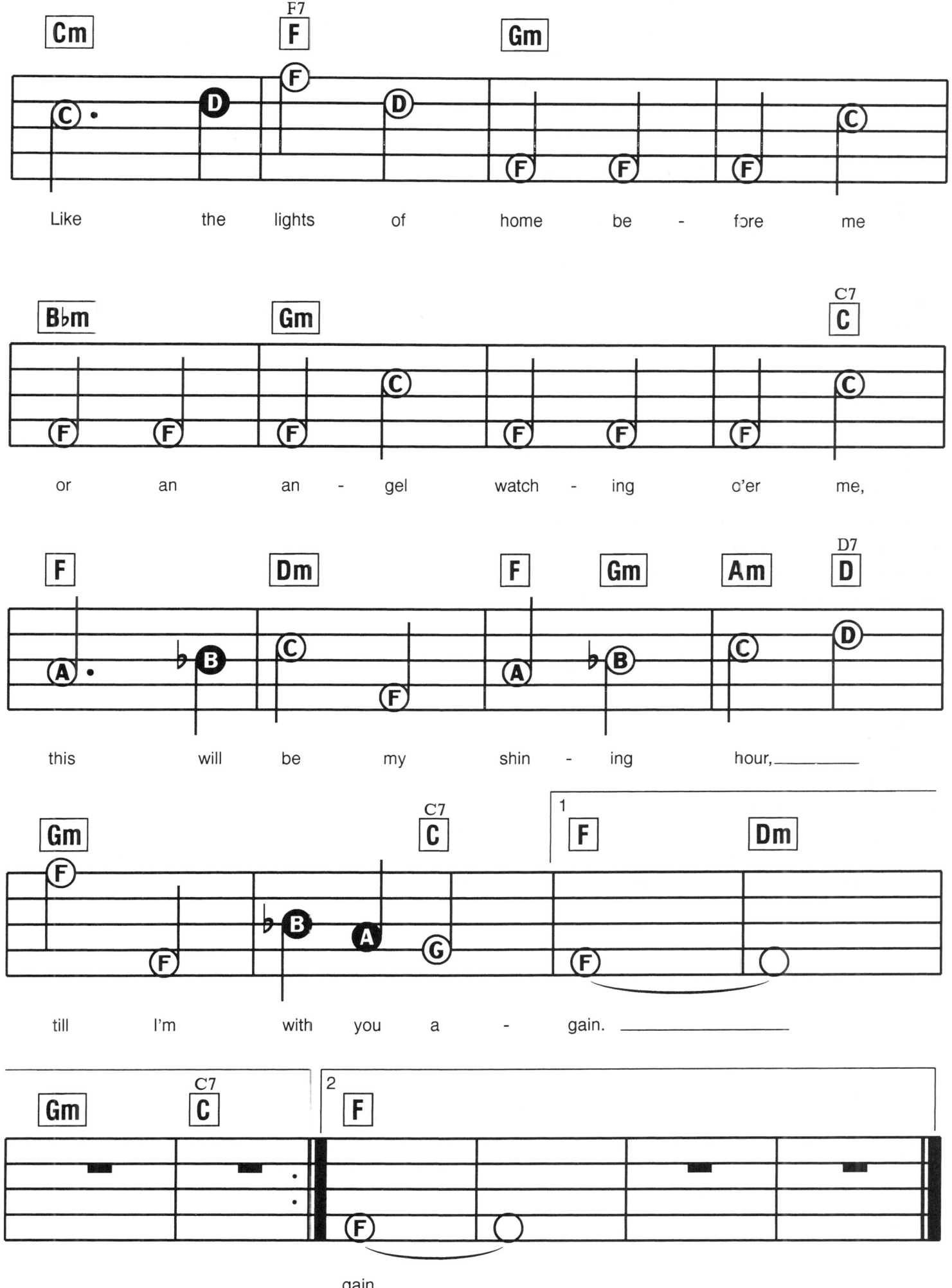

My Ship
from the Musical Production LADY IN THE DARK

Registration 9
Rhythm: Fox Trot or Swing

Words by Ira Gershwin
Music by Kurt Weill

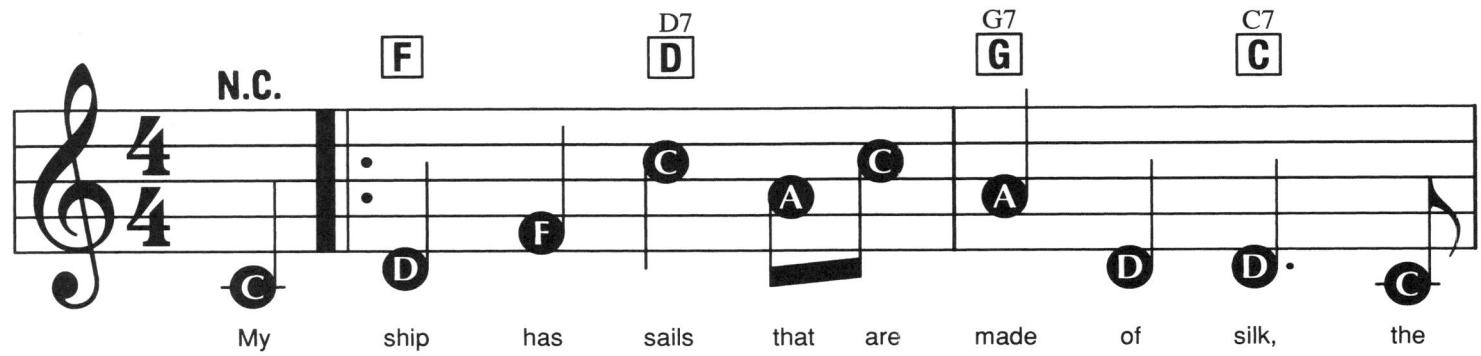

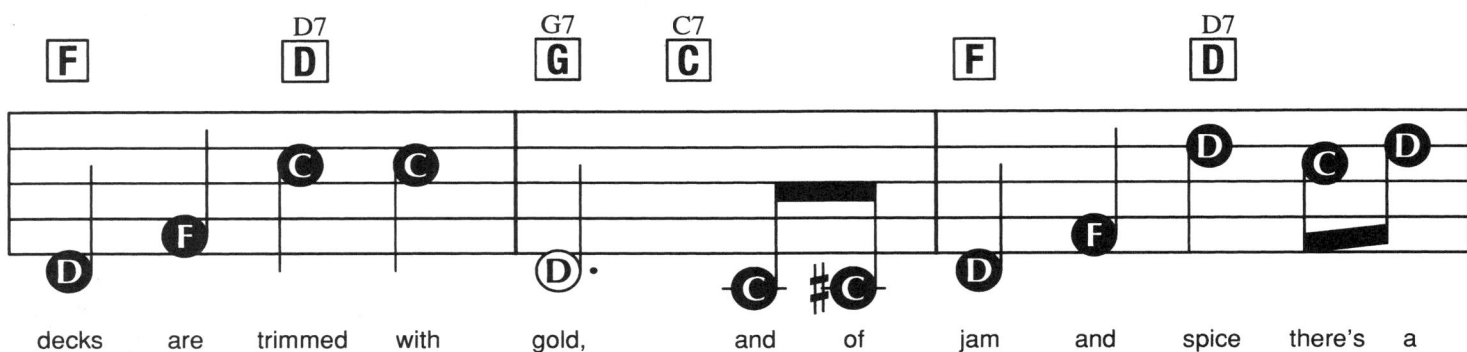

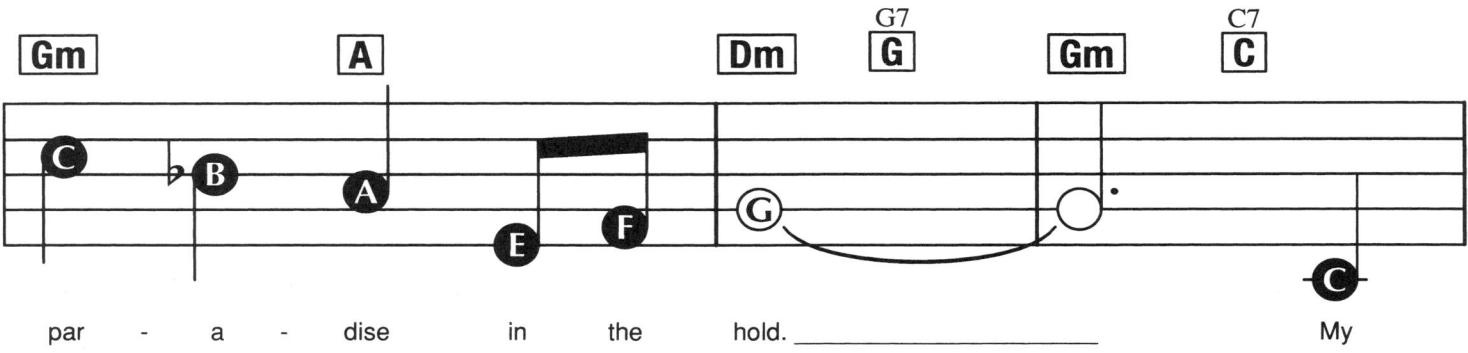

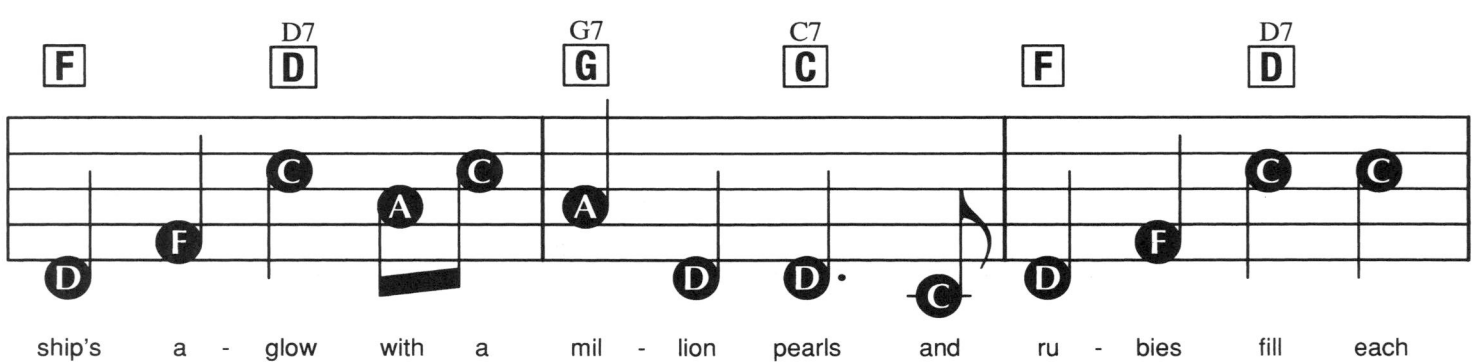

TRO - © Copyright 1941 (Renewed) Hampshire House Publishing Corp., New York and Chappell & Co., Los Angeles, CA
International Copyright Secured
All Rights Reserved Including Public Performance For Profit
Used by Permission

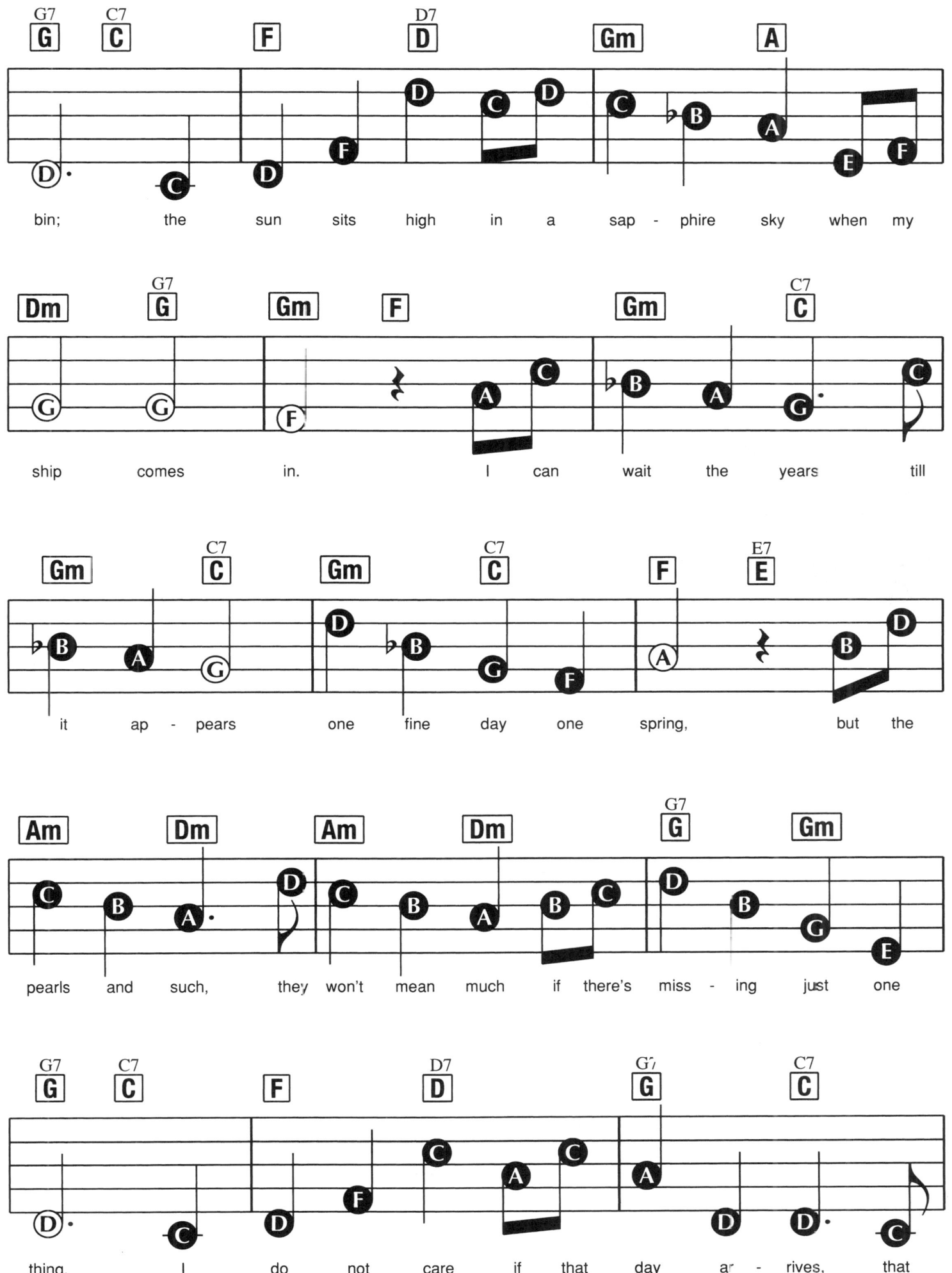

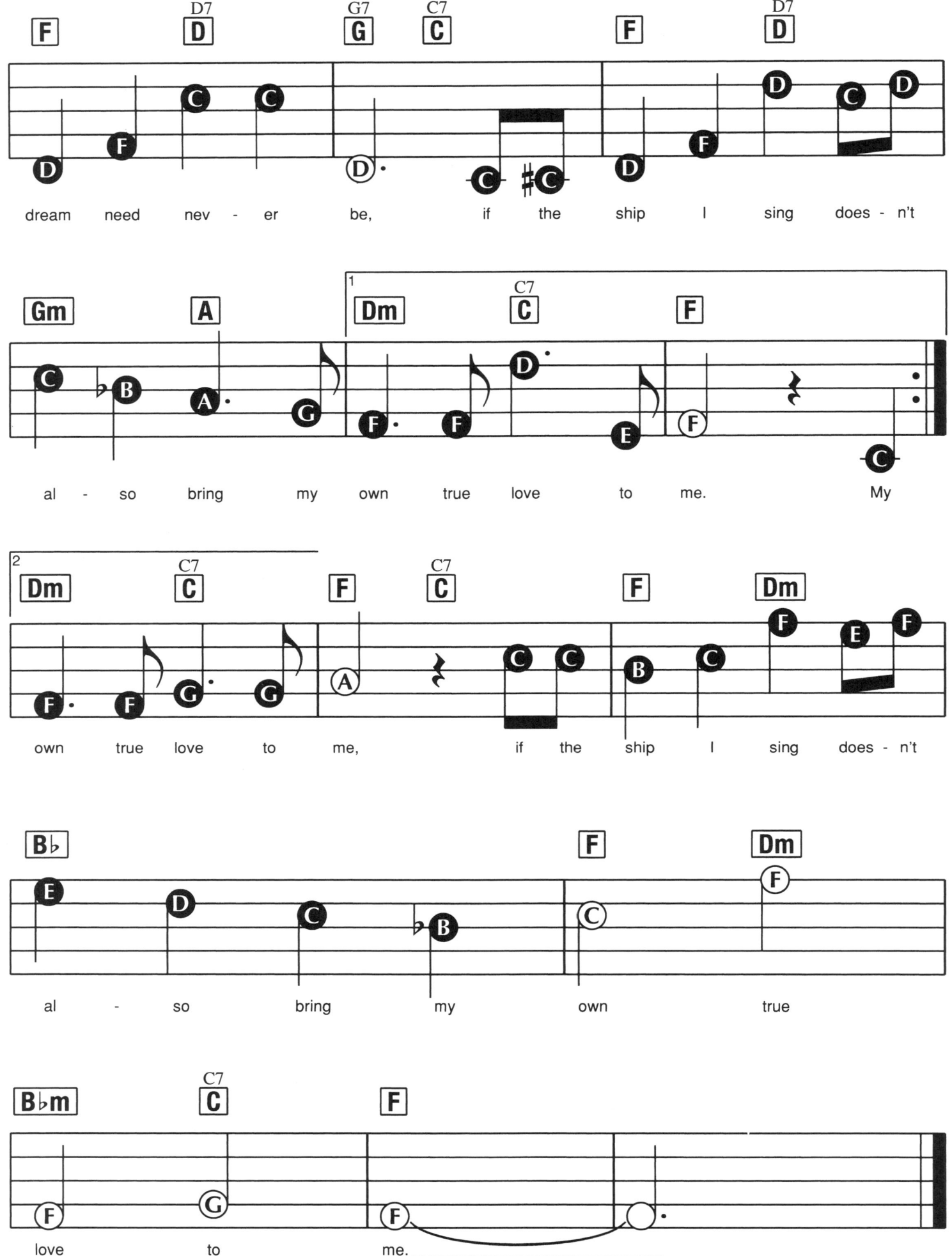

Never Let Me Go
from the Paramount Picture THE SCARLET HOUR

Registration 1
Rhythm: Ballad

Words and Music by Jay Livingston
and Ray Evans

Nev-er let me go! Love me much too much!

If you let me go life would lose its touch!

What would I be with-out you? There's

no place for me with-out you!

Copyright © 1956 Sony/ATV Music Publishing LLC
Copyright Renewed
All Rights Administered by Sony/ATV Music Publishing LLC, 8 Music Square West, Nashville, TN 37203
International Copyright Secured All Rights Reserved

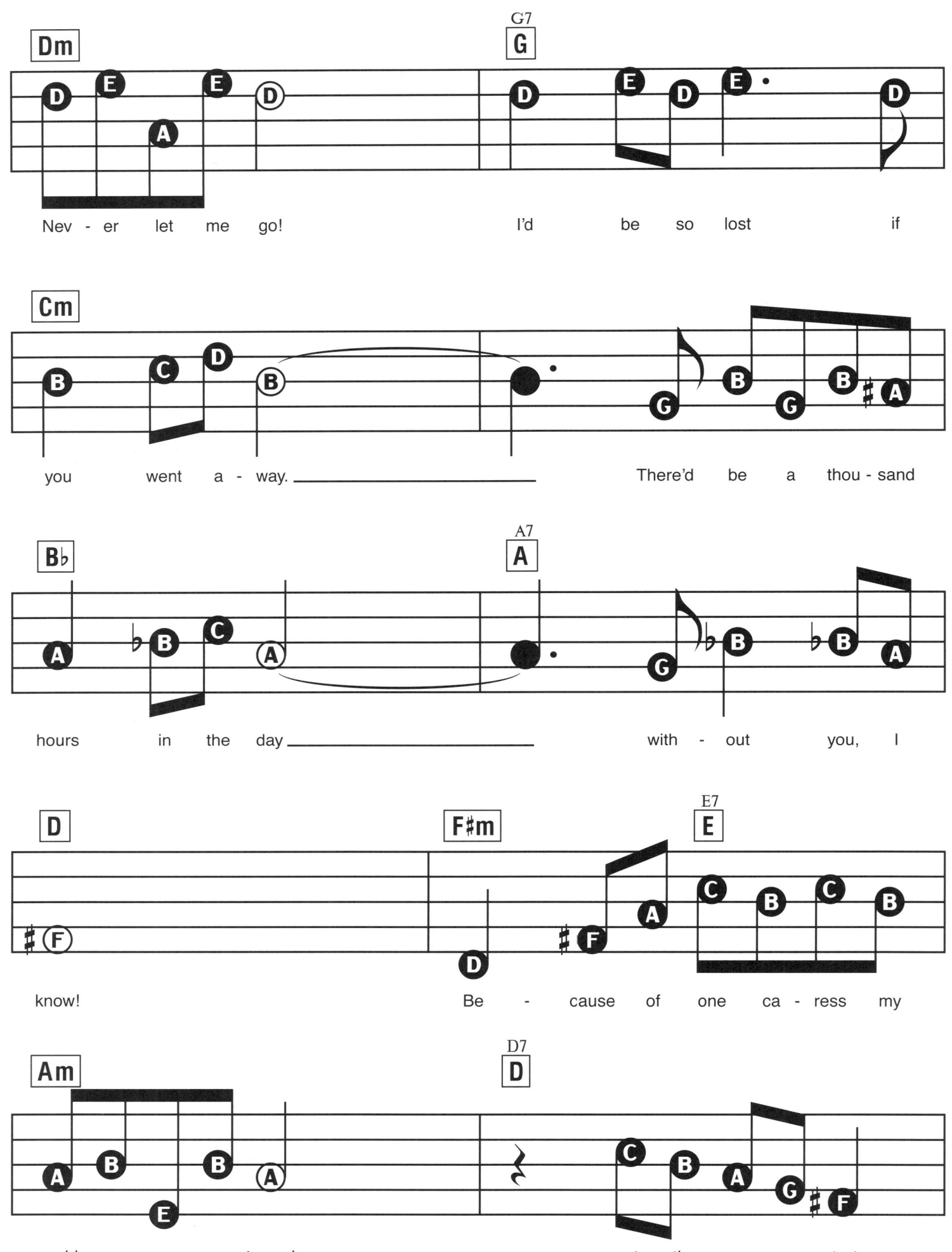

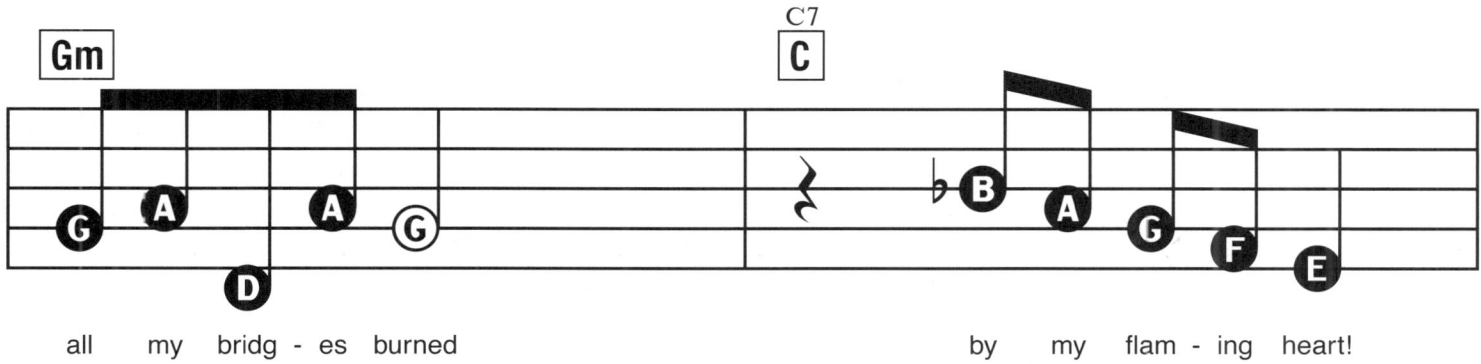
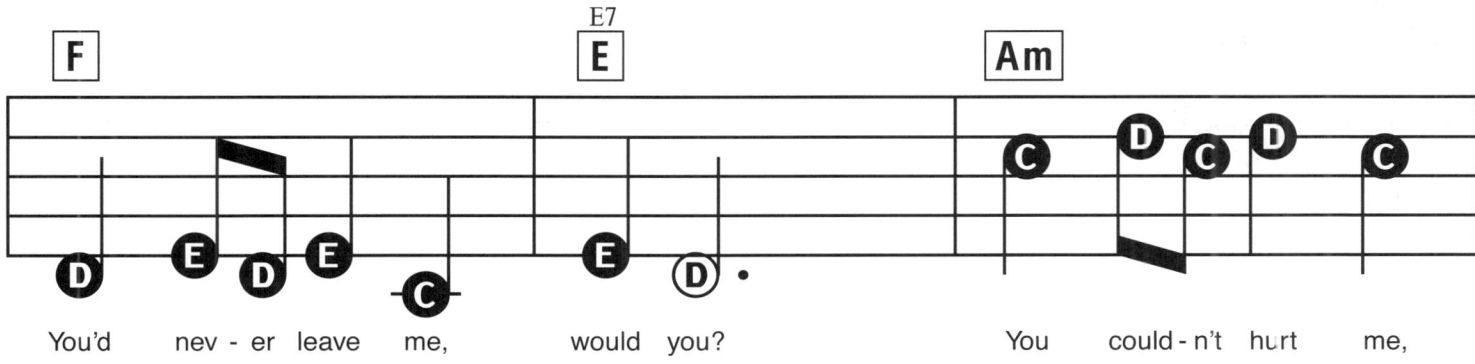
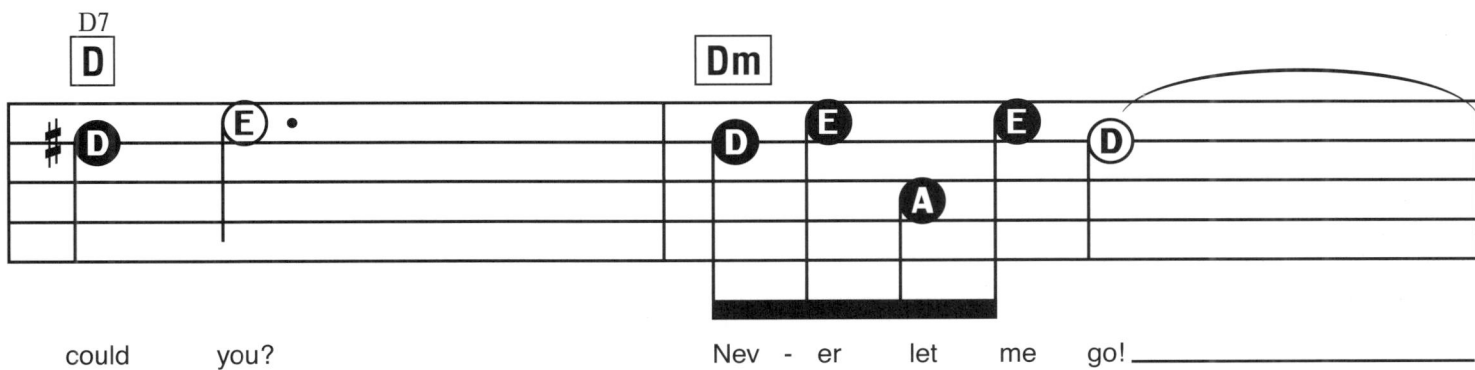
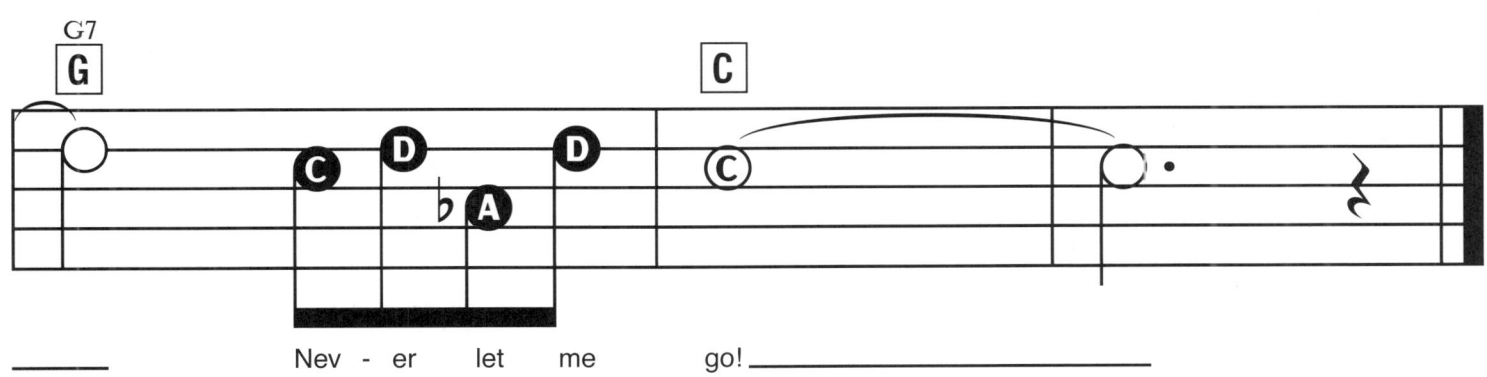

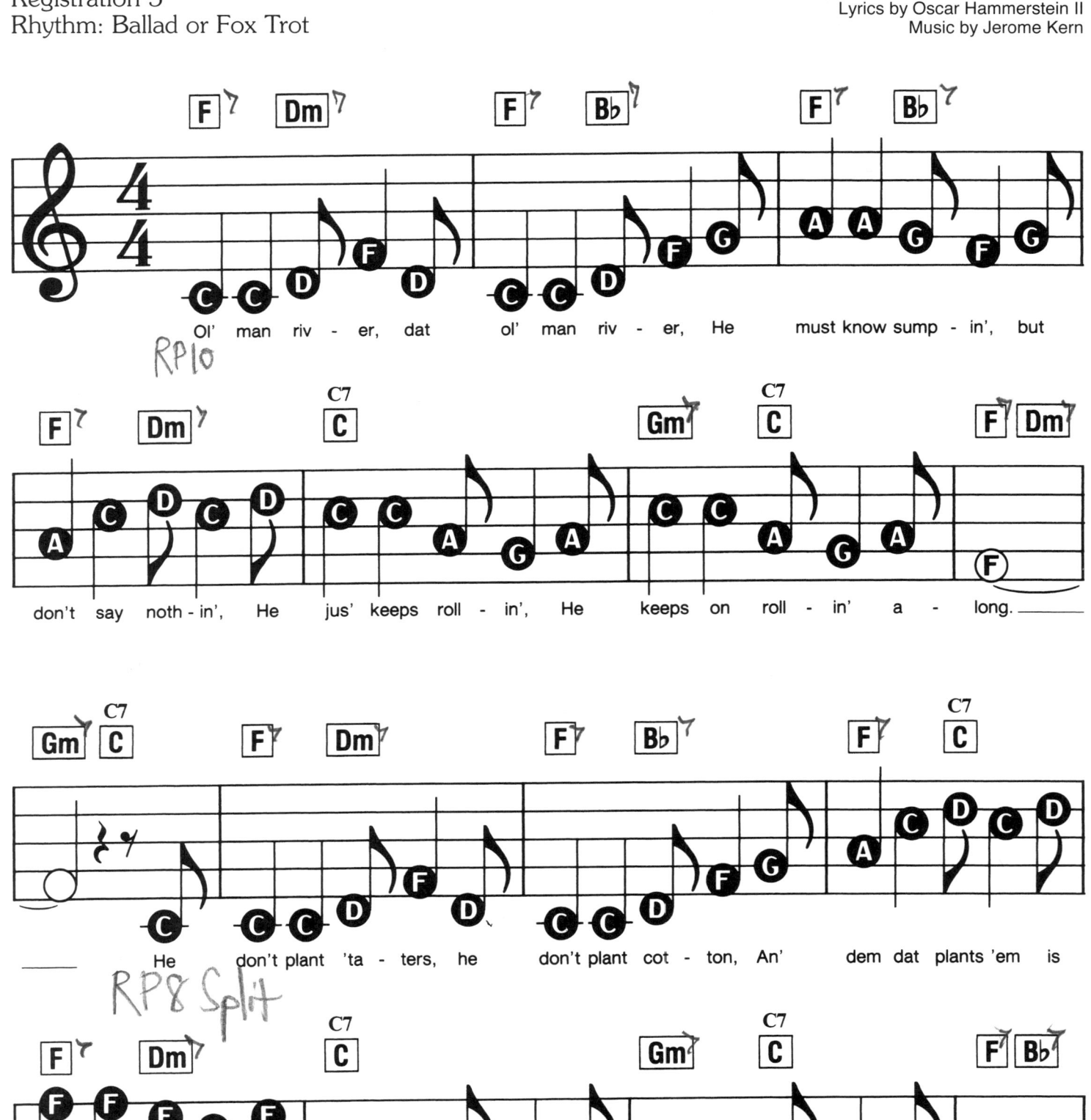

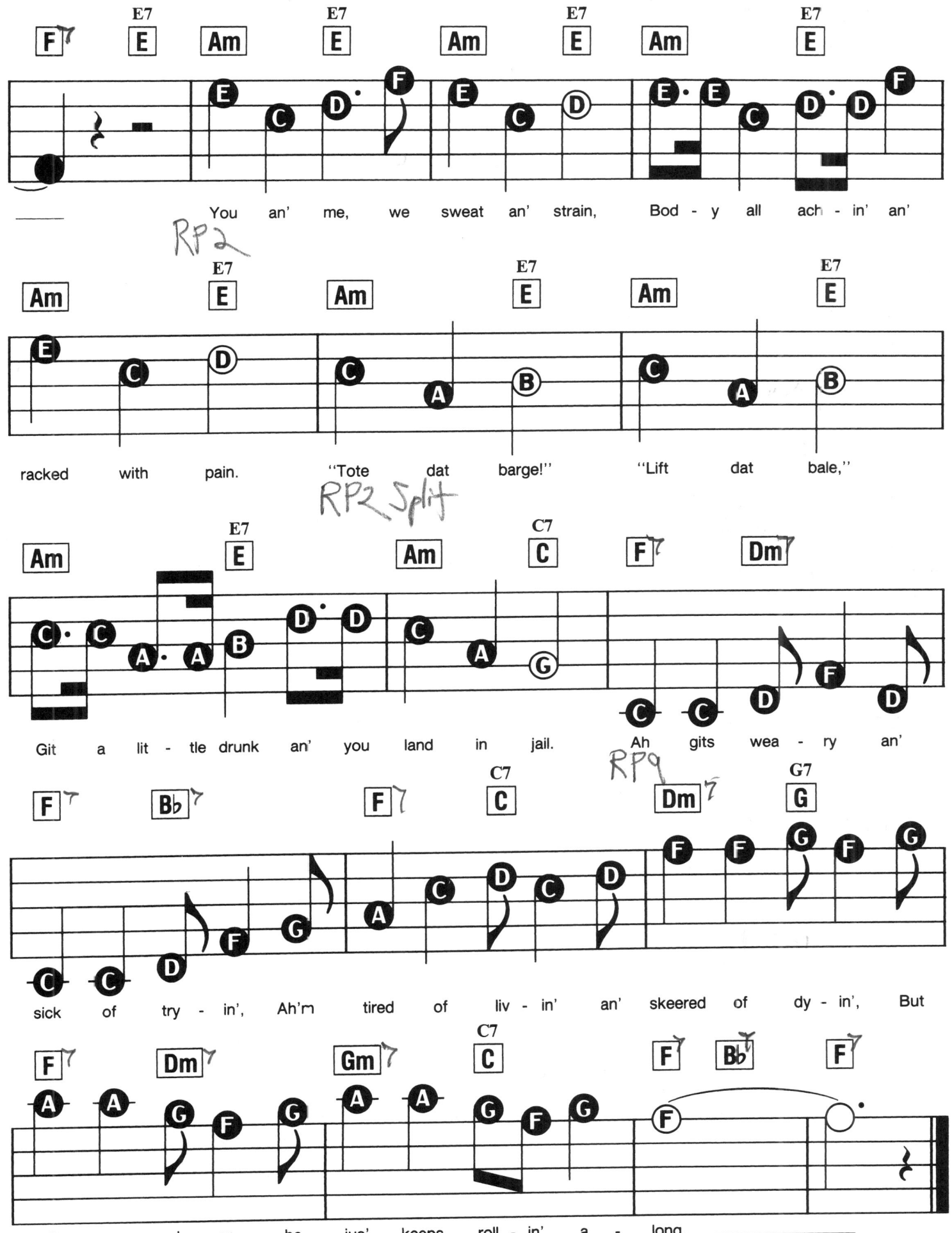

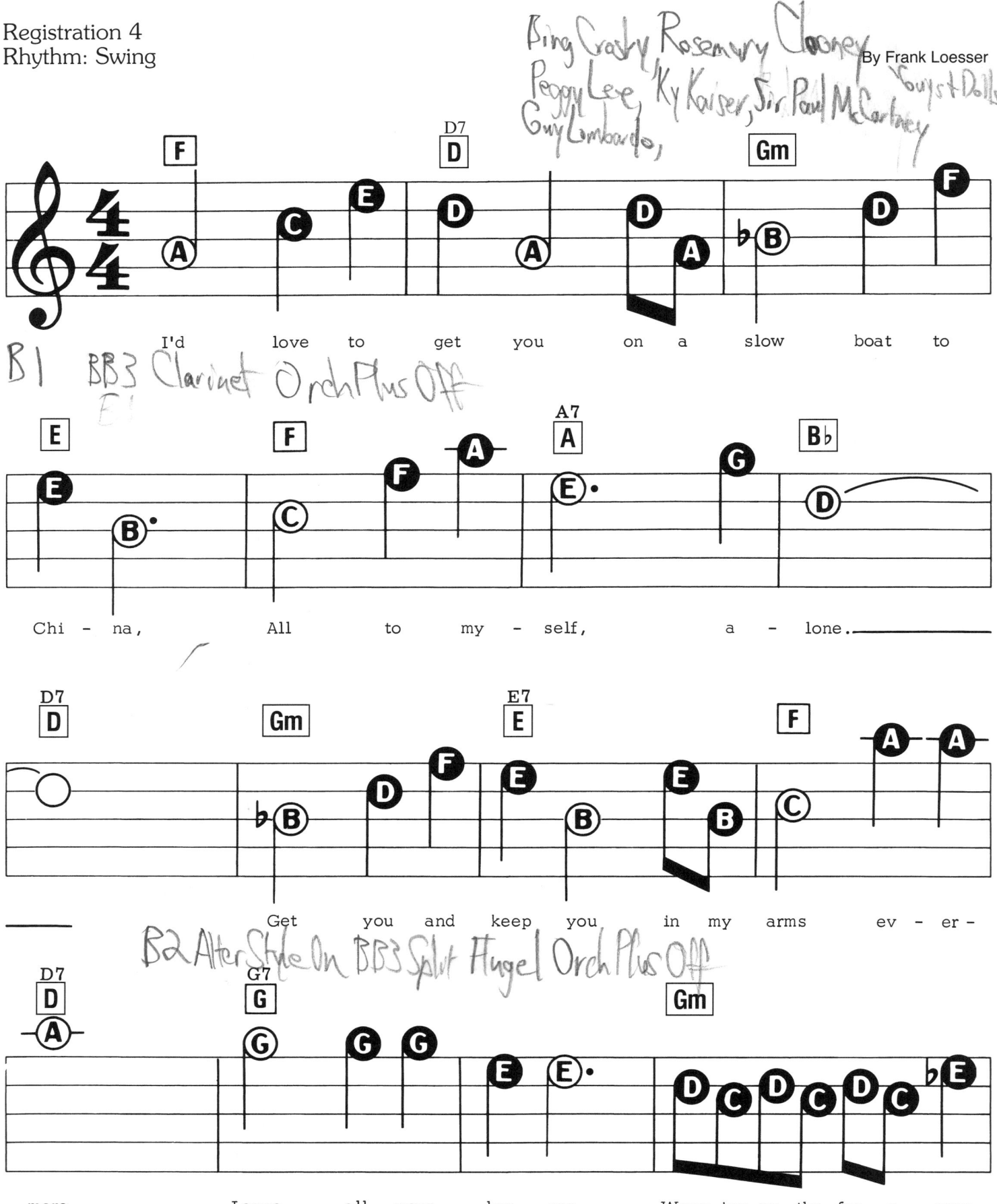

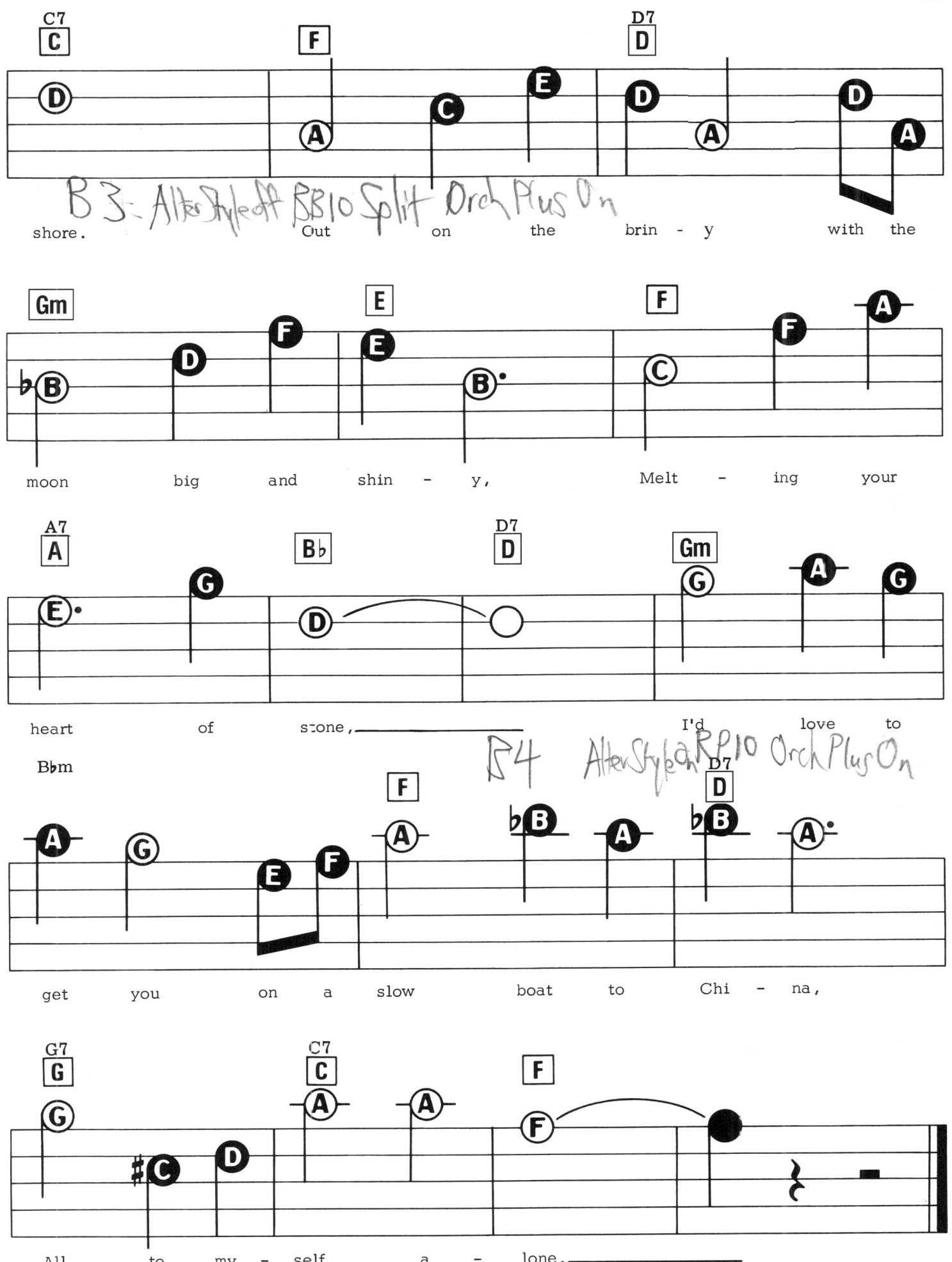

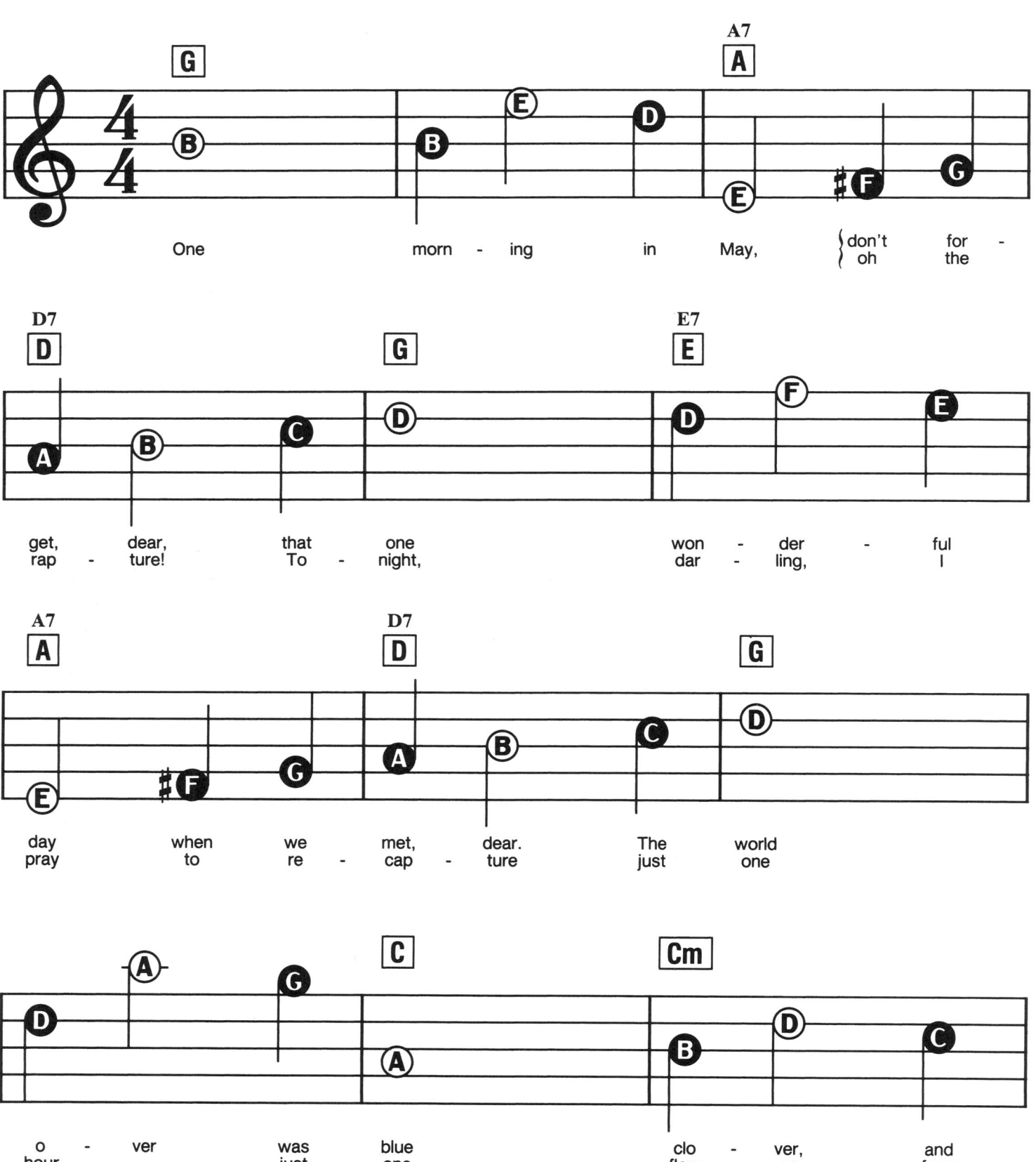

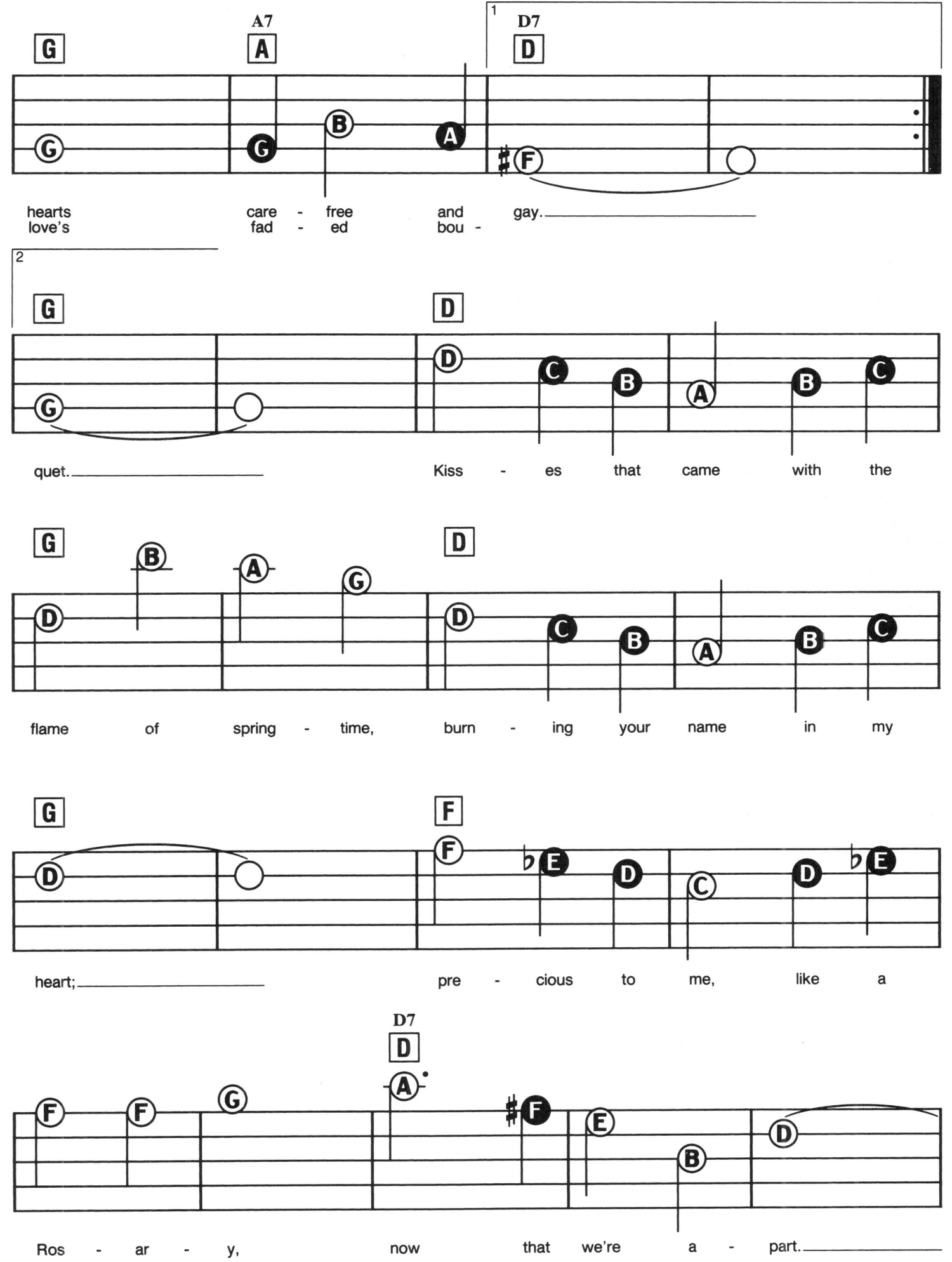

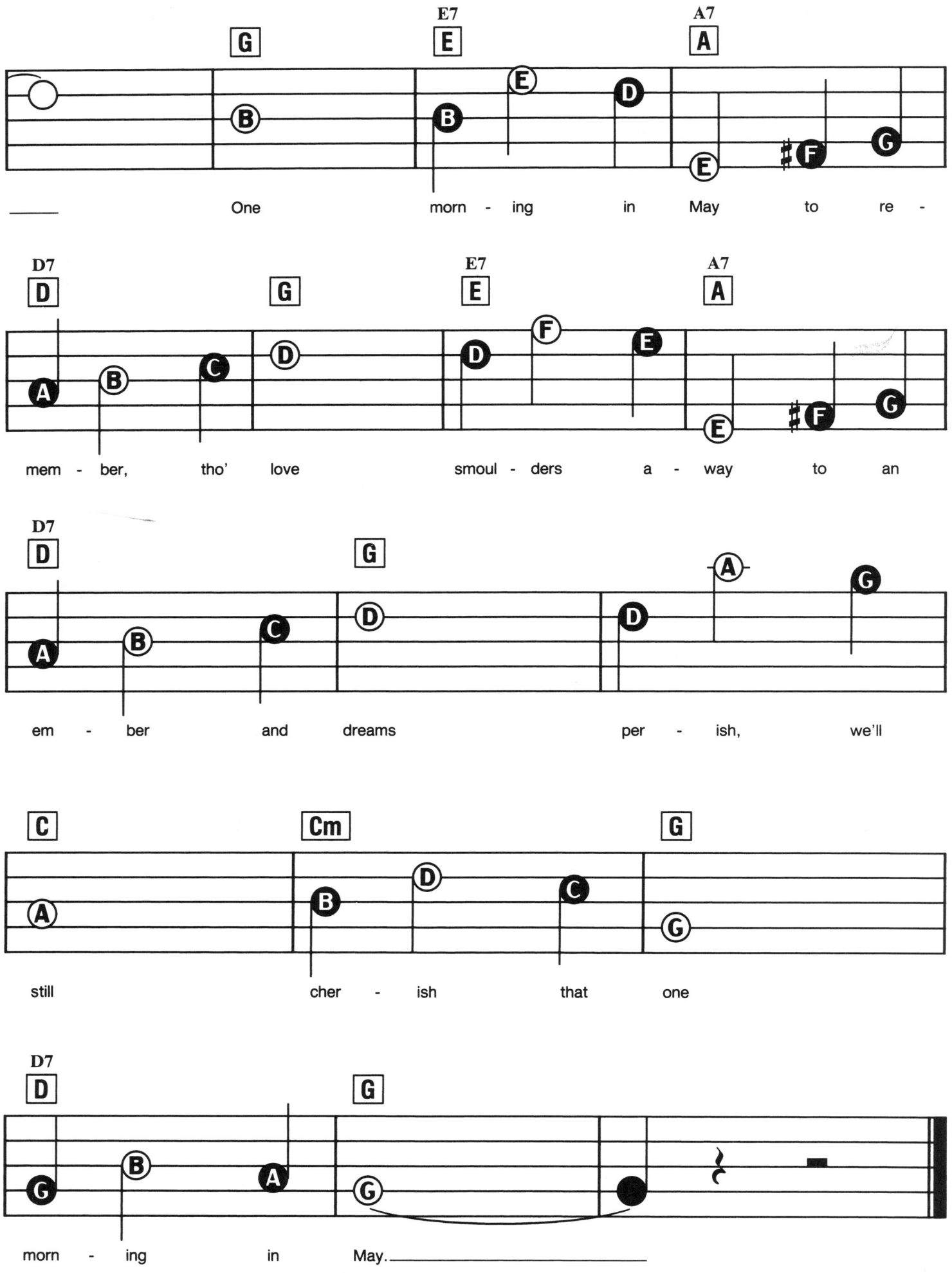

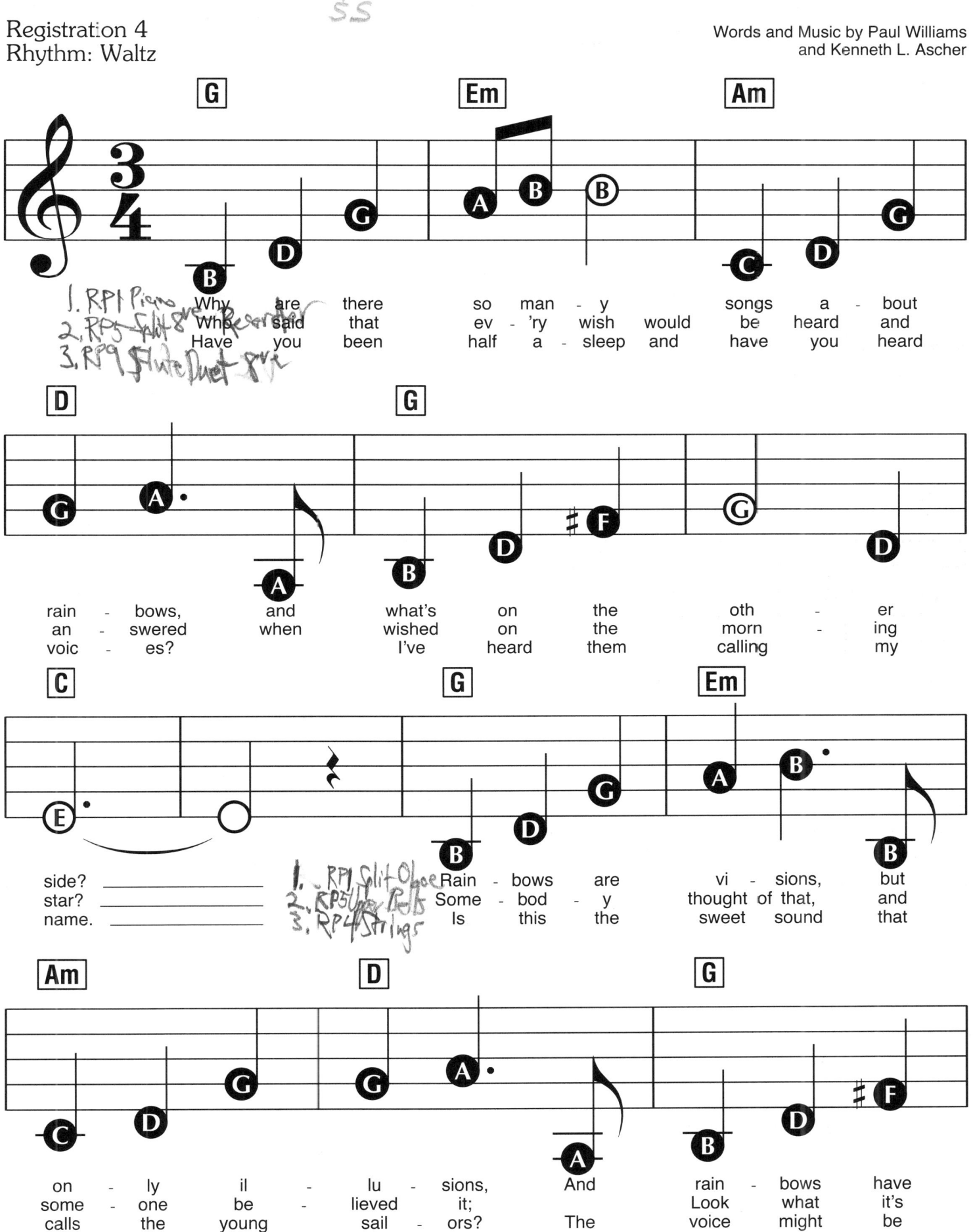

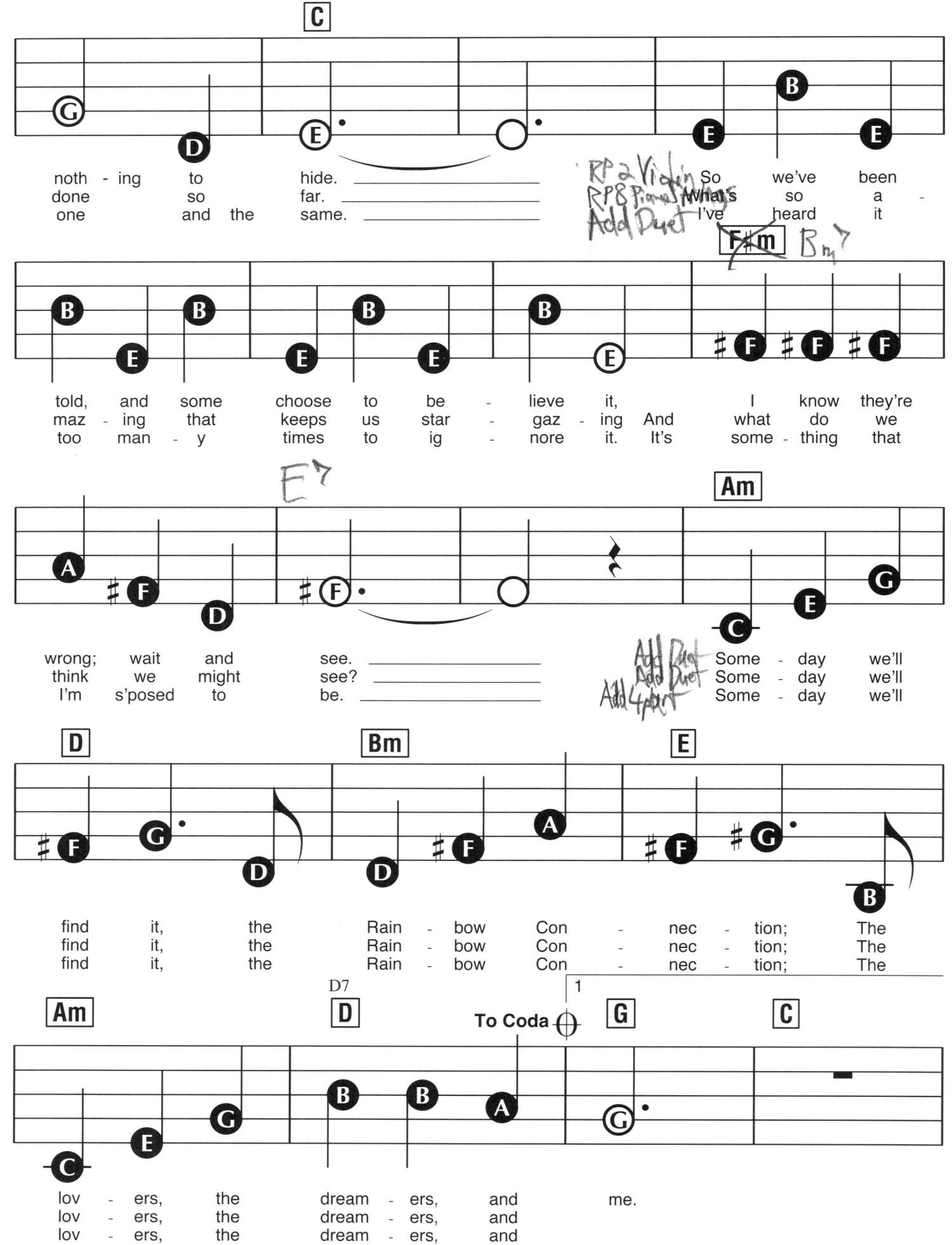

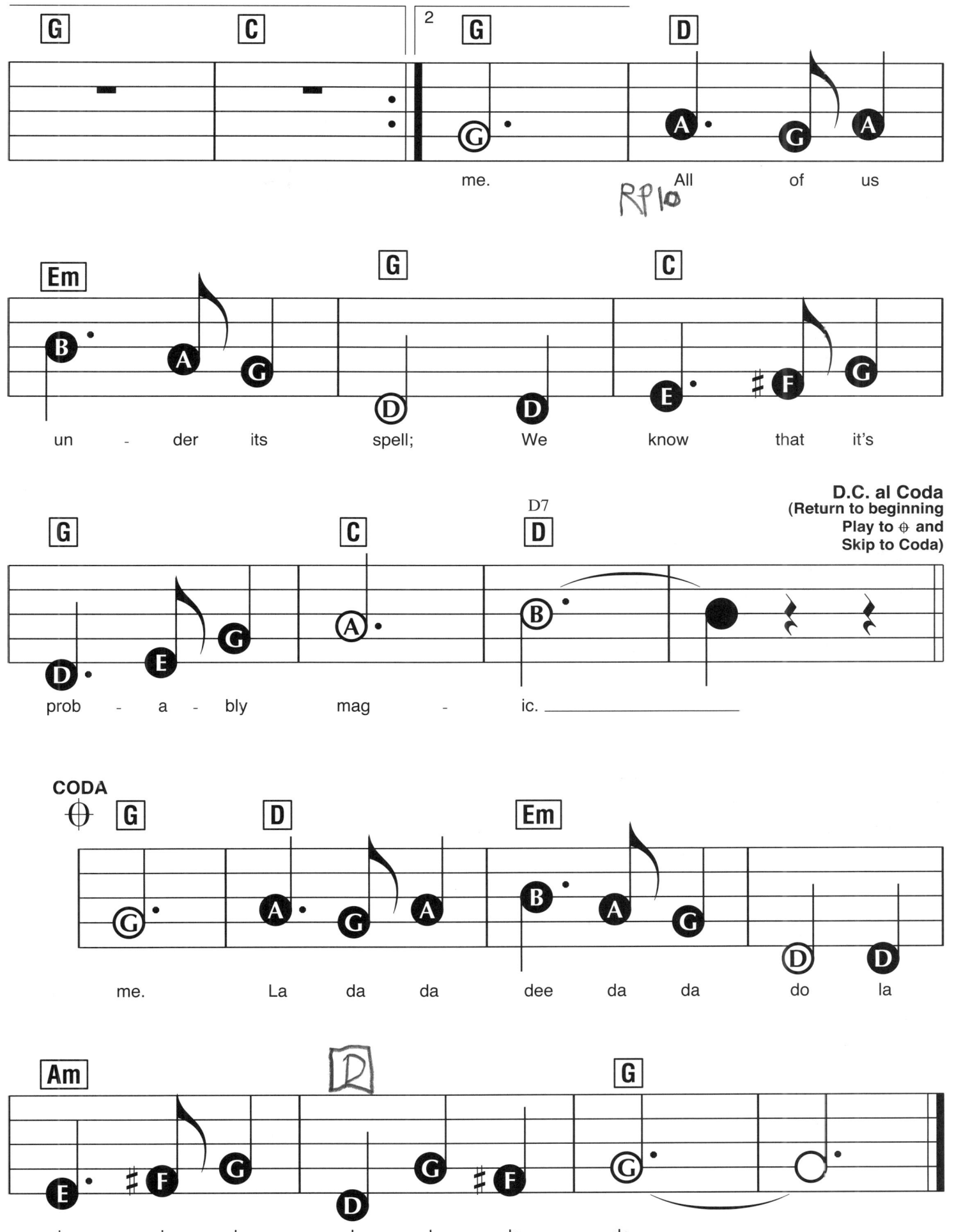

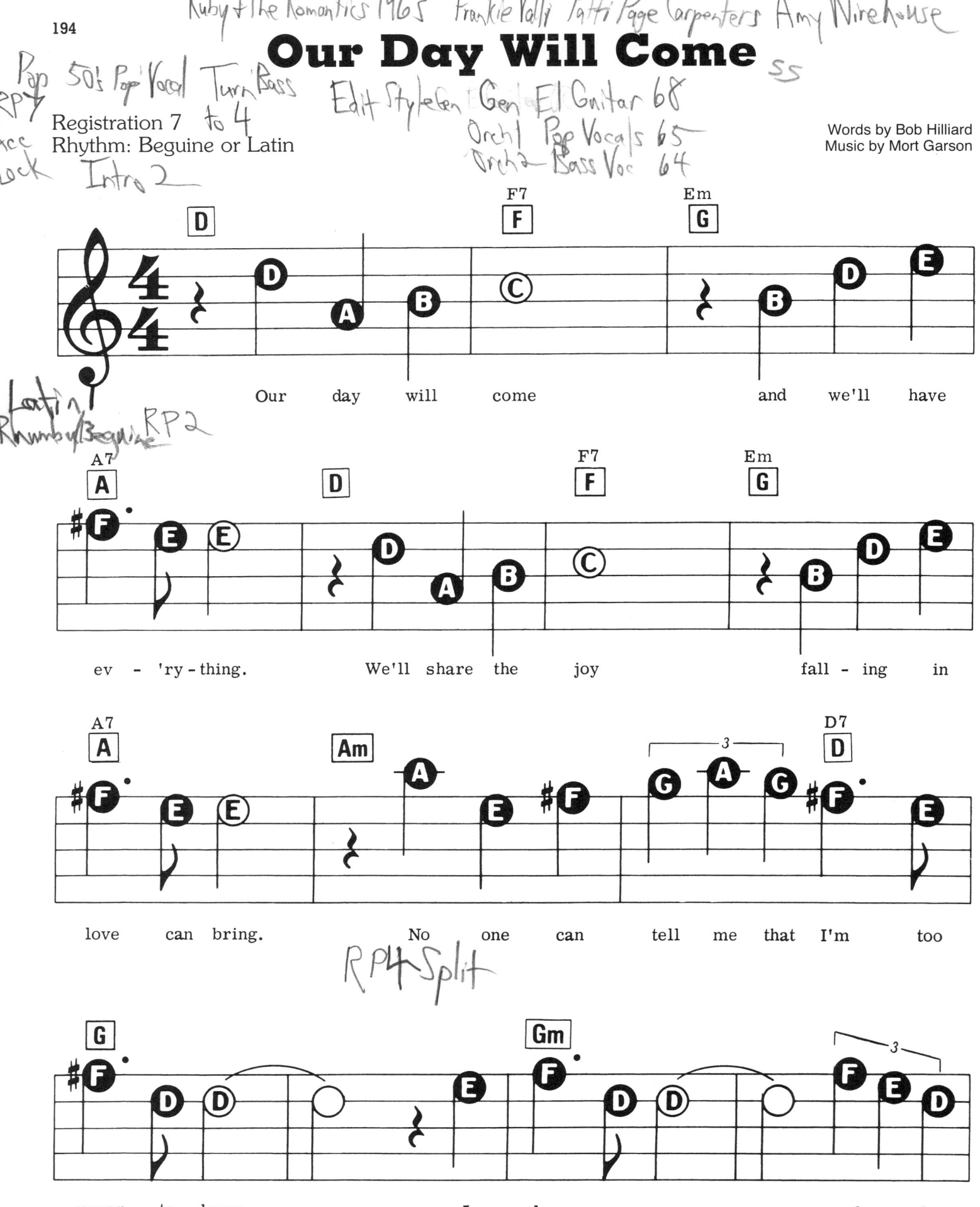

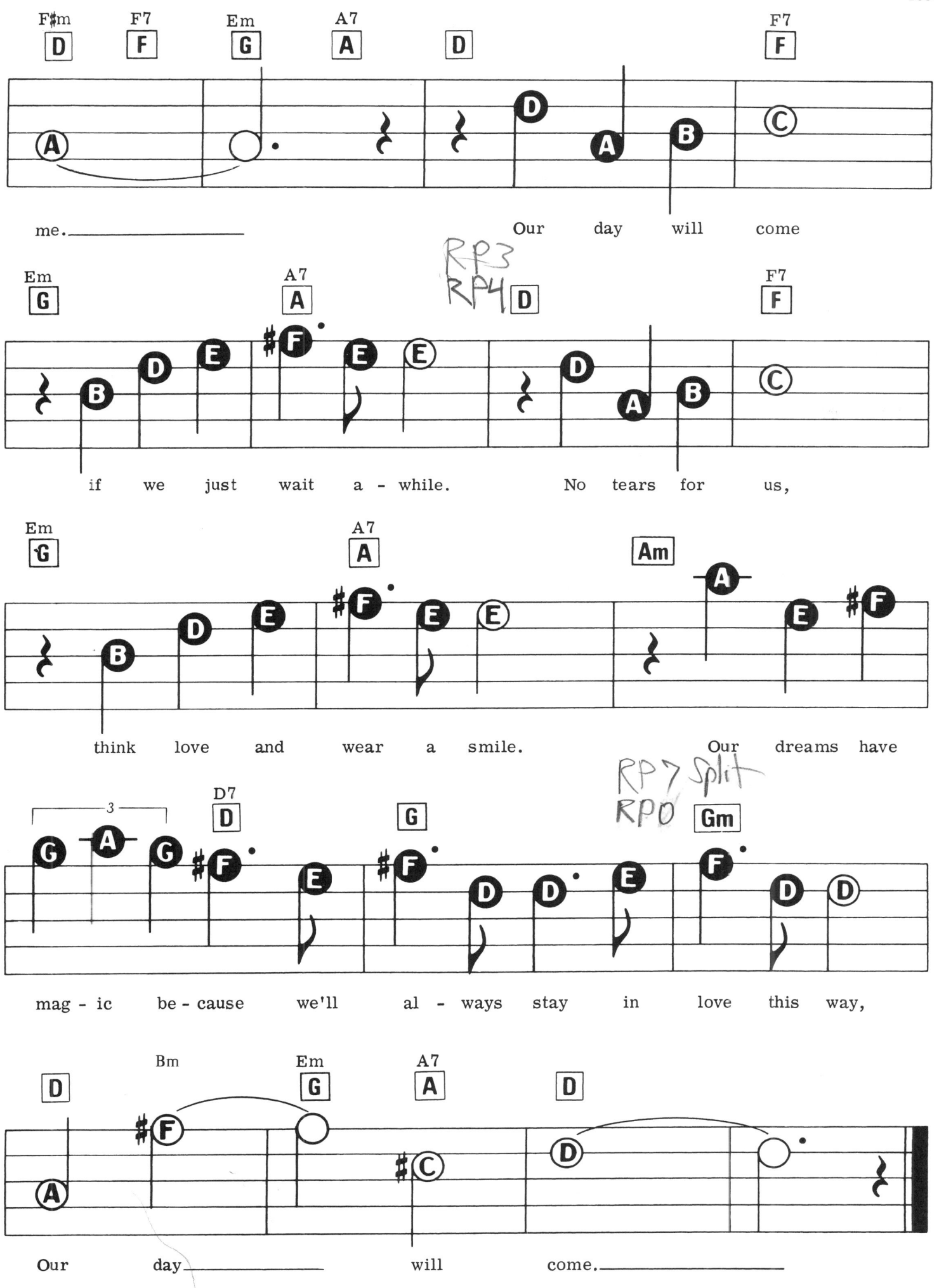

The Party's Over
from BELLS ARE RINGING

Registration 9
Rhythm: Fox Trot or Ballad

Words by Betty Comden and Adolph Green
Music by Jule Styne

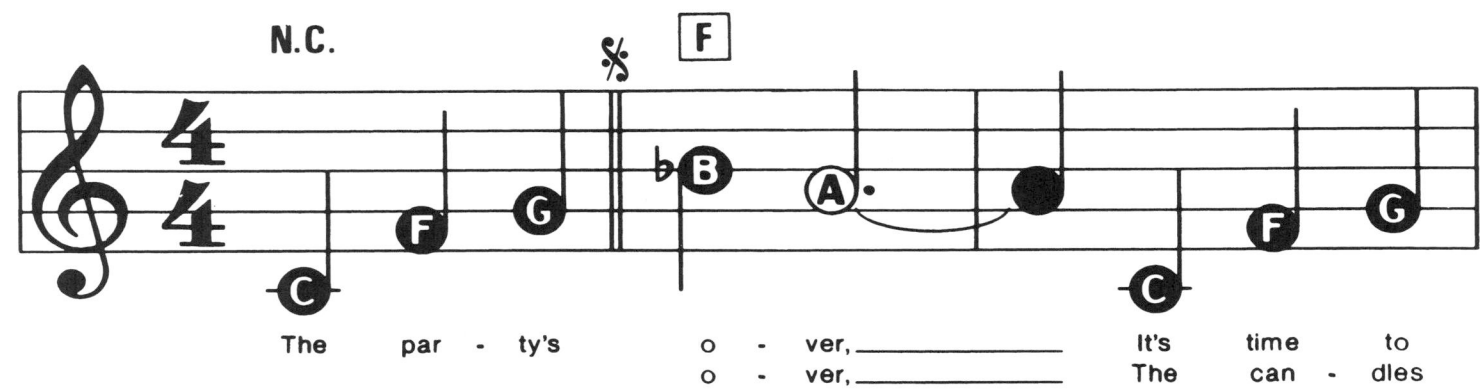

The par - ty's o - ver, _____ It's time to
o - ver, _____ The can - dles

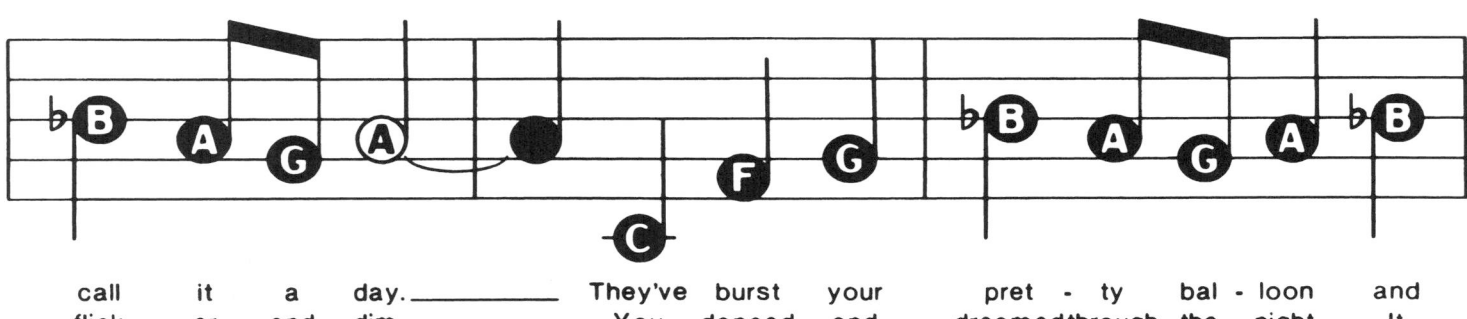

call it a day. _____ They've burst your pret - ty bal - loon and
flick - er and dim. _____ You danced and dreamed through the night, It

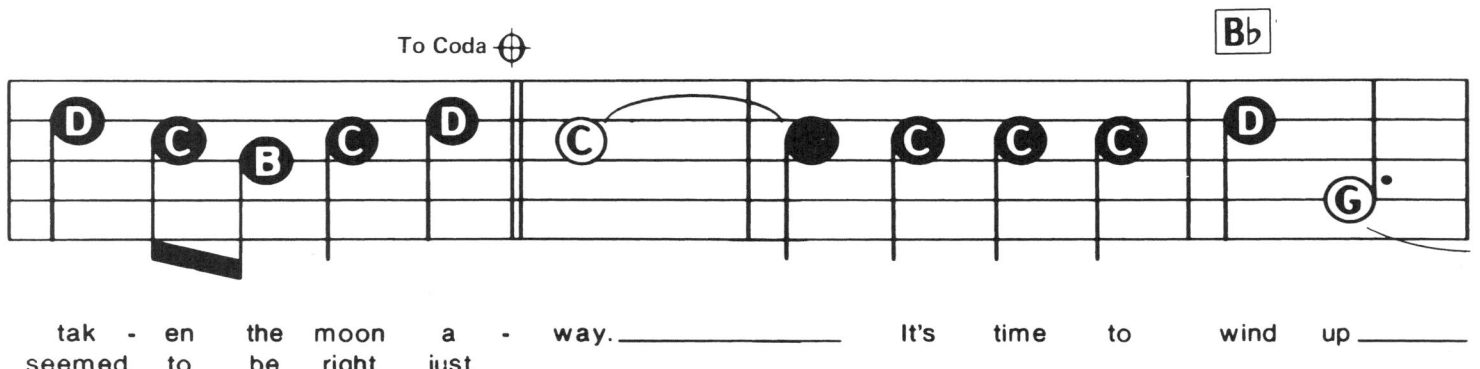

tak - en the moon a - way. _____ It's time to wind up
seemed to be right just

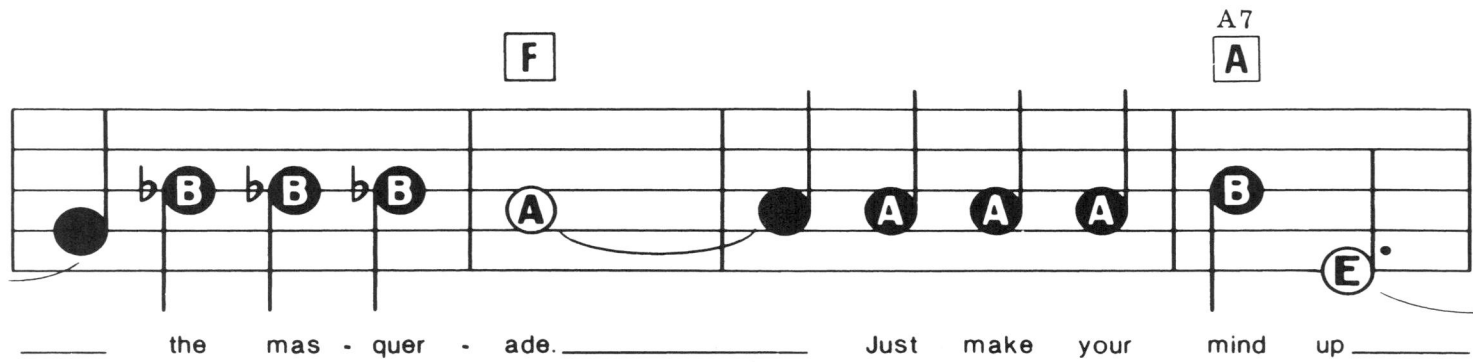

_____ the mas - quer - ade. _____ Just make your mind up

Copyright © 1956 by Betty Comden, Adolph Green and Jule Styne
Copyright Renewed
Stratford Music Corporation, owner of publication and allied rights throughout the world
Chappell & Co., Administrator
International Copyright Secured   All Rights Reserved

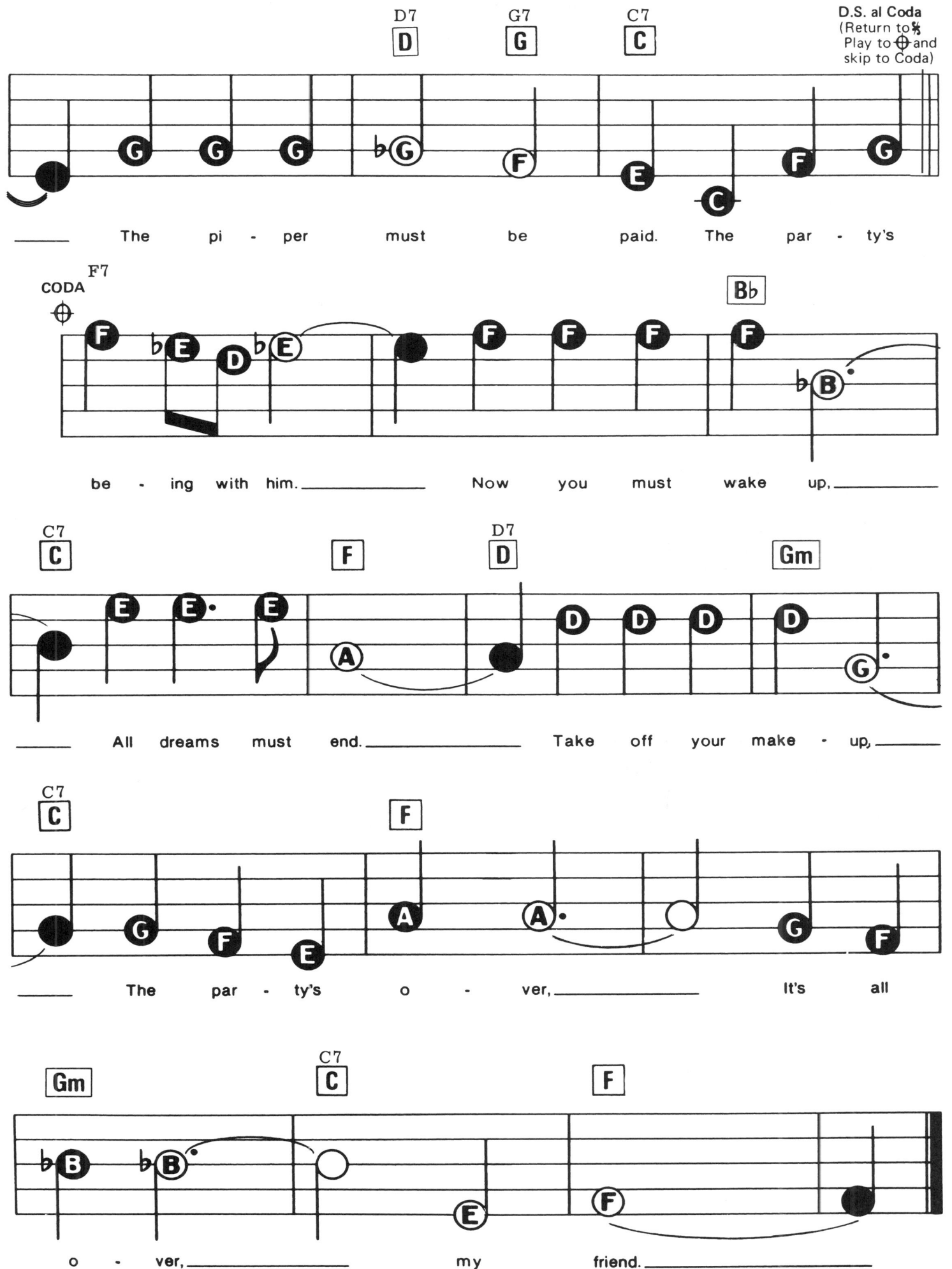

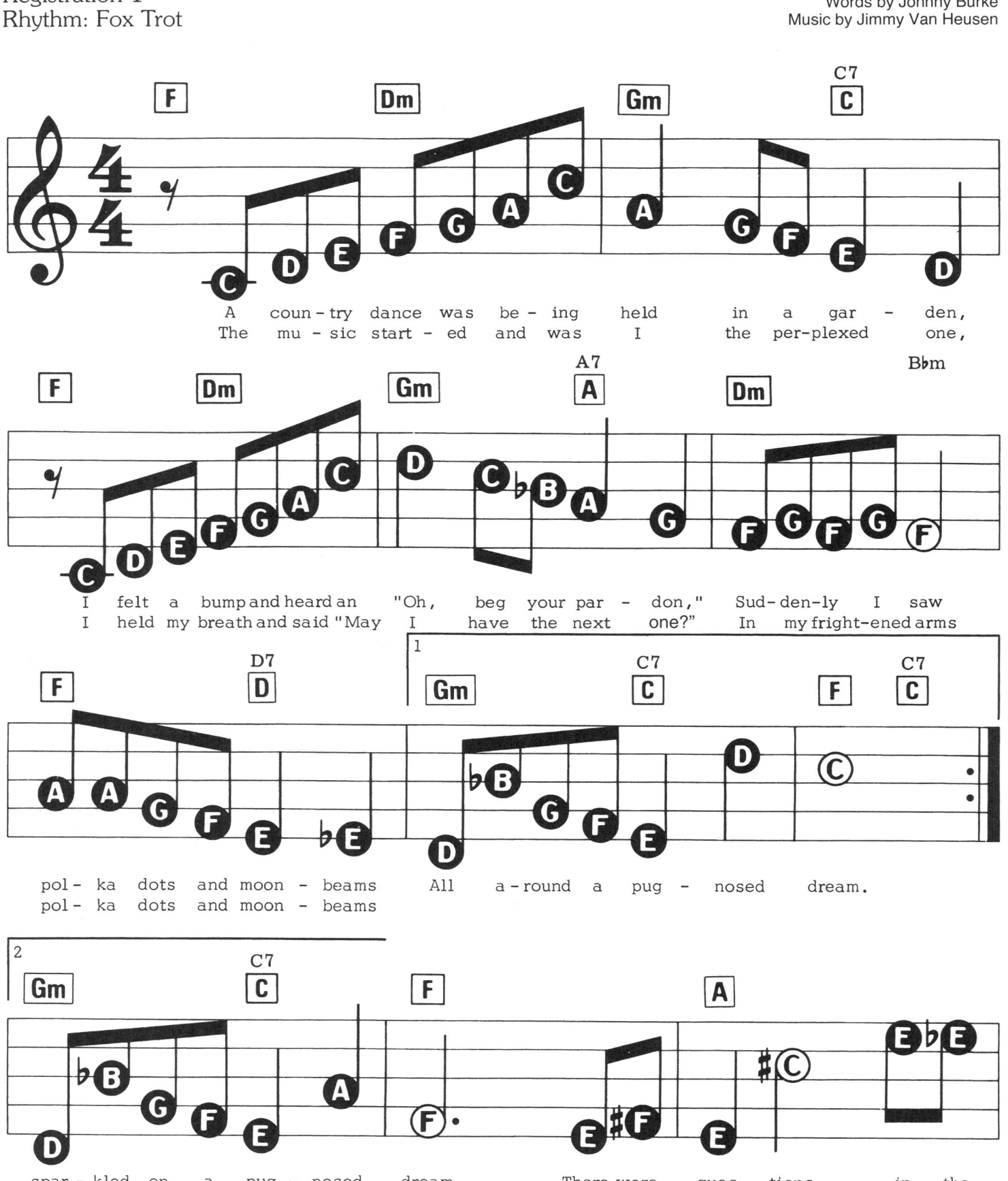

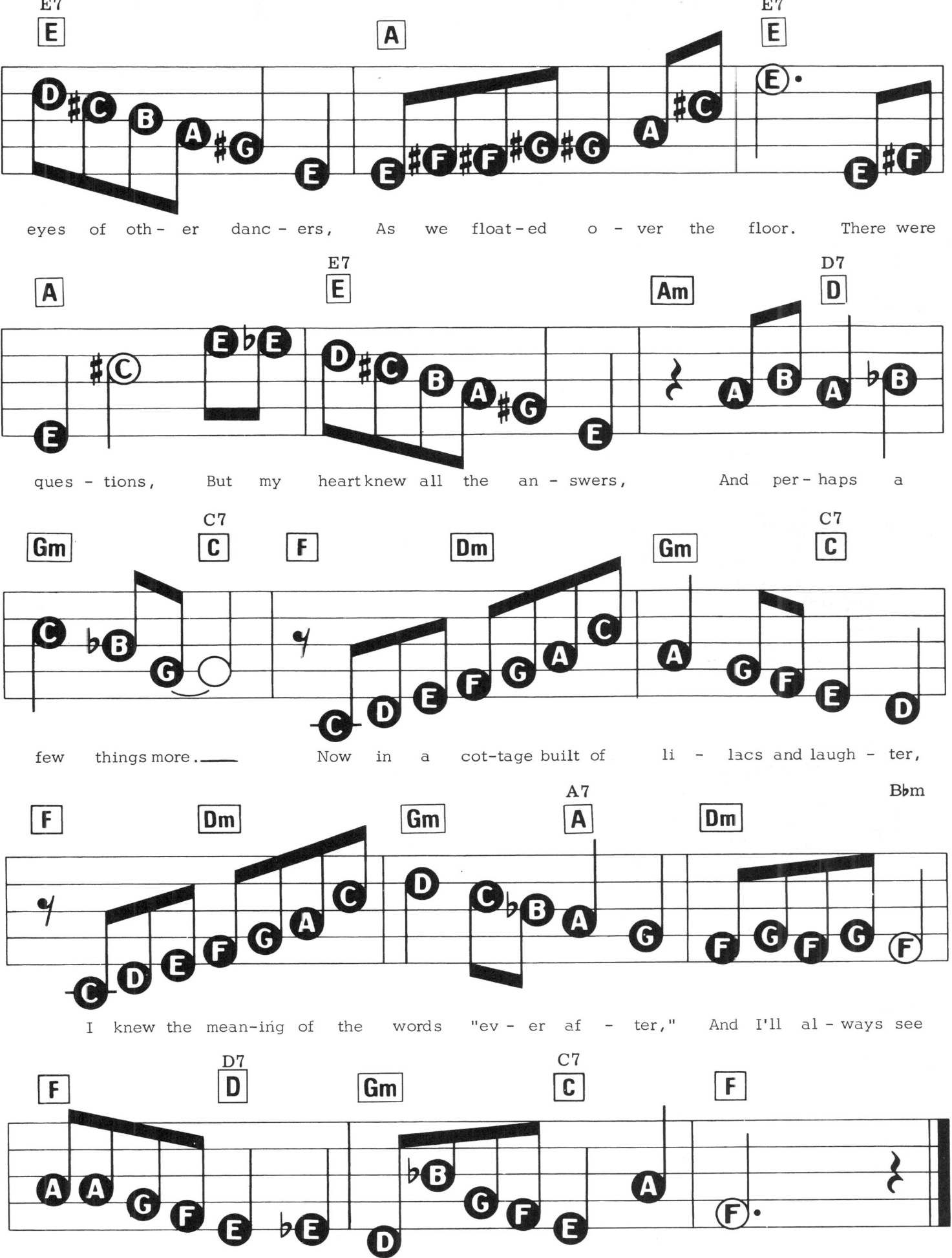

Rockin' in Rhythm

Registration 3
Rhythm: Swing

By Duke Ellington, Irving Mills and Harry Carney

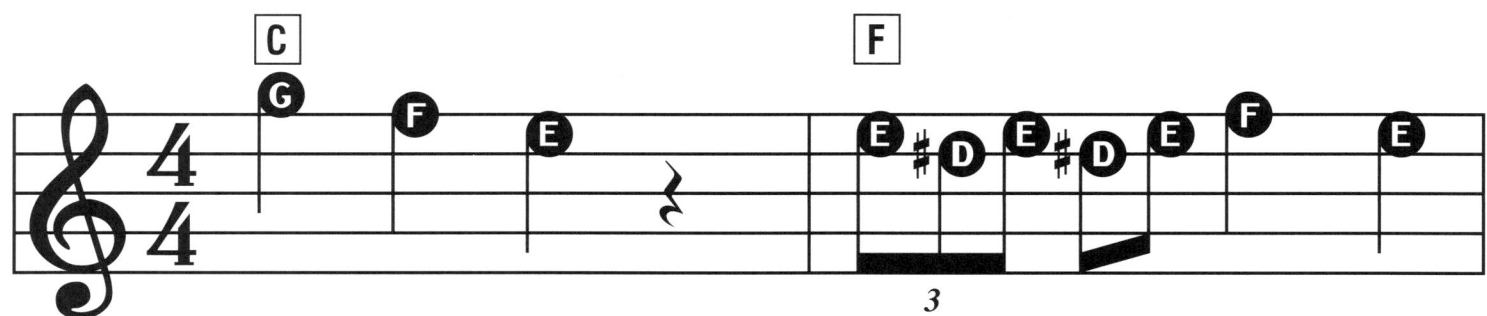
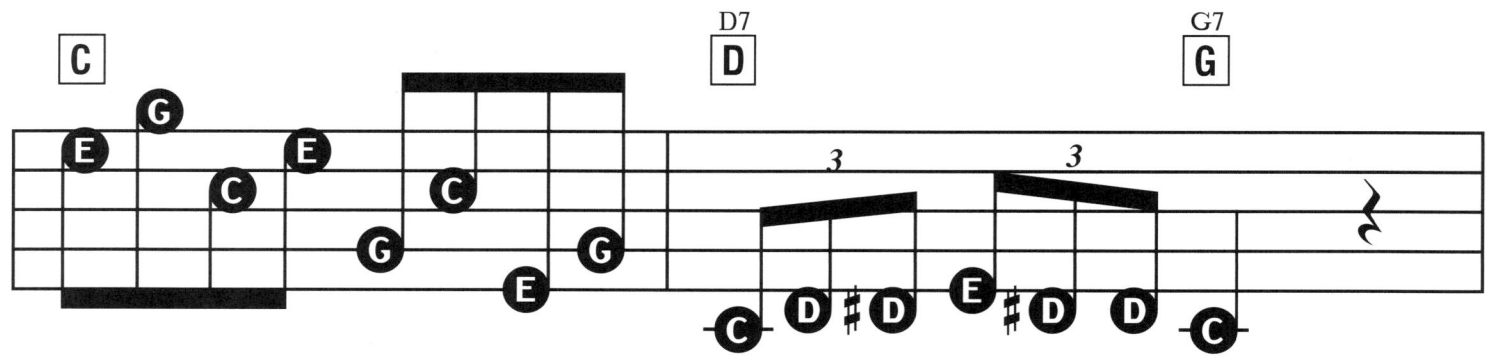
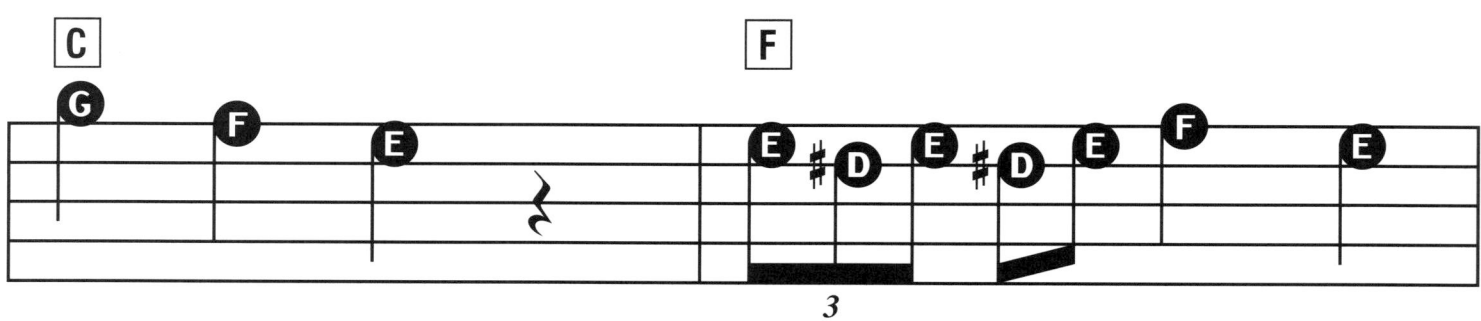
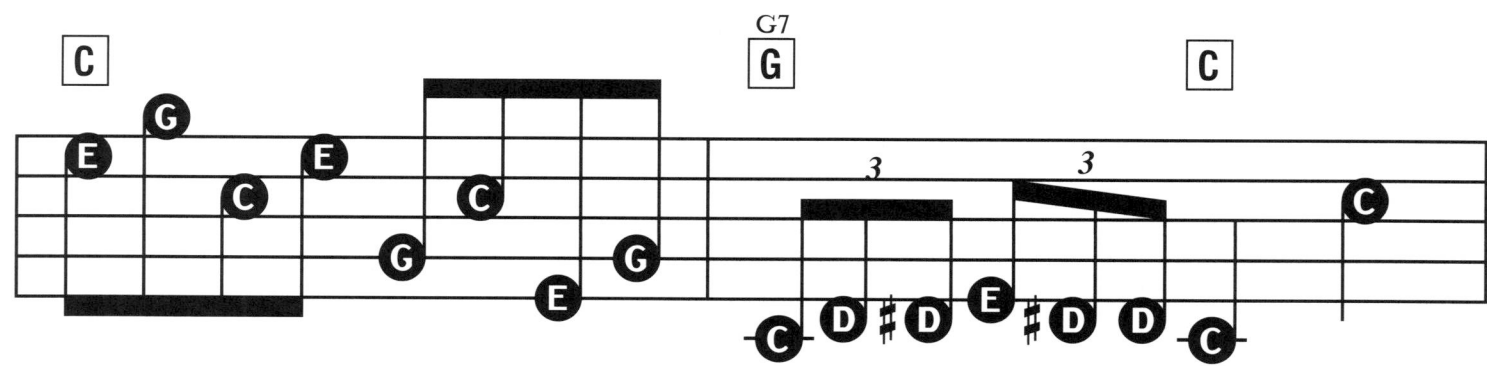

Copyright © 1931 Sony/ATV Music Publishing LLC and EMI Mills Music Inc. in the U.S.A.
Copyright Renewed
All Rights on behalf of Sony/ATV Music Publishing LLC Administered by Sony/ATV Music Publishing LLC, 8 Music Square West, Nashville, TN 37203
Rights for the world outside the U.S.A. Administered by EMI Mills Music Inc. (Publishing) and Alfred Publishing Co., Inc. (Print)
International Copyright Secured All Rights Reserved

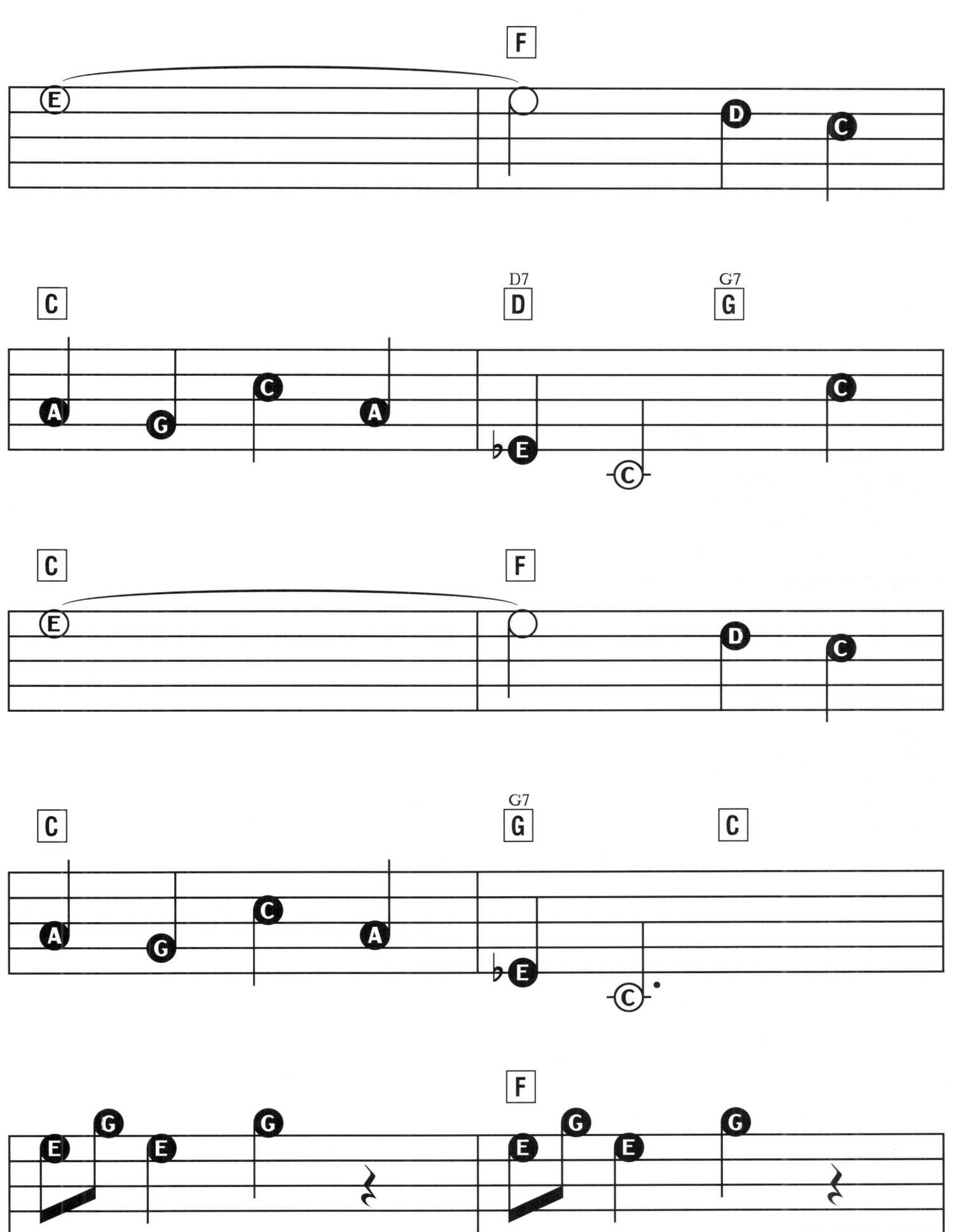

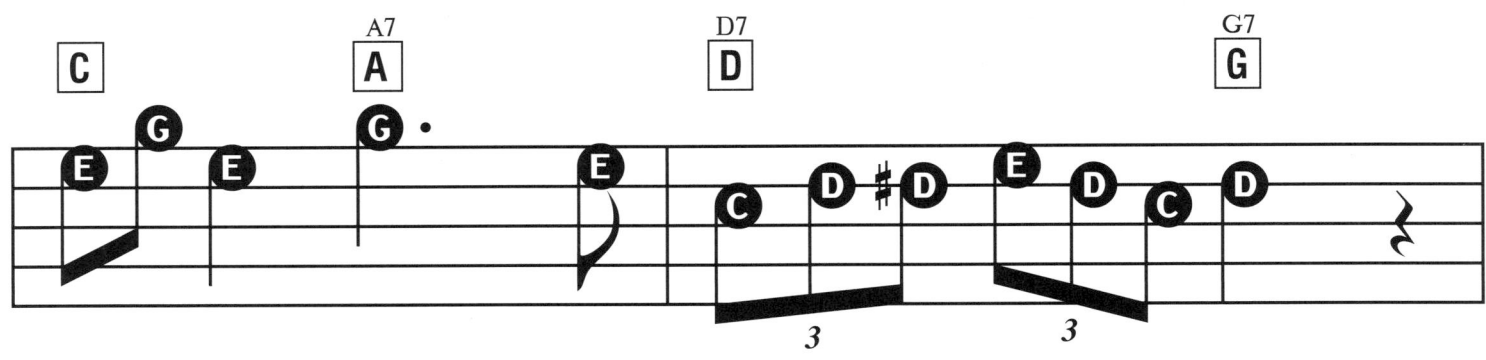
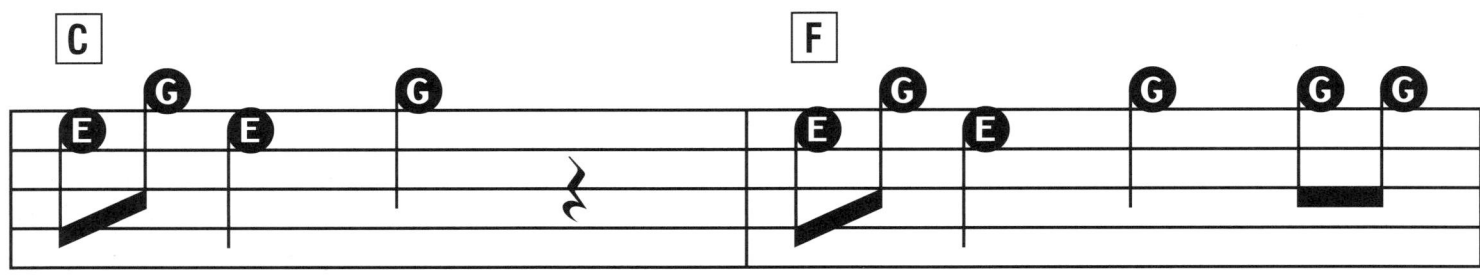
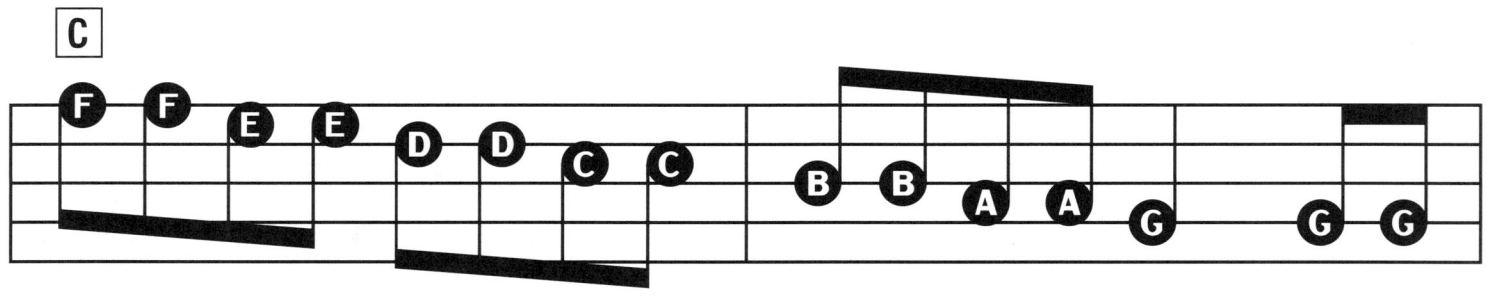
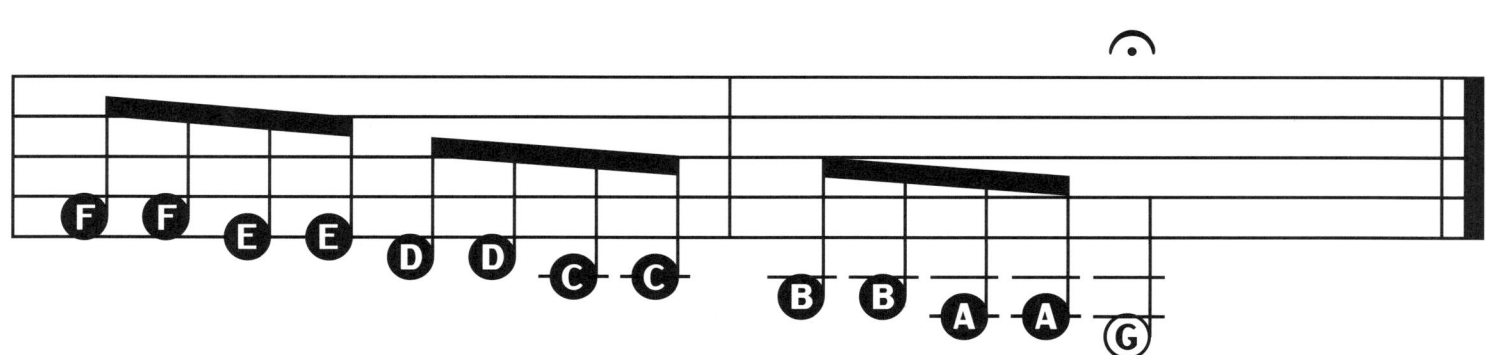

St. Louis Blues
from BIRTH OF THE BLUES

Registration 7
Rhythm: Swing

Words and Music by
W.C. Handy

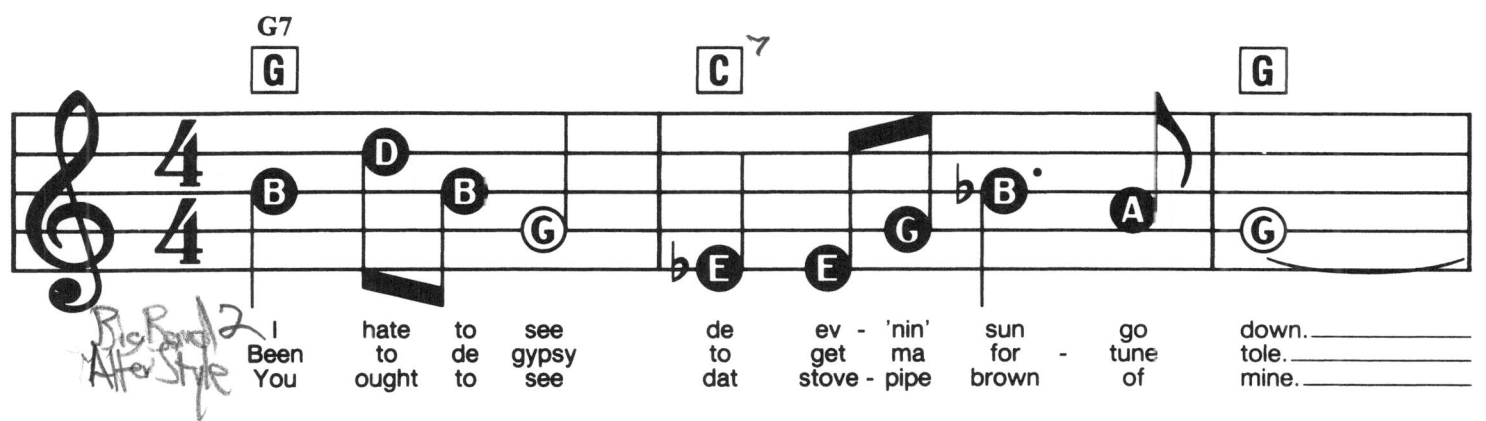

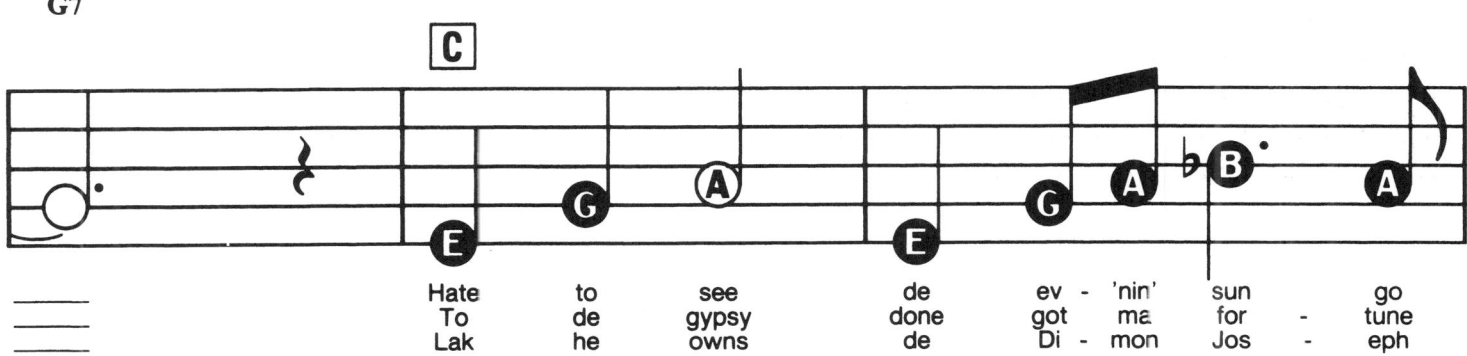

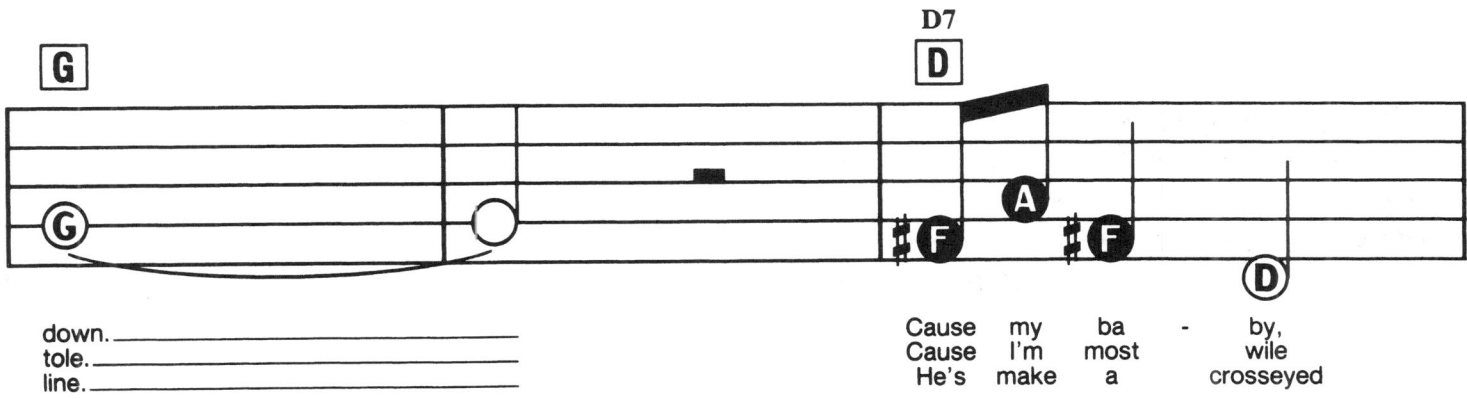

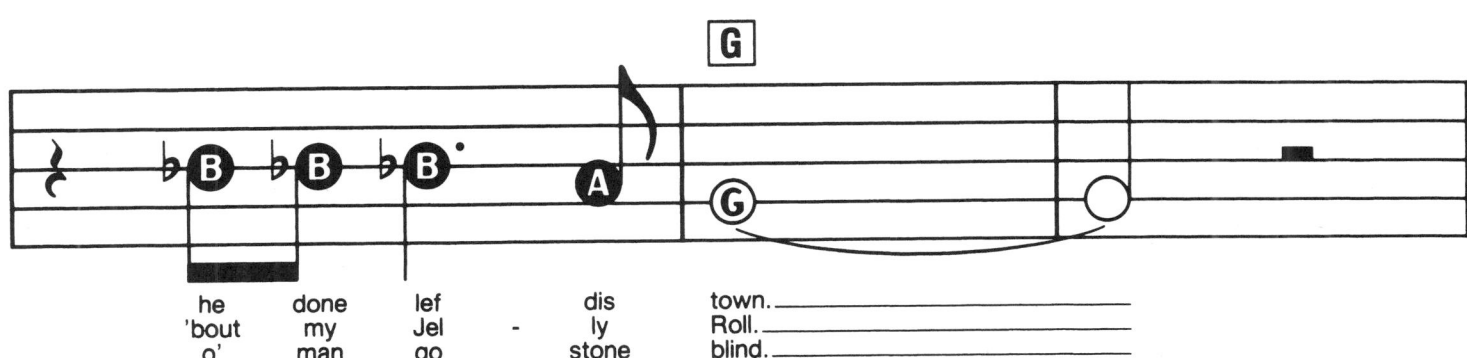

Copyright © 1990 by HAL LEONARD CORPORATION
International Copyright Secured
All Rights Reserved

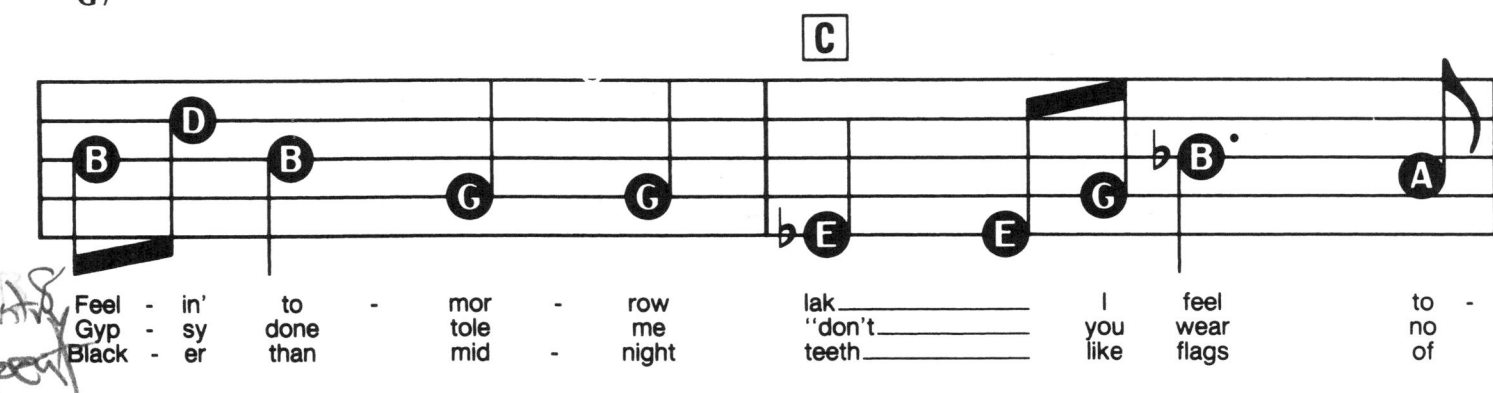
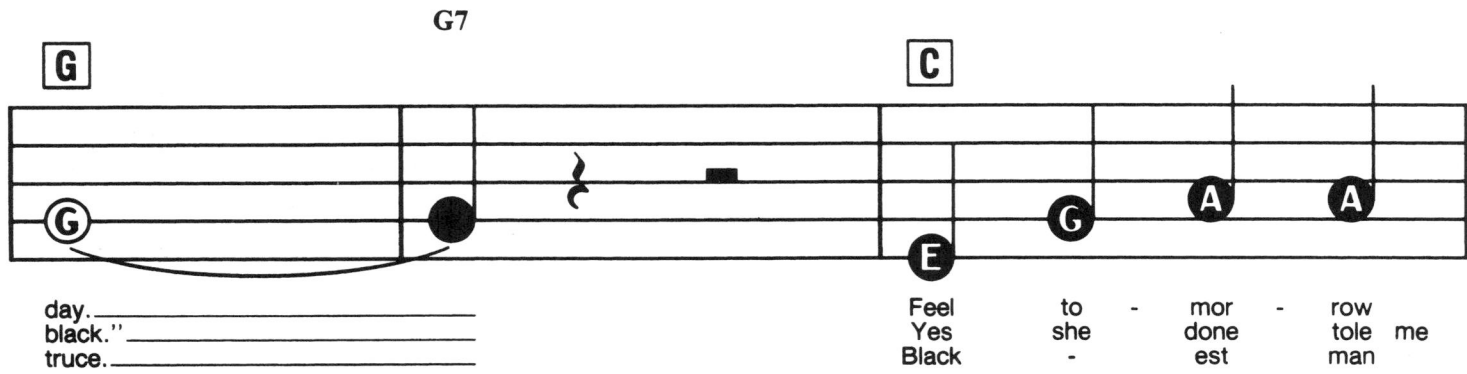
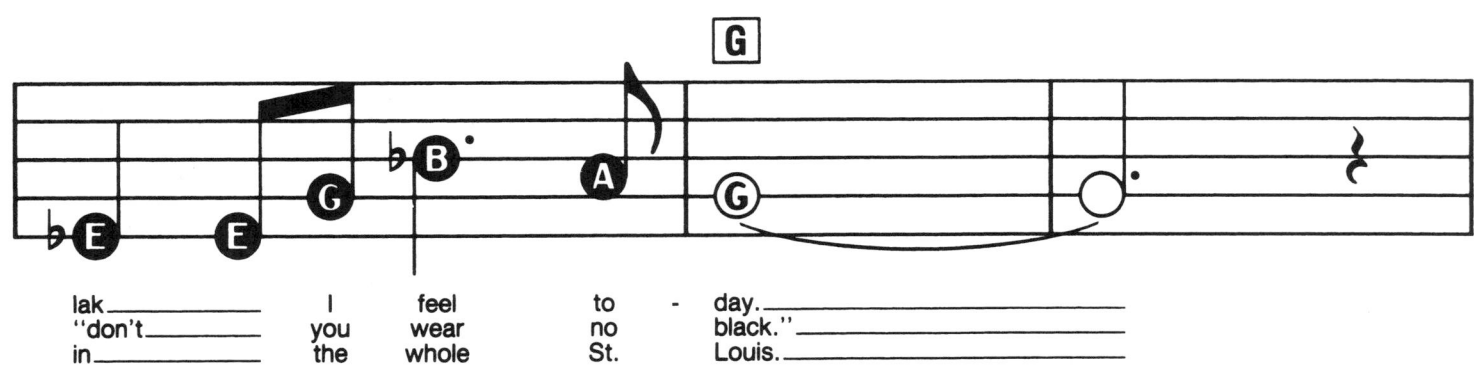
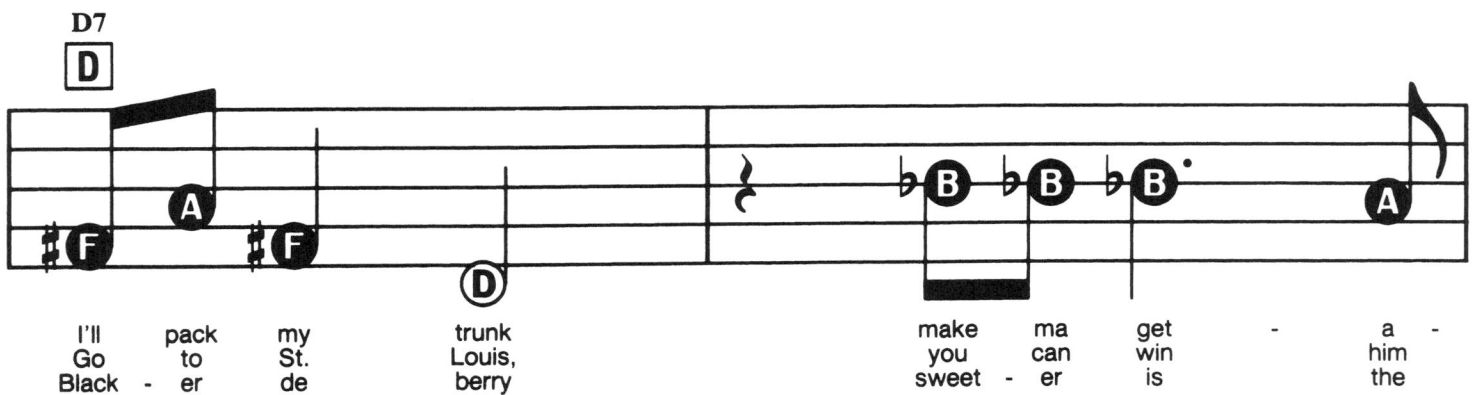

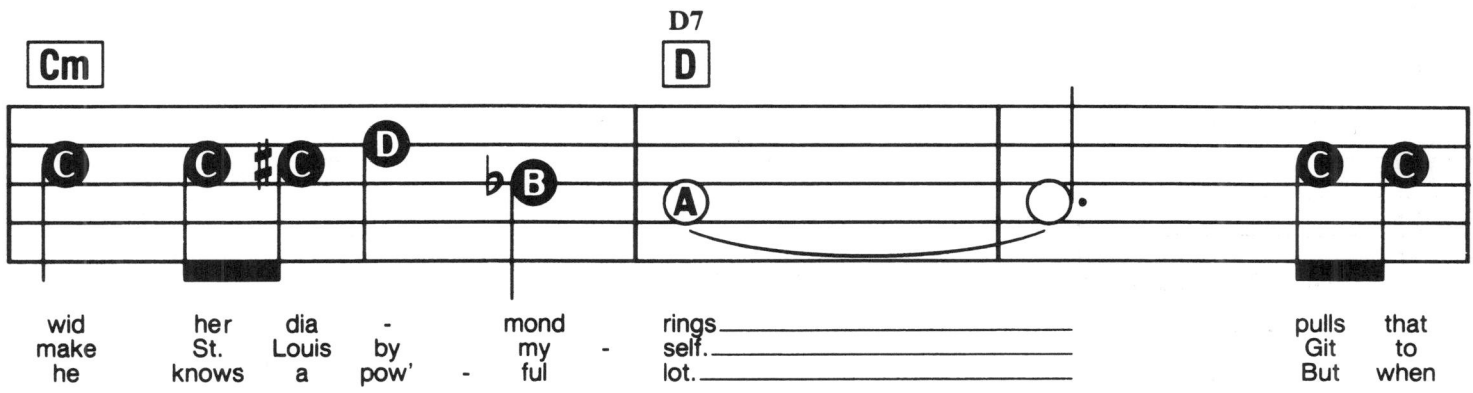
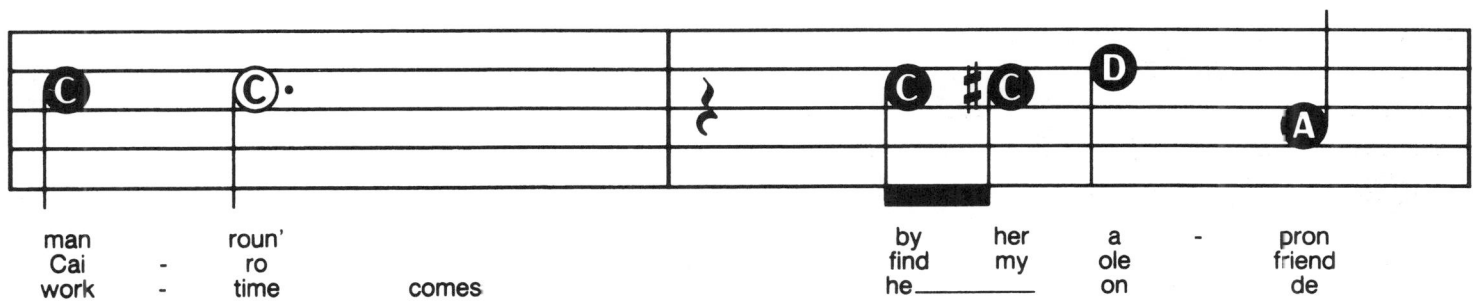
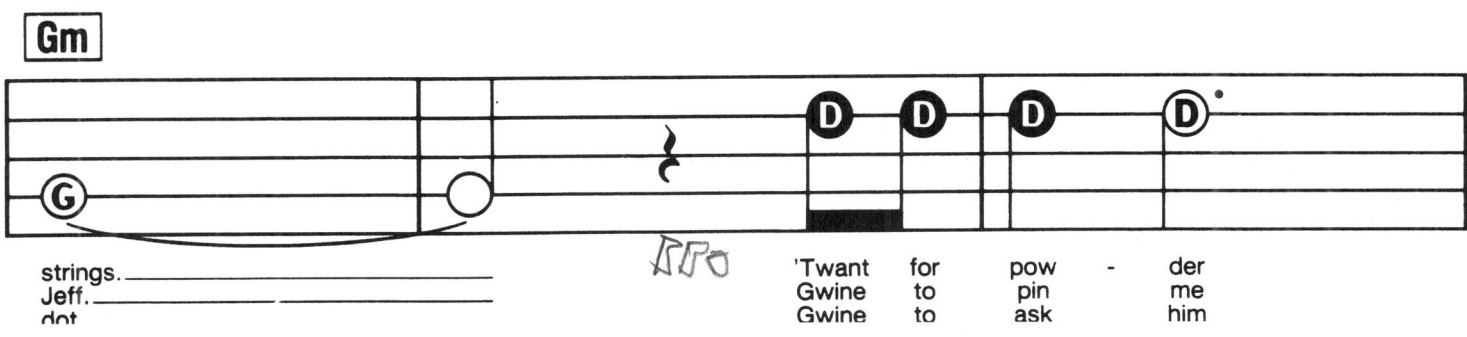

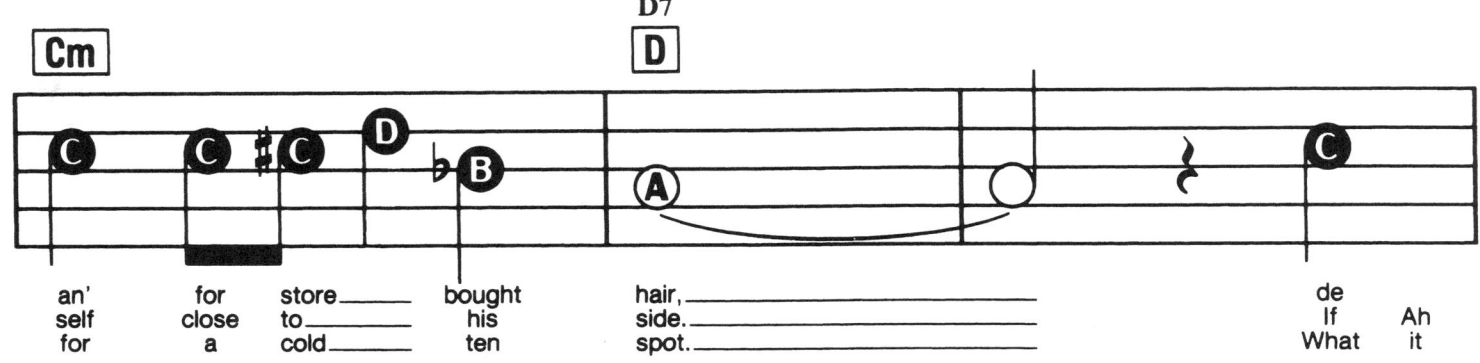
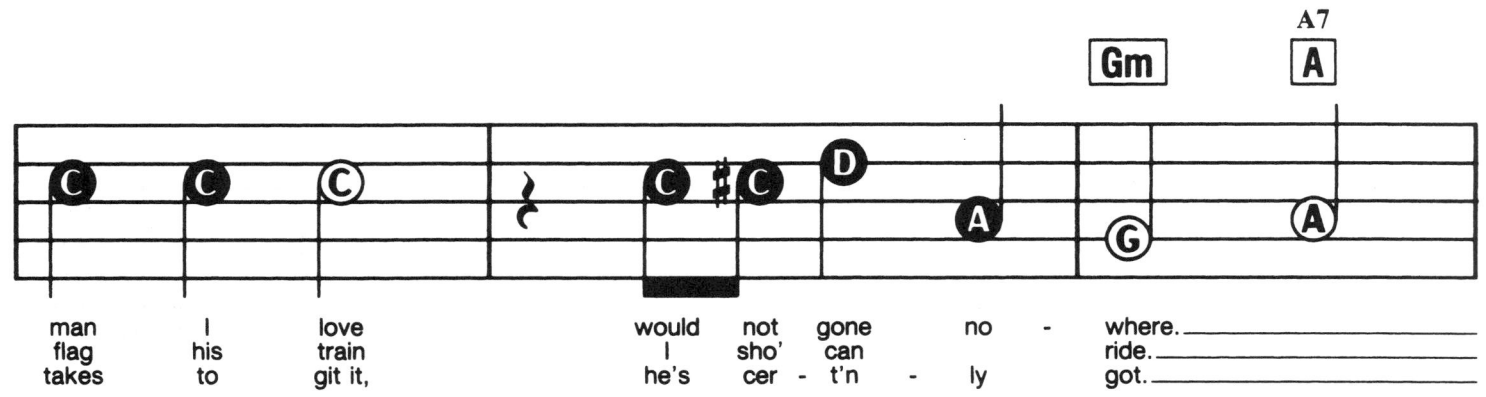
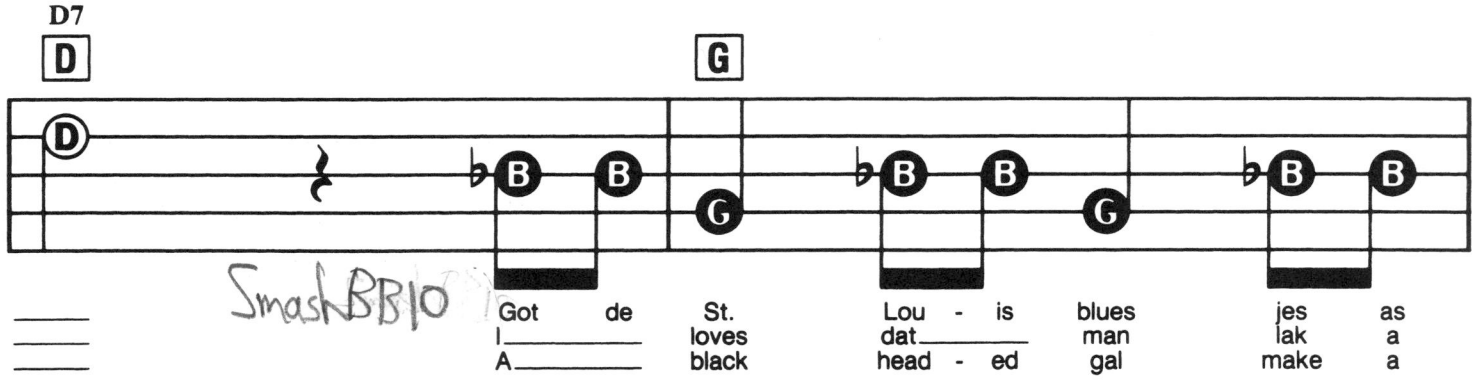
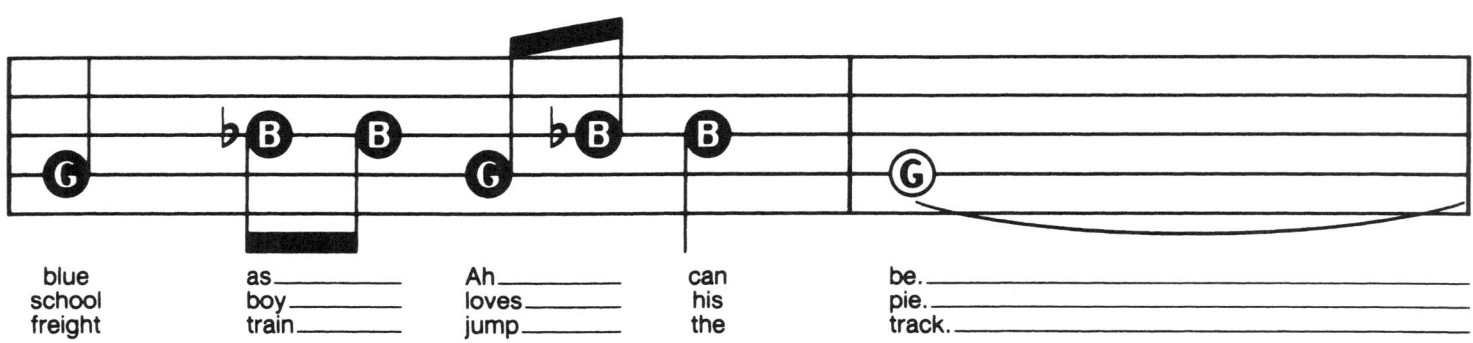

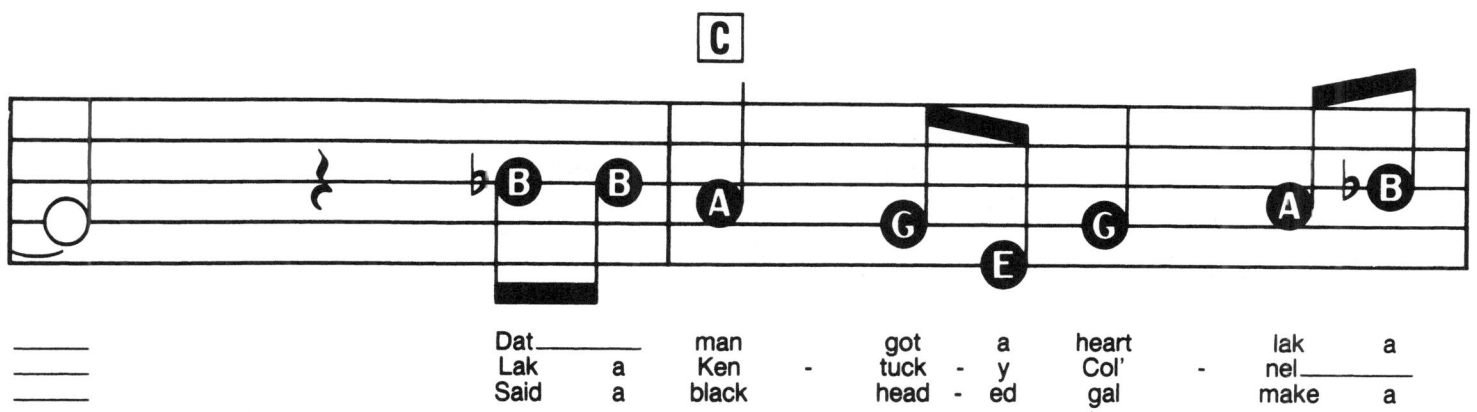
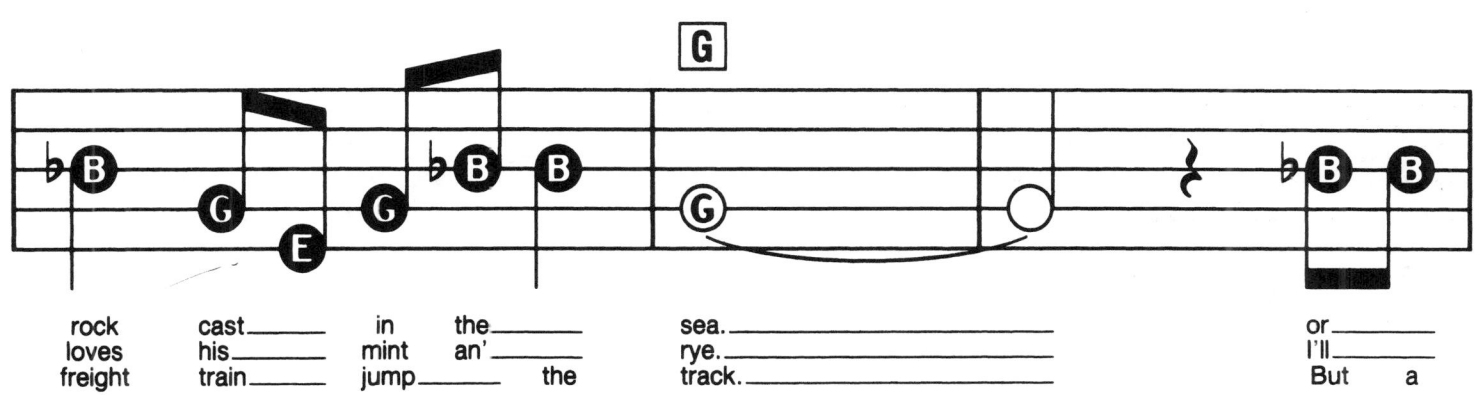
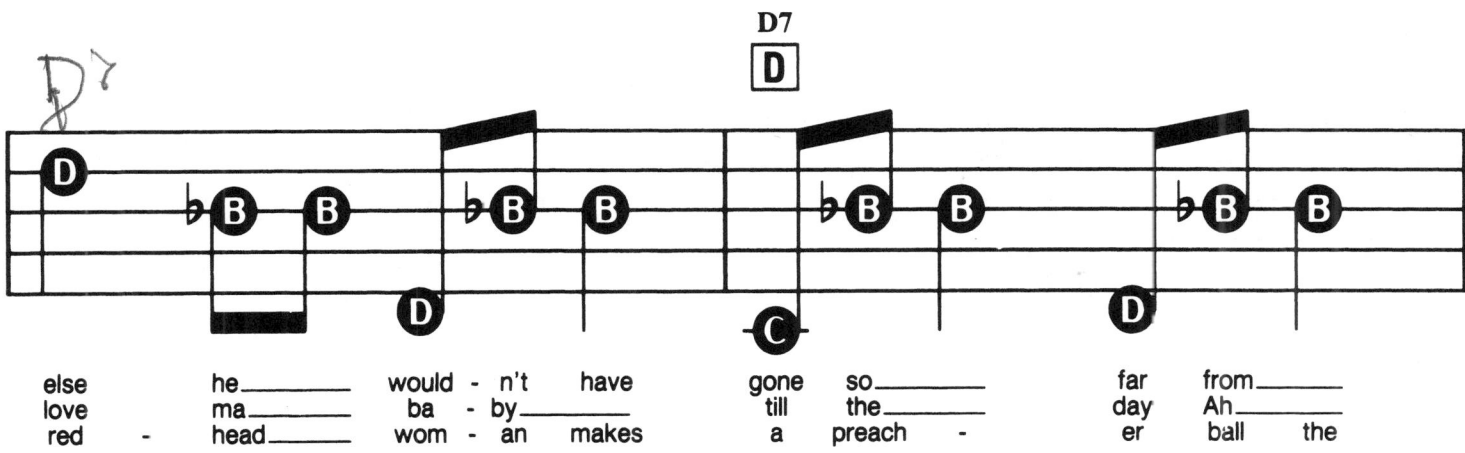
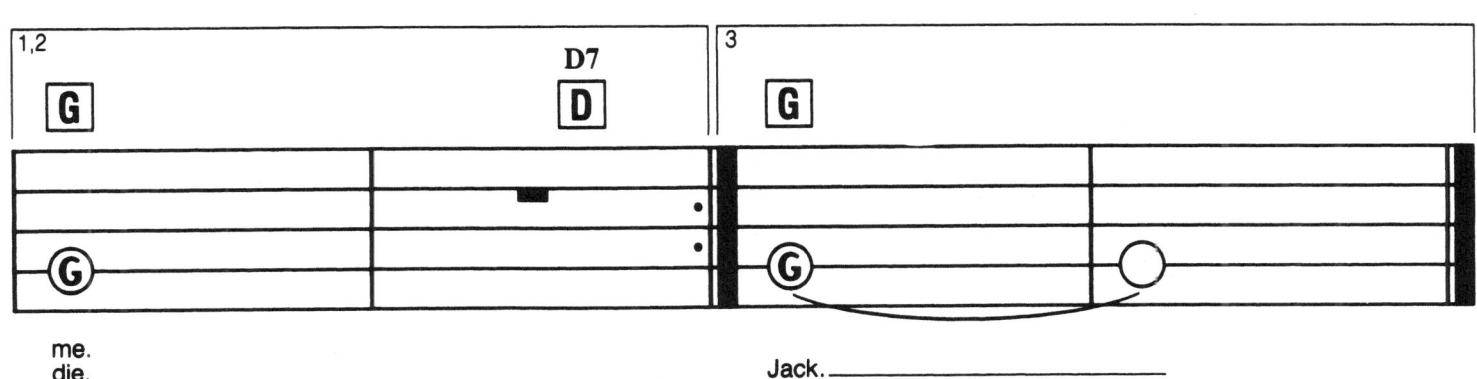

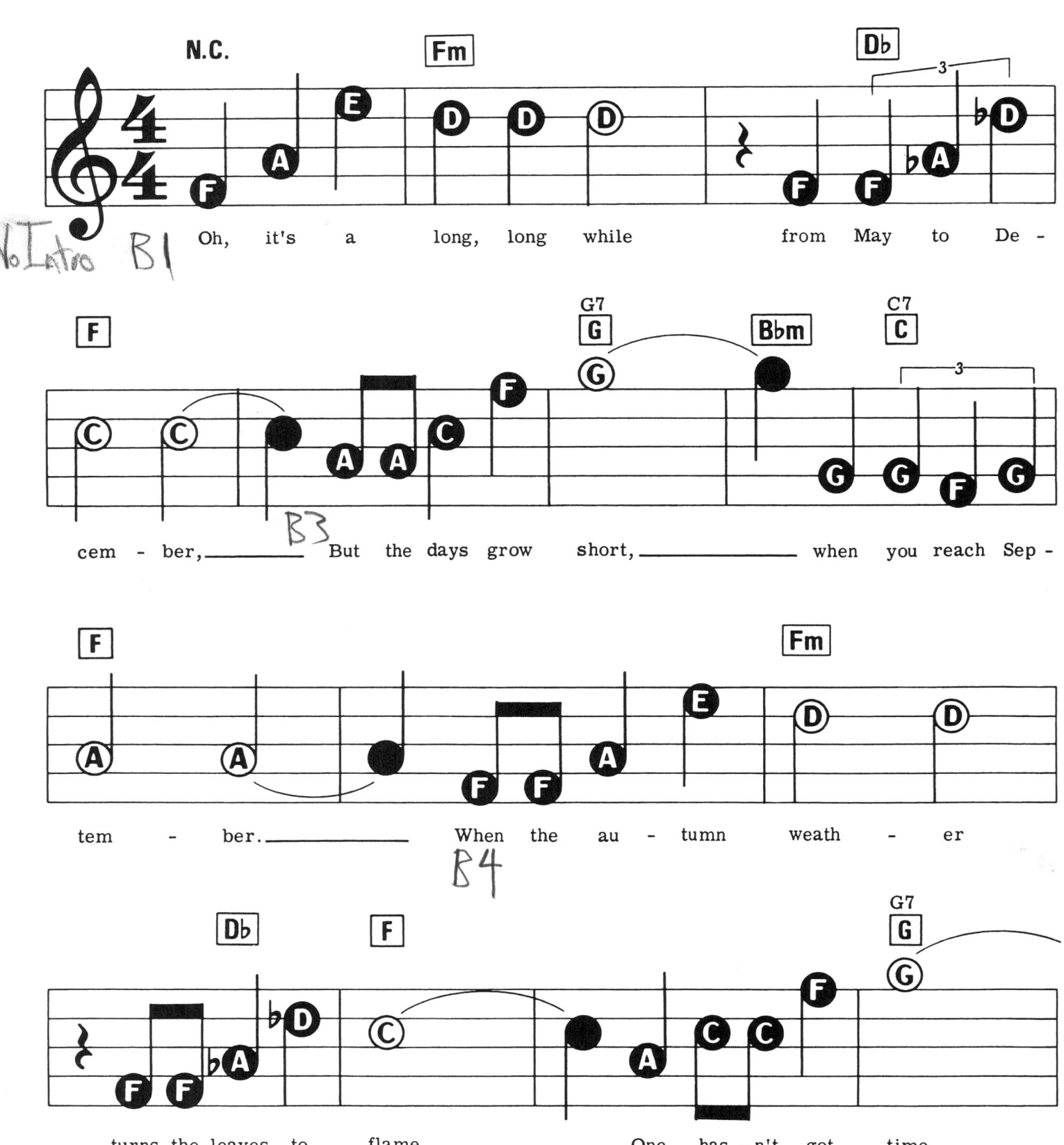

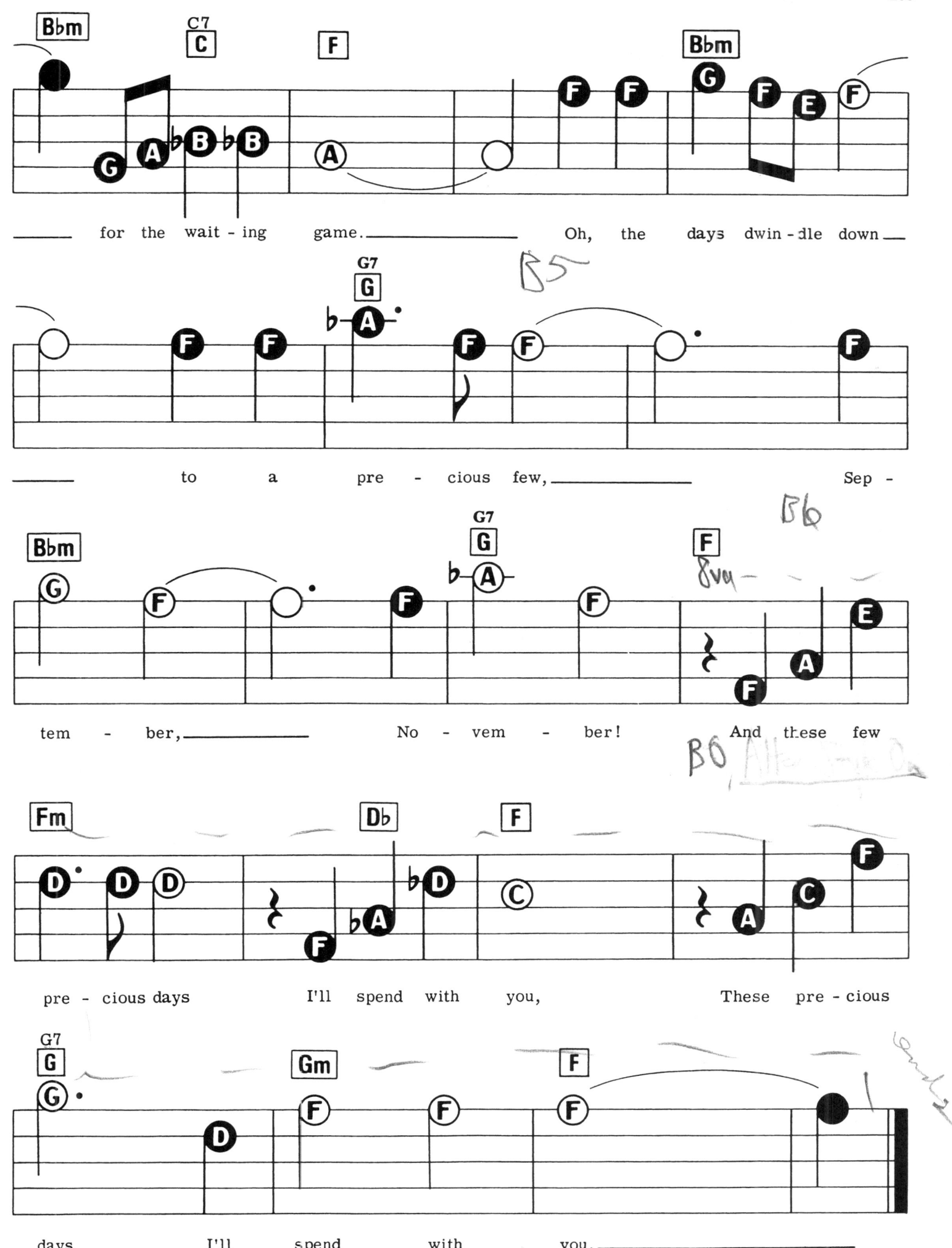

A Sleepin' Bee
from HOUSE OF FLOWERS

Registration 8
Rhythm: Ballad or Fox Trot

Lyric by Truman Capote and Harold Arlen
Music by Harold Arlen

When a bee lies sleep-in' in the palm o' your hand, _____ you're be-witch'd and deep in love's long look'd af-ter land. _____ Where you'll see a sun-up sky with a morn-in' new, and

© 1954 (Renewed) HAROLD ARLEN and TRUMAN CAPOTE
All Rights Controlled by HARWIN MUSIC CO.
All Rights Reserved

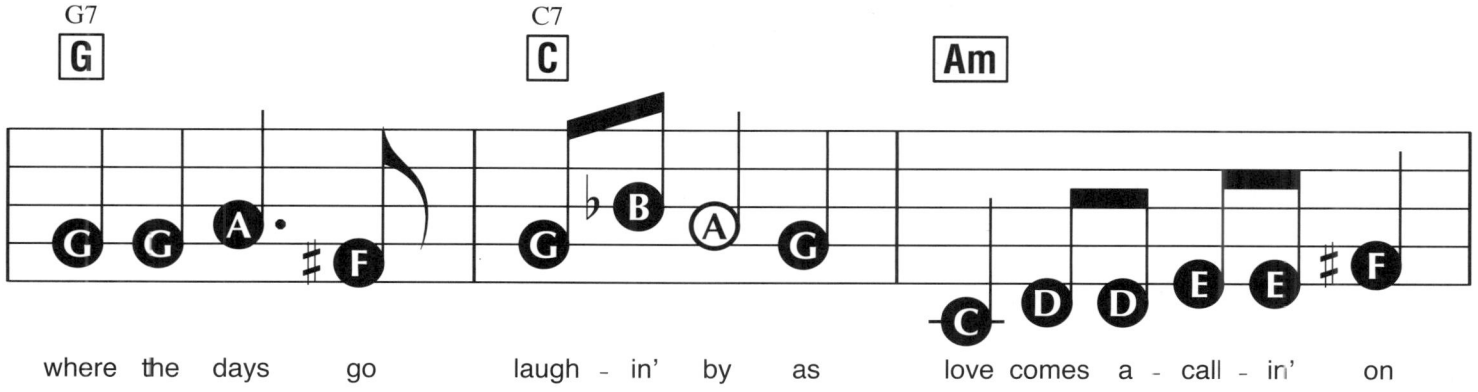
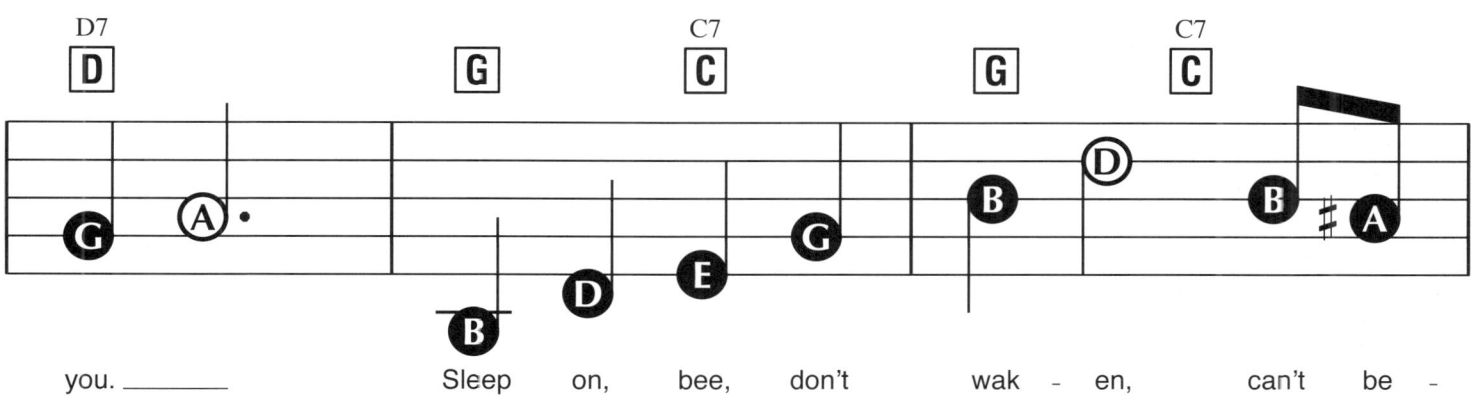
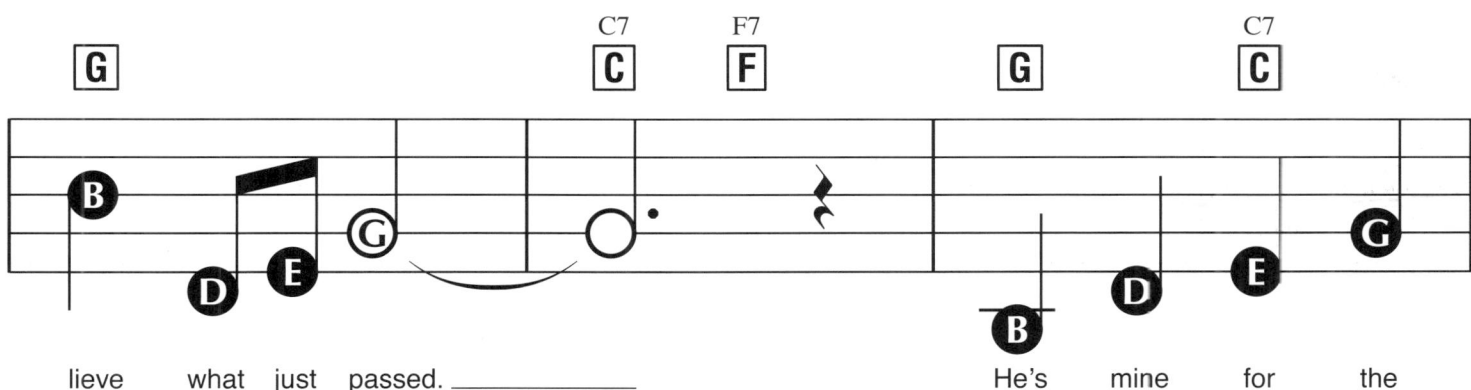
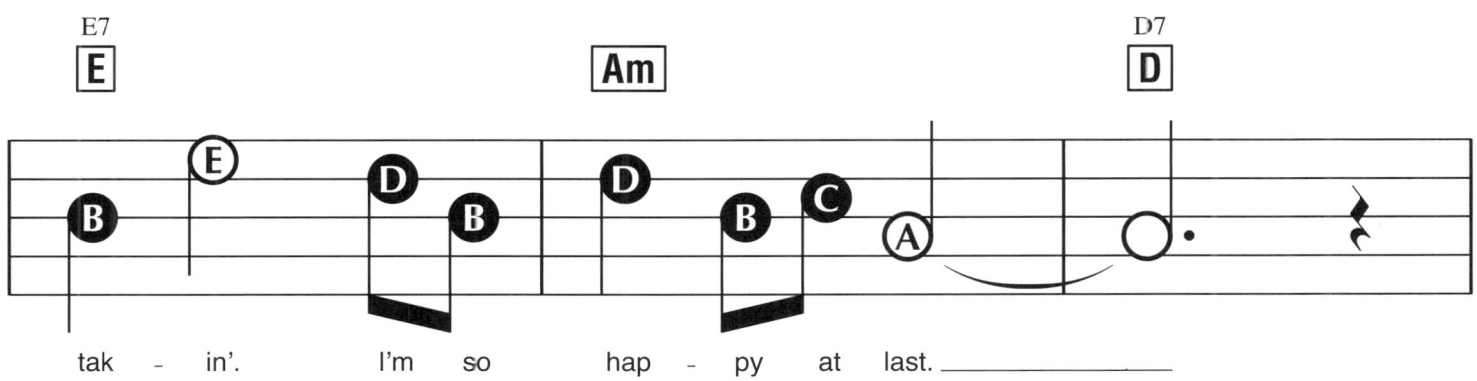

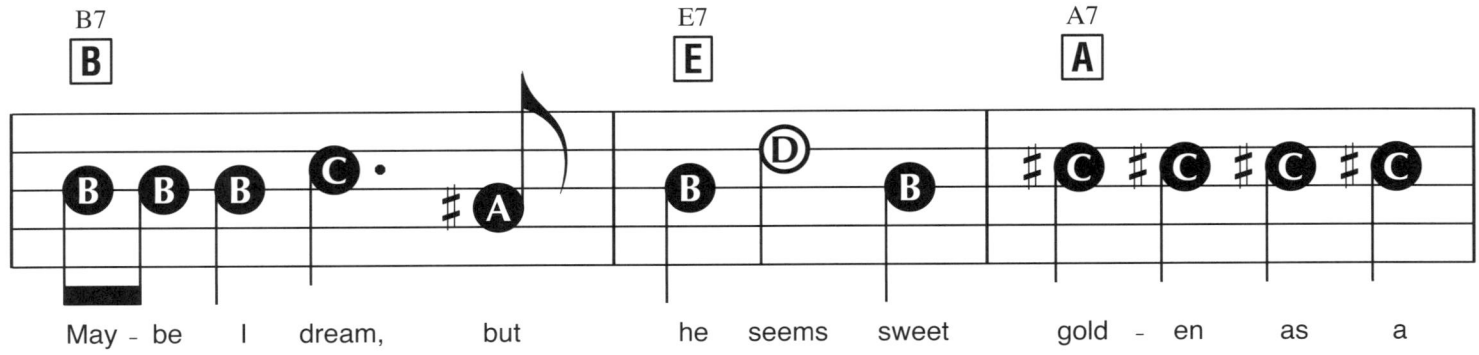
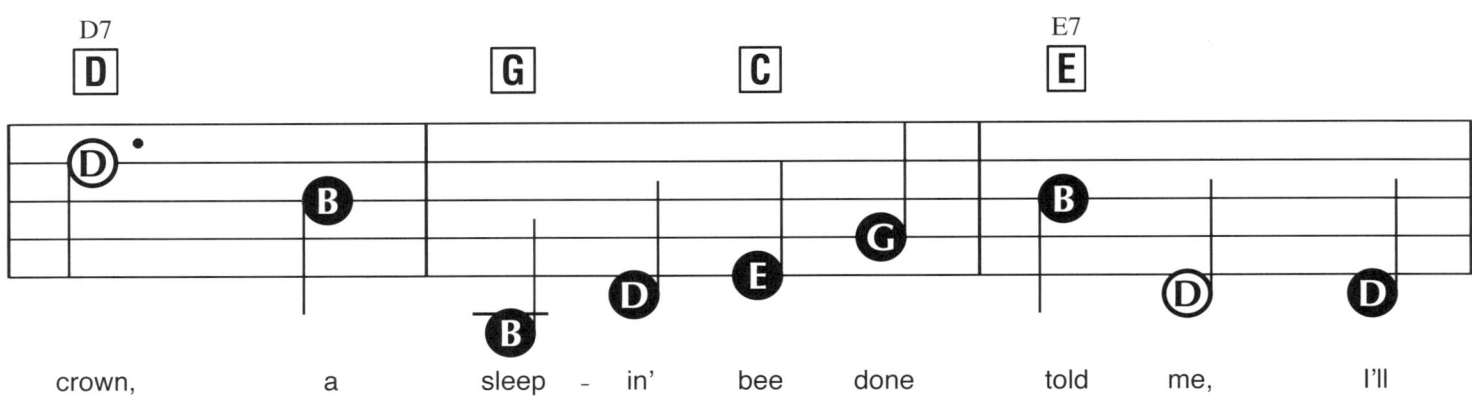
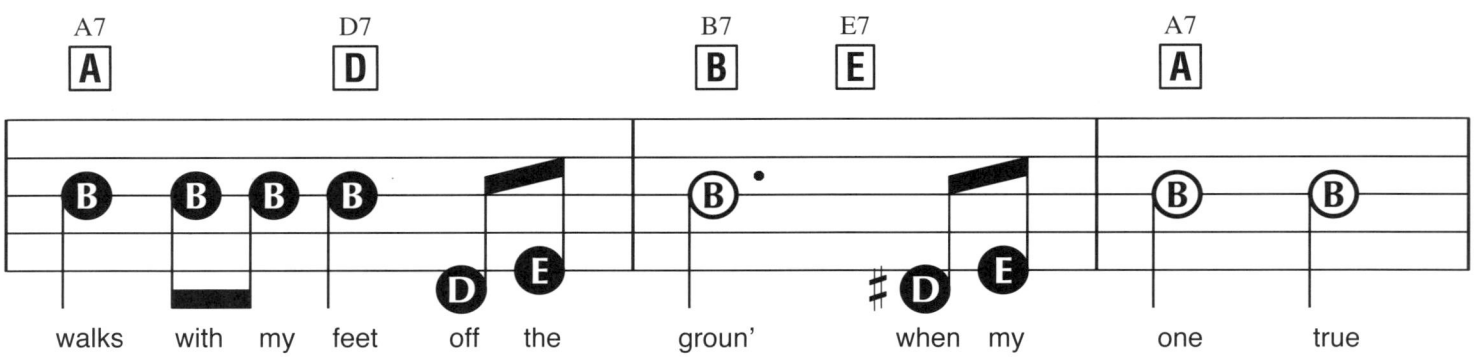
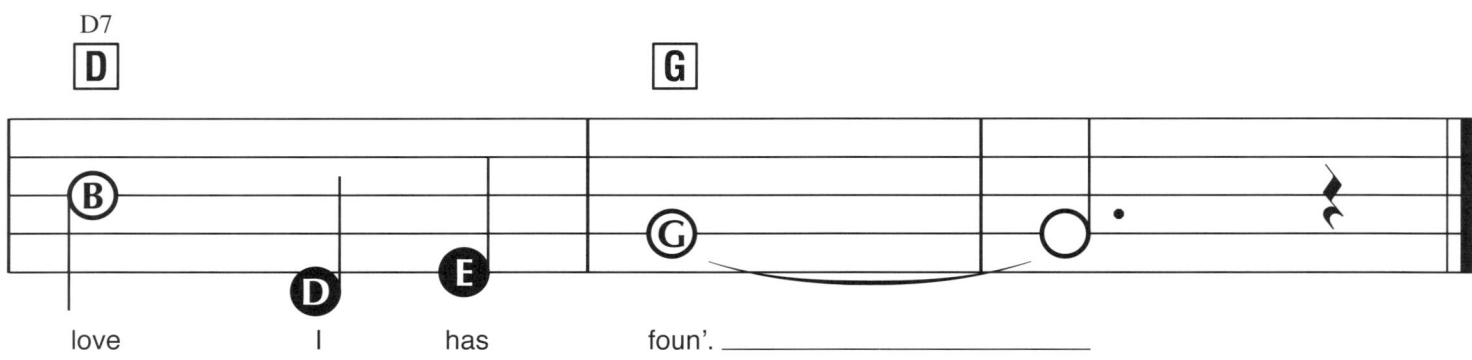

Small World
from GYPSY

Registration 9
Rhythm: Fox Trot or Swing

Words by Stephen Sondheim
Music by Jule Styne

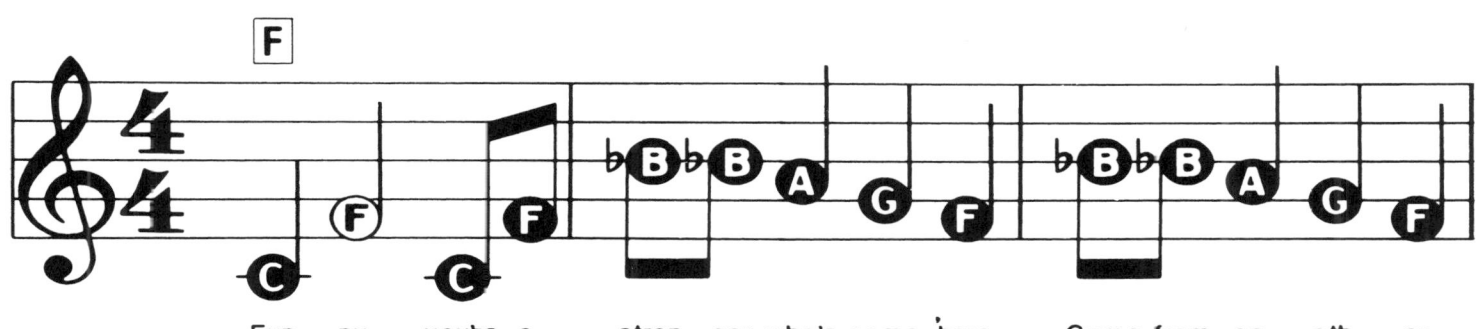
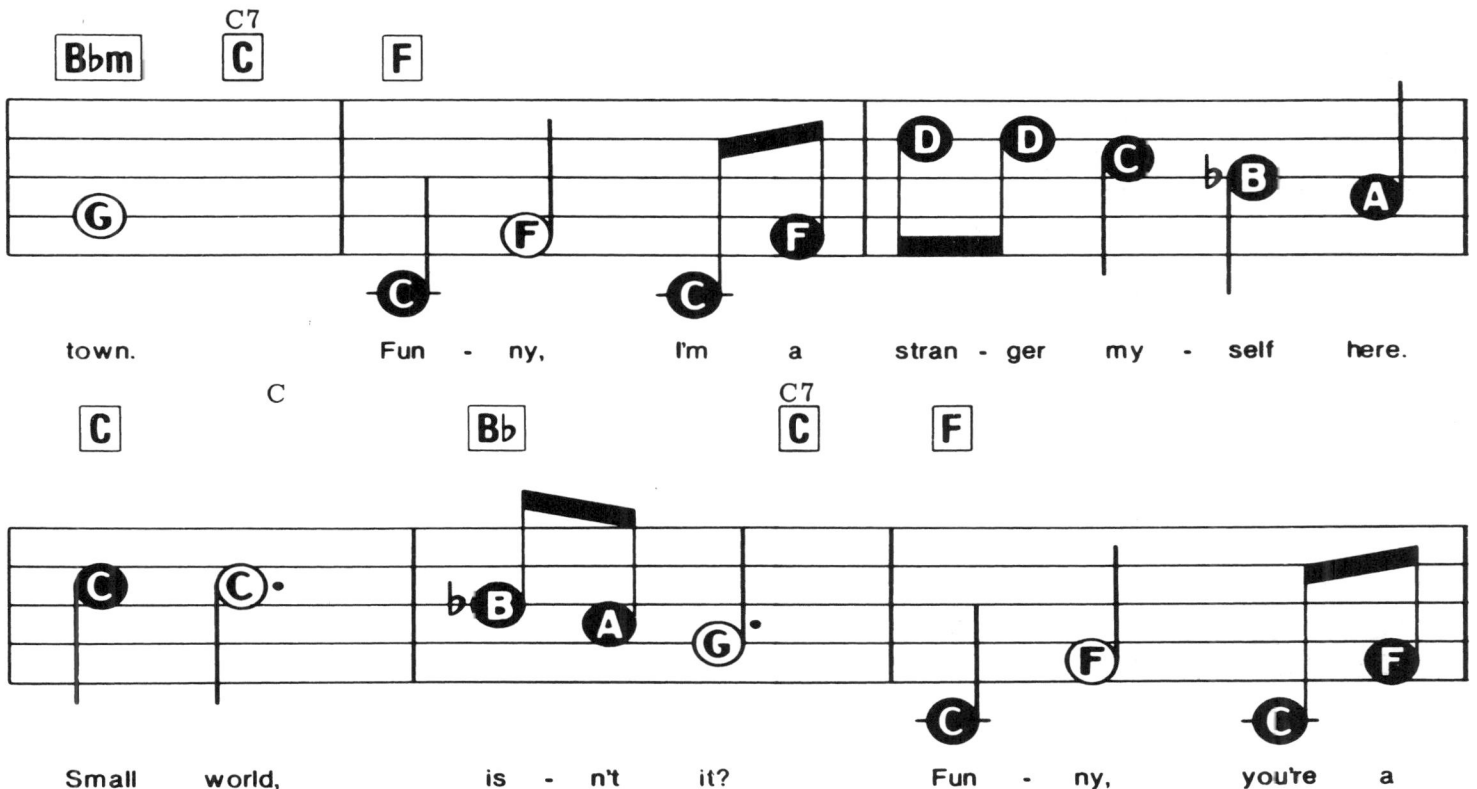
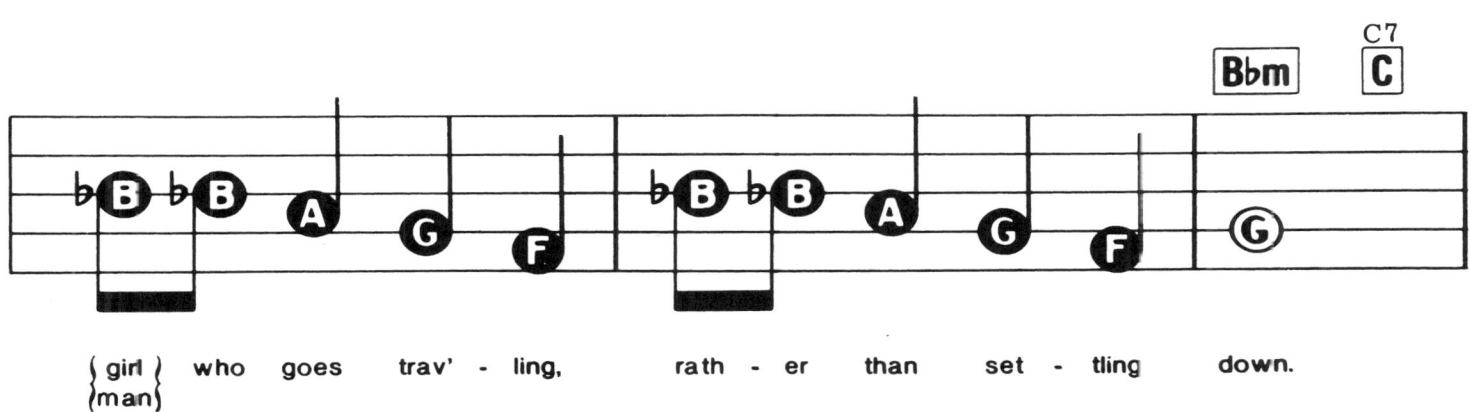

Copyright © 1959 by Stratford Music Corporation and Williamson Music, Inc.
Copyright Renewed
All Rights Administered by Chappell & Co.
International Copyright Secured   All Rights Reserved

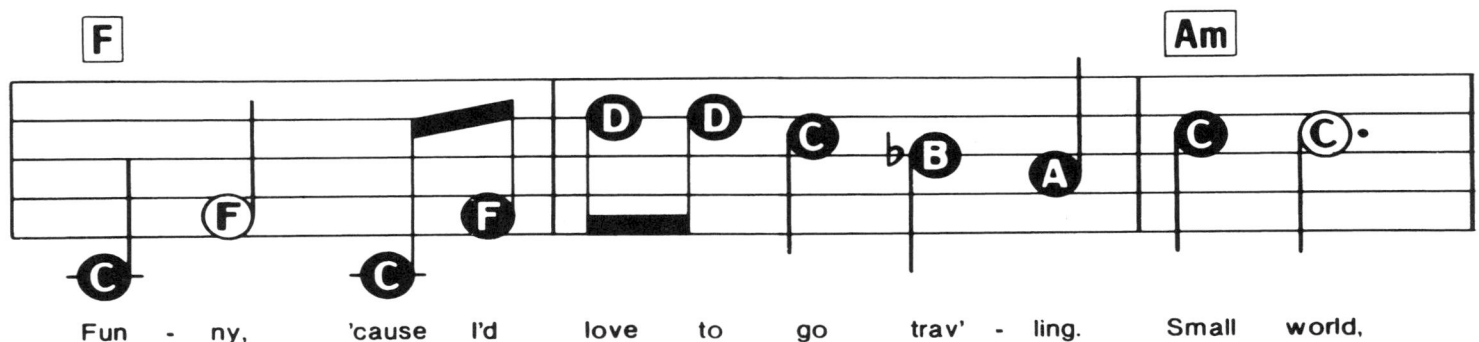
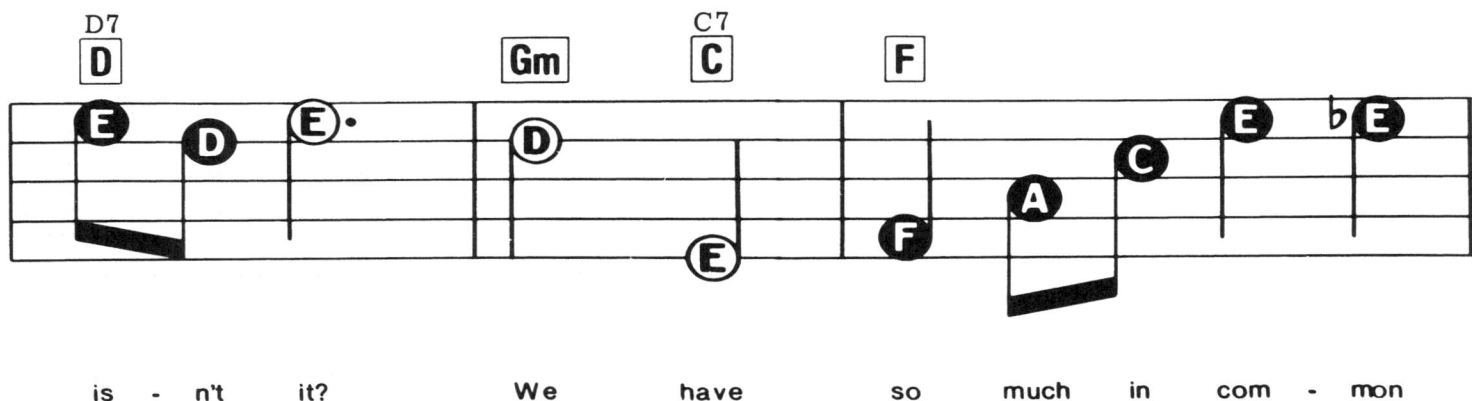
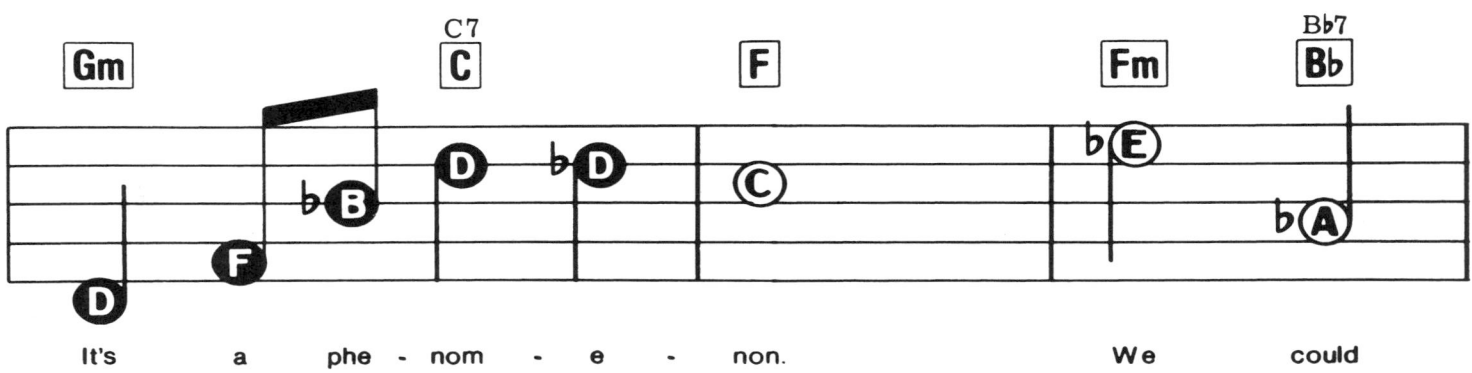
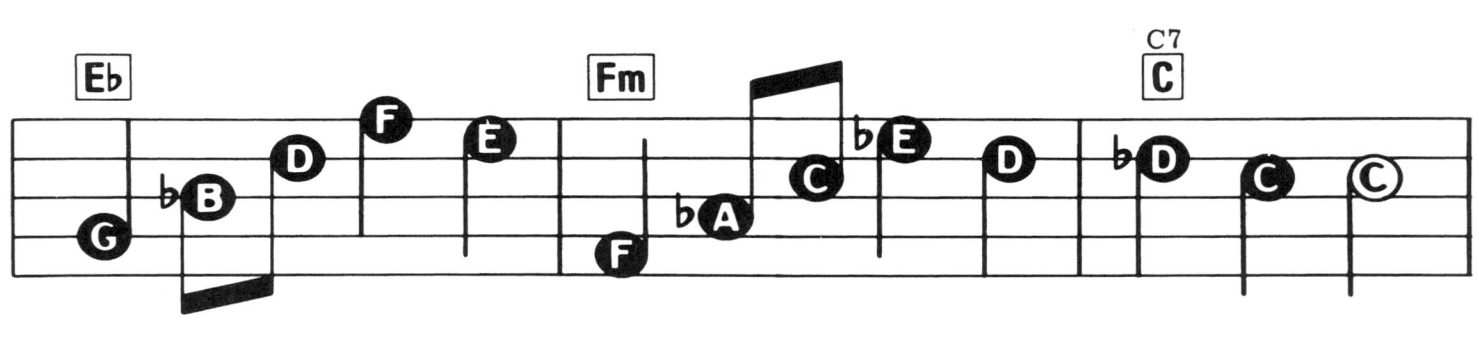

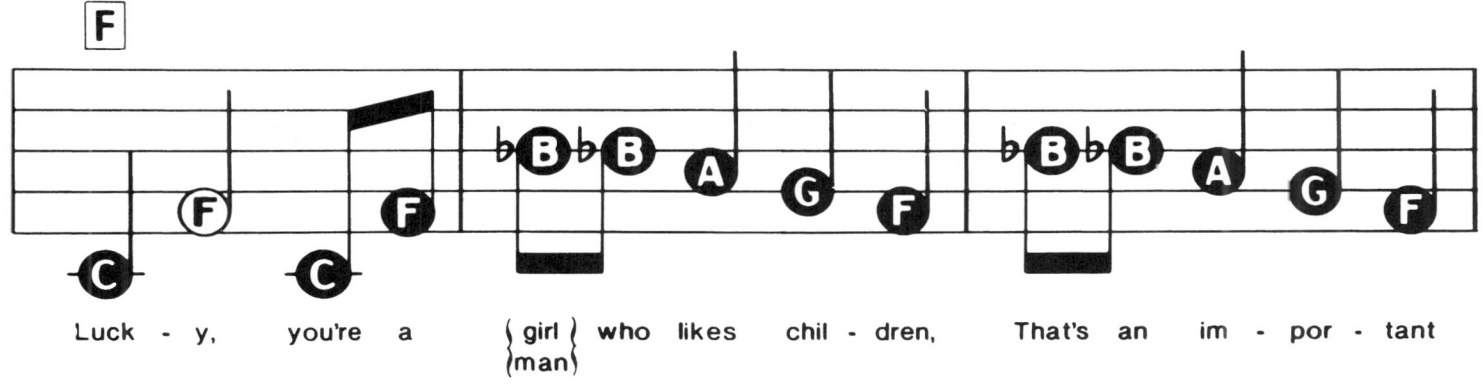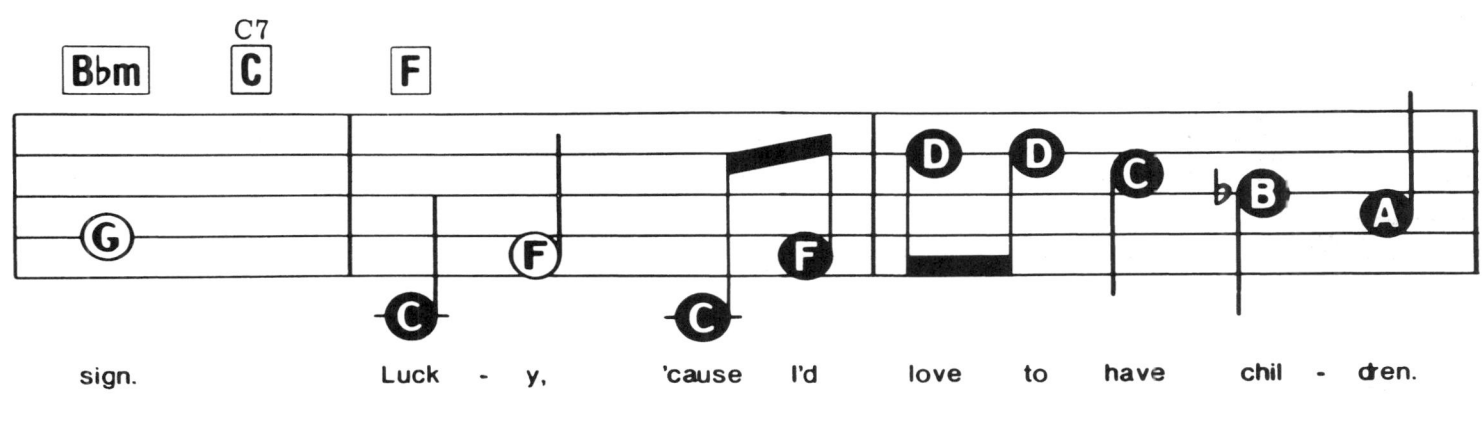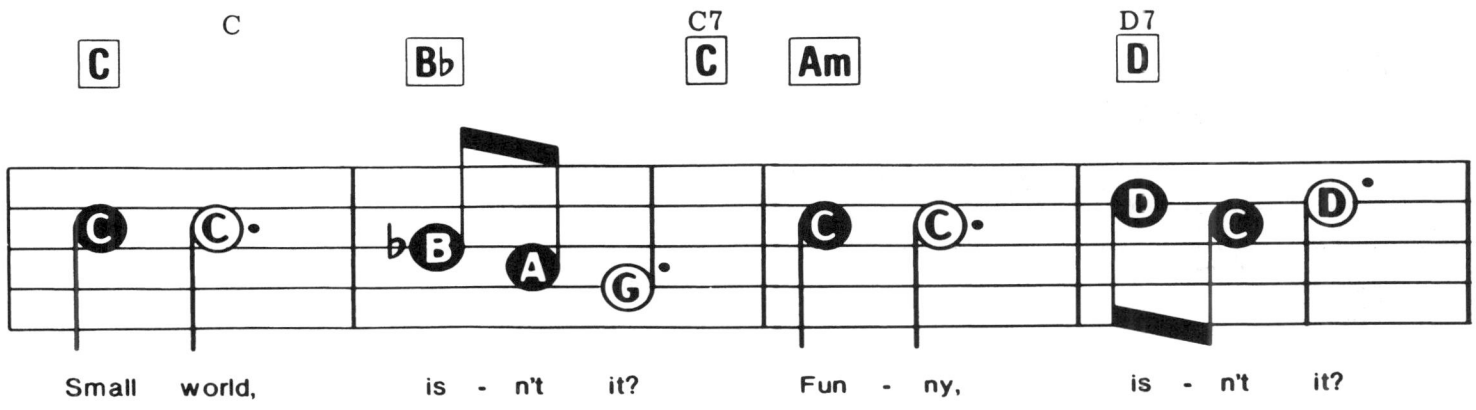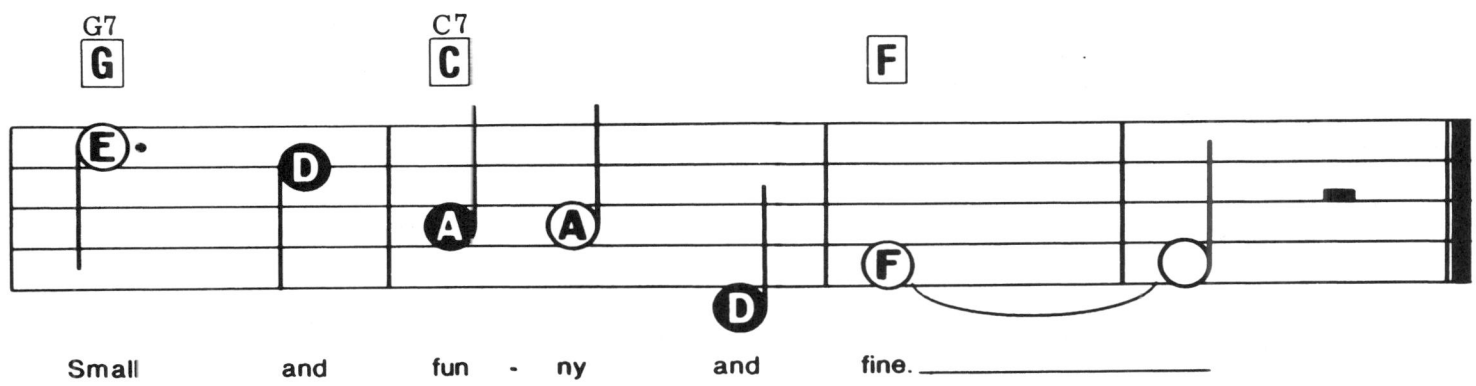

Solitude

Registration 7
Rhythm: Ballad

Words and Music by Duke Ellington,
Eddie De Lange and Irving Mills

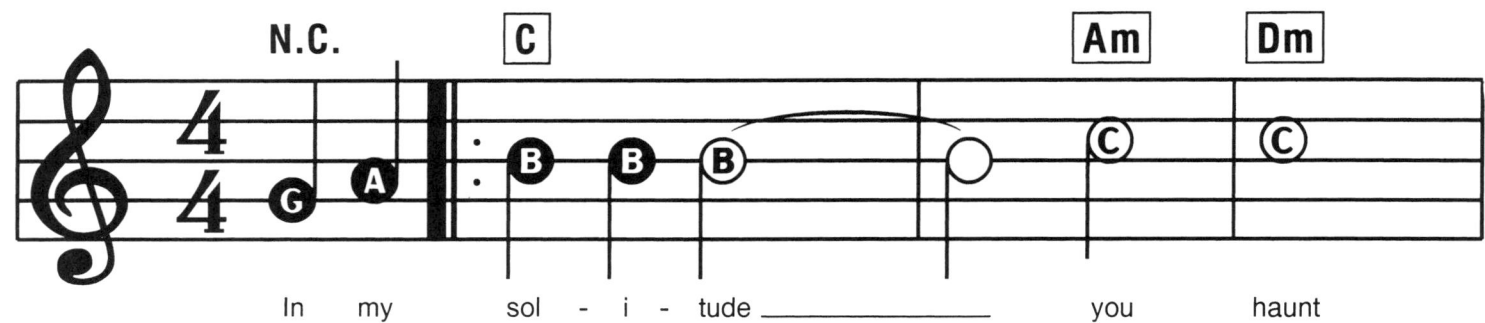

In my sol - i - tude ____ you haunt

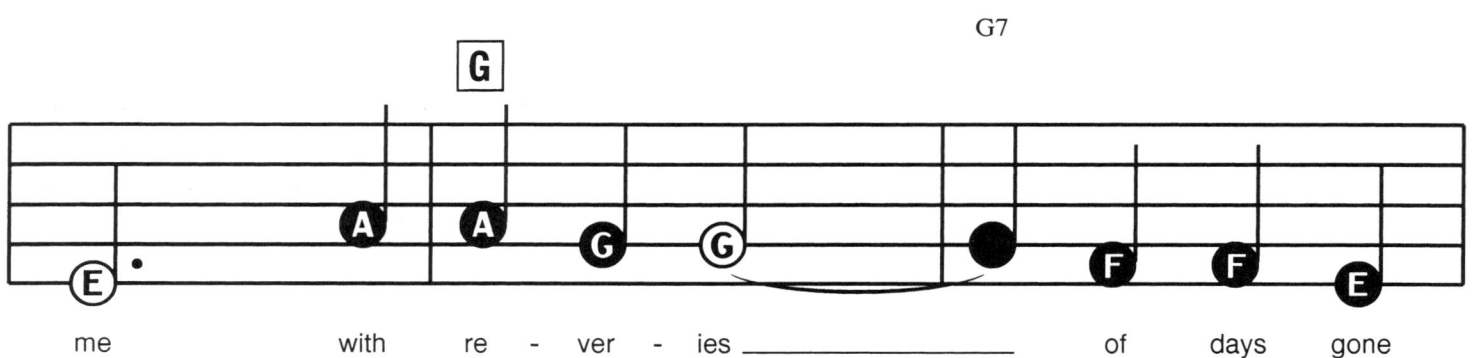

me with re - ver - ies ____ of days gone

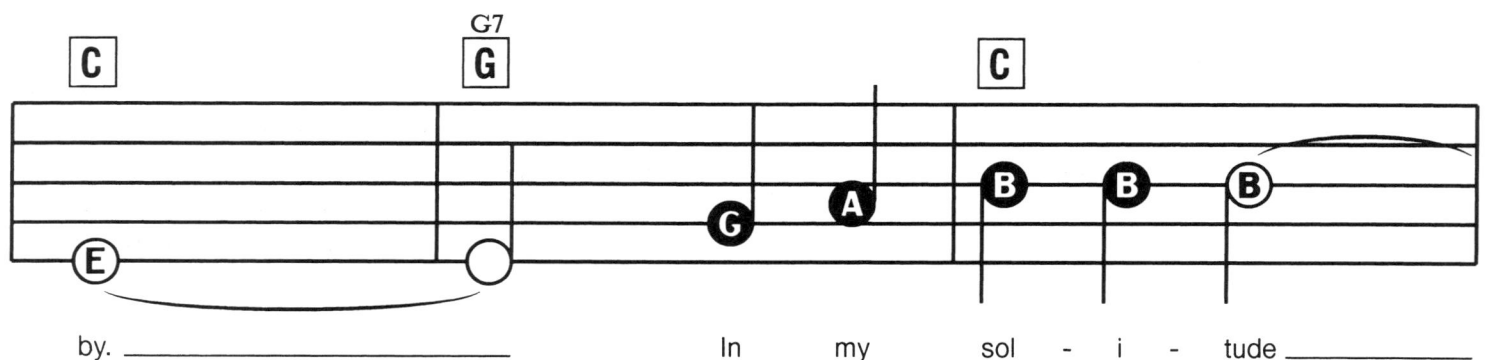

by. ____ In my sol - i - tude ____

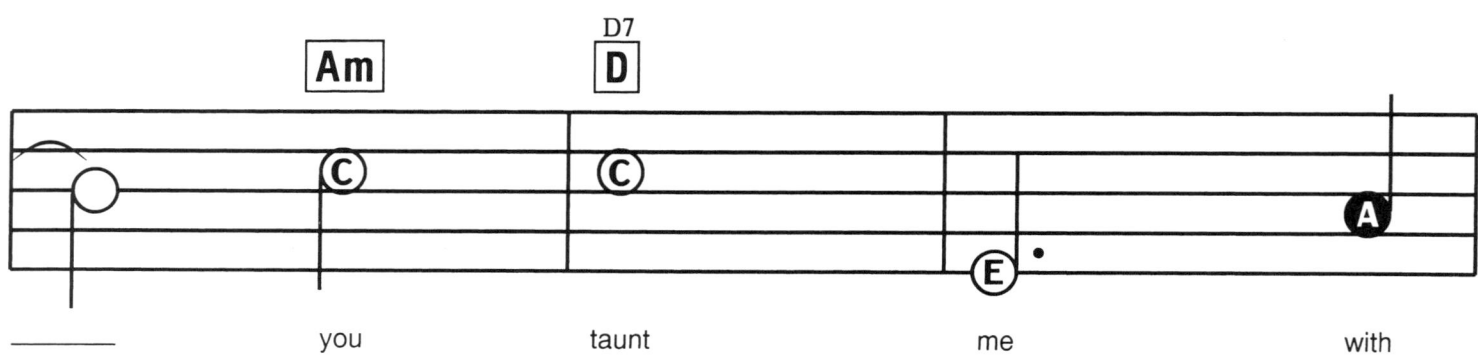

____ you taunt me with

Copyright © 1934 Sony/ATV Music Publishing LLC, Scarsdale Music Corp. and EMI Mills Music Inc. in the U.S.A.
Copyright Renewed
All Rights on behalf of Sony/ATV Music Publishing LLC Administered by Sony/ATV Music Publishing LLC, 8 Music Square West, Nashville, TN 37203
Rights for the world outside the U.S.A. Administered by EMI Mills Music Inc. (Publishing) and Alfred Publishing Co., Inc. (Print)
International Copyright Secured   All Rights Reserved

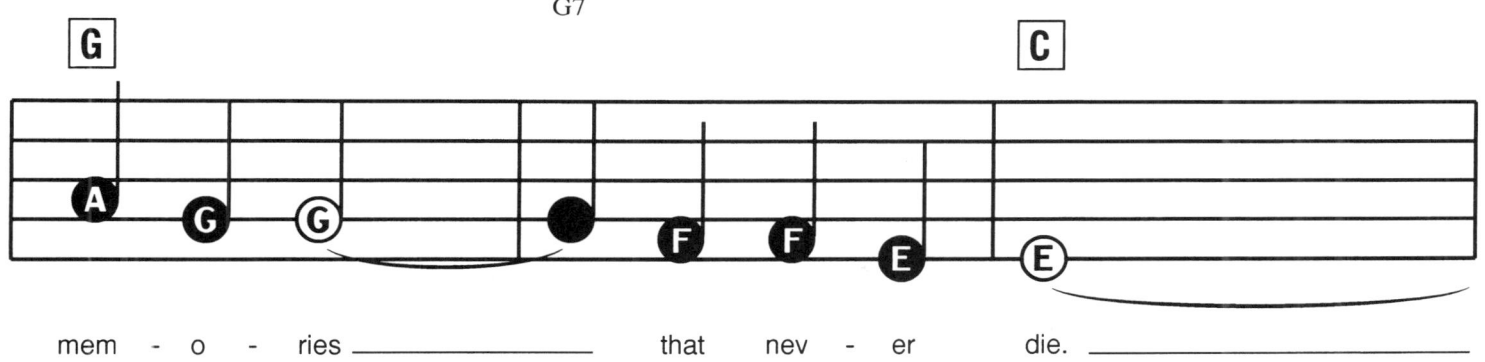
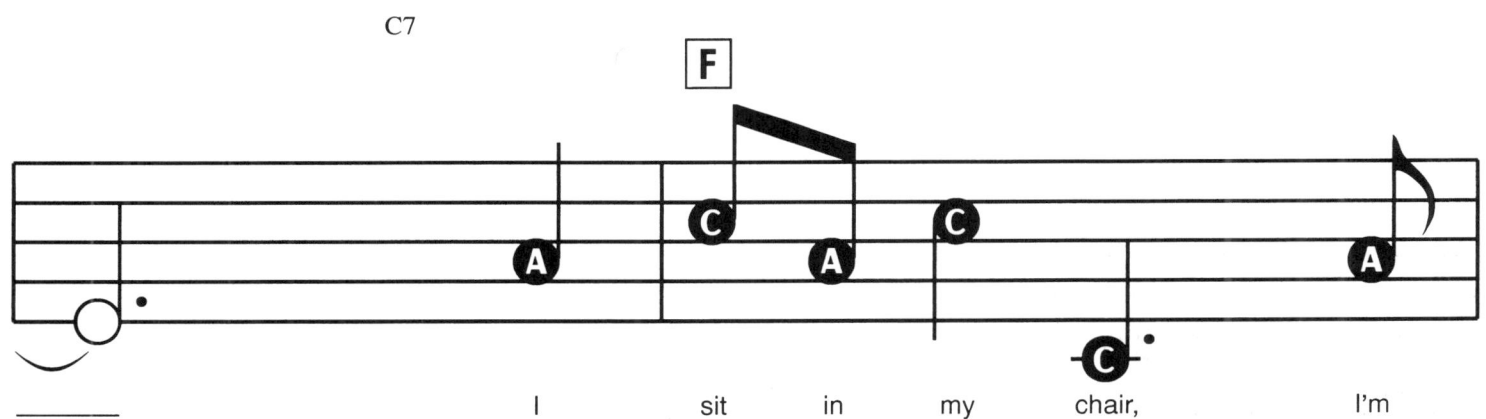
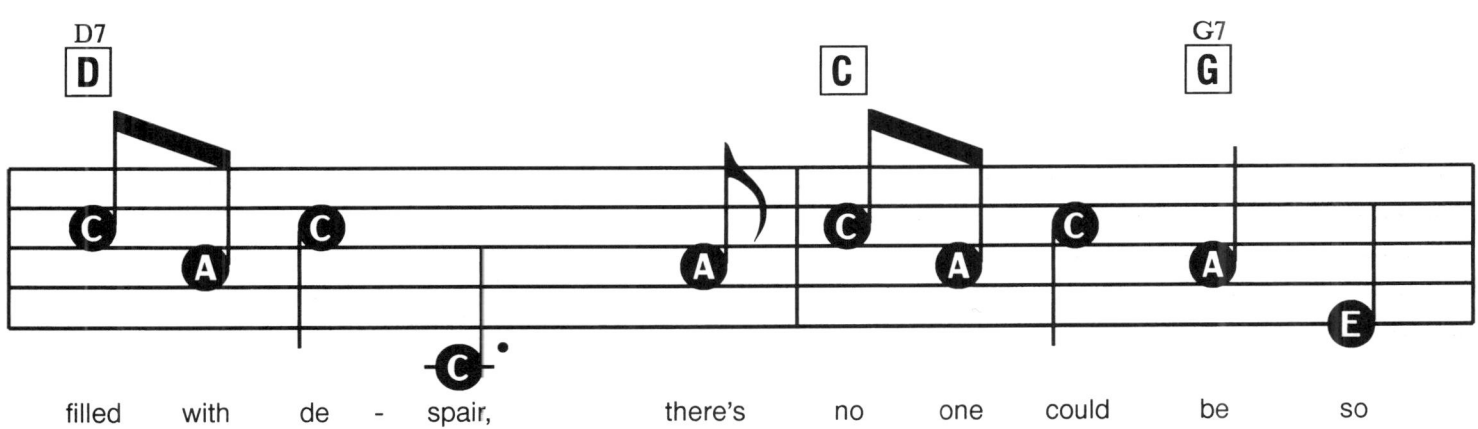
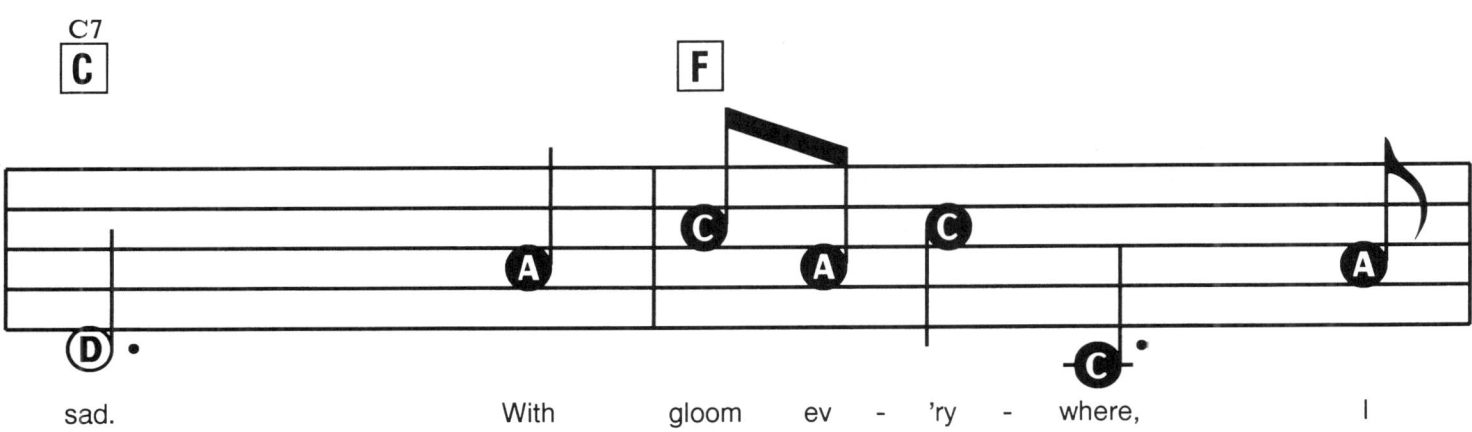

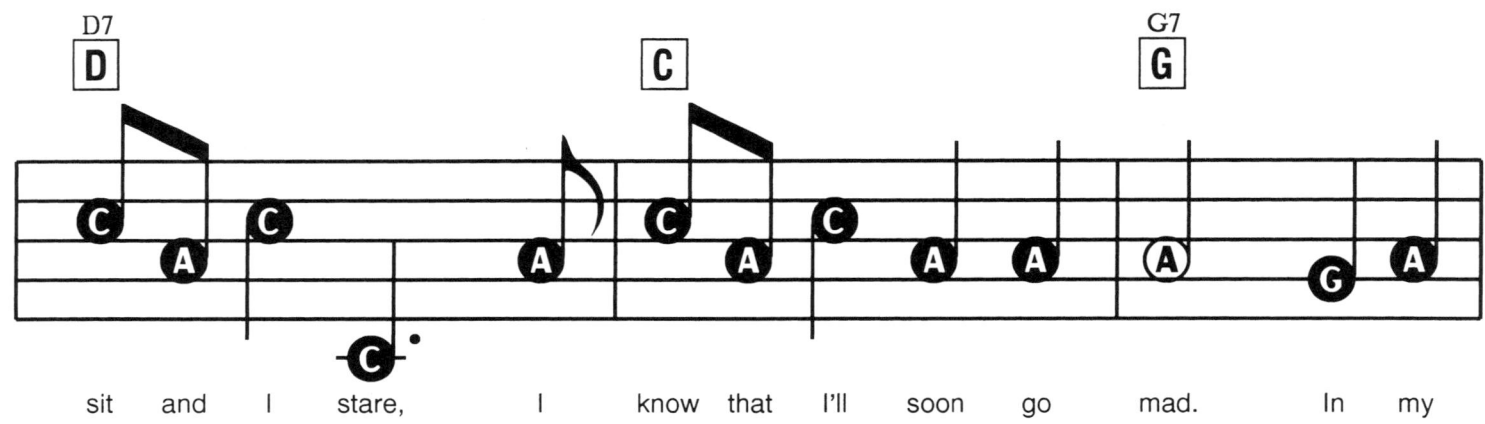
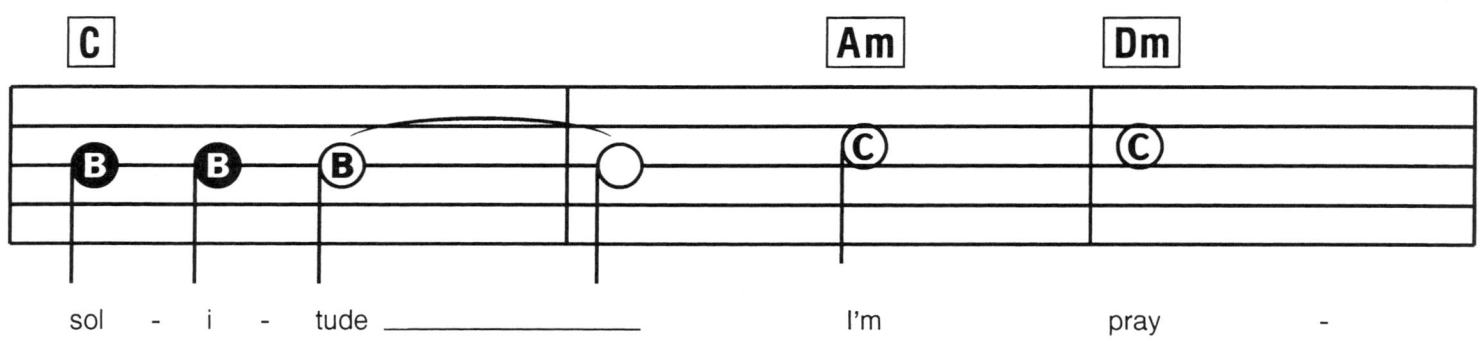
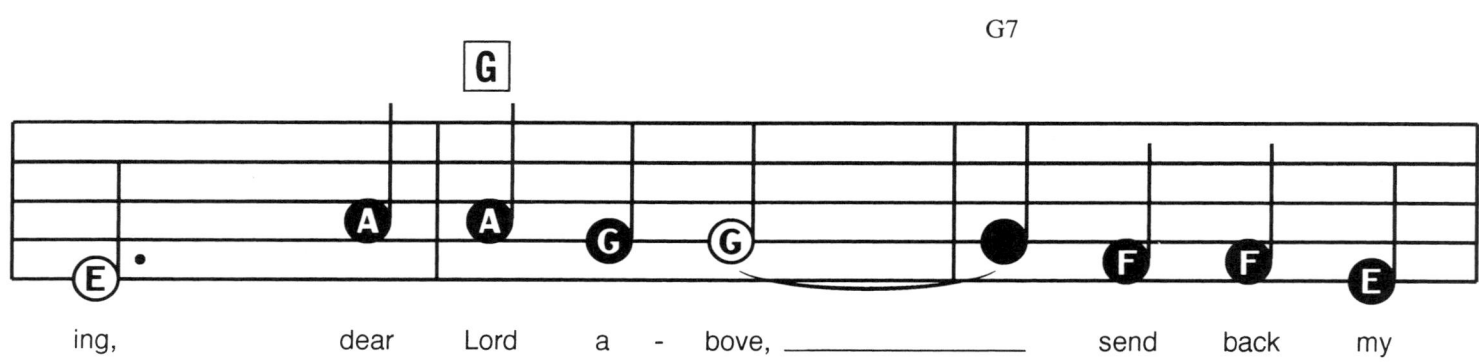
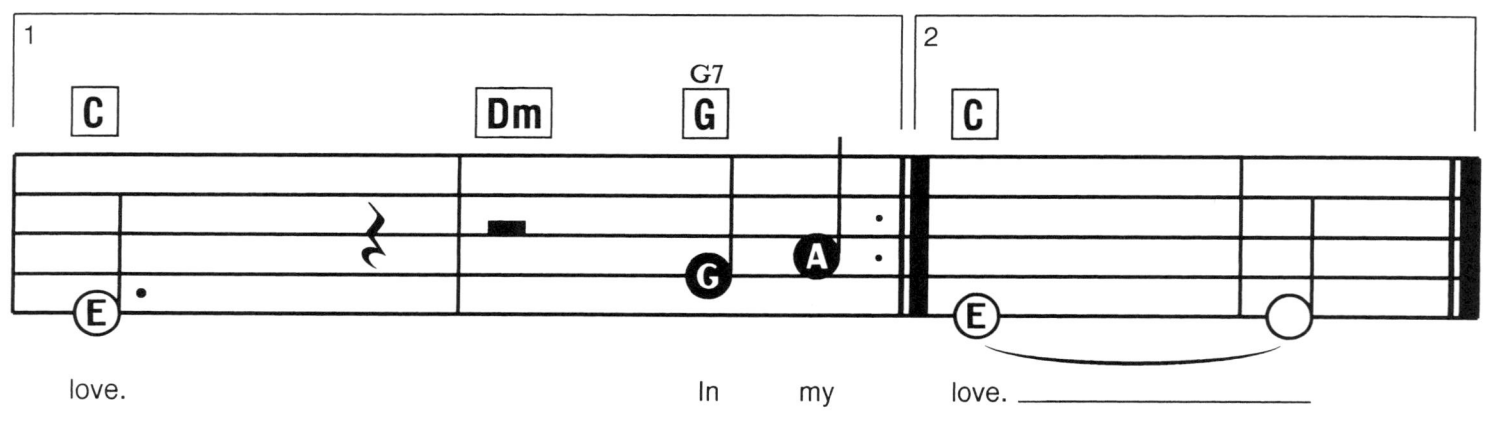

When You're Smiling
(The Whole World Smiles With You)

Registration 9
Rhythm: Swing

Words and Music by
Joe Goodwin and Larry Shay

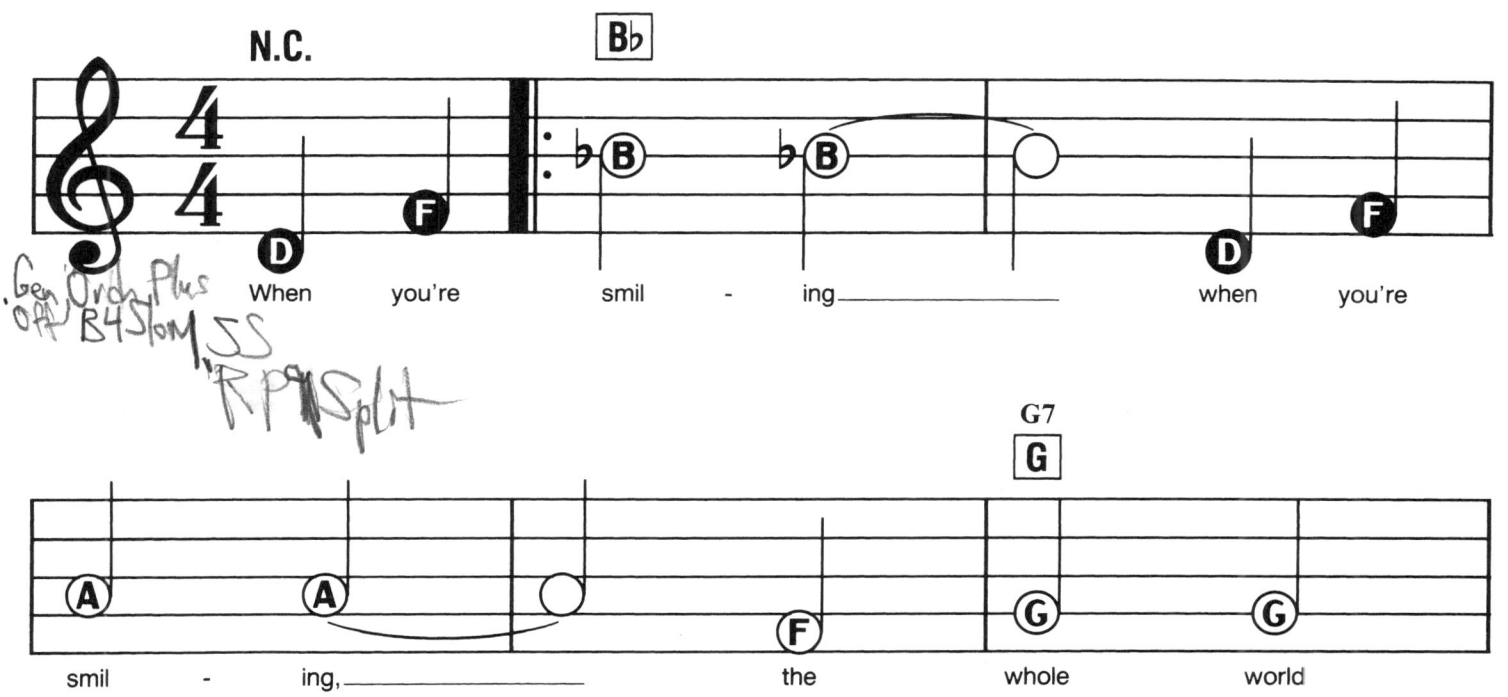

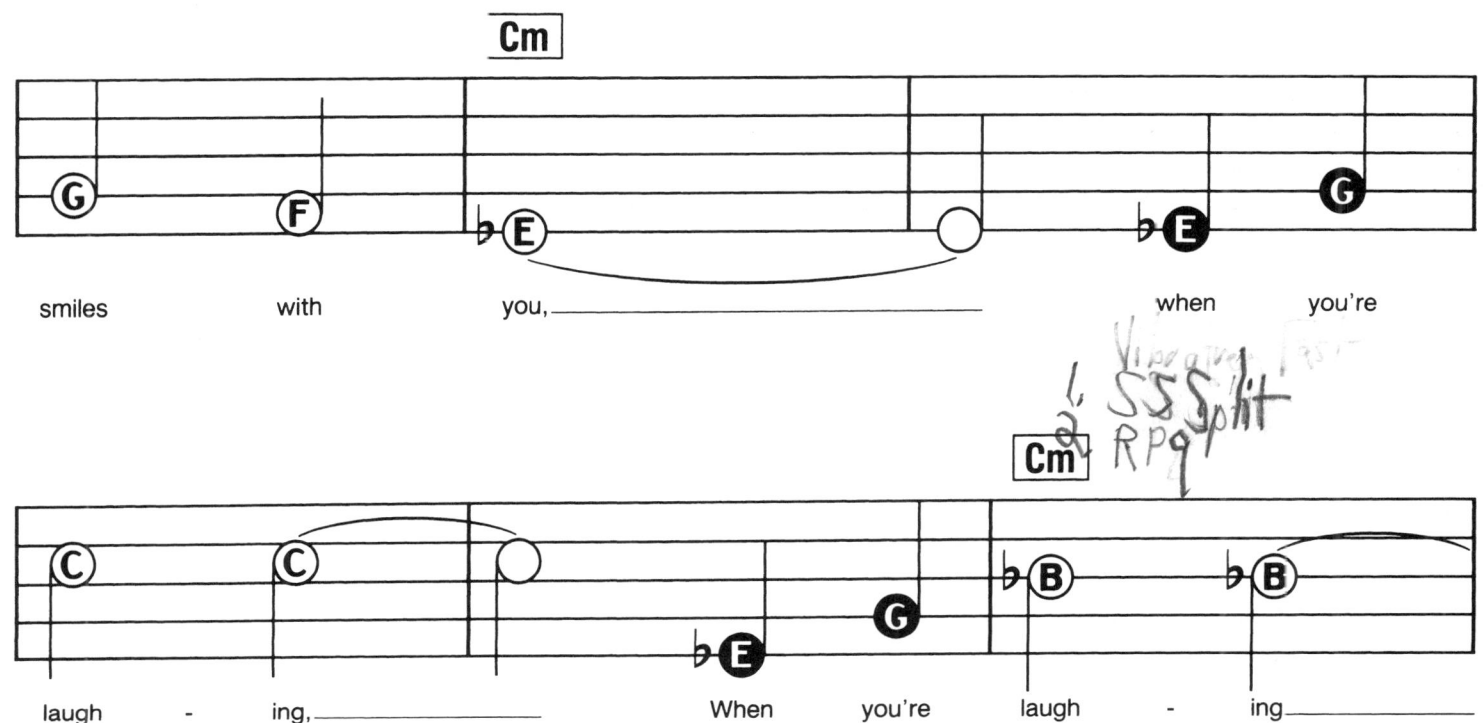

Copyright © 1928 EMI Mills Music Inc. and Music By Shay
Copyright Renewed
All Rights for Music By Shay Administered by The Songwriters Guild Of America
International Copyright Secured   All Rights Reserved

F7
F
G A A A G
The sun comes shin - ing
Bb
Bb7
Bb
F E F G bA bA
thru, But when you're cry - ing
1. RPO Split
2. RP10 Split
Eb
C C bB A bB
you bring on the rain,
C7
C
#F G A bB bB
So stop your sigh - ing

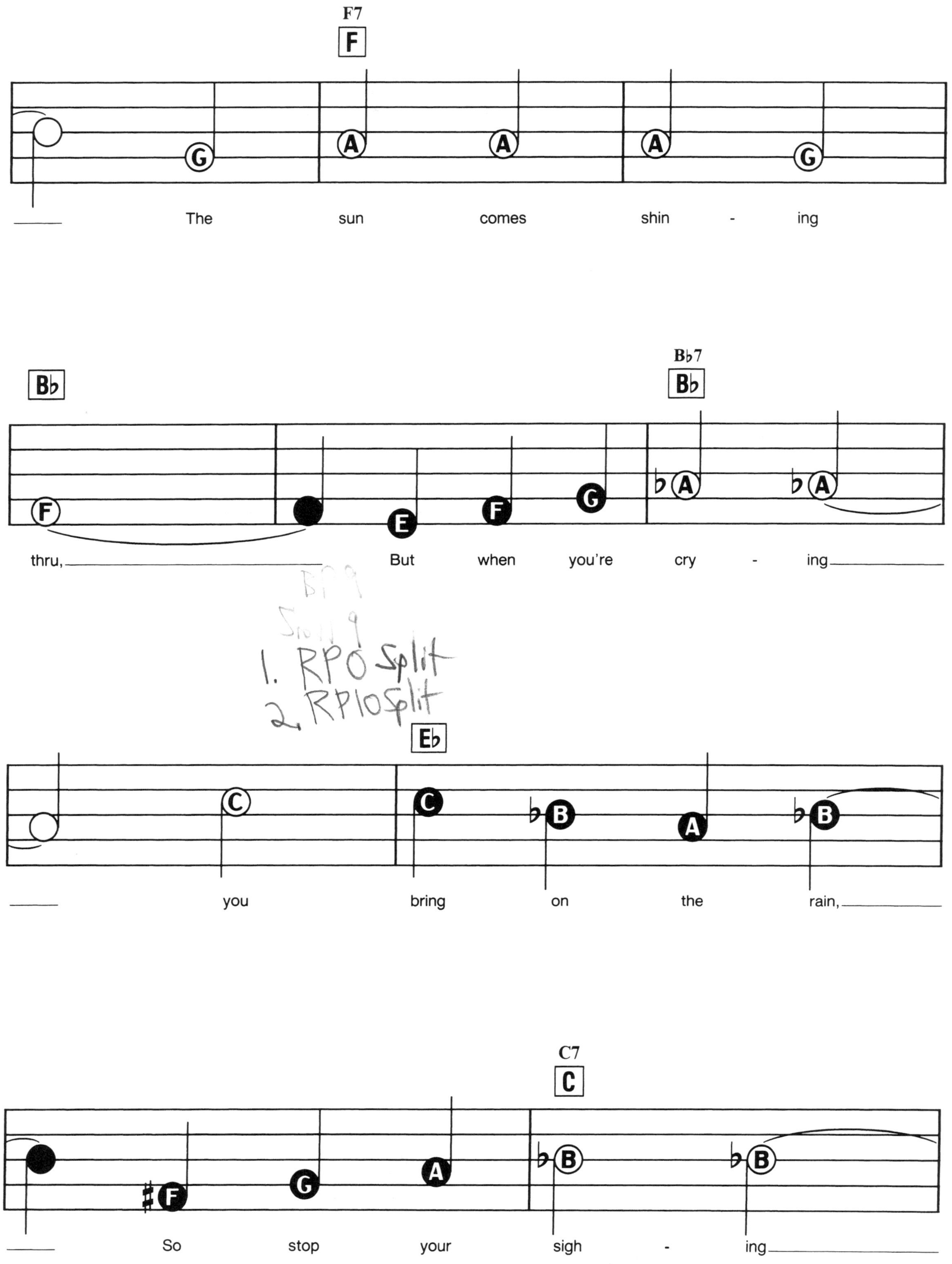

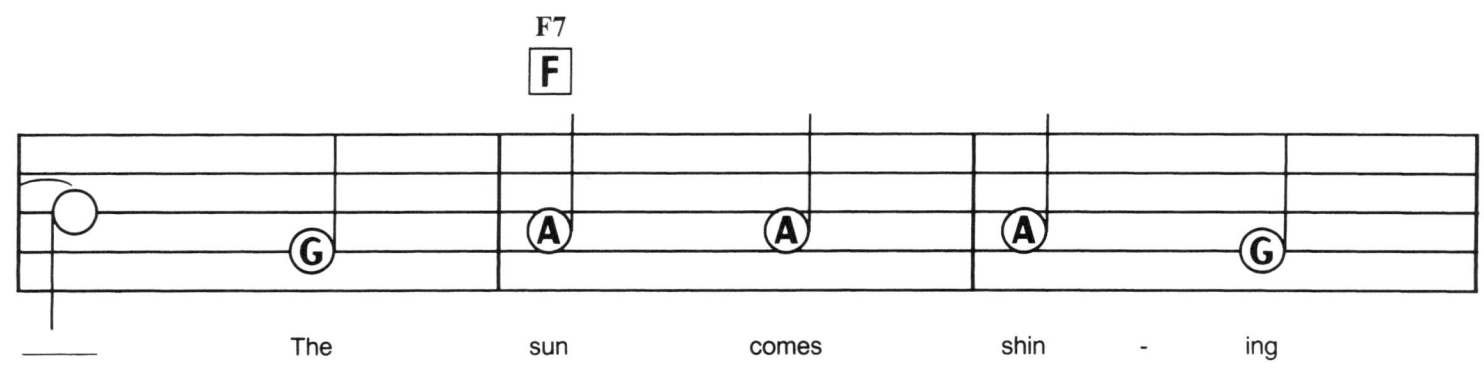

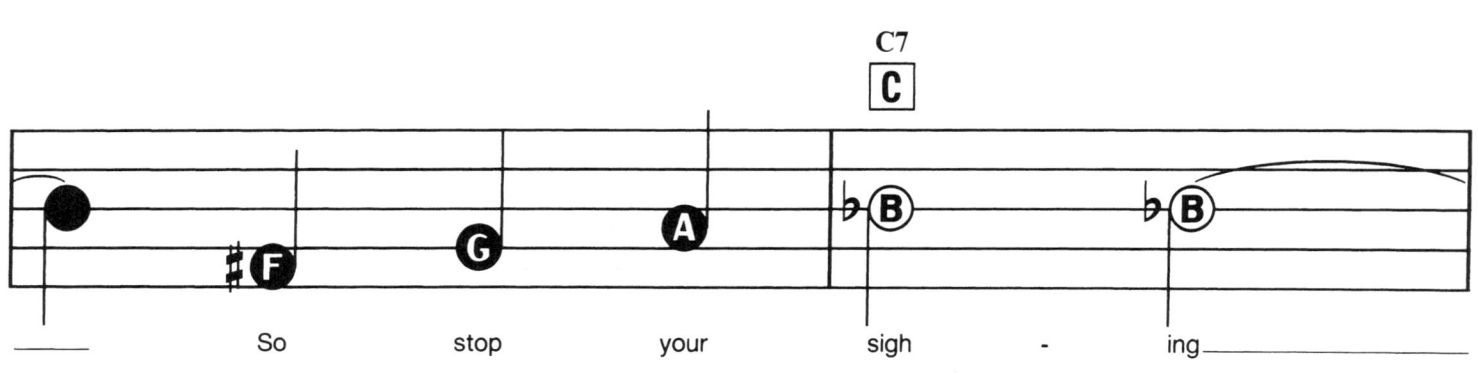

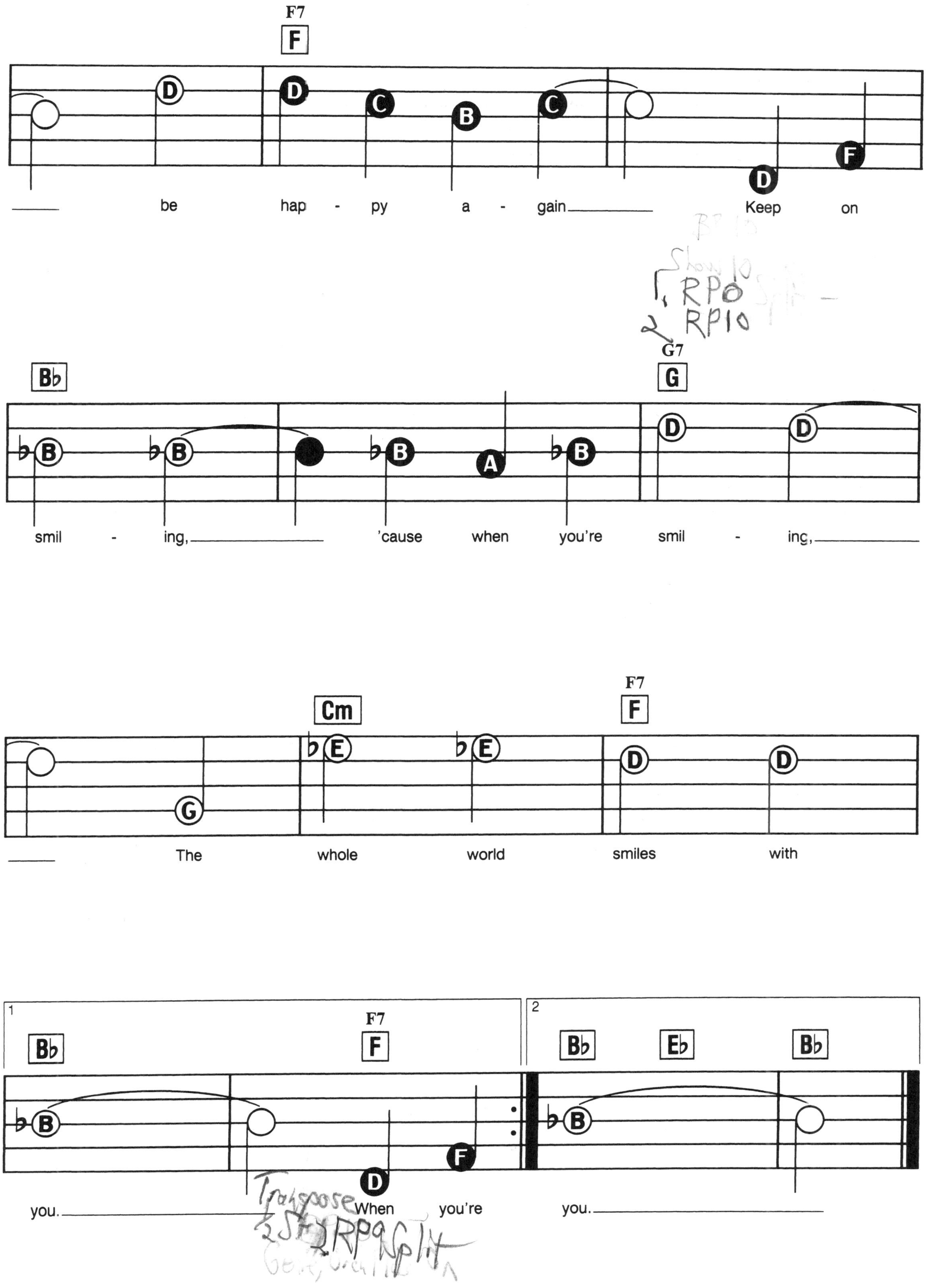
F7 F
be hap - py a - gain Keep on
Bb G7 G
smil - ing, 'cause when you're smil - ing,
Cm F7 F
The whole world smiles with
1 Bb F7 F 2 Bb Eb Bb
you. When you're you.

Some Day My Prince Will Come

Registration 2
Rhythm: Waltz

Words by Larry Morey
Music by Frank Churchill

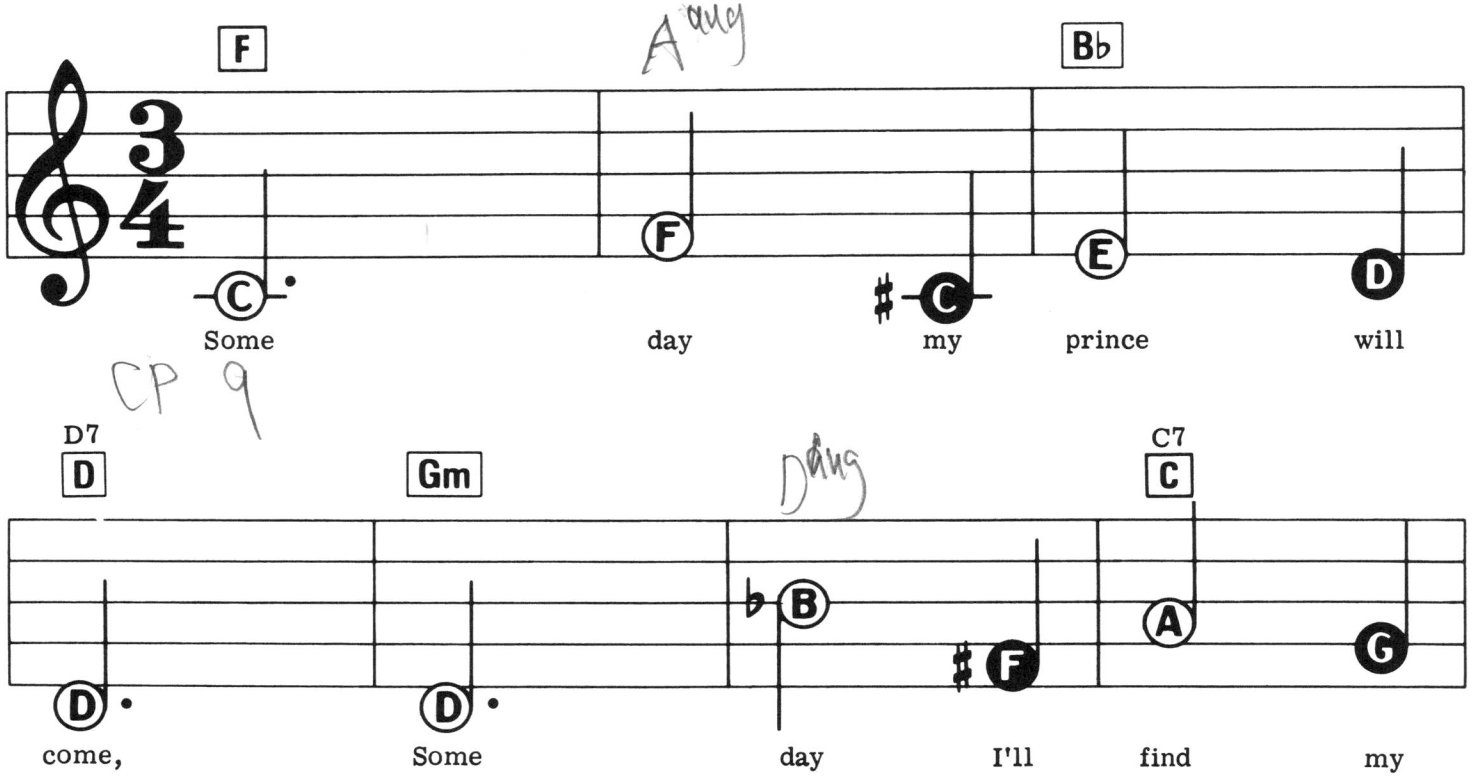
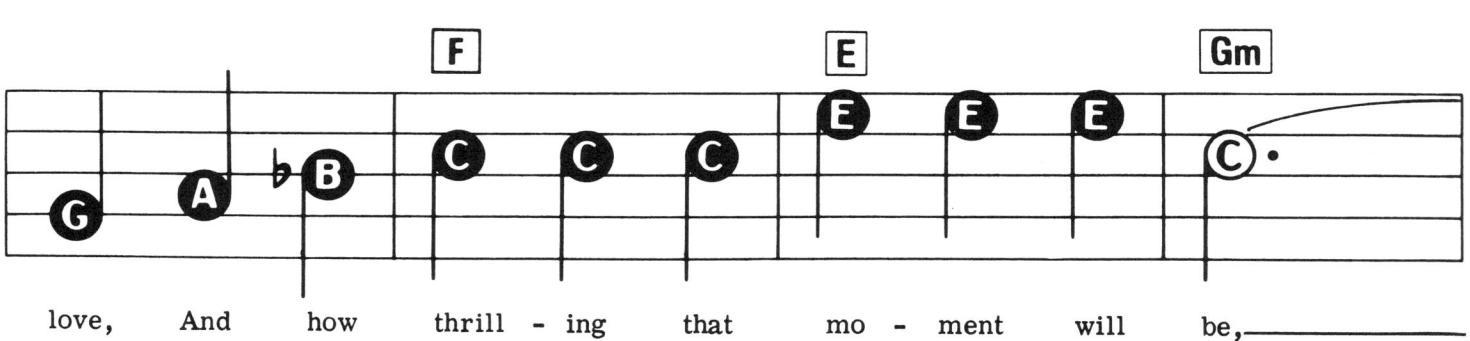
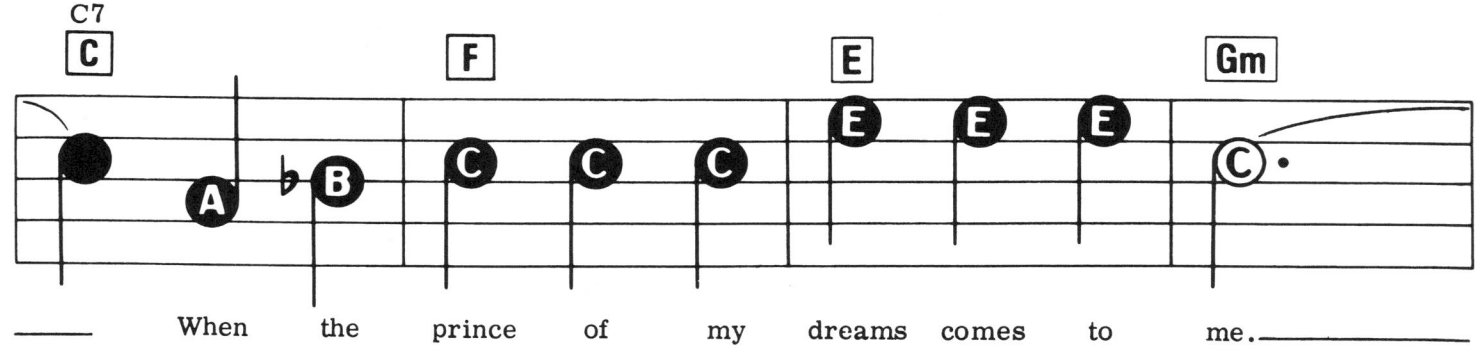

Copyright © 1937 by Bourne Co. (ASCAP)
Copyright Renewed
International Copyright Secured   All Rights Reserved

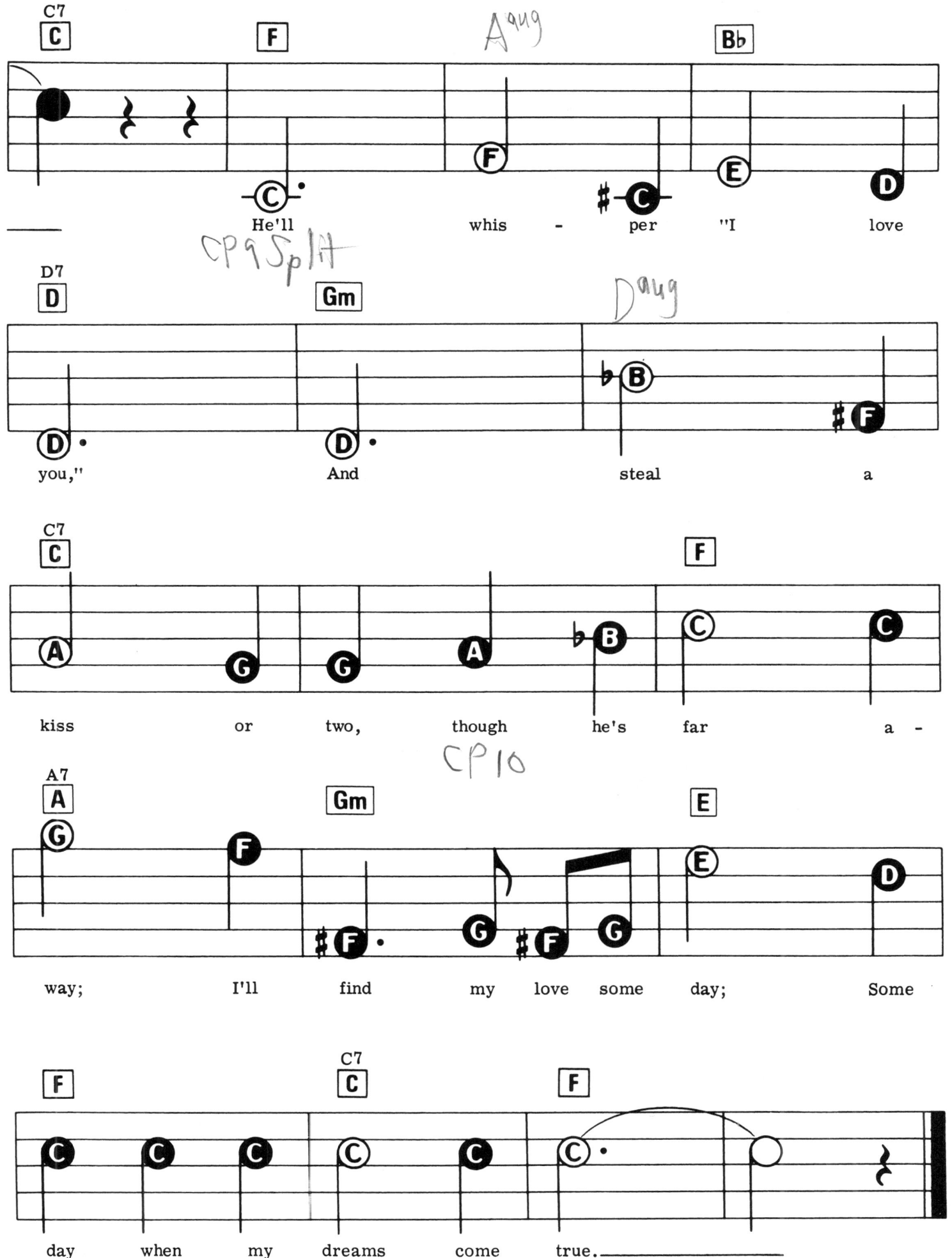

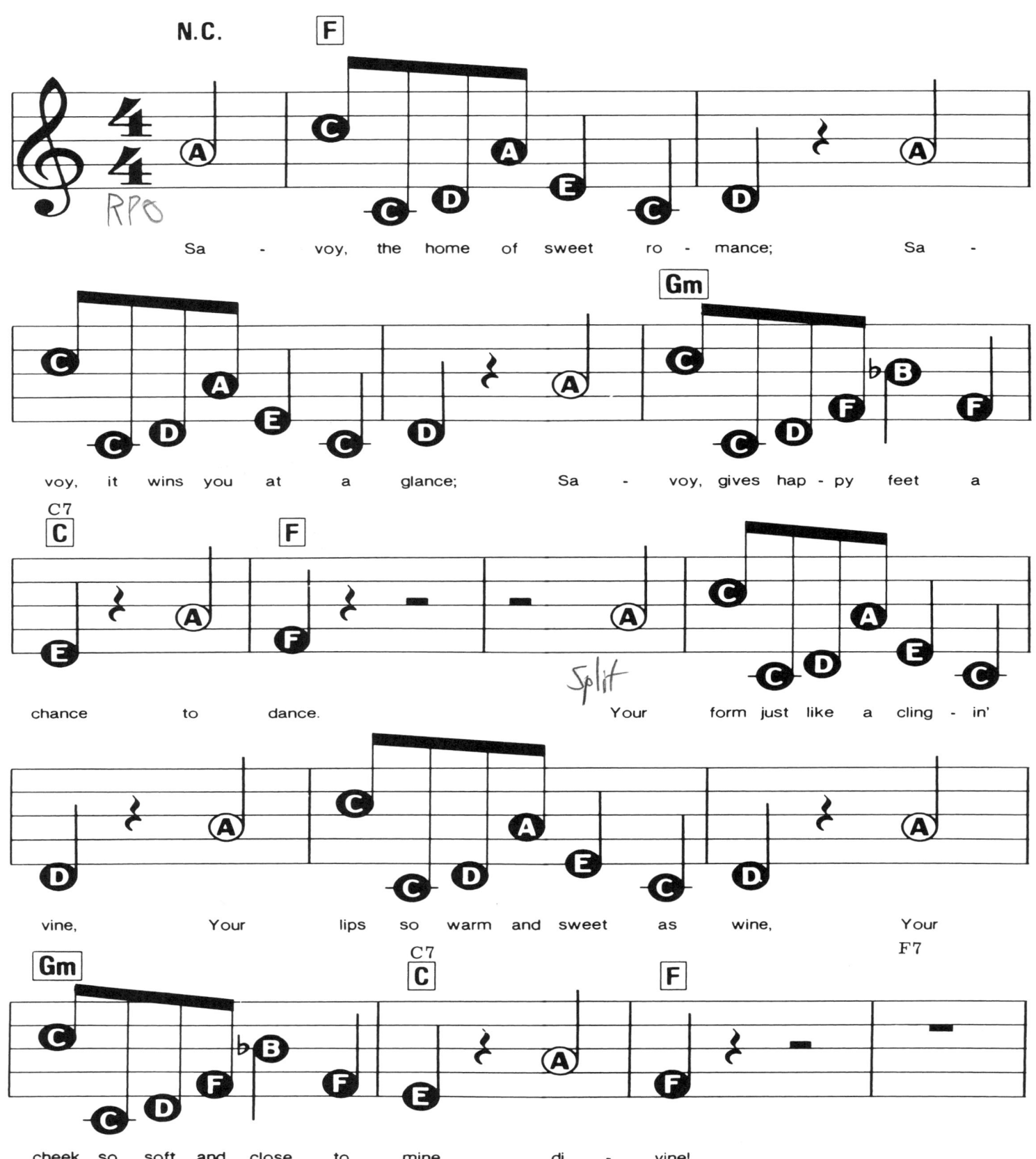

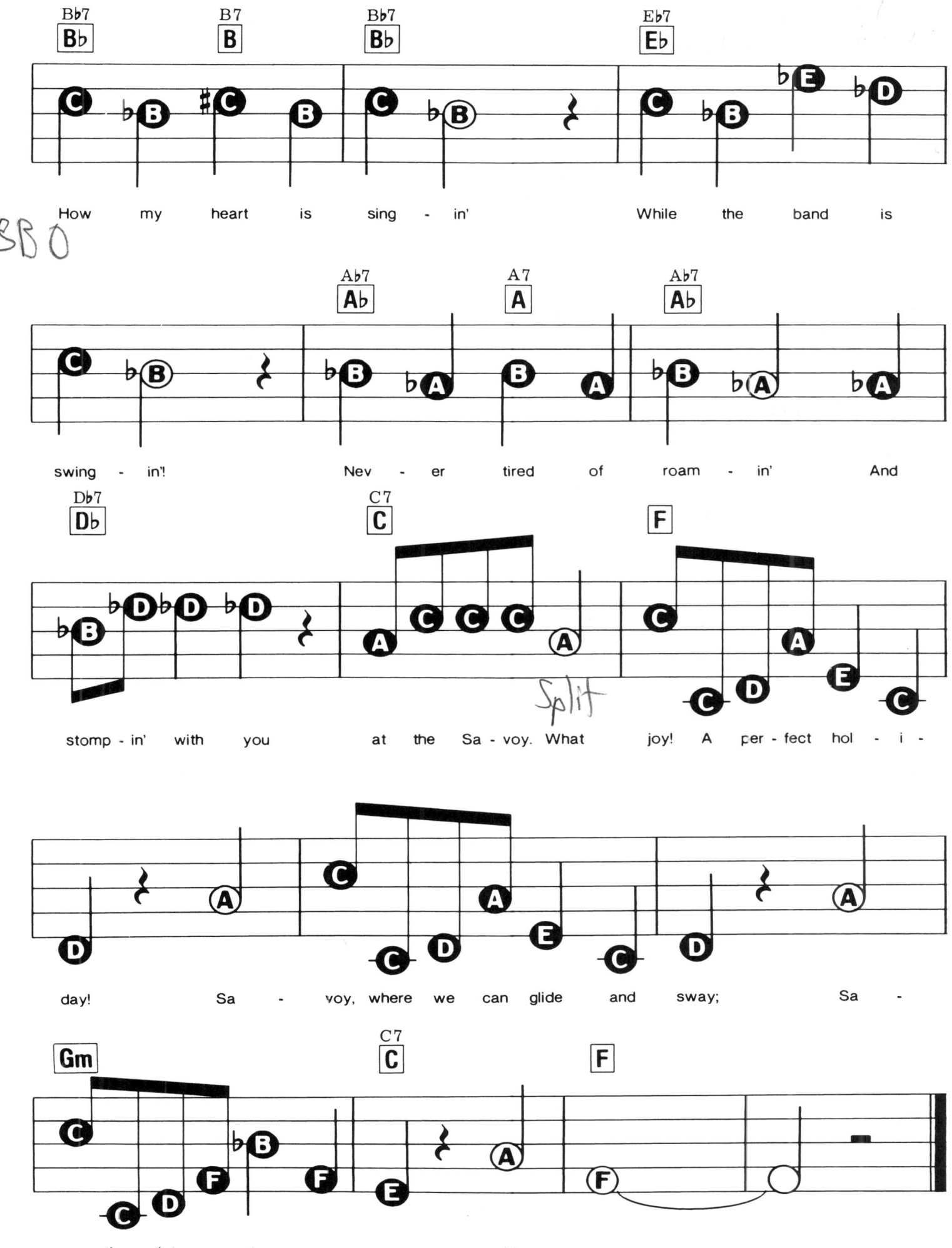

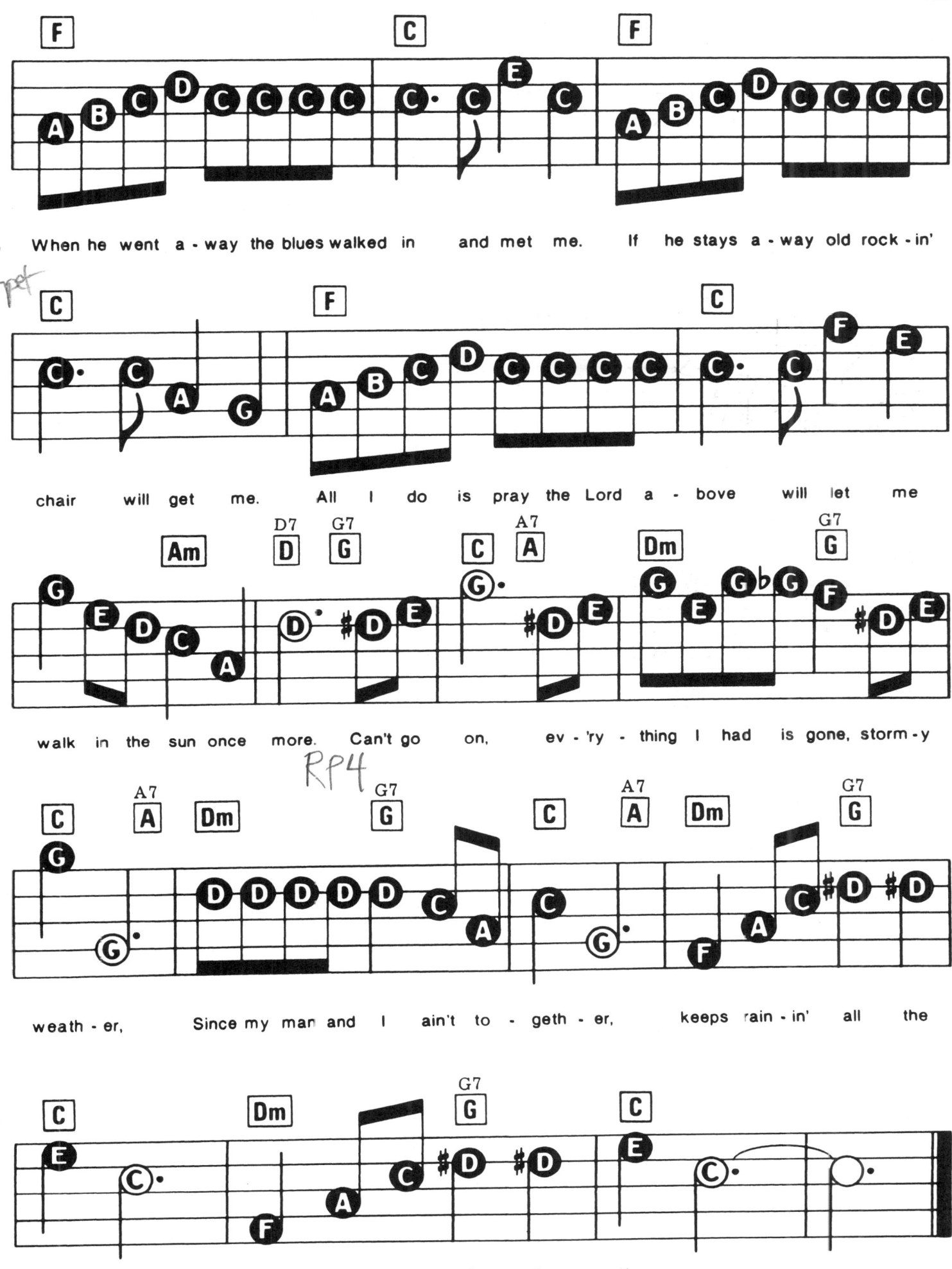

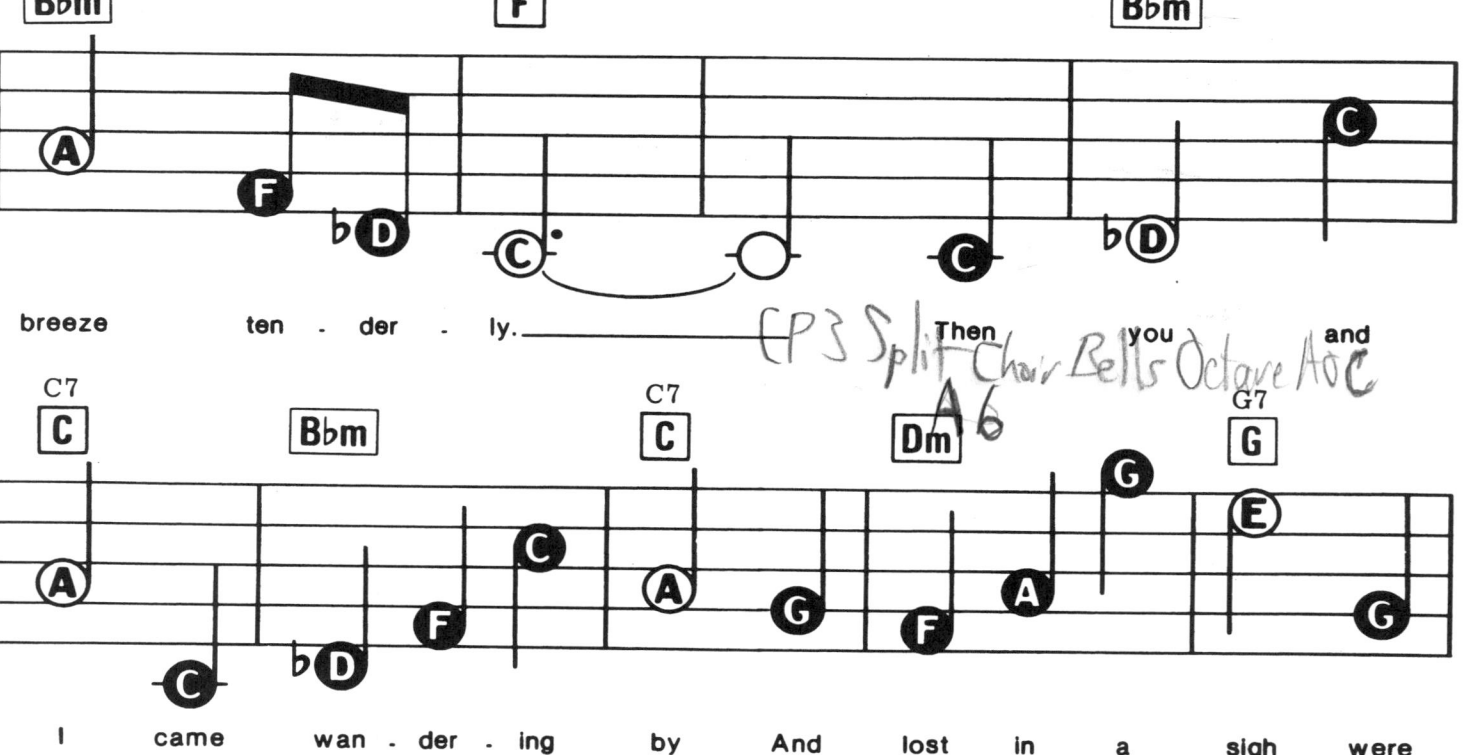

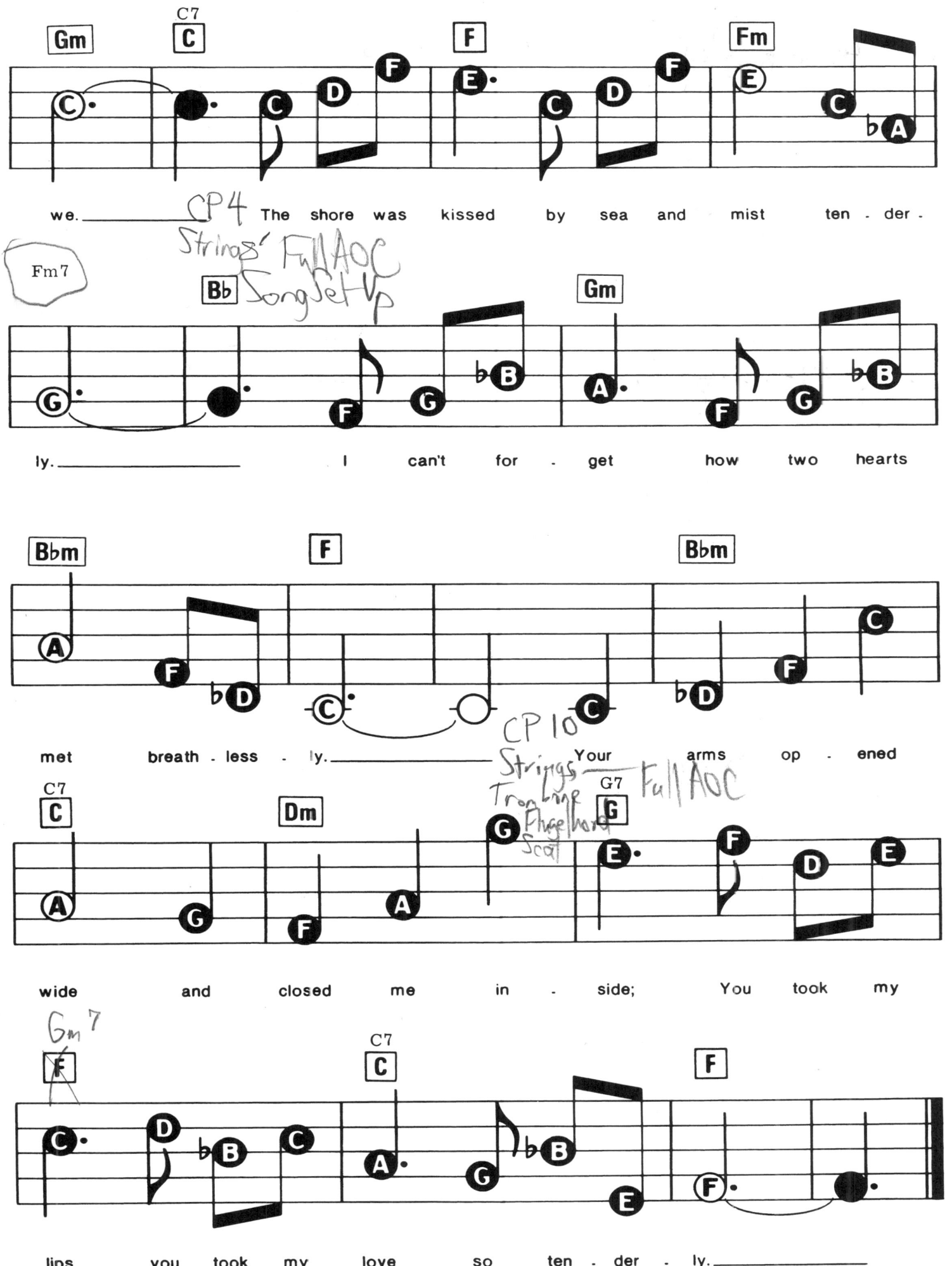

A300 Chicago Swing MM108 Reset Split

There Will Never Be Another You

from the Motion Picture ICELAND

Registration 1
Rhythm: Swing

Lyric by Mack Gordon
Music by Harry Warren

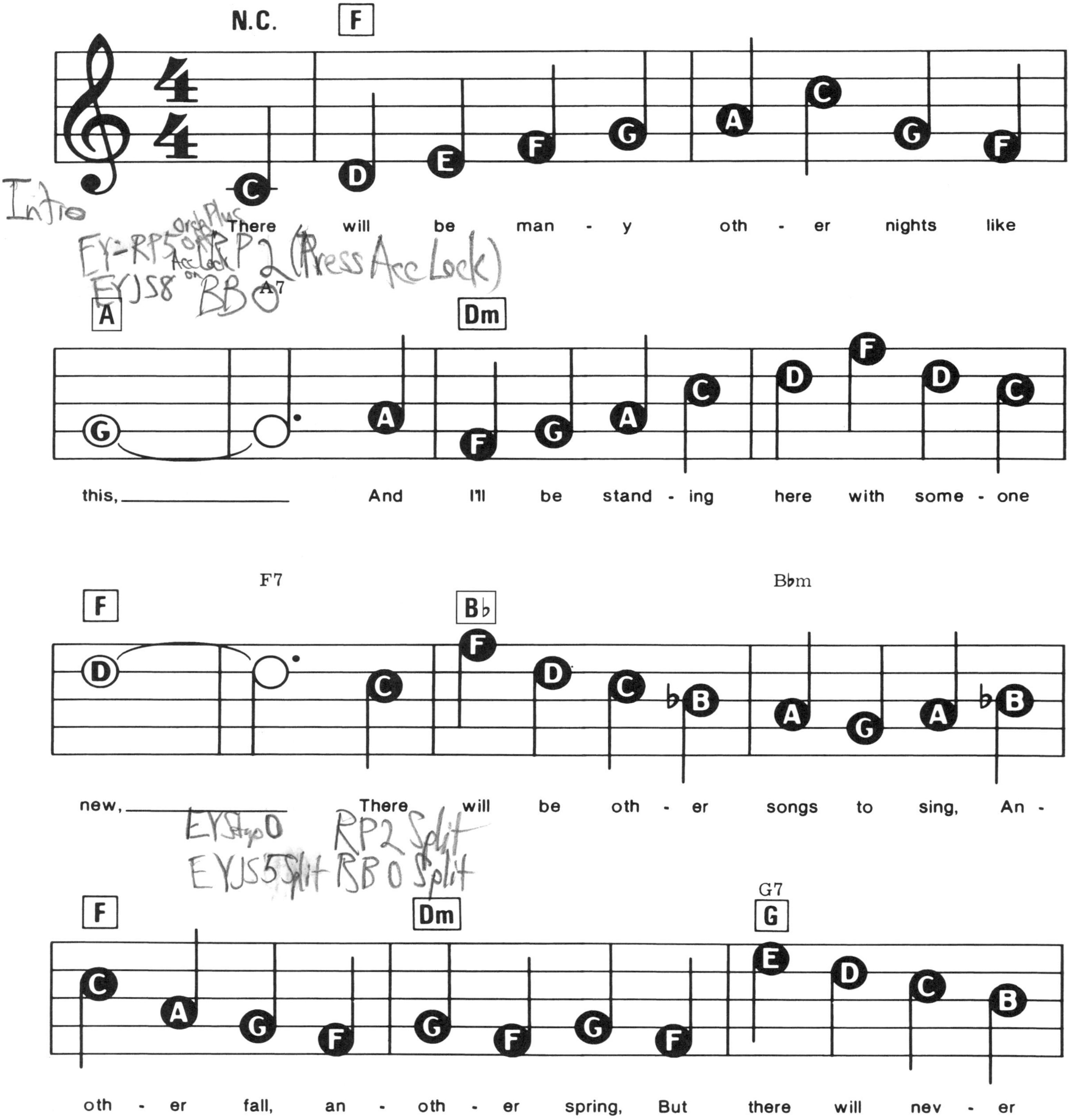

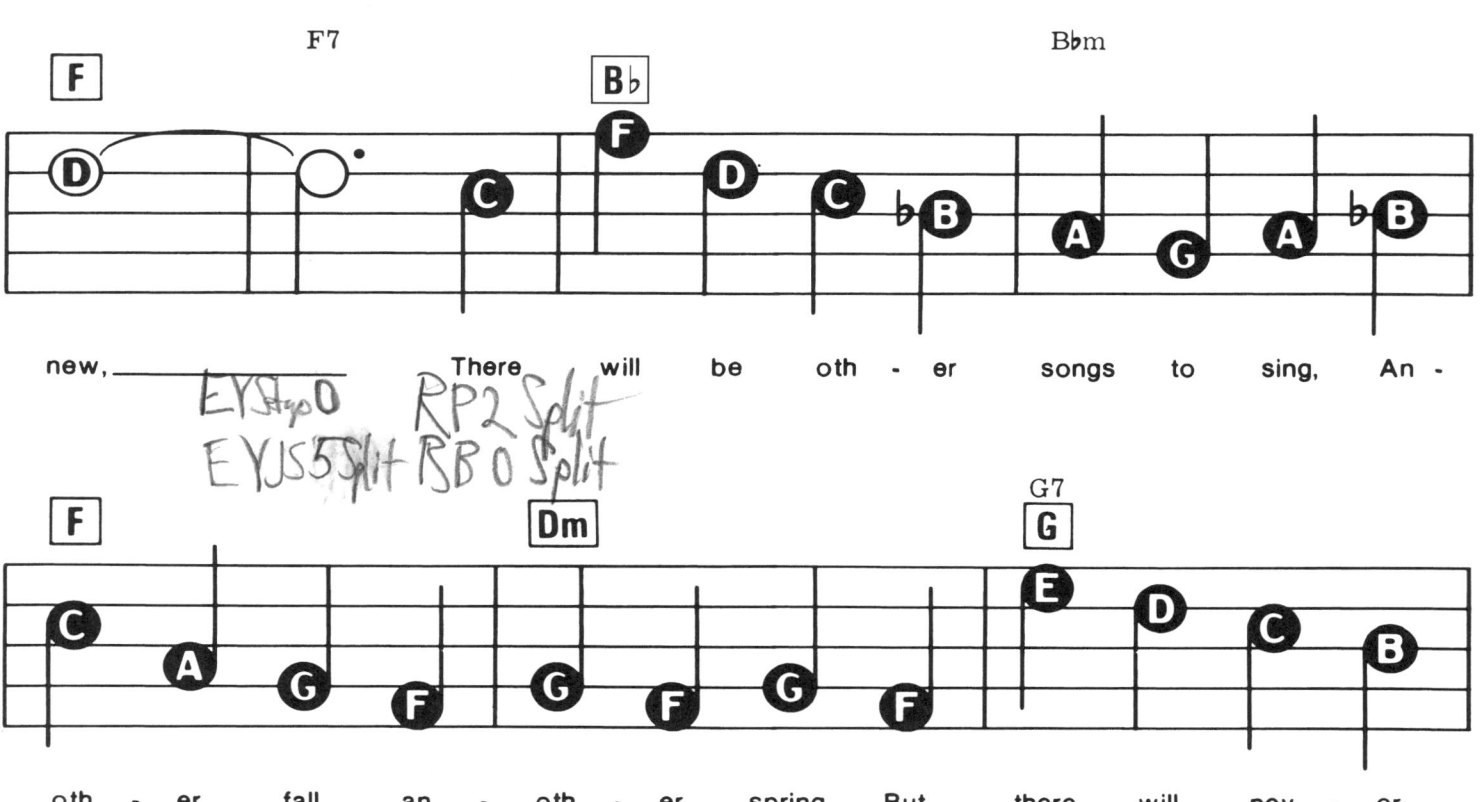

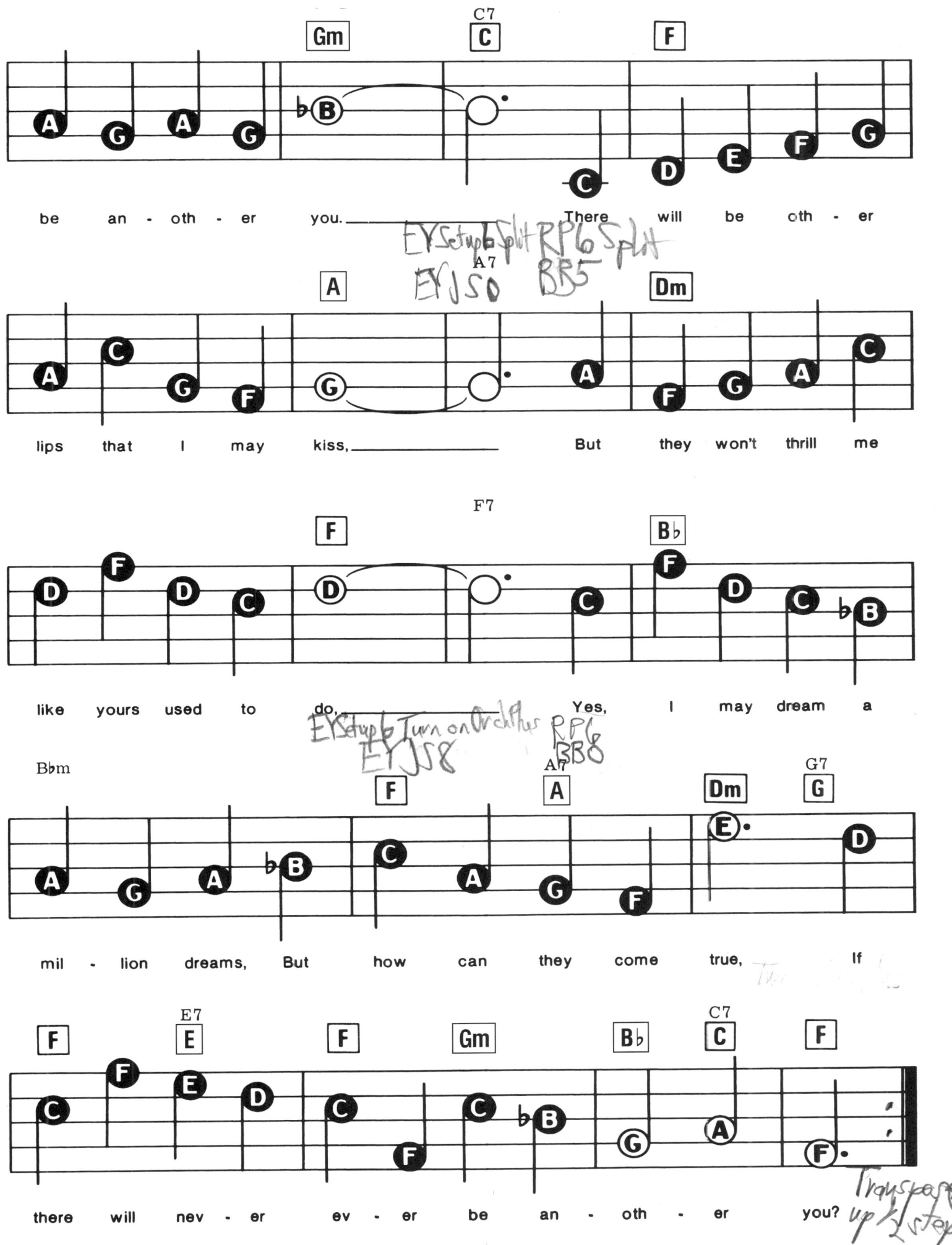

There's a Small Hotel

from ON YOUR TOES

Registration 8
Rhythm: Swing

Words by Lorenz Hart
Music by Richard Rodgers

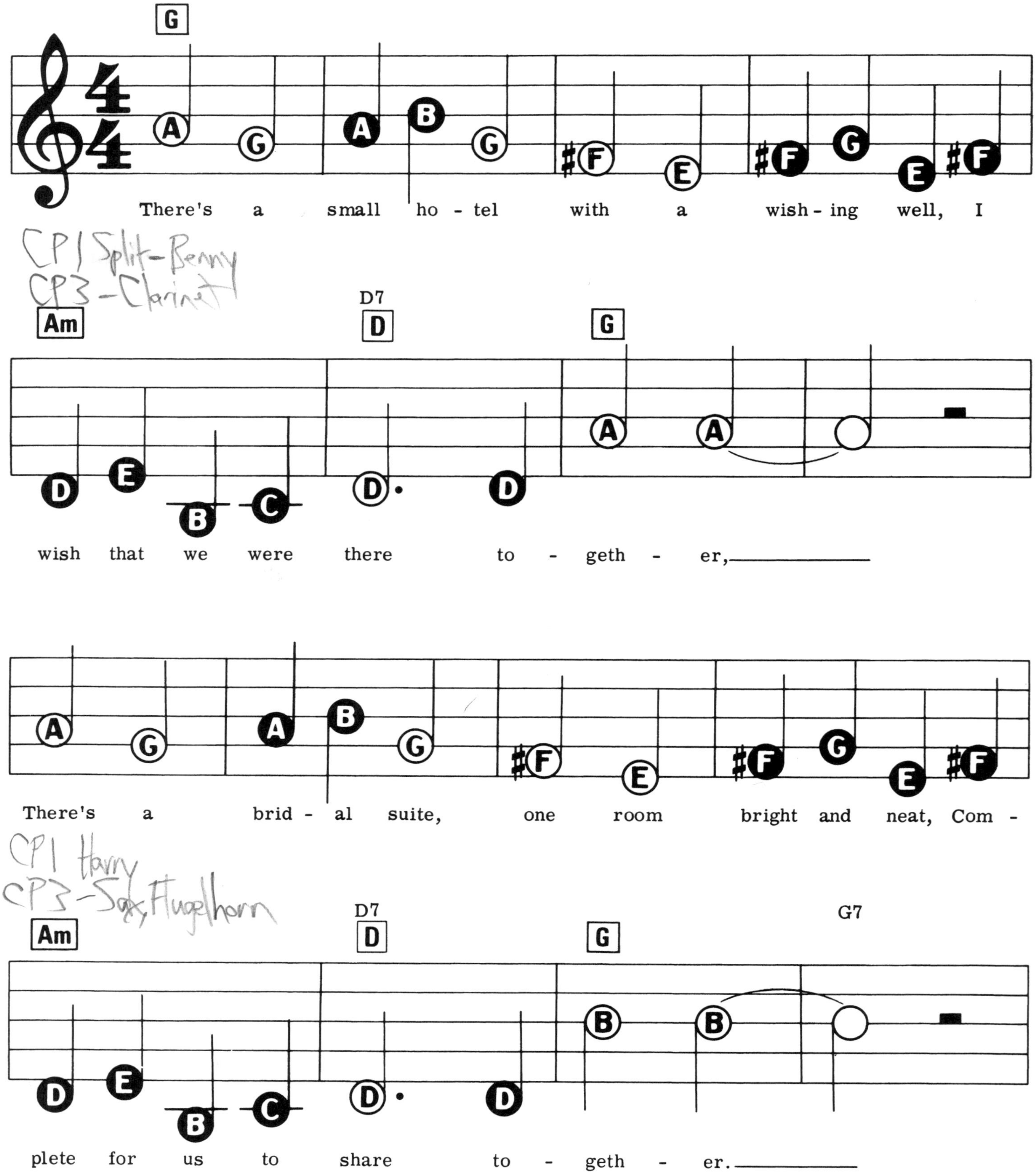

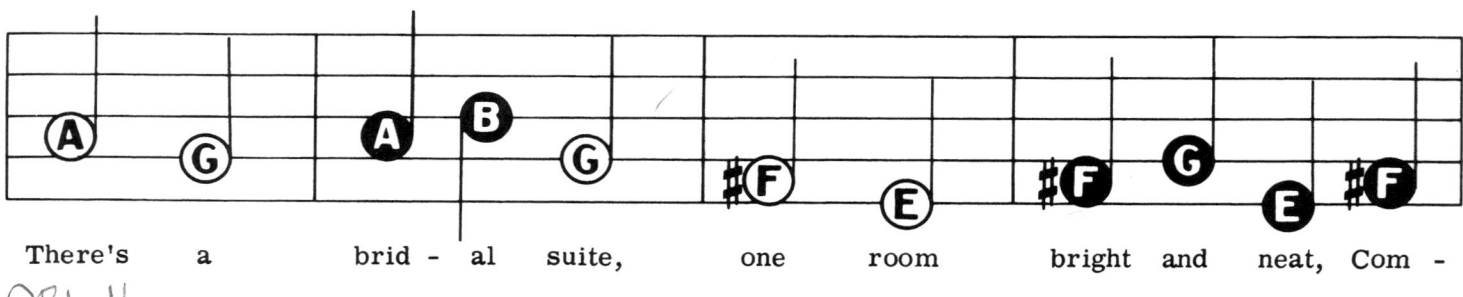

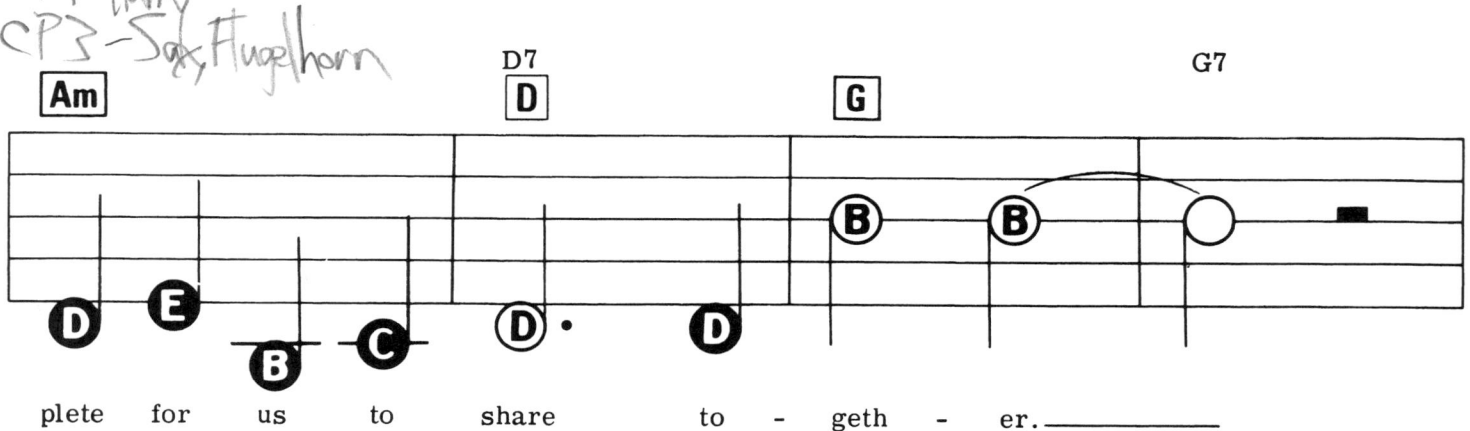

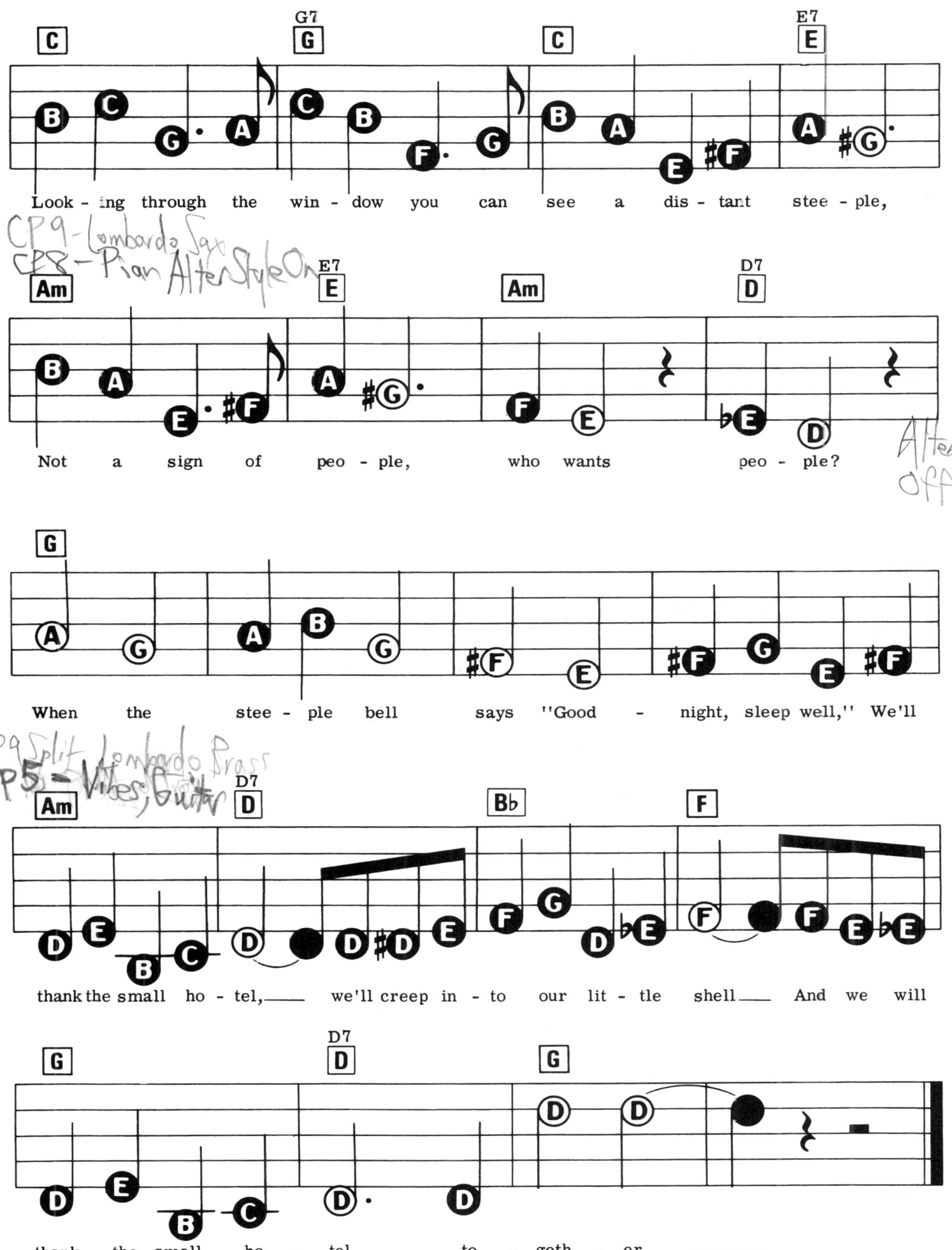

Time After Time

from the Metro-Goldwyn-Mayer Picture IT HAPPENED IN BROOKLYN

Registration 5
Rhythm: Fox Trot or Ballad

Words by Sammy Cahn
Music by Jule Styne

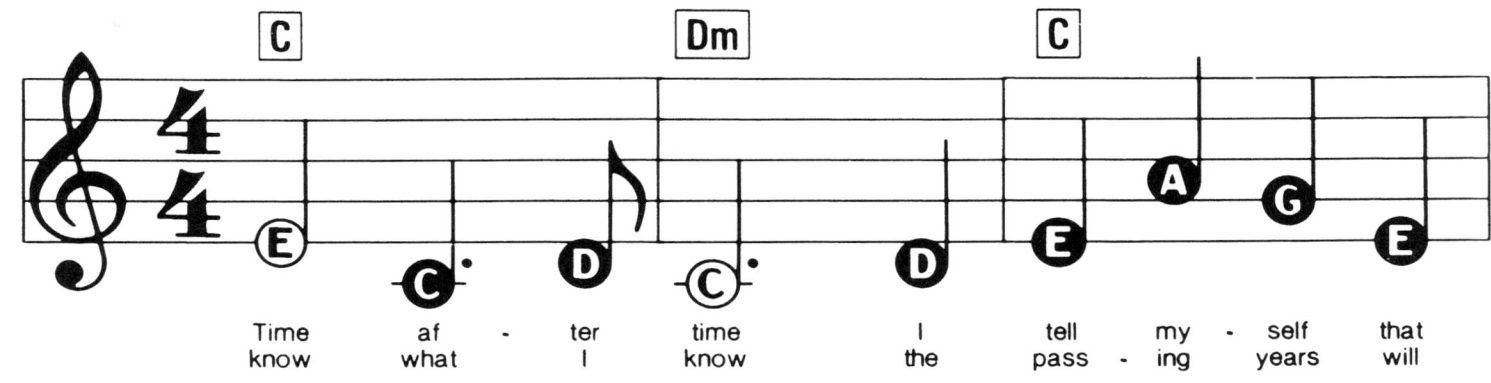
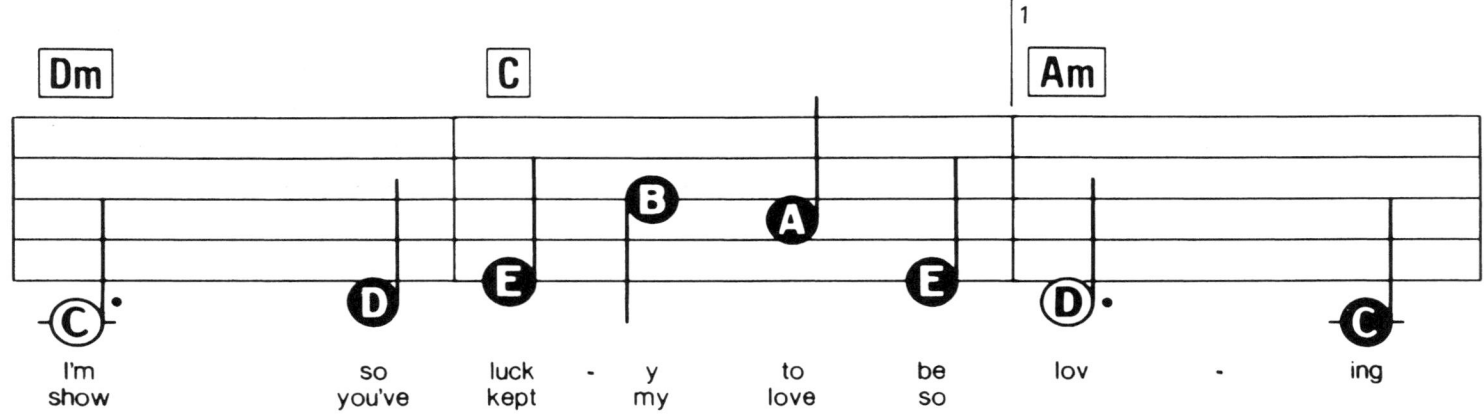
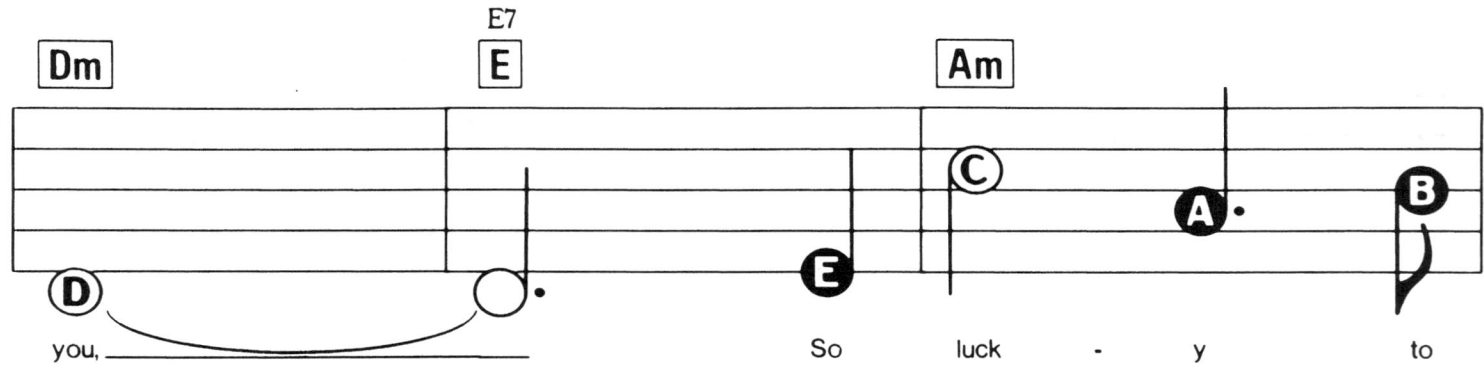
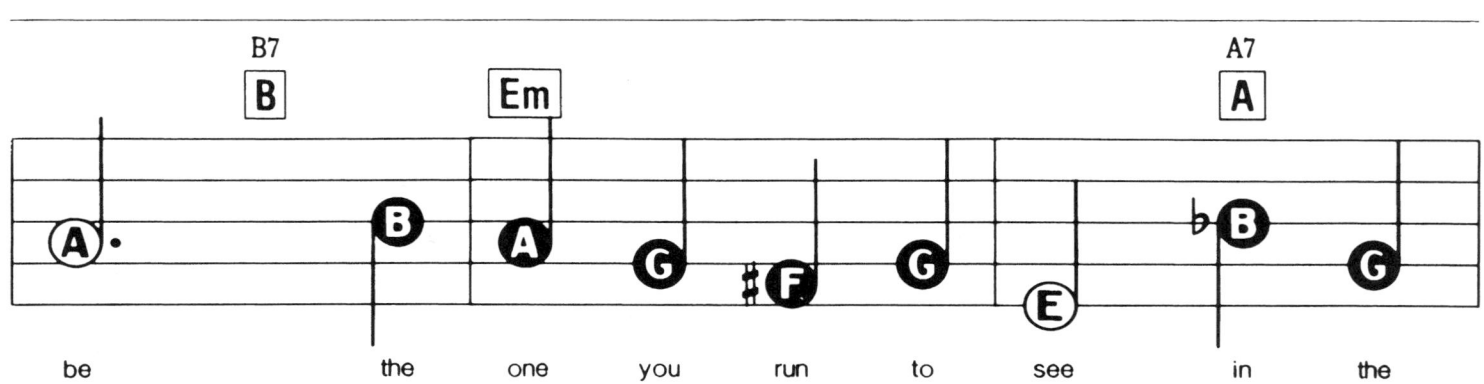

Copyright © 1947 (Renewed) Sands Music Corp.
All Rights Reserved   Used by Permission

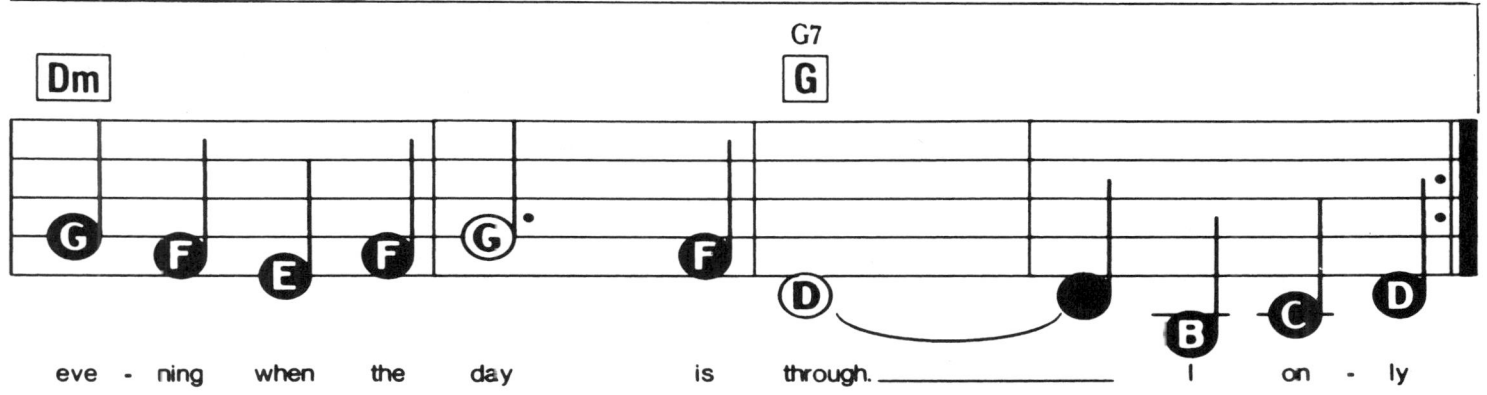
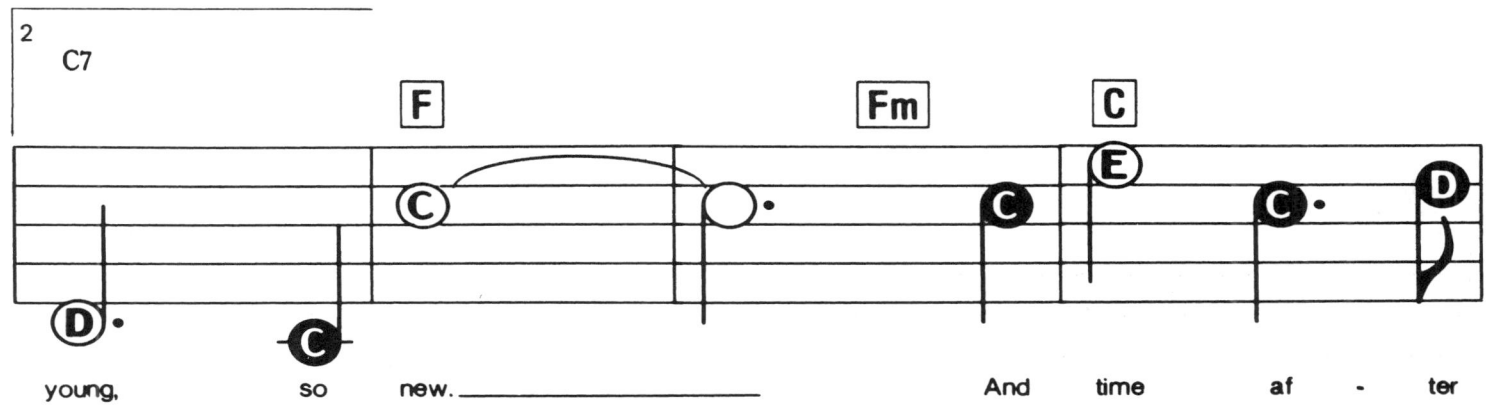
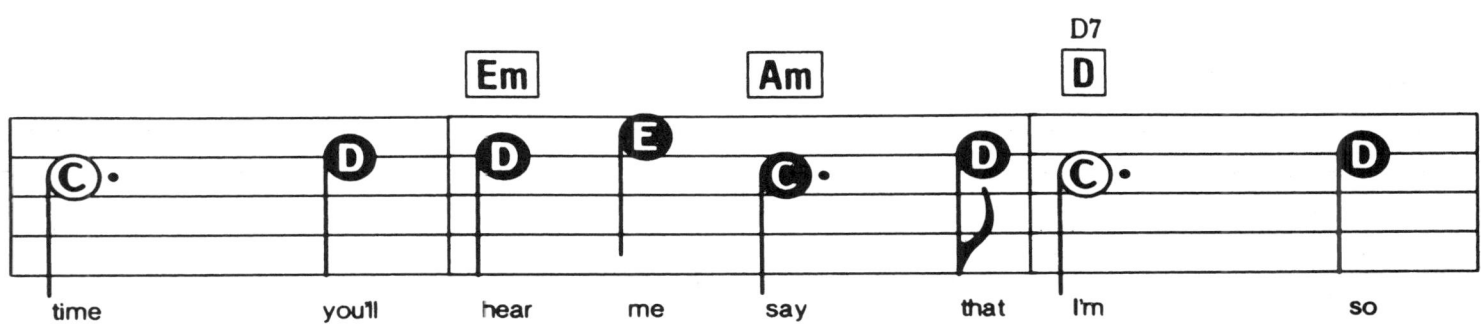
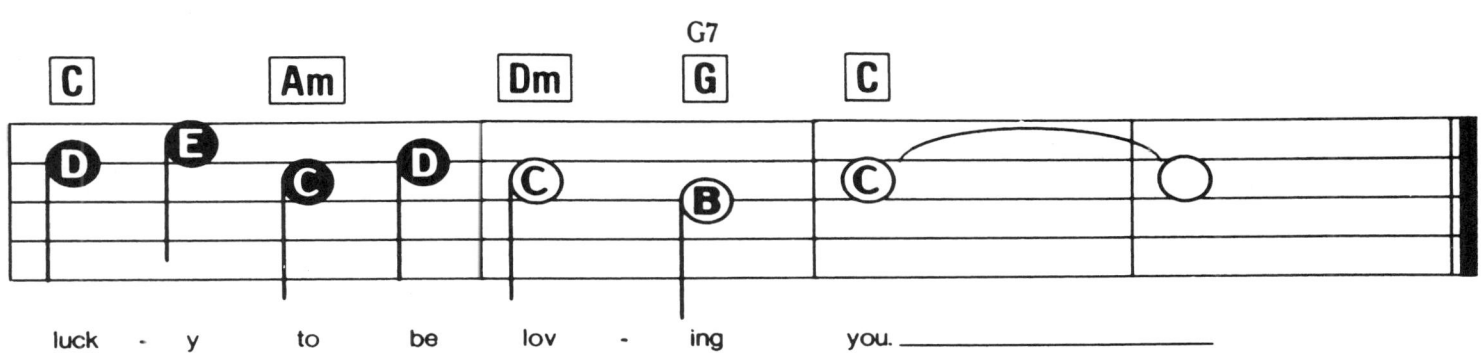

Too Late Now
from ROYAL WEDDING

Registration 1
Rhythm: Ballad

Words by Alan Jay Lerner
Music by Burton Lane

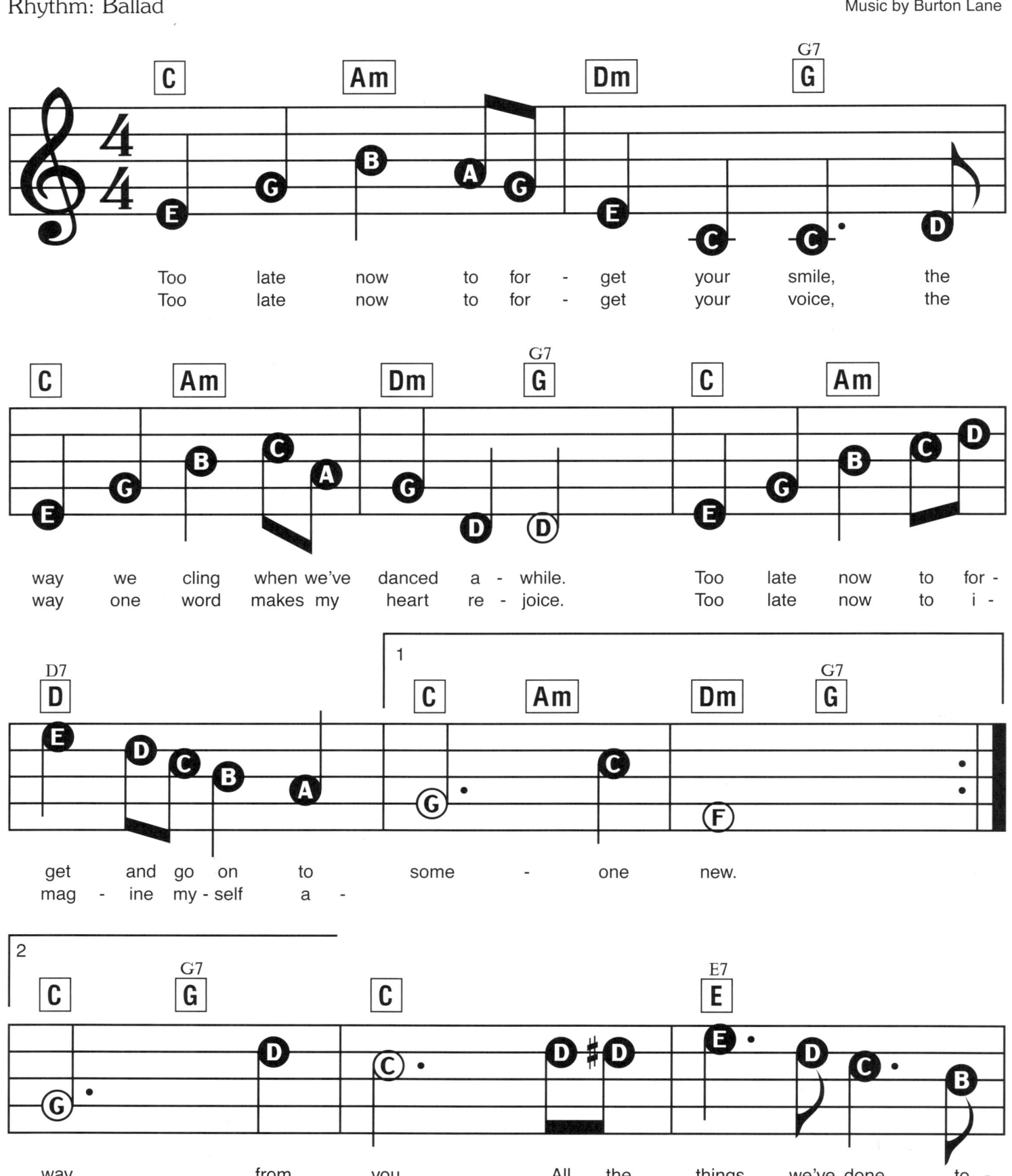

Too late now to for-get your smile, the
Too late now to for-get your voice, the

way we cling when we've danced a - while. Too late now to for-
way one word makes my heart re - joice. Too late now to i -

get and go on to some - one new.
mag - ine my - self a -

way from you. All the things we've done to -

Copyright © 1950 by Chappell & Co.
Copyright Renewed
International Copyright Secured All Rights Reserved

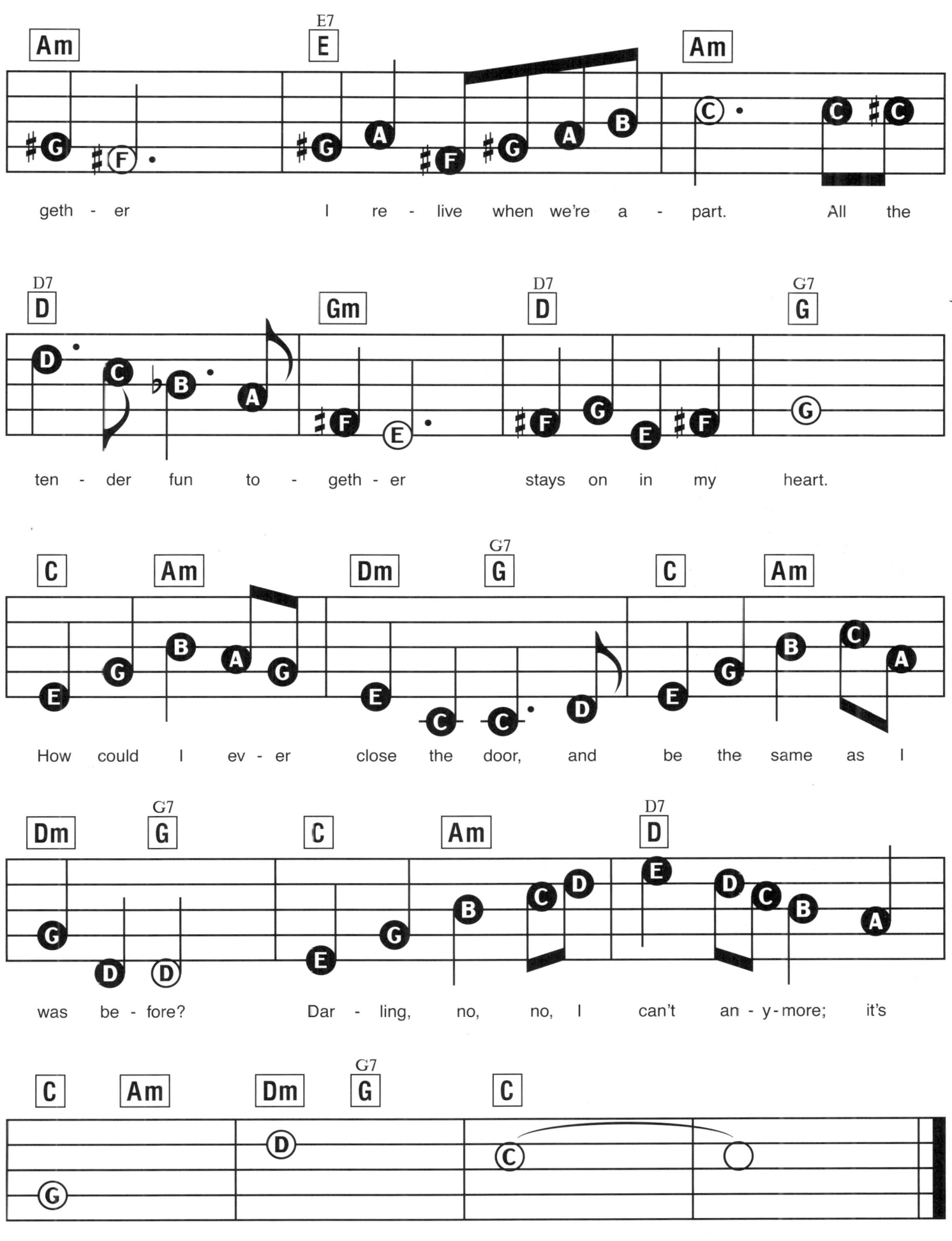

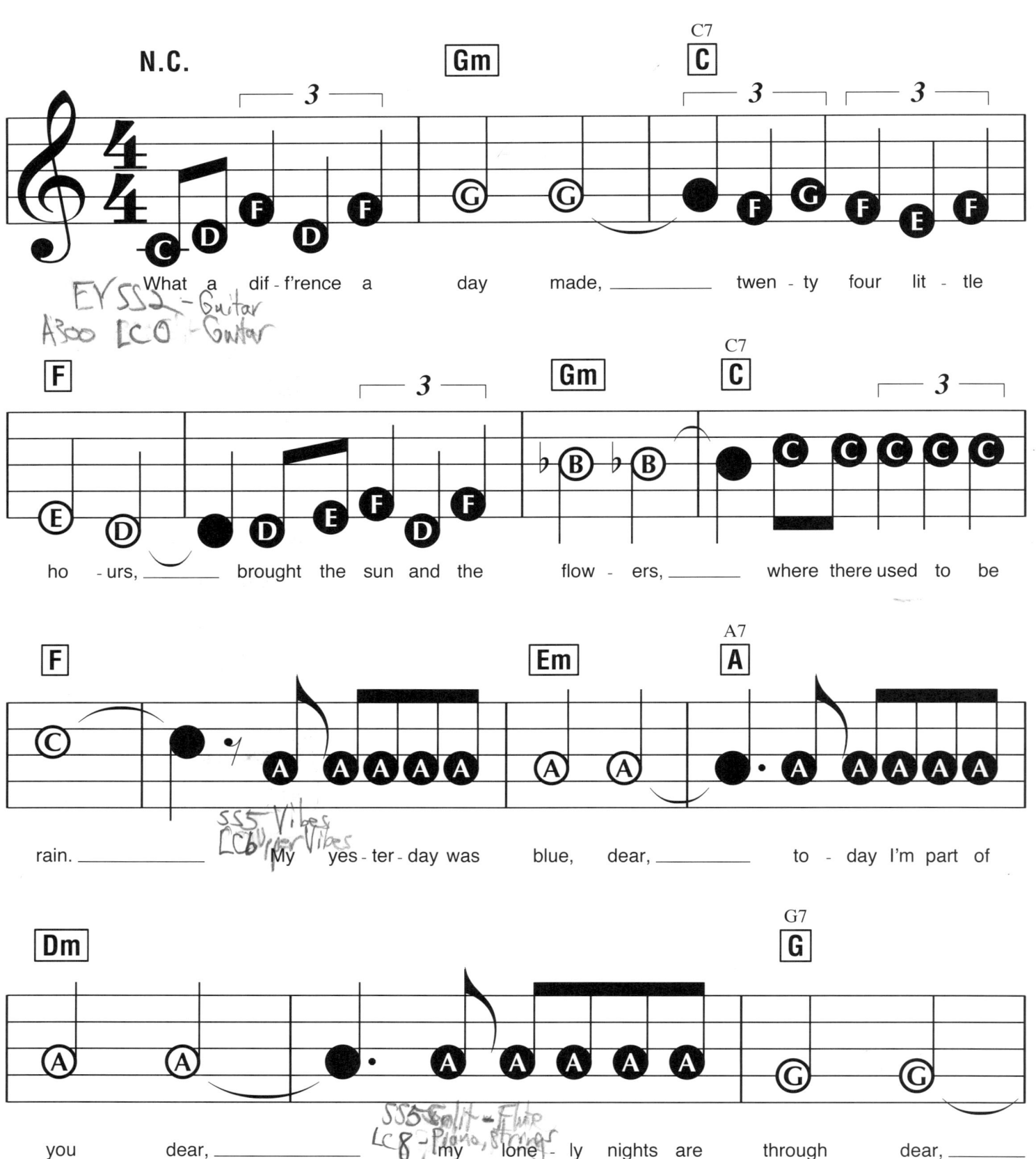

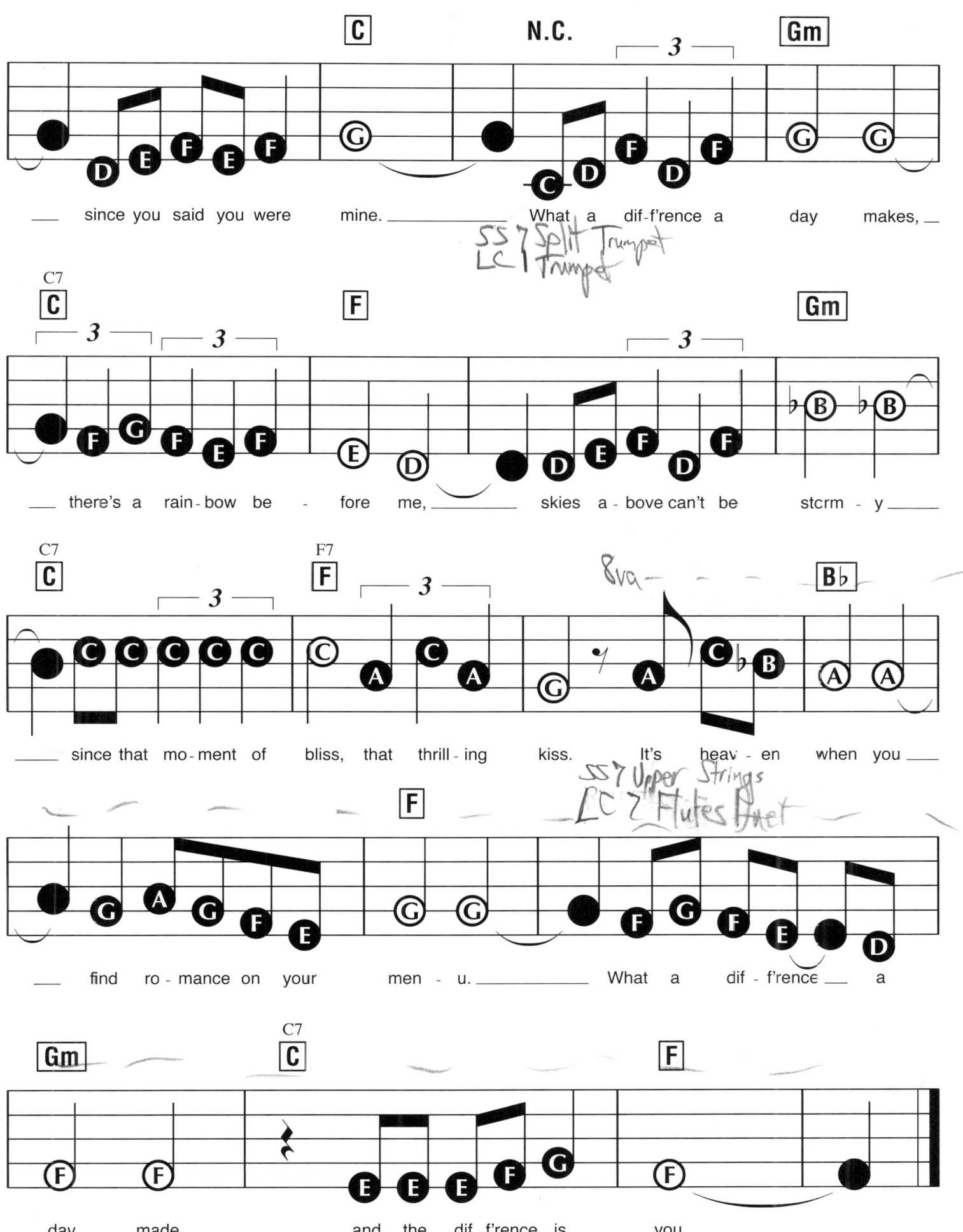

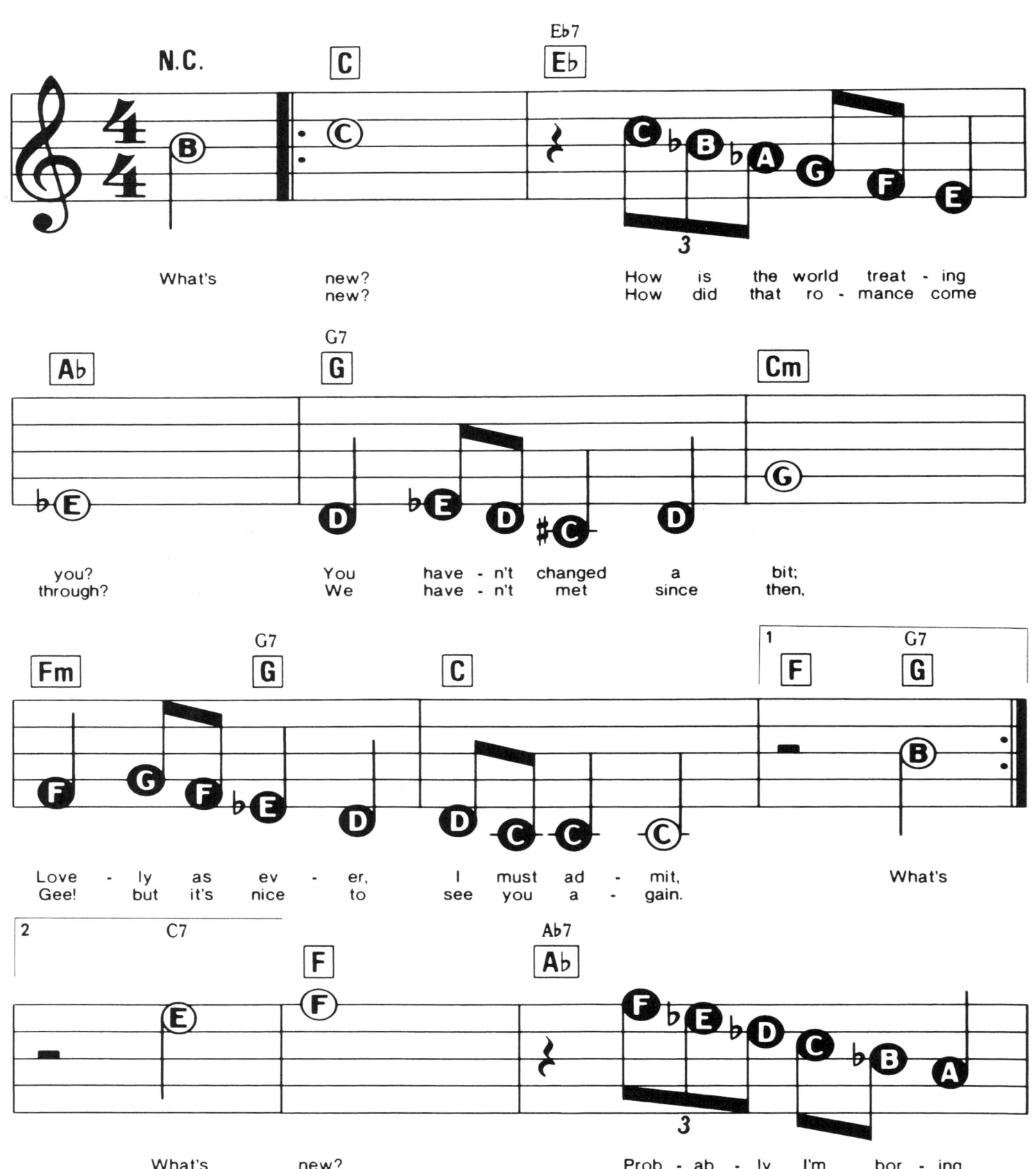

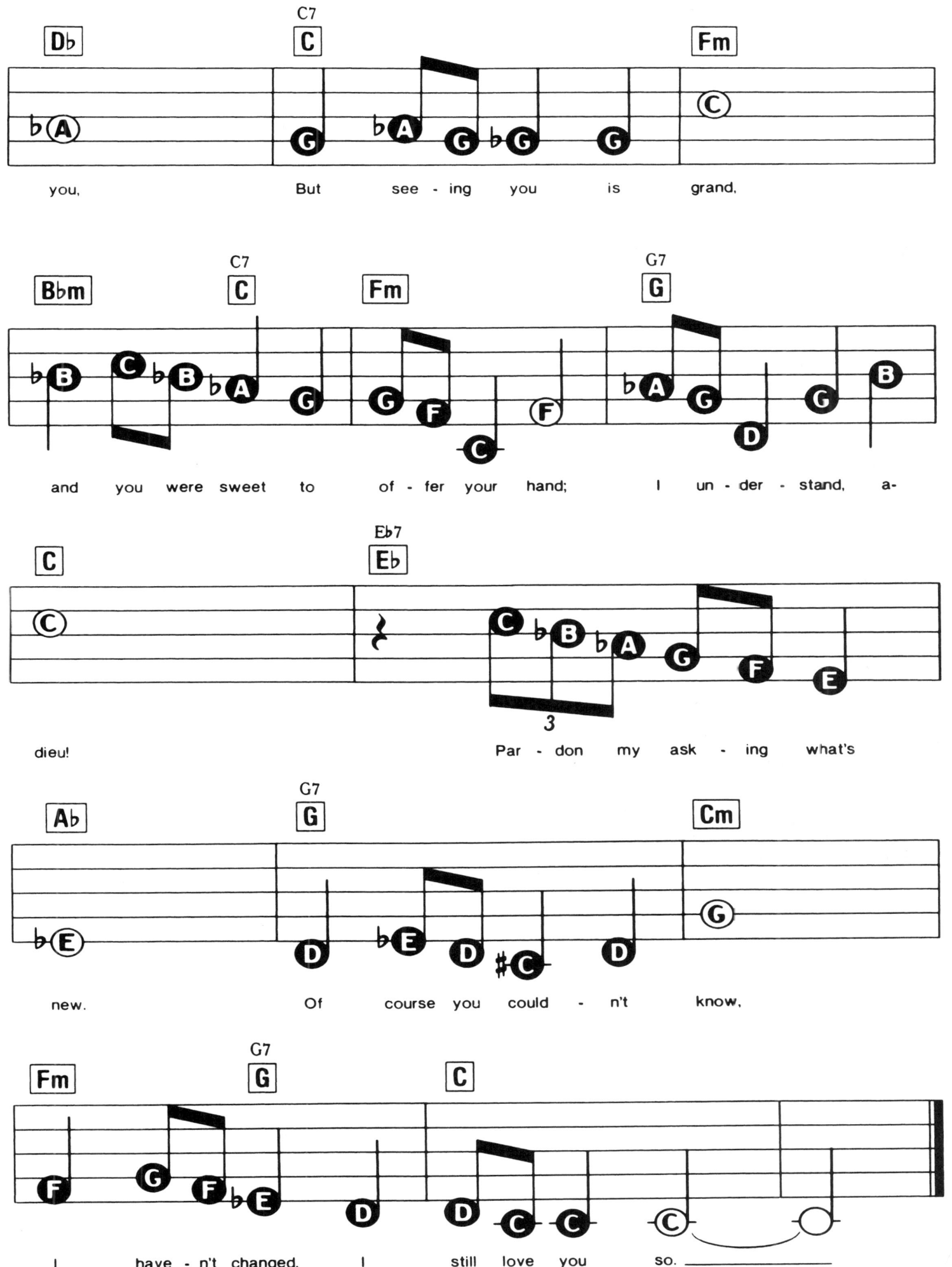

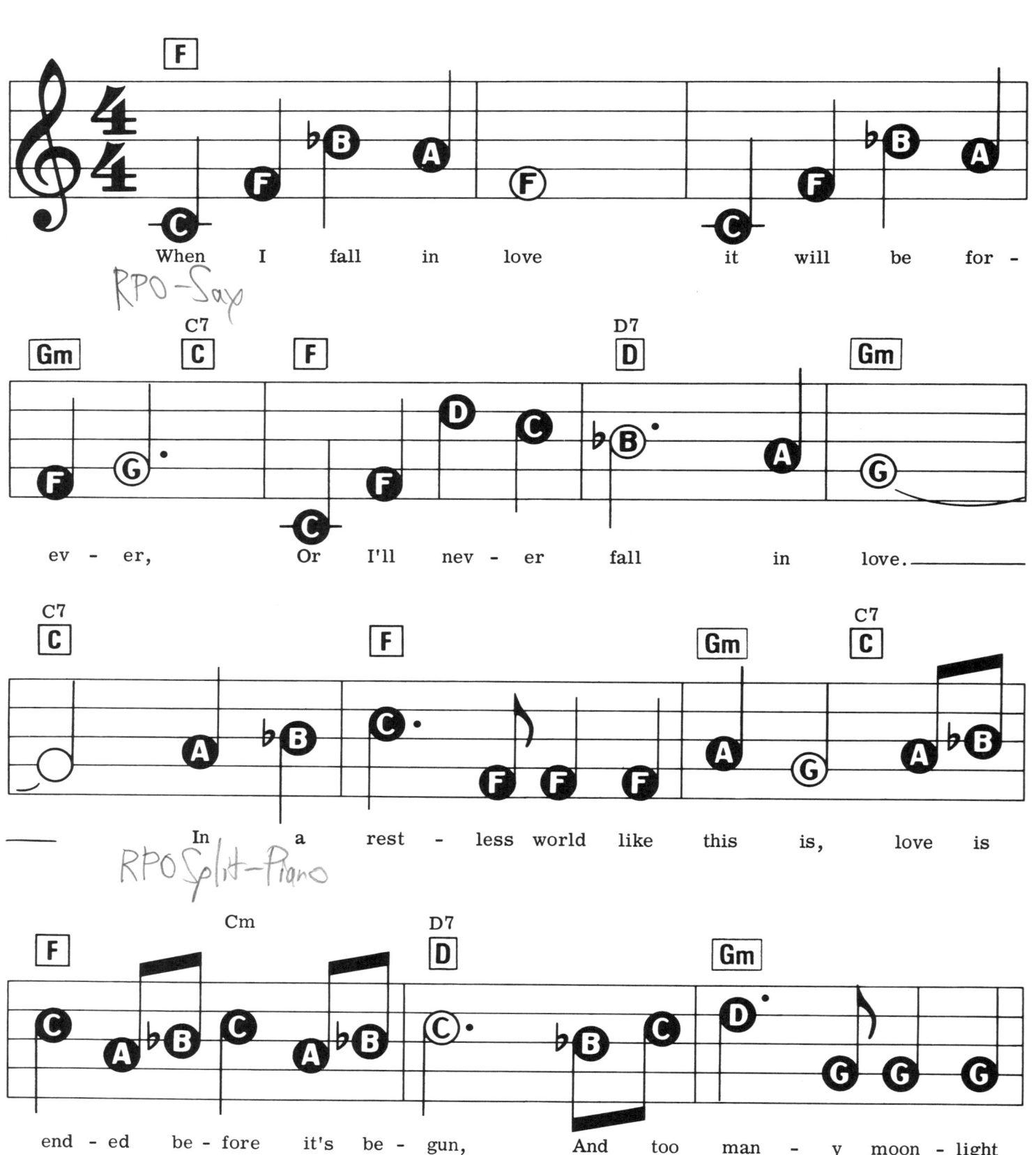

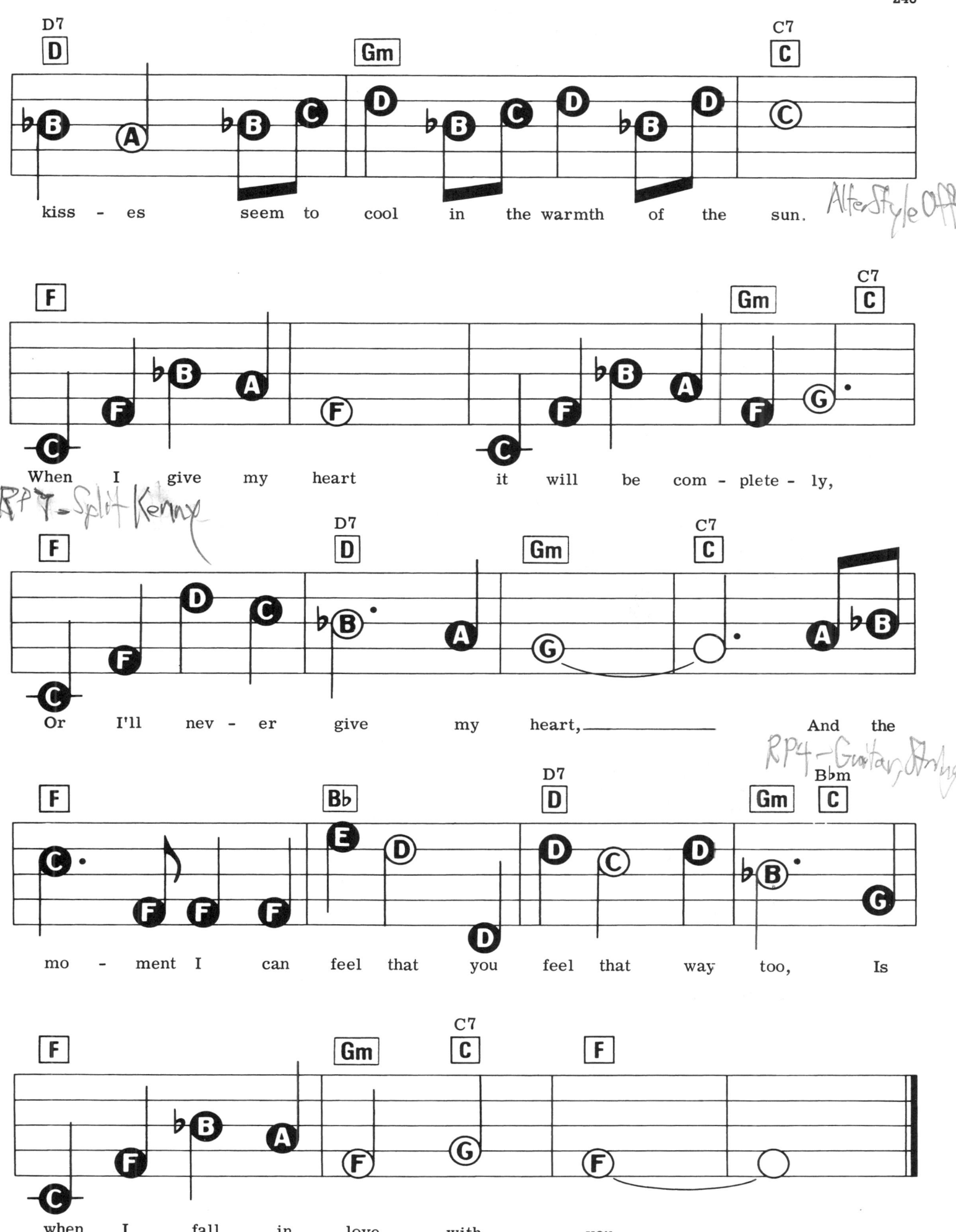

When Sunny Gets Blue

Registration 8
Rhythm: Ballad

Lyric by Jack Segal
Music by Marvin Fisher

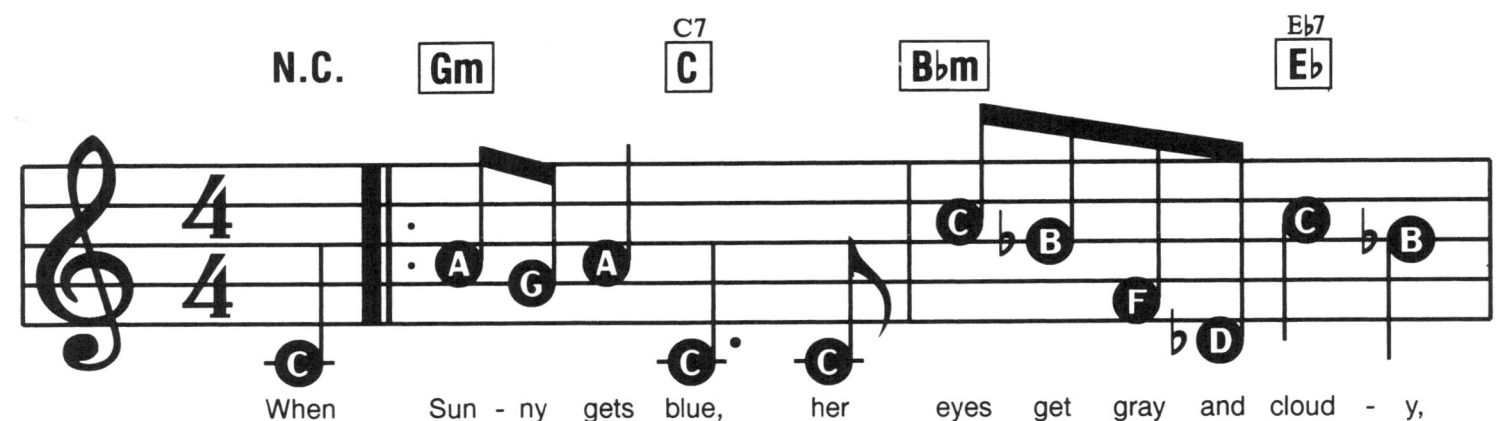

When Sun-ny gets blue, her eyes get gray and cloud-y,

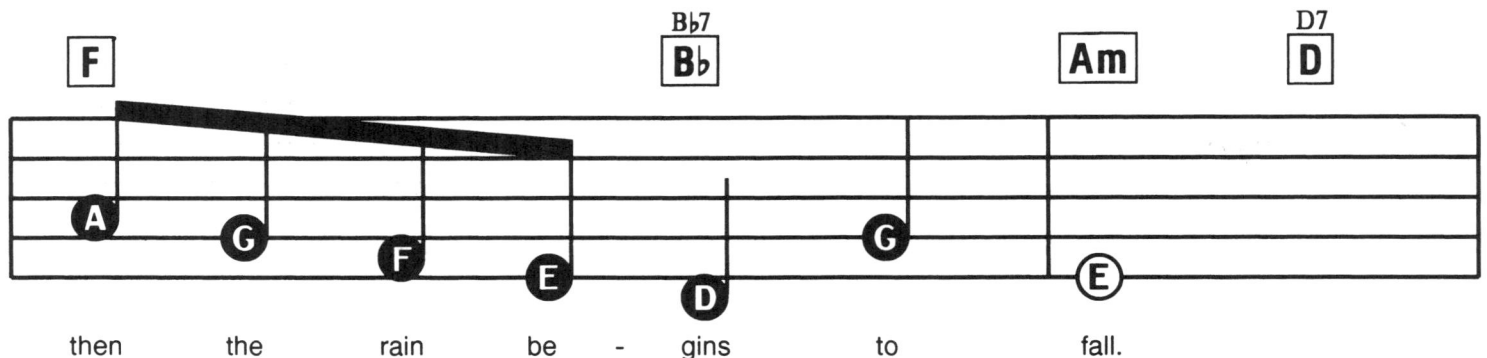

then the rain be-gins to fall.

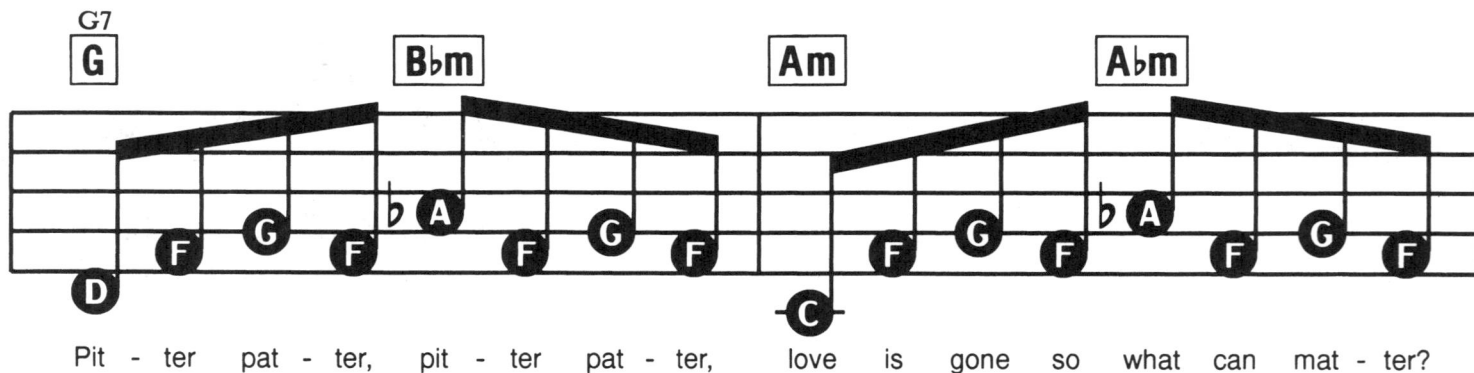

Pit-ter pat-ter, pit-ter pat-ter, love is gone so what can mat-ter?

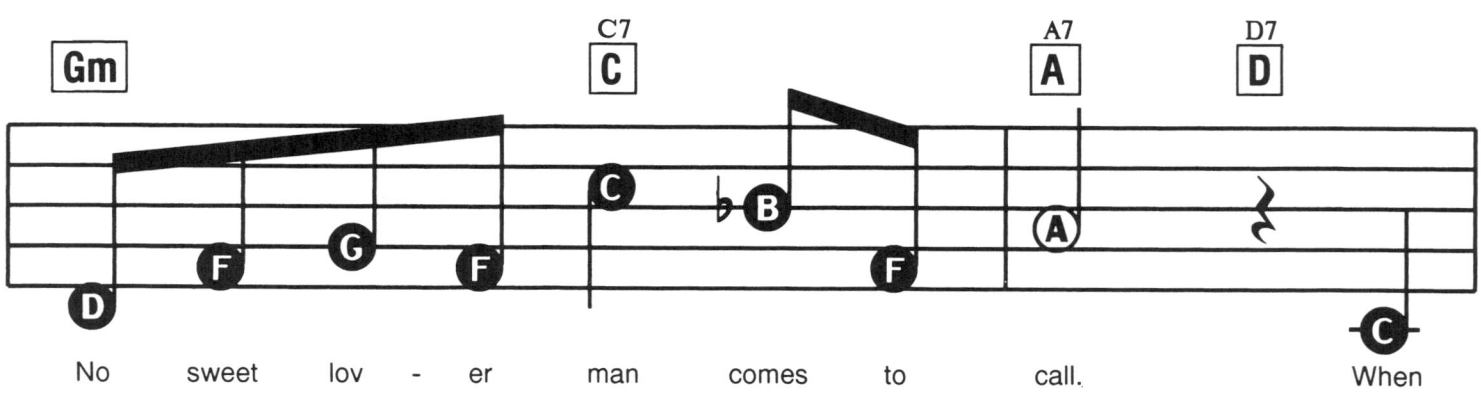

No sweet lov-er man comes to call. When

Copyright © 1956 Sony/ATV Music Publishing LLC
Copyright Renewed
All Rights Administered by Sony/ATV Music Publishing LLC, 8 Music Square West, Nashville, TN 37203
International Copyright Secured All Rights Reserved

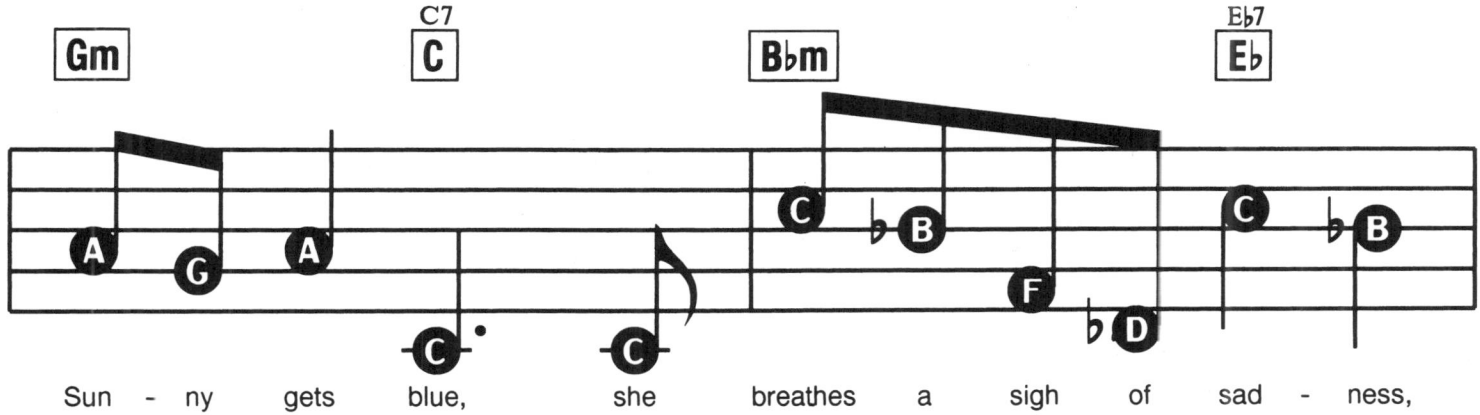
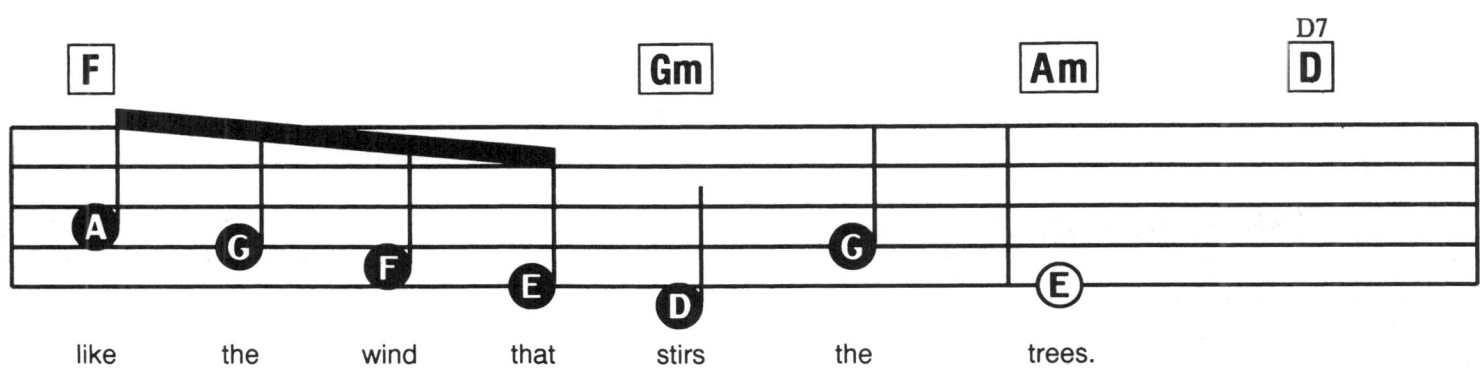
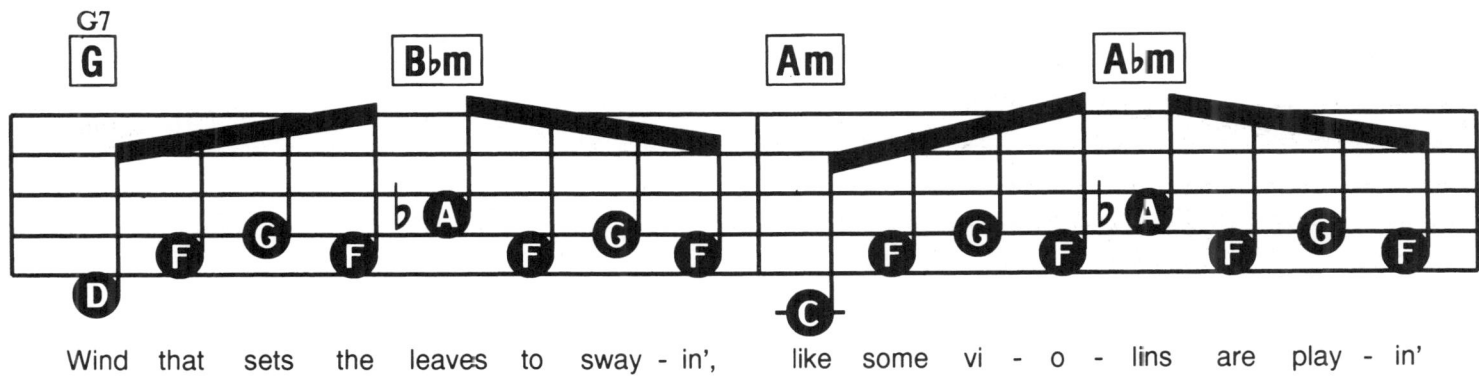
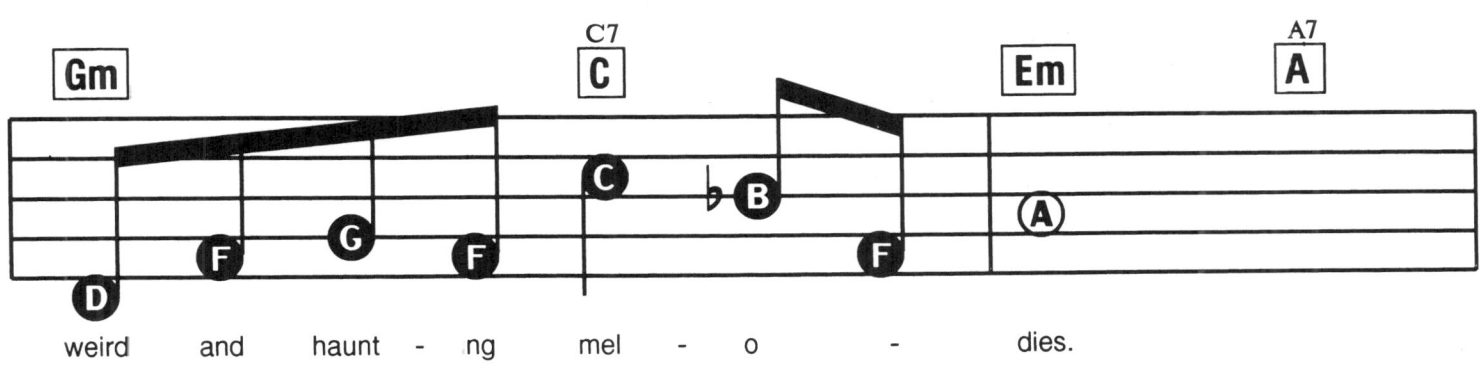

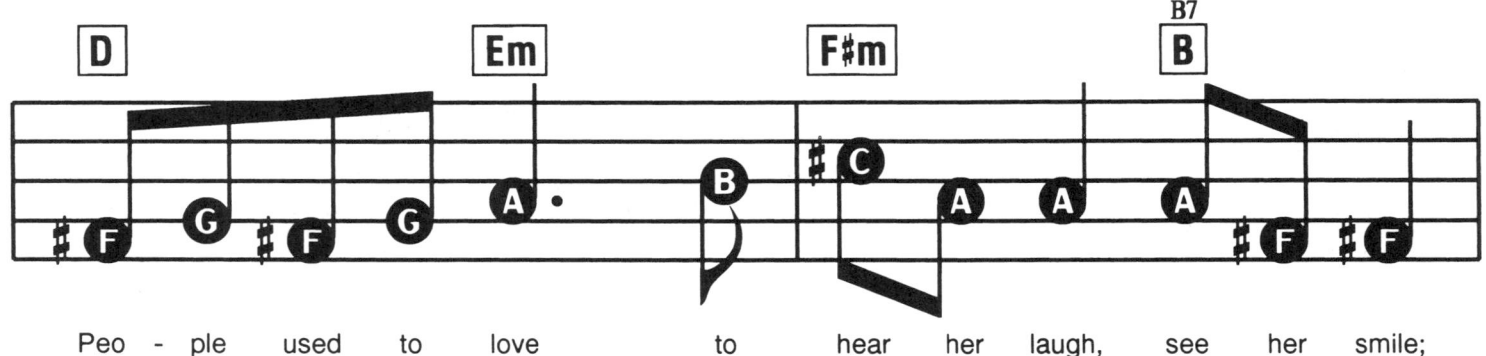
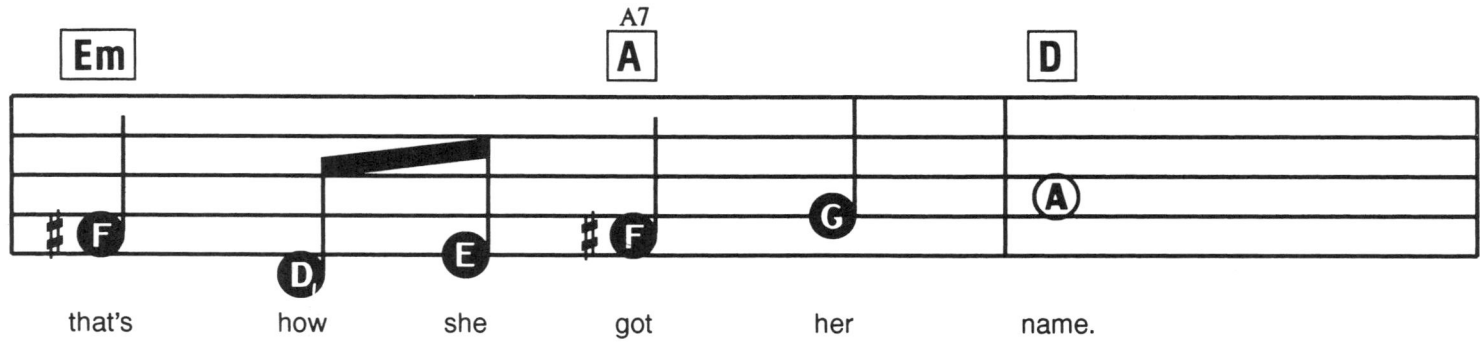
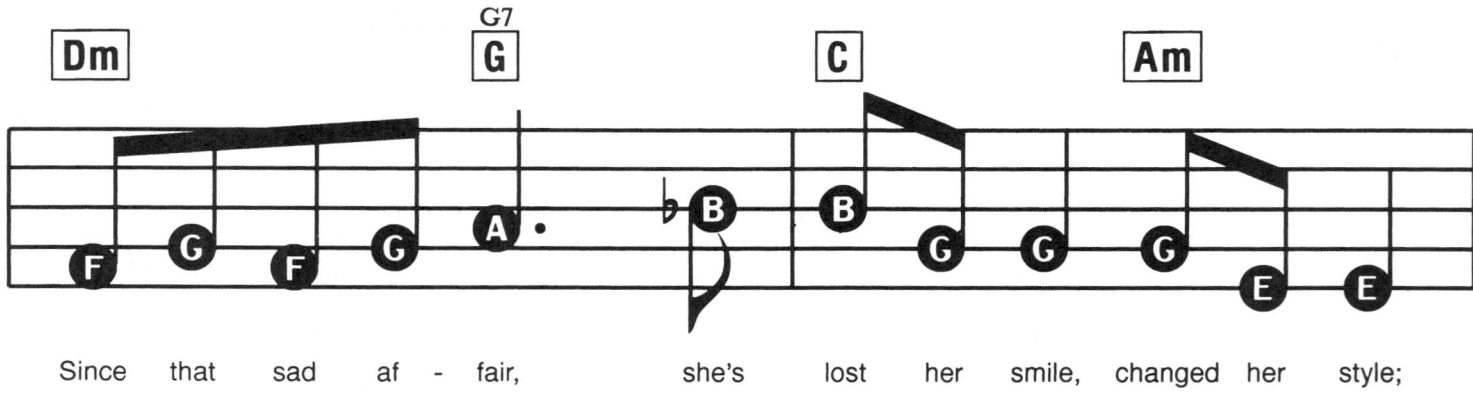
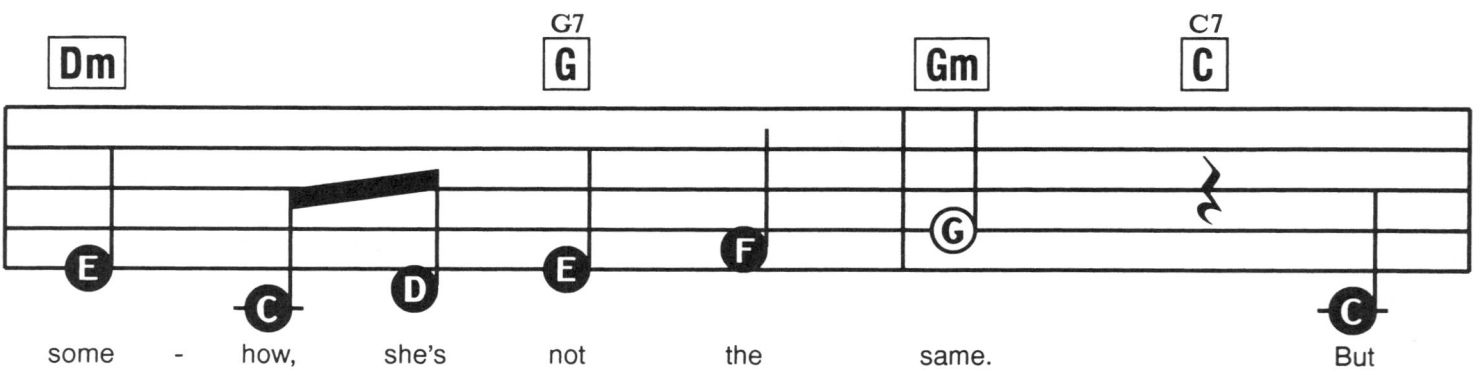

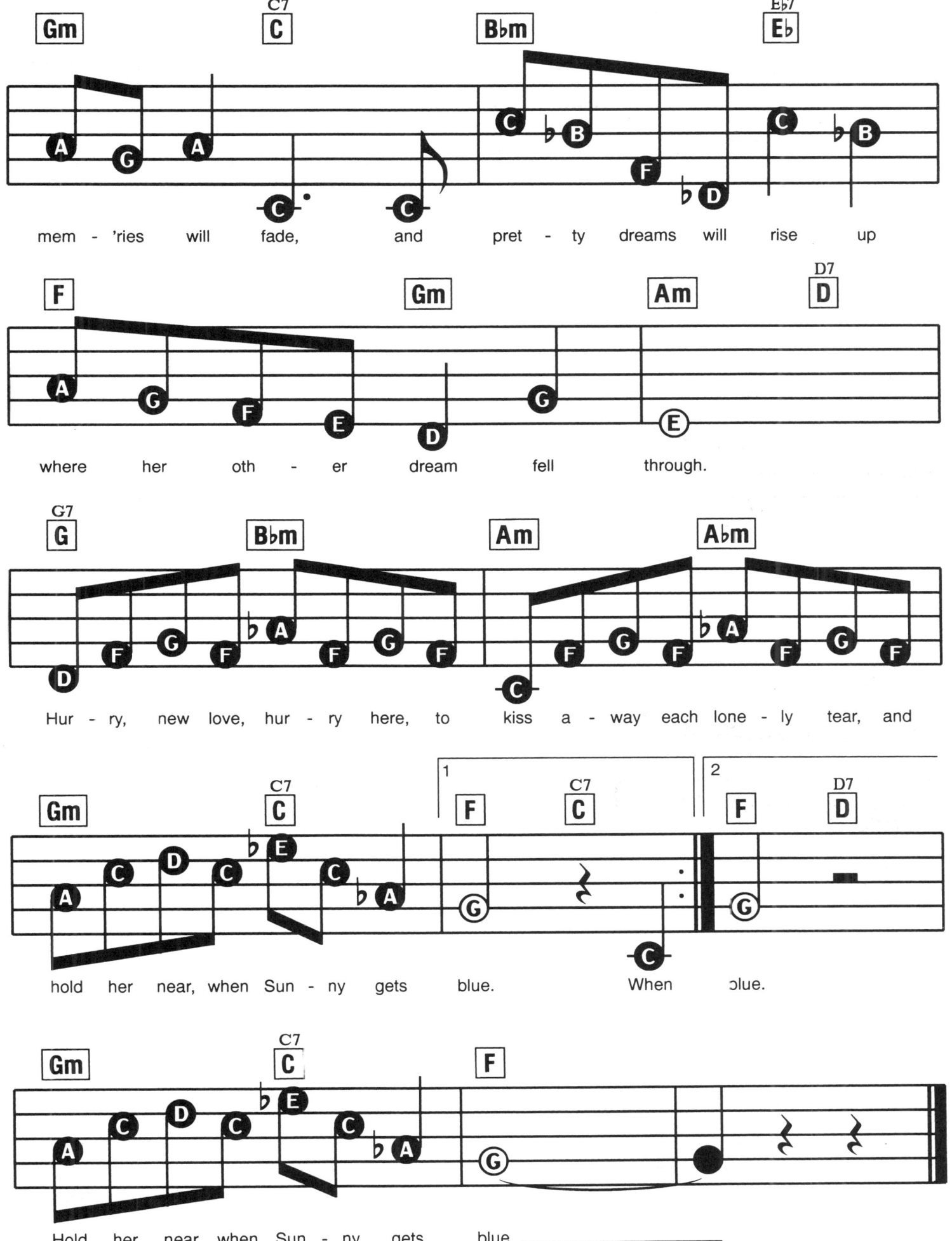

Will You Still Be Mine

Registration 8
Rhythm: Swing or Fox Trot

Words by Tom Adair
Music by Matt Dennis

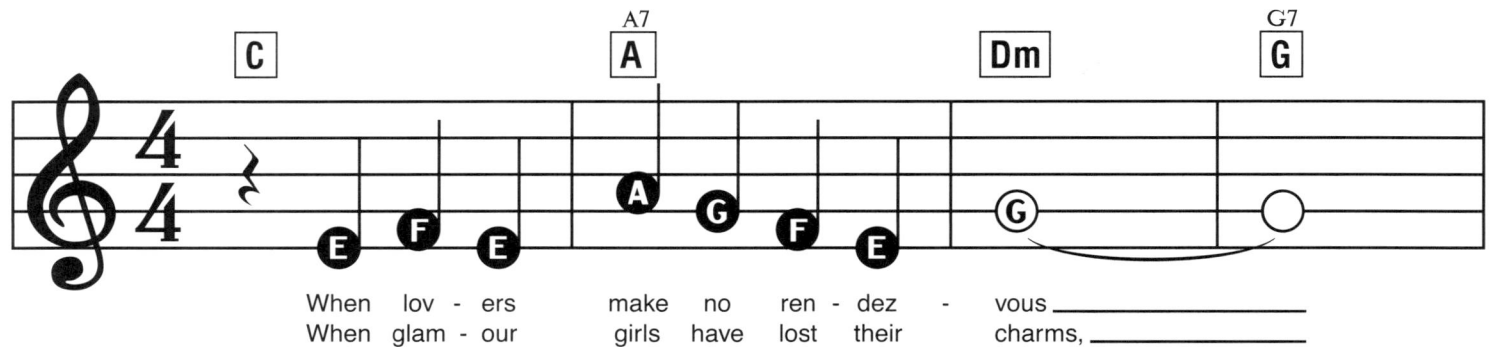

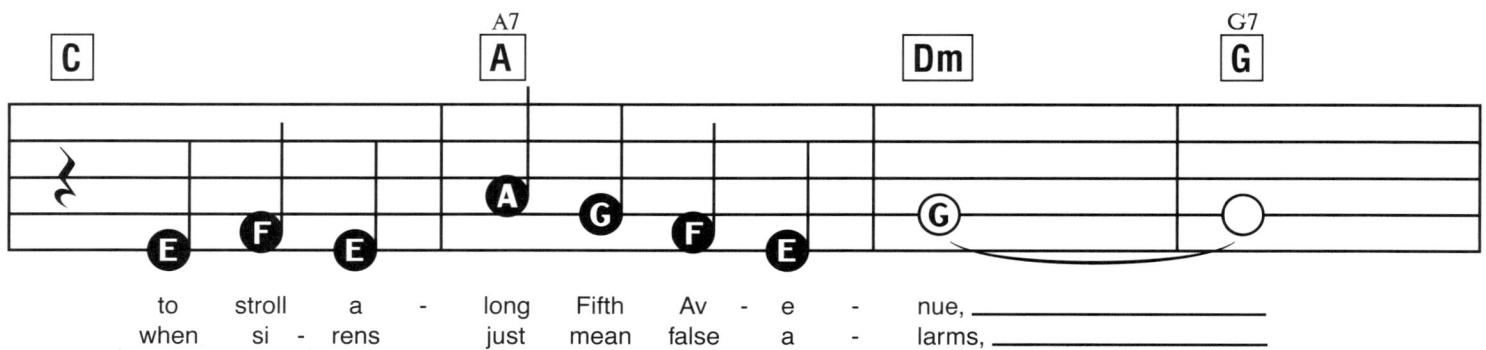

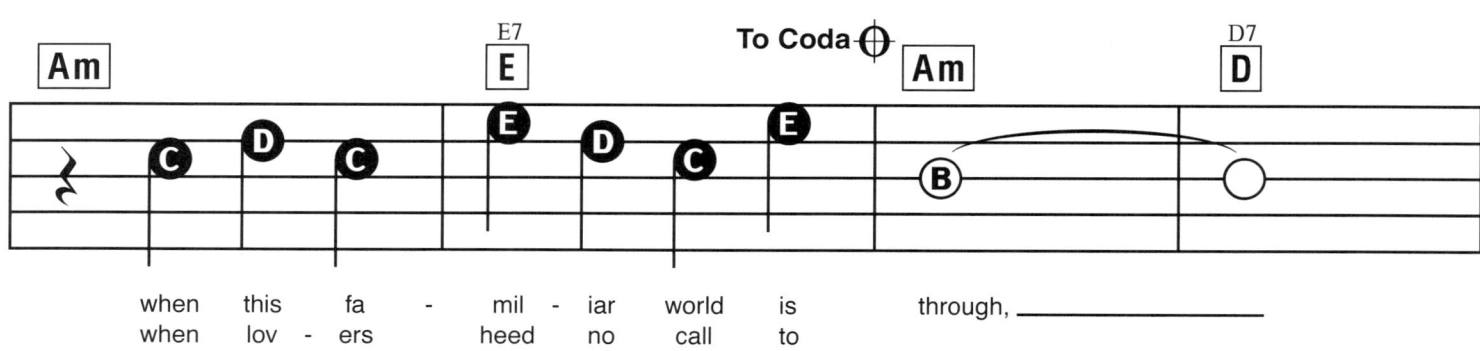

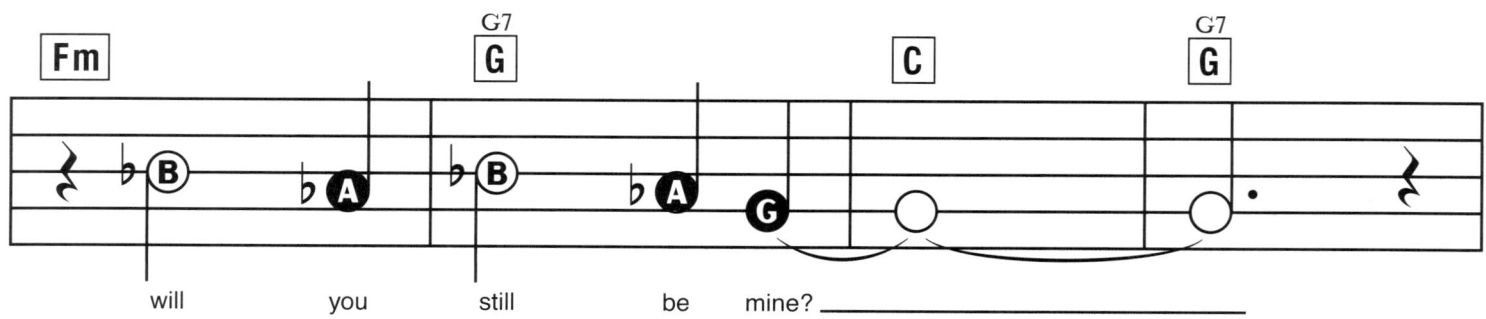

Copyright © 1940 (Renewed 1967) by Music Sales Corporation (ASCAP)
International Copyright Secured   All Rights Reserved
Reprinted by Permission

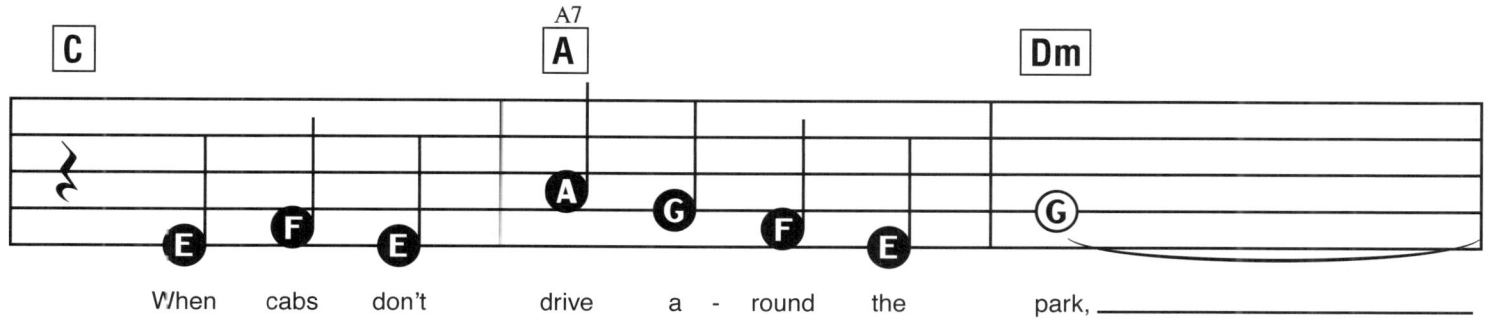
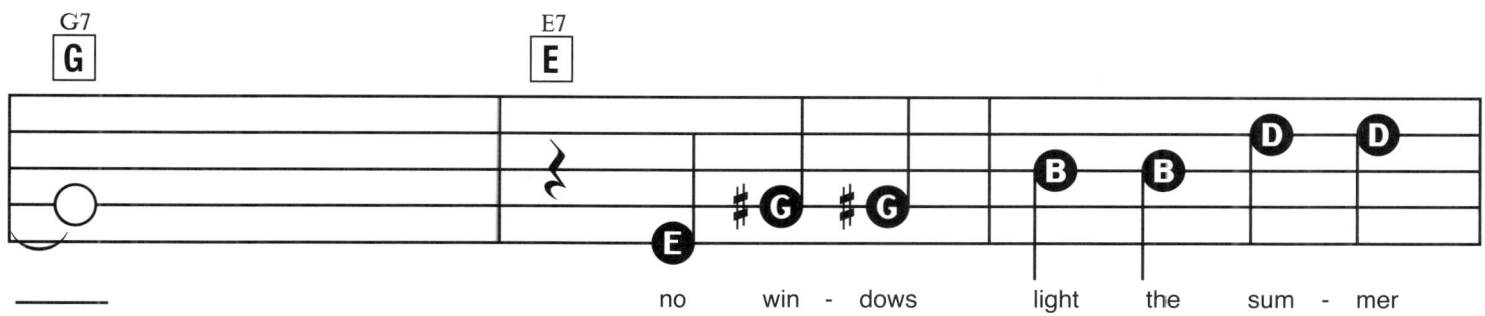
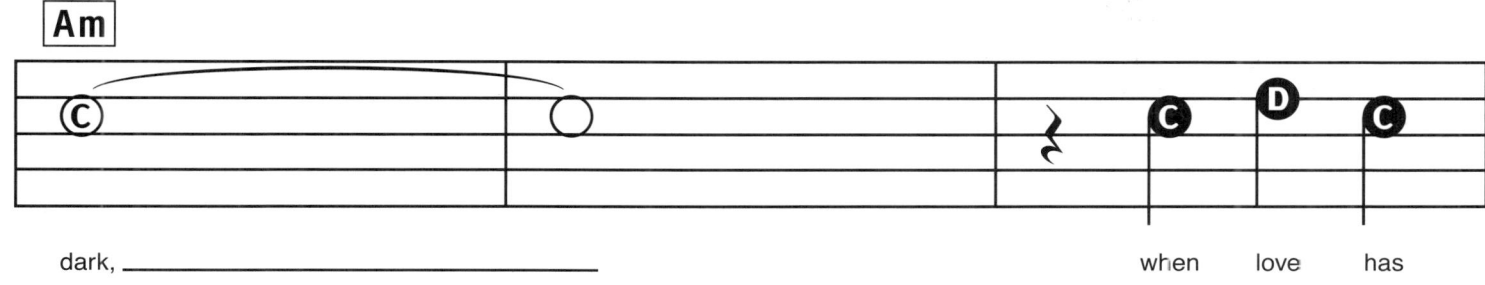
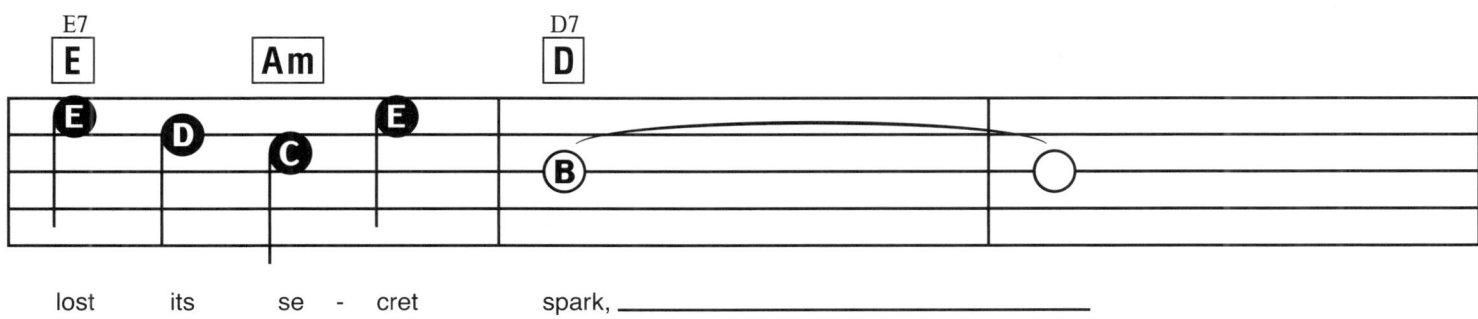
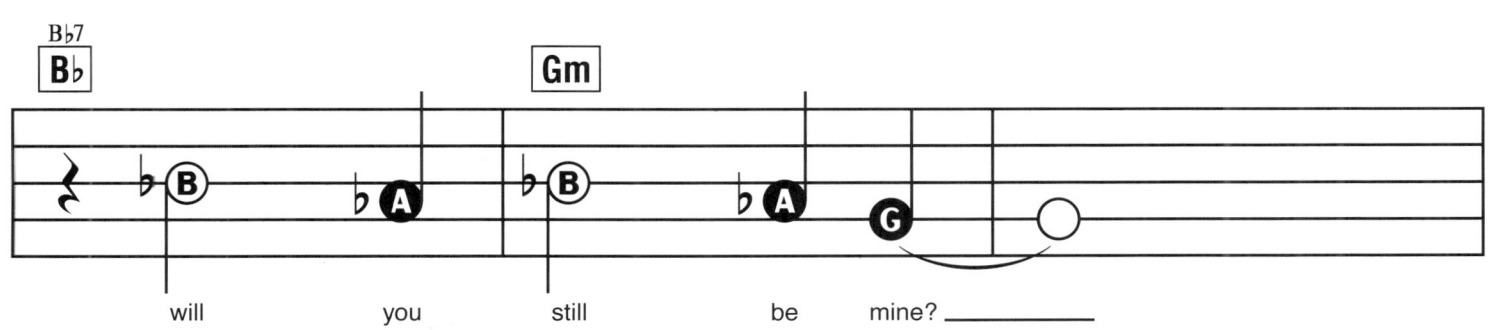

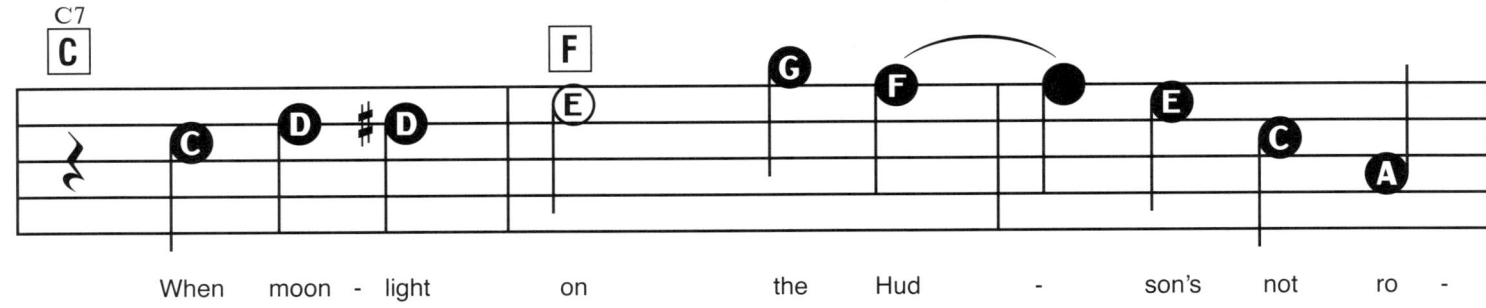
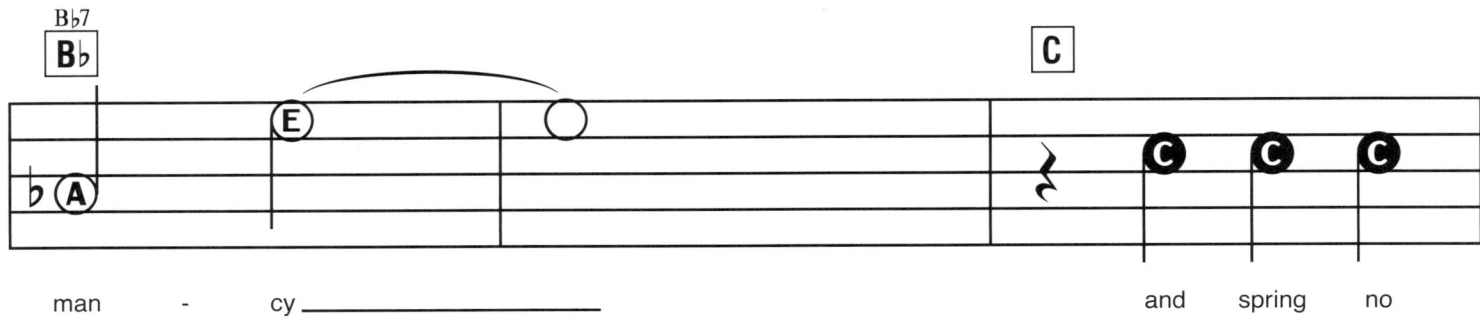
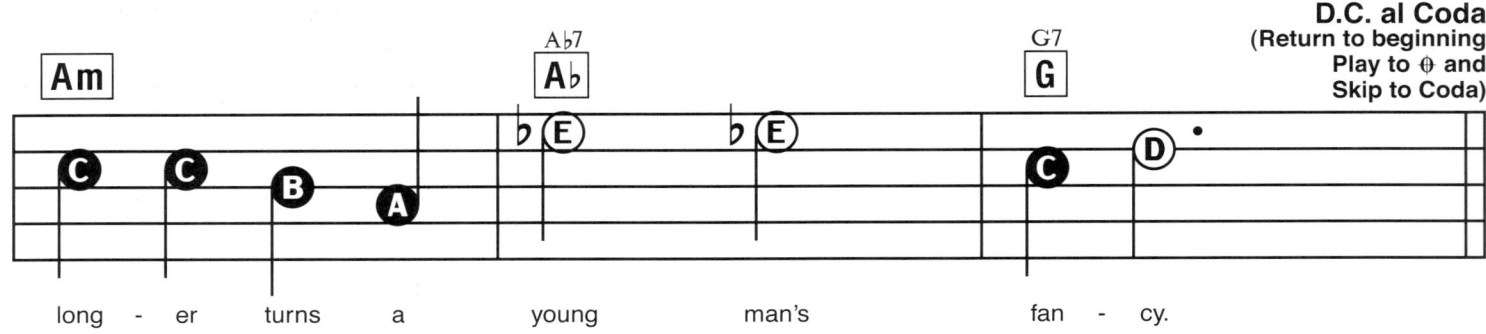
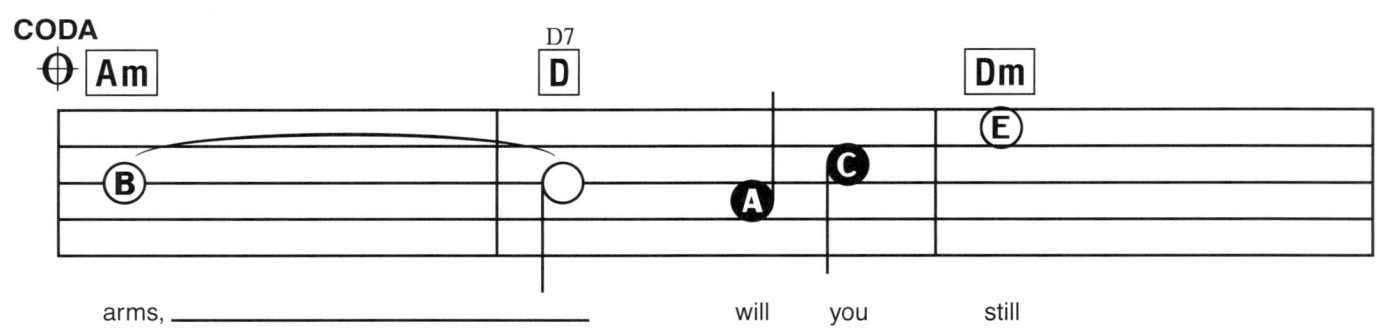
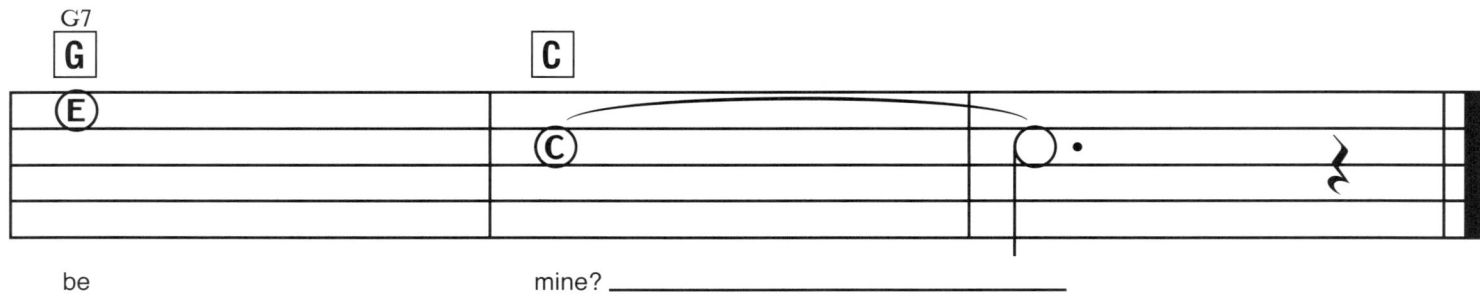

252

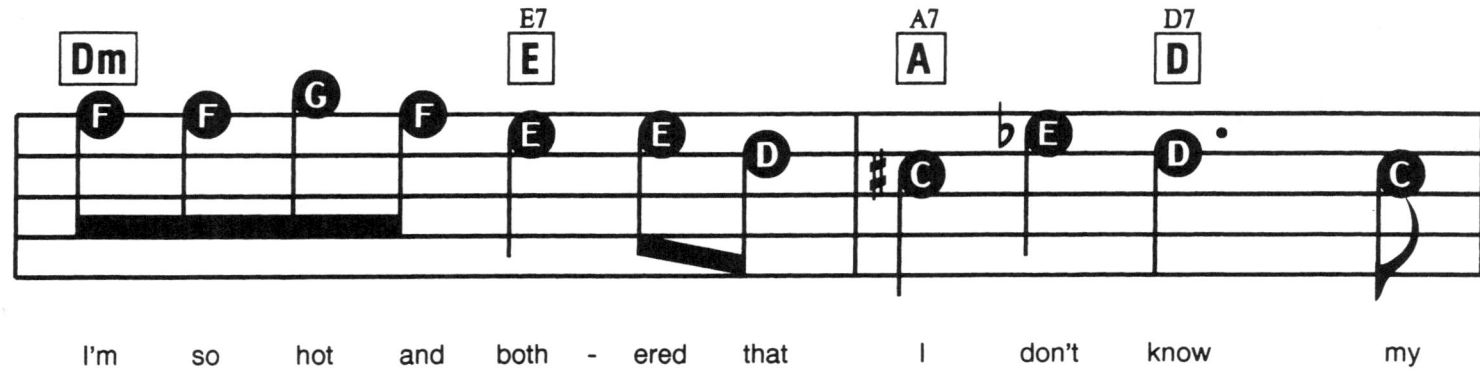

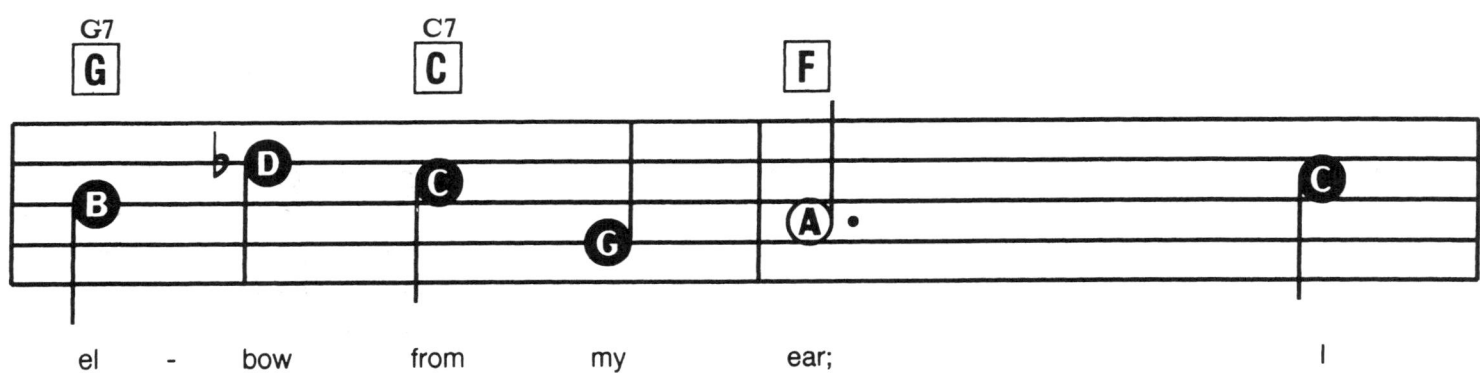

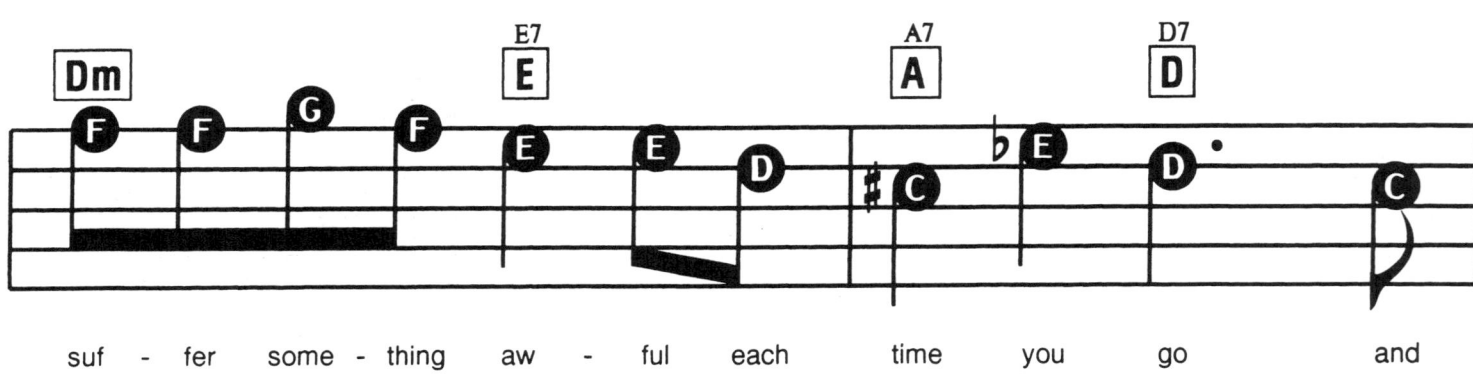

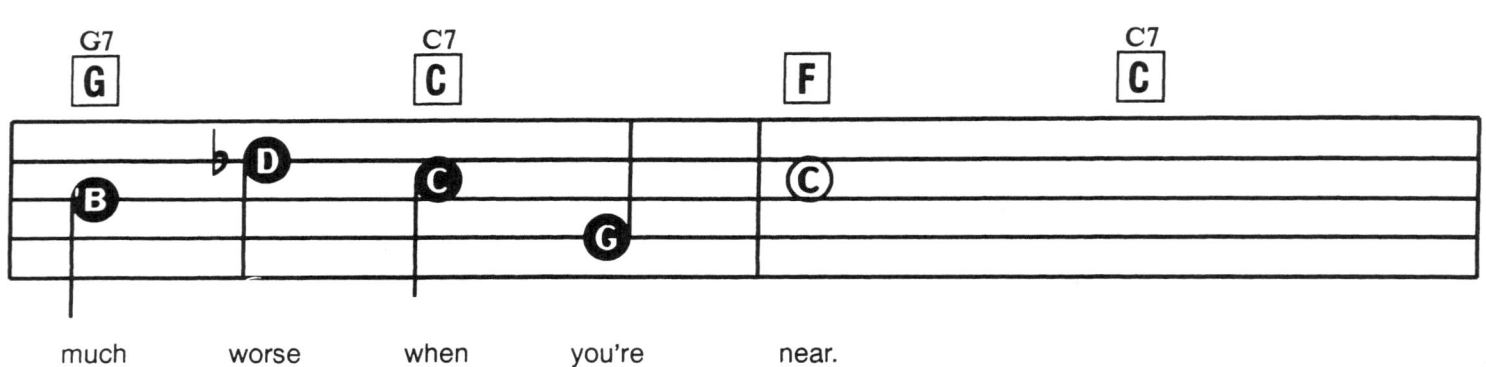

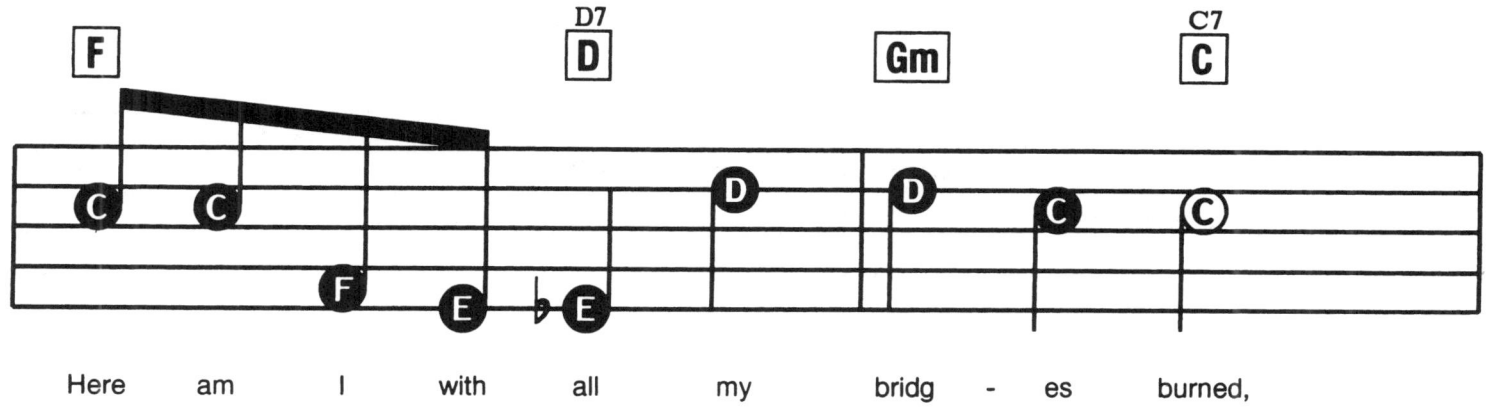
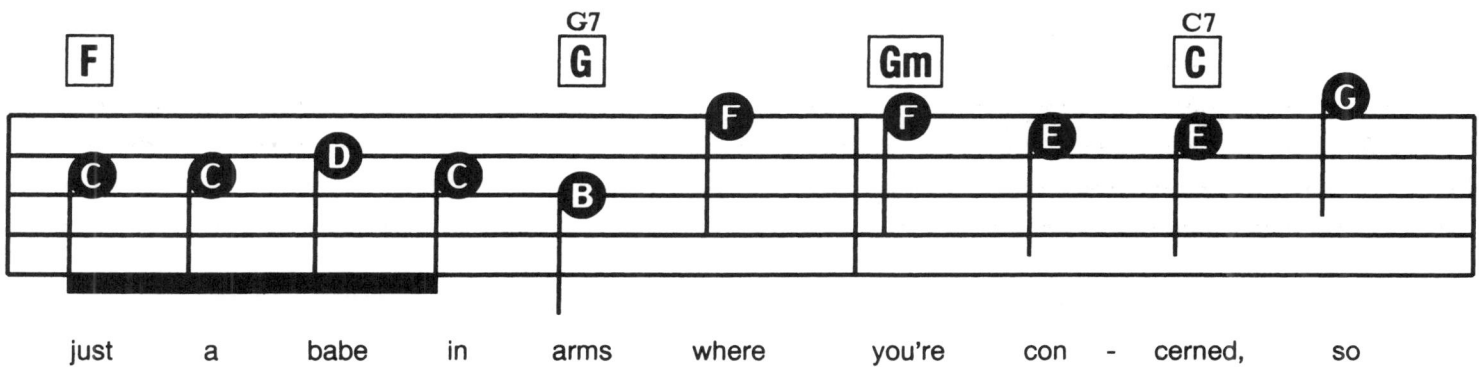
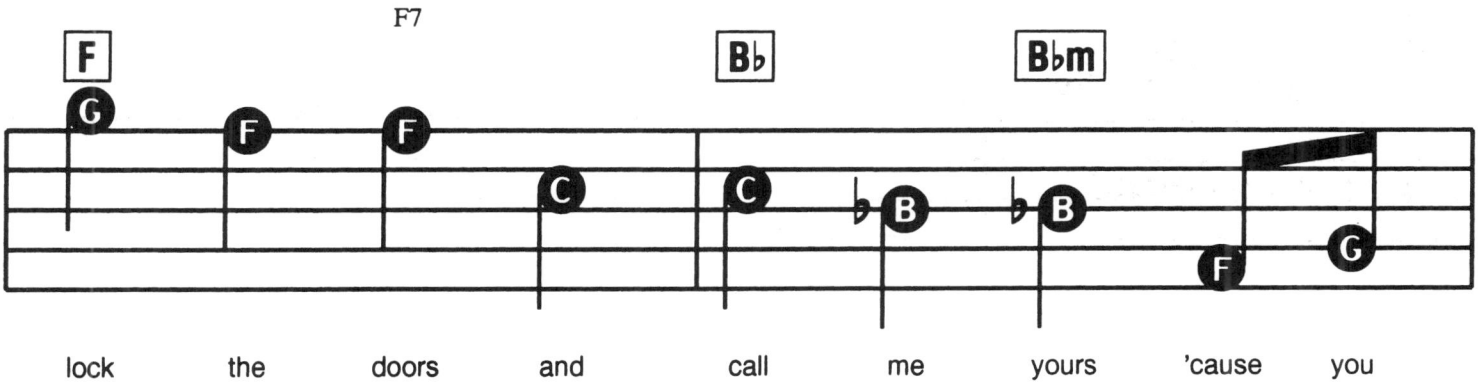
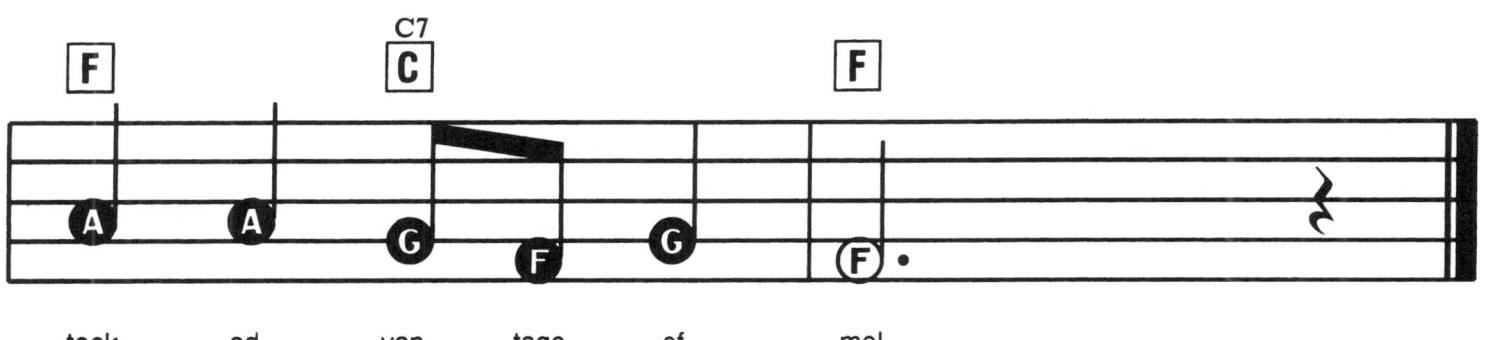

You Are the Sunshine of My Life

Registration 7
Rhythm: 8-Beat or Bossa Nova

Words and Music by
Stevie Wonder

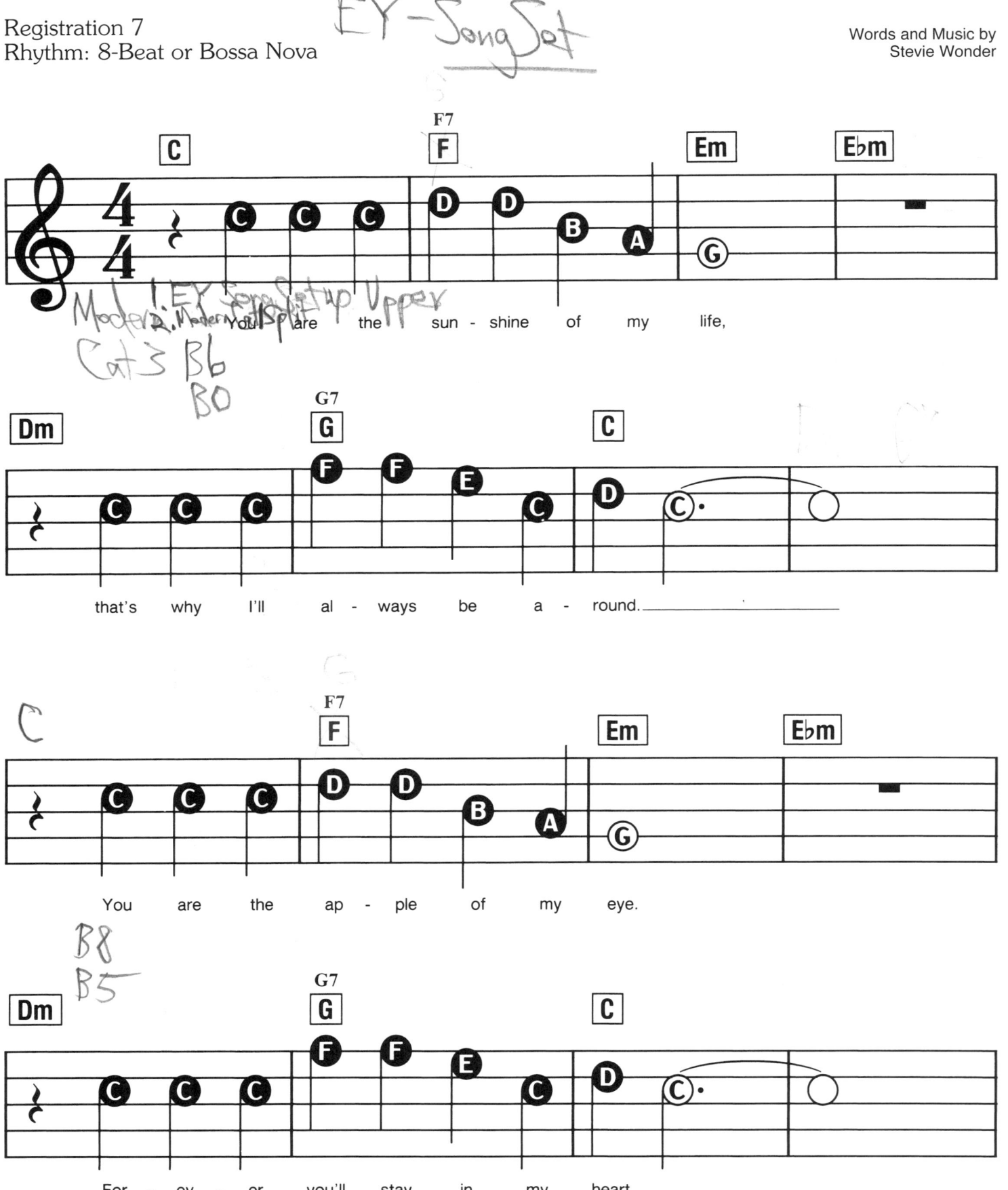

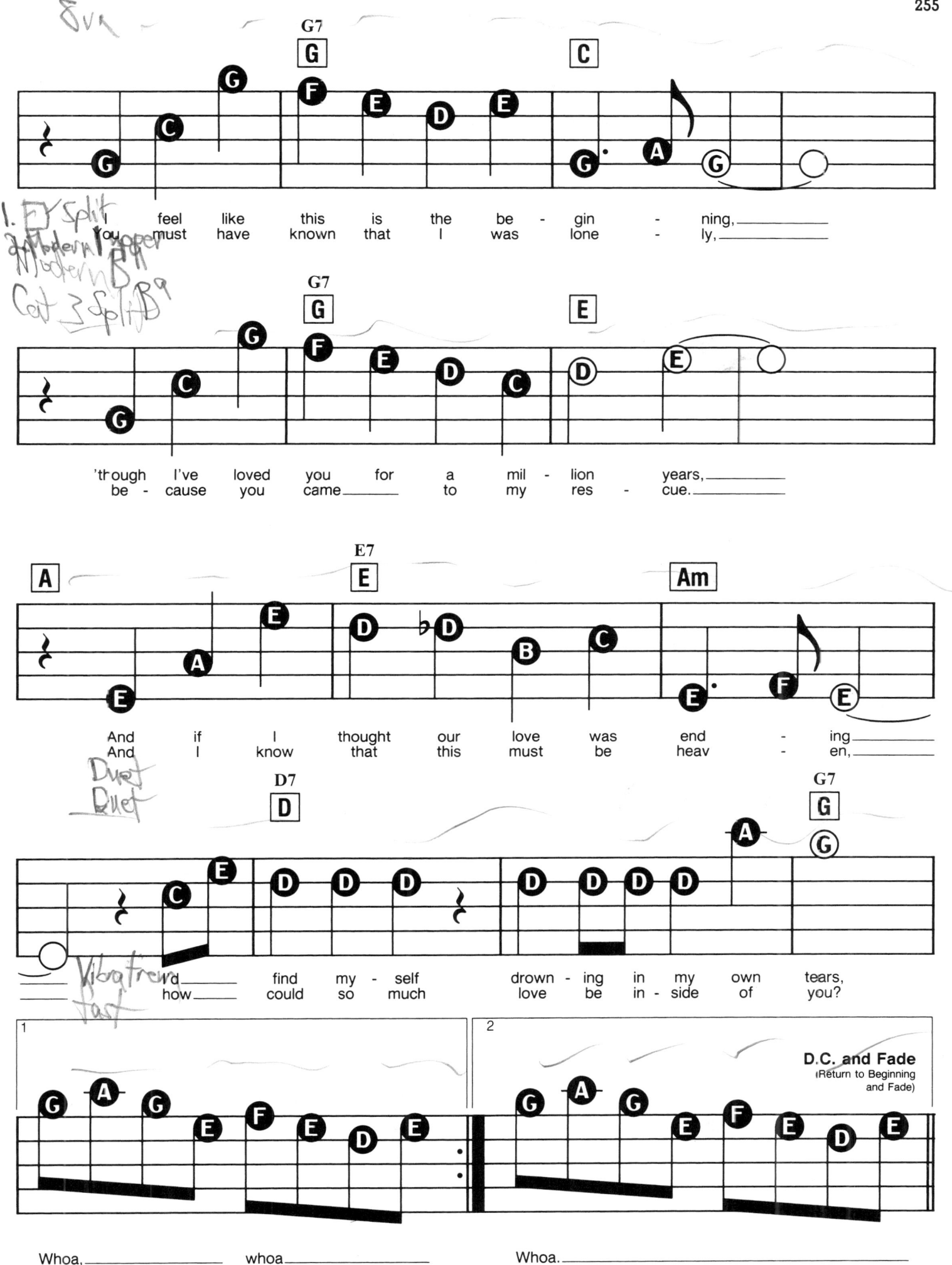

Registration Guide

- Match the Registration number on the song to the corresponding numbered category below. Select and activate an instrumental sound available on your instrument.
- Choose an automatic rhythm appropriate to the mood and style of the song. (Consult your Owner's Guide for proper operation of automatic rhythm features.)
- Adjust the tempo and volume controls to comfortable settings.

Registration

1	Mellow	Flutes, Clarinet, Oboe, Flugel Horn, Trombone, French Horn, Organ Flutes
2	Ensemble	Brass Section, Sax Section, Wind Ensemble, Full Organ, Theater Organ
3	Strings	Violin, Viola, Cello, Fiddle, String Ensemble, Pizzicato, Organ Strings
4	Guitars	Acoustic/Electric Guitars, Banjo, Mandolin, Dulcimer, Ukulele, Hawaiian Guitar
5	Mallets	Vibraphone, Marimba, Xylophone, Steel Drums, Bells, Celesta, Chimes
6	Liturgical	Pipe Organ, Hand Bells, Vocal Ensemble, Choir, Organ Flutes
7	Bright	Saxophones, Trumpet, Mute Trumpet, Synth Leads, Jazz/Gospel Organs
8	Piano	Piano, Electric Piano, Honky Tonk Piano, Harpsichord, Clavi
9	Novelty	Melodic Percussion, Wah Trumpet, Synth, Whistle, Kazoo, Perc. Organ
10	Bellows	Accordion, French Accordion, Mussette, Harmonica, Pump Organ, Bagpipes